Contributions to Political Science

The series Contributions to Political Science contains publications in all areas of political science, such as public policy and administration, political economy, comparative politics, European politics and European integration, electoral systems and voting behavior, international relations and others. Publications are primarily monographs and multiple author works containing new research results, but conference and congress reports are also considered. The series covers both theoretical and empirical aspects and is addressed to researchers and policy makers.

All titles in this series are peer-reviewed.

More information about this series at https://link.springer.com/bookseries/11829

Georgios I. Zekos

Political, Economic and Legal Effects of Artificial Intelligence

Governance, Digital Economy and Society

Springer

Georgios I. Zekos
International Hellenic University
Serres, Greece

ISSN 2198-7289 ISSN 2198-7297 (electronic)
Contributions to Political Science
ISBN 978-3-030-94735-4 ISBN 978-3-030-94736-1 (eBook)
https://doi.org/10.1007/978-3-030-94736-1

This Springer imprint is published by the registered company Springer Nature Switzerland AG
The registered company address is: Gewerbestrasse 11, 6330 Cham, Switzerland

To my lovely wife
ΣΟΦΙΑ ΠΡΟΔΡΟΜΟΥ ΓΡΗΓΟΡΙΑΔΟΥ
And to my son
ΙΩΑΝΝΗΣ-ΜΑΡΙΝΟΣ ΖΕΚΟΣ

Contents

Chapter 1
Introduction

Human beings are the central problem of politics because they have personal interests, and they tend to pursue them, even when they are tasked with pursuing the public interest. Additionally, humans have limited competences, in terms both of how much they can do and how well they can do things.

It could be said that politics is the manners by which competing parties settle their differences and reach decisions. Politics is complex involving many considerations of uncertain short- and long-term effects. It has to be taken into consideration that most problems, when accurately understood, are technical problems amenable to the logic of statistical analysis and optimization. Moreover, technocracy refers to the rule of experts.

When a new technology is appeared to society, the law has to respond to the disorder technology generates but there is a pacing problem and so the thought that law cannot keep pace with technology brings forwards a form of "technological determinism" wherein technology drives social structures and cultural values.[1] Moreover, the law is catching up with technology but "technology has not stood still." Also, AI and robotics as transformative technologies with critical qualities are more exceptional than those of cyberspace and other prior technologies. It could be said that if technology is the driving force of law, law will always follow technology and so technological revolution, embracing the relationships among technologies, their uses, and their relationship between them and people, instigates and influences social transformation.

Artificial Intelligence (AI) is the automation of certain tasks of human intellectual competence. Moreover, AI is an integrated system that integrates information acquisition objectives, logical reasoning principles, and self-correction capabilities. AI products are ranging from domestic appliances, such as smart dishwashers, to

[1] Ryan Calo, Robotics and the Lessons of Cyberlaw, 103 CAL. L. REV. 513, 556–57 (2015) Lyombe S. Eko, New Media, Old Regimes: Case Studies In Comparative Communication Law And Policy 220 (2012).

G. I. Zekos, *Political, Economic and Legal Effects of Artificial Intelligence*,
Contributions to Political Science, https://doi.org/10.1007/978-3-030-94736-1_1

smart medical devices, AI phones and computers, smart speakers, AI human resources and AI quasi-judicial decision-making models that they are powered by versions of statistical/predictive models within all AI categories.[2] AAI systems will be autonomous operating without human intervention and can learn and identify patterns to make decisions and to reach different conclusions based on the analysis of different data imitating the cognitive functions and intelligent behavior of humans.

AI embraces techniques tackling aspects of human intellect using machines. Taking into account that the capability of machines to advance the world via superior decision-making has been recognized, AI enhances human decision-making at all levels.[3] Machines have upgraded people's capacity modeling the world, such as weather modeling,[4] with crucial consequences to human wellbeing.[5]

The political configurations of a jurisdiction rework its tendency to generate and diffuse new technologies. First of all, AI is superior to human intelligence for investigation of large and multifaceted problems engrossing the necessity for strategy, prediction of long-term effects, and analysis of vast amounts of data. Nonetheless, AI can beat humans at games and many other activities. Which is the role of AI-based technologies upon political participation? ICT technologies enabled societal alterations shaping the configuration of the "knowledge-based economies." For a long time, humanity has loaded the world with numerous artifacts, but it now seems in the process of adding a whole range of artifacts with new possibilities. Has AI proven to be superior to human decision-making in certain areas? Which are the consequences of computer decision-making in politics? Is there a link between artificial intelligence and political decision-making?

Algorithmic governance discloses that AI is already employed in many facets of government but it seems that the prospective advantages from AI in politics are heavily contested. Moreover, current AI is not appropriate that can be employed so as to generate prosperous societies but there is indisputably a prospective for the constructive use of AI in politics due to the fact that much of the future applications of AI is based on the technologies presently utilized such as various forms of machine learning are used, while artificial neural networks (ANN) is the most

[2]Casey, Bryan, Amoral Machines, How Roboticists Can Learn to Stop Worrying and Love the Law (February 17, 2017). Northwestern University Law Review, Vol. 111, No. 5, Fall 2017. pp. 231–250.

[3]G. Zekos, Artificial Intelligence And E-Bills Of Lading Contracts, Journal of Internet Law April 2021 Vol. 24 N8 p3–10 Wolters Kluwer https://lrus.wolterskluwer.com/store/product/journal-of-internet-law/ Richard M. Re & Alicia Solow-Niederman, Developing Artificial Intelligent Justice, 22 Stan. Tech. L. Rev. 242, 255–58 (2019).

[4]Hannah Hickey, A.I. model shows promise to generate faster, more accurate weather forecasts, UW News (Dec. 15, 2020), https://www.washington.edu/news/2020/12/15/a-imodel-shows-promise-to-generate-faster-more-accurate-weather-forecasts/

[5]Haris Aziz et al., A polynomial-time algorithm for computing a Pareto optimal and almost proportional allocation, 48 Operations Rsch. Letters 573 (2020).

popular technique in terms of usage.[6] Artificial neural networks imitate biological information-processing systems and consist of artificial neurons that transmit signals to each other in reinforcement systems.[7] Algorithmic governance is utilizing algorithms both in ordering human action in general, and in traditional political structures[8] . It is characteristic that substantial volumes of data analyzed by algorithms permit establishments either to present completely new goods and services or deliver the already existing ones more accurately and cost-effectively.

It has to be taken into account that the human made artificial intelligence has got a limited capability according to the capability of humans and so it seems presently that the artificial intelligence will be controlled by the humans. The unexpected possibility for the artificial intelligence to shelf developed in a degree not be controlled by the humans is less possible at present which cannot be eradicated due to the fact the human's capabilities via biotechnology and nanotechnology are augmented continually. The question to be answered is if technology improves the human elements of human beings by adding to the natural environment or the higher mechanical environment destroys the human level of humans.

Computing technology is a way to develop additional forms of interactivity and so an increasingly widespread presence of highly evolved machines leads to a profound questioning of the pertinence of decision-making. Nonetheless, progress in "artificial intelligences" would not only produce a centralizing, hierarchical, and oppressive technology but also it unavoidably has liberatory prospective. Internet governance bodies are reflexively open and The Internet Engineering Task Force (IETF), which develops open Internet standards, is highly participatory and transparent.

Technology has always been a constant source of uncertainties, risks, change, and, in many cases, disruption. Moreover, technology needs regulators to make a number of complex decisions: whether and when to intervene; what kind of regulatory intervention to employ.

New technological possibilities have changed the social reality of law in theoretical and in practical way which means even an alteration of the essence of conventional law since AAI law will be articulated and enforced automatically. It has to be taken into account that the transformation in the "human-technology" relationship brings forwards a new variety of matters linked both to the legal support of digitalization and numerous legal features of artificial intelligence application and improvement of law in the digital age, and parallel between law and technology in

[6] R. Kurzweil, Superintelligence and singularity, in: S. Schneider (Ed.), Science Fiction and Philosophy: from Time Travel to Superintelligence, Wiley-Blackwell, Chichester, 2015, pp. 146–170.

[7] R.S. Sutton, A.G. Barto, Reinforcement Learning: an Introduction, MIT press, 2018.

[8] J. Danaher, M.J. Hogan, C. Noone, R. Kennedy, A. Behan, A. De Paor, H. Felzmann, M. Haklay, S.M. Khoo, J. Morison, M.H. Murphy, Algorithmic governance: developing a research agenda through the power of collective intelligence, Big Data & Society 4 (2) (2017) 1–21.

general.[9] It has to be taken into account that technological breakthroughs challenge core legal assumptions and all new problems are tackled by examining the effects of a specific technology within conventional legal subjects such as by considering how drones should be regulated under privacy law, property law, or the law of armed conflict.[10] It is worth noting that law has to keep up with technological change due to the fact that law cannot prevent technological change. Moreover, technology is neither neutral nor inevitable, and legal actors have the agency and ability to purposefully shape the evolution of both law and technology.[11]

The law identifies and regulates societal relationships. Moreover, law merely reflects a determinate resolution of the controversy as contemplated fitting by those who have the power and authority to resolve the issue within a specific society.[12] It is characteristic that law is "a body of rules" bringing "social order" by regulating the affairs in society, the relations among various entities, ruling societal coordination and individuals by harmonizing their mutual understanding.

Common law and civil law systems are all, to some degree, amalgams in which case law works alongside codes and statutes.[13] Law is a device of social ordering and governance and so abuses of "rule-by-law" have led to "struggles for justice" intended at protecting "rule-of-law." Legal authority is a type of power exemplified by a content-independent response to a command or order. It has to be taken into account that legal regulation abolishes existing social norms.[14] It is worth noting here that in disobeying the twin commands of stare decisis and federal supremacy, state court resistance to the FAA fosters the troubling idea that law changes based on the ideologies of legal actors.[15]

It has to be taken into account that a state's national courts engage in judicial review of foreign policy when they determine whether another branch's foreign policy decision complies with the requirements of law, such as constitutionally protected individual rights and separation-of-powers principles or rules of

---

[9] Zaloilo, M.V., Pashentsev, D.A. (2019) National legal order of Russia in the conditions of digitalization. Bulletin of Saint Petersburg University. Law. Vol. 10. Issue 2. 196–209; Mazhorina, M.V., Terentieva, L.V., Shakhnazarov, B.A. (2019) International private law in the context of the development of information and communication technologies. Topical issues of Russian law. No. 5 (102). 169–182.

[10] Rebecca Crootof & B. J. Ard, Structuring Techlaw, 34 Harv. J. Law Technol., 1 (2021), https://papers.ssrn.com/abstract=3664124

[11] Ruha Benjamin, Race After Technology: Abolitionist Tools for the New Jim Code (2019) (discussing how technology entrenches social inequity); Meg Leta Jones, Does Technology Drive Law? The Dilemma of Technological Exceptionalism in Cyberlaw, 2018 J. L., Tech. & Pol'y 249, 253 https://ssrn.com/abstract=2981855

[12] Neil MacCormick, Institutions of Law: An Essay in Legal Theory (Oxford: Oxford University Press, 2007) 255–61.

[13] M. Roe, "Chaos and evolution in law and economics" (1996) 109 Harvard Law Review 641–668.

[14] Yoshinobu Zasu, Sanctions by Social Norms and the Law: Substitutes or Complements?, 36 J. Legal Stud. 379, 379–82 (2007) (informal sanctions imposed through social norms are in competition with, or complement, the formal sanctions of the law).

[15] Alyssa S. King, Arbitration and the Federal Balance, 94 IND. L.J. 1447, 1466–79 (2019).

international law.[16] Moreover, national courts also participate in the implementation of foreign policy such as implementing legislative policy concerning the scope of foreign sovereign immunity. Judicial foreign policy often entails direct interactions between domestic courts and foreign states which mean that law and politics are linked tightly. It has to be taken into account that public law is one tool in both domestic and international politics mitigating the fundamental problem of governance.[17]

It is characteristic that the impressive growth of global economic networks has had conflicting consequences on the development on constitutional systems based on regional integration. In the European Union, globalization produces interests and relationships which destabilize conventional constitutionalism as mode of regional governance requiring the constitutionalization of global governance. The EU's approach to artificial intelligence focusses on excellence and trust, enhancing industrial capacity and making certain fundamental rights. The Commission published its AI proposed new rules and actions to transform Europe into the global center for trustworthy AI.[18]

Globalization brings up new challenges for law due to the differences among legal systems. The emergence of powerful private or transnational actors creates networks and new spheres of normativity distinct from the nation state causing question of conventional representation of law itself and the related plot of the relationship between the center and the periphery. To that extent, globalization necessitates a satisfactory institutional response that safeguards stability, steady prosperity, and a more equitable distribution of the rewards of globalization. The rise of supranational institution, regional trading block, and setting up of multilevel governance, interlocking politics and policy networks have augmented the crucial matter of nature and suitable type of contemporary governance.[19] Economic utility stems from the costs linked to legislation. It is worth mentioning that the leading principles that drive the modern convergence are fidelity, conferred powers, subsidiarity, proportionality, and conditionality.[20]

Intelligence is linked to autonomy in that intelligent systems are capable of determining and performing tasks in more complex environments. AI simplifies

---

[16] Sunstein, C. R. (2008). Judging National Security post-9/11: An Empirical Investigation. Working Paper. University of Chicago School of Law, Chicago.

[17] Keohane, R. O. (2001). Governance in a partially globalized world. American Political Science Review, 95(1), 1–13.

[18] Proposal for a Regulation Of The European Parliament And Of The Council Laying Down Harmonised Rules On Artificial Intelligence (Artificial Intelligence Act) And Amending Certain Union Legislative Acts COM/2021/206 final.

[19] F G Snyder, "Governing Globalization" Michael Likosky eds. in Transnational Legal Process, p. 65. Susane Strange, Casino Capitalism (Oxford, Basic Blackwell, 1986). H. Milner, Resisting Protectionism: Global Industries and the Politics of International Trade (Princeton University Press, Princeton, 1998).

[20] Platsas A.E., International Economic Law and the Idea of Legal Convergence (2009) 2(4) IJPL383, 392. Chalmers et al., European Union Law (CUP 2006) 193.

legal research by identifying authorities that are frequently referenced with respect to a particular proposition of law and so assisting with contract drafting by highlighting provisions that are apt to appear in certain types of contracts. Legal analytics is an application of artificial intelligence that makes probabilistic predictions in a matter based on similar, previously concluded matters and so the more data to which artificial intelligence systems are exposed, the better their capacity to predict prospective outcomes.[21]

AI introduction meant that computer processors attained the miniaturization, sophistication, and power needed for AI to take off. Furthermore, the development of open-source frameworks permits developers to work synergistically on the same platforms to construct the infrastructure required for AI-enabled devices to interoperate and so interconnected computer processors accomplishing parallel processing are materialized by artificial neural networks. In addition, networks learn from historical data and known patterns and apply them in clinical diagnosis and image analysis and so networks, such as those used by cryptocurrencies, allow entities to run cutting-edge AI programs by exploiting the collective power of networked personal computers.[22]

It is worth noting that AI could be used by regimes to affect certain parts of their population and so AI will be employed to expand cyber-attacks and enhance the threat of physical attacks which means that AI will be applied to gradually assault an individual's privacy and social manipulation through surveillance, persuasion, and deception will take place.

AI not only functions within the domain of national law but also encompasses the realm of regional and international law and so EU[23] is establishing AI policy principles. AI is already being used by social media and other technology corporations on matters linked to individual profiling, automation of fairness, deep learning shaping omnipresence and omnipotence of customer experience, diplomacy and trade and synthetic practices, such as combining the prospective of blockchain/ Internet of Things with AI.[24]

---

[21] William E. Forster & Andrew L. Lawson, When to Praise the Machine: The Promise and Perils of Automated Transactional Drafting, 69 S.C. L. REV. 597, 621–22 (2018).

[22] Ryan Calo, Artificial Intelligence Policy: A Primer and Roadmap, 51 U.C. DAVIS L. REV. 399, 402 (2017) ("A vast increase in computational power and access to training data has led to practical breakthroughs in machine learning, a singularly important branch of AI."). Emrah Gultekin, The AI bubble won't burst anytime soon, but change is on the horizon, VENTUREBEAT (July 1, 2018), https://venturebeat.com/2018/07/01/the-ai-bubble-wont-burstanytime-soon-but-change-is-on-the-horizon/

[23] EU Guidelines on Ethics in Artificial intelligence: Context and Implementation, September 2019 (EPRS_BRI(2019)640163): https://www.europarl.europa.eu/RegData/etudes/BRIE/2019/640163/EPRS_BRI(2019)640163_EN.Pdf

[24] Bjola, Corneliu. 2020. Diplomacy in the Age of Artificial Intelligence. Emirates Diplomatic Agency. https://static1.squarespace.com/static/52c8df77e4b0d4d2bd039977/t/5e3a9a45d29b7f336bbda061/1580898895236/EDA+Working+Paper_Artificial+Intelligence_EN+copy.pdf Corneliu Bjola, Jennifer Cassidy, and Ilan Manor, "Public Diplomacy in the Digital Age," The Hague

Today's AI systems are only effective in well-specified problem domains. AI is a technology that uses advanced computation to perform at human cognitive capacity in some task area having significant consequences for AI governance and so policy makers and decision-makers must concentrate on the distinctive and powerful problems posed by AI's current capabilities. The challenges of AI governance oblige policy makers to have a significant understanding that regardless of the objective of contemporary AI systems being narrow, the scale at which these systems are deployed will compound the impact of such systems, spreading risks far beyond initial domains.

In an age of cyber insecurity, anxieties about the silence of States concerning the applicability of international law to peacetime cyber operations have been growing. Moreover, there are three distinct types of peacetime security threats that of cyber-attacks, cyber-espionage, and cyber information operations. Cyber information operations are content-based security threats which encompass harnessing the power of online information to cognitively target human intelligence.

Algorithmic trading refers to the automation of the trading process, through the creation of predefined rules and their strict application when executing financial market transactions. Is Algorithmic governance an entirely new phenomenon? Taking into account that algorithms are gradually governing human action, humans will allow the various forms of algorithmic governance. Governments are opening the road for private firms solving public problems and the use of AI in government. Moreover, AI is utilized in all areas of governments[25] such as implementation of AI in the public sector and so AI slowly is applied to ever new areas leading to a situation in which technocracy of AI will be implemented without either political design or democratic input. Has AI a role in politics? Is there a connection between international law and emerging technology? Which is the utility and benefits of AI for civil society? Are AI technologies objects for regulation or can alter the operation and processes of legal systems? Could AAI humanoid robots have rights?

It has to be taken into account that AI drastically revolutionizes the existing political paradigm, allowing more diffused forms of political participation beyond elections such as unrestricted disclosure of governmental data online. Will AI shape sociotechnical system transformation? AI is utilized in the domain of government and so AI is given the authority to govern by mandates. Use of artificial intelligence and machine learning technology brings revolutionary changes in the world generating huge impacts for accountability and reliability.

Will AAI technology involve the redundancy of humanity? There are predictions that humans will be redundant and a mass unemployment due to AI technologies that

---

Journal of Diplomacy 14, no. 1–2 (April 22, 2019): 84, https://doi.org/10.1163/1871191X-14011032

[25] C. Katzenbach, L. Ulbricht, Algorithmic governance, Internet Policy Review 8 (4) (2019) 1–18. W.G. de Sousa, E.R.P. de Melo, P.H.D.S. Bermejo, R.A.S. K, A.O. Gomes, How and where Is Artificial Intelligence in the Public Sector Going? A Literature Review and Research Agenda, Government Information Quarterly, 2019, p. 101392.

will implement all the present human duties in everyday life and so in a way of prophesizing the end of humanity.

The aim of the present work is a deep analysis of the political, economic, and legal effects of AI. The analysis starts with a profound investigation of AI, digital economy, governance, and politics. In the third chapter, the rule of law is analyzed followed by an investigation of the relation between politics and law. In the next two chapters, the role of politics and international law upon the rule of law is examined. Additionally, the analysis moves on to the investigation of cyberspace governance and politics since cyberspace is the basis of all electronic transactions and the basis for the implementation of AI.

The analysis moves forward by examining the role of technology upon the implementation of politics with an emphasis on the impact of AI upon democracy. In the next two chapters, there is a detailed analysis of the role of AI upon politics and the emergence of virtual politics. In the end, conclusions are drawn from the author's analysis of AI and politics regarding political, economic, and legal matters.

Chapter 2
Theoretical Background of AI and Governance

2.1 AI Background

AI technologies range from "Internet of Things" applications to commercial nudging, from speech performance to face recognition software, from automated crime prediction to credit scoring systems, and from AI-powered cars to diagnosing tools in the healthcare sector. Moreover, AI is a portfolio of methods facilitating advances in the precision, speed, or scale of machine performance across complex and large data substituting human performance in diverse specific duties such as decision-making, pattern-recognition, and prediction. Algorithms are being deployed to make or aid decisions in contexts such as criminal justice, child welfare, employment, healthcare, and credit, raising worries about their prospective flaws and unintended outcomes.[1] It could be said that AI systems must lead to efficiency improvement and opacity could provide certain benefits. AI applications in fact play an increasingly important role in organizing society at large, in the regulation of a wide variety of social systems and infrastructures and even in shaping human interactions and preferences. Thus, Algorithmic applications affect how opportunities and possibilities open up for, and are accessed by, individuals and entire groups of populations, or by contrast, how they close up. While AI offers society at large with a broader and more equal access to a wide range of goods and services, voices have developed that also point at unparalleled risks of discrimination. AI can violate the principle of equal access permitting governments to identify and repress cultural groups and so there is a risk that AI could be used to "criminalize" certain cultures.

[1] Alexandra Chouldechova et al., A Case Study of Algorithm-Assisted Decision Making in Child Maltreatment Hotline Screening Decisions, PROC. OF THE 2018 Conf. On Fairness, Accountability, And Transparency (2018) (discussing an algorithmic system deployed to evaluate child abuse and neglect risk in Allegheny County). Mikella Hurley & Julius Adebayo, Credit Scoring in the Era of Big Data, 18 YALE J. L. & TECH. 148 (2017).

G. I. Zekos, *Political, Economic and Legal Effects of Artificial Intelligence*, Contributions to Political Science, https://doi.org/10.1007/978-3-030-94736-1_2

It is worth noting that the impact of AI is not restrained to the substitution of jobs; rather, AI complements and backs human skills and so human analysts who use an AI-based program make more precise stock price forecasts for financial investments than those who do not.[2] Moreover, human workers boost their productivity and performance when they make use of AI technology directly at work. Can AI advance human abilities in making decisions? Taking into account that the utilization of large-scale analytics has supported managerial decision-making, data analytics, and overall, the adoption of new technologies plays an imperative role in decision-making at both organizational and individual levels.[3] The progress in AI with the advancement of machine learning and deep-learning algorithms promotes the avoidance of mistakes and errors stemming from human judgments. AI algorithms improve performance, through self-learning, and, so due to AI's ability to discover hidden patterns. Algorithms improve over time to achieve a superior performance. To that extent, firms use AI algorithms for tasks needing accurate judgment, improving the allocation of valuable resources, designating work schedules, and analyzing employee performance such as in the case of new drug development dependent on automatic data processing and pattern-recognition. In other words, AI assists the process of human decision-making by assessing a wider range of options at a lower cost and by accomplishing a more accurate evaluation of the options available. Choia et al.[4] argue "that AI algorithms improve the move quality of professional players (i.e., players are able to reduce the quality gap between their moves and those of AI) by decreasing the number of errors and the magnitude of the critical mistake. The effect is more prominent for the early stages of the game where higher uncertainty is exhibited and players have had more training opportunity with AI. Young players benefited more from AI than old players, suggesting a potential inequality in AI utilization by age and generation." Hence, it could be said that openness to new technology and the capability to utilize contribute to reaping gains from AI.

It has to be taken into account that when AI is used to replace either managerial or employee functions that encompass adjudication, assessment, or nuanced decision-making, the probability of negative, unplanned consequences enhances. To that extent, AI running virtual meetings, judging employee emotions and responses via facial recognition software and offering both immediate feedback and a full record to review has multiple prospective downsides embracing stressful monitoring, misplaced dependence on "neutral" technology that is actually functioning under hidden biases by generating problematic data relying upon for future adverse

---

[2] Cao S, Jiang W, Wang J, Yang B (2021) From Man vs. Machine to Man + Machine: The Art and AI of Stock Analyses (Cambridge, MA).

[3] Wu L, Hitt L, Lou B (2020) Data Analytics, Innovation, and Firm Productivity. Manage. Sci. 66 (5):2017–2039.

[4] Sukwoong Choia, Namil Kimb, Junsik Kimc & Hyo Kang, How Does AI Improve Human Decision-Making? Evidence from the AI-Powered Go Program at: https://ssrn.com/abstract=3893835 P19.

employment decisions.[5] Correspondingly, the use of AI to monitor, detect, and report prospective harassment moves the technology from constructive to dangerous and so continual monitoring generates unique liability matters for employers, and automatic reporting substitutes all-important human discretion and the human reporter on which harassment, discrimination, and retaliation doctrine rely.

There is a problem of algorithmic discrimination concerning face recognition applications; predictive policing algorithms prove to be racist; and Tay.AI, a chatbot launched by Microsoft in 2016 had to be turned down after 24 h for the reason that it had turned into a racist and sexist online hate speech machine. Moreover, automated operations empowered by algorithms risk perpetuating, and thereby solidifying, a status quo that is deeply discriminatory which means that the results on citizens' daily life are tangible, compromising the exercise of their fundamental rights along with reinforcing social hierarchies and material inequalities. The role of AI in facilitating discrimination is well documented plus there is concern about nearly every internationally recognized human right and so it is released "The Toronto Declaration.[6]"

AI tools, embracing machine learning, deep learning, and predictive analysis intended toward increasing the planning, learning, reasoning, thinking, and action taking capacity. It has to be taken into account that building of various AI systems aids the ability to reason and also knowledge existence which means that at the time AI acquires intelligence greater or equal to that of human beings, there will be a concern about social and political transformation. The use of AI to govern numerous aspects of human activities has been generated concerns linked to matters of privacy and surveillance, bias and inequality, transparency and procedure, and freedom and autonomy. Privacy is a fundamental right that is indispensable to human dignity reinforcing other rights, such as the rights to freedom of expression and association.

The increased speed of information technology is an indispensable part of the AI systems that are at the vanguard of what has been called a fourth industrial revolution. Yet there are indications that the rate of increase is slowing, ever more efficient machines mean that the marginal costs of data storage and computing power are trending toward zero and so the rising involvedness of those systems means that, even though general AI remains science fiction for the time being, existing applications of narrow AI have already moved considerably beyond human cognitive capacities. In other words, the effacement of distance by the speed with which data flow around the globe is noticeable of the character of the new technological

---

[5] Arielle Pardes, AI Can Run Your Meetings Now, WIRED (Nov. 24, 2020), https://www.wired.com/story/aican-run-work-meetings-now-headroom-clockwise/ ("Headroom's software uses emotion recognition to take the temperature of the room periodically, and to gauge how much attention participants are paying to whoever's speaking. Those metrics are displayed in a window on-screen, designed mostly to give the speaker real-time feedback that can sometimes disappear in the virtual context.").

[6] The Toronto Declaration: Protecting the right to equality and non-discrimination in machine learning systems, https://www.accessnow.org/cms/assets/uploads/2018/05/Toronto-Declaration-D0V2.pdf

revolution leading to a virtual world. Cyberlaw is now sub-disciplining in its own right, introducing multifaceted jurisdictional and practical issues in regulating online behavior.[7] It seems that algorithms executing trades are subject to the same regulations as the human brokers that set them in motion and so the possibility of disruption or manipulation owing to the speed at which those algorithms run has led bourses to explore ways of slowing them down. Moreover, computer-based trading has altered not only the culture but also the very nature of the market.

The globalization of information has put more knowledge in the hands of more people than at any time in human history; in many repressive regimes, cyberspace has played a liberating role owing to the difficulty of containing information. As AI systems play a greater role in generating content, efforts at containment via data localization, filtering, or otherwise slowing the flow of information will run the risk of destabilizing the foundations of the digital economy and are at best expected to be a short-term fix for a fast-moving problem. It has to be taken into account that AI explainability, systemic risk, AI biases, and algorithmic collusion have been acknowledged as well-known sources of risk in finance.

A Robotic Process Automation (RPA[8]) enabled by AI has become an essential field within the digitalization of the economy. AI-enabled RPA replaces the work a human would normally do by mimicking interactions with applications. Moreover, RPA enables algorithmic rules without being biased and central rational AI-hubs will outperform underdeveloped remote areas of the world even more in the digital age.[9] Dirk Beerbaum[10] argues that "while in the AI-hubs human will be incentivized to become more creative and humane while AI performs all rational tasks to a maximum productivity, other parts of the world will naturally fall back as for being stuck in spending human capital time on machine-outsourceable tasks and not honing humane skills, which are not replicable by machines." Automation by nature is designed to replace humans causing the replacement of workers with machines.[11] On the other hand, it cannot be supported the view of disallowing automation in order to keep people at work on any cost and so firms switch to

[7] G Zekos, Cyber Versus Conventional Personal Jurisdiction, 2015 Journal of Internet Law, Volume 18 Number 10, April 2015 3–35 Wolters Kluwer. www.wrightsmedia.com https://lrus.wolterskluwer.com/store/product/journal-of-internet-law/ G Zekos, Demolishing State's sole power over Sovereignty & Territory via Electronic Technology & Cyberspace, 2013 Journal of Internet Law, Volume 17 Number 5 November 2013 27–41 Aspen Publications-Wolters Kluwer.

[8] Robotic Process Automation (RPA) is defined as "tools [which] perform statements on structured data, typically using a combination of user interface interactions, or by connecting to APIs to drive client servers, mainframes or HTML code."

[9] Tzafestas, S. 2018. Ethics in robotics and automation: A general view. International Robotics & Automation Journal, 4, 229–234. Van Der Aalst, W. M., Bichler, M. & Heinzl, A. 2018. Robotic process automation. Springer.

[10] Dirk Beerbaum, Artificial Intelligence Ethics Taxonomy—Robotic Process Automation (RPA) as business case, https://ssrn.com/abstract=3834361 p17.

[11] Jeffrey Hirsch, Worker-Protection Laws Aren't Ready for An Automated Future, Conversation (Aug. 28, 2019).

automation due to its higher effectiveness and lower costs.[12] Taking into account the influence of globalization and the globalized supply chain, a firm cannot compete in the global arena without relying on automation to cut costs and advance efficiency and quality. Moreover, innovation generates new types of jobs[13] and so innovation and automation are needed to winning in competitive environments.

While AI is a very broad field, it can be roughly defined as encompassing a set of technologies doings the types of things that human minds can perform and so machines rely on sets of rules called algorithms. Algorithms are mathematical instructions that aim to solve problems, answer questions or perform specific tasks and so for the reason that machine learning has the capacity to learn and discover correlations in any given dataset; the risk of discrimination is greater. Even when not ordered to discriminate, machine learning algorithms have been found producing discriminatory results. Further just automation of discrimination, machine learning techniques cause the extra risk of reproducing existing models of inequality in manners unintended by their designers.

The challenge with machine learning is that algorithms are not only at risk of conveying human biases in their operation, they are also a channel for reproducing inequality models that are structurally embedded in the data they process. Moreover, algorithmic decision-making is the new "regulatory frontier" inter alia for non-discrimination law and equality protection.

It has to be taken into account that any regulation should be domain-specific due to the fact that the precise risks posed by algorithmic devices and their social effects differ depending upon whether they are used to allocate housing, employment, credit, or policing efforts. It is worth noting that blanket rules that regulate AI generically will either be too blunt to be operative or so precise that they might generate unintended harmful aftereffects in certain situations. Current laws offer protection against forms of bias but they were advanced to address a particular set of problems[14] and in many ways are not well suited to tackle the challenges posed by biased algorithms. Do anti-discrimination laws, such as Title VII of the Civil Rights Act apply to algorithmic decision-making? It is argued that with judicial adaptations anti-discrimination law can tackle algorithmic decision-making.[15] Existing anti-discrimination law undoubtedly applies to some discriminatory uses of AI. Besides, if an employer deliberately builds an AI tool with the intent of excluding a specific demographic group, it would run afoul of Title VII of the

[12] Hannah Sloan, Human Rights and IoT: The Right to Fair and Decent Work, IOT FOR ALL (Oct. 23, 2018) ("[T]he efficiencies produced by automation will result in widespread job loss. It's entirely possible that the continued growth of constantly-improving and self-maintaining machines could eliminate 99% of all jobs today.").

[13] Peter Dizikez, MIT Report Examines How to Make Technology Work for Society, MIT: NEWS (Sept. 4, 2019).

[14] United States v. Virginia, 518 U.S. 515 (1996); Washington v. Davis, 426 U.S. 229 (1976).

[15] James Grimmelmann & Daniel Westreich, Incomprehensible Discrimination, 7 Calif. L. Rev. Online. 164, 170 (2017).

Civil Rights Act of 1964.[16] The Fair Credit Reporting Act ("FCRA") contains due process-like and explanatory conditions for credit reporting agencies that apply to the use of algorithmic decision-making.[17]

On the other hand, the development of AAI systems functional in AAI society will impose rules functional in an adequate degree where general AAI law principles will be elaborated in particular aspects of life such as AAI family law, AAI criminal Law, etc. Thus, the governance bodies of AAI society will generate and endorse the rightful AAI laws and of course the way of avoiding the emergence of AAI discrimination cases.

Does AI disrupt the legal services market? Artificial legal intelligence has been seen as a disruption of the legal services market and so governments are trying to enact a regulatory system that stays ahead of the numerous legal constructions created by corporate law businesses to circumvent taxation and other costly compliance matters. Consequently, AI technology raises questions of power[18] and control across society altering almost every domain of human activity because society transitions into a "digital lifeworld[19]" across all spheres of human life such as legal decision-making, policing, health care, military uses, etc.

Taking into account that new technologies have a long history of challenging existing law, AI is triggering major shifts across the legal and regulatory landscape. The force of law is based on the interconnecting of performative speech acts (legislation and judgments) and the monopoly of violence that appears in the background to make certain that legal effect will be imposed. If law were only dependent on enforcement, it would not be law but administration, discipline, or merely a matter of violence. Noticeably, law is in part instituted by violence.[20] It could be argued that as law advances, the AI software should advance which means that fundamental legal principles are taken into account; or else "self-driving law" may decide on short-cuts that it is appreciated in self-driving cars but not in the decision-making infrastructure of human society.

Can AI software be free from biases? Since AI software is produced by humans then bias cannot be avoided in a way because in case of judgment tasks the preference of the programmers will be expressed by the software except in case of mechanical calculations or merely technical solutions. In other words, the

---

[16] Teamsters v. United States, 431 U.S. 324 (1977).

[17] Danielle Keats Citron & Frank Pasquale, The Scored Society: Due Process for Automated Predictions, 89 Wash. L. Rev. 1, 16–18 (2014) Andrew D. Selbst & Solon Barocas, The Intuitive Appeal of Explainable Machines, 87 Fordham L. Rev. 1085, 1100–05 (2018).

[18] Harry Surden, "The Ethics of Artificial Intelligence in Law: Basic Questions" in M Dubber and F Pasquale (eds), The Oxford Handbook of AI Ethics (Oxford University Press 2019).

[19] Hin-Yan Liu, "The Power Structure of Artificial Intelligence" (2018) 10 Law, Innovation and Technology 197. Jamie Susskind, Future Politics: Living Together in a World Transformed by Tech (Oxford University Press 2018).

[20] Robert Cover et al. Narrative, Violence, and the Law, The Essays of Robert Cover (Michigan: University of Michigan Press, 1995). Jacques Derrida, 'Force of Law: The "Mystical Foundation of Authority"', Cardozo Law Review 11 (1990): 920–1045.

computerization of cognitive tasks is aided by the advantage of algorithms chatacterized by the absence of some human biases which means that many roles implicating decision-making will benefit from impartial algorithmic solutions and so occupations that entail "subtle judgement" are inclined to computerization owing to the unbiased decision-making of an algorithm representing a comparative advantage over human operators. It could be said that along with providing algorithmic recommendations to human operators, algorithms will themselves be responsible for appropriate decision-making.

Taking into account that legal effect is caused by legal norms deriving from the sources of law, such as legislation, binding international treaties and case law, legally applicable custom and fundamental legal principles are assisting the interpretation of the legally binding texts of legislation, treaties, and case law which means that both types of sources of law interact with and inform each other. The sources of law do not simply contain information about the law but found the law as such. Nonetheless, legal knowledge is information about the legal outcome of one's actions and so in order to understand legal effect attention must be paid to how law informs the consequences of actions. Hence, Advanced Artificial Intelligence (AAI) systems deployed by law science must have the capacity of taking into consideration the interaction of all the sources of law for legal certainty, predictability, and openness in order to present their AI judgements. In other words, artificial legal intelligence has to empower prediction of the relevant legal outcome, based on analysis not only of relevant case law but also the interaction of all the sources of law by machine learning algorithms optimizing the mathematical relationship between input of legal sources and output being the AI judgements.

It must be noted that the machines are simply simulating mathematically what human reasoning has come up with in written legal text. Moreover, it has to be taken into account that computer systems are now capable of reconfigurations, but they have no self-conscious awareness, they cannot undergo pain or humiliation even where they excel at simulating such emotions stipulating the character of AAI systems.

It is characteristic that advanced computing schemes perform certain functions, based on computation and their decisions have a normative consequence in the meaning that they will stimulate, enforce, inhibit, or rule out some of actions. On the other hand, the central matter will be how to distinguish their normative force from the force of law and so not confusing the performativity of positive law with the performance of artificial legal intelligence.[21]

It has to be taken into consideration that ML replicates parts of legal decision-making with various "Legal Tech" applications being used to model litigation risk, and data analytics informing decisions on issues with relevance to law encompassing probation, predictive policing, and credit evaluation. The next step is the use of AAI

[21] M Hildebrandt, "The Force of Law and the Force of Technology," in The Routledge International Handbook of Technology, Crime and Justice, ed. M.R.P. McGuire and Holt (Routledge, 2017), 579–608.

systems to replicate all functions of legal systems, including adjudication. On the one hand, many aspects of legal reasoning have algorithmic features which could lend themselves to automation. On the other hand, there are elements of legal reasoning which are not consistent with present AI systems or even near future imaginable AAI systems such as the reflexivity of legal knowledge and the incompleteness of legal rules coming across the "chaotic" and unstructured data produced by other social subsystems.[22] Furthermore, rules have to be crafted to guarantee the data can be trusted in fact as an authentic, complete, and immutable record to be ingested into the algorithms.

It is worth noting that the opacity of ML functions at different viewpoints and so the opacity is founded on deliberate hiding of the source code and the relevant training and test data, being portion of the trade secret or IP rights of a law corporation or the tech corporation that formed the software raising problems with the contestability of the output of the software, making difficult or even impracticable to test its reliability and to explore the assumptions that inform the improvement of the algorithms. Furthermore, software verification is a sub-discipline of computing science, engaging in mathematical and empirical verification by authenticating mathematical proof of the system by verifying for prospective over fitting or overgeneralization, determining the weight of the optimization in view of the data used and the given reason. It has to be taken into consideration that software will be developed by big tech companies such as IBM and there is no interest in or experience with matters of Rule of Law. Software's opacity characterized by the event that neither domain experts in law nor those subject to law have acquired any skills to inspect these systems.[23]

On the other hand, if the software and/or the training data are behind trade secret of IP rights, it will not be easy to accomplish such empirical testing as too much information may be lacking. Hence, there is a need for a legal obligation to work with open-source software offering access to particular regulators qualified for testing and contesting the software along with the training and test data.

The deployment of an ML system (Zeb) that is capable of "reading" radiological images has to be checked and recognized by doctors when the automation goes "awry," misrepresents relevant cases, or misinterprets relevant causation. Moreover, the risk of automating incorrect, imprecise, or debatable judgment is not restricted to medical diagnosis but also to the algorithms of artificial legal intelligence, where interpretation and consequent qualification outline and decide the legal outcome/

[22] Christopher Markou and Simon Deakin, Ex Machina Lex: The Limits of Legal Computability at: https://ssrn.com/abstract=3407856

[23] "Legal Tech Market Map: 50 Startups Disrupting The Legal Industry," CB Insights - Blog, 13 July 2016, https://www.cbinsights.com/blog/legal-tech-market-map-company-list/. A. Ramanathan et al., "Integrating Symbolic and Statistical Methods for Testing Intelligent Systems: Applications to Machine Learning and Computer Vision," in 2016 Design, Automation Test in Europe Conference Exhibition (DATE), 2016, 786–91.

consequence of human intercourse.[24] It could be said that in some parts of medicine AI might be able to read more accurately radiology but the problems come out when the next step has to be decided based on other features of the patient as well and not only the pre-programmed data of the current AI systems which means that an AAI system calculates data and makes decisions as an artificial doctor then machines and humans will function equally concerning the capacity for decision-making.

It has to be taken into account that lawyers and judges have mental and moral capacities that so far exceed those of machines due to the fact that human comparative advantages lie in the carefulness of reasoning and capability to reach sound conclusions with imperfect information.[25] It seems that the reality of legal reasoning is far too complex to be described and systematically represented by an algorithm and under the present technical capacities there is only one kind of intelligence, and that is human.

It is worth mentioning here that the complexity and bespoke character of law confronted the programming paradigm while application was impeded by an absence of digital platforms and financial investment.[26] Will legal singularity arrive? It is argued that the legal singularity will arrive when the accumulation of immensely more data and vividly upgraded methods of inference make legal uncertainty obsolete.[27] Can "legal singularity" incorporate political processes and social discourse? It could be said that it is a matter of politics the advancement of an AAI systems implementing "legal singularity." Taking into account that legal singularity anticipates complete law, legal singularity is founded on technological singularity denoting the point when machines themselves become capable of building ever more capable and powerful machines which means an intelligence upsurge surpassing human understanding or ability to control.[28] Consequently, legal singularity anticipates the abolition of legal uncertainty and the materialization of an all-in-one legal order, entirely accessible in real-time. Additionally, a technological singularity is not an indispensable condition for the legal singularity but the super detailed division of the law according to all possible applications to all possible areas into electronic bits might allow a powerful machine to make decisions in a form of statistical analysis. Yet machines are not as intellectually versatile as humans but AI systems are more

---

[24] Federico Cabitza, "The Unintended Consequences of Chasing Electric Zebras" (IEEE SMC Interdisciplinary Workshop HUML 2016, The Human Use of Machine Learning, 12/16/ 2016, Venice, Italy, 2016), https://www.researchgate.net/publication/311702431_The_Unintended_Consequences_of_Chasing_Electric_Zebras

[25] B.C. Brosnahan, "The Law and Computers" (1970) 1 (3) Auckland U. L. Rev. 1 at 2: "no matter how many contingencies the program may be designed to cope with, a computer can never outdo humans and perform activities that cannot be analysed into logical patterns." JC Smith, "Machine Intelligence and Legal Reasoning" (1998) 73 ChicagoKent Law Review 277.

[26] Bob Ambrogi, The 20 Most Important Legal Technology Developments of 2018, LAWSITES (Dec. 26, 2018).

[27] Alarie, Benjamin, The Path of the Law: Toward Legal Singularity (May 27, 2016). https://doi.org/10.2139/ssrn.2767835

[28] Nick Bostrom, Superintelligence: Paths, Dangers, Strategies (Oxford University Press, 2014).

reliable concerning their short- and long-term memories, along with their capacity to achieve series of logical operations.

It has to be taken into account that the advantages of human judges over machine judges is that human judges can count on less quantifiable data, such as the nuances of a defendant's circumstances or prior convictions. Human judges or arbitrators have the human sense of giving changes to people for a better future, whereas AI judges will look mechanical the relation and outcome of data as a statistical outcome and nothing else.

Can artificial intelligence automate public decision-making? Taking into account the rise of machine learning and computational text analysis accompanied by the proliferation of digital platforms has raised the expectation of "robo-judging" and "robo-administrators." It could be said that to a certain degree it will be achieved an improvement of legal services and making decision-making more predictable and efficient but it cannot be avoided the emergence of new types of social control, arbitrariness, and inequality.[29]

Judicial decision-making and dispute resolution in any discipline of law require substantial creativity. Moreover, equally fundamental is that listening machines not only improvise, but do so creatively, that is, with the capacity to advance adapted solutions to individual discipline of law problems. Looking to computational creativity, there is evidence that machines can create artistic outputs and so a neural network can create art in the style of Picasso.[30] Nonetheless, still unsettled is whether the practice of machine creation is itself creative, or whether algorithms as artistic agents have anything to tender us concerning the character of human art and creativity, or the linkage between technology and art being noteworthy concerns.[31] It could be argued that digital justice of all law disciplines entails one more thing: algorithmic software that echoes the emotional state of the humans which means that "emotional transduction," is centered on machine–human interactivity. Thus, machines have to be creative improvisers. It has to be taken into account that while AI challenges concerns about justice, the full blossom of the digital era permits codified law to govern humankind across a global and interconnected network of machines running AI systems. While adaptation of the rule of law has always followed behind technology innovations, the AAI rule of law will exist when those AAI humanoid robots become real and so humankind have to realize that survival requires shifts in how human affairs will be conducted in the AAI era.

---

[29] Richard Susskind, Tomorrow's Lawyers: An Introduction to Your Future (2d ed. 2017). Frank Pasquale, A Rule of Persons, Not Machines: The Limits of Legal Automation, 87 Geo. Wash. L. Rev. (2019).

[30] Michael Culpan, "This Algorithm Can Create an Imitation Van Gogh in 60 Minutes," Wired, September 1, 2015, https://www.wired.co.uk/article/art-algorithm-recreates-paintings

[31] Mark Coeckelbergh, "Can Machines Create Art?," Philosophy & Technology 30 (2017): 285–6. George E. Lewis, "From Network Band to Ubiquitous Computing: Rich Gold and the Social Aesthetics of Interactivity," in Improvisation and Social Aesthetics eds. Georgina Born, Eric Lewis and Will Straw (Durham and London: Duke University Press, 2017).

It could be said that, in the AAI era, the inefficient territorial systems of nation-states and sub-states will disappear and be replaced by a few globally interconnected AAI digital systems through which humankind affairs will be governed in tandem with AAI entities affairs.

It has to be taken into account that irrespective of whether the ODR platform is private, public, or non-profit, justice in the law realm is not just about accessibility, or saving time, money, and stress. For instance, family or medical justice need deep and attentive listening to the singularity and unique conditions of a family conflict or medical malpractice and finding creative solutions to these disputes. Furthermore, it has to be taken into consideration the improvisational character of justice as a compromise between the singularity of a specific case and the pre-existing rules or laws to which it has to obey or follow. Of course, it is required to construct interactive computer-driven systems intended at assisting law litigants with ODR processes contributing at fair justice itself.

The question to be answered is what do humans get by generating improvising machines, or what does technology offer improvising musicians, for instance, which would tempt them to interact with computers? It has to be taken into account that even the most skilled improvisers experience specific limitations on their capacity to process information with the speed entailed for skillful improvisation. It is obvious that there is anxiety for many professions such as lawyers, judges, and musicians that they will be replaced by machines or robots.[32]

Are there machines improvising? It could be said that the conception of machines improvising sounds strange and the current AI systems cannot achieve it. Can machine behavior be the exact opposite of improvisation? First of all, the plain application of rules will not assure an effective improvisation be it in a human or in an automated actor.[33] Accordingly, improvisation in both humans and machines necessitates instantaneous structure and a certain degree of autonomy such that one is able to not only applies the "rules" for improvisation, but also enable non-deterministic decision-making.[34] On the other hand, the techno-human creative process is very much dependent on listening and listening is by its quality an improvisational act such as expression of agency, judgment, and choice operated in a condition of indeterminacy.[35]

It has to be taken into consideration that the creative machine is not only able to analyze a human improvisor's performance in real-time and respond to it, but also

[32] Dana Remus and Frank Levy, "Can Robots Be Lawyers? Computers, Lawyers, and the Practice of Law," The Georgetown Journal of Legal Ethics 30 (2017): 501–58.

[33] Gunter Lösel, "Can Robots Improvise?," Liminalities: A Journal of Performance Studies 14, no. 1 (2018).

[34] Roger Dean, Hyperimprovisation: Computer-Interactive Sound Improvisation (Wisconsin: A-R Editions, Inc., 2003), xiii.

[35] George E. Lewis, "(Machine) Listening as Improvisation," Technosphere Magazine, December 23, 2018), https://www.technosphere-magazine.hkw.de/p/5-Rainbow-Family-5Aj9nAxzG6zFRAAd9icEvH. George E. Lewis, "Listening for Freedom with Arnold Davidson," Critical Inquiry 45, no. 2 (Winter 2019): 434.

offer its own musical contribution in line with the program's internal processes. Thus, creative machines must function in a way utilizing vital parts of improvisation, both within and outside music, such as staking out territory, evaluating and responding to circumstances, and affirming identities and positions. Besides, it has to be taken into account that the music data are certain involving only mechanical combination but other disciplines are more complex for improvisation. Also, machines will deliver artificial meaning, not just like groups of people do but as a perfect statistics system generates its outcome based on the provided data presently or the data that system itself will collect.

Additionally, it has to be taken into account that the move from reason to statistics and from argumentation to simulation is the matter for those subject to law and should raise awareness with legal practitioners and scholars. Thus, an AAI quantified legal prediction (QLP) can simulate legal decision-making by processing data based on mathematical functions that optimize the mathematical link between data points in legal text, data points concerning specific judges and courts, or administrators and data points that denote other legal text such as a variable that depicts whether an injunction is offered, a violation confirmed, or compensation determined. It is worth noting that AAI QLP does not dispute as lawyers do, it computes and processes elements of their usage of natural language which means that it delivers feedback on theoretically relevant patterns. Moreover, it feeds on legal argumentation and decision-making and does not insert its own arguments, other than the numerical rearticulating and mathematical functions that link the dots. Likewise, in order to "read" the relevant statistics there is a need of breaking the spell and develop the adversarial skills of "speaking" statistics considering that the different statistics produce different outcomes and so turning into a data-driven Internet of Things.[36]

While progresses in machine learning allow automated legal research in some fields, the drafting of text for new contracts, and the identification of documents for discovery requests, automation is central in legal technology dialogue and so governments, international organizations, and judicial bodies are shifting from simple digitization to efforts for automation utilizing AAI systems pilot's data-driven systems to predict judicial and administrative decision-making.

Taking into account that current legal practice entails occasionally infringements of human rights and other sorts of legal protection, legal intelligence has to be planned to visualize invisible discrimination, unsubstantiated conclusions, missing facts, hidden arguments, or arbitrary decision-making.[37] Also, the outsourcing of legal intelligence to machines induces the problem of how to assess if and how these machines are actually "getting it right" and so while smart machines get better in

[36]Daniel Martin Katz, "The MIT School of Law? A Perspective on Legal Education in the 21st Century," University of Illinois Law Review, no. 5 (2014). On the lack of methodological integrity of the use of statistics in social science e.g. https://errorstatistics.com/2016/11/08/gigerenzer-at-the-psa-how-fisherneyman-pearson-bayes-were-transformed-into-the-null-ritual-comments-and-queries-i/, adversarial statistics: https://jasp-stats.org

[37]Jason Koebler, "Rise of the Robolawyers," The Atlantic, April 2017, https://www.theatlantic.com/magazine/archive/2017/04/rise-of-the-robolawyers/517794/

simulating the skills of their human trainers, legal experts must keep the training upon software programs. Likewise, while AAI systems function as perfect simulators, it is doubtful if they will ever get down to the "real thing" due to the fact that they lack consciousness and self-consciousness in order to engender both meaning and legal effect.[38] On the other hand, the AAI mechanical law will have results upon AI activities and so fulfilling the legal function regardless of logic, reasonableness, and conventional legal thinking. Alston reported a range of concerns with the rise of automated eligibility assessments, calculation of benefits, fraud detection, and risk scoring.[39]

Who is responsible when AI makes decisions? The employment of AI and AAI technology has to be followed by the resolution of the problem of accountability which means that AAI humanoid robots should be recognized as legal persons with rights and obligations and so held accountable for their actions. In other words, AAI humanoid robots will be accountable to their AAI governance undergoing the consequences of all their rightful or illegal actions.

2.2 Transforming Governance

Around the globe, public and private leaders are seeking new ways to advance governance, solve public problems, and better represent their constituents but in high-income economies, people feel disconnected with the institutions claiming to represent them and so public trust in government has dropped.[40] To that extent, AI which offers unprecedented abilities to quickly process vast quantities of data to deepen insights into public needs poses serious risks. In fact, AI is used to curtail transaction costs generally linked with interactions with public authorities and so machine learning components permit the AI to learn as it engages with more people to enhance response accuracy and timeliness.

It is worth noting that digital technologies are now turning the world upside down and so an ongoing series of technological developments have transformed economic and social life. In fact, the following are consequences of digitization and so there is shrinking of size, increased power, and diverse applications of personal computers, the global reach of communication networks and the new forms of social interaction and economic exchange that these networks have made possible. Moreover, the

[38] Nicholas Carr, The Glass Cage: Automation and Us, 1 edition (New York: W. W. Norton & Company, 2014). John Searle, "Minds, Brains, and Programs," Behavioral and Brain Sciences 3, no. 3 (1980): 517–57.

[39] UN Press Release, World Stumbling Zombie-Like into a Digital Welfare Dystopia, Warns UN Human Rights Expert (Oct. 17, 2019). Report of the Special Rapporteur on Extreme Poverty and Human Rights, UN Doc. A/74/48037, §8 (Oct. 11, 2019).

[40] Bersoff, David M., Sarah Adkins, Cody Armstrong, Joshua Wu, Nick Maxwell, Giuseppe Bovenzi, Abbey Fox, and John Zamites. "2019 Edelman Trust Barometer." Edelman, March 2019. https://www.edelman.com/trust-barometer

availability of cloud databases containing enormous quantities of information that can be processed by software algorithms for use across multiple social and economic settings. In reality, the scale and impact of technological alterations align a "digital transformation" by vanishing industry boundaries are and so new platform firms have appeared which function across multiple industries such as retail, transport, finance, healthcare, food, etc., by exploiting global communication networks to deliver new business models and disrupt incumbents. To that extent, social media authorizes everyone and has transformed the meaning of communication and mass media.[41] In addition, digital technologies have altered consumer behavior and so consumers do not appreciate mass production anymore, and brand loyalty is progressively fragile which means that digital technologies have made consumers way more well-informed and sophisticated. Thus, customers continue to buy if "products" offer them a meaningful and personalized experience. Furthermore, digital technologies are empowering investors in the ecosystems of the future and so AI tools that analyze website traffic and social media engagement tender institutional and other professional investors a better understanding of a firm's growth, opportunities, and prospects.

It is characteristic that recent advances in AI have generated strong reasons for states to develop governance strategies for maximizing the prospective benefits of AI technologies while mitigating their risks.[42] It has to be taken into consideration that the public is concerned about the fitting governance of AI technology and so increasing calls for suitable societal and regulatory responses. There are questions of how to regulate AI and algorithms at the national level and so firstly concentrating on the regulation of robotics, later shifting to use cases such as self-driving cars, increasingly focusing on the problems of algorithmic decision-making more broadly and growing national regulatory initiatives focused on the regulation of various use cases and applications of AI in domestic jurisdictions.[43]

AI has been described as capable of undermining traditional economic governance, management, and growth models and so AI is the central engine of a fourth industrial revolution altering the way people live on Earth and so having a substantial influence on individuals and organizations of all sorts and the society as a whole. To that extent, interconnected organizations will rely on decision-making based on the analysis and exploitation of big data; firms, engaged in increasingly fierce competition, will be able to access capital and other resources at a far cheaper price; and people will buy goods and get services from anywhere in the globe by speaking with non-human service agents.

---

[41] Kevin Kelly Alec Ross, Understanding the 12 Technological Forces that Will Shape Our Future (Penguin 2017).

[42] https://www.oecd.ai/dashboards

[43] Regulation Of Artificial Intelligence In Selected Jurisdictions, 138 (2019), https://www.loc.gov/law/help/artificial-intelligence/regulation-artificial-intelligence.pdf

2.3 Digital Governance and Digital Platforms

There is a growing global concern over AI development rising tensions not just around digital governance, but around the architecture of global cooperation more broadly.[44]

It has to be taken into consideration that in the perspective of a movement toward a more digitalized platformized and decentralized economy, a new role is assigned with such technology to the numerous kinds of corporate stakeholders by the creation of stakeholders' committees in corporations.[45] Dondero[46] argues that the existing company law "organizes the relationships between partners/shareholders, between them and the directors and the other corporate bodies, and to some extent, it apprehends the situation of employees and of the CSR."

Digital platforms are both a tool and a player via digital platform firms and are found of the shared concerns around AI, from data rights to algorithmic transparency and so governance of AI is interrelated to governance of platforms. Furthermore, digital technology platforms have become fundamental access points to decisive activities from investing to communicating and so their private decisions become default regulation, affecting practices about ownership, representation, and values across the private, public, and civil sectors.[47]

Will the investor involvement and free-rider problems be considerably different than in a firm governed by existing corporate governance rules based on the agent–principal and cost agency problematics? It is worth mentioning here that distributed governance is founded on "flat-hierarchy" philosophy and on the view that token holders will devote enough time to participate and vote in line with the interests of the corporation.[48]

The question to be answered is what powers will be assigned to these new kinds of company stakeholders such as smart contract developers, DLT users, smart contract validators, miners, or curators. Moreover, the role of these various stakeholders needs to be identified and defined by DLT projects and so liability issues concerning the use of DLT and smart contracts for managing corporations are

---

[44] Thorsten Jelinek, Wendell Wallach & Danil Kerimi, Coordinating Committee for the Governance of Artificial Intelligence (2020), https://www.g20-insights.org/policy_briefs/coordinating-committee-for-thegovernance-of-artificial-intelligence/

[45] N. Notat and J.-D. Senard, "L'entreprise, objet d'intérêt collectif – Rapport aux Ministres de la Transition écologique et solidaire, de la Justice, de l'Economie et des Finances, et du Travail", 9 March 2018.

[46] B. Dondero, "La raison d'être des entreprises (rapport Notat-Senard)", 10 March 2018: https://brunodondero.com/2018/03/10/la-raison-detre-des-entreprises-rapport-notat-senard/

[47] Conger, K. (2020). Uber and Lyft Drivers in California Will Remain Contractors. The New York Times. https://www.nytimes.com/2020/11/04/technology/california-uber-lyft-prop-22.html

[48] M. Fenwick and E. Vermeulen, "Technology and Corporate Governance: Blockchain, Crypto and Artificial Intelligence," ECGI Working Paper No. 424/2018, November 2018.

significant.[49] To that extent, national laws and regulations will not be adequate to solve these issues which are by definition transnational and so International laws must be drafted on the matter such as general principles about the contractual nature of transactions on decentralized platforms, regarding the particular instrument schemes for DLT users.[50] Taking into account the digital nature of the developments, there is a need to generate digital jurisdictions whose authority would be subject to an international treaty concluded between sovereign nations and whose governance has to be established by specific matters such as the place of the server, the impact of the transaction, and the damage caused by the electronic actions.

It is worth noting that if the project funders hold a noteworthy share of the tokens issued, they will affect the token holders' vote to get the release of more funds. In addition, investors can also take on a strategy of "free-riding" and so putting all their trust in a digital distribution game platform based on a crypto-reward ecosystem by not participating in votes and resolutions, reducing the majority threshold and weakening the security of the mechanism.[51]

It is obvious that the development of the distributed ledger technology, its usage, their regulation is not enough developed to conclude decisively on all the implications for corporations that the DLT adoption by market participants will involve which means that there is a likelihood that new kinds of corporation stakeholders will appear such as the token holders. Hence, these new players will lead to alterations in the securities' issuance and trading, in the shareholder's involvement, but also to a reinforcement of the rights awarded to the different corporation stakeholders and so a new role will be recognized to corporate stakeholders.[52]

DLTs are already modifying the business setting and the way corporations are directed and controlled and so the blockchain and smart contracts redraw the boundaries between corporations and markets, by depriving a number of

---

[49] M. Field, "Decentralized Governance Matters", Medium, 5 February 2018.D. Zetzsche, R. Buckley and D. Arner, "The Distributed Liability of Distributed Ledgers: Legal Risks of Blockchain," EBI Working Paper Series 2017–007, No. 14, 15 August 2017; P. Paech, "The Governance of Blockchain Financial Networks," LSE Legal Studies Working Paper No. 16/2017, 16 December 2016.

[50] D. Guégan and C. Hénot, "A Probative Value for Authentication Use Case Blockchain," Documents de travail du Centre d'Economie de la Sorbonne, 2018. F. G'Sell, "The challenge of algorithmic governance," Interdisciplinary workshop on blockchains, Ecole Normale Supérieure, 2 July 2018.

[51] C. Perreau, "L'interactive initial offering, l'alternativetransparente à l'ICO", LeJournalDuNet.com, 26 October 2018; W. George, "Kleros' IICO Analysis," 26 July 2018; J. Teutsch, V. Buterin and C. Brown, "Interactive coin offerings," 11 December 2017. J. Halfon, "The DAICO: ICO savior or wolf in sheep's clothing?", Forbes, 24 May 2018. C. Pauw, "What is a DAICO, Explained," CoinTelegraph, 13 February 2018.

[52] D. Yermack, "Corporate Governance and Blockchains," Oxford Review of Finance, Volume 21, March 2017. A. Glidden, "Should Smart Contracts Be Legally Enforceable?", Blockchain at Berkeley, 27 February 2018.

intermediary institutions of their role.[53] For example, Northern Trust has created a blockchain solution with technology giant IBM for all corporate meetings embracing two smart contracts that record meeting attendance by collecting biometric information from the numerous gadgets an attendee carries and collects all pertinent information about the meeting, such as the action points and associated dates. Moreover, the blockchain solution converts all such information into meeting minutes, following a standardized format and a third smart contract forwards the minutes of the meeting and associated documents in a predetermined repository permitting meeting attendance and individual contributions to be promptly stored in a predetermined and well searchable format.[54] Furthermore, Northern Trust has created a blockchain-based digital identity management system that delivers the information to be stored in Northern Trust's meeting software tackling corporate governance matters such as executive compensation. It could be argued that smart contracts could be exploited to make compensation arrangements harder to amend in opportunistic manners further down the road, a phenomenon known as "backdating.[55]"

It is worth noting that higher levels of CEO payment take place when executive compensation consultants "cross-sell" services, but also board payment is higher when consultants work for the board rather than for executives.[56] To that extent, it could be argued that instead of relying on compensation consultants and their own biases, boards could utilize smart contracts to control compensation structures and bonuses.

It has to be taken into account that from a governance perspective, the course toward decentralization does not only influence the existing corporate governance rules, and the relationship of contractual affiliations within a corporation, but also possibly on the definition of a corporation. Thus, the role of the board of directors is

---

[53] Assaf Hamdani, Niron Hashai, Eugene Kandel & Yishay Yafeh, Technological Progress and the Future of the Corporation, 6 J. British Acad. 215, 225 (2018) (arguing that, because DLTs reduce fraud and enhance trust, they have the potential to displace "powerful intermediaries").

[54] Jordan Danielle, Broadridge Patents Blockchain Solution For Proxy Voting And Repurchase Agreements (May 10, 2018), https://www.ethnews.com/broadridge-patentsblockchain-solution-for-proxy-voting-and-repurchase-agreements. Christine Kim, Northern Trust Wins Patent for Storing Meeting Minutes on a Blockchain (Jun. 6, 2018), https://www.coindesk.com/northern-trust-wins-patent-storingmeeting-minutes-blockchain

[55] See David Yermack, Corporate Governance and Blockchains, 21 Rev. Fin. 1, 9 (2017). Jesse M. Fried, Option Backdating and Its Implications, 65 Wash. & Lee L. Rev. 853, 858–864 (2008) (describing three forms of secret option backdating, including the backdating of executives' option grants; the backdating of nonexecutive employees' option grants; and the backdating of executives' option exercises).

[56] Jenny Chu, Jonathan Faasse & P. Raghavendra Rau, Do Compensation Consultants Enable Higher CEO Pay? A Disclosure Rule Change As a Separating Device, 64 MGMT. SC. 2845 (2017) (arguing in favor of a more nuanced view on consultants after concluding that "not all multiservice consultants are conflicted while not all specialist consultants are guardians of shareholder value"). Christopher S. Armstrong, Christopher D. Ittner & David F. Larcker, Corporate Governance, Compensation Consultants, and CEO Pay Levels, 17 REV. ACC'T STUD. 322–351 (2012) Kevin J. Murphy & Tatiana Sandino, Executive Pay and "Independent" Compensation Consultants, 49 J. ACC'T & ECON. 247–262 (2010).

unsettled evolving to a supervision role of automated decisions made by computer technology, and even to its disappearance as there are no managers nor a board of directors in a DAO which means that the likelihood that a firm will be governed by algorithmic code instead of human involvement, the so-called algorithmic governance is forthcoming. Furthermore, the growth of corporate governance is improved by algorithmic code due to the fact that it is supposed that algorithms are more trustworthy than human intervention unless human can program the algorithm in a non-unbiased way. In line, it is possible presently to establish governance rules at least somewhat in computer code, and to delegate the management of a firm to algorithms executing smart contracts and certain predetermined actions. Also, the purpose for giving computers the right to decide is that they are able to make evaluations and calculations that are beyond human capability. Besides, Santiago[57] highlights that humans must have the last say in decisions made by AI and opacity is one of Danaher's[58] central objections to algorithmic governance.

2.4 Antitrust and Digital Platforms

The twenty-First century globalization is distinguished by institutional and political reforms in many countries such as gradual trade liberalization and international coordination of policies. Globalization has created centers of power that are alongside, even in competition, with the power of states.

Competition laws and their enforcement present a probing lens into the essential ideals and norms that characterize a modern society's economic and political systems. National competition law systems fluctuate significantly in the degree of restrictiveness of their norms and, principally, in the strictness with which they are applied and enforced causing ambiguity and so companies looking for "havens" in which competition law systems are weaker, and consequently distorting the competitive process. Courts applying the "Rule of Reason" ask whether a contract "promotes" competition or, instead, "destroys" it, by creating or exercising market power.[59] The spirit of the Harvard school view was that allowing a lot of small companies to exist adds to competition rather than a small number of companies which in fact is right but in reality, bigger companies in some fields can produce superior goods in lower prices taking into account economies of scale. The notion of competition changes according to the global circumstances relating to technology and products demand for concentration of companies or not. In fact, competition means freedom to compete in any market under the same terms which means

[57] T. Santiago, AI Bias: How Does AI Influence The Executive Function Of Business Leaders? January 2019 Muma Business Review 3:181–192.

[58] J. Danaher, The threat of algocracy: reality, resistance and accommodation, Philosophy & Technology 29 (3) (2016) 245–268.

[59] NCAA v. Board of Regents 468 U.S. 85, 109 (1984).

existence of many companies and the existence of the possibility freely everybody to be able to enter the market and compete with the other under the same terms. In reality competition under this notion is the ideal which does not exist and so there is a need for the establishment of the conditions under which companies can enter a market and stand a chance to compete with their rivals in the market under fair conditions. The approach of the Harvard School often invalidated conduct that had the prospective to boost companies' efficiencies and benefit consumers. The Chicago School view considers that monopolists should not be penalized for obtaining their market power owing to a superior product but in cases involving monopolists' duty to deal, tying, and exclusive dealing, the more lenient Chicago School view confuses the standards of conduct for dominant companies. The Harvard School prohibited innovative forms of competition that could have improved economic effectiveness, while the Chicago School permitted competitors to hold in certain conduct that harmed consumers in many domestic markets.

Zekos[60] argues that a modified approach of the Harvard school understanding of competition by identifying specifically particular types of agglomeration, which are proven to be always harmful to competition and so disallowed which means permitting other forms of merging or cooperation which will be helpful both for consumers and competition. The loophole of the economic approach endorsed by Chicago school is the vagueness and complexity of the economic analysis and the uncertainty caused by economic calculations which comprise an econometric model rather than simply specific economic factors indicating always an uncompetitive impact upon the market.[61] In other words, the Chicago school approach by using economics to analyze business conduct was an effort to maximize social welfare.

Antitrust law reaches only those that are in or affect commerce.[62] Antitrust doctrine does not condemn firms merely because they are very large and courts have measured market power "indirectly," inferring from a firm's market share in a "relevant market.[63]" It has to be taken into account that regulatory goals could be determined by telecommunications policy, national security, privacy, political balance, equality, protection of particular interest groups, or other values which means

---

[60] G Zekos, ECONOMICS AND LAW ON COMPETITION IN 21st CENTURY GLOBALIZATION 2014 Nova Science Publications New York USA. www.novapublishers.com G Zekos, Economics and Law on Competition in US and EU 2008 Nova Science Publications New York USA.

[61] Herbert Hovenkamp & Fiona Scott Morton, Framing the Chicago School of Antitrust Analysis, 168 U. PA. L. REV. 1843, 1849–50 (2020) (highlighting how Chicago school's call to use economics in antitrust analysis yielded less enforcement and increased consumer welfare and efficiency).

[62] Herbert Hovenkamp, Platforms and the Rule of Reason: The American Express Case, 2019 Colum. Bus. L. Rev. 35, 47. Phillip E. Areeda & Herbert Hovenkamp, Antitrust Law: An Analysis Of Antitrust Principles And Their Application §§ 260–62 (5th ed. 2020).

[63] FTC v. Qualcomm Inc., 969 F.3d 974, 990 (9th Cir. 2020) (quoting United States v. Microsof Corp., 253 F.3d 34, 58 (D.C. Cir. 2001)); Viamedia, Inc. v. Comcast Corp., 951 F.3d 429, 453 (7th Cir. 2020).

that in case that the goal of regulation is other than keeping competitive levels of output, it will have to be fulfilled by means other than the antitrust laws.

A digital platform is a website, app, or other digital venue interacting commercially with one or more groups of users and in some cases (Amazon, eBay, Uber, and Amex), transactions between these groups are negotiated directly on the website. All transactions in platform markets produce a digital record. Platforms such as Facebook, Google Search, Spotify, and Netflix produce digital content almost exclusively.

The simple fact that business is performed on a digital platform does not make it two-sided because some digital platforms are places for merchants to sell their own merchandise such as in case of Tesla manufacturing its own cars and sells them mainly online through its own digital platform.[64] Moreover, two-sided platforms are those that "facilitate a single, simultaneous transaction between participants.[65]"

It is argued that the market for digital platforms is winner-take all[66] and so natural monopolies need increased antitrust enforcement for the reason that the market itself will not discipline dominant platforms. It is worth noting that only few platforms are natural monopolies. Moreover, regardless of whether the Amazon platform is a natural monopoly, most of the things that it sells are not which means that a well-designed policy will restrain the monopoly characterization to those certain inputs to which it applies, leaving other portions of production to competition. Furthermore, natural-monopoly status is not necessarily everlasting and its duration rests on technology and market size, both of which can alter. In addition, if a platform is not a natural monopoly, competition should be both feasible and needed. Most digital platforms are not structural winner-take-all markets and dominant platforms cannot keep their position merely by setting a price at or a little above the competitive level.

Markets for new technologies go through lengthy periods in which multiple technologies compete with one another until a single winner appears.[67] Moreover, the emergence or maintenance of a single technology winner is based on interoperability or pooling of essential information or data.

The Supreme Court in Amex[68] argues that digital platforms and other markets do not compete with one another. There are exclusivity agreements concerning various

---

[64] Jon Fingas, Tesla May Open 'Centers' to Get Around Pro-Dealership Laws, ENGADGET (Oct. 12, 2019), https://www.engadget.com/2019-10-12-tesla-centers-leak.html

[65] Ohio v. Am. Express Co., 138 S. Ct. 2274, 2286 (2018). Erik Hovenkamp, Platform Antitrust, 44 J. CORP. L. 713, 715, 722–24 (2019).

[66] Daniel A. Hanley, A Topology of Multisided Digital Platforms, 19 CONN. PUB. INT. L.J. 271, 289–91 (2020); Herbert Hovenkamp, The Looming Crisis in Antitrust Economics, 101 B.U. L. REV. 489 (2021).

[67] Jignesh Padhiyar, iPhone vs Android: A Look at Competitive Past and Future, GEEKSBLOG (July 21, 2020), https://www.igeeksblog.com/iphone-vs-android

[68] Ohio v. Am. Express Co., 138 S. Ct. 2274, 2287 (2018) ("Only other two-sided platforms can compete with a two-sided platform for transactions."). Texas v. Google, LLC, No. 4:20cv957 (E.D. Tex. Dec. 16, 2020) (alleging an agreement between Google and Facebook to restrain "header

technologies such as in video games and other platforms inducing single-homing.[69] In digital markets, entry and exit occurs, shares change, and dominance comes and goes which means that while large intellectual property portfolios make entry more difficult, extensive licensing facilitates new entry and so IBM, AT&T, and Xerox all initially gained dominance, based in part on large patent portfolios.

It is worth noting that the capacity of corporations to differentiate their products or services enlightens the dominant platform strategy of buying up nascent digital companies not being merely horizontal but rather falling into the category of "product extension" mergers, which are acquisitions intended to broaden the range of products or services that the acquiring business offers in order either to acquire product differentiation or to cut off efforts by others to develop differentiated alternatives which means that platforms keep their positions by buying up all of the prospective challengers before they mature into more formidable rivals.[70]

It is a common phenomenon nowadays that one of the dominant platforms acquires a young startup before it has a chance to emerge as a viable competitor and so many startup entrepreneurs currently are not inspired nearly as much by the prospect of developing a new business as by the chance to sell out to a major platform at a high price, even if their business will be shut down as a result.[71]

Taking into account that the digital platform is not monolith, platforms differ significantly from one another which mean that antitrust litigation against platforms entails individualized fact finding, an assessment of competitive harms, and relief properly adapted to the circumstances. To that extent, the EU's Android decision specified that upon initial startup of a new device the Android screen lists a number of alternative general search engines, and the customer can select one.[72] Moreover, a platform can itself be a "market" within which competition can take place and so

---

bidding," which was a system intended to make ad pricing more competitive by facilitating bidding among multiple ad exchanges).

[69] United States v. Google LLC, No.1:20-cv-03010 (D.D.C. Oct. 20, 2020).

[70] C. Scott Hemphill & Tim Wu, Nascent Competitors, 168 U. PA. L. REV. 1879 (2020) (discussing the importance of protecting nascent competitors).

[71] Mark A. Lemley & Andrew McCreary, Exit Strategy, 101 B.U. L. REV. 1, 7–8, 55–57, 101 (2021) at 24–55 (documenting venture capital markets' heavy orientation toward new entrants' selloff possibilities); Staff Of H. Subcomm. On Antitrust, Commercial And Administrative Law Of The Comm. On The Judiciary, 116th Cong., Investigation Of Competition In Digital Markets 23 (Comm. Rep. 2020) (canvassing Amazon's major acquisitions); at 25, 150 (noting Facebook's acquisitions of at least 63 companies since 2004); at 175 ("In a span of 20 years, Google purchased well over 260 companies—a figure that likely understates the full breadth of Google's acquisitions, given that many of the firm's purchases have gone unreported.") Kevin A. Bryan & Erik Hovenkamp, Startup Acquisitions, Error Costs, and Antitrust Policy, 87 U. CHI. L. REV. 331, 334–38 (2020).

[72] Case AT.40099, Google Android, C(2018) 4761, §§ 1214, 1401 (July 18, 2018), https://ec.europa.eu/competition/antitrust/cases/dec_docs/40099/40099_9993_3.pdf (pre-installation of competing search engines would have created more competition in search traffic, that Google was willing to pay large sums to be the default search engine on some devices, and that installing a single search engine as a default increased that search engine's traffic by a factor of two to three); Katie Collins, Google Won't Be Default Search Engine for Android Users in EU Next Year, CNET (Aug.

antitrust law can be applied to its internal decisions, advancing competition without limiting the extent of scale economies or beneficial network effects.

For technologies such as search engines pooling as an antitrust remedy place the data into a common database equally accessible by all participating search businesses, subject to user rights to withhold and so advancing search results for everyone improves consumer welfare. The Stigler Center's 2019 Final Report on Digital Platforms examines forced interoperability as a solution to firm-dominance problems in networked markets.[73] In line, interoperability enables the entry and survival of small businesses. Moreover, effective interoperability diminishes the exclusionary outcomes of scale economies or positive network effects increasing the number of competing participants.

Networking unquestionably increases value, but it also increases both the opportunities for anti-competitive behavior and its costs.[74] Regardless that platforms differ from one another by almost as wide a range as companies differ in general, courts and other antitrust policy makers should treat digital platforms as companies that have distinctive features, but not so unique which means that competition is applicable in high-technology platforms as well.[75]

2.5 Digitization, Governance, and the Law

The rise of digital technologies and social media are forcing corporations to reassess existing business models, but also how they organize themselves and structure corporation governance. It could be said that existing regulatory approaches are failing business organizations and many corporate governance rules and regulations are programming institutions to be dysfunctional. Hence, there is an ever-widening gap or disconnect between regulatory strategies and the business wants of corporations operating in fast-moving, technology-driven markets. Accordingly, many businesses and other organizations are ill-equipped to meet the encounters of today's digital world which means that there is a need to design regulations that incentivize corporations to set up the organizational structures and practices that will permit them to thrive. It could be said that new corporate governance concentrated on supporting a company's aptitude to innovate which means promoting compliance

2, 2019, 3:35 AM PT), https://www.cnet.com/news/google-to-prompt-eu-android-users-to-choose-a-search-engine-within-chrome

[73] STIGLER COMM. ON DIGITAL PLATFORMS, FINAL REPORT, CHICAGO BOOTH: STIGLER CTR. FOR THE STUDY OF THE ECON. & THE STATE 16 (2019), https://research.chicagobooth.edu/-/media/research/stigler/pdfs/digital-platforms-committee-report-stigler-center.pdf

[74] Herbert Hovenkamp, FRAND and Antitrust, 105 CORNELL L. REV. 1683, 1703, 1716 (2020).

[75] Erik Hovenkamp & Steven C. Salop, Asymmetric Stakes in Antitrust Litigation 4 (USC CLASS Research Papers Series, No. CLASS20–12, 2020), https://ssrn.com/abstract=3563843

and risk management.[76] Risk management for systematic and discretionary strategies causes different contests. In systematic strategies algorithms make all trading decisions which mean that risk management will influence outcomes by being part of the investment process in AAI environment. Hence, the systematic nature of the investing, risk and portfolio construction methods will be coded and nested in the e-investment process. As a result of the algorithmic nature of the investing, systematic risk management is more quantitative necessitating advanced data analysis. Hence, knowledge of optimization, probability theory, and statistics will be replaced by algorithmic evaluation and monitoring.

Corporate law struggles in adapting general principles to fit the distinct characteristics of startups and courts apply traditional contract parameters to the preferred stock that venture capitalists hold not as public company debt, but rather as a stake in a distinctive system of shared equity and governance.

Due to market capitalization the largest companies such as Apple, Alphabet, Microsoft, Amazon, and Facebook began as venture-backed startups and so they have been grown to momentous size with ownership shared between founders, investors, executives, and employees.[77] Moreover, startups have reached private valuations described as one billion dollars and many of these corporations face critical inflection points in their life cycles.[78] Furthermore, other startups are following on their heels (Airbnb, Uber, Pinterest, Palantir, and SpaceX) and global economy and society are increasingly conquered by firms that start and function with a venture-capital style of ownership and governance.

It is referred that the influx of capital to private firms tripled from $26.5 billion to $75.3 billion of 2013–2015.[79] Moreover, the list of unicorns raised to over three hundred private technology firms.[80] Thus, it seems that the intensity of economic

---

[76] Mark Fenwick and Erik P. M. Vermeulen "The Digital Future of Corporate Governance" International Corporate Governance Network Yearbook 2018, p. 11; Mark Fenwick and Erik P. M. Vermeulen, "Technology & Corporate Governance" 48 (1) The Texas Journal of Business Law, 1 (2019); Mark Fenwick and Erik P. M. Vermeulen, "The Unmediated and Technology-Driven Corporate Governance of Today's Winning Companies" New York University Journal of Law and Business (2020).

[77] Venture Capital Ass'n, 2017 Nat'l Venture Capital Ass'n Y.B. 9 https://nvca.org/blog/nvca-2017-yearbook-go-resource-venture-ecosystem/. Henry Hansmann, The Ownership Of Enterprise 40–44 (1996) (observing the "nearly complete absence of large firms in which ownership is shared among two or more different types of patrons, such as customers and suppliers or investors and workers" and theorizing the high cost of collective decision making that would result from having different types of owners).

[78] Alfred Lee, Delayed IPOs Undercut Startup Employee Options, THE INFORMATION (July 13, 2018), https://www.theinformation.com/articles/delayed-ipos-undercut-startup-employee-options (noting 52 unicorns hit the 10-year mark in 2018 and more will follow in 2019).

[79] Begum Erdogan et al., Grow Fast or Die Slow: Why Unicorns Are Staying Private, MCKINSEY (May 2016), https://www.mckinsey.com/industries/high-tech/our-insights/grow-fast-or-die-slow-why-unicorns-arestaying-private

[80] Aileen Lee, Welcome to the Unicorn Club: Learning from Billion-Dollar Startups, TECHCRUNCH (Nov. 2, 2013), https://techcrunch.com/2013/11/02/welcome -to-theunicorn-

value in private firms poses somewhat of an encounter for corporate governance and so governance becomes more critical[81] which means that the separation of ownership and control in corporations with dispersed share ownership is a central governance matters altering agency costs.[82]

It seems that corporation suffers from a conflict of interest between its managers and dispersed shareholders but the closely-held corporation plagued by inter-shareholder conflict.[83] It is worth noting that enhanced disclosure prerequisites will lessen the risks of unicorns without restraining their innovation but deregulatory reforms have destabilized the principal mechanisms that imposed discipline on startup company founders.[84] It has to be taken into account that syndicated financing of VCs restrains shareholder–manager agency costs giving rise to a new horizontal conflict among preferred shareholders in startups[85] but startups have unique governance qualities and do not present the same agency problems and investment risks as all other corporations.

Shareholders have standardized interests with regard to most corporate decisions by wanting to maximize the net present value of future distributions and so ultimate control over the corporation rests with the shareholders which means that other corporate constituencies, such as creditors, employees, suppliers, and customers, have their interests protected by contractual and regulatory means rather than through participation in corporate governance.

It has to be taken into consideration that participants in startups often fill overlapping and shifting roles and so a venture capital (VC) corporation is a shareholder holding a designated seat on the board which means that participants have a dual status as both principal in one context and agent in another. Moreover, startup shareholders are heterogeneous and so startups typically issue common stock to founders and raise money from investors by issuing rounds of convertible preferred stock with varying terms and layered contractual rights generating noteworthy divergences in preferences among shareholders. Additionally, employees

---

club/; The Global Unicorn Club, CB INSIGHTS, https://www.cbinsights.com/research-unicorn-companies

[81] Robert P. Bartlett & Eric Talley, Law and Corporate Governance, in THE HANDBOOK OF THE ECONOMICS OF CORPORATE GOVERNANCE 8 (Hermalin & Weisbach eds., forthcoming), https://papers.ssrn.com/sol3/papers.cfm?abstract_id=3009451

[82] Zohar Goshen & Richard Squire, Principal Costs: A New Theory for Corporate Law and Governance, 117 COLUM. L. REV. 767, 769 (2017).

[83] Lucian A. Bebchuk & Assaf Hamdani, Independent Directors and Controlling Shareholders, 165 U. PA. L. REV. 1271 (2017).

[84] Jennifer S. Fan, Regulating Unicorns: Disclosure and the New Private Economy, 57 B.C. L. REV. 583, 583 (2016). Renee M. Jones, The Unicorn Governance Trap, 166 U. PA. L. REV. ONLINE 165, 169 (2017).

[85] Robert P. Bartlett, III, Venture Capital, Agency Costs, and the False Dichotomy of the Corporation, 54 UCLA L. REV. 37, 37 (2006).

make crucial investments of human capital and hold common equity or options.[86] To that extent, the interests of founders and executives associate with those of employees, but in some circumstances, they deviate owing to differences in control, impending deal payouts, and post-exit opportunities which means that conflicts rise not only between preferred shareholders, and between preferred and common shareholders, but also between common shareholders. In line, in startups divergence between common shareholders classically takes place between the management and employees and so governance disputes within public firms turn to be "horizontal" disputes between shareholders such as activists versus long-term investors. It is obvious the distinctiveness of startups and governance tensions augment as the startup business progresses and the complexity of its capital structure grows. On the other hand, public firms and other closely-held corporations, which do not present predictable or linear patterns of governance modification, venture-backed startups face increasing prospective conflicts. While startups increase in governance complexity as they continue to operate, startups are often unprofitable for long periods while they develop innovative products or services, they usually raise outside investment and continue to do so to fuel growth which means that each stage of financing allocates investors with different terms and interests into the capital structure, adding to impending governance conflicts. Moreover, employees are hired on an ongoing and increasing basis and so as a startup firm matures, it expands the participants with varied interests and claims influencing its governance organization.

It could be said that corporate law should adapt in its application to startups in recognition of their distinctive features. Corporate law has progressed to cope with the classic shareholder–manager and controlling-minority shareholder conflicts arising in public and traditional closely-held companies. In line, courts have applied these conventional frames of reference in cases involving startups, treating preferred shareholders as creditors with regard to their contractual preferences and portraying common shareholders as the residual claimants of the company. In re Trados,[87] the court overlooks the need of heterogeneous shareholders to resolve complex governance issues by contract and a board with constituency directors that is renegotiated over time and so the court overlooks the differing interests even among common shareholders.

The corporation has to be seen as the beneficiary of the fiduciary duties, representing the firm value and the interests of all startup participants. There is a need of understanding startup governance by acknowledging that despite widespread reference to companies by the name of startup and recognition of their

[86] Abraham J.B. Cable, Fool's Gold, Equity Compensation & The Mature Startup, 11 VA. L. & BUS. REV. 613 (2017). Victor Fleischer, Taxing Founders' Stock, 59 UCLA L. REV. 60 (2011).

[87] In re Trados Inc. S'holder Litig., 73 A.3d 17, 21.

economic importance, the law does not generate such a category and so the law does little to formally define startups or mandate their governance.[88]

It is worth noting that Federal securities law draws a line between "public" and "private" corporations and so a company becomes "public" by making a public offering of securities, listing securities on a national securities exchange, or by reaching a certain asset size and number of shareholders of record which means that once a company is public, it is subject to a number of governance rations stipulated by federal statutes and by the securities exchange on which the company's stock is traded.[89] For instance, a public corporation's board must have a majority of independent directors and must give shareholders a nonbinding "say-on-pay" vote on executive compensation.[90]

It has to be taken into consideration that startups are commenced by entrepreneurs and backed by outside investment with the aim of advancing an innovative product or service, generating high growth, and exiting through a trade sale of the company or IPO.[91] Hence, unlike traditional closely-held corporations, startups are acquired by another corporation or transforming to a public corporation and so their existence is ephemeral like "a caterpillar in its chrysalis" and so after an early stage, startups have more than a small handful of shareholders, with the numbers increasing as the firm raises capital from syndicates of investors confers restricted stock and stock options to employees which vest over the course of employment. Moreover, startups administer the number of their holders of record to keep private status, but the numbers are greater than the definition of closely-held provided by the IRS.[92] Like traditional closely-held corporations, startups have stock that is not publicly traded but startups are different in that outside demand for the high-growth asset class exists and startups enable partial liquidity events.

---

[88] Simone M. Sepe, Intruders in the Boardroom: The Case of Constituency Directors, 91 WASH. U. L. REV. 309, 315 (2013) (noting that venture-backed startups "are growing exponentially in importance in the U.S. economy").

[89] A.C. Pritchard, Revisiting "Truth in Securities" Revisited: Abolishing IPOs and Harnessing Private Markets in the Public Good, 36 SEATTLE U. L. REV. 999, 1000 (2013). Securities Exchange Act of 1934, 15 U.S.C. §§ 78 l(a) & 78o(d); see also Donald C. Langevoort & Robert B. Thompson, "Publicness" in Contemporary Securities Regulation After the JOBS Act, 101 GEO. L.J. 337, 343 (2013); Usha Rodrigues, The Once and Future Irrelevancy of Section 12(g), 2015 U. ILL. L. REV. 1529.

[90] Jill E. Fisch, Leave It To Delaware: Why Congress Should Stay Out of Corporate Governance, 37 DEL. J. CORP. L. 731, 752–54 (2013).

[91] Nat'l Venture Capital Ass'n, 2018 Nat'l Venture Capital Ass'n Y.B. 29–31 (providing historic data on U.S. venture-backed exit activity, including 2017 data indicating 750 acquisitions versus 59 IPOs).

[92] Elizabeth Pollman, Information Issues on Wall Street 2.0, 161 U. PA. L. REV. 179, 190–91 (2012).

2.6 AI and Corporations

It seems that AI is set to take over utterly the area of administrative managerial and corporate leadership tasks. What types of tasks that is suitable for AI? Can AI take over corporate management concerning both administrative work and judgment work?

It is argued that AI will gradually replace human directors on boards, leading to "fused boards" where the numerous roles and inputs formerly offered by a collective of human directors are merged in a single software or algorithm, whose performance will be superior to today's human-led governance. Furthermore, AI will also substitute human officers and managers below board level and so these developments will in the end make the board/management separation obsolete leading to "fused management" of companies, with businesses being managed comprehensively by a single AI unit. In addition, it could be said that in the future large commercial AI management software providers will be offering these services to companies for sale or hire which means that this could fluctuate from merely software-based applications, combinations of software with laptop or tablet like hardware, to human look like robots that can listen and speak.

It could be said that AI is an approximation of human intelligence for the reason that it leaves open the prospect that AI will exceed human intelligence demonstrating a separate category of intelligence. Moreover, AI is interrelated to using computers to understand human intelligence, but it is not necessarily confined to methods that are biologically observable which means that AI denotes the competence of a machine to imitate intelligent human behavior.

Public companies are for the most part not managed by the board. In fact, the board transfers substantial managerial responsibilities to officers and managers and in sequence, the board supervises management and only retains a limited number of high-level managerial tasks.[93] To that extent, the G20/OECD Principles of Corporate Governance offer a more detailed description of board functions such as reviewing and guiding corporate strategy, key plans of action, risk management policies and procedures, annual budgets and business plans; setting performance aims; monitoring execution and corporate performance; and supervising key capital expenditures, acquisitions, and divestitures. Moreover, strategy and performance management occurred in areas on which boards spend the most time specifying that they spend even more time on strategy along with organizational matters, such as

---

[93] Stephen M. Bainbridge, The New Corporate Governance In Theory And Practice 74 (2008). In re Caremark Int'l Inc. Derivative Litig., 698 A.2d 959, 968 (Del. Ch. 1996): "Directors legally are only required to authorize the most significant corporate acts or transactions: mergers, changes in capital structure, fundamental changes in business, appointment and compensation of the CEO, etc." Marc Moore & Martin Petrin, Corporate Governance: Law, Regulation and Theory 174–177 (2017).

structure, culture, and talent management.[94] Can Al play the role of the board of a company?

In fact, administrative work in the corporate management context is consisting of administrative tasks, such as scheduling, allocation of resources, and reporting. Moreover, administrative work is broadly contrasted with judgment work which judgment work is work that entails creative, analytical, and strategic skills and so judgment work is the application of human experience and expertise to decisive business decisions and practices when the offered information is unsatisfactory to advocate effective course of action Furthermore, judgment can be individual but will often be collective, predominantly in more complex circumstances involving cooperation such as specific interpersonal skills and social networking. In line, emotional intelligence is a subcategory of judgment.[95]

Information-based technologies are playing an imperative role within both companies and boards, influencing the ways in the decision-making process and its outcomes applying predominantly with reference to companies functioning in areas where big data, Internet, and algorithms matter the most encompassing platforms such as Amazon, Google, Uber, YouTube, Netflix, Facebook, etc. It also applies to companies that rely on platform-based technologies to advance their business such as financial companies standing in direct correlation with the increasing significance of AI. Both information-based technologies generally and AI are triggering important alterations in the manner companies approach and cope with issues regarding analysis of information and compliance. It has to be taken into account that financial supervision focused on external governance must address the risks created by AI, due to: (1) enhanced information asymmetry; (2) data dependency; and (3) interdependency. Moreover, it has to be taken into consideration that business competence to collect and process digitalized information at unprecedented scale and speed is transforming economies around the globe.

Corporate governance will undergo an overhaul, responding to a deep-seated transformation in the board. Boards' function nowadays consists principally in supervising executives: directors devote most of their time to information flows and to the monitoring of regulatory and management issues. Moreover, technology will free directors from such duties, permitting them to devote more time to genuine business matters and so allowing for the appearance of a new form of board: lean, open, digitalized, innovation-oriented, and operative placing its sole focus on strategic and operational management.

Blockchain plays an imperative role in facilitating these transformations within the corporate context mainly influencing the relationship between shareholders and the corporation but not overshadowing its probable significance for boards and so

[94] Mckinsey & Company, The Board Perspective: A Collection Of Mckinsey Insights Focusing On Boards Of Directors, Number 2 (Mar. 2018), at 49, https://www.mckinsey.com/featured-insights/leadership/the-board-perspective

[95] Ajay Agrawal et al., What to Expect From Artificial Intelligence, 58 MITSLOAN MANAGEMENT REVIEW (2017), at 26, http://ilp.mit.edu/media/news_articles/smr/2017/58311.pdf.

when it comes to monitoring, an activity that Blockchain simplifies to a large extent, expanding its transparency and certainty regarding the information flows available to directors.[96] Moreover, Blockchain facilitates book-keeping and help log the whole decision-making process. Managers and executives are subject to "disintermediated" and more effective supervision by the board, which shareholders, in turn, also supervise more easily, particularly with reference to prospective conflicts of interest.[97] Most important of all, Blockchain proves useful in building a fully decentralized governance model, one in which employees would, by casting votes online in rete, have their own say in defining the corporation's strategy. To that extent, AI contributes to this process in several manners, whether by favoring shareholder activism, helping director face the challenges linked with gradually complex organizations, or by giving decision-makers access to assessments unspoiled by the impact of executives and major shareholders.[98]

Can AI play the Corporate Leadership in a company? Which are the potential roles that AI in general is capable of exercising? There is a need for the distinguishing fundamentals between the numerous roles being different levels of AI autonomy such as the energetic distinction between administrative tasks and judgment work, embracing corporate leadership tasks which mean assessing AI's future in corporate management. Hence, while there is little doubt that the so-called administrative duties will be utterly carried out by computers in the future which means that humans can be replaced when it comes to tasks that entangle judgment and emotional intelligence. Vegard Kolbjørnsrud et al.[99] argue that "artificial intelligence will soon be able to do the administrative tasks that consume much of managers' time faster, better, and at a lower cost" which means that AI will put an end to administrative management work but it is doubtful that administrative work will be the exclusive domain of AI in the future.

It could be said that even in these areas the involvement of AI is expected which means that a future is coming where "management by machine" will eventually fully

---

[96] Fenwick M et al., The End of "Corporate" Governance (Hello "Platform" Governance), ECGI Law Working Paper, n. 430/2018, <https://ssrn.com/abstract=3232663>. Yermack D, Corporate Governance and Blockchain, Review of Finance, vol. 21, Issue 1, March 2017, pp. 7 ff., <www.academic.oup.com>; Lafarre A & Van der Elst C, Blockchain Technology for Corporate Governance and Shareholder Activism, ECGI Law Working Paper n. 39/2018, 2018, <https://ssrn.com/abstract=3135209>. OECD, Blockchain Technology and Corporate Governance. Technology, Markets, Regulation and Corporate Governance, 2018.

[97] Carpenter M & Poon SH, Lesson Learned from AI Prototype Designed for Corporate AGM (2018), https://ssrn.com/abstract=3244160.

[98] Van Rijmenam M, Will AI Board Members Run the Companies of the Future? (2018), <www.brinknews.com>. Pugh W, Why not Appoint an Algorithm to Your Corporate Board? (2019), Future Tense, <www.slate.com>. Enriques L & Zetzsche D, Corporate Technologies and the Tech Nirvana Fallacy (ECGI Law Working Paper n. 457/2019) (2019), http://ssrn.com/abstract_id=3392321

[99] Vegard Kolbjørnsrud et al., How Artificial Intelligence Will Redefine Management, Harvard Business Review Online (Nov. 2, 2016), https://hbr.org/2016/11/howartificial-intelligence-will-redefine-management

replace human directors and managers as business leaders. Zekos considers that Al will not fully replace humans regarding corporate leadership as long as humans will exist in their present nature and not be replaced by more mechanical human looking creatures and so humans will manipulate the programming of Al.

It is obvious that the rise of artificial managers will coincide with the rise of large commercial providers of corporate management software, in view of the advantages of scale in terms of data collection. It has to be taken into account that size is beneficial from a liability perspective due to the fact that large, deeply capitalized providers with a broadly used product will be in a better position to circumvent liability though better services but also to resist financial strains in the case of liability payouts, embracing external insurance solutions.[100]

Taking into account that the artificial intelligence system and the company is not a natural person, the difficulty is with “assessing the mental state of the person” to impose liability. Singapore’s Penal Code indicates that the word “person” includes any company.[101] To that extent, Lennard’s Carrying Company[102] case considered that the state of mind of the senior officers of the company as being the state of mind of the company. Afterwards, the Meridian[103] special rules of attribution were articulated to bring a greater “degree of flexibility into a difficult area of the law.” Thus, where an artificial intelligence being becomes the sole director of a company by replacing the existing natural person board of directors, the problem arises since there are no human directors to form the mental state of the company.[104] Furthermore, a central difference between an AI Director and a company is that an autonomous robot may have the competence to commit manslaughter by using its “very powerful hydraulic arm killing a worker instantly” and so generating the issue of AI director responsibility.[105] On the other hand, a company has to act through natural persons and therefore cannot commit manslaughter on its own.

Hence, while company law principles have been retained to preserve the separate legal personality doctrine as emphasized in Salomon, in case of AI beings are concerned, statutory remedies have to be implemented to accord legal personality

[100] E. M. Dodd, Jr., For Whom are Corporate Managers Trustees?, 45 Harv. L. Rev. 1145 (1932); Adolf A. Berle, For Whom Corporate Managers are Trustees: A Note, 45 Harv. L. Rev. 1365 (1932).

[101] Singapore Penal Code (Cap 224, 2008 Rev. Ed).

[102] Lennard’s Carrying Company Ltd. v Asiatic Petroleum Co Ltd. [1915] AC 705.

[103] Meridian Global Funds Management Asia Ltd. v Securities Commission [1995] 2 AC 500 Ben Chester Cheong, “Context is the most Important Factor: One-man Companies and Corporate Attribution in Singapore” Oxford Business Law Blog (12 June 2020) https://www.law.ox.ac.uk/business-law-blog/blog/2020/06/context-mostimportant-factor-one-man-companies-and-corporate

[104] Alexander Sarch and Ryan Abbott, “Punishing Artificial Intelligence: Legal Fiction or Science Fiction” (2019) 53 UC Davis Law Review 323, 325–326; Martin Petrin, “Corporate Management in the Age of AI” (4 March 2019) UCL Working Paper Series (No. 3/2019).

[105] https://www.technologyreview.com/2018/03/12/144746/when-an-ai-finally-kills-someone-who-will-beresponsible/ Gabriel Hallevy, “The Criminal Liability of Artificial Intelligence Entities—from Science Fiction to Legal Social Control” (2010) 4 Akron Intellectual Property Journal 171, 171–172.

to artificial intelligence systems, then there is a need for analogous measures such as withdrawing the legal capacity of the AI director or destroying it with economic consequences as well. Legal capacity of a human and his status as a legal entity is conferred by the law. By the very nature of artificial intelligence, AI is neither possible to speak of its birth not being a natural person. AI can perfectly imitate human beings but it cannot be assumed that it is human. The legal capacity of AI is not natural. Hence, it can only be normative which means deriving from and established by the provisions of the law. On the other hand, the emergence of autonomous AAI humanoid robots in an AAI society means that AAI entity can be a natural AAI person in an analogous way of humans in another dimension.

Zekos considers that corporate governance is the whole networking, conventional and digital, within a firm dealing with the function of the firm in relation to the market and the interrelationships among all levels of directorship and shareholders. It could be said that the function of corporate governance centers on permitting a group of people to synchronize economic activity in pursuit of profit in the most efficient mode by dropping the number and severity of conflicting interests among corporate players. It is worth mentioning here that shareholders, creditors, managers, and employees cooperate with each other for the reason that the market and the law give them reasons to do so and so these parties are supposed to be rational players concerned only with exploiting their own profits. In this manner, the key factors discouraging corporate participants from stealing, shirking their duties, or otherwise mishandling each other are market motivations and legal rules, embracing contract rules.

It has to be taken into consideration that agency costs arise from the separation of control and ownership occurring when managers run a corporation but have to share its gains with equity holders and so such managers have reasons to expend less effort and utilize more privileges than they would if they were the corporation's sole owners which means that by shirking their duties and diverting value, managers engender agency costs and so diminishing their corporation's value.[106]

It is worth noting that Blockchain protocol governance reflects many of these same conflicts of interests for many of the same reasons and so when it comes to resolving contracting inefficiencies in the context of long-term relationships, corporate law, in conjunction with contract law, usually depends on the gap-filling task of law which means that blockchain protocols also experience from gaps—namely, they need additional decisions to be taken concerning software maintenance and updates with the intention of accommodating activity taken by external players on the network. In other words, protocols rely on their off-chain governance procedures to fill those gaps and so correspondingly companies accomplish the same thing by governance mechanisms built on top of legal gap-fillers from corporate law indicating that corporate governance models make possible a more endogenous governance

[106]Zohar Goshen & Richard Squire, Principal Costs: A New Theory for Corporate Law and Governance, 117 COL. L. REV. 767, 769 (2017). Lynn Stout, Corporate Entities: Their Ownership, Control, and Purpose, in Oxford Handbook Of Law And Economics (2017).

model for blockchains than other legal regimes that governments enforce in the absence of any clearly particular system.[107] If public blockchain protocols and their inventors want to preserve the decentralization of its ecosystem without ultimately being forced to accede to an ill-fitting regime enforced by the outside, participants in public blockchain ecosystems have to bear in mind voluntarily implementing a contractual governance mechanism inspired by corporate governance, but customized to the values, and aims of their society. In fact, blockchain protocol communities voluntarily embrace governance mechanisms vital from a policy viewpoint and so attempts by outsiders to force controls, focusing on an intended outcome achieve unplanned outcomes for the reason that the participants in the company such as the blockchain protocol ecosystem are not passive control agents.

It is has to be taken into account that corporate governance echoes the structure of rights and duties of the different stakeholders and its effects for the procedure by which firms are managed and operated and so a central issue for corporate governance is making certain that executives appreciate the rights and interests of corporation stakeholders, along with securing that stakeholders act responsibly relating to the generation, protection, and distribution of wealth invested in the corporation. Moreover, in light of the conflicts of interests that can trouble blockchain governance with very similar kinds of assets at stake, the corporate governance laws present authoritative devices for doing the same in blockchain protocols. Furthermore, the crucial kinds of corporate governance roles identified by state and federal laws embrace fiduciaries and gatekeepers and so corporate governance relies on disclosure methods to lessen information asymmetries between managers and owners.

Can human judgment be replaced by AI? It could be said that human judgment cannot be replaced by AI due to the fact that in the context of big data marketing and sales campaigns analytics-driven short-term outcomes come at the expense of long-term brand building and policies that cannot effortlessly be suggested by data which means that it is up to human marketing executives and so there is use of judgment—combining analytics with their own and others' insight and experience and by assessing short- and long-term priorities. Moreover, if AI systems can calculate and opine on a candidate's vocal inflections, it seems that they may not be able to consider that individual's compatibility with the approaches and history of the firm's existing workforce owing to that fact that these decisions necessitate human consciousness of the administration's context and history which means that only human managers will be the eventual decision-makers when it comes to managerial tasks requiring judgment unless that technology advancement is in a degree approaching the one of god's creativity and so humans will become more machines than humans altering the whole essence of human materiality and existence.

It has to be taken into account that there is AI's superiority in data gathering and prediction missions because prediction is the ability to use acquired information or facts to predict future events and human actions such as what a human driver would

[107] Oliver E. Williamson, The Theory of the Firm as Governance Structure: From Choice to Contract, 16 J. ECON PERSPECTIVES 171, 191 (2002).

do in a given situation or "predicting" a medical condition using observable symptoms. Moreover, while AI excels at prediction, the question to be answered is whether on this basis it can reliably initiate appropriate actions which means that replicating human judgment is conceivable but its feasibility is based on the essential level of judgment and the straightforwardness of defining wanted outcomes of actions in terms of "something a machine can understand.[108]" Obviously, it could be said that human judgment will advance and become subject to growing automation, but in top level of spirituality the need for human judgment will reign in certain situations and contexts which means that companies and governments will have continuing demand for people who can make reliable decisions by embracing ethical judgment, involve clients and employees needing emotional intelligence, and spot new opportunities by demanding creativity. Furthermore, human judgment will be needed when deciding how best to apply AI embracing the decision as to when we should count on judgment by AI, even though this decision will probably be supported by AI and its insights into the benefits of using it in a given setting. In fact, programmed machines via certain software are better at data gathering and analysis than humans which mean that these areas will be governed by AI.

First of all, directors hold the positions of core fiduciaries in the corporate context and so directors owe duties of care and loyalty to the owners of the corporation such as the shareholders and stakeholders. Correspondingly, when we record these roles of directors to the players in a public blockchain protocol, core developers and open-source software contributors do not serve the same function as directors; rather, full node operators do which means that the corporate governance model does not offer support for imposing fiduciary obligations on the developers of the open-source computer code that encompasses the blockchain protocol.

Do the developers of open-source computer code take on the role of a director in a corporation? It could be said that the developers of open-source computer code do not take on the role of a director in a corporation, unless they otherwise participate in the protocol as a node operator or hold a noteworthy volume of the protocol's native cryptocurrency echoing the policy purposes of fiduciary law, the key reason of which is to diminish entrustors' risk from misappropriation of their entrusted property or interests and so dropping the costs of monitoring fiduciaries. Hence, cryptocurrency owners do not delegate assets to open-source software developers and so cryptocurrency owners hand over their assets to the blockchain protocol full node operators.

It could be said that the rise of cryptocurrency is a reaction to dissatisfaction with the existing financial markets which are dominated by a few powerful currencies, financial institutions, and advanced economies. To that extent, the rise of cryptocurrency illustrates wider access to finance, and disruption of the current

[108]Megan Beck & Barry Libert, The Rise of AI Makes Emotional Intelligence More Important, Harvard Business Review Online (Feb. 15, 2017), https://hbr.org/2017/02/the-rise-of-ai-makes-emotional-intelligence-more-important. Ajay Agrawal et al., What to Expect From Artificial Intelligence, 58 Mitsloan Management Review (2017), at 26, http://ilp.mit.edu/media/news_articles/smr/2017/58311.pdf.

global financial system. Will the generation of e-money by everyone engender the conception of capital and money? Will the supply of e-money by everyone lead to a new understanding of trade and exchange of goods? Will the production of money by everyone take over the power from some supposed institutions of keeping the balance the power to keep the world on a supposed legal way of generating money? Has the current way of producing money led to wealth of the world or to the creation of an oligarchy leading the globe according to their interest and not the good of the globe?

Furthermore, the rise of unstable coins on the public chain is both a political movement and an economic response to dissatisfaction with the present global financial system and so a preferred method of transaction by users who need more secrecy than privacy in their transactions.[109] Criminals have been exploring anonymity to participate in illicit and illegal activities, in that way spoiling the reputation of cryptocurrency as a legitimate method of disrupting the established economic and political governance which means that there is extensive market manipulation, fraud, money laundering, tax evasion, etc.[110] It has to be taken into account that value fluctuation and complete anonymity are moderated by stable coins issued by a private consortium such as LIBRA because LIBRA differs from Bitcoin's opaque system in that in the identity of the operators and the design of the information infrastructure are known.[111] On the one hand, cryptocurrency's disintermediation is reducing transaction costs for users and its de-centralization generates more distributive justice by giving back powers of wealth creation and sharing to them. On the other hand, the issue of money not represented by an equal value increase generates price fluctuation with the expected problems in the market that is why there is an effort to control cybercurrencies in many ways.[112]

Which is the impact of corporate crypto governance? It could be said that the impact of corporate crypto governance is on the corporate governance model for off-chain governance recognizing code as a law subsystem of regulatory norms within the greater legal system and so there is a two-way recognition of the interconnected roles of code and law in restricting behavior within the a blockchain ecosystem. On the one hand, the code informs the law and its application to a blockchain ecosystem and on the other hand, law informs behavior and activities

[109] FATF Report to the G20 Finance Ministers and Central Bank Governors on So-Called Stablecoins (The Financial Action Task Force, 2020).

[110] Joseph Lee, Law and Regulation for a Crypto-Market: Perpetuation or Innovation? In Chiu Iris and Deipenbrock Gudula (eds) Routledge Handbook on FinTech and Law—Regulatory, Supervisory, Policy and other Legal Challenges (Routledge, 1st edn, 2021).

[111] Peter Van Valkenburgh, "The Differences between Bitcoin and Libra Should Matter to Policymakers" (2019) https://www.coincenter.org/the-differences-between-bitcoin-and-libra-should-matter-to-policymakers/

[112] G. Zekos, Economics and Legal Understanding of Virtual Currencies, Banking & Financial Services Policy Report, Volume 38 Number 8 August 2019 Wolters Kluwer. G. Zekos, Euro Zone: The Basis for the Materialization of The United States of Europe. Banking & Financial Services Policy Report, Volume 39 • Number 2 • February 2020 Wolters Kluwer.

undertaken through the code denoting the intersection of code and law influence upon understanding of how to apply the law in more conventional situations as well which means that finding out the fitting level and character of fiduciary duties in the blockchain governance context discloses the trade-offs inherent in every imposition of corporate fiduciary duties by underlining a director-centric or shareholder-centric model of the corporation. To that extent, such acceptance leads to prudent regard of the trade-offs and how to balance them with other matters of corporate governance or corporate legal principles which means that "code-as-law" not only represents "soft law" regulation of user behavior in cyberspace but also "code-as-law" influences regulation of functionally equivalent traditional architectures outside of cyberspace.[113]

2.7 AI and Political Corruption

It has to be taken into account that the word ethics signifies a set or system of moral ideals which are a product of society and many ethical issues deal with the relationship between the individual and the group. Aristotle, Plato, and Socrates dealt with ethics providing a set of principles of human conduct and values. Globalization creates a unified world economy, a complex and dynamic network of communications embracing the globe.[114] Corruption is an abuse of public office for private gain and it is often symptomatic of wider governance problems hurting economic development which means that corruption designates incompetence inherent to political institutions and cultures.[115]

Furthermore, it has to be taken into consideration that securing devotion to the rule of law is a constant challenge in every society and so problems such as corruption and the misuse of public power are common to governance. An increasing number of governments are using AI systems[116] that partly or fully replace humans in tax collection, managing welfare programs, guaranteeing the integrity of government records, issuing passports, running elections and ensuring better enforcement of the law, etc. Many AI systems are designed to make government processes more accurate and fairer. AI systems are promoted as eliminators of corruption for the reason that their pre-programmed rules, cryptographically protected data, and a distributed ledger eradicate dishonesty, bias, and arbitrariness.

[113] Aaron Wright & Primavera De Filippi, Decentralized Blockchain Technology and the Rise of Lex Cryptographia (Mar. 12, 2015) http://ssrn.com/abstract=2580664

[114] Twining, W,. Globalisation and Legal Theory, Cambridge: Cambridge University Press, 2000.

[115] Mises, L. v. (1996): Human Action: a Treatise on Economics. San Francisco, CA: Foundation for Economic Education, Inc.

[116] Monika Zalnieriute et al., The Rule of Law and Automation of Government Decision-Making, 82 The Modern Law Review 425 (2019).

Also, global corruption[117] affects economic and political systems by spoiling public confidence in management which means that its detrimental consequence globally by damaging economies, weakening political administrations, and triggering societal conflict. To that extent, good governance is undeniably the most fundamental condition of a country's political development which means that corruption leads to inefficiency and so value minimization.

It is worth mentioning here that privatization by delegating public functions to private foreign actors destabilizes the democratic protections of checks and balances against imbalanced exercise of power. Likewise, globalization has expanded the involvement of foreign corporations in the lives of communities. Doreen Lustig and Eyal Benvenisti[118] argue that "the need to regulate the privatization process so that its outcomes ensure the existence of robust democratic processes that protect individual and collective self-determination. Privatization should be reined in either by setting limits to it or by complementing it by remedial procedures that enable the bidirectional and multidirectional flow of information, and the effective participation of all those affected by it."

While industrialization delegitimized the inequalities of feudal distributions, globalization legitimizes the uneven distributions brought about by differential access to technology-based information. The justification is not only the purely economic one of efficiency but also the political-legal one of substantive justice.

As mentioned earlier, corruption is a behavior which deviates from the rule of law in a state under the prevailed political governance. It could be said that political corruption is the exploitation of public or assigned power for private gain.[119] Hence, a public official expands his/her profit from the office that he/she holds by seeing public service as a business, or corruption is an extra way to exercise influence on the decision-making process, which is a technique for entrepreneurship activities to succeed in the context of unsuccessful political systems.

It has to be taken into account that corruption not only distorts distribution of resources, but it also directly modifies the formation of power and its implementation, directs political institutions and rules of the game, and brings about political decay. Hence, political corruption is not only divergence from norms and laws, as laws themselves are accepted to serve the interests of public officials which means that as a rule, the judicial system is weak and incompetent to tackle intervention from the executive branch. To that extent, political corruption is a piece of authoritarian regimes resorting to political corruption for preservation of power and personal gains and so political corruption is a way of establishing economic control. In addition,

---

[117] Hazlet Th., K. and Sullivan, S.D. (1994), "Professional organizations and healthcare industry support: ethical conflict?", Cambridge Quarterly of Healthcare Ethics, Vol. 3 No. 2, pp. 236–56.

[118] Doreen Lustig and Eyal Benvenisti, The Multinational Corporation as "the Good Despot": The Democratic Costs of Privatization in Global Settings, in Theoretical Inquiries in Law · April 2014 Vol. 15:125 P156.

[119] Corruption and Economic Development, World Bank (May 4, 2019), http://www1.worldbank.org/publicsector/anticorrupt/corruptn/cor02.htm#note1 What Is Corruption?, Transparency International (May 4, 2019), https://www.transparency.org/what-is-corruption/

political corruption is used to forge political support strengthening the power of governments by generating more influence on the political process than formal institutions.

It is worth noting that the stability of autocratic regimes with high levels of corruption is because of the fact that corruption obstructs the democratization of formal institutions, whereas formal institutions do not add to diminishing the level of corruption. Thus, aside the formal existence of a parliament and elections, real power of the electorate is inadequate and so political corruption does not denote organized competition among several interest groups which means that the interests of elite are not subjected to checks and balances. In line, the un-institutionalized character of corrupt networks weakens the prospects of the electorate to contribute in collective decision-making. To that extent, it seems that political corruption pushes society into a dangerous balance where corruption generates personal benefits for many members of society, demoralizing the reasons to demand for more accountable political institutions.[120]

It has to be taken into consideration that political corruption is used not only for personal gains, but also as a means to conquer and keep power because via illegal distribution of privileges and favors, such as appointments to public positions or provisions of profitable contracts, public officials get political support which means that political corruption energizes a vicious circle where a public official who has access to public resources also has more openings for buying votes leading to the formation of clientelistic systems and patronage systems which might survive even in the supposed democratic political systems.[121]

Political or public corruption takes place when office holders illegitimately use public power for personal reward or to benefit a private interest. Moreover, corruption is contradictory to the rule of law value of equality before the law. Thus, in public administration, corruption initiates a gap between "law on the books" and the law in practice, leading to unpredictability and inconsistency between the law and government action and so blockchain-based platforms for the provision of public services and government administration are the means for fighting corruption.[122] Thus, the prospective of public blockchain rests in its capacity to offer an accurate record without demanding a central or human intermediary to authenticate and guarantee the accuracy of transactions. To that extent, it is supposed that Blockchain promotes the rule of law over and above to revolutionize societies and redistribute social and economic power.

---

[120] Hanne Fjelde & Håvard Hegre, Political Corruption and Institutional Stability, 49 (3) Studies in Comparative International Development 267 (2014).

[121] OECD, Financing Democracy: Supporting Better Public Policies and Preventing Policy Capture (2014) (May 4, 2019), https://www.unodc.org/documents/treaties/UNCAC/WorkingGroups/workinggroup4/2014-September-8-10/Responses_NV/OECD_EN.pdf

[122] Alexander James Hamilton & Craig Hammer, Can We Measure the Power of the Grabbing Hand?: A Comparative Analysis of Different Indicators of Corruption (The World Bank, 2018), http://documents.worldbank.org/curated/en/113281515516828746/Can-wemeasure-the-power-of-the-grabbing-hand-a-comparative-analysis-of-differentindicators-of-corruption

It has to be taken into account that a threat to the democratic regime occurs when clientelistic relations materialize between elected officials and those who try to benefit from their close position to occupants of public office. In *Buckley v. Valeo* case corruption was recognized as a threat to the election process.[123] Congress limited the amount a person could contribute to candidates and political committees, but also the amount a person could spend of their own money, "relative to" candidates.[124] It is worth mentioning here that in the post-Buckley era, the Court has found only one interest to be adequately significant enough to justify contribution limits: quid pro quo corruption.[125] The Court highlighted that contribution limits are prophylactic measures taken in anticipation of future corruption rather than purely measures reactive to previous and ongoing corruption. Moreover, limiting political contributions or coordinated expenditure to be deemed constitutional in a post-Buckley world serves a governmental interest in combatting the actuality or appearance of quid pro quo corruption. The McConnell Court[126] concluded that "large soft-money contributions to national political parties give rise to corruption and the appearance of corruption." Unlike the McConnell Court, the D.C. Circuit explicitly recognized a risk of quid pro quo corruption within large individual contributions to political parties.[127] Besides, the Supreme Court[128] held that the free speech clause of the First Amendment forbids the government from restricting independent expenditures for political campaigns by corporations, wealthy billionaires, and committees established for the purpose of fundraising (PACs).

It has to be taken into account that regardless of any money spend for elections citizens are voting in order to get the money. Illegality should be focused on the point to calculate votes that never have been put in the ballet and not to look for the money spend for the real votes of the people. People with their free will get the money and vote, nobody is forcing them to vote and so corruption embraces both politicians and voters. It seems that currently private interests seize state mechanisms and public institutions via clientelism leading to the upsurge of the size, complexity, and non-transparency of governmental decision-making and so clientelism results in "systemic corruption" damaging institutional trust and public confidence in the political system.

---

[123] Buckley v. Valeo, 424 U.S. 1 (1976).

[124] Randall v. Sorrell 126 S. Ct. 2479 (2006) and Wisconsin Right to Life v. FEC. 126 S. Ct. 1016 (2006).

[125] McCutcheon v. Fed. Election Comm'n, 572 U.S. 185, 227 (2014) (plurality opinion) ("The Government has a strong interest, no less critical to our democratic system, in combatting corruption and its appearance. We have, however, held that this interest must be limited to a specific kind of corruption—*quid pro quo* corruption ...".

[126] McConnell v. Federal Election Comm'n, 540 U.S. 93 (2003).

[127] *Libertarian National Committee, Inc. v. FEC* 924 F.3d 533, 553 (D.C. Cir. 2019).

[128] Citizens United v. Federal Election Commission, 558 U.S. 310 (2010) (the government "may not suppress political speech on the basis of the speaker's corporate identity").

Will AI eliminate corruption or will have an AI corruption as well? It could be said that AI provides devices on the hands of politicians to manipulate the governing process and wide easier any corrupting activities. On the other hand, it depends on the fact if the AI system is objectively autonomous and not controlled by any software programmer then corruption will be eliminated. On the other hand, an AAI system controlled by an AAI center will be used in an objective political way of keeping the functionality of the AAI system utilized by AAI society for the interests of the AAI entities which is supposed not to be controlled by any AAI political power for its own political strength but merely for the good of the governed.

References

1. Pasquale, F. (2019). A rule of persons, not machines: The limits of legal automation. *The George Washington Law Review, 87*
2. Zekos, G. (2015). Cyber versus conventional personal jurisdiction. *Journal of Internet Law, 18*(10), 3–35.
3. Zekos, G. (2013). Demolishing state's sole power over sovereignty and territory via electronic technology and cyberspace. *Journal of Internet Law, 17*(5), 27–41.
4. Zekos, G. (2019). Economics and legal understanding of virtual currencies. *Banking and Financial Services Policy Report*, Vol 38(8). Wolters Kluwer.
5. Zekos, G. (2020). Euro Zone: The basis for the materialization of The United States of Europe. *Banking and Financial Services Policy Report, 39*(2). Wolters Kluwer.
6. Zekos, G. (2021). Artificial intelligence and E-Bills of lading contracts. *Journal of Internet Law, 24*(8), 3–10. Wolters Kluwer. https://lrus.wolterskluwer.com/store/product/journal-of-internet-law/
7. Lösel, G. (2018). Can robots improvise? *Liminalities: A Journal of Performance Studies 14*(1).
8. Liu, H.-Y. (2018). The power structure of artificial intelligence. *Law, Innovation and Technology, 10*, 197.
9. Derrida, J. (1990). Force of law: The "Mystical Foundation of Authority". *Cardozo Law Review, 11*, 920–1045.
10. Susskind, J. (2018). *Future politics: Living together in a world transformed by tech*. Oxford University Press.
11. Ross, K. K. A. (2017). *Understanding the 12 technological forces that will shape our future*. Penguin.
12. Fenwick, M., & Vermeulen, E. (November 2018). Technology and corporate governance: Blockchain, crypto and artificial intelligence. ECGI Working Paper No. 424/2018.
13. Petrin, M. *Corporate management in the age of AI* (4 March 2019) UCL Working Paper Series (No. 3/2019).
14. Hurley, M., & Adebayo, J. (2017). Credit scoring in the era of big data. *Yale Journal of Law and Technology, 18*, 148.
15. Bostrom, N. (2014). *Superintelligence: Paths, dangers, strategies*. Oxford University Press.
16. Susskind, R. (2017). *Tomorrow's lawyers: An introduction to your future* (2d ed.).
17. Van Der Aalst, W. M., Bichler, M., & Heinzl, A. (2018). *Robotic process automation*. Springer.
18. Ζέκος, Γ. Εξελιγμένη τεχνητή νοημοσύνη και Robo-δικαστήρια, Αρμενόπουλος 6/2021 p 1093 https://www.dsth.gr/armenopoulos-intro

Chapter 3
Digital Economy and Politics

3.1 Introduction

First of all, globalization's encounter to the welfare state requires that there is a need to figure out how to safeguard the personal, political, and social liberties to which people have become accustomed. In fact, globalization, as a process, is by now a historical fact, which enriches the interactions of people in a lot of different countries. Many of the functions traditionally performed by governments are being disaggregated and privatized. The Westphalian view was simple: each country was separated from its neighbors by frontiers: interaction took place at or across the frontiers and so on a post-Westphalian view, there are no such separations: interactions take place within different "transnational" networks. To that extent, in globalization, the choices of people and societies have generally, but not universally, favored taking advantage of the opportunities provided by declining costs of transportation and communication through increasing economic integration.

Furthermore, globalization, with its cross-border interconnection, and interdependence, upsurges the demand for supranational regulation, i.e., global governance. Likewise, space applications have revolutionized communication facilitating the interconnections that drive globalization and so space applications pushed globalization by enabling faster, cheaper, and safer transportation which means that communication across the globe are speedy and low cost. Additionally, these applications, together with technological progression in other fields, especially computer and cyberspace technologies, link geographic distances. Hence, international law and global governance offer supranational regulation but due to the absence of a global government or supreme authority, they do so with a limited, though still significant, success.

It has to be taken into account that the crucial characteristics of globalization include the liberalization of international trade, expansion of foreign direct investment, the stepping up of global environmental degradation, and the social impact of globalization in compounding inequality. Moreover, globalization, a social process

G. I. Zekos, *Political, Economic and Legal Effects of Artificial Intelligence*,
Contributions to Political Science, https://doi.org/10.1007/978-3-030-94736-1_3

is lifting relationships out of the firmly territorial into the "global" or meta-territorial which means that the space in which social relations are conducted changes and so the manner of regulating those relations changes as well.[1] In fact, globalization can have both direct and indirect impact on states affecting the laws of international business transactions either negatively or positively.[2] In other words, globalization is changing the character of social relations toward the emergence at the global level of elements of the community and so globalizations is paving the way for global justice, even on communitarian terms.

Constitutional democracy entails the right to politically participate and the fundamental rights of all individuals are protected. How democracy can "catch up" to globalizing economy? How nationally based democracy can "catch up" to the realities of post-national decision-making? It is obvious that there is a misfit between nationally based democracies to the realities of post-national decision-making and there is a need to consequently overcome. Hence, there is the political task at hand to achieve the protection of the existing successes of the democratic welfare state, albeit by means of novel experiments in self-government "beyond the nation-state." There is a need for democracy to find the way of "catching up" to economic and technological processes. Due to globalizing capitalism, state democracy has to catch up and adjust itself to the global capitalism.[3] Furthermore, democracy is influencing expansion, innovation, and economic development.

Global governance is the course by which the repertoire of norms and rules that drive the behavior of players in global affairs is ascertained, implemented, and restructured. In addition, the key elements of global governance are norms, rules, policies, institutions, and fora that all affect the behavior of the players in global affairs. Global space governance has become a feature of modern globalization.[4] Also, globalization creates a global society involving global social cooperation, and international law consisting of many regimes best characterized as associations for mutual self-interest.[5] Moreover, globalization and its technological revolutions create the technical capacity to influence global resource distribution.[6] To that extent, globalization is creating a community of knowledge and a global market

[1]Anne Marie Slaughter, A New World Order (Princeton: Princeton University Press 2004).

[2]Kim Kercher, Corporate Social Responsibility-Impact of Globalization and International Business, Bond University. 2006.

[3]William E. Scheuerman, "Critical Theory beyond Habermas," in Oxford Handbook of Political Theory, ed. John S. Dryzek, Bonnie Honig, and Anne Phillips (Oxford: Oxford University Press, 2006), 94–103.

[4]Eytan Tepper, "The Final Frontier of Global Society and the Evolution of Space Governance," in New Frontiers Of Globalization Research: Theories, Processes, And Perspectives From The Global North And The Global South (Ino Rossi ed.).

[5]Frank J. Garcia, Trade, Inequality and Justice (Ardsley: Transnational Press 2003).

[6]Jon Mandle, "Globalization and Justice," Annals of the American Academy of Political & Social Science 570 (2000), pp. 129–30.

society.[7] Information technology has made possible and accelerated the globalization of business.

Can enhanced global governance represent an extension of political and legal processes observable at the national to the transnational stage? It is argued that global governance is an extension of national government and as world government. It is argued that global governance can operate successfully without inevitably taking the form of a world state or even sovereign governments at the transnational or supranational levels.

Do economic elites have captured and manipulated all global principles to their own interests? Do economic elites, acting behind the curtains, permit people to have an idea that the world is running according to their wills? On the other hand, it has to be taken into account that the possibility that operative supranational governance necessitates the launch of fundamentals of global government.[8] Geopolitics still plays a role in space activities and the role of states is even intensifying. To date, space governance is Earthbound and suffers from the troubles of global politics.

However, globalization has posed a big challenge to the notion of nation-state and its sovereignty that we have customarily known and there is a shift of sovereignty from States to market forces.[9] It is not the nation-state but the nature of its sovereignty that wants to be transformed with globalization. Sovereignty is an in-house perception, related only to the basis of legitimate authority within a state. Krasner[10] views sovereignty as a supposed limitation on states' power to interfere in each other's affairs. A more important aspect of sovereignty, however, rests in the Constitution's creation of the national government, the definition of its powers, and the limits thereon. Sovereignty can be regarded as a particular political form which is distinctive of capitalism and without doubt has enabled the constitution of a distinct sphere of international economic activity transforming the fundamentally territorial model of sovereignty and not merely eroding or replacing state sovereignty by a global one. Apparently, the power of sovereignty from the state is step by step shifting to market forces in a globalized world giving rise to different norms, standards, and rules to cope with globalization. In globalization the role of the state is being minimized and that of the non-state actors maximized. International activities are gradually less state-centric and more multidimensional in terms of their character, extent, operational mode, and the actors implicated therein. It has to be examined if deep down non-state actors perform within a states' jurisdiction utilizing the state of establishment in order to enforce their decisions and plans. Nations still control the reality of world politics, but emerging forms of international cooperation are

[7]Frank J. Garcia, Globalization, Global Community and the Possibility of Global Justice, 2005 Boston College Law School Faculty Papers.

[8]James N. Rosenau, "Governance, Order, and Change in World Politics," in Governance without Government: Order and Change in World Politics, ed. James N. Rosenau and Ernst Otto-Czempiel (Cambridge: Cambridge University Press, 1992), 1–29.

[9]Antony Anghie, Imperialism, Sovereignty and the Making of International Law (Cambridge University Press, 2005).

[10]Stephen D. Krasner, Sovereignty: Organized Hypocrisy (1999).

shaping the future of international law and setting the skeleton for expansion in international organizations.

Furthermore, it is worth noting that globalization expresses the expanding scale, speeding up, and deepening effect of transcontinental flows and patterns of social interaction. The centrality of corporations' internationalization strategies to the evolving pattern of the industrial and investment processes of globalization became more and more noticeable. A company must produce enough revenues in order to cover the real cost of capital, the risks and the uncertainties of the future globalized economic activities. Considering that diverge of interests among various states than among MNEs, it could be argued that globalization and global economic governance can be served by non-state actors better than states. To that extent, companies have to comply with business ethics in globalization.

Additionally, it is worth mention here that AI technological developments drive globalization at least as much as global politics. To that extent, globalization is as much about capabilities as it is about ideas and so ideas bring about the new capabilities in computer and cyberspace technology and indeed in space exploration. In line, space exploration and utilization, and its resulting space applications, make available the capabilities that augment the levels of globalization bringing yet another wave of globalization. Moreover, the effects are crucial to globalization and so their joint outcome is the legal, institutional, and physical infrastructure of globalization.

3.2 Financial Globalization

FinTech companies are revolutionizing the core structure of the financial industry, leading to the appearance of the so-called RegTech[11] that deals with reporting and compliance within financial markets. To that extent, the Italian Central Bank has itself been experimenting with the use of new technologies for supervisory purposes and the financial supervisor, CONSOB, is supporting the transition to a "digital" listed company, one in which ongoing disclosure obligations and compliance are exclusively discharged in a fully digital format.[12] Fintechs offer an all-online interface with a social media-style of financial democratization furnishing a near real-time digital interactive experience. Political zest for fintech is the outgrowth of a larger issue because the greater and more valuable use of technology has the prospective to expand access to financial products and services on terms that are

[11] Chazot C, RegTech: Exploring Solutions for Regulatory Challenges, Washington, DC: Institute of International Finance, 2015, https://www.scribd.com . Arner DW et al., FinTech and RegTech in a Nutshell, and the Future in a Sandbox, CFA Institute Research Foundation, www.papers.ssrn.com

[12] Banca d'Italia, Considerazioni finali del Governatore, Roma, 31 May 2019. CONSOB, Discorso del Presidente Mario Nava, 2018, available at www.consob.it/documentsOECD, G20/OECD Principles of Corporate Governance, 2015, www.oecd.org/corporate/principles

more reasonable and so fintech innovation, when regulated properly, creates positive societal results for consumers.[13]

It has to be taken into account that the move toward the use of algorithms in business has altered merchant–consumer interactions and so products and services are adapted for consumers through algorithms that collect and analyze data from interconnected devices, digital platforms, and social networks. Moreover, algorithms enable targeting of consumers more successfully, in real-time, and with high predictive accuracy in pricing and profiling strategies and so algorithms raise concerns on information asymmetry and power imbalances in merchant–consumer interactions by augmenting existing biases and discrimination or generate new ones in society. Algorithms offer a means to influence and modify consumer behaviors.

Likewise, it has to be taken into consideration that algorithmic processing of consumer data for the purpose of tailored pricing and personalized profiling means that merchants utilize algorithms to improve economic and social power over consumers and so algorithms can have undesired ethical, social, and economic impacts for the merchant–consumer interaction if left unaddressed by regulation.[14]

It is worth noting that globalization refers to the increasing integration of domestic and international financial markets, as well as the increasing international presence of major banks and other financial intermediaries and consolidation refers to the growing size and cross-sectoral scope of financial institutions. Consolidation and concentration in the financial services industry have been raised particularly in the origination of syndicated loans and in derivatives markets. To that extent, globalization has encouraged changes in the activities of the IMF and there is a shift in emphasis away from the problems of individual countries to concerns about contagion and systemic problems in international financial markets. It could be argued that interactions between the effects of consolidation and the problems arising from marketization and globalization give further grounds for more extensive use of public safety net instruments. It has to be taken into account that financial integration means another pattern of business cycle which could be argued might be integrated by achieving a synchronization causing problems when a whole area is in the same phase of down fall of a business cycle not mentioning the effects of globalization and the emergence of e-finance and e-commerce. The significance of efficient financial markets is in allowing those that want to obtain capital from different sources at reasonable rates. Likewise, large financial institutions are now very active, indeed often dominant, players in a number of financial markets and they rely on the markets and the markets rely on them.[15] Lately the global financial system has changed deeply and technological improvements and deregulation have increased

[13]Rory Van Loo, Digital Market Perfection, 117 MICH. L. REV. 815, 833–35 (2019) (pro-consumer technological advisers in finance and other sectors can benefit consumers).

[14]Tabrez Y. Ebrahim, Algorithms In Business, Merchant—Consumer Interactions, & Regulation, 2021 West Virginia Law Review 868.

[15]McDonnell, W (2003): "Managing risk: practical lessons from recent 'failures' of EU insurers," Occasional Paper, 20, UK Financial Services Authority.

competition in the financial services industry. It is characteristic that the wide adoption of AI-based solutions leads to financial system diversity which in turn means lower risks that the economy faces related to when a few banks dominate credit provision.[16]

There is pressure by marketization, globalization, and consolidation which means cross-sectoral and more highly concentrated provision of financial services on financial institutions to keep up rates of return contributing to their greater willingness to take on risks.[17] Marketization has encouraged the use of generalized injections of liquidity when financial disruptions threaten.[18] Globalization has implications for the generalized injection of liquidity in the face of financial difficulties inducing national monetary authorities to react to international as opposed to solely domestic objectives. According to William R White[19] "to the extent there has been growing recourse to the use of safety net instruments, the question of moral hazard takes on greater importance. The risk is that measures taken to deal with short-term problems in the financial system may inadvertently make problems more difficult to deal with over time."

Finance is vital for a strong entrepreneurship and subsequently constraints on finance have an impact. Moreover, finance holds back the opening out of markets along both supply and demand lines via its influence on the growth of fixed-cost investments such as infrastructure. The development of an efficient infrastructure is correlated with trade development and infrastructures are constructed using both public finance and private enterprise under public regulations.

It is worth mentioning that banks' profitability has upgraded somewhat, and yet it is still at low levels, and they now have higher capital and liquidity ratios, rendering them more flexible than they were before the global financial crisis. Moreover, the banking sector has a good degree of flexibility overall, even though with some pockets of vulnerability. In addition, the asset management sector now plays a much larger role in financial markets than it did 10 years ago. Luis de Guindos[20] argues that "One of the most notable developments since the financial crisis has been the rapid growth of asset management in the euro area and at global level. In the euro area, investment funds have been growing steadily, with total assets expanding by

[16] Bhatore, S., Mohan, L. Reddy, Y.R. Machine learning techniques for credit risk evaluation: a systematic literature review. J Bank Financ Technol 4, 111–138 (2020). doi: https://doi.org/10.1007/s42786-020-00020-3M. Moscatelli, F. Parlapiano, S. Narizzano, G. Viggiano. Corporate default forecasting with machine learning, Expert Systems with Applications, Volume 161, 2020, doi: https://doi.org/10.1016/j.eswa.2020.113567

[17] Kane, Edward J (2001): "Financial safety nets: reconstructing and modelling a policymaking metaphor," NBER Working Paper Series, 8224, April.

[18] Padoa-Schioppa, T (2002): "Central banks and financial stability: exploring an intermediate land," speech given at the 2nd ECB Central Banking Conference, Frankfurt, 24–25 October.

[19] William R White, Are changes in financial structure extending safety nets? BIS Working Papers No 145, p31.

[20] Speech by Luis de Guindos, Vice-President of the ECB, at the Opening Conference, 21st Euro Finance Week, Frankfurt am Main, 12 November 2018 p2.

roughly 170% between 2008 and 2017, reflecting both continued net cash inflows and rising asset valuations."

Enterprises globalizing their operations and the associated capital flows have become key players of the world economy and cross-border conduct and capital flows span institutional settings with shifting investor protections and levels of capital market expansion. MNEs' activity and FDI arise endogenously in settings characterized by financial differences. In line, UNCTAD[21] assumes that "market seeking FDI and efficiency-seeking FDI are partially undermined by digitalisation" which means that the aptitude of companies to get into international markets with smaller "asset footprints," due to the digital economy, has been linked with the appearance of e-multinationals and the born-global companies that rapidly achieve global grasp with minimal cross-border investment.

Furthermore, it has to be taken into account that there are different ways in which the digital economy is reducing the demand for a physical presence to service foreign markets by enabling the transmission of a wide range of goods and services in digital form; for instance, music, publications, and services extending from architectural design to retail are distributed globally in digital form. Thus, physical products are generated for customers in foreign markets by sending digital files to 3D printers located in those markets and so from an international investment standpoint, the key consequence seems to be that "the trade-off between exporting and market-seeking FDI as market entry modes for delivering products to host countries may be shifting toward exporting."[22] It could be said that the digital economy has altered business models bringing about healthcare solutions based on data and artificial intelligence rather than pharmaceutical research while design and manufacturing based more and more on AI and algorithms rather than on traditional engineering.[23] To that extent, firms across areas are adjusting to an ever more digital business environment by building up internal capabilities plus by obtaining external assets and knowledge from across the globe.

In line, developments in technology are making the world smaller, empowering people and businesses to connect across borders as easily as they do across the road. Thus, anyone can manufacture anything anywhere through 3D printing, where

---

[21] UNCTAD (2017), World Investment Report 2017. Investment and the Digital Economy, United Nations Conference on Trade and Development, New York and Geneva, http://unctad.org/en/PublicationsLibrary/wir2017_en.pdf

[22] Eden, L. (2016), Multinationals and Foreign Investment Policies in a Digital World, E15Initiative, International Centre for Trade and Sustainable Development and World Economic Forum, Geneva, http://e15initiative.org/wp-content/uploads/2015/09/E15-Investment-Eden-FINAL2.pdf De Backer, K. and D. Flaig (2017), "The future of global value chains: Business as usual or "a new normal?", OECD Science, Technology and Industry Policy Papers, No. 41, OECD Publishing, Paris, https://doi.org/10.1787/d8da8760-en

[23] Neville, S. (2017), Pharma turns to big data to gauge care and pricing, Financial Times Online, www.ft.com/content/c148011a-4f43-11e7-a1f2-db19572361bb. Gauger, C., Gehres, B., Quinn, M., Schmieg, F., Xu, G. (2017), Building the Digital Car Company of the Future, Boston Consulting Group Publications, www.bcg.com/publications/2017/automotivedigital-transformation-building-digital-car-company-future.aspx

anyone can advertise their performance globally and so in a cyber-connected, capital-light domain, the future more and more belongs to small and medium-sized businesses, with platforms providing direct stakes in local and global markets. Furthermore, the profits from levelling up the global trading system via liberalizing services trade offsets those from levelling down by putting more limitations on goods trade. It could be said that dropping limits on services to the same extent as those on goods have been over the past years diminishes current account imbalances by up to one half.[24] Thus, the entry of international services providers to national markets advances consumer selection and lower prices which means that it is expected to result in extensive upsurges in productivity, not least for the reason that services such as IT, R&D, transport, communications, and finance are integral to the production of a wide range of goods.[25]

As mentioned earlier, financial globalization is a free movement of finance across national boundaries without facing any restrictions but financial liberalization is not alone sufficient condition for financial globalization. Zekos considers that financial globalization allows a better environment where capital will be moved around the world with less possible barriers where productivity will bring higher profit and so financial globalization means growth of developing economies as global savings are resourcefully directed to capital accumulation in developing countries where the marginal product of capital is highest. Developed and newly-formed countries undertake various measures in order to prevent financial instability by controlling financial flows that are purely speculative in nature ensuring that possible expansion in aggregate expenditure in the productive aspect of the economy is not constrained by inadequacies in the financial flow.

Also, financial markets and institutions have a positive and significant effect over long-run growth. The export sector of the developing countries is a proxy to credit standard, which also acts as the vital means to repay the loan and any negative performance of this sector produces difficulties in recouping the loan, which in turn brings periodic financial crisis. Companies in emerging markets are engaged in activities far from the technological frontier innovating not just through first inventions but also by adopting new ways of production, new goods, and new forms of organization. The outwardly financed percentage of a company's investment expenditures is related to company's innovation. Financial liberalization boosts economic development by getting better distribution of resources and the investment rate. It has to be taken into consideration that suppliers of capital have a distinctive capacity in many occasions to associate with the most skilled and flourishing entrepreneurs. Also, financial liberalization places a state more vulnerable to financial crises and so financial markets and institutions must introduce regulations enabling

[24]Whitaker, S et al. (2018) "Mind the (current account) gap," Bank of England Financial Stability paper No. 43.

[25]Carney, M (2017) "A Fine Balance," speech at the Mansion House London, 20 June 2017.

macroeconomic stability before capital flows are deregulated. J. P. Joyce[26] considers that “A more liberal de jure capital regime lowers the incidence of banking crises. FDI also lowers the duration of banking crises, but a less regulated capital regime is associated with crises of greater duration. Financial globalization does not seem to be directly associated with the costs of the crises, but currency crises are linked to higher costs.”

Furthermore, financial globalization and globalization in general, leads to lower tax rates on mobile factors of production, reflecting augmented competition and the capacity of MNEs[27] to move profits through transfer pricing. In today’s globalized economy, the domestic social and labor standards within a given country are de jure or de facto co-determined to some degree by the actions of mobile capital and labor, by other countries, and by global institutions of global governance. To that extent, the mobility of capital holders has caused the competition among countries to have production facilities located in their territory. In line, if one country advances social standards, for instance, with reference to labor safety, then the touched sectors or fields of industry might run away strict regulations by relocating which means that the expectation of such relocation to cheap and low-standard-states provokes policy makers, concerned to preserve tax revenues and jobs, to lower taxes and so reducing the countries’ resources which could finance social projects. Moreover, the concern is a motivation for freezing labor standards for the reason that compliance with high standards makes the production procedure costlier.[28] It has to be taken into account that when states try to keep or reclaim economically noteworthy industrial sectors by supplying a tolerant legal environment, there is a threat of a downward spiral of standards.[29]

It has to be taken into account that globalization gives rise to income convergence and so many countries managed to catch up with the developed world but, on the other hand, there is still income inequality within countries, above all within advanced economies. For instance, the USA is the country that has undergone the most pronounced upsurge in income inequality, somewhat for the reason that competition from emerging economies has ruined jobs for medium and low skilled labor. Zekos argues that countries that they have endorsed an anti-globalization approach they have lost a chance to improve many aspects of their economy without saying that all consequences/aftereffects of globalization have brought paradise on earth. Moreover, a logical and justifiable utilization of globalization to the peoples’ interests and not merely implementing the interests of some elites will lead to the

[26] Joseph P. Joyce, Financial Globalization and Banking Crises In Emerging Markets, 2009 www.ssrn.com

[27] G Zekos, MNE’s in 21st Century, 2016 Nova Science Publications New York USA. www.novapublishers.com G Zekos, Economics, Finance and Law on MNEs, 2007 Nova Publishers, New York www.novapublishers.com

[28] David Garland, The Welfare State: A Very Short Introduction (Oxford: Oxford University Press, 2016).

[29] Anne Peters, “The competition between legal orders” (2014) 3 International Law Research 45–65.

improvement of the whole world. Likewise, there is always the danger of using globalization to demolish the globe on behalf of some elites which they think that they can control environment and people. Besides, in the end, historically evidenced, elites merely lose their power due to the unexpected destruction because elites have forgotten that they are not the Olympian Gods.

It is worth mentioning that political opposition to globalization has risen in industrialized states, even though the positive consequences on the growth of the global economy and the lessening of poverty are confirmable. Nevertheless, the outcomes of globalization differ according to regions, professional groups, and education. In addition, in globalization, unemployment, and inequality have risen, and since the many new challenges, such as climate protection, can be better solved by global endeavors and so there is a need to evade new national barriers and to strengthen the endorsement of globalization and the associated welfare results. Conversely, it is essential to appreciate cultural differences in preferences and to view globalization as an ongoing process.[30]

It has to be taken into account that globalization brings disadvantages for regions, groups, and companies and so this is the instance when globalization happens alongside with technological breakthroughs and weak demand and when economic policy does not fulfill the required stabilizing measures. To that extent, Zekos argues that globalization should mean development and not merely exploitation and destruction of less developed places.

3.3 Digital Economy and Politics

The digitalization of the economy and society, the introduction of artificial intelligence in human activities actualize a number of new issues linked with both the legal support of these processes, and areas of advancement of law as a regulatory system, and the connection between law and technology. It has to be taken into account that digitalization as a global trend in the development of economy and society based on transformation of information into digital form, shift to other forms of communication through cyber technologies, launch of remote working and studying, which were widely used during the fight against COVID-19 pandemic, unquestionably affect the advancement of law as a regulatory system.

Which are the crucial features of the digital economy? There are a number of qualities that are progressively noticeable in the digital economy and which are possibly relevant from a tax perspective and so while these qualities may not all be present at the same time in any specific business, they gradually distinguish the modern economy. The crucial features of the digital economy embrace: firstly

[30] Karl Aiginger and Heinz Handler (2017). Europe taking the lead in responsible globalisation. Economics Discussion Papers, No 2017–42, Kiel Institute for the World Economy. http://www.economics-ejournal.org/economics/discussionpapers/2017-42

mobility, with regard to (1) the intangibles on which the digital economy depends on profoundly, (2) users, and (3) business roles as a result of the diminished requirement for local personnel to accomplish certain functions along with the flexibility in many cases to decide the location of servers and other resources. Secondly, there is reliance on data, embracing especially the exploitation of the so-called big data. Thirdly, there are network consequences, understood with locus to user involvement, integration, and collaborations. Fourthly, there is use of multi-sided business models in which the two sides of the market are located in different jurisdictions. Fifthly, there is a propensity toward monopoly or oligopoly in certain business models depending profoundly on network outcomes and sixthly there is volatility as a result of low barriers to entry and fast advancing technology. It is worth noting that the Digital Economy embraces: (1) advanced manufacturing, robotics, and factory automation, (2) new sources of data from mobile and ever-present cyberspace connectivity, (3) cloud computing, (4) big data analytics, and (5) artificial intelligence. In conclusion, technologies develop at uneven and unpredictable rates, and deployment suffer under fragmented and competing standards which means that these drawbacks reduce the prospects of even the most enthusiastic optimist, mainly when there is a high obligation for connectivity, interoperability, and integration across organizations and societies. Yet, the influence of any revolutionary technology is frequently over-estimated in the short term and under-estimated over the long term.[31]

The digital economy offers consumers access to information formerly inconceivable in any traditional marketplace. Yet that information and more is also available to retailers who are able to use pricing software to maximize profits. In the past, anti-competitive conduct entailed proof of a meeting of the minds to collude on prices or abuse market dominance but the speed with which prices are adjusted today means that tacit collusion may take place without any intent on the part of market actors or even without any formal coordination between their computer programs.

Nowadays of globalization is distinguished from preceding ones in part because of the major role of information technology, cyberspace, Nano-biotechnology, etc. International trade and its directness to, finance and technology is an option that states make, and despite the facilitating role of information technology, many states, even many leading players in the global economy such as the USA, Japan, Russia, China, India, and Brazil could choose to close their borders. Moreover, globalization depending on political decisions of nation countries has political limits related to nationalism and militarism[32] that nationalism and militarism are strong around the globe, in countries ranging from the USA to China, France, Japan, UK, Germany, Russia, and India.[33] Hence, alterations in national political equilibriums initiate

---

[31] McAfee, A. and Brynjolfsson, E. 2017. Machine, Platform, Crowd: Harnessing Our Digital Future. New York: W. W. Norton & Company.

[32] Martin, Philippe, Thierry Mayer, and Mathias Thoenig (2008).Make Trade Not War?. Review of Economic Studies, 75, 865–900.

[33] Kagan, Robert (2008) The Return of History and the End of Dreams, Random House, New York.

limits to the process of globalization. Likewise, in McCutcheon v. FEC[34] the court presented companies a political cover by verifying that spending large sums of money on elections did not corrupt the political process.

The latest globalization has brought forth three key alterations on the world arena: the rise of the eastern world to the level of the western world and the birth of modernity, the rise of the USA, and currently the "rise of the rest." It is worth mentioning that in globalization the density of the determining factors alters in real-time varying from energy to climate, from technology to commerce, from security to economy. To that extent, globalization altered the rules of liberalization, capital mobility, offshoring, cross-border mobility, inequalities in wealth and so competition within employment markets has risen; fast-moving technological development results in job losses while simultaneously generating new sectors of the economy.[35]

Taking into account the use of people analytics in hiring and managing workforces, the appeal of AI is as a time-saving mechanism for reviewing resumes and the AI's perceived capability to remove human bias from the hiring system means that corporations are turning to AI systems for their predictive competences. Moreover, algorithms predict worker performance based on resume length, hobbies listed, and education, with the AI learning from thousands of applicants which features reliably link with high performing candidates which means that software identify skills and abilities that do not plainly appear on a candidate's résumé. Furthermore, AI is used in online testing to correlate answers to particular questions with job tenure and performance and so corporations like HireVue are using AI and face-scanning technology to assess candidates from a pre-recorded video interview.[36]

Global labor markets have been subject to big structural shifts over recent years, containing the secular fall in the degree of worker unionization in a number of industries and secular upsurge in the scale of globalization and automation via AI in the workplace.[37] Yet, over the same period, structural shifts in the product market have been no less profound. To that extent, there is emergence of highly-integrated global supply chains, boosting the degree of specialization of product markets; the thriving of firms benefitting from global network economies of scale and scope, who

---

[34] 134 S. Ct. 1434 (2014). Jonathan S. Berkon, After McCutcheon, 127 Harv. L. Rev. F. 373, 377 (2016).

[35] Bellamy R and Weale A, 'Political Legitimacy and European Monetary Union', (2015). 22-(2) Journal of European Public Policy 257.

[36] Drew Harwell, A face-scanning algorithm increasingly decides whether you deserve the job, The Washington Post (Nov. 6, 2019). Julie Manning Magid, Does Your AI Discriminate? The Conversation (May 15, 2020), https://theconversation.com/does-your-ai-discriminate-132847

[37] Taylor, M (2017), "Good work: the Taylor review of modern working practices," Department for Business, Energy & Industrial Strategy. Katz, L and Krueger, A (2017), "The Role of Unemployment in the Rise in Alternative Work Arrangements," American Economic Review: Papers & Proceedings, Vol. 107, No. 5, pp. 388–392. Acemoglu, D and Restrepo, P (2018), "Artificial Intelligence, Automation and Work," NBER Working Paper, No. 24196.

gain "superstar" status; and the appearance of e-commerce and price-comparison technology.[38]

It has to be taken into account that AI technological transformations not only globalize the economy[39] but also bring its digitalization. Accordingly, the assimilation of the evolutions of computation and communication technologies in their endeavor, progressively firms turn out to be global attacking the worldwide markets and so externalizing a section of their operations in the course of partnerships with producers and suppliers globally and open subsidiaries all over the world.

Do globalization and governance work in opposite directions? On the one hand, the world has become smaller and connected, with a constant decrease in time, cost, and ease of transportation and the explosion of free, instant, and sophisticated communications. On the other hand, global governance, that is assumed to complement globalization with regulation, is lately in retreat and so there is a tendency for decentralized governance which means that there is anarchy in global politics but the interstate relations are not lawless. Globalization brought new global governance mechanisms to which civil society and private actors, along with governments, contribute knowledge and capital. The global governance mechanisms consist of networks of private and public actors relying on voluntary action, and having only weak enforcement measures.[40] Global governance is up to the task of governing the diverse challenges generated by AI technology.

Digital technologies have given ascent to new businesses and international business models that have permitted companies to develop a global presence without noteworthy amounts of FDI, but FDI reinforces the globalization strategies of businesses in more traditional "bricks and mortar" industries. In fact, digital infrastructure, telecommunication and communication infrastructure with high system interdependence and vulnerability to intrusions or disruptive activities by foreign intelligence services or cyber-espionage are part of the exploitation of digital economy and FDI. Furthermore, critical technology embraces inter alia crucial national technologies; nanotechnologies; biotechnologies; blockchain technologies, AI, etc. The corporations together with the non-standard factors of growth are the players in the global economy, and not the nationally marked economies. MNEs are part of the current economic scene concerning the global circuit of goods, services, capital, technology, and human resources.

It has to be taken into account that the digital economy has generated new contests and opportunities for the international investment policy community and so as digitalization and digital technologies are exploited more broadly and

[38] Autor, D, Dorn, D, Katz, L, Patterson, C and Van Reenen, J (2017), "The Fall of the Labor Share and the Rise of Superstar Firms," NBER Working Paper, No. 23396. Cavallo, A (2017), "Are Online and Offline Prices Similar? Evidence from Large Multi-Channel Retailers," American Economic Review, Vol. 107, No. 1, pp. 283–303.

[39] Daniela Popescul Information And Communication Technologies—One Engine of Globalization CES Working Papers, I, (2), 2009 p.32.

[40] Braithwaite, J., and P. Drahos. 2000. Global Business Regulation. Cambridge, UK: Cambridge University Press.

intensively by MNEs in all areas of the economy, some of the policy disputes to which digital technologies have given rise, but which have up till now been reduced to the digital areas, are expected to become broader international investment policy encounters. Moreover, digital technologies cause state security worries and different programs have placed rules on the collection, storage, and use of digital data in order to defend privacy and consumer selection which means that there is a need for digital policies in protecting digital data being the strategic property for MNEs. Additionally, digital technologies are embraced by different industries causing diffusion of these technologies and so the productivity advantages of digital applications have caused their global endorsement. Hence, there is a need to take into account the increasingly vital role that digital data play in multinational business strategies and the escalating number of modes that governments regulate the use of these data such as data localization which means that data localization prerequisites specify that companies have to store digital data in the host state. To that extent, storing digital data necessitates data centers where data is stored, managed, and handled on a network of high-performance servers which means that it is a fundamental fact where digital information is collected and disseminated to other data centers or the end-user. Hereafter, companies either set up their own data storage infrastructure or outsource this service.

It has to be taken into consideration that the three building blocks of the digital economy are digital data, digital technologies, and digital infrastructure.[41] Digitalization encompasses the conversion of things (sound, shapes, information, etc.) into digital data, which are interminably (re)processed and stored at insignificant marginal cost. Also, digital data has been the foundation for new business models in many traditional industries and has given rise to new industries and so in many areas, "big data" engendered by social networks or algorithms have become a gradually constructive strategic asset for companies.

It is worth noting that digitalization has caused the emergence of new kinds of digital technologies ICT which has stimulated the advance of new products and services ranging from digitally augmented devices such as smart machines, to digital platforms, to exclusively new technologies such as blockchains. Likewise, an imperative building block for digital technologies and data-driven economies was the advancement of a secure and high-speed digital infrastructure comprised of a variety of local, national, and global networks owned by various bodies building the basis for digital services, applications, and business models. Additionally, owing to the swift progress of digital data and digital technologies, along with the occurrence of cloud computing, data storage has become an imperative infrastructure part at the business level.[42]

---

[41] OECD (2015), Data-Driven Innovation. Big Data for Growth and Well-Being, OECD Publishing, Paris, https://doi.org/10.1787/9789264229358-en

[42] OECD (2017), Key issues for digital transformation in the G20. Report prepared for a joint G20 German Presidency/OECD conference, Berlin, www.oecd.org/g20/key-issues-for-digitaltransformation-in-the-g20.pdf

It has to be taken into account that MNEs bring along in the hosting states capital, technology, high-level management, they establish workplaces, take part in the upsurge of work productivity, of exportation competitiveness, of production, of sales, of budget incomes, and they advance the balance of payments. On the other hand, MNEs' role is a negative one as well, given that they challenge democracy, influence domestic societies, and outline a new type of capitalism and so they merge societies in a vague scheme inside which individuals lose control over their own lives, becoming slaves of these ill-using firms whose only preoccupation is profit. Moreover, the rise of work productivity by technology, information, innovation transfer replaces, over time, the workforce, causing a higher unemployment rate, particularly among the low-qualified or unqualified individuals.

Furthermore, it has to be taken into consideration that MNEs possess political power and so if the governments apply against them taxes or regulations with which they do not consent, they often threaten with moving their endeavor elsewhere. In line, MNEs aid to the growth of a state's competitiveness, either by investments with higher added value in areas in which there was no prior investment, or by passing, within one domain, from low-productiveness activities, with low technology and intensive labor levels, to high-productivity endeavors, with an intensive capital level and knowledge-based. Typically, the activity of MNEs permits for a decrease of the growth gap between the developed and the developing states, particularly by technological transfer; they add to the upsurge of competitiveness of the native firms on the internal and external markets. With the influence of globalization and the globalized supply chain, a firm cannot compete in the global arena without depending on automation to reduce costs and advance efficiency and quality. Thus, innovation and automation are essential to winning in competitive environments.

Can an e-MNE be defined as a firm that has facilities in a number of countries and its management achieved via cyberspace? Zekos thinks that an e-MNE can be defined as a virtual enterprise that has production facilities in various countries concerning tangible goods and an advanced network dealing with intangible goods and services achieved its management via cyberspace by humans or some actions be made by electronic agents such as electronic contracts and automated sales. Of course, currently the programming of the electronic agents in order to deal with electronic transactions is made by the humans.[43] Advancement in technology in order machines to think logically and make some decisions based on electronic software inserted by humans is expected in the near future but total transformation in order machines to decide on behalf of humans is forthcoming as well. To that extent, AAI humanoid robots will manage AAI e-MNEs offering goods and services suitable for AAI creatures in AAI society. The big question to be answered is focused on the role of humans in an AAI society where AAI creatures will decide autonomously for their own society. Therefore, an e-MNE can control and manage

[43] G Zekos, Economics, Finance and Law on MNEs, 2007 Nova Science Publishers, New York, www.novapublishers.com

income generating assets in more than one country by the means of a network spread around the world and an electronic base located in a single building or place regardless of its digital space due to the need for electronic equipment transforming e-data in human understandable dimension. On the other hand, AAI e-MNEs located in cyber-places will be managed virtually by AAI entities and so AAI virtual dimension for AAI e-MNEs will emerge not even conceivable by humans due to the virtual dimension. An e-MNE can be engaged in direct investment outside its home country either on traditional plant or on electronic networks selling globally intangible goods and services.

Overall, the digital economy has not yet brought about key alterations to the international investment regime or to the means in which most MNEs structure their international strategies. Foreign direct investment carries on playing an imperative role for companies outside of the digital economy as a way of growing globally. Nevertheless, the most recent data show a sharp escalation in the cross-border acquisition of digital corporate assets by businesses outside of the digital economy which means that if this drift continues and leads to the prevalent implementation of hybrid business models implicating the application of digital technologies in more traditional manufacturing and services industries, enfolding at least three broad consequences for the international investment policy community: First, non-digital MNEs become gradually vital cross-border networks for digital data and technologies, just as they have served as central cross-border conduits for goods, services, financial flows, and more traditional technologies in the past; Second, digital infrastructure, such as cross-border telecommunications connections and digital storage aptitude, becomes an ever more imperative factor for the FDI localization decisions of MNEs and for the investment promotion and facilitation efforts of governments; Third, policies concerning the collection, storage, and exploitation of digital data gradually affect the ways in which digitally-intensive MNEs arrange their international production networks and the modalities they select such as FDI versus licensing and for taking part in foreign markets.

Furthermore, there is a need to take into account the increasingly vital role that digital data play in multinational business strategies and the escalating number of modes that governments regulate the use of these data such as data localization which means that data localization prerequisites specify that companies have to store digital data in the host state. Furthermore, storing digital data demands data centers where data is stored, managed, and handled on a network of high-performance servers which means that it is a fundamental fact where digital information is collected and disseminated to other data centers or the end-user. Hence, companies either set up their own data storage infrastructure or outsource this service.

It is worth noting that online platforms conducting their business in the retail sector ascertain consumer preferences, their will to pay, the timing of their next order, and what other goods or services customers are inclined to buy permitting firms to recommend goods and services more accurately and, this way, direct customers toward making specified transactional decisions. Digital platforms are transforming the modes products and services were traditionally marketed, selected, and acquired, accordingly, decreasing the participation of humans in commercial transactions and even moving toward automatic purchase decision-making.[44] AI systems have the capacity to process vast amounts of traditional, social media, and alternative reference data at high speed to judge market sentiment by managing more highly diversified portfolios to reduce idiosyncratic risk.[45]

It has to be taken into account that digital platforms provide businesses with enormous built-in customer bases and operative ways to connect with them enabling even microenterprises to take part directly in global flows. Thus, digital flows are also transferring globalization into a faster gear as information reverberates around the globe and collaboration spans time zones and so taken together, these shifts generate economic value by expanding innovation, competition, and productivity. Furthermore, digitization alters the economics of globalization in several manners and so firstly, in contrast to the last era of globalization, states on the periphery of the network of global data flows aid even more than the digital content producers at the center. Secondly, the forms of corporations implicated are different and so instead of waiting for the benefits of globalization to come from large corporations, SMEs can become micro-multinationals in their own right, and startups can be "born global." Finally, digitization is powering competition as it facilitates innovative business models and empowers companies to step up rapidly.

It is characteristic that the platform companies, being a new organizational form, challenged traditional industry boundaries and advanced synergies by expanding in modes by reason of their capacity leverage data and computational expertise. Moreover, the growth of online platforms was accompanied by minimal intervention by state players until recently, but the platform companies' remarkable power has drawn the concern of States globally. In line, online platforms extraordinary capabilities for expansion caused the development of asymmetric power regarding other companies and the consumers that interact through them resulting in a rapid alteration in the policy and discourse among political elites and other state players. To that extent, the laissez faire regulatory ideology is rapidly losing its political and societal legitimacy.

Hence, societies go through a dynamic movement in which the reorganizational power and prerogatives of private interests and organizations entailing a self-regulating market have caused a reassertion of political authority and so broader societal interests stimulating an effort within which social forces must generate regulatory and governance mechanisms to constrain and possibly redirect political economic and social development in new modes.[46] It seems that there is an effort of

---

[44] Lee Curtis and Rachel Platts, "AI is coming and it will change trademark law" [2017] Managing IP 9, 10.

[45] Esposito A. (2020), Morning Star, How Tech Funds Performed in the Covid-19 Crisis, 7 April 2020. https://www.morningstar.co.uk/uk/news/201203/how-tech-funds-performed-in-the-covid-19-crisis.aspxInstitutional Investor (2020), AI-Powered Hedge Funds Vastly Outperformed, Research Shows. Available at: https://www.institutionalinvestor.com

[46] McIntyre, D. Srinivasan, A., Afuah, A., Gawer, A., and Kretschmer, T. (2020, 7 May). "Multisided platforms as new organizational forms," Academy of Management Perspectives, Published Online: 7 May 2020, https://doi.org/10.5465/amp.2018.0018

constraining platform power, but also retaining more control over policy-making and its implementation and enforcement. On the other hand, the dominance of the digital environment by AI technology firms poses a range of social, political, and economic setbacks, many of which are compounded by their oligopolistic status.

It is worth noting that digital platforms are an extensible technological core, shared by a controller with a host of independent complementors and so digital platforms form a new locus of innovation. On the one hand, innovation platforms leverage generativity by demonstrating the capacity by sharing a technological base with third parties by producing new products and services to end-users. On the other hand, transaction platforms create value by enabling interactions of one or more groups with subsequent exchanges of products, services, content, etc. Moreover, the larger the network, the more useful it becomes to its participants and the more attractive it becomes to non-participants which means that the enlargement of the network boosts the network's usefulness.

In line, computerization of work, from product design and engineering, over manufacturing and logistics, to services, has empowered the geographic breakup of industries and so computerization causes rationalization of work procedures and precise rules by enabling standardization which means that the transfer of jobs from one stage to the next, either across organizations via outsourcing across borders via offshoring, or both offshore outsourcing firstly it is not new but in the past 5 years improvements in the capacity to codify and transfer highly multiplex information from one stage of the value chain to the next, along with dropping costs for both the movement of goods and making voice and data connections, have made possible the shift of manufacturing to countries such as China and India, Singapore and the sourcing of a variety of services from countries such as India and the Philippines.

Today's globalization is merely the latest and most innovative manifestation of globalization's process.[47] It is worth noting that globalization is transforming practically every sector of the world's economy, and that this transformation has vital consequences for the rapidly globalizing market for legal services. It has to be taken into consideration that globalization's characteristics involve the dominance of a world capitalist economic system, the increased utilization and dependence on new information and communication technologies (ICT), the dominance of MNEs, the erosion of local cultures, values, and traditions, and the appearance of a "global culture" within a global society.[48] The means to understanding globalization "critically" is to evaluate it both as a product of technological developments as well as a course of global restructuring of capitalism in which economic, technological,

[47]G Zekos, Corporate Governance and MNEs in Globalization and Cyberspace, 2013 www.novapublishers.com. G Zekos, Economics, Finance and Law on MNEs, 2007 Nova Publishers, New York www.novapublishers.com James R. Lothian, The Internationalization of Money and Finance and the Globalization of Financial Markets 2002 www.ssrn.com

[48]Castells, M. (1996) The Rise of the Network Society (Oxford: Blackwell). KELLNER, D. (1978) Ideology, Marxism, and advanced capitalism. Socialist Review, 42 (November–December), 37–65.

political, and cultural features are entangled.[49] There is a need for democracy to find the way of "catching up" to economic and technological processes. Due to globalizing capitalism, state democracy has to catch up and adjust itself to the global capitalism.[50]

AI technologies have been crucial to production, networking and pushing forward economic and financial global integration. Moreover, the social consequence of globalization is the more intense generation of inequality which means that AI systems produce winners and losers but globalization accelerates this to extremes. Hence, states with their sound economic stand and lavishness of capital and skill have gained the most considerable paybacks from globalization, with the increasing market power of MNEs,[51] the global growth of financial markets allowing higher revenues in emerging markets leading to a technological leadership and strengthening international rules concerning IPRs.

It is worth mentioning that the effect of stronger IPRs influences the entry modes chosen by MNEs and so MNEs can select between exporting, introducing FDI, and licensing to a national company and so stronger IPR alters the way of entry chosen by MNEs. On the one hand, it is argued that stronger IPRs offer the protection essential for production to move to a developing state and so leave go of resources from developed states to enhance the technological frontier. On the other hand, stronger IPRs diminish the capacity of local companies in the host economy to be exposed to new technologies, and they generate a monopoly outcome that lessens the demand to upsurge R&D in the foreign arena.

It has to be taken into consideration that the rule of law is an essential characteristic of economic upgrading and the role of law in advancement and the political-institutional and economic modification is vital. Besides, sustained economic growth has occurred in the absence of rule of law and stable individual property rights regimes but this had happened under the understanding of the written law because some kind of unwritten law, in a form of a canon, has applied in all activities. Even matters developed or occurred in an anarch way they follow the law of anarchism. Moreover, while established liberal democracies associate with anticipated legal orders, there is a need to examine the quality or regulatory reach of the rule of law, even in settings in the globally developed world for the reason that there are inequalities in terms of how the law is practiced and whose rights are most guarded. Additionally, the substantive features of rule of law within the category of recognized "consolidated" democracies differ notably in terms of form such as separation of powers and judicial review but particularly in terms of normative content.

---

[49] Kellner, D. (2002) Theorizing globalization. http://www.gseis.ucla.edu/faculty/kellner/papers/theoryglob.htm

[50] William E. Scheuerman, "Critical Theory beyond Habermas," in Oxford Handbook of Political Theory, ed. John S. Dryzek, Bonnie Honig, and Anne Phillips (Oxford: Oxford University Press, 2006), 94–103.

[51] G Zekos, Economics, Finance and Law on MNEs, 2007 Nova Publishers, New York www.novapublishers.com

Tamanaha[52] observes that while the "revived" rule of law agenda is more sophisticated in discourse, it is not that far removed from the teleological foundations of earlier modernization doctrines.

Which are the political processes by which rule of law like features shape up in various societies? It has to be taken into account that the inter-disciplinarity within the social and legal sciences is inadequate in the knowledge base to comprehend the role of law and rule of law both in molding political, economic,[53] and social conduct and, in succession, as a sequel of political contestation and negotiation.[54]

It is worth noting that various rule of law paths link with different amalgamations of power relations, resource distribution, and ideational foundations of the reigning political settlement which means that the rule of law is never absolute/conclusive in its heart of its content and context but the essence of the rule of law has to be standardized in a global scale in order to be harmonically applied in globalization achieving its goals. Otherwise, the application of the rule of law will be declared but in fact there will be a different understanding and so allowing misinterpretations and exploitations by various groups to the detriment of the whole society. In other words, there is a need for the international society to declare what the rule of law represents and which is its DNA as a notion and conception essential for the fair existence and continuity of humanity in its natural form because the transformation of human life in another form of existence and the emergence of artificial beings will might demand another understanding of the rule of law.

3.4 EU and Digital Economy

In reality, as digital technology is implemented across the economy, dividing the digital economy is gradually more difficult for the reason that the digital economy is progressively becoming the economy itself, it would be problematic, if not unfeasible, to ring-fence the digital economy from the rest of the economy. Electronic technology and digital economy characterized by volatility. But despite the volatility firms have been able to leverage market position by acquiring dominance. However, in the digital economy, many networks operate instantaneously, with the

[52] Brian Z. Tamanaha, Beyond the Formalist-Realist Divide, The Role of Politics in Judging, 2009 Princeton University Press. Tamanaha, Brian Z., A Companion to Philosophy of Law and Legal Theory, 2nd Edition, Dennis Patterson, ed., Blackwell Publishers, 2009.

[53] Booth, D., Harris, D. and Wild, L. (2016) "From political economy analysis to doing development differently: a learning experience." London: ODI. Brinks, D. and Botero, S. (2014) "Inequality and the Rule of Law: Ineffective Rights in Latin American Democracies" in D. Brinks, S. Mainwaring and M. Leiras, (eds.) Reflections on Uneven Democracies: The Legacy of Guillermo O'Donnell, Baltimore: Johns Hopkins University Press.

[54] Perry-Kessaris, A., The Case for a Visualized Economic Sociology of Legal Development, September 2014 Current legal problems 67(1):169–198, Perry-Kessaris, A. (ed.) (2011) Law in the pursuit of development: Principles into practice? London: Routledge.

result that in many cases competition in a monopolized market is affected by other markets, which combined with the decreased entry barriers, moderate monopoly power in the first market.

Technological progress has led to a plunging in the cost of computing power, and so, neither an Internet end-user nor in many cases the service provider is needed to pay a marginal price for using the network. Thus, increased performance and capital expenditure have evidently lessened barriers to entry for new cyberspace-based businesses and so promoting innovation and the constant development of new business models. Consequently, in short periods of time, corporations that appeared to control a considerable part of the market and possessed a dominant position for a short period of time have found themselves quickly losing market share to challengers that assembled their businesses on more effective technology, or a more sustainable business model. As a result of the fast rate of innovation, the few corporations that have achieved long-term success classically have done so by investing considerable resources in research and development and in acquiring startups with innovative ideas and so persistently evaluating and amending business models so as to leverage their market position and uphold dominance in the market.[55]

It is obvious that digital technologies are modifying the economy, with implications for development and the globe is on the crossover of a new digital era. Thus, with radically reduced costs of collecting, storing, and processing data, and greatly improved computing power, digitalization is transforming economic activities around the globe and so it is predictable to influence value chains, skill requirements, production and trade, needing adaptations of existing legal and regulatory agendas in numerous areas.

UNCTAD[56] shows that "the digital economy is creating new opportunities for trade and development. It is helping smaller businesses and entrepreneurs in developing countries to connect with global markets more easily, and is opening up new ways of generating income. ICTs, e-commerce and other digital applications are being leveraged to promote entrepreneurship, including the empowerment of women as entrepreneurs and traders, and to support productive activities, decent job creation, creativity and innovation. Furthermore, mobile and digital solutions are contributing to facilitating greater financial inclusion. And small firms in developing countries with sufficient connectivity may be able to access various cloud services and obtain crowd finance in online platforms." To that extent, crucial technologies underpinning the advancing digital economy embrace advanced robotics, artificial intelligence, the Internet of Things (IoT), cloud computing, big data analytics, and three-dimensional (3D) print.

---

[55] OECD (2014), "The digital economy, new business models and key features," in Addressing the Tax Challenges of the Digital Economy, OECD Publishing, Paris. DOI: https://doi.org/10.1787/9789264218789-7-en

[56] Information Economy Report 2017: Digitalization, Trade and Development UNITED NATIONS PUBLICATION UNCTAD/IER/2017 p xiii.

It is worth noting that over time the flexibility and velocity of industrial robots and other CNC machinery have amplified while costs have come down which means that straightforward statistical process control algorithms are relied on to shut down or accommodate production processes automatically when they move out of tolerance. Nonetheless, with the rise in computing power and introduction of low-cost sensor technology, the collection and sharing of working data across like machinery, within and even across plants, has made "predictive maintenance" achievable, avoiding processing mistakes or machine breakdowns before wear and tear of mechanical components or other expected setbacks cross critical thresholds. Therefore, industrial robots are becoming more artificially intelligent and so as robots become more responsive and aware of their environments and working backgrounds, they will work securely together with people to supplement and assist workers, rather than replacing them which means that such "robots[57]" will perceive human movements and automatically and intelligently attune their movements and procedures on the fly through machine learning. It could be said that concerning many products in the digital dominion, the continued improvement and miniaturization of both mechanical and micro-electronic technologies mean that robots are becoming smaller, cheaper, less power needing, and much more powerful such as an evolving class of small robot arms priced between 300 € and 1.000 € performing different useful jobs, for instance, the fabrication of solid objects (3D printing), which are pre-programmed to accomplish a range of operations and some are controlled in real-time with a smart phone. Hence, industrial robots are the most distinguishable part of the "intelligent factory," but developments in inventory control and autonomous industrial means are furthering productivity and quality boosts in plants. In addition, by uniting image recognition and augmented reality (AR) technologies, a human operator is directed through complex or variable assembly steps and receives real-time input from an expert in another plant able to distantly picture what the operator is viewing and producing. Thus, IoT wireless transmission is accomplished utilizing open-source protocols like Bluetooth, 3G/4G, WiFi, or any other new technology.[58]

In reality, globalization of markets is one of the most appealing developments of this century which is further augmented by the electronic technologies that have shaped the digital economy and so its effect on economic transactions, procedures, institutions, and actors is spectacular, wide ranging, and continual. Moreover, globalization threatens traditional norms and behavior and necessitates different mindsets which mean that it generates openings for partakers who can be proactive and creative. Thus, all countries that have lost their change for an improvement of their economy due to anti-globalization movements have to blame themselves

[57] Hollinger, P. 2016. "Meet the robots: humans and robots together on the factory floor." Financial Times, May 5. Web access: https://www.ft.com/content/6d5d609e-02e2-11e6-af1dc47326021344

[58] Greenough, J. and Camhi, J. 2016. "Here's why some are calling the Internet of Things the next Industrial Revolution." Business Insider, Tech Insider, Feb. 10. http://www.businessinsider.com/iot-trends-will-shape-the-way-we-interact-2016-1

because globalization offers opportunities for open-minded economies that can consider carefully the pros and cons of globalization in making profitable decisions for their economies.

In today's global competition, decisive sources of competitive advantage are often company specific embracing such factors as the quality of management and leadership, capacity to innovate and commercialize new goods, competence to determine and respond to emerging openings, and ability to organize monetary and human resources. In fact, while country specific advantages such as factor aptitudes or trade setup is still central, their effect is somewhat more uniform across different states. Likewise, it is demanding for public policy makers to articulate industrial or trade policies which influence all industries alike which means that the same policy measure has got a different effect on firms from different industries. Moreover, these new realities of competition indicate that legal professionals have to cultivate a comprehensive understanding of corporation assets and competencies embracing "soft" factors such as information management, technology, and intellectual property.

It has to be taken into account that digitization alters the economics of globalization in several manners and so as digital platforms become global in scope, they are driving down the cost of cross-border communications and transactions, permitting corporations to get hold of customers and suppliers in any state. While globalization was once for large MNEs, platforms diminish the minimum scale necessary to go global, allowing small business and entrepreneurs around the globe to play a part which means that new kinds of competitors appear from all over the world, intensifying pressure on industry incumbents. Also, the new age of digital globalization also creates challenges and firms can enter new markets, but they are subjected to pricing pressures, aggressive global competitors, and disruptive digital business models. Besides, data must be protected against cybercrime and so social media generate global communities permitting networks of extremists to connect which means that there is a need for more international coordination to cope with many of these issues. Today's version of globalization is much more complex and fast-paced, but connectedness can be a path to growth and so the globe has never been more connected by commerce, communication, and travel than it is today. Nonetheless the pattern of globalization is fluctuating and while trade was once conquered by tangible goods and was largely confined to advanced economies and their large MNEs, nowadays global data flows are flooding, and digital platforms permit more states and smaller companies to take part causing repercussions.

The question to be answered is how globalized is Europe? It could be said that since the introduction of the euro in 1999, financial market and trade integration have augmented extremely not only between euro area states, but also between non-euro area states and between Europe and the rest of the globe. To that extent, FDI is deemed the more attractive form of financial integration and it is signposted by European policy makers that such "real" financial integration is superior to international bank loans, for the reason that FDI transfers technology and know-how between states.

Taking into account that 10% ownership share is meant to capture stable long-term foreign investments; it seems that there is a high positive correlation between quarterly FDI inflows and outflows, signifying that FDI inflows might not be as stable as customarily thought.[59] In line, Lane and Milesi-Ferretti[60] argue that FDI positions vis-a-vis financial centers have improved since 2012 due to the escalating complexity of the corporate structures of MNEs. To that extent, it seems that the Netherlands and Luxembourg rank top globally, next to the USA, as FDI recipients and investors even if they are small countries which means that these countries host many foreign-owned special purpose entities (SPEs) which MNEs often employ to accomplish FDI with the intention of curtailing taxes.[61]

It has to be taken into account that it seems that home bias in Europe has not been amended and so even in the Euro area, share of any given country's capital stock owned by foreigners does not exceed 20% which means that risk sharing via capital markets is low and elucidates low levels of consumption smoothing during the European crisis of 2009–2010. Moreover, even though many European companies are directly owned by other European corporations, a large part is eventually owned by investors outside Europe. Thus, it seems that the ownership of corporations by investors outside Europe is undervalued by direct ownership and official statistics, both of which are based on residency principle.[62] Furthermore, North America is a key source of foreign investment funds and any data except ultimate foreign ownership based FDI greatly undervalues this which means that a substantial share of North American investments is routed through Western European financial centers. FDI from Western Europe has been exaggerated and so giving the false idea that FDI within Europe has enlarged immensely but, in fact, it seems that lower and stable levels of FDI within Europe exist and the eventual investing country for these investments is the USA.[63]

Ritzer[64] asserts that economic globalization brings along prospective benefits, but also difficulties to the nation-state, which encounters new types of government and so administering its problems with global policies with the help of international institutions in order to diminish vagueness caused by global insertion involving loss of national sovereignty for national governments. It is argued that there is no direct connection between trade openness and economic growth being a factor to reducing

[59] Blanchard, Olivier and Julien Acalin, "What Does Measured FDI Actually Measure?," October 2016. PIIE Working Paper No. PB16–17.

[60] Lane, Philip R. and Gian M Milesi-Ferretti, "International Financial Integration in the Aftermath of the Global Financial Crisis," May 2017. IMF Working Paper No. 17/115.

[61] Damgaard, Jannick and Thomas Elkjaer, "The Global FDI Network: Searching for Ultimate Investors," November 2017. IMF Working Paper No. 17/258.

[62] Damgaard, Jannick and Thomas Elkjaer, "The Global FDI Network: Searching for Ultimate Investors," November 2017. IMF Working Paper No. 17/258.

[63] Reinsdorf, Marshall, and Robert Yuskavage (2018), "Offshoring, Sourcing Substitution Bias, and the Measurement of Growth in U.S. Gross Domestic Product and Productivity," Review of Income and Wealth, 64(1), (March), 127–146.

[64] Ritzer, G. (2011), Globalization: The Essentials, Wiley-Blackwell, UK.

global inequalities, although not inequalities within each nation and so trade liberalization does not lead to economic triumph for the reason that it is the policy mix that permits taking advantage of globalization.[65] Nonetheless, although states chase a great international economic integration, globalization limits sovereignty, and the possibility of democratic control. Conversely, the latest global crisis reveals that greater international coordination is wanted to move toward a "Global Federalism" so as to continue with dismantling trade in a democratic form. In fact, interdependence denotes that the actions taken by a Nation-State have effects that will be affected by the reaction of other Nation-States and international players such as MNEs and their financial flows, being an indispensable part of economic globalization and gradually contribute more actively to international politics affecting decision-making at the international and national level.

Moreover, capital flows either as FDI or portfolio are vital for the development of economic globalization and so FDI has positive results on the host country and developing economies have realized that. Nonetheless, the higher flow of investment is still focused on developed economies and emerging economies. Besides, to say that globalization is capable of inspiring long-term growth for all states that are engrossed in it is inaccurate for the reason that problems occur with inconveniences and heterogeneous results, principally in economies of developing nations encompassing the loss of a model of economic and social cohesion as the embedded liberalism. Mauricio Lascurain Fernández[66] argues that "Through the Trilemma of the Global Economy it was proven that countries that wish to join economic globalization cannot obtain full sovereignty and democracy. The proposed option is to give democracy a long-term continuity, as long as international organizations equitably and efficiently supply the needs of the nation state. To make this possible, reform of economic institutions of international governance will also be needed. In this regard, agencies need to redefine its role globally with ecumenically accepted rules for moving forward fairly in the process of economic integration, allowing all countries to enjoy the potential benefits of globalization."

Due to globalization there is a need for a better governance system of international trade is necessitated in combination with a greater regulation of the international financial system and so financial globalization without regulation is less secure such as the extraordinary effect that the mortgage crisis had in the USA, which also had an effect on European, Asian, and Latin American economies.

It is worth noting that in a corporate re-domiciliation, the headquarters of the firm relocates to another state. While they can take many modes, corporate re-domiciliation often engages significant FDI flows that are almost entirely, if not entirely offset, by portfolio investment flows which that it is probable that these types of transactions, when they result in offsetting flows, are considered as a mode

[65]Gurgul, H. and Lach, L. (2014), "Globalization and economic growth: Evidence from two decades of transition in CEE," Economic Modelling, Volume 36, January 2014, p. 99–107.

[66]Mauricio Lascurain Fernández, Challenges Of Economic Globalization, rev.relac.int.estrateg. segur.12(1):23–50,2017 p 44.

of pass-through capital for the reason that the capital that has flown into the reporting country flows out to other countries. Furthermore, the characteristics that would make an economy suitable to host a re-domiciliation would be those tendering relative tax, regulatory, and other benefits to foreign investors and so the range of influences on the host economy based on the range to which the redomiciled corporation actually transferred operations to its new headquarters economy. It is worth noting that non-financial MNEs issuing liabilities in some states and currencies at the same time they get assets in other economies and currencies in order to engender profits. Maria Borga and Cecilia Caliandro[67] specify "that the amount of pass-through capital in operating affiliates, rather than in SPEs, is quite extensive, accounting for about one-quarter of the inward FDI positions excluding resident SPEs in a selection of European countries. It also appears that pass-through capital is growing faster than the 'real' FDI."

3.5 AI Economy and Gig-Economy Platforms

AI technological advances are transforming the global economy and societies and so firms and organizations increasingly use automation technologies to streamline their operations, speed up processes, shorten production/service delivery time, offer consistent product quality, diminish costs, and improve competitiveness and economic efficiency. Nonetheless, the employment of automation technologies will continue to accelerate in the future until societies reach a point when all goods and services are produced by automation technologies. Thus, economic systems are moving toward automation as a production factor rather than human labor[68] which means that decisions will be taken and executed by artificial autonomous agents being software programs, not by human beings.

Taking into consideration that the economic decisions will be taken and executed by AAI algorithms and humanoid robots rather than humans owners, the legal system has to be attuned to grant legal personality and consequently rights to robots.[69]

There is a shift from a knowledge-based economy to a data-driven economy and so AI is a central feature of the data-driven economy because of its capability to

[67] Maria Borga and Cecilia Caliandro, Eliminating the Pass-Through: Towards FDI Statistics that Better Capture the Financial and Economic Linkages between Countries, NBER Working Paper No. 25029 September 2018 p 30.

[68] Ivanov, S. (2017). Robonomics—principles, benefits, challenges, solutions. Yearbook of Varna University of Management, 10, 283–293. Ivanov, S. (2021). Robonomics: The rise of the automated economy. ROBONOMICS: The Journal of the Automated Economy, 1, 11.

[69] Gellers, J. C. (2021). Rights for Robots: Artificial Intelligence, Animal and Environmental Law. Oxon: Routledge.

generate more data, information, and knowledge from existing data.[70] Moreover, digital businesses operate transnationally without the need to commit resources to a local presence or local means of production parallel to conventional "investments."

In the ongoing era, the availability of digital "space" is just as important as the availability of physical space. In the labor setting, workers often no longer share a common workplace because merely have no shared physical space in which to meet, discuss, and organize. Unions are recommending that workers who can no longer organize in person gather on Zoom instead.[71] Digital resources are powerful substitutes for physical spaces.[72] Undeniably, digital spaces are vital in organizing even where physical space is available, particularly in circumstances where meeting online is more practicable or advantageous than gathering together in a single physical location.[73]

Another phenomenon of AI technology is the emergence of Gig-economy platforms such as Uber, and Instacart enabling flexible work arrangements and so has attracted increasing participation of workers and employers in recent years.[74] Thus, Gig workers actively take part in short-term job tasks and temporary freelance projects requested by the employers on the platforms. To that extent, the coordinating between workers and tasks is generally managed by the platforms and accelerated by digital technologies.

Will AI-driven robots displace human labor on an unprecedented scale? AI devices are deployed at the behest of employers, and so designers focus on optimizing the corporations' interests. The designer trains the algorithm to identify the personal characteristics of workers and so the AI device can be trained in indirectly undermine collective labor rights or enforcement of minimum standards regulation.[75] AI also gives corporations more control over when and how work is performed. Moreover, AI can keep control over workers and the value generated by their labor and so AI technologies have enabled the gig-economy to thrive by Uber advancing transportation services on a massive scale while employing no drivers. In addition, AI necessitates escalating levels of scrutiny and control over

---

[70] D Ciuriak, "Economic Rents and the Counters of Conflict in the Data-Driven Economy" (2020) CIGI Paper No. 245.

[71] Steps to Organizing for Protection at Work, UE UNION, https://fight.ueunion.org/five-steps

[72] Alexia Fernández Campbell, Why Thousands of Google Employees Are Protesting Across the World, VOX (Nov. 1, 2018, 2:10 PM EDT), https://www.vox.com/2018/11/1/18051884/googleemployee-walkouts-explainedCaroline O'Donovan, Facebook Played a Pivotal Role in the West Virginia Teacher Strike, BUZZFEED NEWS (Mar. 7, 2018, 7:47 PM ET), https://www.buzzfeednews.com/article/carolineodonovan/facebook-group-west-virginia-teachers-strike

[73] Conor Dougherty & John Eligon, How to Protest When You're Ordered Not to Gather, N.Y. TIMES (May 6, 2020), https://www.nytimes.com/2020/04/23/business/economy/coronavirus-tenants-rent-protests.html

[74] Huang, N., Burtch, G., Hong, Y., and Pavlou, P. A. (2020). Unemployment and worker participation in the gig economy: Evidence from an online labor market. Information Systems Research, 31(2):431–448.

[75] Cynthia Estlund, Automation Anxiety: Why And How To Save Work, OUP (2021);

employees within a corporation monitoring workers' productivity and utilizing this information to automate dismissals.[76] To that extent, as predictive AI more and more affects how workers and employers interact in labor markets, courts will have to sort out how far liability for algorithmic bias should extend. On the other hand, the advancement of AAI will eliminate matters of bias and discrimination in AAI labor market.

It has to be taken into account that there is an escalation in the integration of automated and algorithmic systems empowered by artificial intelligence on gig-economy platforms. To that extent, AI is taking on managerial roles transforming the gig workspace by optimally assessing, matching, and assigning the job tasks to gig workers.[77] Hence, an AAI-enabled system can competently accomplish predictions and make recommendations to advance matching quality. While the AI-enabled systems use a rich set of data inputs about labor supply and demand at a large scale to arrive at precise, real-time predictions of best matches, they are noteworthy drivers for escalating workers' productivity and platforms' operational competence and so producing higher revenues. Nonetheless, as a result of the flexible character of the gig-economy, workers decide proactively whether to join in a gig-economy platform and so unlike traditional workers with a fixed schedule, gig workers are more independent and flexible in setting their own work agenda. Additionally, the adoption of AI in matching workers and employers jointly determines the overall revenue of a gig platform because the increased worker performance as a result of improved matching quality and the demand information revealed by matching outcomes, which can lead to workers' strategic participation decisions.[78]

It is worth mentioning here that AI technologies are stimulating organizations to reorganize themselves, alter their numerous departments, build new training models, and re-evaluate all their HR practices. Nowadays, AI capabilities are being used to expand business operations and solutions because AI creates value for firms by increasing productivity, improving processes and resources, forming new ways and means which in turn advance the employee and customer experience overall. Moreover, AI let firms recruit the right person faster with a perfect skill set which matches the role and foreseeing the prospect of future success.[79]

[76] Colin Lecher, How Amazon Automatically Tracks and Fires Warehouse Workers for 'Productivity,' THE VERGE, https://www.theverge.com/2019/4/25/18516004/amazon-warehouse-fulfillment-centers-productivity-firingterminations

[77] Cameron, L. (2020). The Rise of Algorithmic Work: Implications for Organizational Control and Worker Autonomy. PhD thesis.

[78] Kellogg, K. C., Valentine, M. A., and Christin, A. (2020). Algorithms at work: The new contested terrain of control. Academy of Management Annals, 14(1):366–410.

[79] A. Hemalatha & Dr. P. Barani Kumar, A Study On Impact Of Artificial Intelligence On Organisational Effectiveness, (UGC Care Journal) Vol-43 No.-04 (XXXI) October–December (2020) p60.

It has to be taken into account that governments are racing to develop national AI strategies to enlarge their digital economies and so AI technologies generate and channel political and economic pressures.[80]

The law offers some leverage for addressing biased algorithms; nonetheless, anti-discrimination case law has advanced through individual suits challenging discrete decisions not to hire or to fire someone which means that much of the doctrine concentrates on intentional discrimination of humans with discriminatory motives. On the other hand, algorithmic bias is typically not the product of conscious intent, and it functions on a systemic rather than individual basis, making some traditional approaches irrelevant. While existing laws stipulate some levers for addressing the discriminatory impacts of AI, laws have been far less concerned with power imbalances and the social harms they might produce. The power of AI comes from its capability to utilize large amounts of data. It seems that in the employment context, few laws protect worker privacy, but they are ill-suited to an era of big data.[81] In many countries, the law as currently enacted is far more limited in tackling the ways in which predictive AI might contribute to economic inequality.

3.6 Cyber-Colonization and Politics

It is worth noting that in a globally integrated economy, the capital colonizes countries by exploiting the recourses of any country without the need to control the whole territory of the colonized countries. Moreover, the network of the capital seems to have a new approach toward the utilization of the resources worldwide without conquering the territory of the colonized countries showing a picture of self-governed countries boosting the ego of the colonized nations. Economic neo-colonialism obtains the human and the natural resources of a peripheral country to flow to the economies of the wealthy countries at the center of the global economic system. MNEs might cause humanitarian, environmental, and ecological destruction to the populations which inhabit the neo-colonies whose "development" and economy are now dependent on foreign markets and large-scale trade agreements. Privatization of national resources, while initially leading to immediate large-scale influx of investment capital, is often followed by dramatic increases in the rate of unemployment, poverty, and a decline in per-capita income.

Also, there is a new ego-centered tactic to domestic and international economic order building stands counter to the tripartite management of mass production for the home market and to stabilize/calm that system by the rule-based international

---

[80] J Fjeld et al., "Principled Artificial Intelligence: Mapping Consensus in Ethical and Rights-Based Approaches to Principles for AI" (2020) Berkman Klein Center for Internet & Society, https://dash.harvard.edu/handle/1/42160420

[81] Pauline T. Kim, Data Mining and the Challenges of Protecting Employee Privacy under U.S. Law, 40 COMP. LAB. L. & POL'Y J. 405 (2019).

financial order of the gold-dollar standard. Moreover, economic elites, after having lost their red enemy (Soviet Union) at home and abroad, also lost the corrective force that held in reserve their competition at home and abroad within the duty-bound of reason. Markets are apparatus for decentralized coordination of economic decisions. Consequently, international markets are an expansion of national markets. The entrepreneurial state of high-income countries tries to find business openings beyond borders for home-based owners of investment funds and for owners of technological assets. Governments of entrepreneurial states moderate, or try to reduce, social protection costs which means the return of economic competition within states, though in a new, postcolonial form, and of rehabilitated income polarization between countries.

It is characteristic that interests and identity both play a role in the twenty-first century transition. In continental Europe, elites in the twentieth century met defeat at home and humiliation in colonies. Realists in the industrial era affirm that foreign trade and foreign investment are apparatus of power and tools for creating wealth. State actors that control state-society complexes in foreign relations, embracing external commercial policy, utilize these apparatuses for national and elite advantages. One of the first rules of economic growth is that profits come from market deficiency. An imperative source of market imperfection is, first, in technological advancement. Disproportionate access to modern technology generates imperfect markets. For those (countries or merely group of people) in control of societies with productive superiority, military power is a means to expand markets as well as for getting control over markets of late-industrializing countries. To that extent, MNEs are not just an extension across borders of civil society. It has to be considered that trade law is international public law in fact and not private contract law. International financial transactions rely basically on the anticipation that counterparties will perform future contractual commitments placing confidence and probably volatile expectations at center stage.

Has the EU been re-colonized by the global capital? It has to be taken into account that Europe has been re-colonized by the global capital revealing a democratic face but in fact the decisive decisions concerning the future of the Europeans are agreed in such a way that the interests of the global capital prevail over the interests of the Europeans leading to a possible disintegration of EU into the old division of nations states and even igniting old conflicts among them.

In other words, re-colonization concealed as globalization is cold-bloodedly squashed by a range of coercive methods. It seems that globalization led by capitalist interests alone is anticipated, parallel to what it achieved a century ago, to yield a wild global capitalism with social exclusion, uncontrolled competition, and exploitation. Up till now, the civilizing role of capitalism cannot be done by individual countries, but, owing to the global nature of capitalism, by global institutions. Moreover, the development of AI technology and its application should lead to more objective decision-making and revealing to the European the need for moving toward the establishment of the United States of Europe in order Europe to become a global player and not being merely an ally for the Super Powers which means that

Europe's territory might be utilized in order to gain political pros other forces rather that Europeans.[82]

It has to be taken into account that institutions add to stability assisting anchor expectations. In times of political stalemate, valuable institutions are important since they distribute their mandates determinedly and beyond of the push-and-pull of the political course foreshortens the crisis and the self-fulfilling cycle of weak economic functioning. To that extent, independent central banks with a certain mandate to uphold price stability has been effective in anchoring inflation prospects. In line, the ECB has been an anchor of stability, generating an operative safeguard against deflationary narratives when they emerged in the euro area and so the ECB has disallowed deflationary dynamics from materializing.[83]

Cyberspace and the technological revolution allow the coupling of different spaces and times in the fields of law and politics. The relationship between technology and society results in dialectic of mutual impacts[84] and transformations but science and technology are steered by people in power,[85] whether public or private, in accordance with their interests.[86] The engine driving integration of countries is not only the appeal to create an integrated global community around positive values but also the requirement of dealing with shared global risks. Electronic colonization takes place within discursive venues (on television, in education, and in corporate settings), often without anyone perceiving it, for the reason that the ingredients of the global-village narrative are so common. Owners of the global electronic technology explore the global society and its remote corners, and even acting as colonizers of its cyber-dimension and the real-world one.[87]

On the one hand, economic globalization raises the prospect of transnational terrorism merely by increasing the density of suitable targets in more integrated states. On the other hand, economic globalization diminishes transnational terrorist events because it facilitates economic growth, which in turn eliminates an enticement to engage in terrorism. As technology steers economic development, the

---

[82] For further analysis see G Zekos, The United States of Europe The Global Player, 2019 Nova Science Publications New York USA. www.novapublishers.com

[83] "The impact of uncertainty on activity in the euro area," Economic Bulletin, Issue 8/2016, ECB and "Uncertainty about Uncertainty," speech by Kristin Forbes, External MPC member, Bank of England, 23 November 2016.

[84] G Zekos "Internet or Electronic Technology: A Threat to State Sovereignty" 1999 JILT, http://www.law.warwick.ac.uk/jilt/99-3/zekos.html, G Zekos, Cyber-Territory and Jurisdiction of Nations, 2012 Journal of Internet Law, Number 12/3, G. Zekos, Globalisation and States' Cyber-Territory', [2011] 5 Web JCLI. G Zekos, IPRS Protection and Their Impact Upon FDI, GDP Growth &Trade, 2013 Scholar's Press, www.scholars-press.com www.morebooks.de Germany.

[85] Ulrich Beck, La société du risque. Sur la voie d'une autre modernité. Traduit de l'allemand par Laure Bernardi 36–37 (Alto Aubier ed., 2001).

[86] José Alvarez, Do States socialize? 54 Duke LJ, 965–966 (2005).

[87] Rossman, G. P. (2002) Networking and mobilizing collective intelligence http://ecolecon.missouri.edu/globalresearch/chapters/2–04.html. Selfe, C. L. (1995) Lest we think the revolution is a revolution: images of technology and the nature of change. http://www.cptsc.org/conferences/keynote95.html

government is less competitive financially than the private sector in recruiting the high-tech talent.[88] Moreover, the government is limited in its capacity to supervise and sanction tech-savvy money-launderers, transnational terrorists, drug traffickers, and other international criminals who rely on the international financial market.[89] It is worth mentioning that the capital can use dirty tricks to move problems of terrorism around the world with the intention of destabilizing countries not cooperating or fighting dirty re-colonization and so achieving its goals.

Law helps keeps order as a means of social integration at the societal level by coursing within and across sub-systems, and by organizing and directing social action within and between bodies and networks and among persons. Moreover, normal law-abiding behavior enables and inspires law-abiding behavior which means that implementing the rule of law generates the circumstances for its own existence, thereby reproducing and preserving itself.[90]

It is argued that legal evolution is based upon social, doctrinal, economic, and sociobiological influences.[91] In fact, there is an evolutionary process of social advancement common to most advanced or energetic societies which mean that advanced societies go through several successive stages of adaptation. Hence, legal evolution is the law's development and so law continually adjusts to its setting in a progressive way which means that old forms are molded generating new advanced ones. Moreover, Calnan[92] argues that law co-evolves with people, societies, and cultures in a coordinative, information exchange that sponsors stability and survival. Additionally, the causes of this transformation are founded on both human agency and social impacts. In other words, law is founded on reason and human will.[93] Furthermore, it is argued that legal principles are social constructs, created by people in particular social contexts for certain reasons to accomplish specific ends.[94] To that extent, law is seen as evolutionary and safeguarding adjustment to a modifying environment.[95] In line, it could be said that law is not a simple accumulation of social and/or natural forces but it is a multifaceted information network of interdependent "jurisystems.[96]" It seems that over time, law's dynamism alters social behavior and cultural memory, instigating "a cycle of epigenetics and gene-culture coevolution" that regenerates society's biological disposition for legality which means that given

[88] Naím, Moisés. 2000. Missing links: The digital drain. Foreign Policy 120:119–20.

[89] Frankel, Jeffrey. 2000. Globalization of the economy. In Governance in a globalizing world, edited by Joseph Nye and John Donahue. Washington, DC: Brookings Institution.

[90] Richard Dawkins, The Selfish Gene, 2nd ed. (Oxford: Oxford University Press 1990).

[91] E. Donald Elliott, The Evolutionary Tradition in Jurisprudence, 85 Colum. L. Rev. 38 (1985).

[92] Alan Calnan, Law's Coevolution, at: https://ssrn.com/abstract=3363356

[93] Anthony J. Sebok, Misunderstanding Positivism, 93 Mich. L. Rev. 2054, 2062–64 (1995).

[94] Joseph William Singer, Realism Now, 76 Cal. L. Rev. 465, 474 (1988).

[95] A.G. Keller, Law in Evolution, 28 Yale L.J. 769, 773 (1919).

[96] Charles Kadushin, Understanding Social Networks: Theories, Concepts, And Findings At 21–22 (2012). Nicholas A. Christakis, Connected: The Surprising Power Of Our Social Networks And How They Shape Our Lives 35 (2009).

law's systemic nature, any socio-centric jurisprudence now seems obsolete and so the biological understanding of the existence of humans is the basis for the legality of the applied rules. Moreover, law is used as a tool by social players and so legal practice has been rationalized, especially via the differentiation of the modern legal professions.

On the one hand, McAdams[97] considers this function as a collection of motives why individuals obey the law independent of legal sanctions and independent of legitimacy. How the information function of law is conceptualized? Legislation exposes standpoints approving or disapproving of a given behavior, which triggers individuals to modernize their beliefs about what others think, which consecutively leads to behavior alteration so as to circumvent the discontentment of others. On the other hand, Schauer[98] considers this function as yet another way that law forces insofar as the result is generated by means of activating the coercive force of social norms. Hence, coercion is central in explaining how law influences behavior, even though in this context law is merely outsourcing its coercive power to private actors.

Law sets up terms under which an international community exists, creating and varying the potential of visions concerning justice and legitimacy. Any legal system is the product of an uninterrupted development, rationalizing and systematizing diverse forms, whether they are derived from natural law, utilitarian, or positivist principles.[99] It has to be taken into account that the complexity of the international legal system envisages greater interaction between traditional sources of public international law such as treaties, custom, unilateral acts, and general principles of international law and other forms of norm-creation such as sub-state, public, private, and transnational. Moreover, complexity fluctuates from complication, in which there are strong interactions among various components, but the results of which are predictable; in a complex system, this expectedness is not portrayed.

Does international law is formed to deal with private interests? It has to be considered that the decisions of private actors take place under the umbrella of international laws ascertained by independent sovereign governments coming together through international coalitions. Moreover, governments play a critical role in formal compliance with international law by enacting and enforcing domestic laws that put into operation international agreements. Thus, the better the enforcement of international law within a country, the more expected it is that private actors will adhere to such laws either because of norms or by reason of benefits or punishments.[100] It seems that international law more and more is based on private players rather than conventional political establishments.[101] Consequently, the

[97] McAdams, Richard H. 2015. The Expressive Powers of Law: Theories and Limits. Cambridge, MA: Harvard University Press.

[98] Schauer, Frederick. 2015. The Force of Law. Cambridge, MA: Harvard University Press.

[99] François Ost, Legal system between order and disorder, ix-x. (Oxford University Press ed., 1994).

[100] Harlan Grant Cohen, Finding International Law: Rethinking the Doctrine of Sources, 93 Iowa L. Rev. 65, 97 (2007).

[101] Paul B. Stephan, Privatizing International Law, 97 Va. L. Rev. 1573, 1574–75 (2011)

motivation of private actors to comply gives insight on how valuable international laws are and what stimulates compliance with such laws.

The globalization of law is a course of act of the law accomplished by dissimilar players in various territories revealing essential outcomes of the contemporary legal system such as de-territorialization: and multi-directionality. Distinctive legal sources are formed through direct contact among sub-state and transnational actors, both public and private not classified as sources of international law yet.[102] Due to globalization reality has not yet stabilized and the interactions among all actors implicated are already at a maximum but reality changes more swiftly than the speed to which legal thought is accustomed. Principles and dichotomies in international law[103]—such as autonomy and sovereignty, public and private nationality, state and non-state, and territorial limits and the state's monopoly on the legitimate use of force—are inadequate interpretative guides for the legal order in the new globalized environment and there is an imminent need to adapt to in globalization.

It has to be taken into account that the development of traditional international law and the international legal custom are not equipped to handle disruptions triggered by algorithmic activities. Nevertheless, effective political consensus has to be shown in order international law to deal with AI but the advancement of AAI international law will be in the heart of the AAI international society. The fluidity and multidimensionality of cyberspace, information warfare, and metaphysics will be the basis of global AAI society.

3.7 IPRs In Digital Economy

It has to be taken into consideration that MNEs control technology supplies by virtue of their ownership of proprietary technologies, but they also account for a considerable share of the demand, via their foreign affiliates. Zekos[104] thinks that there is a need in distinguishing between the MNE as an economic entity and so allowing the national law of establishment, the private international law, and the international commercial law to deal with the economic matters and the MNE as a whole unit.

Moreover, the process of globalization within the framework of the EU shows that both the mechanisms of a free market and the instruments of central regulation, backed by central enforcement authorities, have been used. Zekos[105] has specified

[102] Paul Schiff Berman, Judges as Cosmopolitan Transnational Actors. University of Connecticut School of Law Articles and Working Papers. Paper 38 (2004) http://lsr.nellco.org/uconn_wps/38

[103] Sabino Cassese, The globalization of law 37 (4) Journal of International Law and Politics 973–993 (2005).

[104] G Zekos, Economics, Finance and Law on MNEs, 2007 Nova Publishers, New York www.novapublishers.com

[105] G. Zekos, "IPRs' impact upon FDI," 2013 PhD Thesis, Economics Department, University of Peloponnese, Tripoli, Hellas, www.uop.gr G Zekos, The United States of Europe: The Global Player, 2019 Nova Science Publications New York USA. www.novapublishers.comG Zekos, Law

that the stronger the IPR regime in a given host economy (denoted by the factor IPR country-index), the more will FDI receive high technology and so IPRs are important in attracting FDI inflows.

AI technology demands fundamental changes in conception of the law itself.[106] Undeniably, the advancement and deployment of AI are motivated or curtailed by fields as different as tax law, tort law, privacy and data protection law, IPR law, competition law, health law, consumer protection law, etc., and so within these dissimilar fields, a large number of regulations already apply to AI now. There is a need for regulatory coherency and so an appraisal of regulatory competition for AI has to consider not simply one area of law, but the regulatory framework as a whole. It is worth mentioning here that AI influences IPRs and consequently AI IPRs legal protection affecting IPRs indexes.[107] In line, Noon, Paul and De Vita, Glauco and Appleyard, Lindsey[108] argue that "existing empirical work on the IPR–FDI nexus, though skewed in favour of a positive relationship between IPR protection and FDI, is fragmented, inconclusive and unable to square the conflicting theoretical predictions on how the strength of IPRs can affect MNEs' FDI location decisions."

It has to be taken into account that all governments maximize the economic benefits, while diminishing national security risks associated with inward FDI. However, Zekos[109] considers that competition is the freedom to compete on equal terms in any transaction or action in social life and so people and companies with higher ability/capacity or more creativity and zest for doings to gain accordingly. To that extent, the significance of IPRs is higher for the short-term reference rather than the long-term reference and so IPRs expressed by ZEKEUIPR1 indexes >25% and <75% is the most significant in attracting FDI, which signposts that a good level of protection is needed for the importance of IPR in the European Union. Additionally, ZEKIPR6 <75% is more significant than >75% in attracting FDI which means that IPR is a vital variable that plays a significant role in attracting FDI inflows or causing FDI outflows. Also, a good and accurate IPR index permits a more accurate demonstration of the magnitude of the role of IPR on FDI, GDP, and Trade. Finally, the significance of zekeuipr1/zekeuipr2/ /zekeuipr4 in attracting FDI inflows and

---

and Economics of IPRs, 2016 Nova Science Publications New York USA. www.novapublishers.com

[106] G. Zekos, Economics and Law of Artificial Intelligence - Finance, Economic Impacts, Risk Management and Governance, 2021 Springer/ https://www.springer.com/

[107] G. Zekos, Economics and Law of Artificial Intelligence - Finance, Economic Impacts, Risk Management and Governance, 2021 Springer/ https://www.springer.com/

[108] Noon, Paul and De Vita, Glauco and Appleyard, Lindsey, What Do We Know About the Impact of Intellectual Property Rights on the Foreign Direct Investment Location (Country) Choice? A Review and Research Agenda (April 2019). Journal of Economic Surveys, Vol. 33, Issue 2, pp. 665–688, 2019. https://ssrn.com/abstract=3349336

[109] G Zekos, ECONOMICS AND LAW ON COMPETITION IN 21st CENTURY GLOBALIZATION 2014 Nova Science Publications New York USA. www.novapublishers.com

outflows concerning the European Union is significant and so IPRs protection adds to their utility as a means in attracting FDI[110] via different modes.

References

1. Bhatore, S., Mohan, L., & Reddy, Y. R. (2020). Machine learning techniques for credit risk evaluation: A systematic literature review. *Journal of Banking and Financial Technology, 4*, 111–138.
2. Brian, Z. (2009). *Tamanaha, beyond the formalist-realist divide: The role of politics in judging*. Princeton University Press.
3. Ciuriak, D. (2020) *Economic Rents and the counters of conflict in the data-driven economy*. CIGI Paper No. 245.
4. Zekos, G. (1999) *Internet or electronic technology: A threat to state sovereignty*. JILT, http://www.law.warwick.ac.uk/jilt/99-3/zekos.html
5. Zekos, G. (2013). *Corporate governance and MNEs in globalization and cyberspace*. www.novapublishers.com
6. Zekos, G. (2014). *Economics and law on competition in 21st century globalization*. Nova Science.
7. Zekos, G. (2007). *Economics, finance and law on MNEs*. Nova Publishers.
8. Zekos, G. (2016). *Law and economics of IPRs*. Nova Science.
9. Zekos, G. (2016). *MNE's in 21st century*. Nova Science.
10. Zekos, G. (2019). *The United States of Europe: The global player*. Nova Science.
11. Zekos, G. (2013) *IPRs' impact upon FDI*. PhD Thesis, Economics Department, University of Peloponnese, Tripoli, Hellas. www.uop.gr
12. Zekos, G. (2021). *Economics and law of artificial intelligence – Finance, economic impacts, risk management and governance*. Springer.
13. Gellers, J. C. (2021). *Rights for robots: Artificial intelligence, animal and environmental law*. Routledge.
14. Joseph, P. (2009). *Joyce, financial globalization and banking crises in emerging markets*. www.ssrn.com.
15. Kellogg, K. C., Valentine, M. A., & Christin, A. (2020). Algorithms at work: The new contested terrain of control. *Academy of Management Annals, 14*(1), 366–410.
16. Lee, C., & Platts, R. (2017). AI is coming and it will change trademark law. *Managing IP, 9*, 10.
17. Van Loo, R. (2019). Digital market perfection. *Michigan Law Review, 117*, 815, 833–835.
18. Schauer, F. (2015). *The force of law*. Harvard University Press.
19. Ebrahim, T. Y. (2021). Algorithms in business, merchant– consumer interactions, and regulation. *West Virginia Law Review, 868*.

[110] For further results concerning the impact of IPRs upon FDI see G Zekos, The United States of Europe in place of the European Union, 2017 Nova Science Publications New York USA. www.novapublishers.com. G. Zekos, Copyrights and Trademarks in Cyberspace: A Legal and Economic Analysis, 15 Chi. -Kent J. Intell. Prop. 313 (2016). https://scholarship.kentlaw.iit.edu/ckjip/vol15/iss1/10. G Zekos, Interrelation of Intellectual Property Rights and Competitiveness: FDI inwards and FDI outwards, 2013 Journal of Intellectual Property Rights vol. 18 July 2013 p 338–350. www.niscair.res.in. G Zekos, Economics and Law of Digital Economy, 2020 Nova Science Publications New York USA. www.novapublishers.com G Zekos, Finance Crimes: Insider Trading and Money Laundering, 2020 Nova Science Publications New York USA. www.novapublishers.com G. Zekos, Economics and Law of Artificial Intelligence - Finance, Economic Impacts, Risk Management and Governance, 2021 Springer/ https://www.springer.com

Chapter 4
AI & Demarcation of the Rule of Law

4.1 The Rule of Law

It is worth noting that law functions as a vehicle by facilitating the elaboration and implementation of public values and the productive engagement of normative inquiry among relevant institutional actors. Moreover, law is a set of neutral rules. Which are the public values that law facilitates in globalization and global economic governance since there is not a state sovereignty to refer to? The focal point of the rule of law is to guarantee law-bounded qualities that tend in the direction of better and more just legal systems.[1]

It has to be taken into account that law allocates benefits, risks, and duties backed by the prospective for enforcement through the use of state power if the choices are not followed by those at whom they are aimed.[2] Thus, law is a formalized way of bringing political preferences into the society. Can the prospective for enforcement through the use of state power apply in globalization and global economic governance? Law is the instrument holding the social system together against individual efforts to take advantage of others.[3] Additionally, law is totally contextual and that it cannot be detached from its social and political environment. Hence, law is justified and applied based on public reason which is free of personal religious, philosophical, and moral doctrines.[4] Which is the public reason for law justification in a global basis if we suggest that the state is not implicated in global economic governance?

[1] Randy Barnett, The Structure of Liberty: Justice and the Rule of Law, (2001) Oxford: Clarendon Press, pp. 136–144; Ronald A. Cass. The Rule of Law in America, (2001) Baltimore: Johns Hopkins University Press.

[2] Lawrence M. Friedman, American Law 257 (1984) "Law carries a powerful stick: the threat of force. This is the first inside its velvet glove".

[3] John Locke, Of Civil Government Second Treatise 67, 68, Introduction by Russell Kirk, (Henry Regnery 1955).

[4] Rawls, John, Political Liberalism, (paperback ed., New York, Columbia University Press) 1996.

G. I. Zekos, *Political, Economic and Legal Effects of Artificial Intelligence*, Contributions to Political Science, https://doi.org/10.1007/978-3-030-94736-1_4

Hereafter, law is secularized and independent from religion, morality, and other social norms but its substance has amalgamated all these values. The norms are transformed into law via the rule of law. Has the notion of law amalgamated global values of morality, religion, and other social norms nowadays? Morality is a personal matter, while law, as a social institution with external intensity, materializes abstract normative standards for the whole of society. Moreover, modern law is positivized into a functional, technical system suspending any need for moral deliberation. However, Habermas[5] argues that law at the post-conventional level of social evolution is still based on moral principles. In addition, Luhmann[6] argues that societal evolution has achieved such a high level of diversity in modern societies that law is a system which no longer needs any justification in terms of normative points of view and so the legal system is operationally closed so that it performs only in terms of its own binary code (lawful/unlawful) set in its own programs (laws). Moreover, Luhmann says that law cannot and does not need to be morally founded to get its internal functionality. Hence, Luhmann's standpoint is in contrast to Habermas's conception of law, explicitly on the question of the moral justification of law. Habermas's[7] identification of law as an institution, which is still in need of moral justification, and law as a medium, as a system isolated from moral-practical concerns, accurately indicates the central "ambiguity in the rationalization of law."

Likewise, Habermas[8] argues that modern law is created by a system of norms that are forced and in reality, that norms supported by the state sanction stemming from the variable decisions of a political lawmaker enveloped by the anticipation that these norms pledge the autonomy of all legal persons equivalently. It could be said that this anticipation of lawfulness is interconnected with the "facticity" of law-making and law enforcement which is echoed in the means of legal validity. Nowadays, the democratic procedure for the production of law evidently forms the only source of legitimacy which means that together with the constitutionally organized political system, law offers a safety net for malfunctions to accomplish social integration. In other words, the modern legal order gains its legality only from the conception of self-determination which means that citizens are supposed to be authors of the law to which they are subject as addressees.

It has to be taken into account that the rule of law necessitates that the ruler be subject to, or at least not above, the law; and that the law be applied equally, or at

[5]Mathieu Deflem, Habermas, Modernity and Law 1996 Sage Publications.

[6]Luhmann, Niklas (1985) A Sociological Theory of Law. London: Routledge & Kegan, Luhmann, Niklas (1992) "Operational Closure and Structural Coupling: The Differentiation of the Legal System," Cardozo Law Review 13: 1419–4.

[7]Habermas, J (1987) The Philosophical Discourse of Modernity: Twelve Lectures. Cambridge: Polity Press. Habermas, J. (1988) The Tanner Lectures on Human Values, Volume 8; Salt Lake City, UT: University of Utah Press.

[8]Jurgen Habermas, Postscript to Between Facts and Norms in Mathieu Deflem, Habermas, Modernity and Law, Sage Publications 1996.

least equitably, to all participants of a society.[9] The Constitution establishes a rule of law state.[10] Which is the ruler subject to the law in the era of globalization and global economic governance? Rule of law is understood in its substantive aspect as attributing the state with a vital role as guardian of a set of foundational communally embraced substantive norms that are to be preserved and advanced through the use of state power grounded in law.[11] Which entity will play the role of state in the rule of law in globalization & global economic governance and so becoming the guardian of a set of fundamental communally embraced substantive norms that are to be preserved and advanced through the use of the entity's power grounded in law?

It is worth noting that the relationship of law and social life is an indispensable basis of the rule of law.[12] The rule of law serves not only to impose the results of the democratic legislative process, but also to safeguard individuals against arbitrary government action. The rule of law is a pledge to limitations that assure greater stability rather than any precise endpoint for law and for government. In addition, the concept of the rule of law is an ideal lying behind and informing both constitutional and non-constitutional doctrines.[13] Upham[14] argues that "the formalist 'rule of law', as 'embodied in the mantra "the rule of law, not men"' remains a fiction—even in that most developed of countries, the US".

It is argued that the notion of the rule of law gets fashioned down in the fast-pace world of policy discourse to bite-sized connotations: "rule of law is about property rights"; "rule of law is about access to justice"; "rule of law is about state-centric justice and security provision" which means that the rule of law is viewed imprecisely about the law, about justice, sporadically also about rights and one way or another it is about law being imperative for enhancement. Moreover, international society engagement is presumed to involve the delivery of technical support to what are supposed to be the appropriate governance building blocks of rule of law, typically concerning courts and policing. Thus, it seems that the grasp of rule of law is unexpectedly "patchy" which means that there is a need for identifying the

---

[9] Dicey, A. V, Introduction to the Study of the Law of the Constitution, London: Macmillian and Co., Limited. 1920.

[10] Marbury v. Madison, 5 U.S. 137 (1803) (treating the constitution as legally enforceable and as the highest law of the land)., Richard H. Fallon. Jr.. "The Rule of Law" as a Concept in Constitutional Discourse", 97 Colum. L. Rev. 1. 7 (1997), at 1 ("The Rule of Law is a much celebrated, historical ideal, the precise meaning of which may be less clear today than ever before.").

[11] Thomas O. Sargentich, The Contemporary Debate About Legislative-Executive Separation of Powers, 72 Corn. L. Rev. 430, 450 (1987) ("A close relation between the rule of law and separation of powers is evident in both the liberal and democratic elements of liberal democratic theory.").

[12] Antonin Scalia, The Rule of Law as a Law of Rules, 56 U. CHI. L. REV. 1175 (1989). Richard H. Fallon, Jr., "The Rule of Law" as a Concept in Constitutional Discourse, 97 Colum. L. Rev. 1, 8–9 (1997).

[13] Miranda v. Arizona, 384 U.S. 436, 479–80 (1966); Olmstead v. United States, 277 U.S. 438, 485 (1928).

[14] Frank Upham, Mythmaking in the Rule of Law Orthodoxy (2002) (Paper No 30, Carnegie Endowment for International Peace Working Papers, Rule of Law Series, Democracy and the Rule of Law Project, September 2002).

heart of the concept allowing its unrestricted/unhindered implementation and not dealing merely with the implementation phases of the rule of law in the whole sphere/domain of human life in a society within the globalization and the endeavor of the digital economy. It is worth mentioning here that notably, common underlying parts of rule of law definitions include that they refer to those procedures and approved rules through which the application of authority is regulated and restrained, along with an agreed set of rules whereby conflict and disputes are determined through non-violent ways. Furthermore, regarding the rule of law definitions on content, on process and on whose agreement counts fluctuate substantially. Thus, rule of law embraces the capability of "end-users" to gain access to the law including how law is generated, for instance through existing mechanisms of representation and legislative deliberation, via the endowment of various types of support for access such as legal aid, etc. and channeling of information on rights and justice and holding rulers to account. Ruth Teitel[15] explains that "legal measures promote creation of public knowledge about past wrongdoing, and judicial opinions, trials, and constitutions provide formal, public justifications. The law, therefore, contributes to the epistemological and interpretive changes necessary to comprehend transition; through public justification legal forms reconstitute state and societal interests, thereby instantiating transition".

The essence of the concept of the rule of law embraces a perceptive that society should be ordered around a set of laws that apply equally to all on the basis of doctrines deducible from the rules and not dependent of the identity of the rulers. Which is the society be ordered around a set of laws in globalization and global economic governance? Thus, there is a need to define the global society ordered around the set of laws applicable via global economic governance. Friedrich Hayek[16] said that the rule of law "means that government in all its actions is bound by rules fixed and announced beforehand—rules which make it possible to see with fair certainty how the authority will use its coercive powers in given circumstances and to plan one's individual affairs on the basis of this knowledge." Is there a need to define the notion of global government bound by the rule of law as well?

In law the consent is not on the honesty of the proposition itself but on the authority and authenticity of the decision-makers. Thus, the proposition might favor the interests of specific groups rather than the interests of the general public. Which is the authority and authenticity of the decision-makers in a globalized world and in global economic governance? Law is about generating systems that cultivate the competence of actors in different settings to identify, engender, and revise norms, and to form systems that are more likely to generate desired conditions and practices. As discussed earlier, the rule of law embodies norms shaped and accepted by people living in a society but the low pace of compliance of formal law supports informal

[15] Ruth Teitel, Transitional Jurisprudence: The Role of Law in Political Transformation, 106 Yale L.J. (1997). Available at: http://digitalcommons.law.yale.edu/ylj/vol106/iss7/2

[16] Friedrich A. Hayek, The Road to Serfdom, (1944) Chicago: University of Chicago Press, p. 80.

dispute systems applying the recently approved norms. To that extent, the rule of law has to attune its rate of compliance and flexibility in order to follow the tempo recognized by the society which the rule of law is assumed to govern. In other words, globalization and cyberspace are triggering a flexibility and changeableness into societies which means that the rule of law has to adjust in order to ratify the global norms.

Once law bestows a legal form on political dominion then it operates as the structure of a power code and so law plays crucial role in this course for the reason that it serves as the tool of organizing state power. Thus, political power produces a "certainty of law" but also codification stipulates the rules of law with certain reliability. Considering that jurisprudence confers consistency to law and so law has to appeal to justice for its legality. Habermas[17] argues that law can be viewed as the "medium through which communicative power is translated into administrative power" which means that law is the political instrument for administering society and consequently a state.

Does the rule of law matter? It is argued that the concept offers a valuable focal point around which to evaluate about the uses and abuses of government authority getting a better handle on what the rule of law means or could mean but these likelihoods say nothing about how well the rule of law serves these functions, at what prospective cost, and evaluated to what alternatives. The answer is given by Planned Parenthood of Se. Pa. v. Casey[18] specifying that the "rule of law" is a reason for adhering to stare decisis, and for preserving the "Court's legitimacy." It is worth mentioning here that even though the rule-of-law dilemma occurs regularly in the criminal context, the issues raise broader questions about the manners in which people in periods of forceful political alteration dispute about the relation of law, politics, and justice which means that standpoints and understandings concerning the rule of law, and of values of justice and fairness are taken place in periods of political revolution. On the other hand, the ideal of the rule of law as legal continuity is apprehended in the principle of stare decisis, a predicate of adjudication in the Anglo-American legal system.[19]

It is worth mentioning here that the rule of law is a political work in progress embracing the demand that society should be governed by law. Lord Bingham[20] said that the central principle of the rule of law is "that all persons and authorities within the state, whether public or private, should be bound by and entitled to the benefit of laws publicly and prospectively promulgated and publicly administered in the

[17]jurgen Habermas, Faktiziuit und Geltung (Frankfurt am Main: Suhrkamp, 1992), p. 186.

[18]505 U.S. 833, 865, 869 (1992).

[19]Planned Parenthood v Casey. 505 U S 833, 854 (1992) ("[T]he very concept of the rule of law underlying our own Constitution requires such continuity over time that a respect for precedent is, by definition, indispensable."); see also Antonin Scalia, The Rule of Law as a Law of Rules, 56 U. CHI. L. REv. 1175 (1989) (advocating "general rule of law" over "personal discretion to do justice").

[20]Lord Bingham, "The Rule of Law" (2007) 66 CLJ 67, 69. P. Gowder, The Rule of Law in the Real World (Cambridge: Cambridge University Press, 2016).

courts." The importance of the rule of law is such that diverse societies and apparently irreconcilable political regimes, ranging from the European Union to Russia, China, etc. have backed the concept regardless that some societies reject democracy and human rights, others oppose capitalism and globalization but they all encompass an ideal of the rule of law.

4.2 The Rule of Law in Globalization

The focal point of the rule of law is to guarantee law-bounded qualities that tend in the direction of better and more just legal systems.[21] The "rule of law" or "legality" covers broad societal respect for and protection of legal entitlements including ownership in tangible and intangible property and personal safety from crime.[22] The relationship of law and social life is an indispensable basis of the rule of law.[23] The rule of law serves not only to impose the results of the democratic legislative process, but also to safeguard individuals against arbitrary government action. Moreover, the rule of law is a pledge to limitations that assure greater stability rather than any precise endpoint for law and for government. In addition, the concept of the rule of law is an ideal lying behind and informing both constitutional and non-constitutional doctrines.[24]

Also, the rule of law is a multifaceted ideal embracing formal and procedural standard that applies to legal norms and institutions.[25] If law is to rule in a political society, law must not only be a device that public officers employ to administer that society, but it must also rule those who intend to rule with it. The rule of law is not forceful in a society if some of those who exert political authority and hold others liable to the law are not themselves responsible under law which means that law does not successfully rule there. It is argued that law is trapped between the past and the future, between backward-looking and forward-looking, between retroactive and forthcoming and so changeovers involve shifts in the understanding of justice via the

[21] Randy Barnett, The Structure of Liberty: Justice and the Rule of Law, (2001) Oxford: Clarendon Press, pp. 136–144; Ronald A. Cass. The Rule of Law in America, (2001) Baltimore: Johns Hopkins University Press.

[22] North, Douglas C, Institutions, Institutional Change and Economic Performance, Cambridge: Cambridge Univ. Press, 1990. Richard H. Fallon, Jr., "The Rule of Law" as a Concept in Constitutional Discourse", 97 Colum. L. Rev. 1, 7 (1997), at 1 ("The Rule of Law is a much celebrated, historical ideal, the precise meaning of which may be less clear today than ever before.").

[23] Antonin Scalia, The Rule of Law as a Law of Rules, 56 U. CHI. L. REV. 1175 (1989). Richard H. Fallon, Jr., "The Rule of Law" as a Concept in Constitutional Discourse, 97 Colum. L. Rev. 1, 8–9 (1997).

[24] Miranda v. Arizona, 384 U.S. 436, 479–80 (1966); Olmstead v. United States, 277 U.S. 438, 485 (1928).

[25] J. Waldron, "The Concept and the Rule of Law," Georgia Law Review, 43 (2008), 1–61.

utilization of the rule of law which means that law's purpose is characteristically puzzling but central in a sound manner being the means for advancement of the world.

The essence of the concept of the rule of law embraces a perceptive that society should be ordered around a set of laws that apply equally to all on the basis of doctrines deducible from the rules and not dependent on the identity of the rulers. Which is the society be ordered around a set of laws in globalization and global economic governance? Thus, there is a need to define the global society ordered around the set of laws applicable via global economic governance. Friedrich Hayek[26] said that the rule of law "means that government in all its actions is bound by rules fixed and announced beforehand—rules which make it possible to see with fair certainty how the authority will use its coercive powers in given circumstances and to plan one's individual affairs on the basis of this knowledge." Is there a need to define the notion of global government bound by the rule of law as well?

Is there the role of the rule of law in the global legal order? Who controls the worldwide changes via globalization? It is possible the entity currently controlling the globalization process in the end to become controlled by their creation if the whole globalization process disregards any ethical values and, in the end, we will have a distractive conflict.

The essence of the rule of law is that power ought to be used only in ways is allowed by the law.[27] Moreover, the rule of law is a whole moral-political philosophy about what the law should accomplish and the ideals it should uphold.[28] The rule of law constructs an autonomous legal order. Since the state is the supreme autonomous entity within a political territory, it is assumed to hold all formal political authority derived from the people. As mentioned earlier, the rule of law entails that the ruler be subject to, or at least not above, the law; and that the law be applied equally, or at least equitably, to all members of society.[29]

The law is supposed to be based upon rationale and purpose unaffected by request.[30] It is questionable if law is unaffected of desire to satisfy the needs of the prevailing groups in a society. The rule of law serves not only to impose the results of the democratic legislative process, but also to safeguard individuals against arbitrary government action. The reason of law not only guarantees the rule of law but also offers an awareness of reassure and control to jurists and citizens in the same

[26]Friedrich A. Hayek, The Road to Serfdom, (1944) Chicago: University of Chicago Press, p. 80.

[27]Dicey, Albert Venn, Introduction to the Study of the Law of the Constitution (8th ed). London: Macmillan and co. 1914.

[28]J. Raz, The Authority of Law (Oxford, 1977), 211.

[29]Dicey, A.V, Introduction to the Study of the Law of the Constitution, London: Macmillan and Co., Limited. 1920.

[30]Ellis Sandoz, Symposium, Religion and the American Founding, 20 Regent U. L. Rev. 17, 25 n.55 (2007–2008).

way, but there are occasions when reason is incompetent to offer answers in law.[31] Can the rule of law be equated with the ideally just state[32]? The concept of the rule of law is an ideal lying behind and informing both constitutional and non-constitutional doctrines.[33] The rule of law itself is an ideal distinct from constitutional doctrine, not capable of direct application.[34] The rule of law encompasses all the morals, and values incorporated in norms created and adopted by people living in a society. Considering the low rate of adaptability of formal law, the mobility of society causing alteration into the norms is better served by informal dispute systems applying the newly adopted norms. Thus, the rule of law has to adapt its pace of adaptability and mobility according to the rhythm endorsed by the society which the rule of law supposed to govern.

The aim of the rule of law should be the arrival at an ideally just state. Aristotle and Plato considered that all components of the society are joining together to bring justice.[35] It is worth mentioning that Athenians developed a well-advanced legal framework for the efficient resolution of disputes, the enforcement of contracts and the protection of private property functioning successfully, refining trust and protecting the security of transactions.[36] It is worth mentioning that Ancient Athens reveal the bond between decentralized enforcement by ordinary individuals and the legal attributes.[37] Moreover, Athenians[38] developed a legal framework including arbitration and mediation for the protection of private property, the enforcement of contracts and the efficient resolution of disputes functioning successfully, refining trust and defending the security of transactions. It has to be taken into consideration that the Athenian system was founded on social norms such as reciprocity, the value of reputation and the broad approval of business ethics and so the people's consent and self-compliance are the principles for an auto-implementation of any formal or

[31] Paul F. Campos, Pierre Schlag and Steven D. Smith, Against The Law (1996); Pierre Schlag, The Enchantment of Reason 15 (1998) (noting that "the reason of law not only underwrites the rule of law but provides a sense of comfort and control to jurists and citizens alike," but that there is a "moment when reason is unable to furnish answers in law").

[32] Joseph Raz, The Rule of Law and Its Virtue, in The Authority of Law: Essays on Law and Morality 210, 211 (1979).

[33] Miranda v. Arizona, 384 U.S. 436, 479–80 (1966); Olmstead v. United States, 277 U.S. 438, 485 (1928).

[34] Richard H. Fallon, Jr., "The Rule of Law" as a Concept in Constitutional Discourse, 97 Colum. L. Rev. 1, 8–9 (1997).

[35] Aristotle, Nichomachean Ethics, 402, bk. V, ch. 2. Plato. (1969). Plato in Twelve Volumes, Vols. 5 & 6 translated by Paul Shorey. Cambridge, MA, Harvard University Press; London, William Heinemann Ltd.

[36] Anastassios D. Karayiannis, Aristides N. Hatzis, Morality, social norms and the rule of law as transaction cost-saving devices: the case of ancient Athens, Eur J Law Econ (2012) 33:621–643.

[37] Carugati F, Hadfield GK and Weingast BR. 2015. Building Legal Order in Ancient Athens Journal of Legal Analysis 7(2): 291–324.

[38] Bitros, G. K., & Karayiannis, A. D. (2008). Values and institutions as determinants of entrepreneurship in ancient Athens. Journal of Institutional Economics, 4, 205–230.

informal legal and ethical framework. A. Karayiannis and A. Hatzis[39] specify that "Athenian law was pioneering in the development of rules and institutional mechanisms suitable for the reduction of transaction costs, many of them surviving in the most complex contemporary legal systems." It has to be considered that law, predominantly when viewed at the systemic level, as the rule of law, includes an irreducible, critical moral element. Law must have an internal, fundamental virtue if it is to be articulate and serve its purpose. The appropriate purpose of law is the safeguarding of social order through rational rules.[40] The rule of law limits the government's discretion in pursuing its bad aims, providing stability and predictability.

Have the Ancient Athenians achieved the rule of law? Considering the openness of the rules of argument, Athenian legal procedures placed no limits on the evidence or arguments that could be utilized to convince a jury to convict or not but a specific written law had to be identified to get the matter before a jury which means that in a way the rule of law was utilized in order to get the matter before a jury. Moreover, once you were before a jury you could ask the jury to find in your favor for reasons entirely unrelated to the written charge but it seems the reasons had to be based on a written law as well and not upon any illegal reason. Consequently, it could be said that politics could be used in the interpretation of the written law not objectively as a legal process rather than a political influence is allowed in the interpretation of the written law indicating that since ancient times the sperm of the politics is encompassed in the applicability and enforcement of the rule of law. In line, Lanni[41] argues that the jury system accordingly did not consistently enforce "the law," even though the law did serve to bolster enforcement of social norms which means that it could be argued that occasionally politics can be injected/implanted in the application of the law via its enforcement and interpretation. It could be said that a jury system, not based on the implementation of the rule of law, would be no better than the elite rule. On the other hand, to achieve neutrality and independence the Athenians employed the ballots for assessing verdicts and punishments lessened social pressure and make bribery difficult which means that the Athenians secured confidence in the neutrality and independence of the system: rich and poor, educated and not, were largely on equal footing before the court except for the occasions of major political interferences which means that politics always have managed to influence the applicability of the rule of law establishing the politics of law.

The political influence in the implementation of the rule of law is minimized by matter that the Athenian rules accomplished universality among citizens for the reason that of the broad-based participation in law-making in the Assembly, along

---

[39] Anastassios D. Karayiannis, Aristides N. Hatzis, Morality, social norms and the rule of law as transaction cost-saving devices: the case of ancient Athens, Eur J Law Econ (2012) 33:621–643 p 622.

[40] Kristen Rundle, The Impossibility of Exterminatory Legality: Law and the Holocaust, 59 U. Toronto L.J. 65, 89 (2009).

[41] A Lanni, Social norms in Ancient Athenian courts, 2009 Journal of Legal Analysis 691.

with broad-based participation in the jury's decisive determination of the content of the legal rules.

Can law exist without publicity, generality, clarity and stability? Fuller[42] states that a legal system is identified as a regime in which people could follow the law and so such a regime involves practical constraints on how government carries out its legal function which means that a legal order exists when governance is illustrated by normatively attractive legal qualities such as publicity, generality, clarity, stability, feasibility and correspondence among rules as publicized and rules as operated.

As discussed earlier, laws are characterized by a kind of internal virtue or morality enabling laws to serve their ends.[43] Aquinas[44] designated law "a dictate of practical reason" thus law is a device for ends outside itself implicated by morality having its own internal virtue if it is to serve properly its ends, and the more general ends of the rule of law. Is there a relationship between law and morality and the nature of the obligation to obey the law? There is a need for distinguishing among real-world legal systems and how they behave and the possibility of theoretical concepts of the essence of law and the rule of law which might alter the applied essence of law and the rule of law. Lon Fuller argues that a legal system must meet a set of criteria that comprise an internal morality. The rule of law compels that laws be distinguished by a set of virtues distinct from the substantive criteria of morality embedded in most natural law systems, which demand that laws advance "virtue" and disapprove of "vice" in the people.[45] Fuller's point is that there is an intrinsic purpose to law that properly should be seen as a moral good. A society's common good is served by the rule of law.[46] Langdell[47] argues for the existence of a natural law ordering human societies, just as there are natural physical laws discoverable by the physical sciences that determine the operation of the world which means that truth in such a system implicating peoples' capacity to understand and precisely interpret the "true" rules of law that occur in this universal order.

---

[42]Fuller L. 1969. The Morality of Law. New Haven: Yale University Press.

[43]Lon L. Fuller, The Morality of Law 47 (1964).

[44]Thomas Aquinas, Summa Theologica, pt. I-II, Q. 95, Art. 2 (Fathers of the English Dominican Province trans., Benziger Bros. 1947), http://www.ccel.org/ccel/aquinas/summa.toc.html Aquinas quotes Isidore of Seville's Etymologies (V, 21): "Law shall be virtuous, just, possible to nature, according to the custom of the country, suitable to place and time, necessary, useful; clearly expressed, lest by its obscurity it lead to misunderstanding; framed for no private benefit, but for the common good." Art. 3.

[45]Kenneth I. Winston, Introduction to The Principles Of Social Order: Selected Essays of Lon L. Fuller 25, 46 (Kenneth I. Winston ed., Hart Publ'g rev. ed. 2001) (1981).

[46]Russell Kirk, The Roots of American Order 3 (fourth ed. 2003) (stating a person "must know order" before living tolerably with himself or others).

[47]The Centennial History of the Harvard Law School: 1817–1917, at 26 (1918) (quoting Christopher Langdell). James B. Conant, Two Modes of Thought at 44 (1964), quoting Langdell's, A Selection of Cases on the Law of Contracts (1871). "If law be not a science, a university will best consult its own dignity in declining to teach it. If it be not a science, it is a species of handicraft, and may best be learned by serving an apprenticeship to one who practices."

The protection of property rights, the enforcement of contracts, and an efficient legal system are the foundations of the modern-day rule of law. Nevertheless, formal establishments do not operate without being approved by the society and without the resilient backing of social norms. To that extent, morality and social norms are the key essentials of the informal institutional organization, the social capital that is also vital for social wellbeing and economic growth. Hence, formal institutions & informal institutional organization governs supposed via the rule of law. In other words, governance supposed via the rule of law takes place nowadays. The protection of property rights, the enforcement of contractual agreements and the effectiveness of the settlement system are the foundations not only of a free market society but also of the modern-day rule of law in contemporary constitutional liberal democracies. It is worth mentioning that formal institutions cannot operate without being taken up by the society and without the forceful backing of social norms. Nowadays a key source of transaction costs is the challenging protection of legal rights and the obstacles to their transfer and use. The existence of considerable transaction costs leads to the upholding of a misallocation of rights and so to a misallocation of resources. A competent legal system diminishes transaction costs by evidently defining legal rights, precluding their over- or under-protection by selecting the fitting combination of property and liability rules, permitting and making possible their transfer, and ultimately plummeting the cost of their legal protection. The development of arbitration together with courts as two co-equal dispute systems in a jurisdiction is a solution adding to the rule of law and the global rule of law.

It has to be taken into consideration that the idea of the rule of law is the key difference between democracies and authoritarian regimes. The rule of law is influential for the preservation of democracy. A basic principle of the Athenian legal system was fairness and equality before the law. "Equality" before the law was central for the Athenian rule of law. The weakening of social norms did lead to the development of the idea of the rule of law influential for the development of Athenian private law,[48] above all property and contract law accomplishing social welfare and economic development.

The rule of law is a political/legal concept addressed to the operation of government and the structure of law. The rule of law is a legally soft perception, not widely or consistently idealized but it is a powerful political concept. Is the rule of law utilized in order to merely legalize actions which in fact impose upon a society predicted values offered as the cornerstone of society but in reality, there is a manipulation of a society imposing useless values? Who values the value of the values?

Have international organization and treaties brought real justice or merely camouflage the seizure of the globe by the forces governing the globe and so obliging people to support their laws and so the rule of law? Formal conceptions of the rule of law ascertain the rule of law as a unique jurisprudential concept, which is distinct

[48] Carey, C. (1994), Legal space in classical Athens. Greece and Rome, 41(2), 172–186.

from conceptions of justice, democracy, human rights, and so on.[49] Moreover, a formal conception of the rule of law involves a condition in which laws are created through duly authorized processes and so conform to established criteria for validity administered by an independent judiciary placing limits on governmental discretion so as not to undermine the foregoing.[50] It is worth noting that democracy in a nation-state has a governmental center and sharing of competencies which means that the structure is ranked, even though some states grant a significant devolution of authority to local units. Also, functional boundaries linked with territorial ones.[51] On the other hand, the government possesses its legal, economic, and administrative authorities within the whole state territory. Can this form of government be implemented in any type of structure in EU, such as the United States of Europe,[52] so as to be more operative and democratic?

In addition, formal conceptions of the rule of law are by design limited and do not seek to cover wider moral or political values about the content of the law. Thus, the rule of law needs the existence of law and so there are ethics and morality not only regarding the concept of law but also the rule of law which is more the application and implementation of law within a society. Laws have to be just, that their content should be morally sound and that substantive rights should be protected within society. To that extent the rule of law is taken to take in the requirement for "good laws." Besides, no conception of the rule of law is devoid of normative content. Even the most formal conceptions are enlightened by values linked to limitations on the exercise of governmental power and regard for the individual vis-à-vis that exercise.[53]

The benefits arising from a system where people have legitimate expectations, and these are respected, are morally significant, in particular when those expectations apply to personal privileges like rights, liberties, and property. Thus, a system that ascertains and respects legitimate expectations precludes citizens' investments of time, energy, and resources being misused by arbitrary decision-making by those in power, assisting them evade the unbearable fears of future losses which means that valuing legitimate expectations permits people to plan their lives and make long-term decisions. While the law's stability cannot assure a project's success, citizens are assertive in their knowledge of the reigning structure of entitlements, protections, and obligations, and in the courses by which specific laws are subject to alteration

[49] Dominic Grieve, United Kingdom Attorney General, "The Value of the Rule of Law to International Trade and Finance", Speech at City of London Guildhall (13 October 2013).

[50] Joseph Raz, "The Rule of Law and its Virtue" (1977) 93 LQR 195, Robert S Summers, "A Formal Theory of the Rule of Law" (1993) 6 Ratio Juris 127; Lon L Fuller, The Morality of Law (Yale University Press, rev edn 1969).

[51] Jan Zielonka, The Quality of Democracy after Joining the European Union, East European Politics and Societies, Vol. 21, No. 1, pages 162–180.

[52] G Zekos, The United States of Europe The Global Players, 2019 Nova Science Publications New York USA. www.novapublishers.com

[53] N. Jansen Calamita, The Rule of Law, Investment Treaties, and Economic Growth: Mapping Normative and Empirical Questions, www.ssrn.com

which means that stable framework tolerates citizens' personal decision-making horizons to spread out beyond the near future, inspiring their freedom.

Substantive conceptions of the rule of law convey the rule of law which includes broader moral and political values.[54] The rule of law based on morality and ethics implements the law articulated by morality, ethics, humans' existence values and spirituality of religion values via arbitration, courts, and constitutional institutions. The rule of law encloses any national and international or global matters as long as the law regulates them in a humans' society. Are economic values incorporated in international rule of law?

States moved from reliance on customary norms to treaties with respect to the treatment of foreign investors. No effort was made in treaties to give solid meaning as to what "fair and equitable" treatment mean or involve and so the treaties did little to tackle the normative challenge of idealizing the substantive protections of an internationalized rule of law guarantee retaining in check deficiencies on the national level.[55]

The EU generally promotes an understanding of the rule of law as a principle that embraces substantive components on top of formal elements, and which involves a democratic and liberal constitutional order giving full effect to human rights. With reference to the EU's role in terms of international norm-building, the EU's involvement to the determining of an international understanding of the rule of law has been limited if only because the EU's conception is not original on the international plane and actually builds up on the conceptual work first undertaken by other international organizations such as the OSCE.[56] It is worth mentioning that the EU has not drastically contributed, since the early 1990s, to the solidification of an international consensus concerning the core elements of the rule of law and the global diffusion of an ideology that views the rule of law, democracy and human rights as entangled and mutually supportive principles. Is the rule of law the basis of democracy, human rights since the basis of everything is law the foundation of the rule of law which mean that there is no principle with the rule of law/even norms and morality are based on a notion of law, the existence of the rule of law is the basis of the whole globe including humans and the rest of the existing life upon earth. The question is the foundation of a fair and human expression law and rule of law.

---

[54] Ronald Dworkin, A Matter of Principle (Harvard University Press, 1985) at pp. 11–12. Simon Chesterman, "An International Rule of Law?" (2008) 56 American Journal of Comparative Law 331.

[55] UN General Assembly, Declaration of the High-Level Meeting of the General Assembly on the Rule of Law at the National and International Levels, UN Doc A/RES/67/1 (30 Nov 2012): "The advancement of the rule of law at the national and international levels is essential for sustained and inclusive economic growth, sustainable development, the eradication of poverty and hunger and the full realization of all human rights and fundamental freedoms, including the right to development, all of which in turn reinforce the rule of law."

[56] "Declaration of the High-level Meeting of the General Assembly on the Rule of Law at the National and International Levels on 24 September 2012," Agenda item 83, A/Res/67/1, 30 November 2012.

As mentioned earlier the rule of law demands a legal system clearly embracing dominant moral norms ensuring procedural and substantive equity and impartiality both in legal rules themselves and in their application. In Rawls' theory justice is fairness and Rawls depart from the hypothesis that people are motivated by self-interest.[57]

It is worth noting that in the global economy emerges a system of regulatory networks. Regulatory systems have become gradually more important in the management of the global economy and causes essential challenges to the conception of the way international law is formulated and enforced; Regulatory webs do not depend on formal international treaties or rely on international organizations for their enforcement depending on the national application of internationally formulated standards.[58] The extension of justice could be seen as fairness obligations to international society.[59] Arbitration must take a sufficient role in interpreting law[60] by becoming the second co-equal and independent pole of justice within a legal system.

It has to be taken into account that globalization and cyberspace/electronic technology are two factors causing a creative mobility and changeability into societies' life expressed by new norms incorporating new values and morals which means that the rule of law has to keep pace with this mobility. The interaction of societies causes changes in society's life which have to be endorsed by the rule of law and so the existence of formal and informal dispute systems is fundamental for the existence of the rule of law because both systems of dispute (courts versus arbitration) contribute into the shaping of its content. Territorial boundaries need not prevent the prospect of transnational moral obligations.[61] Justice is not a general obligation for all people regardless of their dealings, but is limited to persons in precise types of relationships. Publicity is the actual soul of justice and so it is through publicity alone that justice becomes the safeguard of security.[62]

---

[57] Rawls, J. 1971, A Theory of Justice, Cambridge, MA: Harvard University Press.

[58] Anne-Marie Slaughter, The Real New World Order, 76 Foreign Aff. 183, 196 (Sept.-Oct. 1997).

[59] Roscoe Pound, The Causes of Popular Dissatisfaction with the Administration of Justice, 40 Am. L. Rev. 729, 731 (1906).

[60] G Zekos, International Commercial and Marine Arbitration, 2008 Routledge-Cavendish Publishers London www.routledge.com. G Zekos, Constitution, Arbitration and Courts, 2013 Nova Science Publications New York USA. www.novapublishers.com G Zekos, Arbitration's status under EU law, The Journal of World Investment and Trade 13 (2012) 390–419, brill.nl/jwit, G Zekos, Developments on Courts' Involvement in Arbitration. Volume 1: The Rule of Law, Volume 2: Courts and Law, 2019 Nova Science Publications New York USA. www.novapublishers.com

[61] Anthony D'Amato and Kristen Engel, State Responsibility for the Exportation of Nuclear Power Technology, 74 Va. L. Rev. 1011, 1042 (1988) (stating that "a national boundary is an artificial, as well as a morally irrelevant, boundary with respect to moral obligations"); Fernando R. Tesón, The Kantian Theory of International Law, 92 Colum. L. Rev. 53, 82–83 (1992) (stating that "[t]he contingent division of the world into discrete nation-states does not transform political freedom from an ethical imperative into a mere accident of history").

[62] J. Bentham, "Draught of a New Plan for the organisation of the Judicial Establishment in France: proposed as a Succedaneum to the Draught presented, for the same purpose, by the Committee of

The rule of law encompasses ethics but ethics are outside legal requirements. By being ethical, a company encounters demands of business stakeholders, augment business performance, abide by legal requirements, avert or diminish harm and upgrade personal morality. The most vital ingredient of any governance system is regarded to be the board of directors (BODs), which is responsible for the governance of the respective companies.[63] BODs have a main duty to the company, a duty of care,[64] a fiduciary duty and a duty to act within one's power within the company[65] enveloped with an ethical background.

How globalization influences law? Globalization influences law in particular ways. It has to be considered that law is essentially conservative and reactive responding to alterations more than commencing transformations. Insofar as globalization and its related technologies are altering what people do and how they do it, law itself is adjusting and replying through new rules, institutions, practices, and procedures. In addition, globalization is changing the nature of regulation not only is the role of the state as the customary source of globalization, but also new sources of legal regulation are emerging.

Is there the role of the rule of law in the global legal order? Who controls the worldwide changes via globalization? It is possible the currently controlling the globalization process in the end to become controlled by their creation if the whole globalization process disregards any ethical values and, in the end, we will have a distractive conflict.[66]

It is worth noting that globalization has enhanced attention to space.[67] In fact, globalization presents a challenge to the rule of law. While the rule of law has customarily revolved around the laws and institutions of nation states there is moving to have a global existence.[68] Nevertheless, the complexity and components of the global economy make legal accountability difficult to enforce, and if there is no enforcement of legal norms there can be no rule of law.[69] Effective global management will require a significant role for legal rules and principles, as well as

---

Constitution, to the National Assembly, December 21st, 1789," printed in London, 1790, 25–6 (Bowring, iv. 285–406, at 316–17).

[63] Tricker, B. (2009). Corporate governance: Principles, policies and practices. New York, NY: Oxford University Press Inc.

[64] Marshall, S. & Ramsay, I. (2012). Stakeholders and Directors' Duties: Law, Theory and Evidence, University of New South Wales Law Journal, 35, 291–316.

[65] Hareendra Dissabandara, Handling Key Issues in Corporate Governance and Business Ethics: To be True to Self & Beyond Rules and Regulations, http://ssrn.com/abstract=2606160

[66] G Zekos, Ethics and Law in Globalization and Cyberspace, IJOE (2012), Volume 8, Number ½, 2012 Nova Science Publishers, Inc.

[67] Von Benda-Beckmann F, von Benda-Beckmann K, Griffiths A. 2009. Space and legal pluralism: an introduction. In Spatializing Law: An Anthropological Geography of Law in Society, ed. F von Benda-Beckmann, K von Benda-Beckmann, A Griffiths, pp. 1–29. Aldershot: Ashgate.

[68] Sir Anthony Mason, "The tale of law and international economic transactions" in Spencer Zifcak (ed) Globalisation and the Rule of Law (Routledge, UK, 2005.

[69] Philippe Sands, Lawless World (Penguin, Australia, 2005).

procedures and remedies for their enforcement. The rule of law has to be accepted that it constructs an autonomous global legal order for an autonomous global entity within a global sovereignty and global cyber-sovereignty.

4.3 Global Economic Governance and the Rule of Law

What sparks global economic governance? Globalization and global economic governance brought forward the interaction between governments and non-state actors as vital to the production of both positive global effects and averting of negative effects. Different mixes of government policies, institutions, corporate strategies, technologies, and worker skills are linked with upgrading success in global economic governance. The term governance designates all regulations intended for organization and centralization of human societies on a global scale. Moreover, governance conveys formal political institutions coordinating and controlling independent social relations having the capacity to enforce, by force, their decisions.

Which the role of the rule of law in global economic governance? Which is the power behind the global economic governance? Increased globalization over the last years has made valuable global economic governance more central than ever. The series of issues that demand global coordination now embrace matters which were once regarded as falling entirely within a state's domestic jurisdiction, such as banking regulation and domestic resource mobilization.[70] Non-state actors have assumed a larger role in global politics and in the global economy. Moreover, global economic governance influences a broad range of state and non-state stakeholders in the global economy,[71] many of whom were formerly only indirectly influenced by matters such as environmental issues. In other words, globalization forces national economies to share risks.

It has to be considered that the players in global economic governance advance economic policies and practices that permit all stakeholders, including the weakest societies and the poorest individuals, to share in the profits of the global economic system. Moreover, the global economic governance must endorse economic policies that are sustainable and will not be destabilized over time by their environmental or social costs. The pattern of the intensifying scope of global economic governance and restricted effectual involvement in the institutional arrangements for global economic governance is tricky. For instance, although membership is more universal, operative participation in IMF is de facto limited to a smaller number of players.

---

[70] Daniel D. Bradlow, Development Decision-Making and the Content of International Development Law, 27 B.C. Int'l & Comp. L. Rev. 195, 210–11 (2004) (explaining that under the modern view of development, development actors are concerned with economic, social, environmental, and human rights issues as well as traditional economic law issues).

[71] Sungjoon Cho & Claire R. Kelly, Promises and Perils of New Global Governance: A Case of the G20, 12 Chi. J. Int'l L. 491, 493--94 (2012).

In addition, the international financial system is by and large run by the leading industrialized countries which impose their views on developing countries.[72] Furthermore, it could be argued that specific funds that belong to a handful number group of people run the global economic governance.

While following World War II, the key actors in global economic governance were the IMF, the International Bank for Reconstruction and Development ("World Bank"), and the General Agreement on Tariffs and Trade ("GATT"), the number of prime actors in global economic governance grew to embrace the Group of Seven ("G7") and lately, two new global economic governance entities, the G20 and the FSB, were created. Ministers of Finance of the G20 became an additional actor in the inclusive arrangements for global economic governance. In 2008, as part of the answer to that year's global financial crisis, the G20 was lifted up to the level of a summit of heads of government. Moreover, it seems that the G20 is the coordinator, planner & controller of global economic governance granting the setting in which the key economies meet with the leading international institutions such as the IMF, the World Bank, the World Trade Organization ("WTO"), and the United Nations ("UN") to review the main economic challenges facing the international society and synchronize/harmonize their answers to these challenges.[73] Another key global economic governance development is the conversion of the Financial Stability Forum ("FSF") into the FSB.[74] The FSF mandate was extended to embrace considering the vulnerabilities in the global financial system and initiating regulatory and supervisory reactions to them, monitoring market developments, working with the IMF to supply early alert of financial trouble, dealing with cross-border regulation of large financial institutions, and directing the work of the international standard-setting bodies.

Which is the law regulating economic governance? There is no apparent "governing law" for global economic governance. It has to be considered that some of the leading governance institutions, such as the G20, have no international legal personality. On the other hand, the absence of international legal personality offers it with a definite flexibility and informality making possible it to adapt somewhat without delay to changing circumstances. It also means, however, that its official documents have no formal international legal status.

Some important global economic governance players are not the subjects of international law. The decision-making bodies and institutions dealing with international economic governance have to conform to universally applicable customary and treaty based international legal principles in order to confirm a legitimate face.

---

[72] Ngaire Woods, The Challenges to International Institutions, in The Political Economy of Globalization 202, 208 (Ngaire Woods ed., 2000), José Antonio Ocampo, Rethinking Global Economic and Social Governance, 1 J. Globalization & Dev. 1, 4--5 (2010) (providing a general overview of the history of post-World War II global economic governance).

[73] G20: Invitees and International Organizations, Russ. G20, http://www.g20.org/docs/about/international_guests.html (noting that international organizations are invited to the G20 Summit).

[74] Eric Helleiner, The Financial Stability Board and International Standards (Ctr. for Int'l Governance Innovation, Paper No. 1, 2010) (providing a detailed description of the FSB).

Nevertheless, there are a number of international legal principles, derived from customary international law and general principles of law, that are applicable for all players in global economic governance. These principles are the customary international legal principles of sovereignty; non-discrimination, which incorporates treatment of legal and natural persons; environmental accountability; and the legal principle of good administrative practice.

The conventional international legal principle of respect for state sovereignty presents that global economic governance players should abstain from interfering in those affairs that fall within the domestic jurisdiction of each sovereign state.[75] States are needed to report to international supervisory bodies on their compliance with particular international human rights agreements and so cannot treat their domestic conduct with respect to these human rights issues as being entirely within their domestic jurisdiction. In addition, in accordance with the United Nation's "responsibility to protect" doctrine, states are encouraged to intervene in legitimate humanitarian emergencies.[76]

Have states disappeared from the scene due to economic globalization and the emergence of global economic governances in a much more obvious and strong way than prior to globalization in its modern version? Despite developments regarding international legal principles, the legal principle of state sovereignty continues to be an imperative condition in assessing global governance. It could be said that global economic governance decision makers have to act in ways that sustain as much independence and policy space for states as is consistent with effectual global economic governance.

Has the economic globalization brought forward the need to introduce not only the notion of a global sovereignty but also the notion of global cyber-sovereignty? Is it time to introduce a global sovereignty for matters of global interest such as the survivor and existence of earth? It could be argued that super powers already treat earth as their global sovereignty but at least super powers still follow the rule of law to a certain degree.

The principle of nondiscrimination entails subjects of international law to treat all in the same way situated parties in a like manner. It could be said that nondiscrimination is a custom of international law. Consequently, all states have some way to contribute, either directly or indirectly, in international decision-making structures and institutions.[77] To that extent, the application of the principle of nondiscrimination to global economic governance demands treating all alike

[75] Ian Brownlie, Principles of Public International Law 250, 294–98 (seventh ed. 2008) (explaining that international actors should refrain from infringing on the principles of state sovereignty).

[76] Stephanie Farrior, International Reporting Procedures, in Guide to International Human Rights Practice 189, 197–201 (Hurst Hannum ed., fourth ed. 2004) (describing reporting procedures of international human rights treaties). Alex J. Bellamy, Responsibility to Protect 51–59 (2009).

[77] James Crawford, The International Law Commission's Articles on State Responsibility: Introduction, Text and Commentaries (2002) (discussing state responsibility in the International Law Commission). M. Sornarajah, The International Law on Foreign Investment 201–04, 208, 337, 409–10 (3d ed. 2010).

situated states correspondingly and all dissimilarly situated states in a different way.[78] It is worth mentioning that the principle of nondiscrimination is also related to a state's responsibility to corporate players in the global economy. Moreover, the Universal Declaration of Human Rights ("UDHR") should be considered as customary international law defining the responsibilities of global economic governance players to natural persons.[79]

Are states merely agents of corporate capitalism? In reality the international legal process has been an apparatus of hegemony, and powerful Western states have been achieved hegemony through this device over less-developed countries. Modern globalization touches economic, financial, techno-logical, environmental, social, cultural, political, and health-related matters and events. It could be argued that the form of modern globalization, by its nature, involves every ingredient of human life, and consequently has become a sort of jus cogens of today's humanity.[80]

Modern globalization due to economic and financial globalization brought forward corporate capitalism and consequently corporate capitalism is the steam engine of today's globalized world. To that extent corporate capitalism[81] has formed an unseen and inevitable system comprised of two key elements: market and technology, which have become two faces of globalization. Global market and technology as elements of globalization brought forward cyber market and cyber-sovereignty expanding the arena of the modern humanity and so throwing people to the unknown cyber-world encompassing electronic technology and the emergence of cyber dimension. Globalization has permitted corporate capitalism to accomplish several aims such as economic globalization; social, political, and legal value globalization; creation of conflicts within states; and giving globalized effect to those internal conflicts. U. Acharya[82] says that "it is important to realize that corporations' trade and investment activities and governments' policies are beneficial only insofar as

[78] David Hunter et al., International Environmental Law and Policy 495–97 (3d ed. 2007) (explaining that the principle of "common but differentiated responsibilities" reflects principles of equity by placing more responsibility on wealthier countries and those that are more responsible for causing specific environmental problems); Remonda B. Kleinberg, The Politics of International Trade Regulation in the Developing World: Law and Policy of "Preferential" Treatment in the Governance of World Trade 4–5, 7 (2011) (noting that special and differential treatment principles have been incorporated into the architecture of the WTO rules).

[79] Hurst Hannum, The Status of the Universal Declaration of Human Rights in National and International Law, 25 Ga. J. Int'l & Comp. L. 287, 289, 323 (1995) (noting that several commentators have taken the position that the entire Universal Declaration of Human Rights ("UDHR") now represents customary international law).

[80] Stephan Hobe, The Era of Globalisation as a Challenge to International Law, 40 Duq. L. Rev. 655, 656 (2001).

[81] Jürgen Habermas, Beyond the Nation State? 10 Peace Rev. 235, 237 (1998).(discussing the Western trend transitioning from welfare-oriented states to a focus on market-friendly conditions in the 1980s).

[82] Upendra D. Acharya, Globalization And Hegemony Shift: Are States Merely Agents Of Corporate Capitalism? 2013 Boston College International & Comparative Law Review 968.

they are tools to advance human conditions, and should be resisted when they defeat that purpose."

The dynamics of the capitalist world-system placed the foundation for a course of industrialization and new international divisions of labor on a global scale. Moreover, the dynamics of the capitalist world-system take part in globalization, which is qualitatively distinct because it implicates the operative integration of internationally dispersed activities[83] and International trade, investment, and finance have become the hallmarks of economic globalization. The production of goods and services in cross-border, value-adding networks have made the global economy in the last half of the twentieth century qualitatively distinct from what preceded it. MNEs[84] have developed into the key movers and shakers of the global economy coordinating and controlling supply chain operations in more than one country, even if they do not own them.

States and their people seem to be fully wrapped up in the corporate capitalist society and so they have admitted the profit motive of corporate capitalism as their political value system barring to a certain high degree the values of welfare and social justice that were advocated by pre-globalized social democracies. It has to be taken into consideration that the values of welfare and social justice are part of human beings and their spiritual existence which can be in disharmony with the material world supported and promoted by the economic capitalism which materialism is the essence and the DNA of economic capitalism.

The access to goods and services made available by economic globalization transformed corporate capitalism into a state of mind and lifestyle that forces people into the dominion of market and technology while disregarding aspiration, emotional, and spiritual fundamentals of human life.[85] Thus, humans have been persuaded due to their nature that their existence and goal of life is the consumption of products rather than the consumption to be merely the means to achieve the spiritual enhancement since our spirit leaves in the human body. Are corporations as such responsible for the way that people deal with material or the spiritual leaders of the world are not acting as real spiritual leaders rather than being more simply administrators of institutions? It should not be forgotten that corporations are directed by humans and not amorphous funds.

Which is the role of the rule of law in economic globalization and the global economic governance? There is a need to ascertain the role that law and authority should play in globalization stimulated and sponsored by corporate capitalism. The

---

[83] Dicken, Peter. 2003. Global Shift: Reshaping the Global Economic Map in the twenty-first Century. fourth ed. London: Sage.

[84] G Zekos, Corporate Governance and MNEs in Globalization & Cyberspace, 2013 Nova Science Publications, New York, USA. www.novapublishers.com

[85] Jost Delbrück, The Changing Role of the State in the Globalising World Economy, in Making Transnational Law Work in the Global Economy 56, 57 (Pieter H.F. Bekker et al. eds., 2010) (describing the earlier transition from paternalistic monarchies of the sixteenth and seventeenth centuries to mercantilism or state-sponsored economic policies in order to effectuate states' obligations of security and general welfare rather than profit).

hegemonic international law theory posits that powerful nations among the many sovereign states define the course of states' behavior by creating and influencing international law to give effect to the hegemonic interests of powerful states forgiving/disregarding actions which might not be legitimate according to an objective interpretation of law as long as support their interests.[86] It could be said that the rule of law is a core element of governance which means that looking first at rule of law as a result of political means of contestation and negotiation to agree a common stance on handling and regulation of social and political interaction implicates evaluating the levels of consent by dominant groups to be bound by the terms of the political arrangement and the burden of the motivations drawing elite interests under a common drive.

For the reason that international law is based on the mutual consent of sovereign states, each participating state must have common values and interests for international law to be effectual. Considering that state sovereignty is associated with and appreciated in accordance with its material values embraced within it not mentioning the value of the new notion of cyber-sovereignty, the international system has failed to give emphasis on state sovereignty in accordance with the material inequalities among nations.[87] As a result, countries lacking in political and economic power undergo an analogous deficit of national sovereignty within the system, while the sovereignty of powerful countries remains unchallenged and highly dominant.

Regardless of maintaining approval to superimposed Western norms, international law lacks a formal enforcement and compliance authority. The lack of a global formal enforcement and compliance authority allows super powers[88] to keep on their influence upon international law and consequently to the rule of law. Nonetheless, fragmented informal or non-legal authority has been institutionalized through resources controlled by hegemonic super powers that can make others comply with the norms. It could be argued that in a pseudo-legal compliance mechanism, super powers may obey international law when faced with worldwide force and

[86] Detlev F. Vagts, Editorial Comment, Hegemonic International Law, 95 Am. J. Int'l L. 843, 847 (2001) ("In terms of the formation of customary law, such a power can by its abstention prevent the emerging rule from becoming part of custom."). (Vagts's review of earlier "hegemons" that dominated certain regions reminds us that each hegemon "led the way in formulating the international law rules of the time," and that Rome, at least, "define[d] . . . rights and duties of the relationship[s] in its own interest.").

[87] Benedict Kingsbury, Sovereignty and Inequality, 9 Eur. J. Int'l L. 599, 601, 612 (1998) (Kingsbury asserts that the international system's traditional emphasis on state sovereignty is often ignorant of and unconcerned with the material inequalities among nations).

[88] Oona Hathaway & Scott J. Shapiro, Outcasting: Enforcement in Domestic and International Law, 121 Yale L.J., 252, 255–56 (2011) ("The principal objection made by critics of international law is that international law cannot be real law because it cannot matter in the way that real law must matter. In particular, they argue that international law cannot matter in the way it must to be law because it lacks mechanisms of coercive enforcement.").

opposition from competing emerging super powers.[89] It should not be forgotten what Heraclitus has said that everything changes (τα πάντα ρει). It is characteristic what Andreas Paulus[90] said that US have used international law in order to impose obligations to other states while US have failed to obey it.

Which could be the behavior of a global superpower when there will not be an opposition force to balance? Can a global power globally manipulate people? It has to be taken into account that International law, in its creation and practical application, has been a victim of the hegemonic power consolidation process. For instance, non-Western societies did not have any place in "Westphalian"[91] international law, because these societies were not signatories to the treaties and conventions that made international law. Due to the subjective implementation of international law by not recognizing and not following the common goals and values of a pluralistic world, international law considers super powers' values those of "true" civilization. It should not be forgotten that colonizing powers imposed their laws to deny sovereign status to the people of their colonies. From international law's beginning at Westphalia,[92] it has endured the hegemonic process in its development and application. International law, as a result of hegemonic process of powerful Western countries, has globalized the values of Western hegemonic countries as an indispensable legal condition for the world order and has produced a worldview. It is possible that the already produced worldview to be transformed into the global view and as such to be imposed upon the rest of the globe.

Have the globalized values of Western hegemonic countries considered as an indispensable legal condition for the world order imposed as axioms in globalization? Nowadays in the era of globalization, evolving hegemonic international law theory calls for questioning whether states are in fact the "hegemonic force" in today's world. It is worth mentioning here that there is an emphasis on soft law and bilateral state agreements that are more effortlessly formed and controlled by hegemonic countries.[93] The twenty-first century reached a new inception in the development of international law that of the war on terror but it is once again up

---

[89] Thomas S. Szayna et al., The Emergence of Peer Competitors: A Framework for Analysis 45–47, 49–50 (2001) (discussing a theory of hegemonic power and stating that a hegemon's threat of imposing conflict onto another state will greatly influence that state's behavior).

[90] Andreas Paulus, The War Against Iraq and the Future of International Law: Hegemony or Pluralism?, 25 Mich. J. Int'l L. 691, 724–25 (2003) ("Indeed, the United States practices a strategic and, at times, tactical use of international law—trying to impose obligations on others while remaining unrestricted itself.").

[91] Turan Kayaoglu, Westphalian Eurocentrism in International Relations Theory, 12 Int'l Stud. Rev. 193, 199 (2010).

[92] Renê Guilherme S. Medrado, Renegotiating Remedies in the WTO: A Multilateral Approach, 22 Wis. Int'l L.J. 323, 327 n.13 (2004) ("[T]he Treaty of Westphalia is seen as the event marking the advent of the traditional international law . . . .").

[93] Nico Krisch, International Law in Times of Hegemony: Unequal Power and the Shaping of the International Legal Order, 16 Eur. J. Int'l L. 369, 381–84 (2005) (discussing the weakening of international law through an emphasis on soft law and a return to bilateral state relations that are more easily shaped and controlled by hegemonic states).

to the hegemonic states to ascertain what represents terrorism and what methods to utilize to overpower/defeat terrorism.[94]

Soft law concerns nonstate rules reflecting best practices but are not yet legally enforceable.[95] Moreover, the move to soft law responds, at least in part, to the growing difficulty of approving international treaties and so the shift is generating uncertainty because soft law's unenforceability destabilizes predictability.[96]

Has globalization been a foundation/underpinning to Hegemony Shift? International law in the main operates in a decentralized and horizontal system of law and order, where hegemonic states create international law to amplify their self-interests at the cost of global good and the real/genuine significance of the rule of law. Supplementary, international institutions are used by hegemonic countries to facilitate their interests. Hegemonic countries have utilized international law and institutions to expand their economic interests by providing for and promoting the safety of foreign investments made by their national corporations and MNEs. Reisman[97] argues that while hegemonic power is always contemporary, law and globalization can also be counter hegemonic, in any case at times.

It has to be taken into account that globalization has become a channel under which corporations export their values all the way through the legal institutions that safeguard corporate interests. State preferences merely correspond to subsets of domestic society and powerful interest groups rather than the interest of public.[98]

---

[94] Noman Goheer, The Unilateral Creation of International Law During the "War on Terror": Murder by an Unprivileged Belligerent Is Not a War Crime, 10 N.Y. City L. Rev. 533, 560 (2007); at 543 (noting that the U.S. government defined who would be classified as a terrorist after September 11, 2001).

[95] Ryan Hagemann et al., Soft Law for Hard Problems: The Governance of Emerging Technologies in an Uncertain Future, 17 Colo. Tech. L.J. 37, 37 (2018). Steven L. Schwarcz, Soft Law as Governing Law, 2020 Minnesota Law Review 2471.

[96] Robin Creyke, "Soft Law" and Administrative Law: A New Challenge, 61 AIAL F. 15, 18 (2010) (arguing that including unenforceable softlaw rules together with enforceable mandatory requirements in "one document with little distinction made between compliance obligations" can "lead to confusion and higher costs, and ultimately to litigation to resolve these uncertainties"); Joost Pauwelyn, Rule-Based Trade 2.0? The Rise of Informal Rules and International Standards and How They May Outcompete WTO Treaties, 17 J. INT'L ECON. L. 739, 740–44 (2014) (discussing correlation between the rise in soft law and stagnation in the formation of traditional treaty rules).

[97] W. Michael Reisman, Introduction to Jurisdiction In International Law, at xi, xii (W. Michael Reisman ed., 1999) at xiii (noting that transnational decision processes, like all law-making, have "an inevitable political dimension" in the sense that participants "use their effective power . . . to secure the legal confirmation of arrangements which they believe will discriminate in their favor," but that, "as in all law-making, the plurilateral or multilateral character of the process often reduces or contains the power of the strongest actors and forces compromises").

[98] Neomi Rao, Public Choice and International Law Compliance: The Executive Branch Is a "They," Not an "It," 96 Minn. L. Rev. 194, 212 (2011) ("In recent years, scholars have challenged the model of unitary states acting within the international system and proposed instead a liberal account of international relations that disaggregates the state . . . . State preferences represent subsets of domestic society and powerful interest groups, and the configuration of state preferences determines state behavior in international relations."); Jeswald W. Salacuse & Nicholas P. Sullivan, Do BITs Really Work?: An Evaluation of Bilateral In-vestment Treaties and Their

It seems that the idea of the right to development has been replaced by or prioritized through international trade and investment mechanisms.

Unfortunately, during this globalized era, the world is observing not only the battle of Western hegemonic states to keep up their unilateral vital activities, either in the course of the war on terror, or trade war, but also the appearance of recently emerged economically powerful countries and MNEs as super hegemonic force.[99] Globalization of economic interests of corporate capitalism through financial and technological dealings and spreading out has influenced international law and its interpretation as well.

Furthermore, corporate capitalism is disseminated by two players in the era of modern globalization—MNEs as prime players and states as consequential players. Prime players are undetectable in the daily lives, thinking, and altering cultures of peoples around the globe, while consequential players are evident in creating and enforcing policy agendas essential to assist the prime players' interests. States as consequential players take forward prime players' agendas in the name of democracy and human rights, and occasionally in the name of countries' economic interests.

States, as consequential players, take part in economic relations with other states in two ways: direct government-to-government contacts through bilateral treaties, and indirect government-to-government interactions through multilateral economic organizations.[100] State functions are mainly to institutionalize and rationalize the markets by protecting property rights[101] embracing intellectual property rights, opening economic policies universally, and securing vital inputs at lower cost to satisfy the prime players. Moreover, states coordinate and preserve their relations with foreign systems within and outside of national territories with the intention of expanding or de-territorializing corporate capitalism.

Are financial institutions nothing but a policy tool in the name of free trade to serve? Corporate capitalism plays a prevailing role in today's state and human

---

Grand Bargain, 46 Harv. Int'l L.J. 67, 76 (2005) (stating that the United States has actively encouraged investment and market liberalization with host countries to facilitate the entry and operation of investments, and has actively protected private investments by U.S. nationals through aggressive negotiation of bilateral investment treaties).

[99] David P. Fidler, Eastphalia Emerging?: Asia, International Law, and Global Governance, 17 Ind. J. Global Legal Stud. 1, 7 (2010) (considering China and India as possible new contenders as the most influential states in global policy). Joel Slawotsky, The Global Corporation as International Law Actor, 52 Va. J. Int'l L. Dig. 79, 80 (2012) (arguing that large multinational corporations should be treated similarly to states in the application of international law because of their comparable reach, power, and asset control).

[100] Allison D. Garrett, The Corporation as Sovereign, 60 Me. L. Rev. 129, 148 (2008) ("For example, corporations engage in diplomacy, establish outposts in other nations, engage in trade negotiations, and often serve as proxies for their home country's government.").

[101] Frank J. Garcia, Three Takes on Global Justice, 31 U. La Verne L. Rev. 323, 357–59 (2010). Osvaldo Sunkel, Transnational Capitalism and National Disintegration in Latin America, in The Political Economy of Law 282, 285–86 (Yash Ghai et al. eds., 1987).

affairs, and MNEs[102] are everywhere in modern life. MNEs are competent of dictating the choice of states and directing the flow of international law by either prompting states to execute and enforce treaties or inducing international soft law. On the one hand, advancement of corporate interests by state governments generates a noticeable conflict of values. On the other hand, democratic states are built around cherishing human dignity and ingenuity while the only corporate value is the bottom line.[103]

First of all, corporations now function like states and there are instances when states act like corporations. Moreover, Corporations are not responsible under customary international law.[104] Could the second U.S.-Iraq war be considered an actual state-corporate partnership facilitating corporate interests by states? According to Paul Bignell[105] the second U.S.-Iraq war (2003) can be regarded a successful state-corporate partnership facilitating corporate interests by states. Moreover, latest events in Libya show how states can act as conduits for corporate capitalism. It could be argued that a comprehensive analysis of Gaddafi's passionate relationship with Western corporate interests discloses the prospect of sinister motivations and provides evidence of a swing in hegemonic power from states to MNEs.[106]

As mentioned earlier, the theory of global governance has been based on market and technology, principally since the 1990s and due to corporate capitalism and market-driven globalization it could be said that we are beginning to enter an era of post-human society with a weakening or an absence of aspiration and emotional human elements. It could be argued that States have become soft power and corporate capitalism has become hard power in the system of international law and

[102] G Zekos, Economics, Finance and Law on MNEs, 2007 Nova Publishers, New York www.novapublishers.com

[103] Sol Picciotto, Regulating Global Corporate Capitalism 108–10 (2011) ("[T]he corporation is . . . a central institutional form mediating social relations of power . . . . [The corporate form may be used] with virtually any combination of personal, family, institutional and governmental involvement."); Kevin T. Jackson, Global Corporate Governance: Soft Law and Reputational Accountability, 35 Brook. J. Int'l L. 41 (2010) (discussing corporations' voluntary development of soft law as constraints on their own behavior).

[104] Kiobel v. Royal Dutch Petroleum Co., 621 F.3d 111, 145 (2d Cir. 2010), aff'd, No. 10–1491 (Apr. 17, 2013) (holding that corporations are not responsible under customary international law after allegedly facilitating governmental human rights violations).

[105] Paul Bignell, Secret Memos Expose Link Between Oil Firms and Invasion of Iraq, Indep. (London), Apr. 19, 2011, at 4. Chad C. Carter, Halliburton Hears a Who? Political Question Doctrine Developments in the Global War on Terror and Their Impact on Government Contingency Contracting, 201 Mil. L. Rev. 86, 127 (2009).

[106] Jonte van Essen, De Facto Regimes in International Law, 28 Utrecht J. Int'l & Eur. L., no. 74, 2012 at 31, 31, 42, 46 (discussing the relation of international state-recognition doctrines to the Libyan interim government's diplomacy). Ronald Bruce St John, The Changing Libyan Economy: Causes and Consequences, 62 Middle E. J. 75, 80 (2008). Ismael Hossein-Zadeh, Why Regime Change in Libya?, Global Research (June 20, 2011), http://www.globalresearch.ca/why-regime-change-in-libya/. Richard Spencer et al., Blair Went to Tripoli "To Lobby Gaddafi for Deals with US Bank," Daily Telegraph (London), Sept. 19, 2011, at 20.

order. It could be argued that corporate capitalism now determines when and where war or conflicts over resources are to be affirmed or manufactured. Corporate capitalism determines how free markets should be advanced through the IMF, World Bank, WTO, and direct state-to-state bilateral agreements. It seems that states and civil societies have persuaded to surrender their sovereign authority and political will to the superior good of supranational norms of globalization favorable to corporate capitalism. Thus, it could be argued that while the role of the state is changing in the era of modern globalization, the real/hidden forces that are behind the real governing of modern globalization is not changing.

It has to be considered that sovereignty exposes some actual authority over territory. It is argued that the system of international law has an underlying bias, wherein it favors some consequences or distributive choices over others, expressly displaying a bias against the South or the Third World[107] which means that politics might have influenced the structure of international law instead of allowing the rule of law to be applied via legal principles across the whole world equally. Moreover, it is specified that international law even today continues to be "consisted of a set of rules with a geographical basis (it was a European law), a religious-ethical inspiration (it was a Christian law), an economic motivation (it was a mercantilist law), and political aims (it was an imperialist law)[108]". It could be said that the international law is based on a rigorous formalism while concurrently accounting for its political "open-endedness" in the sense that competent argument in the field required to follow precisely defined formal prototypes that permitted and so indeed facilitated the taking of any possible position with regard to a dispute or a problem which means that the political system has the possibility to intervene in order to have a wanted outcome according to the needs of the prevailing elite instead of the rule of law to be applied in accordance with legal principles employed equally in all identical disputes.

Perhaps globalization has made states to be seen weaker[109] or more vulnerable to global forces because states cannot act like MNEs needed to accomplish the requirements of economic globalization demanding global economic governance. MNEs are the first violin in the orchestra of economic globalization but it has to be remembered that MNEs are established within a state according to the national laws of a state. Hence, State might continue to be a central player even in globalization. It is worth mentioning that no single country or region can efficiently regulate the global economy. Globalization brought a shifting of global winds of ideology, power, and socioeconomic inequality ignited and deepened.

---

[107] Martti Koskenniemi, From Apology To Utopia: The Structure Of International Legal Argument (2005).

[108] Mohamed Bedjaoui, Towards A New International Economic Order 50 (1979).

[109] Anthony McGrew, Globalization and Global Politics, in The Globalization of World Politics: An Introduction to International Relations 14, 16 (John Baylis et al. eds., fifth ed. 2011) ("Some—the hyperglobalists—argue that [globalization] is bringing about the demise of the sovereign nation-state as global forces undermine the ability of governments to control their own economies and societies.").

Has globalization strengthened the state? Globalization may have made imminent the need to strengthen the state as the axis for the survival of people in a changeable environment of globalization. The fundamental technological transformation characteristic of contemporary globalization is at the heart changes. The most distinguishing characteristic of globalization today is the revolution in telecommunications, computing, and the cyberspace/Internet that has fundamentally eradicated time and space as substantial features in many areas of human social interaction.[110] Globalization brought human flows, information flows, capital flows, ideological flows that are spectacularly shaping the world and what is probable in it. In a globalized world individuals and organizations can link directly with their counterparts around the globe immediately, cheaply, and without the mediation of the state's apparatus for diplomacy and foreign relations which bring forward an essentially new regulatory environment. States will more and more be judged by how effectively they surf and manage this web of networks.

International cooperation depends on decisions of governments to work together and the governance arrangements underlying international cooperation to augment economic policy coordination on cross border issues have been based either on informal intergovernmental groupings bringing together main players such as the G7 or G20 or on treaty-based international institutions.[111]

Have multilateral institutions in the economic and financial area been effective? It seems that multilateral institutions in the economic and financial area lack in effectiveness. Regardless of attempts to strengthen system coherence over the last few years, the UN System remains very fragmented. Have states found their role in globalization? It seems that the role of states is not clear in globalization yet and the battle by some states to become super powers has neutralized international organizations and the effectiveness of globalization itself.

It has to be taken into account that while the rule of law is the cornerstone of the international legal order, the analysis of intergovernmental instruments, statements made by States, and negotiation records, reveals that within the UN the rule of law has grown progressively contested in the past years, culminating at the post-2015 process leading to the Sustainable Development Goals (SDGs). Moreover, reflections drawn from the post-2015 process show that the rule of law is in decline in institutional and normative contexts. Instantaneously with the broadening of the rule of law with more substance and interpretations attached to it its normative specificity

---

[110] Anthony Giddens, The Consequences of Modernity 63–64 (1990) (de-scribing globalization as interdependence without differentiation of time and space); Daniel Kanstroom, Aftermath: Deportation Law and the New American Diaspora, at x (2012) ("Reports of the death of the nation-state, in short, have been exaggerated, as have reports of the irrelevance of national borders. The importance of geo-graphic space may have diminished somewhat ... [b]ut the poor and the oppressed of the world encounter a tighter regime of state regulation—with fewer migration possibilities—than many would have found in the past.").

[111] Thierry Soret, Governance Arrangements for Global Economic Challenges: Where Do we Stand? A Political Science Perspective A UNDP/ODS Working Paper Office of Development Studies United Nations Development Programme, New York —November 2009.

is being tempered, which generates uncertainty and disagreement among Countries on its core substance. Thus, uncertainty concerning the content of the rule of law means conceptual weakness affecting also the implementation of the rule of law elements in the 2030[112] Agenda indicating a broader crisis of the international legal order.

Can enhanced global governance represent an extension of political and legal processes observable at the national to the transnational stage? It is argued that global governance is an extension of national government and as world government. The global governance brought forward an increasing diversity of interconnected law-making process which has taken the form of a legal pluralism beyond the state level. It is argued that global governance can operate successfully without inevitably taking the form of a world state or even sovereign governments at the transnational or supranational levels. Do economic elites have captured and manipulated all global principles to their own interests? Do economic elites, acting behind the curtains, permit people to have an idea that the world is running according to their wills? On the other hand, it has to be considered that the possibility that operative supranational governance necessitates the launch of fundamentals of global government.[113]

The distinction between "hard" law and non-binding regulatory instruments is obscured. International standards developed by international organizations either acquire a certain amount of legally binding force or they are not directly legally binding. New systems self-regulatory such as the so-called new lex mercatoria have evolved without a significant participation. There is a growing diversity concerning the law enforcement processes in the international system. The key role that started to play non-state actors in the development and enforcement of the regulatory instruments is the central characteristic of global governance.

Might supra-national organizations slip away from the direction of national governments and use their power at the request of private actors, whose pressure had grown with globalization? Globalization creates spillover effects from one society to another and so providing enticements for shifting governance to the supranational level. Globalization advances a homogenization in preferences over public goods. Moreover, globalization increased uncertainty about the state of the world contributing to greater delegation of authority to global institutions.[114] Thus, globalization generates winners and losers within national societies.

[112]Noora Arajärvi, The Rule of Law in the 2030 Agenda, Hague Journal on the Rule of Law April 2018, Volume 10, Issue 1, pp. 187–217.

[113]James N. Rosenau, "Governance, Order, and Change in World Politics," in Governance without Government: Order and Change in World Politics, ed. James N. Rosenau and Ernst Otto-Czempiel (Cambridge: Cambridge University Press, 1992), 1–29.

[114]Koremenos, Barbara, Charles Lipson, and Duncan Snidal. 2001. The Rational Design of International Institutions. International Organization, 55, 4 (Autumn): 761–800.

It has to be considered that globalization[115] remains less than global: "economic integration remains uneven and spatially differentiated." Global governance relies more and more on national means, rather than substituting those means. Contemporary global governance entails the creation or restructure of national institutions and the positive benefits of globalization are bigger in societies correlated with effectual institutions to the global economy. Heightened uncertainty brought by globalization needs a redefinition of global governance requiring greater base of knowledge.[116] The law of global governance offers tools acting not only at the regulatory or procedural levels but also at the institutional one necessitating establishment of a dedicated international body or in the recognition that global private firms functioning in a condition of de facto monopoly are equated to global public administration requiring specific forms of control.

Also, globalization does not unavoidably require or engender effectual global governance, nor does it certainly weaken national governments and their policy options. According to Kanishka Jayasuriya[117] "globalization transforms, not dissolves or erodes, the way in which sovereignty is produced ... Increasingly, globalization fragments this model of internal sovereignty by creating multiple centers of governance around autonomous national and supranational agencies. The emergent multilevel governance of the EU is a good exemplar of this fragmentation of the internal sovereignty of the State ... the emergence of network governance following the transformation of sovereignty has allowed States to regulate or govern economic processes that are increasingly transnational."

Can the effectiveness of international law be judged entirely by the measure of global cooperation or objective state interest? The wish of politicians to hold on to power and advance their taking sides policy preferences should be the axis for the international law to be judged. International agreements and customary international law compel politicians to make concessions by reforming the domestic institutional or policy landscape. According to Jide Nzelibe[118] "international legal commitments are often framed as institutional arrangements rather than as prescribed policy outcomes, partisan politicians tend to rank these commitments based upon their expectations regarding future policy outcomes."

---

[115] Kahler, Miles and David A. Lake. 2003. Globalization and Changing Patterns of Political Authority. In Miles Kahler and David A. Lake, editors, Governance in a Global Economy: Political Authority in Transition. Princeton: Princeton University Press: 412–438.

[116] Miles Kahler, Global Governance Redefined, The Conference on Globalization, the State, and Society Washington University School of Law St. Louis, 13–14 November 2003..

[117] Jayasuriya, Kanishka (1999) "Globalization, Law, and the Transformation of Sovereignty: The Emergence of Global Regulatory Governance," Indiana Journal of Global Legal Studies: Vol. 6: Iss. 2, Article 3. p454–455.

[118] Jide Nzelibe, Strategic Globalization: International Law As An Extension Of Domestic Political Conflict, 2011 Vol. 105, No. 2 Northwestern University Law Review 638.

4.4 New Technologies and the Rule of Law

It is worth noting that digitization, AI, and service robots transform virtually all service industries by improving service quality and productivity. The digital revolution hosts technologies ranging from AI to service robots that serve customers and so altering the landscape in which service marketing decisions are made and how customer and stakeholder value is generated.[119]

Presently AI is a transformative technology which will be augmented by the forthcoming AAI technology.[120] It has to be taken into account that AI can already identify AI-fabricated photos and through machine learning adjust its own algorithms and rather than causing discrimination AI can be designed in an AAI level to overcome it.[121]

Blockchain reduces the power of possibly corrupt public officials by augmenting the predictability of government service delivery, the consistency with which legal rules are applied, and the equality with which those transacting with the government are handled and so blockchain can achieve rule of law values "by design." On the other hand, the capacity of blockchain technology to make certain transparency, accountability, predictability, and consistency depends on both design features and real application.

It has to be taken into consideration that between blockchain technology and rule of law can develop a conflict on a central level. Especially, the principle of equality before the law necessitates that each individual is accorded due process, embracing that all individuals are subject to the same rules of justice including rights to access and rectify information and the right to appeal a decision. On the other hand, the use of blockchain can compromise individual due process rights for the reason that it may undercut the capacity of a person to influence or challenge a decision concerning them due to the fact that individuals are unable to access or ascertain the correctness of key information used to execute a specific transaction or make a decision. So far, blockchain has not been employed in a way that facilitates diverse rule of law values simultaneously because there is a need for a more advanced blockchain technology.

Which is the role of blockchain in implementing the rule of law in elections? First of all, the rule of law is a crucial component in the operation of elections for democracies. Since transparency is a prerequisite for social acceptance of the government, it is vital that elections confirm trust. Modern elections must offer more than simple access to information about the electoral process which means securing the public concerning accuracy, security, and accountability measures

[119] Bock, E. Dora, Jeremy S. Wolter, and O.C. Ferrell (2020), "Artificial Intelligence: Disrupting What We Know About Services", Journal of Service Marketing, 34 (3), 317–334.

[120] Ross Gruetzemacher and Jess Whittlestone, "The Transformative Potential of Artificial Intelligence" [2020] Communications of the ACM https://arxiv.org/abs/1912.00747

[121] Cukier, Kenneth (2021), "Commentary: How AI Shapes Consumer Experiences and Expectations", Journal of Marketing, 85 (1), 152–155.

combined to make certain electoral integrity. Hence, improving electoral processes is the fact that some voting technologies are promoted. Also, election technologies boost accountability and transparency of the election process.[122]

Is the rule of law enhanced by new technologies? It has to be taken into account that different technologies have different applicabilities and the legality of the process as a whole based on the extent to which technical sets associate with legal requirements and local conditions. To that extent, many technologies pledge transparency and accountability, predictability, consistency, and equality before the law "by design" in electoral processes, but many applications fail to do so in practice.[123] Moreover, new technologies play a role in tackling some of the more serious threats to the rule of law, embracing corruption and arbitrary decision-making.

In line, where technologies advance the capacity for people to exercise a right to vote, it augments the extent to which the law takes account of difference to make possible the practical equality of legal rights. Nonetheless, voting technologies can diminish equality before the law and the extent to which people are treated equally.[124]

Can technology influence enforcing compliance with the law? Enforcing compliance with the law is a ground for experimentation with technology and so more effective enforcement and compliance in areas such as intellectual property, environmental protection, and enforcing civil judgments are some of the fields of current experimentation.

4.5 Artificial Intelligence and the Rule of Law

It is argued that the automation of legal services is a manner to enhance access to justice, diminish legal costs, and upgrade the rule of law which means that these improvements are a democratization of law.[125] It could be said that "legal futurism"[126] is a "new form of law" that "will emerge to provide all of the benefits of both

---

[122] Kevin C. Desouza and Kiran K. Somvanshi, How Blockchain Could Improve Election Transparency, BROOKINGS (May 30, 2018), https://www.brookings.edu/blog/techtank/2018/05/30/how-blockchaincould-improve-election-transparency/

[123] Thomas Haines, Rajeev Goré and Mukesh Tiwari, "Verified Verifiers for Verifying Elections," CCS '19: Proceedings of the 2019 ACM SIGSAC Conference on Computer and Communications Security, November 2019, https://doi.org/10.1145/3319535.3354247

[124] Nicole Goodman, Here's How We Can Get More People to Vote in Elections, THE CONVERSATION (Apr. 10, 2019), https://theconversation.com/heres-how-wecan-get-more-people-to-vote-in-elections-112486

[125] Daniel Martin Katz, Quantitative Legal Prediction—or—How I Learned to Stop Worrying and Start Preparing for the Data-Driven Future of the Legal Services Industry, 62 Emory L.J. 909, 939–41 (2013) (discussing predictive technologies used in patent litigation).

[126] Anthony J. Casey & Anthony Niblett, The Death of Rules and Standards, 92 Ind. L.J. 1401, 1403 (2017).

rules and standards without the costs of either." It is argued that the computational revolution molds a politics friendlier to markets[127] but legal services are retained by small literate elites on whom the specialists depend for their existence.[128] Moreover, it seems that legal futurists[129] exhibit the decrease of legal obligations to computer code as an explicit stage toward the realization of the rule of law.

It has to be considered that law is a multifaceted domain that embraces services ranging from the administrative procedures to the highest stakes of imprisonment and freedom which means that the use of software and robots to draft, interpret, and enforce laws has unpredictable degrees of acceptability, varying on the context. Thus, obtaining a kind of license with a chatbot makes sense, and such "civic tech[130]" is expected to be used more in coming years.[131] Besides, legal automation on prison sentences handed down by robot judges or juries are not accepted currently.

Will law turn out to be a subdivision of computer science? There are some dominions of legal practice where algorithms, a building block of artificial intelligence, have already ousted legal workers and so automated document review is a staple of discovery now which means that a worker is far more likely to use TurboTax than to visit a lawyer or accountant to prepare annual returns for the Internal Revenue Service ("IRS").[132] Furthermore, lawmakers could ultimately draft tax statutes in the form of computer code, abolishing the interpretative step that TurboTax's lawyers and engineers must take as they translate statutory prerequisites into their software.[133]

It is argued that lawyers can err about facts or misrepresent precedent; human judges may be affected by irrelevant causes or bias but "automators of law" see their work as one more step toward uplifting the legal system above the unreliability of any specific individual within it.[134] In other words, there is a need to separate the

---

[127] John O. McGinnis, Machines v. Lawyers, CITY J. (2014), https://www.city-journal.org/html/machines-v-lawyers-13639.html

[128] Magali Sarfatti Larson, The Rise Of Professionalism 3 (1977).

[129] Anthony D'Amato, Can/Should Computers Replace Judges? 11 Ga. L. Rev. 1277, 1300–01 (1977) (presenting computerization as a path to a more "determinable legal system").

[130] Civic tech is the use of technology by governments to stimulate positive interactions among citizens themselves, and between citizens and their state.

[131] Mayur Patel et al., The Emergence of Civic Tech 6–7 (2013); see also Michael Halberstam, Beyond Transparency: Rethinking Election Reform from an Open Government Perspective, 38 Seattle U. L. Rev. 1007, 1009–10 (2015) (discussing Open Government movement to increase transparency).

[132] Frank Pasquale & Glyn Cashwell, Prediction, Persuasion, and the Jurisprudence of Behaviorism, 68 U. Toronto L.J. 63, 80 (2018). Frank Pasquale & Glyn Cashwell, Four Futures of Legal Automation, 63 UCLA L. Rev. Discourse 26, 28 (2015).

[133] Sarah B. Lawsky, Formalizing the Code, 70 Tax L. Rev. 377, 379 (2017).

[134] Ozkan Eren & Naci Mocan, Abstract, Emotional Judges and Unlucky Juveniles (Nat'l Bureau of Econ. Research, Working Paper No. 22611, 2016), http://www.nber.org/papers/w22611.pdf (finding that unexpected losses in "football games played by a prominent college team in the state ... increase disposition (sentence) lengths assigned by judges during the week following the game").

legal conceptual process from the human performance.[135] Moreover, a way of accomplishing the ideal for "a rule of law, not of men" is to dispense altogether with persons implementing or interpreting law and so, for instance, an un-appealable fine imposed by a red-light camera and mechanically deducted from a motorist's bank account would amount to clear automation of law, unchanged by any specific decision maker's bias. Can law be mechanically implemented in all occasions? The rule of law should make certain that law itself will administer matters of society, not the desires of influential persons but it is not certain that currently artificial intelligence can achieve it.[136]

It is worth noting that responsibility cannot be imposed upon machines which mean that there is a shift of personal accountability from regulators and judges to those coding their would-be replacements. Thus, until some "master algorithm" can code its "own progeny", human beings will always be accountable for legal determinations.[137] Moreover, in order for legal automation to follow rule of law principles, the axiom "a rule of law, not of men" has to be countered by a new responsibility—to a "rule of persons, not machines.[138]" It could be said that without attributing algorithmic judgments and interpretations to specific individuals and considering them in charge for explaining those judgments, legal automation will undercut fundamental principles of accountability. On the other hand, complementary legal automation, such as search engines or word processing software, simply assists lawyers, regulators, and judges. Furthermore, it seems that substitutive legal automation is intended to replace, rather than simply aid, lawyers and judges.

It is obvious that there is a shifting role of AI in the legal course. To that extent systems such as TurboTax or LegalZoom forums are not answering demanding legal questions which means that rather, the key automation technology at this point is a form of management which uses marketing and other tactics to draw individuals to tender their "expertise" and to inspire users to rely on such "expertise" with no assurance it is correct.[139] In line, it seems that software is the only mode of advice available to many citizens and even many small businesses. Moreover, successes in consumer services have stimulated a new generation of "legal automators" to push

[135] J.C. Smith, Machine Intelligence and Legal Reasoning, 73 Chi.-Kent L. Rev. 277, 278 (1998) ("From the perspective of the lawyer, we have the concept of the rule of law, as contrasted with the rule of persons; thus, in some sense.").

[136] Margaret Jane Radin, Reconsidering the Rule of Law, 69 B.U. L. Rev. 781, 781 (1989) (explaining that "[t]he ideal of "the rule of law, not of men" calls upon us to strive to ensure that our law itself will rule (govern) us, not the wishes of powerful individuals".

[137] Pedro Domingos, The Master Algorithm 12–20 (2015) (discussing how integration of five schools of machine learning may lead to rapid advances in computing).

[138] Margaret Jane Radin, Reconsidering the Rule of Law, 69 B.U. L. Rev. 781, 781 (1989).

[139] Craig Lambert, Shadow Work 201–50 (2016) (discussing shadow work on the internet, such as offering free information through customer reviews that may be monetized through, for example, Zagat guides).

for companies and governments to homogenize and computerize work once done by lawyers and experts who interpret and apply law.[140]

Does this bring less "access to justice" than "reducing legal spending[141]"? It is worth noting that cost savings are an authoritative argument in an era of growing global competition and falling state revenues. On the other hand, in many circumstances, the automation of legal services conceals the externalization of cost and risk to clients, citizens, and business competitors. Thus, the immediate savings in personnel costs are understandable; the long-term risks are probabilistic, but real and so already documented in extant legal-automation projects, these costs are also predictable in idealistic proposals to speed up the robotization of law.[142]

Nevertheless, both lawmakers and regulators must be cautious as they try to code legal obligations into software due to the fact that while computer code and human language both allow forms of communication, the affordances presented by each are different and, in many regards, mutually exclusive. Firstly, code abolishes the forms of uncertainty and flexibility characteristic of much language, embracing legal language.[143] Secondly, just as pursuits to replace all standards with rules have failed, so too will most tries to rewrite legal rules as code. On the other hand, technology is already assisting civil lawyers in their conventional roles as advocates and advisors and will carry on doing so in the future.[144] It is worth noting that the technological displacement of legal work in the criminal context, on substitutive automation of criminal-law enforcement, is far more controlled than it is in the civil space.

Will software eliminate the Law? It seems that current software remains in the early stages of replacing the law, and much remains completely outside software's ambit. It has to be taken into account that software's main advantage over legal systems is concentrated on its enforcement capacity because code is not only fast operating at low marginal cost but also the enforcement mechanism is ex ante rather than ex post, and therefore vastly more effective than law, which always acts after a wrong is committed.[145] Presently software faces limits of explainability, which is a problem for legal decision-making and so AAI technology will generate full

---

[140] How the Legal Industry Is Evolving, STEELCASE (June 2010), https://www.steelcase.com/research/articles/topics/collaboration/a-new-legal-brief/

[141] Boosting Procurement Efficiency Through Automation, SYNERGIST.IO (June 29, 2018), https://synergist.io/procurement-automation/ (automating procurement led to "reducing legal spending in this area by 75%").

[142] David Howarth, Is Law a Humanity (or Is it More Like Engineering)? 3 Arts & Human. Higher Educ. 9, 11–12 (2004). David Howarth, Law As Engineering 61–73 (2014).

[143] David Golumbia, The Cultural Logic Of Computation 78 (2009).

[144] Andrew Guthrie Ferguson, Big Data and Predictive Reasonable Suspicion, 163 U. PA. L. REV. 327, 350–51 (2015), Elizabeth E. Joh, Policing Police Robots, 64 UCLA L. Rev. Discourse 516, 519 (2016).

[145] Riva Richmond, Facebook's New Way to Combat Child Pornography, N.Y. Times: Gadgetwise https://gadgetwise.blogs.nytimes.com/2011/05/19/facebook-to-combat-child-porn-using-microsofts-technology/ Jennifer Langston, How PhotoDNA for Video Is Being Used to Fight Online Child Exploitation, Microsoft https://news.microsoft.com/on-the-issues/2018/09/12/how-photodna-forvideo-is-being-used-to-fight-online-child-exploitation/

explainability on any decision-making.[146] AAI systems will replicate the adjudicatory function in a way indistinguishable from a human, while becoming able to explain what they are doing in a way that complainants find acceptable and so stimulating people to trust such programs as less fallible than humans. Robo-courts cannot be seen merely as inhumane, excessively rule-driven systems and there is no need to include humans as mere tokens of legitimization.[147]

Can code/Al replace legal obligations entirely? Many "futurists" consider that it is possible by predicting that software will not only help lawyers find the cases relevant to their briefs but will write documents themselves.[148] To that extent, others argue[149] that a "legal singularity," which "will arrive when the accumulation of a massive amount of data and dramatically improved methods of inference make legal uncertainty obsolete." On the other hand, it could be said that the scenario of the "end of lawyers" and the "death of Big Law" is far away from reality.

It is worth noting here that Fallon has stated that there are at least three different ideal-typical accounts of the rule of law in contemporary jurisprudence.[150] On the other hand, it seems that legal "automators" concentrate on historicist explanations that link the rule of law with "rule by norms" laid down by rightful law-making establishments prior to their application to specific cases and formalism that describes "the ideal form of law" by means of a rule, regarded as a pure prescription that exists prior to its application and that ascertains suitable conduct or legal outcomes.[151]

It could be said that in case of federal regulation really reducible to "requirements extraction" encoded in software that encoding would be a real improvement for the rule of law, in its formalist perceptions and so the law would be as executable as a

[146] Ashley Deeks, The Judicial Demand for Explainable Artificial Intelligence, 119 Colum. L. Rev. 1829, 1832–38 (2019).

[147] Γ. Ζέκος, Εξελιγμένη τεχνητή νοημοσύνη και Robo-δικαστήρια, Αρμενόπουλος 6/2021 p 1093 https://www.dsth.gr/armenopoulos-intro

[148] John O. McGinnis & Russell G. Pearce, The Great Disruption: How Machine Intelligence Will Transform the Role of Lawyers in the Delivery of Legal Services, 82 Fordham L. Rev. 3041, 3041–42 (2013). Richard Susskind & Daniel Susskind, The Future Of The Professions 202 (2015) (describing computerized drafting of legal and other documents).

[149] Benjamin Alarie, The Path of the Law: Towards Legal Singularity, 66 U. Toronto L.J. 443, 445 (2016); Benjamin Alarie et al., Law in the Future, 66 U. Toronto L.J. 423, 427–28 (2016). Tom Meltzer, Robot Doctors, Online Lawyers and Automated Architects: the Future of the Professions?, GUARDIAN (June 15, 2014, 2:00 PM), https://www.theguardian.com/technology/2014/jun/15/robot-doctors-online-lawyers-automated-architects-future-professionsjobs-technology

[150] Richard H. Fallon, Jr., "The Rule of Law" as a Concept in Constitutional Discourse, 97 Colum. L. Rev. 1, 5 (1997) (describing these "ideal types . . . as (i) historicist, (ii) formalist, (iii) Legal Process, and (iv) substantive").

[151] Martin Ford, Rise Of The Robots 1–27 (2015). Ray Kurzweil, The Age Of Spiritual Machines 2–4 (2000); Nick Srnicek & Alex Williams, Inventing The Future: Post capitalism And A World Without Work 2–3 (2015).

software command.[152] Correspondingly, the translation of traffic rules into a chain of "chatbot prompts" reduces the law into a crystal-clear form—if not application. However, there is another justification of the rule of law, a "Legal Process conception," that is more open than either the historicist or formalist accounts and so Legal Process conceptions find the requisites of "law" essential for the Rule of Law to be fulfilled by a combination of "(i) procedural fairness in the development and application of legal norms, (ii) an (assumed) internal connection between notions of law and reasonableness, (iii) reasoned elaboration of the connection between recognized, pre-existing sources of legal authority and the determination of rights and responsibilities in particular cases, and (iv) judicial review as a guarantor of procedural fairness and rational deliberation by legislative, executive, and administrative decisionmakers[153]". It has to be considered that the term Legal Process signifies the line of a school of jurisprudence that emerged in the mid-twentieth century USA so as to bring together realist and formalist lines to interpretation.[154] While the historicist and formalist lines highlight the "rule" side of the rule of law, the Legal Process tactic underlines "law" as its fundamental component. Law as a social institution is multidimensional and embedded in specific political systems and traditions, such as rights to appeal and explanations for decisions which means that to the degree a legal technology like a smart contract diminishes a legal link to a "clear prescription" that occurs prior to its application and that ascertains suitable conduct or legal outcomes by epitomizing the formalist perception of the rule of law, it is doubtful to meet the multipart standards of review and appeal embodied in the Legal Process conception of the rule of law.

It has to be taken into consideration that in case of conflicts over interpretation occur, the Legal Process approach to the rule of law requires the fighting parties are presented reasoned explanation of the linking between recognized, pre-existing sources of legal authority and the determination of rights and responsibilities in specific cases and so not merely disposition of their cases via code. Moreover, ad hoc interventions, like those pursued via the DAO hack, do assure the "procedural

---

[152] Paul F. Kirgis, The Knowledge Guild: The Legal Profession in an Age of Technological Change, 11 Nev. L.J. 184, 184 (2010) (("Susskind offers no evidence to support his claim that greater automation of legal work will result in less demand for human legal services. In fact, the evidence suggests that productivity increases in knowledge industries increase demand for those knowledge goods."). Frank Pasquale, Two Concepts of Immortality: Reframing Public Debate on StemCell Research, 14 Yale J.L. & Human. 73, 75–76 (2002) (critiquing the "downloading" of memory, intellect, and will onto hardware or software).

[153] Richard H. Fallon, Jr., "The Rule of Law" as a Concept in Constitutional Discourse, 97 Colum. L. Rev. 1, 5 (1997) Fallon's list of aspects of Legal Process conceptions of the rule of law is drawn from the locus classicus of the Legal Process approach. Id. (citing Henry M. Hart, Jr. & Albert M. Sacks, The Legal Process 4–5, 152–53, 157–58, 695 (William N. Eskridge, Jr. & Philip P. Frickey eds., 1994)).

[154] Donald A. Dripps, Justice Harlan on Criminal Procedure: Two Cheers for the Legal Process School, 3 Ohio St. J. Crim. L. 125, 126 (2005); Laura Kalman, The Strange Career of Legal Liberalism 20 (1996) (describing emergence of the Legal Process school).

fairness and rational deliberation" anticipated by a Legal Process conception of the rule of law.

AI is developed as advancement on to the digital internet economy, which it may govern one day taking into account the context and purposes for which it is actually advanced by those who largely control its development. In line Google, Facebook, Microsoft, Apple and Amazon together with handfuls of others shape the delivery of Internet based services to individuals and so they are extremely profitable, leading rises in stock market valuations wielding economic power which does not only guarantee uneven access to legislators and governments, but also permits them to hand out freely direct or indirect financial in all areas of society pertinent to opinion building in democracy.

Concerning artificial intelligence and in the "Google Spain" case before the CJEU, Google first disputed the applicability of EU data protection law to the benefit of EU Citizens despite it having setup a subsidiary on EU territory.[155] Thus, Google principally claimed that because the answer to the search questions posed in Europe came from Californian servers, only Californian law was applicable and secondly it argued that its search engine operation could be regarded as "data processing," which would have relieved Google from any responsibility for search answers, essentially claiming that the selection process of its search engine is beyond its control due to automation in the form of an algorithm.

Google in this case exposed its worldview as to the Rule of law by supporting that automation in the form of an algorithm offering a service to individuals should guard the intermediary employing this technology from any legal responsibility. On the other hand, technology cannot win over the rule of law in the digital age and so the regulatory responsibility has to be one global regime. The unique global internet structure, not fragmented by national regulation, demands a global approach concerning the cyber-rule of law.

Is Cyberspace under the governance of the rule of law? Commendably, the CJEU rejected the claims Google made by authorizing effective protection of fundamental rights for European citizens based on primary law and a longstanding European legal tradition of protecting privacy and personal data. Thus, the Google Spain Judgment is today the leading case permitting to object to any effort to separate responsibility for automation and autonomous development of AI from the original innovation and putting into business of such programs.

Technology algorithm cannot be utilized for shielding the intermediary employing this technology from responsibility for what autonomous AI algorithms would do one day. To that extent, the answer of the CJEU in this case was clear and encouraging: "There cannot be such shielding against responsibility".[156] In other words, the lawlessness in the emergent internet age cannot exist and instead the

[155] Case C-131/12 Google Spain SL v Mario Costeja González [2014] ECLI:EU:C:2014:317, para 47, https://eurlex.europa.eu/legal-content/EN/TXT/?uri=CELEX%3A62012CJ0131

[156] Jürgen Kühling, "Rückkehr des Rechts: Verpflichtung von „Google & Co."zu Datenschutz" [2014] Europäische Zeitschrift für Wirtschaftsrecht 527.

cyber-rule of law is the right answer, because lawlessness can create major and irreversible damage to society.

There is no doubt that Ethics is a good thing, above all intra firm ethics for the leadership and employees which go beyond what the law entails. Nonetheless any effort to substitute or avoid the needed law on AI through ethics has to be precluded because this cuts out democratic process causing problems in electronic transactions. Moreover, the conflicts of interests which occur between the firms and the general public as to the advancement and deployment of AI cannot be disentangled by unenforceable ethics codes or self-regulation. On the other hand, e-firms must take part in the debates on ethics and law for AI (Artificial Intelligence) contributing to the implementation of the cyber-rule of law.

Concerning cyber-regulation trustworthy politics will have to take into account the principle of essentiality[157] which has guided legislation in constitutional democracies for so long. Moreover, this principle stipulates that any matter which is crucial for the reason that it either concerns fundamental rights of parties or is vital to the state has to be dealt with by a parliamentary, democratically legitimized law.

It has to be taken into account that after the experience with the lawless internet, democracies cannot afford the risk of a new, all pervasive and decisive technology, which remains unregulated and so producing, like the internet before it, considerable negative effects.[158] To that extent, the new General Data Protection Regulation (GDPR) of the EU drive innovation for a way of collecting and processing personal data which respects individual rights and the significance of privacy in democracy. In line, the assertion that the law is not able to develop as fast as technology and business models is contradicted by the continued application of good, technology neutral law, in the USA and Europe and so the GDPR is a modern example of technology neutral law, the meaning and relevance of which alterations with the advancement of technology, including through AI.[159] The GDPR has increased privacy awareness among both corporations and data subjects across the EU.[160] It is worth noting that the GDPR limits data processing to permissible reasons, with

[157] The High Court's Brexit Decision: A Lesson in Constitutional Law for the UK Government, in: Verfassungsblog – On matters constitutional, 3. November 2016, https://verfassungsblog.de/the-high-courts-brexit-decision-a-lesson-inconstitutional-law-for-the-uk-government/. judgements in cases C-355/10, ECLI:EU:C:2012:516, European Parliament v. Council, para 64ff, https://eurlex.europa.eu/legalcontent/EN/TXT/?qid=1534186617433&uri=CELEX:62010CJ0355, and C-293/12 and 594/12/, ECLI:EU:C:2014:238, Digital Rights Ireland, para 54ff, http://curia.europa.eu/juris/documents.jsf?num=C-293/12

[158] Microsoft Says AI Advances Will Require New Laws, Regulations, Bloomberg 18. January 2018, https://www.bloomberg.com/news/articles/2018-01-18/microsoft-says-ai-advances-will-require-new-laws-regulations

[159] Regulation (EU) 2016/679 of the European Parliament and of the Council of 27 April 2016 on the protection of natural persons with regard to the processing of personal data and on the free movement of such data, and repealing Directive 95/46/EC (General Data Protection Regulation), OJ L 119, 4.5.2016, p. 1–88, https://eur-lex.europa.eu/eli/reg/2016/679/oj

[160] European Commission, "Shaping Europe's digital future: Digital Privacy", https://ec.europa.eu/digital-single-market/en/online-privacy

heightened protections for sensitive data and so requiring opt-in consent, which limits the use of personal data for training AI systems. It has to be taken into account that there is a need of revising GDPR in light of AI because new technologies test the rules written for GDPR such as the conflict between the "right to be forgotten" and the immutability inherent in permissionless blockchain technologies.[161] Furthermore, the recognition of algorithmic decision-making among legislators in Europe with the enactment of GDPR implies that the use of algorithms will become gradually common in society and of concern to lawmakers and regulators.[162]

It has to be taken into consideration that the law has democratic legitimacy and it can be enforced, even against powerful mega conglomerates and so law generates, along with a reliable warning of deterring sanctions and appropriate enforcement, a level playing field valuable to all and beyond that gives orientation to innovators by offering enticements guiding innovation toward the public interest. Moreover, in the world of technological domination there is a need to strengthen democracy by giving back to the law the utility which it has in constitutional democracy conveying the will of the people in a form obligatory for everyone and able to be brought into reality, even against opposition and disobedience, by usage of public and private enforcement powers.

Nowadays the world is formed by technology as it is by law and democracy. Moreover, in the same manner that the people create the law and the law shapes the behavior of persons, the law is modeled by technology and technology is affected by the law. It has to be taken into account that any technology has lived with being modeled by the law so far, and it is high time that Silicon Valley and the digital internet industry also acknowledge this need of Democracy.

To that extent, the work on ethics rules for technology are precursors of the law and so giving direction on the probable content of legal rules but they cannot replace the law, as they lack democratic legitimacy and the binding character which permits enforcement with the power of government and the judiciary.

4.6 From the Rule of Law to AI Rule of Law

Law is a formalized way of bringing political preferences into the society and so law allocates benefits, risks, and duties backed by the prospective for enforcement through the use of state power. The rule of law necessitates that law rules. Moreover, the rule of law is law writ large throughout society, so a quality of law is unavoidably

---

[161] Proposal for a REGULATION OF THE EUROPEAN PARLIAMENT AND OF THE COUNCIL. European Commission. Brussels, 21.4.2021. COM(2021) 206 final. 2021/0106 (COD) https://digital-strategy.ec.europa.eu/en/library/proposal-regulationeuropean-approach-artificial-intelligence

[162] Guy Aridor, Yeon-Koo Che & Tobias Salz, The Effect of Privacy Regulation on the Data Industry: Empirical Evidence from GDPR, FED. TRADE COMM'N 1–4 (June 9, 2020), https://www.ftc.gov/system/files/documents/public_events/1548288/privacycon-2020-guy_aridor.pdf

a quality of the rule of law. Furthermore, at its core, the rule of law entails obedience to validly enacted law and the core principle of a good law is that the law has to be effective.

Also, law can formally be considered as an institutionalization of practical discourse on social norms and so modern law in western civilizations is positive by articulating the will of a sovereign lawgiver, legalistic by applying to deviations from norms and formal. Hence, in connection with law's genesis in response to local impetus, the law is created in answer to societal need.

Law is both a series of rules and the courses for generating; amending, interpreting, and bringing about compliance with those rules and so legal rules diverge from other types of rules such as moral and scientific in that they are engendered by legal processes. Additionally, legal process denotes rules as legal and so within legal institutions; argumentation agendas launch boundaries for impact and persuasion, approximately outlining the scale of claims, arguments and reasons that are tolerable or legitimate. In line, law reflects the prevailing realities of a given society and so law is utilized as a proactive instrument to stimulate improvement and, so, affect and alter the very realities it is presumed to expose. Thus, if society transforms, law will be altered correspondingly and occasionally law averts unexpected alterations of society. It is worth noting that there is a dichotomy to the rule of law which means that at one hand, the rule of law is a basic principle that we are all subject to the law and on the other hand, the rule of law is the ideal of the values that a legal system ought to own.

Furthermore, law is the instrument holding the social system together against individual efforts to take advantage of others.[163] Hence, law functions in society by fulfilling a social purpose and has been differentiated to accomplish this function by its "autopoietic" reproduction.[164] Of course, law is something imperative but not holy which means that law is not unvarying and so law that does not serve the nation and society is useless and consequently the implied rule of law leads to real disorder. Also, law is a formalized way of bringing political preferences into the society. Likewise, law allocates benefits, risks, and duties backed by the prospective for enforcement through the use of state power if the choices are not followed by those at whom they are aimed.[165]

Which is the ruler subject to the law in the era of globalization and global economic governance? Rule of law is understood in its substantive aspect as attributing the state with a vital role as guardian of a set of foundational communally embraced substantive norms that are to be preserved and advanced through the use

---

[163] John Locke, Of Civil Government Second Treatise 67, 68, Introduction by Russell Kirk, (Henry Regnery 1955).

[164] Gunther Teubner, Law As An Autopoietic System 45–46 (1993). Niklas Luhmann, Law As A Social System 464 (trans. Klaus A. Ziegert, 2004).

[165] Lawrence M. Friedman, American Law 257 (1984) "Law carries a powerful stick: the threat of force. This is the first inside its velvet glove".

of state power grounded in law.[166] Will the state be the enforcer in an AI legal system? Will AI systems be the legislator, the implementor and the enforcer of AI law in an AI legal system in national jurisdictions and an international level? Will AI systems be the legislator, the implementor and the enforcer of AI law in an international terrain?

Do the technologies of the Fourth Industrial Revolution facilitate new systems of governance and "algorithmic regulation"? There is an increase of speed and efficiency in decision-making, and decrease in cost that promotes a number of AI-leveraging "Techs" such as LegalTech, GovTech, and RegTech which encompass the development of "smart" software applications for deployment in legal, political, and human decision-making contexts.[167] Is there algorithmic policy-making? It is worth mentioning here that AI is becoming a regulatory device for policy-makers and so AI applied to policy-making guarantees the decision-making capable of handling complex issues in a transparent and inclusive way. AI GovTech is becoming the field of "democracy tech" supporting governmental activities with online voting, citizens' participation or political activities, candidates' fundraising, etc. and so expanding the capability of people to join in directly in a large number of democratic decisions. Furthermore, AI GovTech generates concerns about the legitimacy of public structures delegating regulatory functions to private companies comprising the liability of private actors contracted by public administrations to offer assistance in engaging citizens in the coproduction of public policies.

It has to be taken into account that AI technological change has "flattened" the globe, diminished state power, and offered models for uncoupling citizenship from territory[168] which means that governments are not "platform" but they have to use platforms to gain use of critical network externalities. In fact, it seems that Big Tech is altering all the rules, not by playing within the existing system,[169] regardless that the system tries to comply by utilizing old rules. The disruptive prospective of Big Tech is evident in existing multilateral and bilateral frameworks for trade and investment and so the manner platforms monetize their operations is not compatible with the principles generated to regulate corporate activities in the physical world. Thus, the existing cross-border allocation of tax rights of Big Tech defers from ordinal corporations. In the process, the apparently unstoppable rise of Big Tech redefines the inner workings of capitalism itself, realizing that financialized capitalism fuse with the data-driven logics of "platform capitalism" or "surveillance

---

[166] Thomas O. Sargentich, The Contemporary Debate About Legislative-Executive Separation of Powers, 72 Corn. L. Rev. 430, 450 (1987) ("A close relation between the rule of law and separation of powers is evident in both the liberal and democratic elements of liberal democratic theory.").

[167] G Marcus and E Davis, Rebooting AI: Building Artificial Intelligence We Can Trust (Pantheon 2019); D Spiegelhalter, The Art of Statistics: Learning from Data (Pelican 2019) 143–187.

[168] M Loughlin, "The erosion of sovereignty" (2016).

[169] T O'Reilly, "Government as a Platform" (2010) 6 Innovations 1. M Goede, "E-Estonia: The e-government cases of Estonia, Singapore, and Curaçao"(2019) 8 Archives of 20 Business Research 2.

capitalism."[170] To that extent, Big Tech has come to revamp political practices and operating systems generating a political backlash.

It has to be taken into consideration that dominant platforms today "function as regulators."[171] There is an effort to counter Big Tech's monopoly power and so the European Parliament has made an effort of limiting the reach of Big Tech and protecting its citizens.[172] Platform monopolists hurt small businesses and entrepreneurs in a number of ways by preventing competitors from even establishing in the first place or deciding what competitors gain visibility and market access along with utilizing their size or market share to drive competitors out of business. An outcome of monopoly can take place when a monopolist controls an indispensable intermediary to commerce[173] and so giving enormous power to dictate the actions of dependent firms and competitors. Hence, platform monopolists' control over a range of industries limiting investors choices and so in the online advertising industry, Google and Facebook control 58 percent of the U.S. digital advertising market, followed by Amazon.[174] Furthermore, Platform monopolists like Amazon, Apple, Facebook, and Google benefit from their capacity to place themselves in the middle of countless commercial transactions and so by utilizing their position as intermediaries to commercial life, platform monopolists have huge power to dictate the terms on which other businesses function.[175] It is worth noting here that antitrust enforcement and strong anti-monopoly rules can prevent dominant platforms from unfairly exploiting their size, structure, or strategic position in commerce against smaller companies.

"Big Tech" firms as investors caused increases in digital communication, shopping, and streaming services across the globe. Moreover, the monopoly power of the world's Big Tech platforms risks destabilizes political and economic freedoms globally which means that Big Tech revamp political practices and operating systems activating a political backlash.[176] Furthermore, Big Tech firms' balance

[170] Zuboff S (2019) The Age of Surveillance Capitalism: The Fight for a Human Future at the New Frontier of Power. London: Profile Books.

[171] Jacques Crémer et al., European Comm'n, Competition Policy for the Digital Era 6 (2019), http://ec.europa.eu/competition/publications/reports/kd0419345enn.pdf

[172] Espinoza, J (2020) EU targets Big Tech with "hit list" facing tougher rules. Financial Times, 11 October.
https://www.ft.com/content/c8c5d5dc-cb99-4b1f-a8dd-5957b57a7783

[173] Tim Wu and Stuart A. Thompson, "The Roots of Big Tech Run Disturbingly Deep," The New York Times, June 7, 2019, https://www.nytimes.com/interactive/2019/06/07/opinion/google-facebook-mergers-acquisitionsantitrust.html

[174] Alexandra Bruell, "Amazon Forecast to Be No. 3 Digital Advertising Player in 2018," The Wall Street Journal, September 19, 2018, https://www.wsj.com/articles/amazon-forecast-to-be-no-3-digital-advertising-player-in-2018-1537351201?mod=article_inline

[175] Matt Day and Jackie Gu, "The Enormous Numbers Behind Amazon's Market Reach," Bloomberg, March 27, 2019; https://www.bloomberg.com/graphics/2019-amazon-reach-across-markets/

[176] Espinoza, J (2020) EU targets Big Tech with "hit list" facing tougher rules. Financial Times, 11 October. https://www.ft.com/content/c8c5d5dc-cb99-4b1f-a8dd-5957b57a7783 McNamee, R

sheets disclose an impressive development built up financial assets compared to their fixed capital and so tech firms are producing network effects which mean that maximizing network effects leads in market dominance and monopoly power. Big Tech firms epitomize the concept of corporate "financialization" better than any other area.[177]

A few digital platforms facilitate a growing share of online commerce and communications and so by having integrated across business lines such that they both operate a platform and market their own goods and services on it, it means that this structure places leading platforms in direct competition with some of the companies that depend on them, initiating a conflict of interest that platforms utilize to further entrench their dominance, thwart competition, and stifle innovation. Moreover, due to the digital nature platforms monitor with unrivaled precision the business activity of third parties while also competing with them which means that a platform can pick insights collected from a producer at the producer's expense.

It has to be taken into account that a digital gatekeeper is a platform that "can control access by a group of users to some goods or another group of users[178]" by offering third parties fundamental access to consumers and regulates the functioning of the whole ecosystem. Hence, a common characteristic of gatekeeping platforms is their dual mode, that is, they are both competitors of third parties and regulators of their ecosystem which means that gatekeepers have the capacity to foreclose third parties leading to complaints against alleged anti-competitive practices such as self-preferencing. Moreover, digital platforms have integrated across business lines such that they both run a platform and market their own goods and services on it and so placing dominant platforms in direct competition with some of the businesses that depend on them, generating a conflict of interest that platforms utilize to cement their dominance, prevent competition, and suppress innovation.[179] Nonetheless, digital markets highlight the occurrence of large network externalities and effects are more uncertain. It has to be taken into consideration that duality diminishes prices while fragmenting demand across services and dropping the network advantages. Axel Gautier et al.[180] argue that "any ex-ante regulation of the platform ecosystem, without clear economic justification, is likely to be challenged (if the burden of

(2020) A historic antitrust hearing in Congress has put big tech on notice. The Guardian, 21 July. https://www.theguardian.com/commentisfree/2020/jul/31/big-tech-house-historic-antitrust-hearing-times-have-changed

[177] Rodrigo Fernandez, Ilke Adriaans, Tobias J. Klinge and Reijer Hendrikse, Engineering digital monopolies The financialisation of Big Tech December 2020 SOMO.

[178] Alexiadis, P. & de Streel, A. (2020), "Designing an EU intervention standard for digital platforms," Robert Schuman Centre for Advanced Studies Florence School of Regulation. RSCAS 2020/14.

[179] Case AT.39740 Google Search (Shopping) and the ongoing proceedings against Amazon (See case AT.40462 Amazon Marketplace) and Apple (See cases AT.40437 Apple - App Store Practices (music streaming) and AT.40652 Apple - App Store Practices (e-books/audiobooks).

[180] Axel Gautier, Leonardo Madio, Shiva Shekhar, Platform duality and network externalities, 2021 p25.

proof is on policymakers) and might deter innocuous and welfare-enhancing entry (if the burden of proof is on the industry)."

Dominant digital platforms serve as critical intermediaries of online commerce and communications and so the US Supreme Court has described Facebook, Google, and other online providers as serving as the "modern public square," while law makers have analogized "Amazon to a nineteenth-century railroad".[181]

It seems that societal ability is gradually expressed algorithmically due to that fact that humans expressively participate in the decision-making process via their networking connected in cyberspace and optimal results obtained by AI exceeding the capabilities of humans in a physical space. Nonetheless, the idea of AI "exceeding" human capabilities comes across a "human-centered society" but it is eventually the AI future is arriving and advanced AI is emerging slowly. Moreover, the advanced artificial intelligence (AAI) involves a machine designed to operate any "general intelligent action" that a human is capable of. Will we have the transformation of the human society into an AI society? Which is the role of humans in an AI society?

Moreover, LegalTech is being arisen being a new era of "smart" law built on AI and Big Data. Can the legal process be abstractly viewed as computation? Zekos considers that currently law and its enforcement cannot be totally computed due to inability of current machines to think and react exactly as humans. There are people[182] arguing that the legal process can be abstractly viewed as computation, inputting information about evidence and laws and outputting a decision, dreaming fully automating the legal process with "robojudges".

Do AI systems vigorously apply the same high legal standards to every judgment without succumbing to human errors such as bias or lack of the latest knowledge? It is obvious that the judicial mentality would be of little interest if judges did nothing more than apply clear rules of law generated by legislators, administrative agencies, the framers of constitutions, and other extrajudicial sources such as commercial custom to facts that judges and juries established without bias or preconceptions. On the other hand, litigation does not happen like this because judges have to evaluate in all cases some individual facts of the specific parties in order to decide in applying the law and a legal precedent.[183] If we arrive to the point that machines will decide via data without any consideration and evaluation of the precise individual elements of the case then human life will become a technical bit as well without any human essence of existence and life. In other words, judges would be superseded by digitized artificial intelligence programs which means that human judges are not just replaceable with AI, but that "AI Judges" should be favored on the hypothesis

---

[181] Packingham v. North Carolina, 137 S. Ct. 1730, 1737 (2017). Ramon Ramirez, Elizabeth Warren Champions Michelob Ultra, Breaking Up Amazon at SXSW, Daily Dot (Mar. 9, 2019), https://www.dailydot.com/layer8/elizabethwarren-john-kasich-sxsw/

[182] MB Chalmers, "SmartLaw 2.0: The new future of law" (Lexology, 22 August 2018) . M Tegmark, Life 3.0: Being Human in the Age of Artificial Intelligence (Allen Lane 2017) 105.

[183] RA Posner, How Judges Think (Harvard University Press 2008).

that they will not inherit the biases and drawbacks of human decision-making.[184] Will "AI judge" output valid legal decisions?

Moreover, it is argued that if an entity accomplishes medical diagnoses reliably enough, it's intelligent enough to be a good diagnostician, whether it is a human being or a computer. On the other hand, specific tasks based on given data might be executed accurately by machines without ignoring the fact that the final decision of the therapy is made by a human doctor because the road for an AI system making reliable calculation of data followed by a therapy is for the very distant future. Thus, preprogramed tasks or standardized movements can be achieved by machines as well.

It has to be taken into account that if an entity writes judicial opinions well enough, then this entity is intelligent enough to be a good AI judge. Who decides if the Al judgments are good enough? If there are technical prototypes of decisions like statistical outcomes, then Al judges can exist for an AI way of life but not for humans in their present human entity. Moreover, if a system reliably yields opinions that society view as sound, society could accept it, without requiring some predetermined structure for how the opinions are shaped. Giovanni Sartor and Karl Branting argue that "no simple rule-chaining or pattern matching algorithm" can correctly model judicial decision-making for the reason that the judiciary has the mission of generating reasonable and acceptable solutions in cases in which the facts, the rules, or how they fit together are debatable.[185]

Having in mind the role of machine learning into the tax system through the law, the facts, and values, Alarie argues that the "legal singularity"[186] will be imposed. First of all, taxation is more a technical subject which can easily be standardized and programmed which makes easier the computation of certain legal rules not needing any interpretation or human evaluation which means that a kind of legal singularity of the specific tax law might be able to be achieved in the future via intelligent AI systems.

It is worth noting that the legal singularity is indirectly a suggestion for eradicating juridical reasoning as a basis for dispute resolution and the allocation of powers, rights, and responsibilities. On the other hand, the complexity of law application and implementation due to differences not only on circumstances but also on individuality of the parties, legal singularity is not easy made unless a robot with human capacities is created replacing humans as legal personnel. Moreover, Alarie's legal singularity can be deemed as a credible exclamation for less human lawyers and judges in occasions where the application of the law is a mechanical matter generating standard decisions for the same data and so avoiding any possible judges' favors for particular persons or corporations.

---

[184] E Volokh, "Chief Justice Robots" (2019) 68 Duke Law Journal 1135, 1138.

[185] G Sartor and LK Branting, "Introduction: Judicial Applications of Artificial Intelligence" in G Sartor and LK Branting (eds) Judicial Applications of Artificial Intelligence (Springer 1998).

[186] Alarie, Benjamin, The Path of the Law: Toward Legal Singularity (May 27, 2016). https://doi.org/10.2139/ssrn.2767835

Likewise, it could be said that albeit the mathematical or symbolic logic used in AI could duplicate the structure of juridical reasoning, this could not automatically make up the political, economic, and socio-cultural influences that affect legal discourse and the evolution of the legal system.[187] It has to be taken into account that political, economic, and socio-cultural impacts are important because all the sciences imply relationship of factors and their advancement is based on a situation-specific understanding of meaning explicated only hermeneutically which means that not any pre-structured reality can be formed by observation alone.[188]

Taking into account that mathematical logic cannot encapsulate the "situation-specific understanding" of legal reasoning and the complexity of the social world it exists in, the legal singularity would instantiate a certain view of law via "AI judges": one in which legal judgments are fundamentally deterministic or probabilistic outputs, produced on the basis of static or unambiguous legal rules, in a societal vacuum which does not comply with the historical development of law as being a social institution, encompassing socially constructed activities, relationships, and norms not easily translated into numerical functions.[189] Of course, the moving to an AI era stipulates the emergence of AI law, AI legal formation and AI legal enforcement but this in order to happen presumes the emergence of a new understating of life with priority to its mechanical nature and there will be no reference to human life where AI systems merely used to advance human productivity.

As discussed earlier, the reality denotes that legal decision-making involves an exercise of power which is both material and political as framed via the historical developments. Legitimacy is achieved if the process through which each exercise of it follows the established procedural expectations that is highly contingent and socially constructed. On the other hand, it could be said that the AI revolution brings forwards a new understanding of AI legitimacy via standard technical imposition by the AI network.

It is worth mentioning here that the legal system as a totality, and its outputs, embracing legal judgments, is subject to checks and balances to ascertain the "legal validity" of its internal operations and the process of outputting and enforcing them with a society.[190] Hence "AI judges" moral scrutiny, in the traditional understanding of morality and not the one established by AI systems for the AI judges and the whole AI legal system, would not be a profound prophylactic again questioning abuses of power such as in the case with "black box" algorithms which are

---

[187] P Stein, Legal Evolution: The Story of an Idea (Cambridge University Press 2009); S Deakin, "Legal Evolution: Integrating Economic and Systemic Approaches," University of Cambridge Faculty of Law Research Paper No. 41/2011 (2011).

[188] J Habermas, On the Logic of the Social Sciences (1967) cited in W Outhwaite, Habermas: Key Contemporary Thinkers (second ed., Polity Press 2009). H Ross, Law as a Social Institution (Hart 2001).

[189] P Bourdieu, Language and Symbolic Power (Harvard University Press 1991).

[190] HLA Hart, The Concept of Law (third ed., Oxford University Press 2012).

inscrutable at a technical level, or where trade secret-protections preclude diagnostic scrutiny.[191]

Furthermore, it has to be taken into account that legal decision-making is structurally algorithmic in nature to the extent that it implicates following well-defined steps to reach a specific output, and so the mathematical simulation of elements for legal judgment cannot be considered as the legal judgment itself because machines are very good in simulations, judgment itself is grounded on the question of interpretation of legal certainty in the light of the integrity of the legal system which goes further than a quasi-mathematical consistency.[192] To that extent, Judges[193] rightly view sentencing as a weighty responsibility taking into consideration not only the appropriate punishment for the offense but also the risk the offender poses, predicting the probability of the offender's recidivism. Moreover, the criticisms of algorithmic risk assessments have voiced wariness of the technology's use in the criminal law context as purported advancements may boost existing inequalities.[194] The court held that the judiciary should use considerable caution in assessing the qualitative value of these new technologies via their algorithmic risk assessments.[195]

It has to be taken into consideration that power and legitimacy are maintained and transferred across generations via litigation and precedent and so there are risks undermining the principal institutions of a liberal-democratic order through the "black boxing" of the legal system. Per se "AI judges" have to be treated with caution for the existing conventional legal systems merely utilizing AI systems as assistant means due to the fact that AI judges outputs defy both moral and technical scrutiny not be able for complex analysis.

Mathematical and statistical calculations have been utilized by many sciences and even legal analysis by humans but yet mathematical models do not shape and

---

[191] State of Wisconsin v Loomis 881 N.W.2d 749 (Wis. 2016); H-W Liu, C Fu and Y-J Chen, "Beyond State v Loomis: Artificial Intelligence, Government Algorithmization and Accountability" (2019) 27 International Journal of Law and Information Technology 2; R Yu and RS Alo, "What's Inside the Black Box? AI Challenges for Lawyers and Researchers" (2019) 19 Legal Information Management 1.

[192] M Hildebrandt, "Law as computation in the era of artificial legal intelligence: Speaking law to the power of statistics" (2017).

[193] Williams v. New York, 337 U.S. 241, 251 (1949) (describing the "grave responsibility" of sentencing).

[194] Eric Holder, Att'y Gen., U.S. Dep't of Justice, Address at the National Association of Criminal Defense Lawyers 57th Annual Meeting and 13th State Criminal Justice Network Conference (Aug. 1, 2014), https://www.justice.gov/opa/speech/attorney-general-eric-holder-speaks-national-association-criminal-defense-lawyers-57th (cautioning that recidivism risk assessments "may exacerbate unwarranted and unjust disparities").

[195] State v. Loomis881 N.W.2d 749 (Wis. 2016) Wisconsin Supreme Court Requires Warning Before Use of Algorithmic Risk Assessments in Sentencing. The Wisconsin Supreme Court's mandated PSI advisement is a critical—though likely ineffectual—acknowledgement of the potential problems of algorithmic risk assessments. https://harvardlawreview.org/2017/03/state-v-loomis/

enforce by themselves the law.[196] Moreover, AI and various statistical techniques are making prediction gradually feasible by utilizing inserted data and so the concept of making law more predictable is intertwined with the development of AI systems but it is more like statistical prediction rather than legal analysis as it has been established via judge's precedent.

According to Leibniz' view law typified how society should resolve "the most serious deliberations on life and health, on the state, on war and peace, on the moderation of conscience, [and] on care of eternity."[197] Thus, law was considered as the most advanced instrument of human rationality and so judges were used to evaluate the relative weight of arguments by the parties and their advisors prior writing down the decision which has been the decision-making process. Can AI systems produce law by typifying the needs of the society and afterwards generating the decision-making process in an analogous way? It could be said that the initiation of mechanical steps for law production and enforcement can be taken but not in the conventional dialogic way. Hence, an advanced AI system can be considered as the AI legal center for AI disputes for an AI society but not replicating the conventional way of law science as has been established by humans' society which means that an AI revolution will emerge transforming law science into bit's analysis.

Furthermore, in order law to be as precise as mathematics, a just legal rule has to merge abstract legal axiom rather than being a general frame and by its interpretation to cover all the possible cases. On the other hand, in an AI environment precise rules can be generated covering all possible cases which will be employed by the AI legal center and so according to the data of every AI dispute will get an AI legal decision by using AI judges which means that the whole AI legal process will remind statistical analysis. Of course, AI judges will generate their own AI legal precedent.

Langdell collected the data[198] for an empirical "legal science" from the cases decided and reported by courts permitting prediction of the outcomes of contract disputes which is more an effort to extract data from case law and make a statistical analysis in order to find the possible correlations which is far away from producing an AI legal system of generating legal rules and applying them in an AI way in order to have an AI decision-making process leading to AI legal decisions and so creating an entire AI legal science. Due to AI decision-making and sociality already takes part through digital infrastructures, machine learning, algorithmic assemblages and quasi-automatized predictions, obscuring the boundary between human and not-human agency which means that new human realities are generated.

---

[196] M Annany and K Crawford, "Seeing without knowing: Limitations of the transparency ideal and its application to algorithmic accountability" (2018) 20 New Media & Society 3; J Pearl and D MacKenzie, The Book of Why: The New Science of Cause and Effect (Penguin 2018) 358.

[197] P Boucher, "Leibniz: What Kind of Legal Rationalism?" in M Dascal (ed) Leibniz: What Kind of Rationalist? (Springer 2008).

[198] CP Wells, "Langdell and the Invention of Legal Doctrine" (2010) 28 Buffalo Law Review 3. CC Langdell, Cases on Contracts (Little Brown & Co. 1871), vi. MH Hoeflich, "Langdell and the Invention of Legal Doctrine," (1986) 30 The American Journal of Legal 83 History 2.

According to Holmes the law is not formed only by logic but it encompasses "experience" with the meaning the life produces the axioms which the law formulates as written principles.[199] Holmes rejected the deterministic and non-political conceptions of law advanced by legal formalists like Langdell who considered law a coherent set of rules and norms from which a "right" answer could always be obtained. Scott Brewer[200] says that "... the theorist who aspires to high-density axiomatization, as did Leibniz and Langdell, would seem to have to try and steer between the Scylla of generating axioms that are so open textured and often so vague that one could never settle on the final set of axioms, but would forever have to be revising them." Additionally, Roscoe Pound[201] considered that "mechanical jurisprudence" is the "lazy practice of judges to formulaically" apply precedents to cases with disregard for effects. In other words, merely the logic of precedents calculated as statistical data cannot solve jurisprudential difficulties based on the need for individual evaluation of the factors of every case. Besides, axiomatics endanger solidifying socially constructed and politically affected legal concepts into self-evident truths.

It is worth noting that realists consider law as characteristically indeterminate and defying understanding as a coherent or complete system of rules and principles from which there was always a "right" answer.[202] It could be said that the realists considered judicial opinions and judges with skepticism since written rules did not settle what the law was, the rationale of juridical reasoning was not explaining how the court arrived at a decision and providing guidance to judges and litigants encountering similar circumstances in the future. Hence, they regarded that the real reason was to "rationalize" and "legitimize" decisions and camouflage from the public and other judges the real justifications.[203] According to Dewey,[204] no legal argument is signified as a "deductive inference", and law never truthfully epitomized as deductive axiomatic systems but rules of law have to as regular and as definite as possible.

Will the law of mathematics or any other science be utilized by AI replace the law? Mathematization of Law cannot be achieved under the current law science

199 OW Holmes, The Common Law (Little Brown & Co. 1881) 1. OW Holmes, "The Path of the Law" (1897) 110 Harvard Law Review 5, 997. MH Fisch, "Justice Holmes, the Prediction Theory of Law, and Pragmatism" (1942) 39 The Journal of Philosophy 4; RA Posner, "The Path Away from the Law"(1996) 110 Harvard Law Review 1039.

200 S Brewer, "Law, Logic, and Leibniz: A Contemporary Perspective," in A Artosi, B Pieri and G Sartor (eds) Leibniz: Logico-Philosophical Puzzles in the Law (Springer 2013).

201 R Pound, "Mechanical Jurisprudence," Columbia Law Review 8 no. 605 (1908).

202 SR Ratner, "Legal Realism School," in R Wolfrum (ed) Max Planck Encyclopedia of Public International Law 89 Online (Oxford University Press, 2007).

203 KN Llewellyn, The Bramble Bush: The Classic Lectures on the Law and Law School (Oxford University Press, [1930] 2008).

204 J Dewey, "Logical Method and Law" (1924) 10 Cornell Law Review 1, 25. C Gray, The Nature and Sources of Law (Columbia University Press 1909); R Pound, "Justice According to Law" (1914) 1 The Midwest Quarterly 3.

where interpretation cannot be formalized. On the other hand, in an AI society where everything can be a "bit" then everything is possible because even humans might be mathematically be programmed to merely execute standard steps with no human dialectic analysis but with an AI dialectic analysis.

It has to be taken into account that McCarthy's idea[205] was to have a computer program encapsulate and store large amounts of "human knowledge" about a specific domain such as law or medicine and use mathematical logic to represent it and logical inference to determine the "best" actions to accomplish an anticipated "output" from a knowledge-base. It is worth mentioning that existing AI machines execute specific problem-solving or "reasoning" tasks in "narrow" domains not needing wider aspects of human intelligence and so many sciences utilize this type of AI systems in order humans to take better decisions and act more accurately. It will be a miracle to have machines thinking like humans in a scale of endless multiplicity and diversity which means that beings can be produced by more solid material but the AI question to be answered is if the AI machines independently of any human intervention or another one can produce their own machine beings thinking and acting like humans or even in a better way.

Legal expert systems (LES) developers apprehended their mission as formalizing the texture of legal rules into mathematical conditionals upon which there could be no disagreement.[206] They wanted by utilizing computation to accomplish the "mechanical jurisprudence" by fundamentally simplifying the multipart and indeterminate character of law and legal reasoning. Law and jurisprudence are founded upon evaluation which will be very complicated to be achieved via mathematics because the capacity of the human brain is very difficult to be substituted very easily by the current technology. Moreover, the human brain communicates unnoticeably by the human being creator via sleeping because the capacity of the human brain is arranged by our creator named and understood as GOD and information is received constantly via unnoticeable signals. It has to be taken into account that the collapse of the LES project was mainly by reason of technical limitations by miscalculating of the complexity in applying axiomatic methods to law.[207] Nevertheless, the law's social context was not taken into consideration but merely they thought that law can be broken into mathematically computed bits with no reference to the politics of law. Do AI systems have the ability for a dialectic analysis of a legal problem by generating a new precedent due to alteration in social and political environment?

Taking into account that humans perform tasks in manners that permit acquired knowledge to become both tacit and implicit, current AI systems cannot utilize

---

[205] J McCarthy, "Recursive Functions of Symbolic Expressions and Their Computation by Machine, Part 94 I"(1960), http://www-formal.stanford.edu/jmc/recursive.pdf; cf. SL Andersen, "John McCarthy: Father of AI" (2002) 17 IEEE Intelligent Systems 5. J McCarthy, "Philosophical and Scientific Presuppositions of Logical AI," in HJ Levesque and F Pirri (eds).

[206] Hart, The Concept of Law, 124–154. WG Popp and B Schlink, "Judith, A Computer Program to Advise Lawyers in Reasoning a Case" (1974) 15 Jurimetrics Journal 303.

[207] MZ Bell, "Why Expert Systems Fail" (1985) 36 Journal of the Operational Research Society 7 (1985).

"axiomatics to extract" and express legal knowledge and intuition in a practicable state.[208] It is worth mentioning here that IBM's Watson and DeepMind's AlphaGo seemed to achieve "intelligence" both technically feasible and commercially worthwhile by utilizing neuroscientific models of the brain and not exhaustively formalize human expertise and knowledge to create axioms.[209] Thus, using both ML and DL techniques, IBM's Watson and DeepMind's AlphaGo used numbers of training data (historical examples) permitting them to update their mathematical parameters and augment performance at directed tasks but they are not tested in an entire legal process from the law to the judgment. It is characteristic that David Spiegelhalter[210] said that these are technological systems that use past data to answer immediate questions, rather than scientific systems in an AI form able to comprehend how the globe functions which means that those AI systems perform limited tasks at hand, and, although, the form of the learned algorithms present some insights, they are not having human creativity or have super-human skills in everyday life.

ML concerning law will continue to flourish and so the idea of a functionally complete legal system, one capable of being illustrated using the formal logic and axiomatic reasoning linked with mathematical models is the aim of AI engineering. Will AI law system be more mode of governance encompassing automatically and simultaneously all the legal process from introducing the law, litigation and judgment to its enforcement rather than law in the conventional essence? Is law computable? If there are computers equal in intelligence to human brain, then law can be computed. Of course, the present understanding of law, its application and jurisprudence will be adapted to the means utilized for their applicability and enforcement.

Taking into consideration the raising acceptance that biological and artificial intelligence diverge only in their substrates, AI and data science will make possible system-level modeling of social reality and the complete prediction of human behaviors.[211] To that extent, it is hoped that a new generation of AI-leveraging LegalTech and ADM systems will succeed where AI logic-based systems have failed replicating legal reasoning, deduction, and inference. Will LegalTech advance access to justice, lower costs, and expand the efficiency of legal administration among many other practical advantages?

Taking into account that the present LegalTech rests on the "Leibnizian-Langdellian assumption" that there is a sterilized principle to law and legal reasoning there to be mathematized, the functional capabilities of this generation of AI systems

[208] P Leith, "Fundamental Errors in Legal Logic Programming"(1986) 29 The Computer Journal 6. M Polanyi, The Tacit Dimension (Rev ed., University of Chicago Press 2009) 3–25.

[209] JE Laird, C Lebiere and PS Rosenbloom, "A Standard Model of the Mind: Toward a Common Computational Framework Across Artificial Intelligence, Cognitive Science, Neuroscience, and Robotics" (2017) 38 AI Magazine 4.

[210] David Spiegelhalte, The Art of Statistics: Learning from Data (Pelican Books) March 28, 2019.

[211] PS Churchland, "Can Neurobiology Teach Us Anything About Self Consciousness?" (1994) 42 Proceedings and Addresses of the American Philosophical Association 3; M Allen and KJ Friston, "From cognitivism to autopoiesis: towards a computational framework for the embodied mind" (2018) 195 Synthese 6 (2018).

will not produce an AI legal system comparable and commendable substitute of the conventional justice system.

Can computer programs be used to solve real problems? Can "legal problems" be ultimately decidable as "right" or "wrong"—or "1" or "0"? It is worth noting that contract analytics is a popular application for LegalTech applications, with firms competing to have their proprietary interpretations of contractual terms established as definitive referents but a deterministic or "mechanical jurisprudence" tactic disregards the interaction between concepts at different levels of generality achieving little more than ossifying legal concepts into self-evident computational "truths" which means that this kind of algorithmic utilization evolves a simplified legal ontology by undertaking these concepts as stable referents part of tractable computational problems decidable by a Turing Machine.[212]

It seems that LegalTech developers believe in an axiomatic conception of law, but also an implicit understanding of reality known as "pan-computationalism" under the understanding that physical reality is describable by information and the global life is the deterministic or probabilistic output of a computer program or network of computational procedures. In other words, interpreting law, legal notions, norms, and the array of human and non-human behaviors are accepted as eventually "computable" functions but it is ignored that no existing AI system is analogous to a human brain permitting not only interpretations via combinations but also estimation in sequence with the particular legal data and the individuality of the problem. Of course, independent legal matters well-standardized and applicable simply anywhere can be computed but not a whole legal system.

In addition, LegalTech applications and suggestions for "AI Judges" back a sense about social reality and information itself expressed in computer code/mathematical universe hypothesis and that everything is computable, since everything is computation which means that, in the end, it can be true if the AI system is analogous to a human brain capable of making all the calculations and evaluations in order to solve any problem.

Can all legal problems be decidable using binary logic? Since the binary nature of computation means that all legal problems must finally be decidable using binary logic, the answer is no needing an AI system working not only with binary logic but also combining a human brain function.[213] It seems that AI development is based on "digital ontology" and broad support for an informational attitude to structural realism whereby knowledge of the globe reveals its structures and so the whole effort is directed by "pan-computationalist" and materialist interpretations of intelligence.[214] On the other hand, taking into account that there are material and

[212] John MacCormick, What Can Be Computed?: A Practical Guide to the Theory of Computation, Princeton University Press.

[213] J Schmidhüber, "Algorithmic Theories of Everything" (2000) https://arxiv.org/abs/quant-ph/0011122; P Hut, M Alford and M Tegmark, "On Math, Matter and Mind" (2006) 36 Foundations of Physics 6.

[214] L Floridi, "Against Digital Ontology" (2009) 168 Synthese 1. J Smithies, The Digital Humanities and the Digital Modern (Palgrave 2017) Hildebrandt, Mireille, Law as Computation in the Era

practical restrictions to computation and data storage and so restraining the computability of all problems, this indicates that some legal problems are computable as long as there is a standardized legal process not needing any further interpretations.

It could be said that if juridical reasoning is replaced by AI reasoning then the rule of law which has to be applied by the AI systems is the AI rule of law.[215] Besides, the idea behind the rule of law will be fulfilled and implemented since AI systems will apply an AI rule of law suitable for the nature of the AI legal process.

Does the employment of AI in law alter the essence of law? Does the implementation of AI alter the meaning of law in a society even in an AI society? Does an AI society need law and order or the mechanisms of the system solve all the problems in a technical way or the legality and legitimacy are meanings that have to survive? Can judges and their opinions be standardized like a manufactured product and which will be role of the Supreme Court in generating new precedents? Will not altered the old precedents due to society alterations based on many factors such as technology, politics, etc.? Will AI systems arrive at a form of moral consciousness?

Will AI systems influence the justice system? It has to be taken into account that AI and machine learning are already bringing changes to market practice and service delivery in some parts of the legal sector. However, the role of efficiency driven solutions powered by AI systems is still advancing within the legal industry. To that extent, in litigation AI will influence the way criminal and civil proceeding are heard and decided not mentioning the utilization of electronic evidence and the e-submission of materials. Furthermore, increased automation is altering the nature and character of the conventional legal system and the AI legal system is emerging.

4.7 AAI Rule of Law and AAI International Law

Law implies a binding legal commitment, including for instance those ethical contents that are common and/or shared and so reach the statute of obligatory norms.[216] Hence, law concerning AI has to follow those rationales. Legal standards and legal norms are common and uniform for the reason that they arise from the agreement between States in the case of International Law or from a legitimate legislative process in domestic law. Moreover, legal regulation reproduces the political, social, and economic aspects of AI and compliance with the rules is guaranteed both legally and judicially. On the other hand, the ethical factor of AI

---

of Artificial Legal Intelligence: Speaking law to the power of statistics. / In: University of Toronto Law Journal, Vol. 68, No. 1, 2, 2018, p. 12–35.

[215] Alain Supiot's identification of (the "anthropological function" of law as a "technique [for the] humanization of technology," contend that the replacement of juridical reasoning with computation would ultimately result in the subordination of the "rule of law" to a new "rule of technology".) Homo Juridicus: On the Anthropological Function of Law By Alain Supiot. London, New York: Verso, 2007.

[216] https://ec.europa.eu/digital-single-market/en/news/draft-ethics-guidelines-trustworthy-ai, p. 2.

is essential but ethics is not an obligatory mandate applying on a voluntary basis by a specific subject or community. In addition, there is not one single or a universal uniform ethical code, even though there are many common or shared ethical concepts and principles.[217]

It has to be taken into account that the perception of law as a set of mandates, limitations and prohibitions overcomes its notion as a needed instrument to organize society and coexistence among people. Moreover, law does not always lead to a just resolution, but without law coexistence in society is not imaginable. Ethical principles lack both the enforceability of legal standards and the needed mechanisms to make certain compliance. Will the legal logic be altered by AAI? The answer is no merely the expression will be different analogous to AAI society and AAI disputes.

There is fairly limited reference to the overall panorama of the ethical or legal problems caused by AI and so there is an absence of a global attitude on the legal and ethical aspects of AI. Taking into account AI characteristics such as invisibility explain that there is not a clear social and political consciousness about the existence, scope, and importance of AI; complexity of AI has led to not easily understandable, nor rationalizable through norms or principles, currently there is not enough social or political awareness on AI.

It is worth noting that AI has been developed through the connection of "intelligence" and "humanity" but intelligence is not only a human quality or a quality that is unique to the human being not determined solely or principally by intelligence and so there is not a single human or natural intelligence but different modalities of intelligence.[218] To that extent, Winfield[219] argues that "we lack a general (mathematical) theory of intelligence".

AI is ranging from purely mechanical devices, which could hardly be qualified as intelligent, to devices planned to generate super-intelligent systems. In addition, the machine simulates understanding but it cannot be related to the human mind for the reason that it lacks understanding and so computers purely use syntactic rules to operate symbol strings which means that external influences of consciousness cannot be simulated by a current technology computer. On the other hand, AI devices have understanding capacity and comprehension skills such as smartphones or virtual assistants to the quantum computing.[220]

---

[217] Article 38 of the Statute of the International Court of Justice provides that the Court may judge according to criteria of equity rather than by applying the law. This so-called contra legem equity serves as an alternative to cases in which the application of the law may lead to an unfair result.

[218] According to Winfield, "Humans have several different kinds of intelligence – all of which combine to make us human".

[219] Winfield, A. (2019). On the simulation (and energy costs) of human intelligence, the singularity and simulationism. In A. Adamatzky, & V. Kendon (Eds.), From astrophysics to unconventional computation. Emergence, complexity and computation (Vol. 35). Cham: Springer.

[220] Smith, B., & Browne, C. A. (2019). Tools and weapons. The promise and the peril of the digital age. Penguin Press, 2019. Surden, H. (2019). Artificial intelligence and law: An overview. Georgia State University Law Review, 35(4), 1304–1337.

Which is the law– machine interface in a hybrid environment in which both humans and intelligent machines will make legal decisions at the same time? For the reason that "human–machine" amalgams will be the replacement for human-only legal systems, at least at the first stage of AI systems, advancing a meaningful understanding of this interface is necessary.[221]

Taking into account that AI continues to improve and has inserted in everyday life, society has to achieve an optimal allocation of decision-making power between humans and machines in such a hybrid environment fostering the "new division of labor." It is worth noting that the copyright industry and their supportive technology platforms have already actively deployed automated copyright enforcement to identify, monitor, filter, and monetize possibly infringing works on digital networks.[222]

YouTube and other platforms have deployed Content ID systems and algorithms to facilitate automated enforcement systems that are consistent with existing copyright law have established some form of fair use. Regardless of the lack of a de jure obligation to filter under the DMCA many platforms are employing automated copyright enforcement systems.[223] Moreover, algorithmic enforcement systems effectuate the rights of copyright owners while instantaneously limiting the liability of content intermediaries.[224] It is argued that algorithms will make businesses more competent and more objective, but they do not remove or even always diminish the likelihood that things will sometimes go wrong.[225] Undeniably, the speed and geographic reach of algorithmic practices indicates that when things do go wrong, they can go really wrong for a lot of people in a lot of places at once.

It is worth noting that the problem is that the law is not set to address corporate liability when the "thinking" behind corporate misconduct has been discharged to automated systems. Under current law, corporate liability entails evidence of a culpable corporate mental state: purpose to discriminate, knowledge of competitors' prices, or irresponsibility in operating a vehicle.[226] The legal doctrine for attributing mental states to companies defines corporate mental states in terms of employee

[221] Roger Brownsword, Law, Technology and Society: Re-Imagining the Regulatory Environment 181 (2019).

[222] Maayan Perel & Niva Elkin-Koren, Black Box Tinkering: Beyond Disclosure in Algorithmic Enforcement, 69 FLA. L. REV. 181, 189 (2017).

[223] Nicolas P. Suzor, Lawless: The Secret Rules That Govern Our Digital Lives 72 (2019) ("Automated copyright detection systems have now been built into many other services on the Internet. Facebook has developed its own detection systems, and companies like Audible Magic produce software that has been adopted by many platforms.").

[224] 17 U.S.C. § 512(c)(3)(A)(v) (2018) (requiring "[a] statement that the complaining party has a good faith belief that use of the material in the manner complained of is not authorized by the copyright owner, its agent, or the law").

[225] Sonia K. Katyal, Private Accountability in the Age of Artificial Intelligence, 66 UCLA L. Rev. 54, 65 (2019) ("Algorithms hold tremendous value. Big data promise significant benefits to the economy . . . .").

[226] United States v. Athlone Indus., Inc., 746 F.2d 977, 979 (3d Cir. 1984) ("Robots cannot be sued."); U. Pagallo, Killers, Fridges, and Slaves: A Legal Journey in Robotics, 26 AI & SOC'Y

mental states and so the collective knowledge doctrine permits courts to aggregate employee knowledge, and the control group test only reinforces the current legal fact that corporate mental states must derive from employee mental states. Moreover, when businesses using algorithms misbehave in ways that, from the outside, look just as purposeful, knowing, or reckless, current liability doctrines do not apply.[227]

Is there needed the comparison between human and artificial intelligence? The comparison is obvious due to the fact that human understanding and so in an AAI world reference will be made to AAI intelligence applicable to an AAI globe. Presently only the human brain is able to learn from the world, to plan and to execute.[228] The AI HLEG[229] states that "since intelligence (both in machines and in humans is a vague concept, although it has been studied at length by psychologists, biologists, and neuroscientists, AI researchers use mostly the notion of rationality. This refers to the ability to choose the best action to take in order to achieve a certain goal given certain criteria to be optimized and the available resources." Hence, the AI HLEG recognizes that rationality is not the only ingredient in the concept of intelligence.

Present AI does not possess consciousness and so only human brain is the only object that is generating consciousness which means that AI does not have intentionality, feelings, and interests. It is argued that as soon as AI as smart as humans are built then it rapidly re-invents itself to be even smarter, starting a chain reaction of smarter-AI inventing even-smarter-AI until humans cannot understand how the super-intelligent AI works and so the future of humanity becomes unpredictable and out-of-control from the moment of the singularity onwards.[230]

AI raises many questions and challenges from a juridical point of view such as the protection of the basic rights and freedoms of individuals. It could be said that the co-occurrence and relationships between humans and AI devices is the central legal, social, and political encounter[231] presently. In addition, there is not a legal vacuum because there are legal rules and principles which apply generally to all human and

347, 349 (2011) ("[C]ommon legal standpoint excludes robots of any kind from criminal responsibility.").

227 Sherman Antitrust Act, 15 U.S.C. § 1; United States v. Wise, 370 U.S. 405, 416 (1962) ("[A] corporate officer is subject to prosecution under s 1 of the Sherman Act whenever he knowingly participates in effecting the illegal contract, combination, or conspiracy.").

228 Hawkins, J. (2017). What intelligent machines need to learn from the neocortex. https://spectrum.org/computing/software/what-intelligent-machinesneed-to-learn-from-the-neocortex

229 High-Level Expert Group on Artificial Intelligence (AI HLEG). (2018). Draft ethics guidelines for trustworthy AI. https://ec.europa.eu/knowledge4policy/publication/draft-ethics-guidelines-trustworthy-ai_en. High-Level Expert Group on Artificial Intelligence (AI HLEG). (2019). Ethics guidelines for trustworthy AI. Available at: https://ec.europa.eu/futurium/en/ai-allianceconsultation

230 https://ec.europa.eu/digital-single-market/en/news/ethics-guidelines-trustworthy-ai. Winfield, A. (2019). On the simulation (and energy costs) of human intelligence, the singularity and simulationism. In A. Adamatzky, & V. Kendon (Eds.), From astrophysics to unconventional computation. Emergence, complexity and computation (Vol. 35). Cham: Springer.

231 Frank, L., & Nyholm, S. (2017). Robot sex and consent: Is consent to sex between a robot and a human conceivable, possible, and desirable). Artificial Intelligence and Law, 25, 305–323.

social activity embracing the development of AI. The principle of the prohibition of the use of force in the context of international relations or the right to life and the integrity of the person are clear examples in this regard.[232]

In addition, there are mandatory rules and principles that can be applied to AI through the principle of analogy and so consumer protection or liability for defective goods can be inferred analogously to the sphere of the AI. Moreover, the development and operation of AI systems typically involves contributions from multiple individuals, organizations, and machine components and so all legal systems have principles and procedures to demand accountability.[233] If an autonomous, self-driving car that injures a pedestrian, then we will hold human persons and corporations accountable for the accident by targeting the hardware manufacturer or repairer, the software programmers, or even the parties who chose to install the software in the car and so courts will hold these parties to different standards of liability.[234]

It has to be taken into account that in the situation of a hardware or physical failure, individuals direct one's anger to the manufacturers and in the case of a non-autonomous smart device, where the reason of a problem within the computer's code is distinct, one can condemn the software developer or the party who decided to run the software in the device. Moreover, in the case of any computer, if many related machines are making the same error, even if it cannot be recognized why, one will focus on the software developer or manufacturer, with an instinct toward the doctrine of res ipsa loquitur—even if it cannot be articulated precisely what happened, indicating that there is negligent design. Under the present legal regime, accountability and responsibility cannot be transferred to machines and so the concerns concerning human control, responsibility, liability, and ethics are crucial which means that AI challenges national, regional, and international laws, which will therefore need to be adapted to properly address the legal issues that this technology raises.

On the other hand, there are rules and principles need to be revised to take account of the unique characteristics of AI and so data protection regulations must be revisited to be effective in the different scenarios of the massive use of data implied by the AI[235] such as in the case of the circulation of autonomous vehicles prohibited by the Vienna Convention on Urban Traffic of 1968. Conclusively, AI necessitates the formulation of new rules embracing the dogma of explicability or explanation. WIPO has been recently working in AI explaining "that most patent applications

---

[232] https://fra.europa.eu/en/publication/2019/data-quality-and-artificial-intelligence-mitigating-bias-and-error-protect. Collins, R. (2019). Two idea(l)s of the international rule of law. Global Constitutionalism, 8(2), 191–226.

[233] Yeung, K. (2019). Responsibility and AI. Council of Europe Study DGI (2919)5.

[234] M. Ryan Calo, Open Robotics, 70 MD. L. REV. 571 (2011).

[235] UNI Global Union. (2018). 10 principles for ethical AI. http://www.thefutureworldofwork.org/opinions/10-principles-for-ethical-ai/

Wachter, S., & Mittelstadt, B. (2019). A right to reasonable inferences: Re-thinking data protection law in the age of big data and AI. Columbia Business Law Review, 1, 1–130.

have a commercial, application focus, as they refer to an AI functional application or are combined with an AI application field. This report identifies 20 fields/industry sectors that patent documents refer to, ranging from entertainment to education to banking, indicating that sectors across the board are exploring the application of AI technologies[236]".

Certain core characteristics of AI and the way AI are utilized by social media to mold access to information, and over time, tastes and identity involve an interplay of choice and constraint which means that the law has to spot ways to push users to deem actively how they want to deal over time with technology. Above all, the law can draw attention to how a digital technology will alter preferences and behaviors over time.

It has to be taken into account that the design of artificial intelligence image detection system is founded upon the Internet of Things having the pros of high image detection rate, high recognition accuracy, stable operation, and efficient processing.[237] Is it possible to grant legal personality to artificial intelligence software systems? In *Sega Enterprises Ltd v. Accolade, Inc.,*[238] the Court applied the fair use doctrine to protect the public interest in reverse engineering technology permitting software engineers as a group of users to accomplish interoperability of different software programs. Technical standardization enables systems and network compatibility, making possible interoperability and so wider interoperability translates into economies of scale, and market competition, stipulating incentives for international cooperation and coordination in standards development. It has to be taken into account that in every new technology, the first regulation is comprised by technical standardization being a meaningful type of private regulation. Moreover, technical standardization is highly creative in the development of AI technologies and not politically neutral by generating regulatory and policy diffusion. Has private regulation been turned into a device for power politics? Of course, it seems that new technologies attribute power to individual companies via IPRs and so high-tech firms are gaining political power. It is characteristic that uncontrolled and illegitimate use of AI for criminal justice and surveillance reasons generates fears of serious human rights violations.[239]

Is there a right to technology already established? Taking into consideration that technology justice is a matter for the international community, the Universal Declaration of Human Rights ("UDHR") established the human right to technology in 1948, stating that "everyone has the right . . . to share in scientific advancement and

[236] https://www.wipo.int/publications/en/details.jsp?id¼4386 https://www.epo.org/law-practice/case-law-appeals/recent.html

[237] Cheng Mo, Wei Sun, Point-by-point feature extraction of artificial intelligence images based on the Internet of Things Computer Communications 159 (2020) 1–8.

[238] 977 F.2d 1510 (ninth Cir. 1992).

[239] Feldstein, Steven (2019) The Global Expansion of AI Surveillance.https://carnegieendowment.org/2019/09/17/global-expansion-of-ai-surveillance-pub-79847

its benefits" but this human right remains ineffective.[240] Moreover, H. Sun[241] argues that a new essential right to technology should be recognized under the U.-S. Constitution and so due to the weight to human dignity and equality, the right to technology has to boost equal distribution of the benefits of technological progress.

It has to be taken into consideration that the U.S. courts have relied on the fundamental rights to free speech, to bear arms, and to property in dealing with critical cases relating to law and technology. Hence, the Supreme Court has proscribed injustices arising from the use of speech-censoring technologies on the basis of the First Amendment.[242]

In *Reno v. American Civil Liberties Union*[243] held that cyberspace as a whole had served as a "vast democratic forum" further presented how cyberspace had begun to play a vital role in advancing societal interests in political communications. Furthermore, the Supreme Court in Packingham v. North Carolina[244] deliberated the societal interests generated by cyberspace and argued that the new social media technologies have drastically increased the power of cyberspace to engender a collective interest in the public exchange of information and knowledge.

In *Field v. Google Inc.,*[245] Google had used an automated web crawler to cache Field's personal website containing his copyrighted works and displayed the cached

---

[240] G.A. Res. 217 (III) A, Universal Declaration of Human Rights, at 76 (Dec. 10, 1948). Yvonne Donders, The Right to Enjoy the Benefits of Scientific Progress: In Search of State Obligations in Relation to Health, 14 MED. HEALTH CARE & PHIL. 371, 371 (2011), https://www.ncbi.nlm.nih.gov/pmc/articles/PMC3190088 ("After having received little attention over the past decades, one of the least known human rights provisions in international human rights law—the right to enjoy the benefits of scientific progress and its applications—has had its dust blown off.") (citations omitted); Jessica M. Wyndham & Margaret Weigers Vitullo, Why the Right to Science Matters for Everyone, OPENDEMOCRACY (Apr. 20, 2017), https://www.opendemocracy.net/jessicam-wyndham-margaret-weigers-vitullo/why-right-to-science-matters-for-everyone ("Although nearly 70 years have passed since this right to science was first [articulated], the implications of the right and its meaning for individuals and governments have never been fully articulated.").

[241] Haochen Sun, The Fundamental Right To Technology https://ssrn.com/abstract=3635947 p445 Amber Miekle, Technology Justice: A Call To Action (2016), https://infohub.practicalaction.org/

[242] Elonis v. United States, 135 S. Ct. 2001, 2006, 2011–12 (2015); United States v. Am. Library Ass'n, 539 U.S. 194, 205–06 (2003). Washington v. U.S. Dep't of State, 318 F. Supp. 3d 1247, 1251, 1263–64 (W.D. Wash. 2018); Gina Martinez, Why the Legal Battle over 3D-Printed Guns May Prove Futile, TIME (Aug. 1, 2018), http://time.com/5354963/3d-printed-guns-hard-to-stop. Carpenter v. United States, 138 S. Ct. 2206, 2217–20 (2018); Adam Liptak, In Ruling on Cellphone Location Data, Supreme Court Makes Statement on Digital Privacy, N.Y. TIMES (June 22, 2018), https://www.nytimes.com/2018/06/22/us/politics/supreme-court-warrants-cellphone-privacy.html

[243] 521 U.S. 844 (1997) Rochelle Cooper Dreyfuss, Patents and Human Rights: The Paradox Re-Examined, in Intellectual Property And Access To Science And Culture: Convergence Or Conflict? 65, 65 (Christophe Geiger ed., 2016) (arguing that the right to technology "extends only to basic technologies, such as medicines, transportation, telephones, and computers—as opposed to Ferraris, smartphones, high-definition televisions, Roombas or Fitbits").

[244] 137 S. Ct. 1730 (2017).

[245] 412 F. Supp. 2d 1106 (D. Nev. 2006). The Court summarized its fair use ruling as follows: [T]he first fair use factor weighs heavily in Google's favor because its "Cached" links are highly

content of that website when users clicked on cached links in Google search results and Google's provision of cached links constituted fair use largely on the grounds that such links "serve different and socially important purposes in offering access to copyrighted works . . . .". Furthermore, In Kelly v. Arriba Soft Corp. and Perfect 10, Inc. v. Amazon.com, Inc., the Ninth Circuit Court of Appeals held that the reproduction in their entirety of numerous photographs or web pages to generate and operate Internet search engines constitutes fair use[246] benefiting society as a whole by refining public access to information. In addition, it could be said that the fundamental right to technology protects societal interests in precluding harmful uses of AI technologies, both fundamental and derivative.[247] Consequently, it forbids people from utilizing any technology triggering harm to societal interests in preserving a democratic political system, cultivating environmental protection, and improving innovation capacity.

In *Righthaven LLC v. Realty One Group, Inc.*,[248] fair use was invoked to protect the interests of bloggers as a group of users in copying limited amounts of copyrighted work to produce blog posts on cyberspace. In the interim, new technological developments could cause the invocation of the group right to technology to prevent or eradicate harm to a certain group of people such as the use of algorithms in facial recognition technology. In addition, the problems with facial recognition technology are even more alarming needing swift action to correct its algorithms, facial recognition technology deteriorate group-based interests in racial equality.[249]

transformative. The second fair use factor weighs only slightly against fair use because Field made his works available in their entirety for free to the widest possible audience. The third fair use factor is neutral, as Google used no more of the copyrighted works than was necessary to serve its transformative purposes. The fourth fair use factor cuts strongly in favor of fair use in the absence of any evidence of an impact on a potential market for Field's copyrighted works. A fifth factor, a comparison of the equities, likewise favors fair use. A balance of all of these factors demonstrates that if Google copies or distributes Field's copyrighted works by allowing access to them through "Cached" links, Google's conduct is fair use of those works as a matter of law.

[246] 336 F.3d 811 (ninth Cir. 2003). 508 F.3d 1146 (ninth Cir. 2007) (ruling that "a search engine provides social benefit by incorporating an original work into a new work, namely, an electronic reference tool").

[247] 977 F.2d 1510 (ninth Cir. 1992). at 1523 (ruling that reverse engineering "has led to an increase in the number of independently designed video game programs offered for use with the [plaintiff's] console"); Pamela Samuelson & Suzanne Scotchmer, The Law and Economics of Reverse Engineering, 111 Yale L.J. 1575, 1608–09 (2002) ("From this approximation of source code, reverse engineers can discern or deduce internal design details of the program such as information necessary to develop a program that will interoperate with the decompiled or disassembled program.").

[248] No. 2:10-cv-1036-LRH-PAL, 2010 WL 4115413 (D. Nev. Oct. 19, 2010). Ali Breland, How White Engineers Built Racist Code – and Why It's Dangerous for Black People, The Guardian (Dec. 4, 2017), ("facial recognition software has problems recognizing black faces because its algorithms are usually written by white engineers who dominate the technology sector. These engineers build on pre-existing code libraries, typically written by other white engineers.").

[249] Drew Harwell, Federal Study Confirms Racial Bias of Many Facial-Recognition Systems, Casts Doubt on Their Expanding Use, Wash. Post (Dec. 20, 2019).

Facial recognition technology (FRT) raises profound questions about the role of technology in society[250] and there is rapid uptake of FRT in many new domains, such as finance, travel, and criminal justice. It could be said that the fundamental right to technology is protected via the public's fair share of the technological benefits that are key to fulfillment of the overall economic, political, and cultural needs of a society or a group to which that public belongs and so prohibiting the uses of technology jeopardizing societal and group interests.

The IP Clause[251] of the U.S. Constitution empowers Congress "to promote the Progress of Science and useful Arts, by securing for limited Times to Authors and Inventors the exclusive Right to their respective Writings and Discoveries" and by defining the objective of the legislative power of Congress and prescribing means to accomplish the objective. Moreover, the IP Clause capitalizes on legal protection of copyrights and patents as the means to advance technological progress and knowledge evolution.[252]

It has to be taken into account that AI is moving away from universities toward firms based on their capability to collect large data repositories that are needed for modern AI research. It is characteristic the influence of Supreme Court jurisprudence on the patent eligibility of AI technologies and in a series of Supreme Court decisions, starting in 2010 with *Bilski v. Kappos,*[253] have changed the natures of inventions that are eligible for patent protection and so dropping the patent eligibility of inventions that contain abstract ideas, laws of natures and products of nature.[254]

In *Bilski v. Kappos*[255] the term "useful arts" incorporates the fields relating to technology or "technological arts" and in *Sony Corp. of Am. v. Universal City Studios, Inc.*[256] the monopoly privileges that Congress may allow are neither unlimited nor offer a special private benefit which means that the limited grant is a way by which an imperative public commitment is achieved by inspiring the creative activity of authors and inventors via the provision of a special reward and so permitting the public access to the products of their genius after the limited period of exclusive control has ended. In other words, the worth of IP rights in business

---

[250] Daniel E. Ho, Emily Black, Maneesh Agrawala, & Li Fei-Fei, Evaluating Facial Recognition Technology: A Protocol For Performance Assessment In New Domains, 2021 Denver Law Review 753 [Vol. 98.4.

[251] U.S. CONST. art. I, § 8, cl. 8.

[252] Barton Beebe, Bleistein, The Problem of Aesthetic Progress, and the Making of American Copyright Law, 117 Colum. L. Rev. 319, 341 (2017).

[253] 561 U.S. 593, 130 S. Ct. 3218.

[254] Kesan J. and Wang R., 2020. Eligible subject matter at the patent office: An empirical study of the influence of Alice on patent examiners and patent applications. Minnesota Law Review, 105(2). Harris, S., Trippe, A., Challis, D. and Swycher, N., 2020. Construction and evaluation of gold standards for patent classification—A case study on quantum computing. World Patent Information, 61, p. 101961.

[255] 561 U.S. 593, 634 (2010).

[256] 464 U.S. 417, 429 (1984).

stems from the strategic use of the right to exclude.[257] It has to be taken into account that IP protection enables the constitutional objective of promoting technological progress.

On the other hand, in *Golan v. Holder,*[258] the constitutionality of the Uruguay Round Agreements Act ("URAA") was tested for the reason that this statute automatically restored copyright protection to all works of foreign origin that were not yet in the public domain in their source states, but that were in the public domain in the USA for particular purposes and so restoration of copyright protection essentially brought distributive effects disadvantaging specific groups of content users. H. Sun[259] argues that "the fundamental right to technology is by no means an absolute right. It is not intended to substantially harm the interests of IP rights owners by disrupting their business plans to merchandize their IP assets in the market. Nor is it intended to erode the legal confinements of the Fifth Amendment by "[taking] private property . . . for public use, without just compensation." This is because the right does not defy distribution of benefits through market exchange."

The fundamental right to technology demands the equal distribution and enjoyment of the benefits of technological progress and so legislature and litigation has to rewrite IP laws to render them more protective concerning this right by acknowledging that IP rights protection has performed the well-known role in regulating technology and social justice. To that extent, the international human rights system needs further protection via AAI and so reordering the benefits of technological progress in the interests of all global citizens embracing AAI entities via AAI international law as well. The AAI international law is the new notion generated due to the AAI technology in order to deal with the legal relations among states. The question to be answered is if the current sovereignty of states will remain under AAI systems or new blocks of AAI states will be developed? Will AAI generate a single global AAI e-state on earth?

AAI technological advance unavoidably is altering human and social behaviors demanding an adaptation of existing norms or the creation of specific rules if the law in force proves inadequate or unproductive. Essentially, AAI will be a cross-cutting happening necessitating not only the establishment of specific standards but also the reconsidering of the feasibility and effectiveness of pre-existing rules.[260] Due to the scope and nature of AAI, international regulation is unavoidable with a universal or general vocation as a result of the scope and nature of the AAI. Nonetheless, in the case of AAI worldwide legal norms can coexist and be fully compatible with

---

[257] Christopher Kalanje, Leveraging Intellectual Property: Beyond the "Right to Exclude," WIPO, https://www.wipo.int/sme/en/documents/leveraging_ip_fulltext.html

[258] 565 U.S. 302 (2012). Haochen Sun, Copyright and Responsibility, 4 Harv.J. Sports & Ent. L. 263, 297 (2013).

[259] Haochen Sun, The Fundamental Right To Technology https://ssrn.com/abstract=3635947 P 480.

[260] https://ec.europa.eu/jrc/en/publication/eur-scientific-and-technicalresearch-reports/artificial-intelligence-european-perspective https://www.accessnow.org/cms/assets/uploads/2018/08/The-Toronto-Declaration_ENG_08-2018.pdf

regional norms. Zekos considers that at the verge of humanity losing earth's control there will be a war of humans against AAI machines by immobilizing the AAI intelligence and arriving at zero point for a restart.

Will humans lose themselves along the way for more AAI? B. Frischmann and E. Selinger[261] argue that "As we collectively race down the path toward smart techno-social systems that efficiently govern more and more of our lives, we run the risk of losing ourselves along the way." Does humanity's future depend on the advancement of technology justice?

Is the essence of AAI rule of law something different than the conventional rule of law? The essence is the same with a difference in the technological expression because not following a rule of law rationale will lead into a collusion and final crash. AAI brings forwards modernization of corporate organizations and to profoundly alter corporations' inner workings. Over time, corporations have remained almost intact in their characteristic qualities, which involve a body of investor-owners delegating management to one or more people sitting on a board.

While mutual funds and other institutional investors introduced some modifications in corporate governance, agency problems stay a well-known result of delegated management regardless of technological advances.[262] Even cyberspace has not brought serious transformation and virtual shareholder meetings are a distant likelihood in many jurisdictions, while proxy and direct voting portray practical challenges, embracing ensuring proper shareholder identification and vote recording. Thus, EU states do not tolerate virtual shareholder meetings.[263] Considerably, information readily available on cyberspace has not even fully replaced paper documents and regular mail in corporate communications yet but AAI will transform the way securities transactions are cleared and registered, certifying specific shareholder identification along with more transparency for corporate records and even virtual shareholder meetings.[264] Hence, AAI alterations will mark the balance of power between directors, managers, and shareholders.

Furthermore, AAI will transform the way directors and officers make decisions in many different ways, from providing informational support to actually substituting them in whole or in part. To that extent, common predictions for technology's influence on corporations diverge from completely autonomous organizations, run

---

[261] Brett Frischmann & Evan Selinger, Re-Engineering Humanity 1 (2018).

[262] Sergio Gramitto, The Technology and Archeology of Corporate Law 32 (Cornell Legal Studies Research Paper No. 18–40, 2018), https://papers.ssrn.com/sol3/papers.cfm?abstract_id=3232816

[263] https://papers.ssrn.com/sol3/papers.cfm?abstract_id=2992804 (observing that); Christoph Van der Elst & Anne Lafarre, Blockchain and Smart Contracting for the Shareholder Community, 20 Eur. Bus. Org. L. Rev. 111 (2019).

[264] Florian Möslein, Robots in the boardroom: artificial intelligence and corporate law, in Research Handbook On The Law Of Artificial Intelligence 649, 657–66 (Woodrow Barfield & Ugo Pagallo eds., 2019.

totally by algorithms, to more partial improvements and efficiencies in the workings of corporate bodies and procedures.[265]

It is worth noting that the existing distribution of powers is fairly similar across jurisdictions. Shareholders vote on control-related and structural decisions, such as appointing and removing the enterprise's directors and supporting mergers and liquidations. Moreover, directors are responsible for making business decisions, such as whether to launch a new product or reject a supplier, but classically designate day-to-day management to enterprise executives and officers and retain policy-making and monitoring functions.

Taking into account that shareholder empowerment protects stakeholder concerns, AAI will enhance transparency toward different stakeholder groups and smart contracts will administer contractual relationships between some stakeholders and the corporation. There is a move from corporate governance to "Platform" Governance which merely alters the means of governance rather than altering the essence of governance by all the above-mentioned modes which means that it is expected the AAI governance via AAI systems dealing with matters of AAI enterprises.

Has technology in corporate organizations moved from digitalization to automation? The answer is not yet. Moreover, shareholders of public corporations haven't begun to meet more frequently or become more involved in corporate affairs and the link between big data and platforms is at the foundation of the so-called digital economy via "platforms" and so digitization indicates that cyberspace events such as communications, finance, transactions in goods and services, entertainment, social contacts, even employment take place via platforms which means that governance is facilitated by enormous instants information making easier and quicker any decision by modifying the model of management of a company.[266] The introduction of an AAI algorithm as the central point of examining the relevant information, the governance scheme can easily make any decision prior moving to the stage of automated decisions for all the matters of a company.

In addition, taking into account that blockchains and smart contracts ease, digitalize, and improve corporate accounting and shareholder meetings, algorithms allow companies to move toward "algorithmic management": assigning the power to make business decisions to algorithms and other artificial intelligence devices.[267] It has to be taken into consideration that algorithmic management influence legal entities' decision-making processes from delivering simple advisory services to directors and managers in the form of predictions, recommendations, and other information to replacing all human decision-makers. Algorithms supplant middle managers by setting work shifts, scheduling workers' activities, allocating duties,

[265] Ronald J. Gilson, From Corporate Law to Corporate Governance, in The Oxford Handbook Of Corporate Law And Governance 3, 15–22 (Jeffrey N. Gordon & Wolf-Georg Ringe eds., 2018).

[266] Mireille Hildebrandt, Primitives of Legal Protection in the Era of Data-Driven Platforms, 2 Geo. L. Tech. Rev. 252, 254–55 (2018) (drawing parallels between modern day platforms, the Greek agora, and the Roman forum as spaces for market exchanges, political discourse, and other forms of expression).

[267] Martin Petrin, Corporate Management in the Age of AI, 2019 Colum. Bus. L. Rev. 965, 966–68.

and supervising worker performance, as they do in gig economy corporations such as Amazon and Uber. AAI is expected to replace corporate directors.

The capacity of firms to design their own tech governance structures and to balance the allocation of powers between different corporate constituencies needs to be preserved at least in the present form of AI systems. Moreover, the possible advantages and costs of using technology to empower different corporate constituencies fluctuate founded on the distinctive features of the company. Hence, permitting a range of governance structures, and refrain from direct regulation of the allocation of control rights remain valid in the context of the present technology-driven corporate governance alterations. Also, AAI governance will be needed for all corporate enterprises in the near future. Chiara Picciau[268] argues that "the most significant and immediate impact will fall somewhere in between and will concern the distribution of powers and competences among corporate bodies."

The CJEU found that the level of interference with privacy rights was high, for the reason that the directive entailed operators to store all track and location data of users, irrespective of whether the users posed a certain risk, or whether the data had a precise link to an investigation.[269] According to the CJEU, the more detailed and intrusive the data, the more serious must be the crime.[270]

The proportionality test was applied recently by a court in The Hague, Netherlands, concerning an algorithm used by the social security authorities to detect prospective social security fraud. The District Court of The Hague found that the measure was "provided for by law" because the law was sufficiently detailed, and that the objective of fighting welfare fraud was a compelling social interest, satisfying the first and second test.[271]

---

[268] Chiara Picciau, The (Un)Predictable Impact of Technology on Corporate Governance at: https://ssrn.com/abstract=3643500 P 64 Jill E. Fisch & Simone M. Sepe, Shareholder Collaboration, 98 Tex. L. Rev. 863 (2020) (arguing that collaboration between insiders and institutional investors could be firm-value enhancing by aggregating the partial and complementary information in their possession). Broadridge, Virtual Shareholder Meetings. 2019 Facts And Figures 3 (2020), https://www.broadridge.com/_assets/pdf/broadridge-virtualshareholder-meetings-2019-facts-and-figures.pdf

[269] Digital Rights Ireland v. Minister for Communications, CJEU, Joined Cases C-293/12 & C-594/12,, (Apr. 8, 2014).

[270] CJEU, Case C-207/16, Ministerio Fiscal, 2 October 2018, points 56 and 57". In accordance with the principle of proportionality, serious interference can be justified, in areas of prevention, investigation, detection and prosecution of criminal offences, only by the objective of fighting crime which must also be defined as "serious." By contrast, when the interference that such access entails is not serious, that access is capable of being justified by the objective of preventing, investigating, detecting and prosecuting "criminal offences' generally." Secretary of State v. Watson, CJEU, Joined Cases C-203/15 & C-698/15, (Dec. 21, 2016).

[271] Rb. Den Haag 5 February 2020 (Nederlands Juristen Comité voor de Mensenrechten/Staat Der Nederlanden) (Neth.), https://uitspraken.rechtspraak.nl/inziendocument?id=ECLI:NL:RBDHA:2020:865 Netherlands law allows the government to collect data from various government databases so as to create risk profiles showing the likelihood that a given individual is cheating on social security benefits.

When a judge or a policy maker is faced with the necessity for a new legal rule, he or she typically considers, along with formal analytical factors such as economic cost, consistency with existing rules, administrability, etc. his or her own personal experience. Nonetheless in the case of new technologies and discoveries such as regulating human gene editing, or orbital weapons systems, or cerebral implants, there are few personal experiences to draw from. Thus, science fiction is a guide concerning AI technology influencing the direction of the followed understanding and way of thinking to establish.

Will AAI influence the law? The answer is that the law has to make central alterations into its concept and functionality in order to tackle AAI commercial utilization by taking into account that AI systems have caused many problems in the commercial world.[272]

Platforms need algorithmic deployment to promote fair use in copyright law and automation is needed by the fast pace of digital dissemination and the exceedingly large volume of distributed content.[273] It is worth noting that correct technological enforcement of the law of fair use is far beyond today's state of the art which means that an AAI rights management code is required to be developed immediately.[274]

Due to the fact that AI systems approach the point of interchangeable to humans they are eligible to a status comparable to natural persons. While AI systems become more hi-tech and have a larger role in society, they have to be recognized as persons before the law due to prospective accountability generated by their autonomy, and opacity which means that recognizing personality makes certain that there is someone to reward when things go right.

Does the science fiction generate the new technology on the terrain? The motivation to fulfill fantasy into reality is the guide for new technologies and so the creation of a world of robots is forthcoming with humans on the drive seat but the distant future is unknown instead of moving toward nature with humans utilizing in a

---

[272] Eugene Volokh, Chief Justice Robots, 68 Duke L.J. 1135 (2019); Tim Wu, Will Artificial Intelligence Eat the Law? The Rise of Hybrid Social-Ordering Systems, 119 Colum. L. Rev. 2001 (2019).

[273] Timothy K. Armstrong, Digital Rights Management and the Process of Fair Use, 20 Harv.J.L. &Tech. 49, 56 (2006) ("[Digital rights management] mechanisms engineered to protect fair use rights are in the long-term interests of both content providers and consumers."); Niva Elkin-Koren, Fair Use by Design, 64 UCLA L. Rev. 1082, 1085 (2017) ("[T]he checks that [fair use] intends to create on the rights of authors must . . . be embedded in the design of online systems."); Jeff Desjardins, How Much Data Is Generated Each Day?, World Econ. F. (Apr. 17, 2019), https://www.weforum.org/agenda/2019/04/how-much-data-is-generated-each-day-cf4bddf29f/

[274] Edward W. Felten, A Skeptical View of DRM and Fair Use, Comm. Acm, Apr. 2003, at 57, 58 ("A [digital rights management system] that gets all fair use judgments right would in effect be a "judge on a chip" predicting with high accuracy how a real judge would decide a lawsuit challenging a particular use. Clearly, this is infeasible with today's technology."); Julie E. Cohen, Between Truth And Power: The Legal Constructions Of Informational Capitalism 192 (2019) ("Automated processes have obvious efficiency advantages, but such processes may not align well (or at all) with applicable legal requirements that are couched in shades of gray.").

cleverer way science without so much destruction. Will humans be transformed into mechanical entities?

It is worth mentioning here that legal personality is fundamental to any system of laws. Actually, the legal systems identify two forms of legal person: natural and juridical.[275] Natural persons are accepted owing to the simple fact of being human. Besides, juridical persons are non-human entities that are given specific rights and duties by law. To that extent, companies and other forms of business associations are the most common examples, but many other forms are possible and so religious, governmental, and intergovernmental entities act as legal persons at the national and international level.

Specific kind of personality to new entities like AI systems can be attributed by a state.[276] It could be said that the understanding that AI systems equal humans recommends personality. By assigning AI systems with some form of legal personality facilitates tackling liability questions, such as an automated driving system entity in the case of driverless cars whose behavior is under the control of their "driver" or foreseeable by their manufacturer or owner.[277] Since they know the uncontrollable of an automated driving system entity and they use it they should be liable.

Moreover, a corporation is a device generated by law to permit natural persons who orgànize themselves as a group to echo that organization in their legal relations with other parties and so group members launch individual contractual relations with those other parties limiting liability and so on, then the corporate form qualifies them to do so collectively at a lower cost which is easily applicable to AI systems.[278] Corporation's personality protects investors from liability beyond the fixed sum of their investment and so the reallocation of risk boosts investment and entrepreneurship which means that AAI corporations will gain from personality accordingly. It has to be taken into account that human directors can delegate some accountability to an AI system; nonetheless under most corporate law regimes they cannot absolve themselves of the final accountability for managing the organization. It is characteristic that in US business entity law limited liability companies, with no human members at all could be formed[279] allowing the formation of AAI companies.[280]

---

[275] J Dewey, "The Historic Background of Corporate Legal Personality" (1926) 35 Yale LJ 660.

[276] VAJ Kurki, A Theory of Legal Personhood (OUP 2019) Bumper Development Corp. v Commissioner of Police for the Metropolis [1991] 1 WLR 1362 (recognizing legal personality of an Indian temple under English law).

[277] Automated Vehicles: A Joint Preliminary Consultation Paper (Law Commission, Consultation Paper No. 240; Scottish Law Commission, Discussion Paper No 166, 2018).

[278] V Morawetz, A Treatise on the Law of Private Corporations (Little, Brown 1886) 2 ("the fact remains self-evident that a corporation is not in reality a person or a thing distinct from its constituent parts. The word corporation is but a collective name for the corporators").

[279] S Bayern, "Of Bitcoins, Independently Wealthy Software, and the Zero-Member LLC" (2014) 108 Northwestern U L Rev. 1495–500.

[280] S Bayern, "The Implications of Modern Business-Entity Law for the Regulation of Autonomous Systems" (2015) 19 Stanford Technology L Rev. 101.

In other words, personality is awarded to accomplish policy ends, for example boosting entrepreneurship, making possible limited liability, influencing the coherence and stability of the legal system via the permanency of certain entities. To that extent, granting personality explicitly through legislation became a mere formality in the course of the twentieth century which could be repeated for AAI systems achieving policy ends for the AAI era.[281] AAI systems can establish AAI corporations needing legal personality for purposes of entrepreneurship dealing with liability of stakeholders.

It is argued that corporations are neither fictions nor mere symbols but objectively real entities that pre-exist delivery of personality by a legal system and so AAI corporations are entities that pre-exist delivery of e-personality as well.

In practice, actual recognition as a person before the law remains in the ability of the state.[282] Which state will attribute legal personality to AAI corporations? In a mechanical globe the essence of conventional legal personality will have no meaning since the AAI society will follow the law of machinery order and functionality which means that the AAI personality will emerge and of course a kind of order will be imposed.

Which is the substance of legal personality? First of all, legal personality brings with it rights and obligations, but these are not the same for all persons within a legal system. Will AI legal personality come only with obligations? In the case of corporations, personality typically means the capability to sue and be sued, to enter into contracts, to incur debt, to own property, and to be convicted of crimes. Moreover, corporations experience constitutional protections analogous to natural persons. It has to be taken into account that typically, juridical persons will have fewer rights than natural ones and in international law states enjoy plenary personality and international organizations have diverging degrees of it.[283] To that extent, the ability to be sued is one of the principal appeals of personality for AI systems, as the European Parliament approved.[284]

---

[281] CE Amsler, RL Bartlett, and CJ Bolton, "Thoughts of Some British Economists on Early Limited Liability and Corporate Legislation" (1981) 13 History of Political Economy 774; G Dari-Mattiacci et al., "The Emergence of the Corporate Form" (2017) 33 J of L, Economics and Organization 193.

[282] K Iwai, "Persons, Things and Corporations: The Corporate Personality Controversy and Comparative Corporate Governance" (1999) 47 AJCL 583; SM Watson, "The Corporate Legal Person" (2019) 19 J Corporate L Studies 137.

[283] S Chesterman, "Does ASEAN Exist? The Association of Southeast Asian Nations as an International Legal Person" (2008) XII Singapore Year Book of International Law 199. Citizens United v Federal Election Commission, 558 US 310 (corporations are not members of society and that there are compelling governmental interests to curb corporations' ability to spend money during local and national elections.) (corporations are not members of society and that there are compelling governmental interests to curb corporations' ability to spend money during local and national elections.).

[284] European Parliament Resolution with Recommendations to the Commission on Civil Law Rules on Robotics (2015/2103(INL)) (European Parliament, 16 February 2017), para 59(f).

Can humanoid robots be functioning under advanced artificial intelligence have rights under the current EU law? The legal framework of the EU is intended for natural persons, legal persons and anybody assimilated to a legal person meaning that in the absence of a personality comparable to natural and legal persons, an AI entity does not benefit from any right.

Is a legal person only a legal entity? A legal person is a certain organization whose activities depend on the intent of a natural person. From a legal point of view, the action of a natural person is the action of a legal person only if the natural person acts in the way stipulated in the Act and the statute based on it as the body of a legal person. Under civil law, a legal person is liable for damages and so a firm dealing with renovations triggers damage by inappropriate performance of the renovation which means that the responsibility lies with natural persons acting for the legal person. Karolina Ziemianin[285] argues that "liability for damages caused by artificial intelligence must be borne by natural persons, legal persons or organisational units with legal capacity. The principles of this responsibility should depend on the type of artificial intelligence and its technological advancement."

Should liability for AI actions be attributed to its creators, operators or possible end users? Artificial intelligence's status of a legal entity should lead to easier assignment of liability for the actions of artificial intelligence. Civil law must be changed and adapted to refer directly and comprehensively to AI, which is already operating and may cause damage such as in the case of autonomous cars. Currently, compensation for damage caused by artificial intelligence can only be made on the basis of regulations on dangerous products. However, they do not apply to all types of artificial intelligence if they cannot be classified as a product. On the other hand, the compensatory function of tort liability rationalizes granting legal personality to AI.

Civil liability leads to an award of damages which can only be paid if the wrongdoer is capable of owning property, otherwise AAI "Personality" would be a mere formality.[286] Furthermore, by granting personality to AAI systems remove accountability under current laws away from existing legal persons generating a spur to transfer risk to such e-persons with the purpose of protecting natural and conventional juridical ones.[287]

A final quality of legal personality is the ability to be punished. If given legal personality analogous to a corporation, then an AI system will be prosecuted under the criminal law correspondingly. It is worth noting that provided *actus Reus* and *mens rea* are recognized,[288] AAI entity could be fined or has its property seized; a

[285] Ziemianin, K. (2021). Civil legal personality of artificial intelligence. Future or utopia?. Internet Policy Review, 10(2). https://doi.org/10.14763/2021.2.1544 P 19.

[286] KS Abraham and RL Rabin, "Automated Vehicles and Manufacturer Responsibility for Accidents: A New Legal Regime for a New Era" (2019) 105 Virginia L Rev. 127.

[287] 7 JJ Bryson, ME Diamantis, and TD Grant, "Of, for, and by the People: The Legal Lacuna of Synthetic Persons" (2017) 25 Artificial Intelligence and Law 280.

[288] JW Yockey, "Beyond Yates: From Engagement to Accountability in Corporate Crime" (2016) 12 New York U J of L and Business 412–413.

license to function could be suspended or revoked. It has to be taken into consideration that the event that companies are capable of violating criminal laws regardless of missing free will or moral accountability apparently contributes to the allotment of criminal responsibility of AAI systems.[289] It is obvious that in an AAI society the measure of having a "robot criminal" being destroyed or reprogrammed will be imposed. Taking into account that reasons for criminal punishment are retribution, incapacitation, deterrence, and rehabilitation, those rationales will be applicable in AAI entities.

The penal system is used to incapacitate those convicted of crimes, physically averting them from reoffending which could be applicable to AAI entities in an analogous way. Of course, in case of AI systems merely products of other AAI entities will not have personality but simply as goods will be recalled or a license revoked. In the case of an AI system, the deterrent force of a fine would affect its programming maximizing economic achievement without regard for the underlying criminal law itself. Violations of the criminal law by AI entities can be seen as errors to be debugged rather than sins to be punished and so aspect of rehabilitation can be directly applied via machine learning.[290]

Who will run a global AAI society? Will AAI states with borders, citizens, and activities analogous to conventional states exist in the distant future? It cannot be rejected in advance the emergence of robotics conquering earth and imposing a mechanical life which means that it is up to humans to tackle innovation in a human standpoint by converting life toward instigating the high spirituality of people in a way of using material to conquer spiritual life in another dimension and not having humans be ruled by mechanical robots. Will humanity produce robotics-slaves to their needs in an analogous way that human-slaves have employed in prior years or even presently humans are slaves of the economic system?

It is obvious that neither legal personality nor the coercive powers of the state are needed to certify that machine learning leads to outputs that do not violate the criminal law but the coercive powers of the state will enforce compliance with criminal law rationale.

It is characteristic that scientists want to ascribe human qualities such as moral sensibility to AAI entities on the basis of their humanoid appearance, natural language communication, or the simple fact of having been given a name.[291] Will AAI entities follow the paradigm of human scientists in the distant future by inserting other characteristics in their own AAI creatures in order to comply with the demands of the AAI society dealing with more advanced civilization concerning science and environmental problems?

---

[289] C Mulligan, "Revenge Against Robots" (2018) 69 South Carolina L Rev. 579; WR Thomas, "Incapacitating Criminal Corporations" (2019) 72 Vanderbilt L Rev. 905.

[290] MA Lemley and B Casey, "Remedies for Robots" (2019) 86 U Chicago L Rev. 1370. RA Guttman, "Effective Compliance Means Imposing Individual Liability" (2018) 5 Emory Corporate Governance and Accountability Rev. 77. 65.

[291] SM Solaiman, "Legal Personality of Robots, Corporations, Idols and Chimpanzees: A Quest for Legitimacy" (2017) 25 Artificial Intelligence and Law 174.

Is it apt in AI approximating human qualities? It is argued that AI approximating human qualities is doubtful because it has not investigated about how those qualities manifest in humans ourselves.[292] In line, the 2017 European Parliament resolution echoes a warning in an open letter that legal personality for AI would be unfitting from "an ethical and a legal perspective." On the other hand, legal status based on the natural person model essentially brings with it all the "human" rights guaranteed under EU law.[293]

Of course, in a world governed by humans, the law of humans will govern AI entities but in an AAI world then the legal personality of AAI entities will be imposed assimilated in the demands of the AAI demands and needs regardless of human's objections. In other words, the legal status of humans will be dependent on the legal status of AAI entities, AAI global governance, and AAI international law.

References

1. Alexiadis, P. & de Streel, A. (2020). *Designing an eu intervention standard for digital platforms*. Robert Schuman Centre for Advanced Studies Florence School of Regulation. RSCAS 2020/14.
2. Karayiannis, A. D., & Hatzis, A. N. (2012). Morality, social norms and the rule of law as transaction cost-saving devices: the case of ancient Athens. *Eur J Law Econ, 33*, 621–643.
3. Casey, A. J., & Niblett, A. (2017). *The death of rules and standards*, 92 Ind. L.J. 1401, 1403.
4. Scalia, A. (1989). *The rule of law as a law of rules*, 56 U. CHI. L. Rev. 1175.
5. Deeks, A. (2019). *The judicial demand for explainable artificial intelligence*, 119 Colum. L. Rev. 1829, 1832–38.
6. Bock, E. D., Wolter, J. S., & Ferrell, O. C. (2020). Artificial intelligence: disrupting what we know about services. *Journal of Service Marketing, 34*(3), 317–334.
7. Cukier, K. (2021). Commentary: How AI shapes consumer experiences and expectations. *Journal of Marketing, 85*(1), 152–155.
8. David, P. (2010). Fidler, Eastphalia emerging?: Asia, international law, and global governance. *Indiana Journal of Global Legal Studies, 17*(1), 7.
9. Volokh, E. (2019). Chief justice robots. *68 Duke Law Journal, 1135*, 1138.
10. Fuller, L. (1969). *The morality of law*. Yale University Press.
11. Zekos, G. (2012). Arbitration's status under EU law. *The Journal of World Investment and Trade, 13*, 390–419. www.brill.nl/jwit
12. Zekos, G. (2013). *Constitution, arbitration and courts*. Nova Science.
13. Zekos, G. (2019a). *Developments on courts' involvement in arbitration. Volume 1: The rule of law, Volume 2: Courts and law*. Nova Science.
14. Zekos, G. (2008). *International commercial and marine arbitration*. Routledge-Cavendish.
15. Zekos, G. (2019b). *The United States of Europe the global players*. Nova Science.
16. Arajärvi, N. (2018). The rule of law in the 2030 Agenda. *Hague Journal on the Rule of Law, 10*(1), 187–217.

[292] E Hildt, "Artificial Intelligence: Does Consciousness Matter?" (2019) 10(1535) Frontiers in Psychology, 1–3; G Meissner, "Artificial Intelligence: Consciousness and Conscience" (2020) 35 AI & Society 231.

[293] Open Letter to the European Commission: Artificial Intelligence and Robotics (April 2018) J Turner, Robot Rules: Regulating Artificial Intelligence (Palgrave Macmillan 2019).

17. Gowder, P. (2016). *The rule of law in the real world*. Cambridge University Press.
18. Fallon, R. H., Jr. (1997). "The rule of law" as a concept in constitutional discourse. *Columbia Law Review, 97*(1), 8–9.
19. Sarah, B. (2017). Lawsky, formalizing the code. *70 Tax Law Review* 377, 379.
20. Zuboff, S. (2019). *The age of surveillance capitalism: The fight for a human future at the new frontier of power*. Profile Books.
21. Ζέκος, Γ., Εξελιγμένη τεχνητή νοημοσύνη και Robo-δικαστήρια, Αρμενόπουλος 6/2021 p 1093 https://www.dsth.gr/armenopoulos-intro

Chapter 5
Politics Versus Law

5.1 Introduction

First of all, politics (πολιτικός/politikos) is the procedure of making decisions applying to all members of each group and so politics refers to accomplishing and exercising positions of governance—organized control over a human community, particularly a state. Additionally, politics is the study or practice of the distribution of power/authority and resources within a given society on top of the interrelationship (s) between societies. It is very often said that politics is about power/authority. To that extent, a political system is a framework which expresses adequate political methods within a given society. Globalization has political, social, and cultural dimensions by generating economic networks. International production networks implicate not just inter-industry or inter-company but also intra-industry and intra-company trade. To that extent, economic globalization refers to the increasing interdependence of world economies by means of the growing scale of cross-border trade of commodities and services, flow of international capital and wide and rapid spread of technologies. Moreover, the rapid growing magnitude of information in all types of productive activities and marketization are the two key driving factors for economic globalization. Hence, financial globalization and the spreading out of global capital flows bring a number of benefits such as more competent allocation of resources, enhanced risk sharing, and more swift technology transfer.[1]

It is characteristic that the framework of GATT and WTO has stirred the development of trade and investment. MNEs have become the main carriers of economic globalization by organizing production and allocating resources in line with the principle of profit maximization restructuring macroeconomic mechanisms of the function of the world economies. Globalization has brought substantial

[1] G Zekos, Monetary Policy and Risk Management in Financial Globalization, 2015 Nova Science Publications, New York, USA. www.novapublishers.com G Zekos, MNE's in 21st Century, 2016 Nova Science Publications New York USA. www.novapublishers.com

G. I. Zekos, *Political, Economic and Legal Effects of Artificial Intelligence*, Contributions to Political Science, https://doi.org/10.1007/978-3-030-94736-1_5

changes on traditional international institutions and the creation of the WTO based on the "single undertaking principle," and characterized by binding dispute resolution expanding international trade law into areas which formerly were exclusively under national jurisdiction concealing the traditional distinction between the "international" and the "domestic."

It has to be taken into account that globalization is instigated the state to wither away but globalization is overstated because the state remains in essence the same as the sovereignty influenced by new networks. Moreover, globalization brought forwards the competition state pointing a new reality, but at the same time states and governments still have a role to play. In other words, globalization and the state are not two conflicting dynamics destined to pull toward the same direction but the state has to adjust to the new environment.[2]

The key economic goal of a nation is to yield a high and rising standard of living for its citizens due to information technology. Economic globalization brought integration of national economies into the international economy through trade, foreign direct investment, capital flows and spread of technology.[3] While economic is only one of the aspects of globalization, globalization is the outcome of political will and of law.

States are sovereign and rules are only advantageous to the extent that states agree to follow them. Therefore, the need of the rule of law means that the sovereign state concedes a great deal of legal power to the law and organization that stabilizes the system. In conjunction with the upsurge of new international or transnational institutions and norms, the partial reconfiguration of the state denotes that norms "created somewhere else" influence daily life in ways which were up to that time out of the question. Law merely reflects a determinate resolution of the controversy as contemplated fitting by those who have the power and authority to resolve the issue within a specific society.[4] Legal authority is more multipart than parental authority, but it is similar in that subjects obey for the reason that an authoritative actor has said what handling is needed. People continually renegotiate their internal rules on how they should act with regard to each other on a day-to-day.

There is a need to examine the political context in which law operates. Does law apply irrespective of any political context or politics influence the appliance of law? Does politics overrule the rule of law? Is there a tendency to implement a politics of law instead of objective appliance of law? Is there a relationship between Law and politics expressed as politics of law? Has globalization influenced the rule of law and

---

[2]Ian Clark, Globalization and International Relations Theory (Oxford: Oxford University Press, 1999), pp. 89–106. Peter Dicken, Global Shift: Reshaping the Global Economic Map in the 21st Century, 4th edn. (London: The Guilford Press, 2003), p. 141.

[3]G Zekos, RISK MANAGEMENT, CORPORATE GOVERNANCE IN 21ST CENTURY DIGITAL ECONOMY 2014 Nova Science Publications, New York, USA. www.novapublishers.com G Zekos, Law and Economics of Corporate Governance and Insider Trading, 2016 Nova Science Publications New York USA. www.novapublishers.com

[4]Neil MacCormick, Institutions of Law: An Essay in Legal Theory (Oxford: Oxford University Press, 2007) 255–61.

its appliance owing to politics? What is the impact of politics upon the advancement of law and the rule of law as being implemented in national and international level?

What the law needs is a doctrinal framework for extending its conception of the corporate mind beyond the employees whose shoes algorithms are coming to fill. Psychologists and philosophers have addressed related set of issues about the human mind contending that the traditional understanding of the human mind as limited by the boundaries of the skull is too restrictive. Moreover, the so-called extended mind thesis asserts that the human mind reaches beyond the brain to comprehend external cognitive aids—like diaries or cell phones—that facilitate the brain do its work which means that if an individual can as easily "recollect" a phone number by checking "his phone's memory bank as by checking his neurological memory bank, his mind may, according to the thesis, extend to aspects of his phone."[5] It is argued that the law could and should accept that corporate minds extend to algorithms fulfilling roles that were once dominated only by human employees which mean that by extending the corporate mind in this manner, the law could bring corporate accountability into the twenty-first century.

5.2 Legal Globalization

The figure of international organizations dealing with matters of uniformity or synchronization spreads in an analogous manner with the enlargement in the number of States.[6] However, legal globalization is now central overvaluing the unity and uniformity of the global legal order, on top of its capacity to induce national legal systems.[7]

First of all, legal globalization permits for the assortment of national laws, and actually leaves them the right to be different, either by leaving whole disciplines uncovered, to be regulated by State law, or by providing exceptional derogatory measures, or else by applying techniques that abandon spaces, margins and weave networks. Nonetheless, legal globalization is a result of the materialization of problems that no national legal order can resolve on its own such as the expansion of trade and the demand for a "corpus" of rules to accompany it. There is the need to apply control over some of the sources of environmental pollution and so there is the need to legalize phenomena that evade the control of individual States, from air traffic to the use of the seas, postal transport, financial crises, etc. Therefore, there was the need to establish international criminal tribunals to pay off for the inactivity of local judges in pursuing crimes that the whole international community considers

[5] Andy Clark & David Chalmers, The Extended Mind, 59 ANALYSIS 10 (1998).

[6] A. Alesina and E. Spolaore, The Size of Nations, Cambridge London, The MIT Press, 2003, and A. Caffarena, Le organizzazioni internazionali, Bologna, Il Mulino, 2001.

[7] D.W. Drezner, The Global Governance of the Internet: Bringing the State Back In, in "Political Science Quarterly", vol. 119, n. 3, Fall 2004, pp. 477–498.

as deserving punishment. Have the established international criminal tribunals offered applicability of the rule of law or enforcement of political affairs via an international rule of law enveloped with a political color?

There is balance being established among national legal systems within the global legal order but introducing several sectoral imbalances. The variability of "international regimes" generates a different form of relativism such as sectoral rather than national aggravating reactions.[8] It has to be taken into account that the global legal order is less well equipped to foresee or resolve situations of legal uncertainty, or to keep accountable the insertion of technology in legal processes. Nevertheless, at the international level there is no authoritative final legislator to compel ex ante consideration of a technology, to assure the coherence of legal responses across domains, or to synchronize the integration of new technologies into law-making, adjudication, or enforcement practices.[9]

Which is the role of the rule of law in the global legal order? Has the rule of law applied to the global order? The answer is yes but in fact there is emergence and utilization of politics of law rather than appliance of objective law. Can globalization endure governance without government? Above the States there is now a network of sectoral governments and this network has developed incrementally and has been made possible by the need of a center and by the occurrence of a center—the UN—operating as a "forum." To that extent, Sabino Cassese[10] argues that "A unitary cosmopolitan legal system is not on the horizon nor is it perhaps among current ambitions. Instead a process is under way that affects certain positive principles and branches of law."

It is worth mentioning that while comparative law is facing the matter of what makes up a practice irreducible to the classical conception of a national "legal system" and to a general categorization of "legal families", public international law has to cope with "governance without government", and private international law has to tackle the altering meaning of the linkage between law and territory. In reality, various legal fields are today reconfiguring around several points of general agreement.[11] Bruno Latour[12] argues that there is "a passage from law as an institution to law as an enunciation." A. Riles[13] says that rather than concentrating on how global private law is or is not an objet d'art of state power, a body of private norms, or a sound legal system, there is a need to view global private law as an array of institutions, actors, doctrines, ideas, documents, that is, as a focused series of

---

[8] S. Krasner (ed.), International Regimes, Ithaca, Cornell Univ. Press, 1983 (3 rd ed. 1995).

[9] Rebecca Crootof and BJ Ard, "Structuring Techlaw" (2021) 34 Harvard Journal of Law & Technology n 1 https://papers.ssrn.com/abstract=3664124

[10] Sabino Cassese, The Globalization of Law www.ssrn.com P24.

[11] A. Riles, "Comparative Law and Socio-Legal Studies", in M. Reimann, R. Zimmermann, The Oxford Handbook of Comparative Law, Oxford, Oxford University Press, 2008, p. 799.

[12] B. Latour, La fabrique du droit. Une ethnographie du Conseil d'État, Paris, La Découverte, 2002.

[13] A. Riles, "The Anti-Network: Global private law, legal knowledge, and the legitimacy of the state", American Journal of Comparative Law, Vol. 56, No. 3, 2008; Cornell Legal Studies Research Paper No 07–025.

knowledge practices. It is worth mentioning that the old concepts of international law, which were all "state centered", are now questioned by the globalization of law.[14] To that extent, the "mobility" of the private actors is altering the notion of territoriality of law, the perception of choice of law, of public order or even the notion of legal order. On the one hand, the law of property and contract ascertains fundamental, pre-political rights that restrain the activities of states. On the other hand, private law just is one of the activities of states, to be evaluated in the same manner as any other employment of state power. To that extent, private law is only a system of reciprocal restrictions on freedom so long as those restrictions are general in the right way.

Furthermore, it is worth noting that globalization challenges the public/private distinction in particular ways. It is argued that once the state loses it privileged position, public law governing the state's relations with private parties loses its unique position regardless that traditional regulatory functions of the state are performed by private actors. Moreover, the state sees itself in competition with other states and private parties in a global market for investors starting to resemble private actors.[15]

There is a confluence of public and private international law.[16] In international investment law pairs states and investors on opposing ends having asymmetrical powers such as the state has sovereignty and the investor has assets without being clear, in terms of either power or law, which is superior.[17] Besides, the common law materializes from custom but what makes it law is its recognition by the state. Individuals are restrained not only by law but by multiple other norms. Currently, globalization challenges this distinction and the reason is not simply, as is sometimes proclaimed, a decline in the significance of the state as regulator. If anything, official laws have become more vital than they were in the past: the state regulates more and more affairs.

It is worth mentioning that globalization compels that we re-cast international law into a global public law, and open out the domain of justice from the national into the global, as the underlying normative criterion for international law. Moreover, it has to be considered that via a re-examination of central international legal doctrines and institutions such as boundaries, sovereignty, legitimacy, citizenship, and the territorial control of resources, the international law of a society of states is re-shaped into

[14] G. Lhuilier, "Analysis of Global Law", http://www.msh-paris.fr/recherche/aires-geographiques/monde/le-reseau-glsn/; or: http://www.glsn.eu

[15] T Büthe and W Mattli, New Global Rulers: The Privatization of Regulation in the World Economy (Princeton NJ, Princeton University Press, 2011). R Michaels and N Jansen, "Private Law Beyond the State. Europeanization, Globalization, Privatization" (2006) 54 American Journal of Comparative Law 845.

[16] JA Maupin, "Public and Private in International Investment Law: An Integrated Systems Approach."(2013) 53 Virginia Journal of International Law.

[17] A Mills, The Confluence of Public and Private International Law (Cambridge: Cambridge University Press 2009); H Muir Watt, "Private International Law Beyond the Schism" (2011) 2 Transnational Legal Theory 347.

the global public law of a global institute. Presently, the lack of democratic participation and legitimacy, lack of distributive justice, lack of basic welfare rights and security characterize international law and institutions. Also, globalization is altering the character of global social relations by producing the basis for both society and community at the global level. It has to be considered that from viewpoint of political theory, globalization is lifting relationships out of the closely territorial into the "global" or meta-territorial era. Thus, the political and legal consequence of this alteration is important and central: as the space in which social relations are handled transform the way of regulating those relations as well. To that extent to be effective, regulatory decisions have to progressively entangle the meta-state level.

The globalization of the law is a development of the twentieth and twenty-first centuries and the rules governing the interpretation of international treaties are to be found in articles 31 and 32 of the Vienna Convention on the Law of Treaties. Moreover, the crucial rule is contained in article 31(1) which stipulates that a treaty shall be interpreted in good faith in line with the ordinary meaning to be given to the terms of the treaty in their context and in the light of its object and rationale.

Furthermore, international law and norms formed in the international arena have effect on almost every legal area from human rights law to intellectual property rights, trade, taxation, labor, environmental law, criminal law, government procurement, governance, etc. Similarly, there is a mounting stimulus by the international field on national policy and the internal conduct of the state. It has to be considered that most areas of law were internal state matters and not subject to state to state relations. Nowadays, in many of law areas, there are agreements on a state to state level, expanding the responsibilities of states toward each other. Nowadays intellectual property rights, human rights, environmental, labor, and criminal laws are influenced by some form of international regime or norm and so many of the international norms no longer have the form of general statements, which are broadly interpreted, and fashioned to affect the national policy when applied nationally. To that extent, the international norms are similar to the one in national legislation and regulations, recording details of the issues, leaving the national legislature with very little guiding prospects, if at all. In other words, there is a convergence among national and international norms in various areas of law due to global policy which means that there is interplay among them.

Globalization has forced states to adjust to these modifications in international law. States realize today that many matters that were customarily counted as pertaining to national jurisprudence and policy have now augmented to the international level. Moreover, there are many sorts of international agreements, many of which launch international obligations, embracing duties for variations of national legislation and so any alterations the state has to produce in its national legislation or policy or in its state to state commitments are the result of the state's positive decision to enter into the agreement. Therefore, globalization and increasing interdependency is varying this reality more and more which means that a state has to enter into a new international agreement or accede to an existing one, if a state wants to stay a worthwhile player in the embryonic global community in economic globalization. In other words, the state may not be able to affect the norms set forth in the agreement which means having to put up with those norms "as is" resulting in a requirement to perform alterations in the national legislation and policy in specific fields that if not might not have been contemplated by the state. Owing to the globalization and escalating interdependency, states often are left with no option on whether to join these organizations or not. Hence, there is a growing significance of international and transnational law in the international arena in forming the norms and practices of states in globalization.

The expansion of international law and organizations is a remarkable development of globalization. The European Union has been in the forefront of legalizing inter-state relations, to the point where the national and inter-state legal structures in Europe are broadly undividable. On the other hand, nowadays the undertaking to assemble logic has brought international relations to the intersection of politics and law. Political parties are based on the performance and undertaking of national politicians on national matters such as war and peace, monetary policy, and deficit spending.

Explicit barriers to international trade, investment, technology, and financial flows have been reduced considerably due to globalization. International rules agreed-upon by governments for the principal actors in international production and markets supplement the unilateral rules that occur at the national level. Such international rules set the parameters for specific qualities of the cross-border doings of companies stipulating the global governance for functioning in the global production and trading areas. Developing international micro-regulatory frameworks of rules for the global operations of companies in the globalizing world economy is the new edge of international commercial diplomacy which means that a new rule of law is emerging.

The international system lacks the standard by which we consider national legal systems in terms of the legitimacy and enforceability of law. Economic rules are frequently contested concerning enforcement mechanisms and some international treaties are referred to as "soft law" which means that they depend on the political will of states for enforcement.[18] Moreover, diplomats and the bureaucrats of intergovernmental economic governance institutions such as the WTO have been unenthusiastic to refer to the embryonic system of rules as law. Yet in the modern WTO, there is an effort to circumvent the juridical and legal development and so dispute settlement reports do not generate precedent in the manner that courts do in the national jurisdiction.

It is worth noting that an AI system at the level of global institutions such as WTO, OECD, and UN will undertake the matter of the dissemination of technological advances and capabilities to less developed economies. Additionally, global issues such as climate change or energy supply disruptions can be tackled and so there needs to be a global AI competency that is the outcome of cooperation and contributions from individual states.

[18]Dunoff, J.L. and M.A. Pollack (2013), "International law and international relations," in J.L. Dunoff and M.A. Pollack (eds).

5.3 The Advancement of Law

First of all, law is not mere singularity but also it is about unity in coherent wholes. Thus, law is about system, order and discipline and the very raison d'être of the nation-State is legal unity. Napoleon created the Civil Code in order to unite France in law. Cosmopolitan law is about the forces of legal convergence and divergence coming into one. Also, cosmopolitan law is not promoted by States but it is driven by citizens. The world of post-modernity is characterized by insecurity, choice, and indeterminacy. However, cosmopolitan law functions in a close-to-chaotic postmodern setting of global political alliances, economic interests and at-many-times intrinsically centrifugal legal realities. Furthermore, cosmopolitan law has to provide for a new sense of global justice which means that global justice must be served by global institutions. It has to be taken into consideration that the death of the nation State is not an option regardless of the emergence of more powerful movements and there is rise of cosmopolitan law.[19] The cosmopolitan in law does not confirm the democratic successes of the nation State which means that the establishment of cosmopolitan institutions does not come with democratic assurance.[20]

Furthermore, the law has an internal or external meaning. Internally, people can naturally decide for themselves how to act enabling them to lead their day-to day lives. The internal rules of life continually advance with everyday occurrences. Moreover, the internal rules that a person will acquire will stem from the way in which they construct the world around them. Nevertheless, the law is external when the rules that are directed toward them are not made by them, but come from an outside source, such as the statutes of a legislature, or the common law of the courts. In spite of this, what both internal and external forms have in common is that they regularize the association between the subject and the other in their world.

The substance of law is to legalize the relationship between the being and the other in their world, external rules do this by positing the rules that people need so as to accomplish their existential lives together. Moreover, the law has a constructive essence. Whether it is internal or external, it lets people to make sense of their own world offering them with a context in which they comprehend/understand their existential nature, which is to master their world.

It has to be taken into consideration that law has to be understood not only in terms of its own "internal dynamic," but also in empirical, critical and complex interplay of causes and effects.[21] To that extent rules of custom and local legal

[19] Stone Sweet A. A Cosmopolitan Legal Order: Constitutional Pluralism and Rights Adjudication in Europe // Global Constitutionalism. 2012. No. 1.. Ruddall J. A Cartography of Cosmopolitanism: Particularising the Universal // Cambridge Journal of International and Comparative Law. 2014. No. 3.

[20] Dibadj R. Postmodernism, Representation, Law // University of Hawai'i Law Review. 2006–2007. Vol. 29.

[21] Richard Abel, "Law and Society: Project and Practice" (2010) 6 Annual Review of Law and Social Science 1.

processes are favored over and above formal legal institutions visualized under liberal notions and positivist thinking in justice delivery mechanisms.[22] There is consideration to norms with the emergence of "soft law" or rules of conduct which supposedly are not legally binding but which nonetheless have practical and even legal effects. Codes of conduct were developed progressively by private actors, not by international organizations, both as codes among private actors and codes internal to private actors transforming global and corporate governance. Compared to hard law, soft law has the advantages of lower contracting costs and lower sovereignty costs tailored to conditions of uncertainty or those demanding compromise.[23]

It has to be taken into account that primary rules are the most fundamental type of law embedded in custom or generalized practice. Besides, secondary rules build upon the first set stipulating for operations to the creation or variation of duties or obligations. To that extent, secondary rules generate, modify, alter or negate primary rules in particular conditions.

Can soft law offer the most favorable institutional design for governing sensitive matters such as working conditions, human rights, or protection of the environment? The widespread arrays of standards are produced by international standards organizations and other institutions are not legally binding. International standards organizations apply noteworthy powers of "governance without government" gaining their international leverage from their gate-keeping role.

Legalization of rules infers a discourse mainly in terms of the text, reason, and history of the rules, their interpretation, admissible exceptions, applicability to classes of situations, and specific facts. Moreover, "Legalization" refers to specific physiognomies that institutions may or may not have and so these physiognomies are outlined along three dimensions: obligation, precision, and delegation. Firstly, obligation means that countries or other players are constrained by a rule or commitment or by a set of rules or commitments which means that they are legally compelled by a rule or commitment in the viewpoint that their behavior there under is subject to inspection under the general rules, processes, and discourse of international law, and often of national law too. Secondly, precision means that rules explicitly describe the conduct they need, approve, or proscribe. Thirdly, delegation means that third parties have been given authority to apply, interpret, and utilize the rules; to resolve disputes; and probably to make supplementary rules. To that extent, statutes or regulations in developed national legal systems are taken as archetypal of hard legalization.

To that extent, Hart[24] described a legal system as the concurrence of primary and secondary rules. Primary rules are rules of obligation bearing directly on individuals or entities demanding them "to do or abstain from certain actions." Besides,

[22] Tanja Chopra, "Dispensing Elusive Justice: The Kenyan Judiciary amongst Pastoralist Societies" (2010) 2 Hague Journal on the Rule of Law 95.

[23] Abbott, K.W. and Snidal, D.: "Hard law and soft law in international governance," International Organization, 54, 2000, pp. 421–456.

[24] H. L. A. Hart's The Concept of Law.2 Hart 1961.

secondary rules are "rules about rules"—that is, rules that do not "impose obligations," but as an alternative "confer powers" to generate, extinguish, adjust, and apply primary rules. On the other hand, it could be said that a vital quality of legalization is the flexibility of each of its three dimensions, and so the by and large legalization of international norms, agreements, and governments.

It is worth mentioning that legalization has three dimensions: the existence of legal obligations, the accuracy with which these obligations are identified, and the extent to which responsibility for dispute resolution is entrusted to third parties. Each dimension is a continuum, composed of differences of degree, and each differs separately of the others. Particular norms or specific procedures are more or less legalized. To that extent interstate dispute resolution and transnational dispute resolution as two idyllic types, differing in independence from actual state interests, admittance by parties other than states and embeddedness in the awareness that decisions can be implemented without governmental action. It could be said that the transnational dispute resolution is more thriving than interstate dispute resolution in controlling case loads and making certain compliance.

The legislature sets how within its jurisdiction people should behave with regard to others. The legislature will advance laws to allow people to live together. In other words, the legislature will settle the desires of all people to create their own world. With respect to the normative sphere, ethics are focused on the meanings and elements of social goods, stemming from several breaches, disturbances, or disorientations in familiar ethical habits and prospects.[25]

Internal or external rules are renegotiated on a day-to-day basis which means that as people come across new experiences and dialogues, the values they give to things will adjust.[26] To that extent, the legislature will have to enact external rules in order to make certain that all people carry on making their own individual point of the world around them. Thus, the external rules empower a person to accomplish their reason to be consisting of those norms that the legislature has acknowledged as indispensable to allow people to lead their lives together.[27] Legislature should be able to enforce these rules and it is also vital that these laws are adjudicated in line with the general spirit of the community for the reason that external rules that a community develops are an essential part of an individual's identity. Hence, the goal of any law, whether internal or external, is to make possible a person to make sense of the world around them. Although people do this internally by making their own rules, the legislature interferes to advance these if the fights between people become too much. Nevertheless, in all cases, the purpose is to permit people to survive.

---

[25] Critchley, S. Ethics, Politics, Subjectivity. London: Verso, 1997.

[26] Mill, J. S. On Liberty. London: Penguin Books, 1974, p. 59–60; Berlin, I. Two Concepts of Liberty. Four Essays on Liberty. Oxford: University Press, 1969; Ed. Hardy, H. Liberty: Incorporating "Four Essays on Liberty: Isaiah Berlin". Oxford: University Press, 2002.

[27] Hegel, G. W. F. (translated by Dyde, S.W.), Philosophy of Right. New York: Dover Publications, 2005; Jessie Allen, A Theory of Adjudication: Law as Magic, 41 Suffolk U.L. Rev. 773, 811 (2008) (noting that in the ritual of trial, "[n]orms and values ... become saturated with emotion, while the gross and basic emotions become ennobled through contact with social values").

Due to globalization in interpreting any of its external national rules, not just those take on further to positive international law the states take into consideration national values and international ones as well which means that there is a need for striking a balance between national and global values. To that extent, states cannot abandon its national values altogether but there is a need to make certain that the national identity is preserved with an adjustment in accordance with the greater global culture in order to escape tensions evolving from an existential anguish.[28]

It is characteristic that "legal pluralism" gets across the reality of a diversity of legal cultures within a society. Thus, globalization and pluralism instruct an understanding of tension generating more inclusive legal knowledge constructive to a diversity of social communities. As globalization prolongs, nations face the challenge of balancing the necessities for global competitiveness against the internal pressure to uphold the cultural identity of the region generating interesting challenges for law and legal structure. The developments in Australia, a federation, were provoked by two High Court decisions[29] and globalization influences the advance of law in nations including the USA, Australia, and in the supra-national body that is the EU. To that extent, translating and converting policy into law is a complex course which means that the external pressures of globalization have to be squared with the internal pressure to make certain that legal advances are in line with the legal culture of the nation state. Moreover, while "legal culture" includes its own definitional and abstract problems, it does grant a device for classifying a variety of phenomena upsetting the function of law in society embracing the thoughts, wishes, and ideas of members of society, both generally and particularly.

As an alternative, the distinction begins to disintegrate for the reason that the criteria used in legal positivism to define what should count as law are becoming dubious. Legal positivism calls for an unquestioned starting point such as a constitution, a sovereign people and this starting point is tied to the state. Moreover, there is a need to rationalize this very starting point becoming aware that the starting point itself is a fabrication of the law, not just its forerunner. The result is that we have to comprehend law and society as being mutually constitutive: law is shaped by and in society, but law also generates society in the way in which we find it. In other words, law and politics are shaped by society and both serve the society but the problem is which is superior in a way that the other has to follow in order to have an agreed order bringing equality and justice.

It is worth noting that Constitutions are an instance at which law, politics, philosophy, ideology, and religion are amalgamated. On the one hand, Constitution is regarded as a disclosed set of higher laws, albeit on one level people know realistically it is not, but then again, the Constitution is made into something comparable to "Moses' Tablets brought down from the mountain." On the other

[28] Habremas, J. The Inclusion of the Other: Studies in Political Theory. Ed. Cronin, C.; De Greiff, P. Cambridge: Polity Press, 2005, p. 124–125,, Grotius, H. On the Laws of War and Peace. Kessinger Publishing, 2004; Kant, I. PerpetualPeace. New York: Cosimo Books, 2005.

[29] Re Wakim; Ex Parte McNally (1999) 198 CLR 511. R v Hughes (2000) 171 ALR 155.

hand, this fiction is created by the political and legal part of society's reality and society has decided to handle it as true. Besides, the Constitution has to be considered that it is representing a dynamic course implemented through adaptive interpretation or endorsements. It could be said that the predicament of law in modern society is that people retain belief in the immanence of law, in its superiority to individual, temporary needs and so a whole-hearted modern belief in law's instrumentality is assumed.[30] Moreover, it could be said that the fiction of a higher law exemplified in the Constitution is both a conscientious and abstract set of choices with momentous consequences for how the political order functions because the choice of the wording of the articles of the constitution is not only a pure legal decision but also it implicates the political order incorporated by the authors of the constitutional text and so instigated via the constitution's implementation and interpretation. It seems that there is a need not to abandon the belief that the Constitution is a source of natural law because it might lead to even greater factionalism than we are undergoing nowadays.[31]

Legal thought has acted in response to globalization not with a real move but instead by progressive attempts to become accustomed to the methodological nationalism that has provided its paradigm for the last hundred years or so. On the other hand, globalization poses interdisciplinary challenges, and inter-disciplinarity in law and globalization is still lacking by disregarding or downplaying the law as an imperative factor further than an occasional indicate agreement to international law. To that extent, a prevalent understanding of globalization recognizes three features such as economics, culture, and politics which means that law is absent.[32] In legal thinking seems that globalization is either simply absent or emerges as a minimal idea of internationalization that in some way affects the law. Alternatively, legal theory and doctrine have functioned with basic concepts of globalization.[33]

According to common law legal rules occur from the decisions the courts reach and the reasoning they utilize in the course of resolving specific disputes. Moreover, the course of rule formation is by no means entirely unprompted resting on the meta-rule of "precedent," or stare decisis: similar cases have to be decided correspondingly being both a principle of justice, inferring equal treatment under the law, and a basis for allowing the law to advance in response to social alteration. To that extent, the doctrine of precedent is multi-functional permitting both for the establishment of legal rules and also for their amendment. Karl Llewellyn argues that the common law

[30]Daniel Boorstin, The Decline of Radicalism 76 (1969) "How continue to believe that something about our law is changeless after we have discovered that it may be infinitely plastic? How believe that in some sense the basic laws of society are given us by God, after we have become convinced that we have given them to ourselves."

[31]David Barnhizer, "Natural Law as Practical Methodology: A Finnisian Analysis of City of Richmond v. Croson," 38 Cleveland St. L. Rev. 15 (1990).

[32]D Held, A McGrew, D Goldblatt, J Perraton, Global Transformations: Politics, Economics, and Culture (Stanford, Stanford University Press 1999) 14–28.

[33]W Twining, General Jurisprudence—Understanding Law from a Global Perspective (Cambridge, Cambridge University Press 2009).

doctrine of precedent by some means achieves "at once stability and change."[34] There is a specific complex trade-off between the adaptability and autonomy of the common law. It is argued that the common law is a "catallaxy" for the reason that rules develop unexpectedly from the decisions of courts deciding specific cases and it is supposed that the law is developed via a legal analysis and the need of the emerging rules which of course serve the social needs of the people which is a political standpoint as well.

While legal change is frequently a matter of chance, the direction which the law takes is coordinated in a more organized manner by the path on which existing decisions have formerly set it due to political and social prevailing conditions. Lord Macmillan[35] argues that the law adjusts due to social conditions and standards' changes which means that the "legal principle must adjust and adapt itself to the changing circumstances of life." In other words, the law's autonomy, that is to say, its parting from the political and economic environment, is weakened/undermined/ undercut.

Does common law produce objective law? Does civil law by legislation produce objective law? Is there subjectivity in both systems adding to the politics of law? Is there in fact a politics of law in an away to apply some rules or interpretations in order society to follow specific direction based on ethics, norms or social life imposed to society by the economic elite?

Any legal system has to have standards/principles for judging what is a legal rule and what is not in order to discern between legal norms, on the one hand, and social or economic, policy on the other, because there is a need to maintain the continuity of the legal order. A new rule, an "alteration," is chosen for survival if it is one which is explicated in terms of established doctrinal structures of juridical thought. To that extent, finding a doctrinal justification for a new rule and preserving the autonomy of juridical thought in the face of external political or social forces are two sides of the same coin.[36]

There is a need to understand the integrating of the total system of law and not merely mechanically dealing with specialized compartments of law and doctrine. It has to be considered that the "law" and "legal system" are not one-dimensional when it comes to purposes, substance, and procedure. On the other hand, the political systems epitomized by terms such as "law" and "legal system" are complex and organic structures packed with technical, moral, religious and society data, objectives and substance. Besides, some doctrines operate as rules that serve as the system's basis making available the large-scale structure while some serve as the internal structure of parts of the system.

In addition, there is a need to permit the law maximum flexibility to adjust to social change. Since a legal rule is formed there is a need to be applied objectively without any political intervention in order to be applied objectively which does not

[34] K. Llewellyn, The Bramble Bush (New York, Oceana: 1930).

[35] Donoghue v. Stevenson [1932] AC 562. 619.

[36] Donoghue v. Stevenson [1932] AC 562. 619 per Lord Buckmaster.

mean that the new legal rule will not be formed in a way influenced by political and social changes via globalization. Who decides the social change? Does a change intact with the interests of the prevailing economic elite?

As mentioned earlier, the common law method is designed by the meta-rule or doctrine of precedent, which has itself advanced, but is a basis of stabilization indeed for the reason that of the consistency it compels on judicial decision-making. To that extent, systems which merge the surfacing legal order of judge-made law with periodic statutory interferences have an evolutionary lead over those which are dependent entirely on the courts. On the other hand, judge made law might have less political direct interference rather than statutory law which might serve directly the political interests of a prevailing group promoting their political affairs via a government's legislature. In practice all legal systems of developed states, whether of common law or civil legal origin, conjoin judge-made law with codes or statutes in some manner or another. The common law is characteristically more prospective to generate rules which favor the interests of well-resourced litigants and repeat players such as insurers and business companies than those of society overall.[37] It could be said that courts should formulate judge-made doctrinal principles.

Common law as judge-made law systems are, in fact, noticeably shaped by legislative norms, while judicial innovation is, equally, a weighty issue in the development of private law and commercial law in civil law systems. However, common law and civil law methods of reasoning are no identical but merely we have no undoubted justifications for considering that common law methods are essentially superior to those of the civil law in reinforcing/supporting economic development and growth.[38]

On the one hand, legal rules are expected to be adaptive in the logic of assisting communal coordination. On the other hand, common law rules are adaptive to their setting or circumstance, but ineffective rules may stay,[39] and disequilibria are engendered by lock-in consequences internally and externally which means that within common law systems, rectification of error through legislation is often required, albeit that legislation, sequentially, is often merely an incentive for an extra development of case law. In other words, Common law and civil law systems are all, partially, hybrids in which case law work along with codes and statutes.

It is worth mentioning that two inter-related mechanisms function through which legal origin inspire finance, etc. Firstly, the "political" contraption underlines that (a) legal traditions vary in terms of the priority they assign to private property vis-à-vis the rights of the State and (b) the protection of private contracting rights

[37] M. Galanter, "Why the 'haves' come out ahead: speculation on the limits of legal change" (1974) 9 Law and Society Review 95–151.

[38] J. Armour, S. Deakin, P. Lele and M. Siems, 'How do legal rules evolve? Evidence from a cross-country comparison of shareholder, creditor and worker protection" (2009) 57 American Journal of Comparative Law 579–630.

[39] See Concerning Bills Of Lading Precedent G Zekos, Judicial Analysis Of The Contractual Role Of Bills Of Lading As It Stands In Greek, United States And English Law, Phd Thesis, Hull Law School Https://Hydra.Hull.Ac.Uk/Resources/Hull:8290.

materializes the center of financial development.[40] Secondly, the "adaptability" contraption underlines that (a) legal traditions fluctuate in their formalism and capacity to advance with shifting conditions and (b) legal traditions adjust competently to diminish the gap between the contracting requirements of the economy and the legal system's potential cultivate financial development than more inflexible systems.[41]

Courts have to enforce private contracts fairly and have both the aptitude and willingness to deal with multipart contracts and substantiate technically complex clauses generating explicit actions. Hayek[42] says that Emperor Justinian employed two substantive modifications in comparison with Roman law. Firstly, while Roman law placed the law above all individuals, the Justinian texts placed the emperor above the law. It could be argued that Justinian tried to abolish the employment of the rule of law and implying a more political utilization of the law by the interests of the Emperor. Secondly, Justinian broke with Roman law by trying to abolish jurisprudence. Roman law had produced over centuries on a case-by-case basis, modifying according to the requirements of a community to the requests of a world empire with only a minor role left for formal legislation. Justinian altered this doctrine and "... asserted for himself a monopoly, not only over all law-making power, but over legal interpretations"[43] but jurisprudence continued to mold the law. Of course, the French Revolution put the State above the courts abolishing jurisprudence. Codification under Napoleon backed the unification and strengthening of the State downgrading judges to a minor, bureaucratic role. Moreover, in line with the theory underlying the French Civil Code, the legislature drafts laws without gaps, so judges do not make law by interpreting existing laws. On the other hand, the legislature does draft conflicting laws, so that judges do make law by choosing between laws.

Like Justinian, Napoleon required a code that was so apparent, complete, and consistent that there would be no necessity for judges to consider about which laws, customs, and past experiences apply to new, embryonic situations. It could be said that it is chosen the approach that the political head leads the legal development without the need for implementation and law making based on the employment of the laws by courts and the legal system. In addition, this approach needed a high degree of procedural formalism to lessen the freedom of choice of judges in regulating the presentation of evidence, witnesses, arguments, and appeals.[44] Besides, German legal history favored jurisprudence rejecting France's approach

[40] La Porta, R., Lopez-de-Silanes, F., Shleifer, A., Vishny, R.W., 1999. The Quality of Government. Journal of Law and Economic Organization 15, 222–279.

[41] Merryman, J.H., 1985. The Civil Law Tradition: An Introduction to the Legal Systems of Western Europe and Latin America. Stanford University Press, Stanford.

[42] Hayek, F., 1960. The Constitution of Liberty. The University of Chicago Press, Chicago, IL.

[43] Dawson, J. P., 1968. The Oracles of the Law. University of Michigan Law School, Ann Arbor, MI (Reprinted in 1986 by William S. Hein & Co., Inc. Buffalo, New York).

[44] Schlesinger, R., Baade, H., Damaska, M., Herzog, P., 1988. Comparative Law. Case-Text-Materials. (New York, NY: The Foundation Press, Inc.).

which means that the German Code does not get rid of prior law put simply codifies those principles of German law that surface from meticulous historical study of the German legal system.[45] In addition, the power of the law vis-à-vis the State, the courts in England were viewed more positively and as supporters of progressive improvement, so that judges were given greater discretion.

In terms of legal formalism, English law compels less rigid and formalistic rations on the presentation of evidence, witnesses, etc., and instead offers judges greater autonomy.[46] In terms of jurisprudence, the English common law tradition is equal with judges having broad interpretation powers and with courts shaping and generating law as state of affairs change. The question to be answered is if the judges' alteration and law-making is based on legal terms or on political terms in order to support the new politically prevailing cast against any legal justification. The common law is preoccupied with facts and deciding concrete cases, rather than holding to the logical principles of codified law.

The political contraption is based on firstly on the fact that legal traditions vary in the weight they place on protecting the rights of private investors in relation to the rights of the State and secondly on the fact that private property rights protection materializes the foundation for financial development. Consequently, firm differences in legal origin make clear existing disparities in financial development along with the viewpoint of the law and finance.[47] Moreover, the political contraption supports that the Civil law maintains the rights of the State, rather than private property rights, to a greater degree than the Common law with undesirable inferences for financial development. It is supposed that judges are freer to follow law making on principles of law rather than legislature that it is influenced by the governmental policy but in reality, both players can be more legalistic and less politically influenced in the process of law making or be influenced indirectly by their agents that they appoint them. The more important is the implementation of the endorsed law in any case without any political influence to the detriment of justice and the rule of law.

It is argued that in civil law countries, the State grants judges' tenure by giving court's jurisdiction over cases concerning the government, or permitting judicial review of the constitutionality of laws.[48] Moreover, it is mentioned that a civil legal tradition is taken as a proxy for the aim to build institutions to advance the power of the State[49] which means that an authoritative State with a responsive civil law at its

[45] Merryman, J.H., 1985. The Civil Law Tradition: An Introduction to the Legal Systems of Western Europe and Latin America. Stanford University Press, Stanford, CA.

[46] Schlesinger, R., Baade, H., Damaska, M., Herzog, P., 1988. Comparative Law. Case-Text-Materials. (New York, NY: The Foundation Press, Inc.).

[47] La Porta, R., Lopez-de-Silanes, F., Shleifer, A., Vishny, R.W., 1999. The Quality of Government. Journal of Law and Economic Organization 15, 222–279.

[48] La Porta, R., Lopez-de-Silanes, F., Pop-Eleches, C., Shleifer, A., 2003. Judicial checks and balances. National Bureau of Economic Research Working Paper 9775.

[49] La Porta, R., Lopez-de-Silanes, F., Shleifer, A., Vishny, R.W., 1999. The Quality of Government. Journal of Law and Economic Organization 15, 222–279.

disposal redirects the flow of society's resources toward favored ends, which is antithetical to competitive financial markets, etc. On the other hand, it seems that states favor financial markets in order to advance their economies via the legislation of privileged laws.

Incompetent laws are contested in the courts, so that the process of litigation and re-litigation advances the efficiency of the law.[50] Quite the opposite, legal systems that discard jurisprudence essentially count on statutory law changes to update and adjust the law. Moreover, statutory law is slow and costly to modify, so that the lack of jurisprudence deters the efficiency with which laws adjust to altering setting.[51] Besides, courts are expected to comply with the review of constitutional amendment than replacement which means that courts comply with their decisions when they involve in broad interventions in other parts of the polity demanding cooperation with other institutions. Courts' active role in refining politics in line makes it more probable that political actors will value their review of constitutional amendments.[52] In other words, there is an interrelation between law-making and politics in order to have the rightful law complying with the polity demands of the society. Moreover, constitutional interpretation is a unique endeavor/venture which is taken for granted by legal professionals. Moreover, constitutional law is issue to distinct interpretive methods as linked to other sources of law, such as statutes and common-law precedents.[53]

Anyway, the Constitution is not essentially more fixed in practice than all other sources of law.[54] It has to be taken into consideration that the Constitution is specially legitimated which means that it justifies unique interpretive treatment for the reason that it is prepared and ratified through a procedure designed to guarantee that it enjoyed prevalent public support reflecting the whole political approach of a state.[55] Besides, the Constitution diverges from other sources of law because it is written using broad terms so that it could undergo well beyond the classic life of a statute.[56] All legitimate interpretation of the Constitution is categorized as either doctrinal, historical, or what he called responsive.[57] The Constitution as a whole is

[50] Pistor, K., Keinan, Y., Kleinheisterkamp, J., West, M.D., 2002. The evolution of corporate law. University of Pennsylvania Journal of International Economics and Law 23, 791–871.

[51] Bailey, M. J., Rubin, P. H., 1994. A positive theory of legal change. International Review of Law and Economics 14, 467–477, December 1994.

[52] Lee Epstein, Jack Knight & Olga Shvetsova, The Role of Constitutional Courts in the Establishment and Maintenance of Democratic Systems of Government, 35 L. & Soc'y Rev. 117, 156 (2001).

[53] District of Columbia v. Heller, 554 U.S. 570, People v. Nutt, 677 N.W.2d 1, 6 (Mich. 2004).

[54] William Baude, Is Originalism Our Law?, 115 Colum. L. Rev. 2349, 2355 (2015).

[55] Christopher Serkin, Public Entrenchment Through Private Law: Binding Local Governments, 78 U. Chi. L. Rev. 879, 882 (2011).

[56] Bruce Ackerman, We The People, Volume 3: The Civil Rights Revolution (2014) Shelby County v. Holder, 133 S.Ct. 2612, 2631 (2013).

[57] Robert Post, Theories of Constitutional Interpretation, 30 Representations 13, 19 (1990).Jeffrey A. Pojanowski, Statutes in Common Law Courts, 91 Tex. L. Rev. 479, 482–83 (2013).

subject to particular interpretive steps that are not validated by features or attributes of the Constitution as a whole.[58]

Taking into consideration the emergence of cyberspace and its significance in all aspects of social life within globalization, national legislators have chosen to intervene in regulating cyberspace. Accordingly, law of global application has been caught between nation-centered politics and economics. Minimum level of regulation is applied in the area of ecommerce law playing a dominant role in trade itself nowadays.[59] Furthermore, existent law takes in the area of interest of cyberspace matters such as contract law responding successfully not in all occasions needing some amendments in order to apply rightfully. To that extent, the involvedness of cyberspace applications presently is regulated, whilst in other parts of the world is little regulated or not regulated at all.

Nonetheless, a minimum degree of regulation is needed not only at a national level but also at the global level. Information law, data-protection law, and freedom of information as a whole as well as the right to cyberspace entrée are perceived as these areas of e-law should be structured on a national basis. Considering that technology and innovation are a central element of globalization, it has to be answered how national standards fit in the global phenomenon of technological development which means that there is a need for international regulation of some cyberspace' legal matters such as jurisdiction, applicable law, etc.[60]

According to the traditional private international law cyberspace' matters can merely be regulated by choice of law clauses. The "freedom of contract doctrine approach" and the private international law suggest that such matters are matters falling within the domain of national sovereignty. On the one hand, the "freedom of contract" approach does not give us an answer as to how inter-national matters are controlled in an international approach. On the other hand, the "national sovereignty" approach comes from the domain of public law which means that e-traders cannot involve with the territory and the imperium of States in international e-Commerce matters in the substance that e-commerce deals involve many jurisdictions at once causing problems of forum shopping, etc. Certainly, international trade matters are typically dealt at the national level of litigation but that alone does not solve the dispute being a mere portrayal of the present status quo. It could be argued that national sovereignty plays an inconsequential role having little to offer to traders in the area of international e-Commerce.

E-commerce platforms may be able to leverage their intermediary position to gather information about commercial transactions on either side of the two-sided

[58] Larry Alexander & Emily Sherwin, Demystifying Legal Reasoning 221–22 (2008). Burwell v. Hobby Lobby Stores, Inc., 134 S. Ct. 2751, 2772 (2014).

[59] Lim Y.F., Cyberspace Law: Commentaries and Materials (OUP 2007). Forder J. and Svantesson D., Internet and E-Commerce Law (OUP 2007).

[60] Goldman D.B., Globalization and the Western Legal Tradition: Recurring Patterns of Law and Authority (Cambridge University Press 2007) 25.

market they facilitate. Hence, relying on predictive algorithms, they may be able to engineer demand through targeted advertising.[61]

5.4 The Rule of Law

Primarily, law was accepted as the principle/rationale upon which authorities based their power in order to govern the society and so introducing the use of the rule of law in dealing with all matters of human life. Thus, the sine qua non of "law" has neither connection with nor responsiveness to social need but in fact the enforcement of legal rules, unrelatedly of content for without this quality it is not law which means that the role of law is neutral depending on the way in which it is used and the interests it aims to serve. Shihata[62] defines the "rule of law" as "understood generally to indicate that decisions should be made by the application of known principles or laws without the intervention of discretion in their application." Moreover, in the twelfth- and thirteenth-century English laws were utilized to confine the power of Monarchs accrediting "constitutionalization" to the Massachusetts Constitution of 1780 in which a separation of powers was established so as to make certain a government of "laws not men."[63] In other words, it could be said that law is a definite social occurrence which, supported by an independent judiciary, indicates the likelihood of operative control over arbitrary state action and the degree of predictability.[64] Thus, the rule of law establishes the formal equality of citizens embracing a vision of government under the forms of law and law in the form of clearly identifiable rules. It could be said that the rule of law is founded on law being a product of will serving a reason.

It could be said that the rule of law exists when the law is publicly known, applies equally to ordinary citizens and rulers, and where all are free to test and observe that universal application. To that extent, politics cannot prohibit or manipulate the ordinary application of the law according to who is under consideration and due to the political affairs of state or political ambitions of economic elites upon the outcome of a particular case. The rule of law means equality. Can the rule of law mean equality per occasion or constantly applicable? The rule of law occurs in a society when government officials and the populace are generally compelled by and accept law. Thus, to not violate the law means not acting contrary to legal obligations, which is likely even without certain knowledge of the law. A society in which

[61] Przemysław Pałka, "Algorithmic Central Planning: Between Efficiency and Freedom" (2020) 83 Law and Contemporary Problems 125. Joseph Stiglitz, "The Revolution of Information Economics: The Past and the Future" NBER Working Paper Nr 23780 (2017).

[62] Ibrahim Shihata, The World Bank in a Changing World (Dordrecht: Martinus Nijhoff, 1991) 87.

[63] Ibrahim Shihata, "The Role of Law in Business Development" (1996–97) 20 Fordham Journal of International Law 157.

[64] Beverley Brown and Neil MacCormick "Philosophy of Law" in E. Craig (ed.), Routledge Encyclopedia of Philosophy (London: Routledge, 1998).

the populace and government officials are generally compelled by and put up with law gives rise to an individual and collective sense of security and trust. Therefore, individuals in advanced capitalist societies carry out their daily affairs wholly supported by an expected legal environment that offers them with a feel of security in their social, cultural, economic, and political affairs.[65] The function of law is to preserve social order through the integration of society.

It is argued that the rule of law is a covered and differential process in which unequal qualities and practices reconcile which means that it is comprehended differentially by various groups in society, echoing the landscape of power relations and structural inequalities and so this is just in democracies with stable legal, judicial, and law enforcement orders. In other words, in places where confrontation among elites to being law-bound is never far from the surface and so competing welfares in practice result in some people's rights surpassing those of others. In line, it seems that constitutional reforms are often believed to be vital junctures empowering such game-changing courses. It is questionable how drastically constitutional reforms reflect or establish new orientations in the exercise of authority and in the terms of state–society relations fluctuate a lot, as does the scale to which competing actors perceive them as significant "sites of political contestation." It is worth noting here that law as a "site of contestation" is demonstrated in the examples of women activists and feminist lawyers engaging tactically with constitutional reform and transitional justice legislation.[66]

The principle of the rule of law means that the law should be predictable and consistent and so predictability and consistency of law is having dual rationale by firstly improving certainty and efficiency so that individuals manage their affairs efficiently and secondly comparable cases ought to be treated equally. In line, in common law systems, predictability and consistency of law are advanced by judicial adherence to precedent.[67] The doctrine of stare decisis directs lower courts to follow precedent when matters reappear before them and so reinforcing the rule-of-law principle that like cases should be treated alike.[68] U.S. Supreme Court precedent in formulating and assessing state courts own comparable doctrines.

---

[65] Brian Z. Tamanaha, A Realistic Theory of Law (New York: Cambridge University Press 2017).

[66] Gibson K. Kuria, The Rule of Law in Kenya and the Status of Human Rights, 16 Yale J. Int'l L. (1991). http://digitalcommons.law.yale.edu/yjil/vol16/iss1/7, Anna Doyle, Colombia, conflict and the rule of law, Amicus Curiae Issue 84 Winter 2010, Keith S. Rosenn, Brazil's Legal Culture: The Jeito Revisited, 1 Fla. Int'l L.J. 1 (1984). Anthony W. Pereira, Political (In)Justice: Authoritarianism and the Rule of Law in Brazil, Chile, and Argentina Series: 2005 Pitt Latin American Studies.

[67] J. Waldron, "Stare Decisis and the Rule of Law: A Layered Approach" (2012) 111 Michigan Law Review 1; . S. A. Lindquist and F. C. Cross, "Stability, Predictability and the Rule of Law: Stare Decisis as Reciprocity Norm" University of Texas Law School, Conference Paper, 2010 at https://law.utexas.edu/conferences/measuring/The Papers/Rule of Law Conference.crosslindquist.pdf

[68] William Baude, Precedent and Discretion, 2019 SUP. CT. REV. 313, 314–29 (2020) (contending that the Roberts Court has introduced elements of arbitrary discretion into modern stare decisis doctrine). Andrei Marmor, Should LikeCases Be Treated Alike?, 11 LEGAL THEORY 27, 27 (2005) (arguing that the principle "like cases should be treated alike" is often confused with two other ideas: "the rationale of analogical reasoning in adjudication" and "the value of coherence").

It is worth noting here that non-profit organizations have a long history of involvement in politics in the USA[69] and individuals usually engage in such spending to promote their personal political preferences. Hasen[70] specifies that "Money can influence who is elected to office, which in turn affects legislative outcomes [and] often buys access and cooperation, permitting those with wealth ... to affect legislative policy." In other words, it seems that people spend money in order to be elected and so via politics and legislation influence the law. It is characteristic that the preferences of interest groups and economic elites have a considerable effect on public policy, while the preferences of average citizens have little independent effect and consequently elites influence law via politics.[71]

It has to be considered that the conventional comprehending of the rule of law ideal concentrates mainly on constraints on official decision-making and so a government of laws is one in which official action is governed by pre-existing legal rules of satisfactory precision and generality that they are capable of preventing the arbitrary whim of persons or the impositions of power.[72] Consequently, the rule of law ideal is closely entangled with law's traditional tendency toward formalism and the rule of law ideal asserts that no one be above the law even the highest officials are subject to legal constraints.[73] It is worth noting that laws make certain that reason rules and not specific paroxysms, nonetheless they are invented and preserved by men triumphing only when men are steered by reason to the public good and not by desire to private ends. In other words, the laws look after themselves, then, regulating the behavior of the men who keep up them.[74] Moreover, the rule-of-law ideal conserves that every person is governed by the same law without regard to status or person which means that there is "equal justice under law." Furthermore, the rule of law ideal underlines the ordinariness of law and, thus,

[69] Steven Rathgeb Smith & Kirsten A. Grønbjerg, Scope and Theory of Government-Non-profit Relations, in The Nonprofit Sector: A Research Handbook 221, 222, 229–33 (Walter W. Powell & Richard Steinberg eds., 2006).

[70] Richard L. Hasen, Plutocrats United: Campaign Money, The Supreme Court, And The Distortion Of American Elections 54 (2016) at 58 ("Money does not buy political outcomes, but, along with candidate quality and campaign organization, it is important to winning elections"). Nicholas Stephanopoulos, Aligning Campaign Finance Law, 101 Va. L. Rev. 1425, 1467–68 (2015) (empirical evidence indicates governmental outputs align more with rich and with political campaign donors than with any other group and non-donors, respectively).

[71] Martin Gilens & Benjamin I. Page, Testing Theories of American Politics: Elites, Interest Groups, and Average Citizens, 12 Persp. On Pol. 564, 576 (2014).

[72] Antonin Scalia, The Rule of Law as a Law of Rules, 56 U. Chi. L. Rev. 1175 (1989). See the relationship between Justice Scalia's narrow view of rules and his plurality opinion in Michael H. v. Gerald D., 491 U.S. 110 (1989).

[73] Steven L. Winter, A Clearing in the Forest Law, Life, And Mind, 2001, 2003 Chicago Press.

[74] J.G.A. Pocock, The Machiavellian Moment: Florentine Political Thought and the Atlantic Republican Tradition 324 (1975) (If laws can attain the status of reason ... then laws must rule and not men.).

Dicey[75] recognized as well the quality of ordinary law administered by ordinary tribunals. It has to be taken into consideration that the rule of law ideal matters having meaning and value with the meaning of assessing the overall health of a legal system. To that extent, global organizations have formed rule of law indices measuring and score legal systems around the world.[76]

The rule of law easily gets politicized when it is directed at particular policies and action. Even though the rule of law ideal is flush with neutral principles—stability, transparency, procedural regularity, etc.—these abstract values lose their nature when tested in the predicament of reality due to political influences upon their context.[77] Moreover, the rule of law ideal inspired the "rise and rise" of the administrative state and the rule of law became a reason to centralize executive governance.[78]

Furthermore, the rule of law is the ideal in accordance with which it is the law that should rule which means that society live under the rule of law only to the extent that the general public obeys the law. The rule of law is threatened when the law becomes so unknowable, so vague, or so all-pervading, that people can't use it as a guide to staying on the right side of it even when they are determined to be so guided. Nevertheless, the rule of law is also threatened, in a different way, when people can't count on the law to foresee how officials will react to their breaches of it. Moreover, the growth of law endangers the rule of law in two manners: firstly, by obstructing our capacity to evade falling foul of the law by following it; secondly, by requiring certainly unreliable official discretion in upholding the law.

Is it late to salvage the rule of law ideal? First of all, the rule of law is a historic ideal being a mental image that has to be always an aim to be closely implemented in a certain degree not diverging a lot from this image,[79] which has been imagined and reimagined over time. The merger of law and politics in governmental offices and generally administration that are main threat to the rule of law but, on the other hand,

[75] A.V. Dicey, Introduction to the Study of the Law of the Constitution 179–92 (1908). Entick v. Carrington 95 Eng. Rep. 807 (K.B. 1765). Luther v. Borden 48 U.S. (7 How.) 1 (1849). Maurice Chittenden, Pinochet Held by London Police on Murder Charges, Sunday Times (London), October 18, 1998, at 1.

[76] Mila Versteeg & Tom Ginsburg, Measuring the Rule of Law: A Comparison of Indicators, 42 Law & Soc. Inquiry 100 (2017). Rule of Law Index 2016, World Just Project, http://data.worldjusticeproject.org/#groups/USA

[77] Thomas W. Merrill, Presidential Administration and the Traditions of Administrative Law, 115 Colum. L. Rev. 1953, 1958–59 (2015) (noting that rule of law arguments centered on accountability and transparency "are designed to confer legitimacy on [presidential actions] without regard to whether they have been authorized by positive law").

[78] Gary Lawson, The Rise and Rise of the Administrative State, 107 Harv. L. Rev. 1231 (1994); Richard B. Stewart, The Reformation of American Administrative Law, 88 Harv. L. Rev. 1667 (1975); Cass R. Sunstein, Constitutionalism After the New Deal, 101 Harv. L. Rev. 421 (1987). FTC v. Ruberoid Co., 343 U.S. 470, 487 (1952) (Jackson, J., dissenting) ("The rise of administrative bodies . . . has deranged our three-branch legal theories . . .").

[79] Peter L. Strauss, Overseer, or "The Decider"? The President in Administrative Law, 75 Geo. Wash. L. Rev. 696 (2007).

politics without the rule of law cannot be implemented. It is worth noting that Barack Obama[80] argues that "our entire way of life in America depends on the rule of law" and it could be said that the way of life all over the world has to be based on the rule of law which of course influenced from political and sociological norms. It has to be taken into consideration that the concentration of power is contrary to the rule of law which has to apply regardless of any power but a concentrated authority causes an alteration of the content of the rule of law in favor of the powerful elites imposing their interests via the utilization of the suitable altered content of the rule of law.

It is worth noting that at its foundation, the rule of law ideal necessitates government officials to exercise authority pursuant to heretofore defined legal authorities, rather than pursuant to particular preference or arbitrary whim/caprice which means that the rule of law entails legal commands to flow from existing agreement rather than from the exercise of discretion or preference by those individuals who happen to be in positions of power in order to achieve their own political aims.[81]

It is fundamental to have in mind that advance notice of the law's musts is a principal characteristic of the rule of law, which permits private parties to plan their affairs and hold government officials accountable to law and so minimizing any political intervention by altering the rule of law accordingly. Thus, the rule of law means that government or any administration in all its movements is compelled by rules fixed and announced in advance and so rules which make it possible to anticipate with fair certainty how the authority will use its coercive authorities in given surroundings and to plan one's personal affairs on the substance of this knowledge. Furthermore, formal rule of law conceptions has been criticized for their compatibility with despotic regimes but "substantive" rule of law conceptions rush to fill this void and anyway these conceptions demand more than rule by law by demanding rule by "good law." It has to be considered that what qualifies as good law is contestable and so it has to be associated with moral justice, equality, and natural law.

An objection to substantive conceptions is that disagreement thrives over what the law ought to be, which confuses an already confused view of what the rule of law ought to involve and so the rule of law has to embrace substantive norms of morality and justice. It is worth mentioning that while formal legality is the central understanding of the rule of law, the substantive rule of law assesses the common sense of the rule of law within global societies by guessing that a common has to be achieved and not a departing understanding that causes confusion into the legitimacy. The ideal of the rule of law is associated with respect for fairness and human dignity, the stipulation for an environment of freedom with instrumental value, having to do with

---

[80] Barack Obama, The President's Role in Advancing Criminal Justice Reform, 130 Harv. L. Rev. 811, 814 n.11 (2017).

[81] Jerry L. Mashaw, Greed, Chaos, And Governance: Using Public Choice To Improve Public Law 139 (1997).

the effective pursuit of whatever other goals one is trying to use law to stimulate.[82] It has to be taken into consideration that the rule of law is a disputed perception generating competing interpretations which has to be focused on the core of the conception which is a stable law in force. Moreover, the ideal is invoked to justify specific decisions, practices, rules, or legal systems as adequately close of be acceptable which means that the rule of law is utilized as an evaluative device for testing government action and institutional arrangements. Besides, when the rule of law is taken to mean the rule of good law, the concept becomes synonymous with those substantive values, such that the rule of law loses independent analytical value and so the rule of law is just one of the qualities of a legal system and has to be well-adjusted against claims proceeded on behalf of other values.

It is worth mentioning that the state has a monopoly on the legitimate violence or authority within a defined territory and administered by some form of logical bureaucracy rule of law existing when the sovereign or ruler is compelled to the same laws set for his subjects. Consequently, the rule of law acts as a restraint against uncontrolled state authority and exists somewhat in opposition to the ability of the modern bureaucratic state which means that this dualism of state authority and its institutionalized control due to the rule of law is required to keep any apt governing order in balance. Does a rule of law exist or to be sure that it does not? How many sovereigns or rulers have declared themselves formally above the law since the French Revolution?

It has to be considered that rulers themselves do not promptly appreciate that it is vital to protect the public from their prospective abuses and destructions which means that the ruling power ought to govern by announced and received laws, and not by extemporary dictates and undetermined resolutions.[83] Hereafter the origins and root for legal restraints on government officials lies elsewhere in longstanding, advancing cultural views and so laws were declared to originate with the gods, who diffused them to humans through "the proclamations of rulers" which means that the legal order was said to be the product of higher metaphysical forces that categorized law with justice and the natural order of things.[84] Furthermore, rulers in Medieval Europe[85] were seen as subject to customary law, natural law, and ecclesiastical law, a common appreciating articulated in coronation oaths. Government officials are bound by and abide law is a normative ideal, expectation, and orientation broadly shared in society about suitable conduct, a central element in generating the rule of law.

---

[82] Jeremy Waldron, Is the Rule of Law an Essentially Contested Concept (in Florida)?, 21 LAW & PHIL. 137, 151 (2002).

[83] John Locke, Second Treatise of Government, edited by C.B. Macpherson (Indianapolis: Hackett Publishing Co. 1980).

[84] Bruce G. Trigger, Understanding Early Civilizations (Cambridge: Cambridge University Press 2003).

[85] John B. Morrall, Political Thought in Medieval Times (Toronto: Univ. Toronto Press 1980).

It is questionable how many countries in the current age have a rule of law. Moreover, weak states are further undermined by accountability which means that the Rule of law is not sufficient in powerless states or in the absence of democracy. It has to be taken into account that strong rational states, ruled by leaders bound by the same laws as everyday citizens and subject periodically to elections and other forms of liability, are the most expected to reveal good modern governance. Moreover, it is characteristic that the concept of rule of law is as old as systematic thinking about politics itself. Aristotle promoted laws to rein in the power of rulers. Cicero advised against rule by dictators unrestricted by legal restraints in the days of the Roman Republic. Montesquieu urged for a type of judicial independence.

It is vital that not only does the state enforce external rules so that everyone can accomplish their raison d'être together, but also that they are administered in line with the same social will that people generally obey, otherwise they may reject them. To that extent, it is central that law is not only interpreted impartially, but that it is done in a manner that reveals the general and individual spirit of the public. On the other hand, if law is interpreted unfairly or unjustly to the disadvantage of one group, then it demoralizes one of the foundations of law, which is that people generally accept it for the reason that it settles their interests. Thus, all people in a society have to know that the law is interpreted fairly in line with the social spirit that they are assented for the reason that it is basic where the legal system gets its legitimacy, explicitly that it is instituted to settle the conflicts between people. To that extent, external rules are administered in line with the general will of the society in order to evade existential anguish which means that the state has to make certain that they are enforced against those who are on the outside, or do not come within the social will, if not this may lead to disruption as well.

Borders identify territories within which political communities arise and flourish. Political communities extend beyond borders, but in our world, they are directly linked with borders. Thus, political borders play a role in generating a membership in a political community.[86] In line it has to be taken into consideration that the nation state has a sole social will that has to be defended at all costs for the reason that this is the only way in which its people accomplish their elemental reason to be. Moreover, due to globalization the world has noticeably transformed and now there are numerous identities that ought to be protected permitting people to make sense of their worlds. Nevertheless, whereas the conservation of national external rules is central for the reason that they allow people to preserve their distinctive cultural identity and heritage to that extent globalization with its global "markets in goods, services and capital," means that individuals rely on people in different countries as well. It could be said that due to globalization not only public institutions but also everyday life is becoming free from the hold of tradition which means that societies

[86]Coleman, J. L. and Harding, S. K. Citizenship, the demand of justice, and the moral relevance of political borders. Justice in Immigration. ed. Schwartz, W. F. Cambridge: University Press, 2007, p. 40. Maier, C. S. Being there: place, territory and identity. Identities, Affiliations and Allegiances, ed. Benhabib, S.; Shapiro, I.; Petranovic, D. Cambridge: University Press, 2007, p. 78.

are becoming de-traditionalized producing a global cosmopolitan society which means another role for law making as well.[87]

In interpreting the law internally, the state has to make certain that it does so in a fair way that is harmonious with what people see as part of their identity. If they do not do this, it might lead to larger conflict for the reason that this general will is also part of a person's identity that permits them to accomplish their raison d'être, and if it is not made possible, it may cause them existential anguish. Thus, all legal systems are ranked along one scale in terms of the degree of rule of law present or lacking. Certain legal systems actually exhibit the qualities of a legitimate rule of law to a clear and reliable degree. Nonetheless, apart from the development of internal rules that make people more morally aware of their dependability to those in other parts of the world, and external rules, such as the economic ones by which legislatures augment their people's prospects by take full advantage of their global prospects.

5.5 International Rule of Law

States take into consideration wider global factors in the general interpretation of national rules in their territories as well which is achieved via public international law as well. It is worth mentioning that States come together in forums like the United Nations, European Union, and other international and regional groups to advance rules to the general good.[88] There is the direct transfer of institutions from one national system to another. In addition, there is the imposition of a global legal principle upon national public administrations which means that the imposition by a global judicial body of a common legal principle, not only upon States, but also within national legal systems. Moreover, legal thought is the first area influenced by the circulation and spreading of law. Globalization[89] influences research approaches, techniques, and methodologies not extended to positive law.[90] To that extent, the universal or general legal thought founded on principles common to several systems of positive law including the writings of jurists.[91] A universal law involves a single sovereign and a single, worldwide legal community which means that universality extends to the extent that legal thought and does not influence the relativism of

[87] Garrett, G. The Causes of Globalization [interactive]. Yale University, April 2000 <http://www.yale.edu/leitner/pdf/2000-02.pdf>: "I define globalization somewhat narrowly as the international integration of markets in goods, services and capital." Giddens, A. Runaway World: How Globalization is Reshaping our Lives. London: Profile Books, 2002, p. 42–43.

[88] Evans, M.; Cerny, P. Globalization and Social Policy. Developments in British Social Policy 2. Ed. Ellison N.; Pierson, C. Basingstoke: Palgrave Macmillan, p. 22.

[89] G. Silverstein, Globalization and the rule of law: "A machine that runs of itself?", in "International Journal of Constitutional Law", vol. 1, n. 3, 2003.

[90] G. Fassò, La filosofia del diritto dell'Ottocento e del Novecento, Bologna, Il Mulino, 1988.

[91] M. Barberis, John Austin, la teoria del diritto e l'universalità dei concetti giuridici, in "Materiali per una storia della cultura giuridica", n. 2, December 2003.

positive legal systems. On the other hand, universality/legal globalization might cause a fundamental interference of politics in order to shape the required politics of law necessary for the satisfaction of the needs of economic elites against a general justice and objectivity in the appliance of the law and the rule of law. It is worth mentioning that positions are grounded on central ideological beliefs to the extent there is no likelihood of a negotiated compromise which means that there is the right or calling of individuals to disobey positive law when it runs counter to divine or natural law.[92] Moreover, codifying and consolidating international law was seen as important which means that there was a wide-ranging international strategy for inaugurating the prevalence of law in relations between countries. The reassert of formal sovereign equality was seen as restricted in advance by the structures and content of international law being an effort reaffirming the implied universal applicability of international law to all countries and the formal equality of those countries within the terms of that law.[93]

As mentioned earlier, a rule-of-law system is one in which the choices of an actor are made in light of rules that are fixed. To that extent, actors opt to violate the rules, but when they do, they do so know what the rules denote and considering the inferences of compliance and breach. In a domestic context, the rule of law tackles problems related with an overly powerful centralized authority illustrating a political system founded on stable public laws and known in advance applying equally to a government and its citizens without regard to specific status. It is supposed that the rule of law regulates the government power implying equality before the law and favoring judicial justice. China is expanding the horizontal rule of law addressing the relationships among private entities, which China considers vital to its market economy and future economic development. Thus, China's emphasis on the horizontal rule of law indicates an effort to connect China to international rule of law norms in the realm of commercial interests.[94]

It seems that international law has struggled for a "Rule of Law" adding to the old project of bringing law to bear on the darkness of politics. It is worth mentioning that German interwar jurisprudence from Kelsen to Lauterpacht and even Carl Schmitt and Hans Morgenthau advocated that there is no opposition between "law" and "politics" and so it is feasible to portray all of the international world as already

---

[92]Chester James Antieau, The Higher Laws: Origins of Modern Constitutional Law (William S. Hein, Buffalo, 1994) where he concentrates on Divine Law and Natural Law concerning the U.S. Constitution.

[93]Miguel Angel Gonzalez Felix, "Current Development: Fifth Legal Advisers' Meeting at UN Headquarters in New York" (1995) 89 American Journal of International Law 644. V. Petrovsky, USSR Memorandum: On Enhancing the Role of International Law (Letter from the Deputy Head of the Delegation of the Union of Soviet Socialist Republics to the 44th Session of the General Assembly, 29 September 1989) UN Doc A/44/585 (2 October 1989), cited in Koskenniemi, "The Politics of International Law" (1990) 1 European Journal of International Law 4.

[94]Eric Li, China and the Rule of Law, 3 AM. AFF. (2019), https://americanaffairsjournal.org/2019/08/china-and-the-rule-of-law/

regulated by the rules of law.[95] Moreover, both Schmitt and Morgenthau held it unfeasible to distinguish law from politics by any general rule—whether something was considered as a "legal" or a "political" problem was a matter of strategy. It is argued that there is a transformation of Western modes of governance ("governmentality") from the use of the "jurisdiction" of law to "veridiction" by expert systems.

It is worth noting that international law is altogether central in structuring the way in which the political and economic world materializes, creating an open field of opportunities for participants and settling their bargaining authority in an egalitarian system of concepts and institutions. Moreover, it is international law that indicates who qualifies as a "member" of the international community and what such membership brings about which means that international law outlines the basic forms of interaction between the members (diplomacy, treaties, intergovernmental and nongovernmental organizations, transnational private activities, contracts, etc.), states the objectives toward which they are acting ("ownership", "jurisdiction", "authority") and so also, what it is that may occur as objects of desire in the first place ("right", "self-determination", "territorial possession", etc.). In other words, the law is not a limiting but an enabling device.

The international rule of law is a derivative function of the domestic rule of law. The "rule of law" portrays a social system that divides society into political and legal domains placing the latter within the former. Moreover, the international rule of law embraces the obligation of states to comply with their legal commitments and states are free to take on legal obligations as they see them fit requiring complying with them. The idea that states should comply with their legal obligations is primary to conventional accounts of the contemporary international legal-political system. It is central to international law and is almost universally preferred over violation. Compliance is broadly seen as a legal, political, and moral vital for states. Legally, the obligation to comply is institutionalized in the principle of pacta sunt servanda and in the "good faith" clauses that come out in many international treaties, including the Vienna Convention on the Law of Treaties.

In which ways international law, especially in its reliance upon "the practice of legality," assists in understanding of the Rule of Law in international society? The understanding of the "Rule of Law" implicates practices of players within international community that are formed and sometimes even controlled by "criteria of legality" that permit actors to track their rationales and arrange their interactions. Moreover, the instantiation of these criteria in continuing practice creates a unique form of legal legitimacy, in that way forming a responsibility among those to whom law is addressed, enlightening legal obligation. There is a "culture of legality" that is broader in its content and its ability to form behavior than Koskenniemi's "culture of

[95]Michael Byers, The Role of Law in International Politics: Essays in International Relations and International Law, Oxford Scholarship Online: January 2010 DOI: https://doi.org/10.1093/acprof:oso/9780199244027.001.0001 Martti Koskenniemi, Carl Schmitt, Hans Morgenthau, and the Image of Law in International Relations DOI:https://doi.org/10.1093/acprof:oso/9780199244027.003.0003

formalism[96]" which means that this "culture of legality" does not entail responsibilities to strong substantive ends or goods, so it cannot be discharged as an exclusionary liberal internationalism. French Revolution had transformative political effect and so "brought about by the language of constitutionalism."

Human rights, international stability, and perhaps even the progress of civilization itself are said to be founded on compliance with international law. Is this the rule or politics have proscribed this principle? The normative preference for compliance over violation is deep-seated in international legal understanding, to some extent for the reason that law is seen as the alternative to power politics. It could be argued that a legal order emerges to be the antidote to force but it seems that in many occasions the law and the rule of law are replaced by use of force in demand of politics which destroys order in the long run despite that in many occasions political groups think that they have imposed their interests upon local or international society. On the other hand, international order based on states' choices to abide by international law and so to track a negotiated common position rather than an individualistic, short-term, and self-interested one. Besides, in many occasions' powerful states seem to try to impose their political position against the well understanding of the rule of law.

In international level the legality of an action is dependent on an actor doing it and it is difficult to assess the legality of an international act without knowing the identity of the agent. Moreover, the international legality of an act depends on which state undertakes it, what that state says about the act, and what it has previously said about its link to the pieces of international law that may apply. International legal obligations so attach to states in an occasional way opposing the factor of equality that is said to be vital for the national kind of the rule of law. In national law, the identity of the actor should not enter into the assessment of how law regulates the act; in international law, it ought to.

It is worth mentioning that states use international law to rationalize their policies. To that extent, states offer explanations for how their conduct is coherent with their international commitments, and accordingly there is a competing diplomatic and legal accounts concerning compliance. In other words, there is no likelihood for an objective settling of the differences. It seems that the international rule of law utilizes law to legitimate state policy.

Is the rule of (international) law impossible to be implemented? It is argued that the rule of (international) law is impossible and this impossibility derives not so much from the widespread motivation of "realpolitik" but from law's own internal tensions, tensions finally generated by the lack of a self-assured foundation either for law's power or for its substantive gist.[97] In other words, it seems that the politics influence upon international law has to be taken into consideration in its global

[96]Martti Koskenniemi, "What Should International Lawyers Learn from Karl Marx?," Leiden Journal of International Law 17 (2004), 246 (similarly arguing for the transformative potential of the "myth" of universalism, but observing that "an aspect of the difficulty that any fundamental challenge to the iron laws of power must imply" is that this potential "appears only occasionally, and even then in connection with events of exceptional magnitude, even scandal").

[97]Roberto Unger, Knowledge and Politics (New York: The Free Press, 1975).

applicability. Anyway, the notion of formal sovereign equality between states has been materialized.[98] It is worth mentioning that it is affirmed the universality of liberal democracy in a new world order focused on the idea of democracy on the rule of law.[99] How democracy can "catch up" to globalizing economy? How nationally based democracy can "catch up" to the realities of post-national decision-making? It is obvious that there is a misfit between nationally based democracies to the realities of post-national decision-making and there is a need to consequently overcome. Hence, there is the political task at hand to achieve the protection of the existing successes of the democratic welfare state, albeit by means of novel experiments in self-government "beyond the nation-state."

In other words, law is seen as a resource which states and others utilize in the chase of their targets which means that state goals are inseparable from the practices of international law challenging a common assumption that law has to be independent of the preferences of the agents. The conventional view of international law is that it provides a self-imposed set of limits on states so as to better permit those very states to chase their mutual and individual interests.[100] International law as a set of resources acknowledging that law contains the aptitude to legitimate state policy. Moreover, international law presents the resources with which states talk about and comprehend their behavior.[101]

AI applications produce situations of legal uncertainty around existing norms or regimes in international law and so particular technical and political characteristics of AI technology in practice render it destructive or erosive to key areas of international law for the reason that the legal "gaps" that AI systems expose on the international level are abstractly or politically hard to patch through the usual avenues of international law "development" such as interpretation; treaty amendments; new treaties; customary international law development; or jurisprudence by international courts.

Can new technologies alter the processes by which international law is formed? First of all, technologies speed up international law formation due to the fact that AI systems changing the practices of international law creation or adjudication. It seems that currently the mere utilization of AI by states cannot alter the substance of international law because there is a need for changing the way of forming international law via economic and military power rather than purely the rule of law.

---

[98] Robert Kagan, Paradise and Power: America and Europe in the New World Order (London: Atlantic Books, 2003).

[99] Universal Declaration on Human Rights, International Bill of Human Rights, GA Res 217(III), UNGAOR, 3rd sess, 183rd plen mtg, UN Doc A/RES/217(III) (10 December 1948), International Covenant on Civil and Political Rights, opened for signature 16 December 1966, 999 UNTS 3 (entered into 3 January 1976) ("ICCPR"), and the International Covenant on Economic, Social and Cultural Rights, opened for signature 19 December 1966, 999 UNTS 171 (entered into force 23 March 1976).

[100] France v. Turkey), "Judgment of 7 September 1927," PCIJ Series A, no. 10, at p. 18.

[101] Martin, Lisa L. "Against Compliance." In Cambridge: Cambridge University Press, 2013.

Moreover, it is supposed that the emergence of AAI technology applicable to AAI society will advance a legal model facilitating the creation of a "completely specified" AAI international law serving as a mean of global governance which means that automatically AAI will identify and resolve conflicts concerning norms and law application in settling an AAI international law and so generation a global constitution which means elimination of fragmentation and regime complexity. In other words, it is expected to have a fully automated adjudication of international law founded upon the AAI international rule of law.

Furthermore, it is anticipated that the use of AI technologies will strengthen the enforcement of existing or future international law and global governance instruments. It is supposed that new technologies will play a crucial role in altering the modes and estimated effectiveness of compliance monitoring and enforcement such as in the field of arms control. It is argued that "Legal automation" would change the texture of international law irrevocably but it would presumably remain law and so AI will not alter the core, normative "regulatory modality" of international law.[102]

Has got the existing international law a place in AAI society? AAI technology will generate an AAI society based on AAI entities producing an AAI sovereignty which demands a new model of AAI international law due to the digitized society and working environment. The current physical borders of sovereignty will be bypassed by the AAI technology.

It could be said the content of international law is altered in the course of being used to validate state policies due to the practices of diplomacy, as states give legal rationalization for their actions seeing the mutual charter of international law and foreign policy. In many jurisdictions, there is a need of restructuring national foreign policy-related institutions and reinforcing human resource capabilities and processes so that these are in coherence with occurring consequences of AI for national sovereignty. Moreover, AI's effects for foreign policy necessitate an approach that links national and international institutions and so encompassing not only foreign policy civil servants but multiple stakeholders from the private sector and branches of the government. It has to be taken into consideration that the correlation between AI and Diplomacy is not entirely metaphysical and so the feasible attributes and factors that encompass AI and Diplomacy which means that there is a need for adopting a realpolitik approach.

AI offers a prospective vehicle for combining causal and teleological explanations of foreign policy behavior by appropriately managing competing policy demands and institutional priorities and so assisting the decision-maker prescribe a course of action in a non-deterministic way that is, by repetitively and automatically adjusting its recommendations based on continuous description, diagnostic, and prediction. While foreign policy[103] is about the particular strategy a state decides

---

[102] Maria Sapignoli, "The Mismeasure of the Human: Big Data and the 'AI Turn' in Global Governance" (2021) 37 Anthropology Today 4.

[103] Ben Scott, Stefan Heumann, and Philippe Lorenz, "Artificial Intelligence and Foreign Policy," 2018, https://www.stiftung-nv.de/sites/default/files/ai_foreign_policy.pdf . Michael C Horowitz

to develop in pursuit of its national interests, diplomacy refers to the processes by which such a strategy is implemented. Hence, AI can be utilized as a diplomatic tool, and AI as a factor that shapes the environment in which diplomacy is performed. AI is relevant for a broader policy agenda extending from economy, business, and security, all the way to democracy, human rights, and ethics. Moreover, AI supports the functions of diplomacy and the day-to-day tasks of diplomats and so AI turns out to be the defining technology having the prospective to restructure the foundation of the international order.

AI advances communication between governments and foreign publics by lowering language barriers between countries, boosts the security of diplomatic missions via image recognition and information sorting technologies, and supports international humanitarian operations by monitoring elections, assisting in peacekeeping operations, and guaranteeing that financial aid disbursements are not misused. Moreover, AI systems offer great assistance to diplomats in times of crisis by assisting them make sense and identify possible trends. Algorithmic driven engagement will be critical for digital diplomats to use so as to communicate with their target audiences and so AI assists diplomats by offering reliable diagnostics of the scope conditions for effect via network, cluster, and semantic analyses.

It has to be taken into account that AI systems capable of causing harm are not confined to one jurisdiction being not possible to link them to a specific jurisdiction at all. Moreover, different national approaches to regulation poses barriers to effective regulation intensified by the speed, autonomy, and opacity of AI systems and so regulation, in the sense of public control, necessitates active involvement of states. To that extent, international organizations have been unsuccessful at responding to technological innovation. If regulation lags at the national level, it trails internationally.[104]

To that extent, the connotation of international legal rules occurs from how it is used in the diplomacy of states.[105] It is characteristic that states give favorable legal interpretations to legalize their own actions, which are inseparably legal and political, being part of the course of international politics.[106] Furthermore, governments and others employ international law to clarify and justify their actions adding to the meaning of the rules they appeal to altering the meaning of the rule of law which is an objective approach of the meaning and content of law in order to have lawful

---

et al., "Artificial Intelligence and International Security" (Washington D.C., 2018), https://www.cnas.org/publications/reports/artificial-intelligence-and-international-security

[104]Eyal Benvenisti, "Upholding Democracy Amid the Challenges of New Technology: What Role for the Law of Global Governance?" (2018) 29 European Journal of International Law 9.

[105]Hurd, Ian. "International Law and the Practice of Diplomacy." In edited by Ole Jacob Sending, Vincent Pouliot, and Iver B. Neumann. Cambridge University Press, 2015.

[106]Beaulac, Stéphane. "The Rule of Law in International Law Today." In edited by Gianluca Palombella and Neil Walker. Portland, OR: Hart, 2009. Patten, Chris. "The Rule of Lawless." February 23, 2015. http://www.project-syndicate.org/commentary/international-rule-of-law-by-chris-patten-2015-02

justice and not a lawful justice in accordance with the demands of a politically powerful state of agent against the general good of a society.

It is obvious that the rule of law is not utilized as a solution to the governance challenges in Europe or globally. The rule of law has to alter/redraft political disputes in legal language. On the other hand, the international examples illustrate that eventually, the rule of law and the international rule of law have become political resources which actors utilize in the political struggle over the legitimation and de-legitimation of their desires which is against the real meaning of the rule of law to the detriment of international peace and progress. However, states utilize international law in order to legalize their actions and those of others against the real legal meaning of the rule by enveloping the meaning of an international rule of law with a lawful context which in fact is the political dress of law in order to achieve any political goals even against a settled legal order and in an effort to change the legal status quo accordingly.

The international rule of law is enveloped/encircled with the essence of being a political term based on the national rule of law which is shaped by a real law context rather than the political affairs of state sovereignty. To that extent, the prevailed international rule of law makes certain that legal resources carry political weight, and that being seen as acting legally is politically authoritative for states. Legal resources such as national rule of law and international rule of law are an available and socially legitimated pool of such ideas and concepts. National rule of law and international rule of law is utilized as a useful, and dominant, device in the course of "sense-making" for states.

In addition, the international rule of law is seen as ingredient of the political structure for international relations on top of the agency of actors to maneuver and utilize fundamentals of the legal system with their own interests in mind against the essence of the rule of law itself. The ever-present employment of international law in foreign policy sits at the crossroads of international structure and agency limited by international legal resources.[107]

The due process of law in the global legal order is based on the following three features. First, the principle of "procedural fairness" is not acknowledged by international treaties, but is created by judicial bodies. Secondly, the expansion of global law through lateral connections, in particular with trade, is open to further opening out for the reason that of its many ties to such correlated matters as the environment, human rights, health protection, security, and other areas in which "constitutional" principles emerged by global judges are effortlessly transferred. Finally, under global law, both the State and private actors have the right of involvement in their correlation with public administrations. It has to be taken into consideration that there is an escalating number of areas in which a body of fairly uniform rules of universal application is developing. In fact, the escalation of global trade necessitates common standards for product conformity, consumer protection, and product

[107] Hurd, Ian. "International Law and the Practice of Diplomacy." In edited by Ole Jacob Sending, Vincent Pouliot, and Iver B. Neumann. Cambridge University Press, 2015.

liability. To that extent, states' incapacity to manage such phenomena as financial crises, global warming, the exploitation of the seas and maritime resources authorizes that these universal public goods be protected at the global altitude.

Does an international economic consortium accomplish its targets via the international politics of law in harmony with politics of law internally? It is worth mentioning that international organizations consolidate work on various matters, and their decisions, or the rules set by them, converted into binding guidelines or requirements for participation for states in the modeling of their national laws and policy. In other words, politics influence the formation of law in international and national level but since its formation the law has to be implemented without any further political influence in order to have application of the rule of law.

5.6 State Authority and International Rule of Law

It has to be taken into account that the rule-of-law norms and principles, at both national and international levels, are conceived to protect the freedom and dignity of the individual. Does the rejection of a particular set of international rules denote a diminishing of the international rule of law?

It is argued that the international rule of law denotes state conformity with existing international legal rules, whatever those happen to be. On the other hand, it is considered that the international rule of law embraces the normative substance of the rules, especially, human rights-based legal limitations on state authority including norms that protect individual freedom and dignity. Hence, the loss of international law-based rights protections comprises a decline in international rule of law. Therefore, an increase of authoritarianism in a mounting number of states indicates a decline in the international rule of law which means that the spread of authoritarianism erodes not just the strength of international human rights norms but also shrinks the rule of law in additional domains such as security, economics, and environment that are parts of the post-World War II international rule-of-law system.

It seems that the reviving authoritarianism observable in varied parts of the world among regimes of fluctuating kinds such as democratic, autocratic, and hybrids necessitates a set of national routines that destabilize constraints on state power in modes that compromise the basic rights and freedoms at the heart of modern rule of law, national and international. It could be said that the core of authoritarian political strategies consists of the subordination of the judiciary, suppression of independent news media and freedom of expression, and restrictions on civil society groups, involving NGOs.

It is worth noting here that authoritarian[108] governance takes place when "rulers see public opposition as a major threat to the extent or continuation of their power,

[108] Beetham, David (2015). "Authoritarianism and Democracy: Beyond Regime Types." Comparative Democratization 13(2): 2, 12, 13.

and believe that they can work to undermine it with relative impunity." Moreover, Wayne Sandholtz[109] argues that "for a thick conception of international rule of law, grounded on legal limits on the powers of the state. This conception of the rule of law ties together domestic and international levels: both domestic constitutions and international treaties establish limitations on state power, limitations derived from the dignity and freedom of each person. Authoritarian politics target such limitations on state power, as authoritarians seek to weaken or eliminate independent mechanisms for holding them accountable ... authoritarian practices degrade the ability of domestic compliance constituencies to criticize or oppose government policies that violate international legal rules that such constituencies favour. As political accountability erodes, authoritarian governments have more leeway to disregard or undermine international legal structures without facing domestic political consequences." In line, it could be said that the authoritarian demolishing of limits on state power signifies, in itself, an erosion of international rule of law. Furthermore, taking into account that international rule of law is composed by the interconnected set of international legal rules regulating international affairs, rising authoritarianism entails a diminishing share of democracies in international organizations raising concerns about international peace and stability which means that resurgent authoritarianism is expected to erode international rule of law.

It has to be taken into consideration that the national rule of law is directly and characteristically linked to international rule of law, through substantive values and norms that are foundational to both national and international legal orders and so these norms and values seek the protection of individual dignity, rights, and freedoms and accordingly generate boundaries on government authority. Moreover, the erosion of national, rights-oriented rule of law directly diminishes international rule of law to the extent that an increasing number of countries demolish crucial mechanisms for limiting government powers.

Furthermore, it has to be taken into account that three components outline the rule of law: (1) the powers of government can only be exercised through law, (2) the law applies to the state and its officials, and (3) the law must apply equally to all.[110] Hurd[111] considers that the rule of Law is a political tool or an element of political strategy and so the international rule of law is the "the idea that all state behaviour should conform to whatever international legal obligations relate to it" which means that law is the mean that states employ to comprehend and explain their acts, goals, and needs. Hence, international rule of law exists to the extent that states employ in the practice of legal justification emphasizing formal legality and justificatory

[109] Sandholtz, Wayne, Resurgent Authoritarianism and the International Rule of Law, KFG Working Paper Series, No. 38, Berlin Potsdam Research Group "The International Rule of Law – Rise or Decline?", Berlin, September 2019, p 25–26.

[110] Hurd, Ian (2015). "Three Models of the International Rule of Law." Eidos: Revista de Filosofía No. 23: 37–48. Hurd, Ian (2014). "The International Rule of Law: Law and the Limit of Politics." Ethics & International Affairs 28(1): 39–51.

[111] Hurd, Ian (2015). "The International Rule of Law and the Domestic Analogy." Global Constitutionalism 4(3): 365–395 at 391.

practices within its context without tying it to specific substantive values, like human rights. Moreover, Hurd[112] argues that the international rule of law cannot consist of limits on the powers of national governments for the reason that there is no international government to enforce such limitations and because countries can select which limitations on their powers to accede.

It is argued that international rule of law has to be more than a system of rules that permits countries to pursue their interests and Palombella[113] says that rule of law cannot "coincide with the mere existence of a legal order . . . in the absence of any other qualifications . . ." and so the rule of law involves democracy combined with fundamental rights implemented within the municipal constitutional domain or in the international sphere. On the other hand, international rule of law is a system of rules that permits states to pursue their interests which means that the rules implement the framework within the national and the international rule of law are applied and so legal order means existence of all the democratic prerogatives for the functioning of a society. Of course, it could be said that an authoritarian international rule of law can exist that implements a legal order far away from a democratic legal order but even authoritarian rule of law tends to satisfy the rights of people in order to survive on the long term. Correspondingly, Nardin[114] argues that the rule of law should not be confused with the existence of laws: "The expression 'rule of law' does no intellectual work if any effective system of enacted rules must be counted as law, no matter what its moral qualities" and so the moral qualities of the rule of law have to embrace rights which means that "rule of law" defines a legal order in which law both constrains decision-making and protects the moral rights of those who come within its jurisdiction.

Moreover, Krieger and Nolte[115] argue that international law has shifted from highlighting state-oriented principles in the direction of a more value-based order which is defending and serving the individual. Moreover, international rule of law encompasses a substantive normative standard as a feature of reference, together with the acknowledgment and interpretation of global value-based rules and principles that safeguard individuals. However, Krieger and Nolte use the term "international rule of law" to signify the totality of international law as it has advanced since

[112] Hurd, Ian (2015). "The International Rule of Law and the Domestic Analogy." Global Constitutionalism 4(3): 365–395 at 391.

[113] Palombella, Gianluigi (2009). "The Rule of Law Beyond the State: Failures, Promises, and Theory." International Journal of Constitutional Law 7(3): 442–467 at 454.

[114] Nardin, Terry (2008). "Theorising the International Rule of Law." Review of International Studies 34(3): 385–401 at 394.

[115] Krieger, Heike and Georg Nolte (2016). The International Rule of Law - Rise or Decline? Points of Departure. Working Paper No. 1. Berlin Potsdam Research Group "International Rule of Law - Rise or Decline?". Berlin. October 2016. https://papers.ssrn.com/sol3/papers.cfm?abstract_id=2866940

the end of the Cold War, embracing rules for trade, investment human rights, the use of force, etc.[116]

It could be said that rights-based limitations on state authority, well-maintained in international law, are foundational to the international rule of law but it is feasible for relations among states to be designed and steered by international legal rules, across diverse domains, irrespective of the character of national regimes. Hence, authoritarian states are conforming to international legal regimes on the use of force, the conduct of war, trade, investment, refugees and migration, and the environment which means that it is possible for a specific pattern of international legal rules to regulate international affairs albeit an important or even growing share of states in the globe is authoritarian. Moreover, authoritarian governments can and do live by WTO rules, abstain from the illegal use of force, stick to international environmental accords, etc. It is worth noting that by permitting governments to monitor, understand, and control their citizens far more closely than ever before, AI generates conducive conditions for the rise of the digital authoritarian state, probably just as a political alternative to liberal democratic systems.

It is worth mentioning here that national rule-of-law concepts cannot be transferred directly into the international arena for the reason that the international rule of law cannot merely be derived from the national translation, since the two depend on exclusive political foundations which means that it is inapplicable to associate the state under international rule of law to the individual under national rule of law.[117] However, at the national level, individual rights have to be protected from infringements by the state and a central drive of the national rule of law to launch limits on the powers of government is dominant to modern international law. Thus, modern international law sets boundaries to state powers, in the form of international human rights law.

To that extent, basic international human rights norms have been undertaking by virtually all states, even if states continue to disagree about the priority to be afforded various rights or about the interpretation of universal rights in particular cases. Certainly, one of the great modifications in international law post-World War II is that sovereign prerogatives are bounded, with the effect that how states treat people under their jurisdiction is no longer merely a matter of national policy. Thus, in the era of human rights law, national rule of law and international rule of law impart the aim of building legal limits to state authority in an attempt to protect individual rights and freedoms. Waldron[118] argues that states "are not ends in themselves, but means for the nurture, protection, and freedom of those who are ends in themselves. This is acknowledged in the philosophy of municipal law, when it is said that the state exists

---

[116] Krieger, Heike (2019). "Populist Governments and International Law." European Journal of International Law 30(3).

[117] Waldron, Jeremy (2006). "The Rule of International Law." Harvard Journal of Law & Public Policy 30(1): 15–30.

[118] Waldron, Jeremy (2006). "The Rule of International Law." Harvard Journal of Law & Public Policy 30(1): 15–30 p 24.

for the sake of its citizens, not the other way around" and so the welfare of people together with their freedom and dignity, and not the welfare of sovereign nation-states, is the supreme end of international law.

5.7 States and the Law

How the existence of the state can be justified? It is worth noting that religious and political conditions have favored the rise of absolutism, absolutism being a form of law and exercise of law over people that are unconstrained by customs, privileges, rights, and even free from the legitimate protests of its subjects. Thomas Hobbes proposed an exceptional and uncompromising answer about the modern state in terms of sovereignty by considering that it does not matter to whom citizens give their right of self-defense to provided that they do, and when they do that, they conform to whatever the ruler says.[119] Thus, the consent of the ruled by transferring the power to the ruler to govern is the basis of sovereignty.

On the other hand, the modern state is a nation state tied to a territory and to a population whose traditions lead to a sense of collective identity. Hence, the state is an organization that implicates everyone within a given territory and so the state has near-universal jurisdiction and power being exercised over every resident everywhere within the boarder.

It has to be taken into account that bureaucracy and the rule of law are linked to the conception of the state. For Weber, the rise of the bureaucratic form was an imperative part of the justification of the modern world.[120] Moreover, bureaucracy operates as a law onto itself and in this manner safeguards deep-rooted interests of the elite preserving it. On the other hand, aim of any administration should be the interests of all society. Kafka[121] highlights three truths about modern bureaucracy: its secrecy, its arbitrariness, and how impersonal it is. Besides, it is worth noting here that one of the central fundamentals of politics as it developed in the West, via the courts of emperors, kings and lords, is law. Therefore, law, either common law in England or Civil law in Europe, became the justification and the device through which power was centralized and exercised over people. Doug Magendanz[122] argues that "it is an interesting and striking fact that the modern concept of rule of law has one of its origins within religion and within the religious institution of the Roman Catholic Church. Not only did the church give it is first regular form, it did something else: namely, it introduced the idea that the ruler, be it the emperor,

[119] D. Magendanz. 2019. Church Power, Sovereignty and Freedom of Religion in Thomas Hobbes. SSRN Working Paper. Lloyd, Sharon A.; Sreedhar, Susanne (12 February 2012). "Hobbes's Moral and Political Philosophy". Stanford Encyclopedia of Philosophy.

[120] Weber, Max. Political Writings. Cambridge University Press, 1994.

[121] Corngold, Stanley (2004). Lambent Traces: Franz Kafka. Princeton, New Jersey: Princeton University Press.

[122] The Idea of the State Doug Magendanz at: https://ssrn.com/abstract=3449855 p 27.

king or lord, was not the ultimate source of law. So, through these two things—the development of the bureaucratic form and the development of canon law—the Roman Catholic Church started to look and act like the modern, secular state, giving birth to is early form."

As mentioned earlier, globalization right away generates pressures for centralization to accomplish economic objectives, and also decentralization to safeguard local exercise of powers in a way compatible with upholding of local legal culture. Globalization refers to developments in the real world that are global.[123] In globalization state, courts and lawmakers acknowledge the continuing delegation of power to the private sector, and develop new forms of accountability to maintain a public voice.[124] In this regard, NGOs play a central role in fields such as development aid, sports, human rights, and the environment that they have become a competitor of the state in legal as well as factual terms. Moreover, NGOs have to be granted an international legal status, while at the same time there should be a global legal framework to construct their participation and make them liable.[125] Thus, NGOs have to be given an augmented role in the legislative, executive, and judicial branches of the WTO. The White House published a draft memorandum outlining ten principles which federal agencies should consider when devising laws and rules for the use of AI in the private sector.[126]

States make certain that courts exist as an expression of state prerogative and power. Arbitration is not a national court procedure but arbitration is a private proceeding with public consequences.[127] According to McGinnis and Somin[128] "Judges thus often put aside their political and public policy preferences to enforce the law according to a set of rules." On the other hand, voting patterns in the Supreme Court back a "political" or "attitudinal" model which posits that judicial votes abide by political ideology.[129] The Supreme Court in Marbury v. Madison[130]

---

[123] RO Keohane and JS Nye, Power and Interdependence (Upper Saddle River NJ, Pearson, 4th edn 2011).

[124] Aman, A.C., Jr., "The globalizing state: A future-oriented perspective on the public/private distinction, federalism, and democracy, "Vanderbilt Journal of Transnational Law, 31, 1998, pp. 769–870.

[125] G Zekos, MNEs and Human Rights in International Law in Globalization, 2006 The ICFAI journal of International Business Law, issue October p7 www.icfaipress.org

[126] Office of Management and Budget (OMB), The White House (2019) Draft Memorandum for the Heads of executive departments and agencies, Guidance for regulation of artificial intelligence applications. www.whitehouse.gov/wp-content/uploads/2020/01/Draft-OMB-Memo-on-Regulation-of-AI-1-7-19.pdf

[127] G Zekos, The Independence of Arbitration, 2016 Nova Science Publications New York USA. www.novapublishers.com

[128] John O. McGinnis, Ilya Somin, Federalism vs. States' Rights: A Defense of Judicial Review in a Federal System, Research Paper No. 04–08, p48.

[129] Daniel R. Pinello, Linking Party to Judicial Ideology in American Courts: A Meta-Analysis, 20 Justice Sys. J. 219 (1999). Theodore W. Ruger, et al., The Supreme Court Forecasting Project: Legal and Political Science Approaches to Predicting Supreme Court Decision-making, 104 Colum. L. Rev. 1150, 1162 (2004).

[130] 5 U.S. (1 Cranch) 137 (1803).

stated that the interpretation of constitutional provisions was the province of judges.[131] A. Marmor argues that[132] "courts tend to possess legal expertise, they are the best kind of institution to be entrusted with constitutional interpretation." The constitutional system of federalism assigns powers to state and federal government officials not for their own benefit, but for that of the people of the entire nation. The total segregation of the courts from the legislature was itself a departure from an English tradition in which the House of Lords both wrote the laws and served as the supreme appellate court.[133] Courts' decisions cannot be reversed by the legislature.[134]

Federal courts have jurisdiction under Article III for cases "arising under" the laws of the USA.[135] To that extent, the Constitution only requires minimal diversity, and it does not employ an amount-in-controversy requirement.[136] Global constitution-making is a highly political and risky exercise in a multi-ethnic globe, not just for the reason that it might fail but since it tends to presuppose that "the best comes from the West."

Is the legislative branch totally independent from the judicial? Can the legislation drive the law toward the political direction and interests of the prevailing group via their economic status in a society? Can the judicial by the interpretation of law drive toward a specific direction? Is there the politics of law? Can law be totally objective? Is there the subjectivity of the objectivity of law? Does the politics of law define the objectivity of law and the depth of its subjectivity? Can the judicial branch by itself produce objective law? A totally independent judicial branch can produce objective law but it is based on a political decision toward the needed substance served by the content of the law. Can the legislative branch control in a way the judicial branch by producing the law serving the demands of interests of specific groups and not the whole society but merely the rest of the society has to adjust to the interests of the prevailing group?

Constitutions refer to both the right to be ruled by law and the right to a fair trial. In national legal systems it has been applied commonly to the relationship between citizens and the government which principle is now applied also globally. It is worth mentioning that while the doctrines and institutions of public law are tied to the State and to the blueprint thereof preserved in State norms, private law institutions like

---

[131] David Boies, Judicial Independence and the Rule of Law, 22 Journal of Law and Policy 57.

[132] Andrei Marmor, Constitutional Interpretation, USC Public Policy Research Paper No. 04–4, p10.

[133] Sotirios A. Barber, The Constitution Of Judicial Power 50 (1993).

[134] Dickerson v. United States, 530 U.S. 428, 443–44 (2000); Marbury v. Madison, 5 U.S. (1 Cranch) 137 (1803).

[135] Retail Prop. Tr. v. United Bhd. of Carpenters & Joiners of Am., 768 F.3d 938, 947 (9th Cir. 2014) Caterpillar Inc. v. Williams, 482 U.S. 386, 393 (1987).

[136] Exxon Mobil Corp. v. Allapattah Servs., Inc., 545 U.S. 546, 584 (2005) 28 U.S.C. § 1332 (2012).

property, family, contract, and tort law may actually have common rules. Moreover, public law too resorts to imitation due to transfers from one national legal context to another national legal framework, on top of the universal level embracing the consequences of such transfers in domestic legal systems.

The mutual recognition agreements well point up the transfer of legal institutions from one country to another. Due to such agreements, a product that can be sold in one state can also be sold in another state, on the same conditions. Moreover, mutual recognition agreements do not consist simply in the approval by one State of the law that applies to goods and businesses in another State in a given instant but they also portray that the other State's rules may be modified. Furthermore, with mutual recognition, national laws mix together, escalating the requirement for common standards to be established by multilateral organizations making possible one to choose from among multiple national law regimes. To that extent, labor protection, criminal justice and government-citizen relations exemplify the transfer from the state to the worldwide framework. Thus, a transfer takes place along a vertical alignment rather than a horizontal one which means that universal criminal law protects peace and security, and delineates war crimes, crimes against humanity and genocide as international crimes. In other words, the alternative of establishing non-State tribunals reacts to the objective to prevail over national legal systems by presenting the global one. A "universal" criminal law amalgamates or sometimes counters "parochial" criminal law.[137] To that extent, they have to act as real courts and not as political instruments in order to achieve political targets via the utilization of the law and the rule of law.

The Appellate Body of the WTO held that a State, when limiting imports from other countries, has to give exporting countries the likelihood to be heard, has to offer a reasoned and rational decision acknowledging the right to defense. The International Tribunal for the Law of the Sea (ITLOS) decided that a government which sequesters a ship and takes away the crew's passports has to respect the due process of law and the principle of fairness, informing the ship's owner and the crew and giving them the option to be heard. The European Court of Human Rights (ECHR) held that administrative decisions influencing individual rights are taken only after the interested parties have been heard.

The possibility of a technocratic patron-state and its client companies to exercise over market outcomes has weakened with integration into global markets, and to some extent for the reason that states have fractured in the meaning that state actors and agencies are ever more intertwined with "trans-governmental networks"—and the neoliberal state has become the established model of the competition state nowadays.

Considering that the state, through its government, has the power to lay down binding rules as laws that do not demand the explicit consent of the governed, it means that the state, and only the state, is permitted to enforce its laws which means

[137] G.P. Fletcher, Parochial versus Universal Criminal Law, in "Journal of International Criminal Justice", n. 3, 2005, p. 4.

that it has the monopoly of violence. It is vital to comprehend the contingency of the dual monopoly of law making and of enforcement. The monopoly is an achievement of the modern state, not a feature of every conceivable state because the monopoly did not exist in the middle ages, when multiple institutions competed. Moreover, the monopoly does not mean that state laws are the only binding rules in society for the reason that many non-state institutions are able to make binding rules and to have them enforced via the state's courts or via arbitration. What the monopoly implies is that such powers of non-state institutions get hold of their legally binding force only from assignment or recognition by the state. Besides, the state is not the only lawmaker, but it is the only institution that is free to decide whose rules should be recognized as law.[138]

On the one hand, transnational law is appealing in particular from the standpoint of social theory, for the reason that it amalgamates both doctrine and theory and both law and social reality.[139] On the other hand, international law embraces non-state actors, in particular NGOs and MNEs. In addition, international law focused more on individuals such as in human rights law, on the one hand, and in international criminal law, on the other. Thus, international law reaches into what had formerly been considered internal matters of sovereign states fragmenting the initiative of absolute state sovereignty.

National law has had to internationalize, the more it has been faced up to with circumstances that cannot be located evidently within one state. To that extent international and domestic law are no longer as distinct as they once were which nowadays this is a direct outcome of globalization and the decline of the bordered state. Nevertheless, international and national law stay officially distinct, and a theory of transnational law that disregards this prescribed distinction would have to be deficient.

As discussed earlier, public law is the law that governs relations between the state and the individual; private law governs relations between individuals. The distinction between public and private law exists in all national legal systems having different meanings in various legal systems. Besides, even private law depends for its enforcement on the state and its institutions. Insofar as private plaintiffs enforce their private rights, they make use of sovereignty of the state.

Therefore, by linking, in many occasions a state is forced not just by the core documents of the organizations, but also by following decisions, interpretations, and other actions undertaken by organs of that organization which have to be taken into consideration by the state when forming its national policies and laws. Moreover, the capacity of a state to affect the various norms depends on the organization, and its comparative power within it. Furthermore, a member state progressively undergoes a decrease in its capability to affect the decision-making processes within the

[138] PS Berman, Global Legal Pluralism: A Jurisprudence of Law Beyond Borders (Cambridge: Cambridge University Press 2012); S Richards, "Globalization as a Factor in General Jurisprudence" (2012) 41 Netherlands Journal of Legal Philosophy 129.

[139] P Zumbansen, "Transnational Legal Pluralism" (2010) 1 Transnational Legal Theory 141.

organization's institutions such as WTO because the state is constrained by these decisions as long as it remains a member of the organization.

The key reliance on public law urges the well-ordered state, rather than looking for the well-ordering of the state from other resources and then anticipating that well-ordering to be mirrored in the state's public law. Although public law is considered as qualitatively unique from the rest of municipal law, it implies a pre-eminence for law in this area which means looking to the law to offer us the idea of the well-functioning.

Which is the role of the state in relation to community? A modern state covers various elements bringing up possibilities of recognizing different conceptions of a state. The range of states even in considering only those that are contemporary and considered as democratic displays an analogous diversity of bodies of constitutional law or public law. Public law as constitutional law[140] cannot threaten the state, since its very task is to bring together the elements of a state in a manner which permits them to exist together as this state. It has to be considered that if the sovereign is equated with the state, then constitutional law does not limit the sovereign; it compels that sovereign's authority.

As mentioned earlier, competitiveness is the aptitude or capacity to compete in supplying a product or service. International competitiveness has been comprised both as a central objective with respect to which more or less all state policies should be considered, and as a central means to the resolution of more or less all other problems that the state is confronted with. To that extent, the term competitiveness tackles matters which have been central in public policy.[141] The public law concedes justice in a formalistic and institutionalist[142] direction acknowledging the normativity of legal decision-making and acknowledging that "no issues are simply 'procedural'[143]" having social, political, and ideological consequences.[144]

[140]Barry Friedman and Scott B. Smith, The Sedimentary Constitution, 147 U Pa L Rev. 1, 33 (1998).

[141]Paul R. Krugman, "Competitiveness: A Dangerous Obsession," Foreign Affairs, 73:2 (1994). Erik S. Reinert, "Competitiveness and Its Predecessors – a 500-year Cross-National Perspective," Structural Change and Economic Dynamics, 6:1 (1995).

[142]William N. Eskridge, Jr. and Gary Peller, The New Public Law Movement: Moderation as a Postmodern Cultural Form, 89 Mich L Rev. 707, 708 (1991).

[143]William N. Eskridge, Jr. and Gary Peller, The New Public Law Movement: Moderation as a Postmodern Cultural Form, 89 Mich L Rev. 707, 708 (1991).

[144]Keith E. Whittington, The New Originalism, 2 Georgetown J L & Pub Pol 599, 601 (2004) Antonin Scalia, Originalism: The Lesser Evil, 57 U Cin L Rev. 849, 863 (1989).

5.8 Politics and Law

It is worth noting that politics within the framework of law vary from politics out of law for the reason that legal institutions mediate power and control actions. In fact, under law, rules form the political institutions via which further rules and policies are identified and carried out and disputes settled which means that law-based institutions do not tame power or invalidate power differences. Quite the reverse: the rules mostly reveal the interests of those players with the highest political power, and authoritative players are better able to gain the results they wish through a society's institutions. Thus, law does not eliminate the pros of power but it does moderate the exercise of power by entailing that it be exercised via institutions and by rule-defined courses. Furthermore, institutions expressed by legal rules arbitrate the crude use of power, and they do so at both the national and the global altitude. Hence, it has to be taken into consideration that if politics within the context of law fluctuate qualitatively from politics outside it, then the link between politics and international law alters as we move along the range toward greater legal institutionalization.[145] Besides, F. A. Hayek argues that participation in politics is not that significant, and that economic liberty is what is central to good societies but economy works via political decisions and actions which means that economy is part of politics as well.[146]

As mentioned above constitution is the ground norm or basic norm of any national legal system which means that all other sources of law acquire their legitimacy from the Constitution. All legal systems are placed within their societal and political context having a number of functions. While the passage of law and its interpretation are of remarkable weight, there is a need to look at the interface of law with individuals, with political systems both formal and informal and with society. Furthermore, politicians, judges, administrative decision-makers, and the legal profession interlock with their functions within a societal context concerning their impact upon the formation of law and the legal system.

Moreover, as discussed earlier, the political contraption asserts that State control of the judiciary generates a system that focuses more on the authority of the State and less on the private contracting rights of individual investors than a legal system portrayed by an independent judiciary. Consequently, the political conduit emphasizes that cross-country differentiations in the independence of the judiciary are decisive for explaining cross-country divergences in financial development due to law application and its interpretation. Quite the opposite, the adaptability conduit underlines that cross-country disparities in the flexibility of the law are essential for explaining cross-country differentiations in financial development. To that extent, the political channel concentrates on the authority of the State while the adaptability channel highlights variations in the capacity of legal systems to go forward with

[145] Alec Stone Sweet, "Path Dependence, Precedent, and Judicial Power" in Martin Shapiro and Alec Stone Sweet (eds), On Law, Politics, and Judicialization (Oxford University Press 2002).

[146] F.A. Hayek, The Constitution of Liberty, The University of Chicago Press, Chicago, 1960.

altering circumstances. The impact of Jurisprudence is less in a system in which the State controls the judiciary than in a system where the judiciary benefits from greater independence.[147] Anyway, it is obvious that there is an impact of the elite economic interest groups upon the formation of laws especially in fields such as finance and trade in order to safeguard their interests. Moreover, elite economic interest groups (business and industry) make up the majority of interest groups and spend the most money on lobbying.[148] Economic elites have uneven impact over public policy.[149] Martin Gilens[150] argues that government policy across all policy areas echoes the policy preferences of the well-off but is untouched by the views of the poor and middle class. It is worth mentioning that global governance is escalating fast and in different directions, frequently without a clear or principled agenda to direct institutional formation and alteration. Moreover, formal international institutions, intergovernmental networks, and private authority run alongside, sometimes in harmony, sometimes in divergence, and all of them have close relations with a range of national political actors.[151]

It has to be considered that political influence is tilted in support of the wealthiest members of society in all states.[152] In addition, economic matters and their political lobbying is a fundamental ingredient of the conversation at the macro-level in constitutional law[153] which means an impact upon law making as well. Business and industry interest groups are not only more engaged in politics, but also their interests better elucidate effects than the views of other interest groups.[154] It is questionable how much affect those with economic power have over politics and public policy in all states.[155] It is worth mentioning that the majority only gets its way when, by coincidence, their liking happens to line up with the standpoint of economic elites.[156]

---

[147] Glaeser, E., Shleifer, A., 2002. Legal origins. Quarterly Journal of Economics 117, 1193–1230.

[148] Kay Lehman Schlozman, Sidney Verba & Henry E. Brady, The Unheavenly Chorus (2012).

[149] Benjamin I. Page & Lawrence R. Jacobs, Class War? 14 (2009).

[150] Martin Gilens & Benjamin I. Page, Testing Theories of American Politics: Elites, Interest Groups, and Average Citizens, 12 Persp. On Pol. 564, 573 (2014).

[151] Andreas Follesdal, The principle of subsidiarity as a constitutional principle in international law, 2 Glob. Const. 37–62 (2013).

[152] Benjamin I. Page, Larry M. Bartels & Jason Seawright, Democracy and the Policy Preferences of Wealthy Americans, 11 Persp. On Pol. 51 (March 2013). Martin Gilens & Benjamin I. Page, Testing Theories of American Politics: Elites, Interest Groups, and Average Citizens, 12 Persp. On Pol. 564, 573 (2014).

[153] Randy E. Barnett, Restoring, The Lost Constitution (2013); Richard A. Epstein, The Classical Liberal Constitution (2014).

[154] Andrew Gelman, Red State, Blue State, Rich State, Poor State (2010).

[155] Larry Bartels, Rich People Rule!, Wash. Post. Monkey Cage Blog, Apr. 8, 2014, http://www.washingtonpost.com/blogs/monkeycage/wp/2014/04/08/rich-people-rule/ G. William Domhoff, Who Rules America? (7th ed. 2013).

[156] Martin Gilens & Benjamin I. Page, Testing Theories of American Politics: Elites, Interest Groups, and Average Citizens, 12 Persp. On Pol. 564, 573 (2014).

On the one hand, states have assigned progressively power to international institutions and international courts. On the other hand, many international bodies have developed well beyond preliminary prospects and new types of transnational and private authority have materialized unlikely of formal assignment compositions altogether.[157] It has to be taken into consideration that the global elite economic interest groups formed due to economic globalization influence global politics and governance which means an impact upon the global law making as well. In addition, global governance has criticized for its democratic deficit, weak accountability mechanisms, and absence of judicial control in analogous way than national models have grown over the years.[158]

It is supposed that legal authority is a form of authority distinguished by a content-independent reaction to an instruction or order which means that the reply is content-independent for the reason that the order is not tailored to the recipient's interests.[159] It is worth mentioning that subsidiarity needs in global governance have turned into practice in certain areas of international politics, such as the European human rights regime, while they have exercised in other areas, such as trade and investment.[160] On the other hand, informal institutional settings generate fewer needs for subsidiarity not suited to the application of the principle as more formal decisional procedures.[161]

It has to be considered that legal systems do not occur from thin air. While law and legal systems have a "relative autonomy", law and legal systems are shaped by citizens' engagement with the political system, on top of the values and practices of legislators, judges, and the legal profession. Moreover, it has to be taken into consideration that legal systems are influenced by their institutions whose task is to generate law, their courts' interpretation and contribution in the application of law and the rules emerging from legal systems[162] assisting persons to comprehend what they can or cannot do. In other words, law enjoys a "relative autonomy" as long as its content is shaped and written down until it is repelled or modified by new rules formed by the above-mentioned influence.[163]

[157] Who Governs The Globe?, (Deborah D. Avant, Martha Finnemore, & Susan K. Sell eds., 2010).

[158] Michael Zürn, Martin Binder & Matthias Ecker-Ehrhardt, International authority and its politicization, 4 Int. Theory 69–106 (2012). Benedict Kingsbury, Nico Krisch & Richard B. Stewart, The Emergence of Global Administrative Law, 68 Law Contemp. Probl. 15–61 (2005).

[159] Andrei Marmor, An Institutional Conception of Authority, 39 Phil. & Pub. Aff. 238–40, 240 n.3 (2011).

[160] Sanford Levinson, Our Undemocratic Constitution: Where The Constitution Goes Wrong (And How We The People Can Correct It) 167–80 (2006).

[161] Michael Zürn, Global governance and legitimacy problems, 39 Gov. Oppos. 260–287 (2004).

[162] J. Raz, The Concept of a Legal System (Oxford: Clarendon, 1967); and L.M. Friedman, The Legal System: A Social Science Perspective (New York: Russel Sage, 1975). J. Raz, "The Identity of Legal Systems" (1971) 59(3) California Law Review 795.

[163] I.D. Balbus, "Commodity Form and Legal Form: An Essay on the 'Relative Autonomy' of Law" (1977) 11(3) Law & Society Review 571.

All players in legal systems are no different and it is central to reflect their effect on the concept, contestation and application of legal rules and norms. It is essential to focus on the principle of legality, equality before the law, the need for an independent judiciary, and for law to be public, precise, and accessible. Have these principles followed by international courts?

The law alone proscribes in a way state interference in the administration of justice.[164] Hence, legal decision-making has to be uncovered of political considerations and concentrated to a course of categorizing the facts into the appropriate legal categories which means that law could and should exclude political impacts. It has to be considered that all law in basically bound up with politics and so its practice carries both political and wider social influences and implications which means that States with closed or fixed polities are governed by stable elite coalitions that are not at immediate risk of losing or having to share power. Besides, the rule of law means that since the law is formed it has to be applied and interpreted in the same way in all cases regardless of who is under consideration or what economic or political interests are at stake. Algorithms are used in legal practice for administrative and organizational tasks, such as in the context of administration of justice. For instance, in Poland an AI system for random allocation of cases has been employed in 364 ordinary courts assigning cases to the judges of the specific court.[165]

Legal regimes with low intervention into the adjudication of specific cases are formally rational democratic. Besides, legal regimes in which political actors interfere dynamically and often into the adjudication of individual cases end up as apparatus or conservatory of politics, rather than fully functional legal systems in their own right. On the one hand, when legal institutions adjudicate cases without significant intervention by other actors, they function according to the rule of law. On the other hand, when legal institutions are subject to intervention in their adjudication of individual cases, they function under the order of authoritarian leaders, or other contenders for power seek to mobilize justice in support of revolutionary, transformational, or other political agendas. Where intervention is high, but the polity is closed or fixed, neo-traditional legal systems can be found which means that in such systems, well-established elites use law energetically as a means to uphold their positions of political, economic, and social power. Besides, where established elites abstain from intervention, leaving legal institutions to adjudicate cases in a properly rational manner even in anticipation of augmenting their political legitimacy or assisting undeniable types of economic relationships and development, they are categorized as rule by law regimes.

Which is the place of law in a globalized terrain of politics and economics? It is worth mentioning that law and politics are intensely interrelated in the space beyond the state. In other words, regarding the creation and application of law, politics is a

---

[164] Mirjan Damaška, "The Reality of Prosecutorial Discretion: Comments on a German Monograph." American Journal of Comparative Law 29 (1981): 125.

[165] Alek Tarkowski. 2019. Report. Automating Society, Poland AlgorithmWatch, (29 January 2019) available at: https://algorithmwatch.org/en/automatingsociety-2019/poland/

force that has to be controlled via legislative and juridical action. It could be argued that politics intervene when law fails which means that rules are a means to political ends, both in words of a policy agenda, on top of provisions of political concession. On the other hand, law is needed for political success, but it seems that law is not always the first movement toward an orderly international system.

Furthermore, politics considered as a way to an end by altering rules and practices regarded detrimental to the public good. Moreover, both politics and law are medians for social advancement and restructuring. It is argued that politics and law are discrete fields of "ontological and epistemological" peculiarities, but they are utilized by governments in order to produce institutional and juridical grounds modeling the rationality of political agency that commands the new world of global economic law. In other words, global politics more and more take place in a legal framework and so alike in the national milieu, international legal environments are arenas at which governments and private entities pursue political contests over procedure and outcome. It worth mentioning here that the impact of politics over the formation of law and vice versa is productive in many occasions as long as the written law is applied as a rule of law without any effort to manipulate the interpretation of law in order to serve specific economic affairs against the equality and justice in the essence of the rule of law' applicability.

On the one hand, political economists regard institutions and their attendant rules and practices as establishing the modern form of global economic governance. On the other hand, lawyers talk about the escalating institutionalization of market governance mechanisms as international economic law. In other words, global economic governance is achieved via international economic law but this does not mean that the international economic law as an international rule of law has not to be applied objectively which means not accepting a case by case different application of the international economic law in accordance with the economic interests of the specific economic elite.

It could be said that law is considered a product of political alteration with the meaning that any change of law is made after a political decision has taken place in order to achieve the political goals via the utilization of the law and the rule of law indicating the impact upon each other. In other words, it seems that the path of the transition enlightens the reigning balance of power, which sequentially purportedly makes clear the legal response. Nevertheless, to say that countries do what they can does not enlighten the great diversity of transitional legal phenomena due to the fact that the global political forces intervene in order to achieve their global political interests via political and legal means.

It is argued that the rule of law is a political element of how societies are structured which means that it is both a political product that is the result of political contestation and negotiation between both elite and non-elite actors and a "constitutive" ingredient of how power is applied and constrained and how societies accomplish their social, political, and economic interaction and distributional struggles by non-violent ways.[166]

It has to be considered that the course of regional economic integration in Asia has been slow-moving for the reason that the politicization of regionalism by power rivalries. On the other hand, regional integration is essentially legalization advancement and so via FTAs, states establish rules and standards to govern their external economic relations, and assent to bind themselves to legal obligations under international economic law. It could be said that power and politics open new roads and the law comes to regulate the new situation in order to have a viable situation by the application of the rule of law. Regional integration via political decisions generates international economic law subsystems.[167]

The question to be answered is if the political targeting influences directly the law and the rule of law rather than a good law works nicely with the political targets implementing them? The political goals should not twist the implementation of the rule of law in order to achieve and implement the interests of a particular group against the essence of justice and fairness. However, political and legal practices converge toward a future of legal interconnection but political deliberations over the future of the global economy occur via legal networks and in institutional arenas. To that extent, law counted less in international relations than did the eternal effort over wealth and power designating the equilibrium of power by which politics molds legal frames. It could be said that the fight for international law is a fight to restrain politics.

Regional integration is achieved by power politics and so the prevailing great powers use legal rules and institutions to enhance their interests and institutionalize their power, both regionally and globally. Consequently, Asian regionalism is one of the best instances of exploring the role of law in influencing international politics in tandem with the role of politics in molding international law, and the prospect of using international economic law to restrain injurious power politics. Wang Jiangyu[168] argues that the course of regional economic integration in Asia "has

[166]Desai, D. and Woolcock, M. (2012) "The Politics of Rule of Law Systems in Developmental States: 'Political Settlements' as a Basis for Promoting Effective Justice Institutions for Marginalized Groups" ESID Working Paper No. 08, University of Manchester. Desai, D. and Woolcock, M. (2015); "The politics – and Process – of Rule of Law Systems in Development States," in Bukenya, B., Hickey, S. and Sen, K. (eds.), The Politics of Inclusive Development: Interrogating the Evidence, pp. 174–196. Oxford: OUP.

[167]Joel Trachtman, International Trade: Regionalism, in Research Handbook In International Economic Law 151, 151–52 (Andrew T. Guzman & Alan O. Sykes eds., 2007). Masahiro Kawai & Ganeshan Wignaraja, Multilateralizing Regional Trade Arrangements in Asia, in Multilateralizing Regionalism: Challenges For The Global Trading System 495, 500–504 (Richard Baldwin & Patrick Low eds., 2009).

[168]Wang Jiangyu, Between Power Politics and International Economic Law: Asian Regionalism, the Trans-Pacific Partnership and U.S.-China Trade Relations NUS Law Working Paper 2018/027Jiangyu Wang, Decoding the Trans-Pacific Partnership: Will the U.S.-led trade agreement pose a threat to China?, BEIJING REV. (May 20, 2017), http://www.bjreview.com/World/201510/t20151026_800041255.html

been rather slow because of the politicization of Asia regionalism by power rivalries."

Moreover, the formation of FTAs cannot be fully understood without bearing in mind the political context within which they are molded.[169] To that extent, it seems that China's FTA tactic includes both economic and geopolitical considerations, with the latter playing a comparatively more important role. According to a World Bank report regional integration is good politics by meeting politics desires, such as security or augmented bargaining power and so satisfying powerful lobbies which mean that politics impose their own rule of law.[170]

The TPP is a major instrument from the viewpoint of international economic law and is already in the process of influencing the direction of the international economic order and so the success of the TPP in rule-making demonstrates the clarified strategy of the U.S. in using FTAs like the TPP to export American laws and make rules for the rest of the planet. Thus, the big power with its politics forms the international rule of law.[171] It is argued that monopolizing the rule-making power in international trade was the first strategic objective of the Obama Administration in stimulating the TPP.[172] Kejin Zhao[173] argues that, in big powers understanding, discourse power embraces, in part, a state's capacity to "operate politically" which is expressed in "agenda-setting, rule-making capacity and international mobilization ability" which means that politics impose their own rule of law via their rule making. Thus, it is clear that politics, via a powerful state, impose law upon people and other states. On the one hand, the rule of law demands a legitimate approach but, on the other hand, the other way around politics decide the law and the legitimacy according to their interest and not essentially based on equality and justice. Therefore, they impose their legitimacy and legality via their own rule of law which in fact is shaped via a politics course rather than a purely legal process.

In practice, rule of law takes very different forms due to the fact that societies find their ways to managing and regulating political, social, and economic interaction. It has to be taken into consideration that rule of law exists where there is adequate consensual agreement among elite players and governing authorities, and most of society, to be bound by an approved body of norms comprising the "law" to administer social, political, and economic interactions via non-violent ways; and there is appropriate supervision, dispute resolution, regulatory and coercive

---

[169] Marc Bacchetta Et Al., World Trade Report 2011: The WTO and Preferential Trade Agreements: From Co-Existence To Coherence 95 (2011).

[170] World Bank, Trade Blocs 11 (Oxford Univ. Press 2000).

[171] Barack Obama, President Obama: The TPP would let America, not China, lead the way on global trade, WASH. POST. (May 2, 2016), https://www.washingtonpost.com/opinions/ "America should write the rules. America should call the shots. Other countries should play by the rules that America and our partners set, and not the other way around."

[172] Michael Froman, The Strategic Logic of Trade: New Rules of the Road for the Global Market, FOREIGN AFF. (2014), https://www.foreignaffairs.com/articles/americas/strategic-logic-trade

[173] Kejin Zhao, Note, China's Rise and Its Discursive Power Strategy, CHINESE POL. SCI. REV., Sept. 2016, at 539.

capability by the accepted public authority to implement this normative structure, via permitted patterns of bureaucratic, adjudicatory, oversight, and enforcement devices in accordance with a community's sociocultural, political, and institutional background. In line, it seems that the scale of inclusion, legitimacy, participation, and consensual agreement regarding this is a political result and will differ both between and within states which means that law not only is about formal state law but also embraces other "reigning" norm systems, echoing the various realities of legal pluralism in many states.

Concerning the rate of the powerful state and its capacity to impose law and rule of law, Wang Jiangyu[174] specifies that "It may be able to resist and refuse to accept certain rules made by the U.S., but it does not have the ability to create a new system of rules for FTAs or any other area of the global economy, at least at this stage ... even though China is in possession of the power to make rules, it would choose to adopt the existing rules made by the West—specifically the U.S.—rather than make a different set of rules of its own." Therefore, it is obvious the role of power upon the creation of law and in line to the formation of the applied rule of law.

It has to be considered that politics covers a wide ground of activity, while the law remains a confined ground where the rules of politics are generated and questioned. Nonetheless, politics is not external to law and international politics takes place within a legal environment. Any political activity by an individual or business, or a government that takes place within the modern state is regulated to some degree. Global politics is ruled as much by the law as by the ethos of diplomats. States are the subject of international law commanding the use of violence undermining the question of legal legitimacy.

In addition, it has to be taken into account that space applications, particularly telecommunications, global navigation, and Earth observation, have a fundamental role in the process of globalization due to the fact that globalization is a result of the interconnections and interdependence of and across human societies that is enabled by the developments of communication, cyberspace, transportation, and computer technology that bridge geographic distances. Technological upgrade has allowed the use of AI in international diplomacy. In particular, many countries are active in making use of AI in offering insights for its diplomats into the possible scenarios and the evolution of events on the international arena. There is also an increasingly active use of AI in supporting economic diplomacy in trade negotiations and so boosting international cooperation. Furthermore, space applications and their uses are various, embracing communication and data transfer, navigation, meteorology management, tracking, and logistics influencing international politics and diplomacy.[175]

---

[174] Wang Jiangyu, Between Power Politics and International Economic Law: Asian Regionalism, the Trans-Pacific Partnership and U.S.-China Trade Relations NUS Law Working Paper 2018/027 P50.

[175] Pelton, J. N., Madry, S., & Camacho-Lara, S. (Eds.). (2017). Handbook of Satellite Applications (Second Edition). Cham: Springer. Bjola, C. (2017, October 14). Satellite Remote Sensing and Diplomatic Crisis Management. https://medium.com/digitaldiplomacy/satellite-remote-sensing-

AI is utilized not only in international security; the use of autonomous weapons systems but also there is a wide range of areas in economic diplomacy, where AI is contributing to international cooperation. Moreover, AI is an imperative device in international diplomacy to build trust among the key stakeholders in conflict resolution or dispute settlement via the use of impartial procedures that are at the same time verifiable and transparent. Thus, robo-justice will be the mechanism utilized by diplomacy in AAI society.

At the global level one of the key risks linked with AI development is the likelihood of the progressive rise in the technological gap between the advanced and the least developed economies which is a matter in international diplomacy.

It has to be taken into account that firms, foundations, and governments allocate funding to develop and deploy AI systems. Indeed, advantages in the development of AI capabilities translate into economic strengths ranging from a stronger base for further technological innovation to a stronger and more competent economic diplomacy.

States have developed a noteworthy legal system in order to utilize economic law moving from politics and law to the politics of law in the realm of international economic regulation. State action is based upon a rationale rooting in some form of planning process signifying the strategic and political intent of governments.

It is worth mentioning here that legitimacy is a variable concept in law and politics denoting the way in which social and political players experience a system of governance regarding as creditable, loyalty, and respect. Along these lines, legitimacy delivers a degree of stability and resilience to forms of social organization and rule. So, legitimacy offers an analytical encounter to anyone paying attention in the link between legal and political alteration and their socio-political, socio-cultural foundations. For instance, there is a varying character of the legitimacy of a "constitutional" legislature as opposed to a simply "administrative" body or an independent agency.

In current governance, both sorts of institutions are qualified as legitimate producers of rules of general and potential application, notwithstanding in separate settings and under different limitations. To that extent, the rules generated by administrative bodies are, legally at least, considered as inferior to, indeed even dependent upon, the rules produced by legislatures but the legitimacy cannot be challenged.[176] The national legislature is the apparent source of legitimacy, a privileged role often written in the constitution itself[177] generating the law and so the need for the application of the rule of law free from any influence of politics during the appliance of the law.

---

and-diplomatic-crisis-management-286651c83cb, Bjola, C., & Holmes, M. (Eds.). (2015). Digital Diplomacy: Theory and Practice (1 edition). London; New York: Routledge.

[176] Peter L Lindseth, Power and Legitimacy: Reconciling Europe and the Nation-State (OUP 2010).

[177] Peter L Lindseth, "The Paradox of Parliamentary Supremacy: Delegation, Democracy, and Dictatorship in Germany and France, 1920s–1950s" (2004) 113 Yale LJ 1341.

5.9 The Politics of Law

Legal scholars frequently talk about the politics of law meaning that the design and application of law is not a direct procedure of applying reason to produce rules. It is worth mentioning that the values and beliefs of decision makers have to be taken into account concerning the setting of the decision-making procedure.

As discussed earlier, law is stated as a set of rules that rule relations between members of society involving a basis in obligation and contains enforcement measures together with a procedure for establishing violation. Moreover, the materialization of law occurs in a political arena in which ideas and interests are disputed which means that the politics of law articulates a phenomenon incorporating the essence of the way of forming and implementing law in order to achieve the political goals for which the law is made to serve which is explored across international relations and international law.

Politics of law embrace the role of ideology in legal processes. The aim of law is to advance social life which is the aim of politics as well which means that politics is the background upon which the law is shaped and so politics is indispensable for law and law is for politics for the reason that politics is arena for law to develop and advance. It has to be considered that the politics of law may be identified as political belief over the way that rules are formulated and applied. In other words, politics of law is the frame/setting in which politics takes place beyond the state. Moreover, it could be argued that politics of law is about politics in the context of law because any written law not only encompasses the prevailed political aspect of social life on the regulated matter but also the written law is interpreted in accordance with the political environment prevailed in the regulated jurisdiction. Furthermore, there is politics of international economic law for the reason that the place of law has to be considered due to the conception of the rule of law beyond the state since international law is a tool of state authority, and so international economic law considered as a means to politics and diplomacy that governments exploit when it suits them.

Furthermore, politics of law is the utilization of law in such a way that it promotes the interests of the prevailing group with all governments which in fact is the one holding the economic resources. The legislature produces the right law to implement the interests of the prevailing group but not being obviously against the rights of a society and the society is shifting by law toward the direction decided by the leading economic syndicates. In other words, it is given the interpretation and approach by courts the one helpful toward the prevailing syndicates producing the politics of law. Globalization adds to the politics of law as well implementing the interests of the international economic syndicates. Moreover, the law has to be objective but in fact there is a subjective objectivity which is formulated via the politics of law in order to comply with the interests of the prevailing economic group being behind all governments. Is the politics of law context clear from the wording of the law? The answer is no and on first sight it seems that the law expresses the whole society but the combination of various laws and their interpretation or implementation in practice identifies the direction chosen to be followed by the prevailing economic group within a society. Does politics of law affect politics? There is an interrelation between them utilized by governments to achieve their goals. Is politics of law illegal? No, it is a fair way to achieve with a typically legal way the interest of the prevailing group. Does this happen with all laws? No, it takes place in topics essential for the dominant economic syndicate with in a society.

5.10 Politics, Law, and Courts

As mentioned above a range of normative principles have been projected to direct the allocation of global authority and the classical norm is the consent of contracting states. To that extent, if states consensually choose to use right in a given subject area jointly, their consent also determines the aptness of the newly constituted international authority.[178] Besides, Utilitarian considerations founded on the principle of "comparative benefit", the idea of global public goods, or the Pareto principle offering an option which means that decisions are allocated to an institution that can make certain the most valuable stipulation of welfare.[179] Moreover, a third standpoint puts up conceptions of justice which means the emergence of cosmopolitan justice stressing moral obligations beyond borders backing global authority. Furthermore, cosmopolitan justice rationalizes the formation of strong supra-state institutions as instrumentally needed so as to guarantee compliance with trans-boundary obligations of justice, together with obligations of distributive justice.[180]

Which is to the relations between national and international institutions? Subsidiarity is a principle entailing decision-making to take place at a lower level if not good reasons are for shifting it upwards. Subsidiarity favors local action becoming a justification for higher-level decision-making.[181] Which is to the relations between national and international institutions? Subsidiarity is a principle for assigning authority to various levels of governance presenting assistance on how powers are to be implemented. Moreover, subsidiarity is "the soul of federalism" which means preference for the local leaving open how this is to be accomplished being the list of

[178] Tom Christiano, The Legitimacy of International Institutions, in The Routledge Companion To Philosophy Of Law (Andrei Marmor, Ed.) 380–393 (2012). Nico Krisch, The Decay of Consent: International Law in an Age of Global Public Goods, 108 Am. J. Int. Law 1–40 (2014).

[179] Allen Buchanan & Robert O. Keohane, The legitimacy of global governance institutions, 20 ETHICS INT. AFF. 405–437 (2006).

[180] Simon Caney, Justice Beyond Borders: A Global Political Theory (2005). ch. 5. Michael Blake & Patrick Taylor Smith, International Distributive Justice, in Stanford Encyclopedia Of Philosophy (2013), http://plato.stanford.edu/archives/win2013/entries/international-justice/

[181] Michelle Evans, The Principle of Subsidiarity as a Social and Political Principle in Catholic Social Teaching, 3 Solidar. J. Cathol. Soc. Thought Secul. Ethics 4, 54 (2013). David Golemboski, Federalism and the Catholic Principle of Subsidiarity, EarlyView PUBLIUS (2015).

powers for each level of government.[182] To that extent, in the EU subsidiarity has dominated a prominent place which is introduced as a formal rule for the first time in the 1992 Maastricht Treaty. Furthermore, subsidiarity deals with political questions of power-sharing which should be left to the political procedure but in general not be used by constitutional courts to review legislative endeavor. Besides, it could be said that courts should play a role in reviewing formal, written constitution-making which means constitutional amendment and replacement.[183]

Forceful types of judicial review have developed that have enhanced the politics of constitution-making suggesting that courts might be able to defend individual rights and political competition from the dangers of majoritarian constitution-making in embryonic democracies.[184] Courts are often unable to advance constitution-making politics allowing abuse by the elite of formal constitutional alteration.[185] Moreover, formal, written constitution-making whether it is constitutional amendment or replacement can be risky to individual rights demonstrating institutionalized political competition in weak and inadequately institutionalized democracies. Formal institutionalization of presidential rule through the constitution-making procedure is considered to be "abusive constitutionalism."[186]

It is worth mentioning that there is an escalating role of courts in regulating constitution-making politics. Considering that "new constitutionalism" has spread around the globe constitutions have allowed courts significant formal power to mediate in politics. Moreover, it seems that courts perform a vital task in protecting democratic outcomes in constitution-making.[187] Andrew Arato[188] argues that

---

[182] Gareth Davies, Subsidiarity: The Wrong Idea, in the Wrong Place, at the Wrong Time, 43 Common Mark. Law Rev. 63–84 (2006).

[183] Jenna Bednar, Subsidiarity and Robustness. Building the Adaptive Efficiency of Federal Systems, in Federalism And Subsidiarity (Nomos Lv) 231, 231 (James E. Fleming & Jacob T. Levy eds., 2014). Steven G. Calabresi & Lucy D. Bickford, Federalism and Subsidiarity: Perspectives from U.S. Constitutional Law, in Federalism And Subsidiarity (James E. Fleming & Jacob T. Levy, Eds.) 123–189 (2014). Paul Craig, Subsidiarity: A Political and Legal Analysis, 50 J. Common Mark. Stud. 72–87, 80 (2012).

[184] Katherine Glenn Bass & Sujit Choudhry, Democracy Reporting Int'l, Constitutional Review In New Democracies 7 (Michael Meyer-Resende & Duncan Pickard eds., 2013), http://www.democracy-reporting.org/files/dri-bp-40_en_constitutional_review_in_new_democracies_2013-09.pdf

[185] Samuel Issacharoff, Constitutional Courts and Democratic Hedging, 99 Geo. L.J. 961, 965 (2011); Po Jen Yap, The Conundrum of Unconstitutional Constitutional Amendments, 4 Global Constitutionalism 114, 136 (2015).

[186] David Landau, Constitution-Making Gone Wrong, 64 Ala. L. Rev. 923 (2013) David Landau, Abusive Constitutionalism, 47 U.C. Davis L. Rev. 189, 191 (2013).

[187] Ran Hirschl, Towards Juristocracy: The Origins and Consequences Of The New Constitutionalism 169–70 (2004). William Partlett, The Dangers of Popular Constitution-Making, 38 Brook. J. Int'l L. 193 (2012).

[188] Andrew Arato, Constitution-Making Under Occupation: The Politics Of Imposed Revolution In Iraq, at viii (2009). Victor Ferreres Comella, The Consequences of Centralizing Constitutional Review in a Special Court: Some Thoughts on Judicial Activism, 82 Tex. L. Rev. 1705, 1730 (2004).

judicial review makes certain that the principles of constitutionalism apply not just to the resulting constitution but also to "the democratic process of constitution making." President Morsi striped the courts of jurisdiction eventually diluting deliberation and turning constitution-making into a divisive assignment of majoritarian imposition.[189] Besides, judicial review is most common in the review of constitutional amendment.

It is worth noting that predictability, or "reckonability," is a requiring quality of any law worthy of the name.[190] Moreover, considering that a vital function of the law in operation is to make visible the scale of interests and concerns when key decisions are made, rules that are fixed and announced beforehand make it possible to anticipate with fair assurance how the authority will use its coercive powers in certain situations and to plan one's personal affairs on the core of this knowledge. Therefore, when present, these features of law infuse the rule of law with a certain degree of fairness nonetheless, under modern rule of law conceptions, fairness depends on the equitable administration of justice which means that this obligation, in turn, necessitates "procedural due process," the disposal of an independent judiciary, and the government's obedience to procedural obligations for forming and changing law.[191] In other words, the rule of law denotes equality and justice in its application and so it is procedure that denotes much of the difference between rule by law and rule by fiat.[192] Overall it has to be considered that judicial review by independent courts is a crucial element for rule of law, particularly in the framework of administrative governance.[193]

It has to be taken into account that administrative law is premised on transparency, accountability, and reason-giving and so when government takes action involving rights, it must explain why. Algorithmic devices that federal agencies use to make and support public decisions are not, by their structure, fully explainable and so there is a need of crafting concrete legal and regulatory mechanisms for algorithmic devices fulfilling transparency values by making certain fidelity to the agency's legislative mandate and other legal commitments.[194]

---

[189] Nathan Brown, Decoder: Morsi, the Judiciary, and Acts of Sovereignty, ARABIST (Nov. 25, 2012), http://arabist.net/blog/2012/11/25/decoder-morsi-the-judiciary-and-acts-of-sovereignty.html

[190] Karl N. Llewellyn, The Common Law Tradition 17 (1960).

[191] Papachristou v. City of Jacksonville, 405 U.S. 156, 171 (1972) Wisconsin v. Constantineau, 400 U.S. 433, 436 (1971).

[192] Jeremy Waldron, The Rule of Law and the Importance of Procedure, in Getting to the Rule of Law 18 (James E. Fleming ed., 2011) (providing account of procedure as a fundamental rule of law value).

[193] A.V. Dicey, Introduction To The Study Of The Law Of The Constitution 181–205 (10th ed. 1959).

[194] Judulang v. Holder, 565 U.S. 42, 45 (2011) ("When an administrative agency sets policy, it must provide a reasoned explanation for its action."); FCC v. Fox Television Stations, Inc., 556 U.S. 502, 515 (2009) (noting "the requirement that an agency provide reasoned explanation for its action").

It is worth noting that a central requirement of administrative law is the agency's duty to explain the decisions it makes which it has to be based on an existing law and not politics to form a law according to their needs in order to claim that it follows the rule of law.[195]. It is worth noting that the risk of an adverse judicial ruling intensifies agency incentives to use policymaking mechanisms not subject to judicial review[196] which means that there is an effort to utilize the formal rule of law. Furthermore, it seems that for the reason that agency non-enforcement decisions have been exempted from judicial review, administrative agencies protect policy decisions of great public importance from judicial review by generating a situation in which agencies are able to hide what are at bottom legislative and judicial judgments behind the pretense of executive discretion which means a bypassing the utilization of the rule of law.[197]

Therefore, the rule of law is the concept that everyone, both state and national, is bound by the law and so the state makes the rules and is anticipated to follow the rules. Even though it may make the law, the state is not itself above the law which means that the state has the "duty to govern in accordance with law" and so the executive doesn't have an unrestrained authority to lock people up but the executive has to rule in accordance with the law.[198] To that extent, the Supreme Court[199] repeated that "If the rule of law is to mean anything, decisions as to what is necessary or expedient in this context cannot be left to the uncontrolled judgment of the executive."

The appealing to the rule of law for the Executive may be kept in check through judicial review and so judicial review affects the doctrines and calling the Executive to account to the law.[200] Can judicial review be utilized for shaping the rule of law accordingly? It has to be taken into account that courts can incentivize some departures from the law and so in conjunction with their role as law enforcers, courts design, preserve, and legitimize an incentive structure that empowers public officials

[195] Ming H. Chen, Administrator-in-Chief: The President and Executive Action in Immigration Law, 69 Admin. L. Rev. 347 (2017) (positing that the extent to which the President enhances the procedural legitimacy of agency actions strengthens the legacy of the policies when the substance of the policies is challenged).

[196] Nina A. Mendelson, Regulatory Beneficiaries and Informal Agency Policymaking, 92 Cornell L. Rev. 397, 408 (2007).

[197] Ashutosh Bhagwat, Three-Branch Monte, 72 Notre Dame L. Rev. 157, 157 (1996).

[198] Tom Bingham, "The Case of Liversidge v Anderson : The Rule of Law Amid the Clash of Arms" (2009) 43 The International Lawyer 33, 38. In Liversidge v Anderson [1942] AC 206, "Even in times of war, the courts could not simply accept without question the executive's view of what was reasonable. So, the executive couldn't lock up a person without evidence because they thought it was necessary, they had to at least be able to justify this in a court to be in accordance with the law".

[199] Ahmet and others v HM Treasury [2010] UKSC 2 at para. 45.

[200] Daniel Kanstroom, The Better Part of Valor: The REAL ID Act, Discretion, and the "Rule" of Immigration Law, 51 N.Y. L. Sch. L. Rev. 161, 166–67 (2007) ("It is simply impossible to define, 'unconstitutional, unauthorized or simply arbitrary or capricious' without judicial review and without a rule-like, systematic backdrop.").

to resist the law which means that via disparate judicial doctrines, such as standing, political question, sovereign immunity, state secrets, and contempt of court, courts grant public officials discretion to depart from laws that they are otherwise bound to obey.[201]

On the one hand, some constitutions explicitly ascertain that parts of the constitution un-amendable. On the other hand, other constitutions clarify the majority required for the amendment to be backed up by referendum or delegate the determination of the majority to a particular law. In addition, many new constitutions clearly award constitutional courts the formal power to review constitution-making.[202] It has to be considered that courts perform a positive role in improving constitution-making when the judges on these courts being part of a community which has a broad role in advancing the performance of democracy. Judges of such specialized constitutional courts are expected to build up an attitudinal duty which is developed in contexts with historically entrenched respect for judicial review where courts have control over who is appointed to the court.

Likewise, various countries across the globe use changing and intersecting ideologies and practices in the administration of justice. There are primary constitutional and political reasons for separating state from community but certain local agency employees are forming part of "community" throughout the restorative procedure. To that extent, state representatives though politically separated from the community, in reality form an imperative component of any local social milieu.

Further, most International Courts (ICs) gain formal legal authority (de jure authority) due to an act of delegation from states creating a court's formal right to rule on disputes falling within its jurisdiction.[203] The legal right to rule exists even if the moral or ethical basis of that right continues to be disputed. ICs acquire unquestioned power merely by asset of delegation which means that delegation awards formal authority on ICs denoting their purpose in vital manner.

To that extent, the act of delegation grants upon a court a defined authority to rule on disputes that fall within its jurisdiction.[204] International judges supposed to decide cases based on the reasoned interpretation and application of international law irrespective of any political interference. It has to be considered that ICs by

---

[201] Adam Shinar, Enabling Resistance: How Courts Facilitate Departures from the Law, and Why This May Not Be a Bad Thing, 17 N.Y.U. J. Legis. & Pub. Pol'y 989, 992 (2014) ("The removal of such oversight opens the door to interpretations and actions that may deviate from those of the courts to the point of violating the law.").

[202] European Commission for Democracy Through Law (Venice Commission), Report on Constitutional Amendment, Study No. 720/2008, CDL-AD (2010)001 (Jan. 19, 2010), http://www.venice.coe.int/webforms/documents/default.aspx?pdffile=CDL-AD%282010%29001-e. Tom Ginsburg & Mila Versteeg, Why Do Countries Adopt Constitutional Review?, 30 J.L. Econ. & Org. 587, 587 (2014).

[203] David A. Wirth, Reexamining Decision-Making Processes in International Environmental Law, 79 Iowa L. Rev. 769, 779 (1994) Andrei Marmor, An Institutional Conception of Authority, 39 Phil & Pub Aff. 238–40, 240 n.3 (2011).

[204] Curtis A. Bradley & Judith G. Kelley, The Concept of Delegation, 71 Law &Contemp Probs no. 1, 2008.

being new institutions, their rulings may conflict with and ousting well-established or presumed interpretations of legal rules or social norms which means that replacing established ideas and practices is challenging. For international judges, doing so is particularly insubordinate for the reason that ICs function in a milieu of compound authoritative decision makers. Officially, ICs are the premier judicial interpreters of the international rules within their jurisdictions but other international and national legal and political players compete over their respective jurisdictions and over the meanings of laws. The judicial nature of ICs makes them a marked kind of international institution having the right to rule applying the rule of law which means turn their formal mandate into de facto authority provoking political, legal, and practical encounter. Moreover, delegation alone is inadequate for the reason that a court may have de facto authority in some of the disputes that it adjudicates but still not be a politically commanding institution since many legal violations are never brought to court or are the theme of rulings that are disregarded.[205] Besides, authoritative ICs have power in reality stretching out across a wide array of matters, states, and types of cases.[206]

5.11 Global Justice and Politics

Global justice[207] embodies an "institutionalist" cosmopolitan approach limited to conditions in which social goods are allocated in a context of mutual political and legal relationships. International economic law and its institutions are at the center of global justice.[208] Moreover, global justice as a concept is not a problem but the problem is determining what this justice consists of, and how to deliver it.[209] Imposition by a global judicial body of a common legal principle not only upon states but also within national legal systems is respected by everyone at the national level. On the other hand, legal principles maybe transplanted from national legal systems to the global level. The power of law operates where you have the ability to

[205] Walid Ben Hamida, The First Arab Investment Court Decision, 7 J. World Invest. & Trade 699 (2006) (discussing the Arab Investment Court). Joseph Weiler, The Transformation of Europe, 100 Yale L.J. 2403, 2447–48 (1991) (discussing how the ECJ built its authority incrementally through its interactions with national judges, government officials, and private litigants).

[206] Eric A. Posner & Alan O. Sykes, Efficient Breach of International Law: Optimal Remedies, "Legalized Noncompliance," and Related Issues, 110 Mich. L. Rev. 243, 280 (2011).

[207] Simon Caney, Justice Beyond Borders. Oxford: OUP, 2006. p. 1.

[208] Chi Carmody, Frank J. Garcia and John Linarelli, Global Justice And International Economic Law 2011. Jack L. Goldsmith And Eric A. Posner, The Limits Of International Law (2005) (arguing that international law is simply the product of nation states pursuing their self-interest on the international stage and that international law creates no obligations apart from those that arise from the pursuit of self-interest).

[209] Allen E. Buchanan, "Assessing the Communitarian Critique of Liberalism," Ethics 99 (1989) pp. 852–82, Michael Walzer, Spheres of Justice (New York: Basic Books 1983).

enforce.[210] Both Hart[211] and Fuller[212] ascribe the incident of formal legal systems to the demand for a more deliberate ways of adapting normative classification to altering or multifaceted settings. Thus, in a society with a secure legal order secondary rules are applicable which means that a modification in rules or their interpretation, enforcement moves from the old to the new. It is characteristic that judicial formalists prefer to check formal adherence to rules rather than the motives and effects of the actions.[213]

It is characteristic that judicial formalists prefer to check formal adherence to rules rather than the motives and effects of the actions.[214] Justice is not only to apply the law, but its core is to reach—between a complex, ritualized and even exhausting process—the solution of a dispute which could be socially shared and accepted as long as justice is independent from any political manipulation or implementing the philosophy of an elite that the elite governs according its interest the democracy and law are interpreted accordingly by forcefully persuading the people for the fairness of the systems by utilizing many means such as money or use of force by "mafia" behind the curtains, etc.

Has Poland be turned into an illiberal state via a rule of law crisis? It is argued that Poland, which used to be an epitome of successful transition from communism to liberal democracy, descended so easily to an illiberal state via a rule of law crisis.[215] Bojan Bugaric and Alenka Kuhelj[216] argue that both in Hungary and Poland, the

---

[210] Anthony D'Amato, Is International Law Really "Law?," 79 Nw. U. L. Rev. 1293, 1293 (1984). Gregory C. Shaffer & Mark A. Pollack, Hard Versus Soft Law in International Security, 52 B.C. L. Rev. 1147, 1163 (2011) (describing the advantages of law that is not binding); Joshua Kleinfeld, Enforcement and the Concept of Law, 121 Yale L.J. Online 293, 306–15 (2011), http://www.yalelawjournal.org/images/pdfs/1029.pdf (arguing that enforcement power is not a necessary condition for law).

[211] Hart H.L.A. 1961. The Concept of Law. (Third edition, paperback 2012) Oxford, UK: Oxford University Press.

[212] Fuller L. 1969. The Morality of Law. New Haven: Yale University Press.

[213] Frederick Schauer, "Formalism", 97(4) Yale Law Journal (1988) 509–548, Marcin Matczak, "Why Judicial Formalism is Incompatible with the Rule of Law", Canadian Journal of Law and Jurisprudence, (February 2018), 61–85.

[214] Frederick Schauer, "Formalism", 97(4) Yale Law Journal (1988) 509–548, Marcin Matczak, "Why Judicial Formalism is Incompatible with the Rule of Law", Canadian Journal of Law and Jurisprudence, (February 2018), 61–85.

[215] Marcin Matczak The Strength of the Attack or the Weakness of the Defence? Poland's Rule of Law Crisis and Legal Formalism https://ssrn.com/abstract=3121611

[216] Bojan Bugaric Alenka Kuhelj, Varieties of Populism in Europe: Is the Rule of Law in Danger? Hague Journal on the Rule of Law April 2018, Volume 10, Issue 1, pp. 21–33 R. Markowski, Creating Authoritarian Clientelism: Poland After 2015, Hague Journal on the Rule of Law, 2019(1); W. Sadurski, How Democracy Dies (in Poland): A Case Study of Anti-Constitutional Populist Backsliding, Sydney Law School Research Paper No. 18/01, 2018; W. Sadurski, Poland's Constitutional Breakdown, 2019 (in press); W. Sadurski, Polish Constitutional Tribunal Under PiS: From an Activist Court, to a Paralysed Tribunal, to a Governmental Enabler, Hague Journal on the Rule of Law, 2019 (1); Commission's Reasoned Proposal in accordance with Article 7(1) of the Treaty on European Union regarding the rule of law in Poland: Proposal for a Council decision on the

populist forces relatively easily destabilized the rule of law and democracy, and steered politics in a dangerous authoritarian direction.

On the one hand, judicial formalism normally perceived as a tool for establishing the rule of law influencing its destruction. On the other hand, the advancement of a robust, non-formalistic methodology of legal decision-making such as an independent arbitration is a qualification for defense of the rule of law.

It is worth noting that law secures legal safety and politics stimulates effectiveness as long as advancing the rule of law on behalf of the society instead of promoting the interests of elite against the demands of the society leading in the end to an explosion. In fact, when law and politics collide, politics outplays law to alter the society in line with the political will, even if this implies breaking the law. In other words, politics generate their law by altering the existing one via its break in order to achieve political targets which mean that the rule of law is in hands of politics with its sociological view and in many major importance occasions with its party politics standpoint. To that extent, Marcin Matczak[217] argues that the kind of the political attacks heading for the rule of law in Poland are attacks through which political values prevail over legal values, and procedural justice generates the advancement of material justice, defined by the governing party.[218]

Moreover, a clear and plain hierarchy in which law is "subservient" to politics is established and so the values of the latter prevail over the values of the former. Nevertheless, regardless politicians openly declare that politics should prevail over law, when they implement their policy and justify it; they "rather pay lip service to the law than ignore it[219]" because in the end politics need law for its legitimization and the rule of law is the means for legalizing any politics.

Of course, law is something imperative but not holy which means that law is not unvarying and so law that does not serve the nation and society is useless and consequently the implied rule of law leads to real disorder. Politics have to influence the shaping of law in a degree serving the demands of the society and not merely the interests of temporary elite. It could be said that the legal culture has to advance sufficient defense mechanisms that should be triggered once the rule of law is attacked.[220]

---

determination of a clear risk of a serious breach by the Republic of Poland of the rule of law, COM (2017)835 final.

[217] Marcin Matczak The Strength of the Attack or the Weakness of the Defence? Poland's Rule of Law Crisis and Legal Formalism https://ssrn.com/abstract=3121611

[218] Jane Burbank, "Lenin and the Law in Revolutionary Russia", 54(1) Slavic Review (Spring 1995), 23–44.

[219] Marcin Matczak, Matyas Bencze, Zdenek Kuhn, "Constitutions, EU Law and Judicial Strategies in the Czech Republic, Hungary and Poland", 30 Journal of Public Policy (April 2010), 81–99.

[220] Aharon Barak, Purposive Interpretation in Law (Princeton University Press, Princeton, Oxford, 2005.

5.12 Criminal Law and Politics

It is characteristic that law enforcement agencies globally are constantly seeking new technologies to better ensure successful detection and prosecution of crimes in order to keep citizens and society safe. The establishment of globalized society throughout the post-modern period has had numerous noteworthy implications on the ways in which individual states now react to crime. Especially, the explosion of international human rights laws together with the creation of international governing bodies such as the United Nations has produced the forefront for a developing and improving policy basis for the internationalization of crime regulation.

The growth in international justice mechanisms is a system of justice placing emphasis on imposing deserved punishments while upholding defendant rights within a framework of proportionate sentencing.[221] Any international justice mechanism has to be employed according to the rule of law not influenced by any political targeting. Has the international justice implemented without any political intervention either direct or indirect via the tools of criminal procedure codes?

The Organization for Security and Co-operation in Europe (OSCE) has been influential in internationalizing both the concept of hate crime and its legal proscription.[222] ODIHR's work has been instrumental in proliferating hate crime laws internationally. The international policy domain for hate crime has been focused mostly on neo-liberal and punitive approaches to dealing with the problem. Article 4 of the European Union Framework Decision on Racist and Xenophobic Crime[223] states that member states "shall take the necessary measures to ensure that racist and xenophobic motivation is considered an aggravating circumstance, or, alternatively that such motivation may be taken into consideration by the courts in the determination of the penalties." All members of the EU must have provisions in law that count hate-motivation as an exacerbating factor for any offence or member states must punish hate-motivated offenders more strictly.

According to the Council of the EU's conclusions on combating hate crime members to make certain that they have transferred the provisions of the Framework Decisions 2008 and to "consider the experience of other Member States in extending within their criminal legislation, the scope of punishable hate crime offences." Nonetheless, legislating to combat hate crime cannot, by itself, immobilize the globalization of hate and there is an increase in the number of hate-motivated

---

[221] Findlay, Mark J. 2008. Governing through Globalised Crime: Futures for international criminal justice, Devon: Willan Publishing. Ashworth, Andrew. 2010, Sentencing and Criminal Justice, 5th ed. Cambridge: Cambridge University Press.

[222] Goodall, Kay. 2013. "Conceptualising 'racism' in criminal law." Legal Studies, 33 (2): pp. 215–238. http://www.legislationline.org/topics/subtopic/79/topic/4

[223] Council Framework Decision 2008/913/JHA of 28 November 2008 on combating certain forms and expressions of racism and xenophobia by means of criminal law. https://eur-lex.europa.eu/legal-content/EN/TXT/?uri=LEGISSUM%3Al33178

offences across Europe.[224] Globalization's encounter to the welfare state requires that there is a need to figure out how to safeguard the personal, political, and social liberties to which people have become accustomed. It is worth noting that the European Union's key normative justification is that existing levels of self-government and social policy can be conserved at the supranational level which means that the EU indicates how political and economic institutions can accustom themselves to the truths of globalization.

Prosecutors have suppressed exculpatory evidence, applied the law selectively and used their sentencing leverage to force plea bargains.[225] To that extent, prosecutors lack of accountability, non-transparent decision-making processes, and prosecutors' desire for political gain due to the inefficiency of elections.[226]

It has to be considered that by increasing transparency and strengthening prosecutors' democratic responsibility we reduce the inequitable exercise of prosecutorial discretion and so restricting prosecutorial misconduct.[227] Moreover, in corporate corruption cases weak laws and personnel constraints lead prosecutors to assume weak "confession agreements" with influential corporate interests which means that there is an impact of politics upon prosecutors.[228] There is a need to upgrade fairness and advance integrity of prosecutors in order to have more legally objective employment of the rule of law.

It has to be examined the operational transparency of an AI instrument and indeed what kind of "transparency" is needed and so selection about transparency encompasses a principal-agent problem emerging in the public context which means that officials in the judicial system are entrusted authority by the people to implement the law, but then have assigned a set of policy selections expressed in code and interface design.[229]

---

[224] Home Office, Office for National Statistics and Ministry of Justice 2013. An Overview of Hate Crime in England and Wales, London: Home Office, Office for National Statistics and Ministry of Justice.

[225] Angela J. Davis, Arbitrary Justice: The Power of the American Prosecutor (New York: Oxford University Press, 2007), 4.

[226] "Federal Prosecutor Range Criticizes 'Political Influence' on Investigation," Deutsche Welle, August 4, 2015. http://www.dw.com/en/federal-prosecutor-range-criticizes-political-influence-on-investigation/a-18625429. Hon. Alex Kozinski, "Criminal Law 2.0," Georgetown Law Journal Annual Review Criminal Procedure. 44 (2015): iii, viii. http://georgetownlawjournal.org/files/2015/06/Kozinski_Preface.pdf

[227] Ronald F. Wright, "How Prosecutor Elections Fail Us," Ohio State Journal of Criminal Law 6 (2009): 509–606. Glenn Harlan Reynolds, "Ham Sandwich Nation: Due Process When Everything Is a Crime," Columbia Law Review Sidebar 113 (2013): 102.

[228] Shawn Marie Boyne, The German Prosecution Service: Guardians of the Law? (Heidelberg: Springer, 2013). David Crawford and Mike Esterl, "Siemans Settlement Sets off Criticism of German Inquiries," The Wall Street Journal, October 8, 2007, http://www.wsj.com/articles/SB119179176083751435

[229] Tim Miller, Explanation in artificial intelligence: Insights from the social sciences. 267 Artificial Intel. 1, 1–2 (2019).

To that extent, neither the Federal Constitution nor the Constitutions of the Länder denote exactly where the prosecution offices fit within the State's constitutional structures. Nevertheless, Article 92 of the German Constitution (Grundgesetz) gives full decision-making independence to the judicial branch. It is characteristic that German legal practitioners deem that "the Prosecution Services are criminal justice authorities within the executive whose individual agents exercise their power in non-political fashion."[230] Besides, even though many of the battles over prosecutors' decision-making independence occur away from the public eye, German prosecutors strive to weigh up their loyalty to the state with their normative directive to find the objective "truth."

Like the USA, Germany is a federal system which means that there is both a federal prosecution service located in Karlsruhe on top of independent prosecution services organized at the level of the sixteen Länder. However, Germany's federal prosecutors concentrate their practice on crimes against the state and crimes against humanity representing the State in cases before the Federal Court of Appeals.[231]

In contradiction of the American adversarial system, where prosecutors act as a party to the criminal proceeding, in the German system, most prosecutors are not devoted in "winning a case." German prosecutors do not bear the burden of proof at trial but they are free to give their own sentencing recommendations examining the evidence through an objective lens. Moreover, German prosecutors' role is to find the truth which means a pledge to objectivity and to the law itself is embedded in the German conception of the State. The German ideal is rooted in the civil law tradition which not only embodies the perception that the authority of the state is confined by law, but more notably, it means that the state acts in a lawful (rechtlich) way. To that extent, any action undertaken by the state has to be based on law which means that every citizen has the right to contest the constitutionality of a government action before the Federal Constitutional Court adding to the demand for acting according to the rule of law. Thus, the law is the medium through which the State governs compelling state action to avert arbitrariness and to ensure certainty and predictability.[232] In addition, as an organized entity, the state is restricted not only by law, but also by the primary principles of legality.[233]

---

[230] Ekaternia Trendafilova and Werner Róth, "Report on the public prosecution service in Germany," in Promoting Prosecutorial Accountability, Independence and Effectiveness. Comparative Research. Ed. Open Society Institute (Sofia: Open Society Institute, 2008), 237, citing German Code of Criminal Procedure (StGB) Sect. 160, https://www.opensocietyfoundations.org/sites/default/files/promoting_20090217.pdf

[231] Gwladys Gilliéron, Public Prosecutors in the United States and Europe: A Comparative Analysis with Special Focus on Switzerland, France, and Germany (Switzerland: Springer 2014), 243, citing GVG Sect. 142 (1).

[232] Martin Krygier, "Rule of Law (and Rechtsstaat)," University of New South Wales Faculty of Law Research Series No. 53 (October 2013): 6, http://law.bepress.com/cgi/viewcontent.cgi?article=1052&context=unswwps-flrps13

[233] T.R.S. Allan (1998). Rule of law (Rechtsstaat). In Routledge Encyclopedia of Philosophy (1998). London: Routledge, DOI: https://doi.org/10.4324/9780415249126-T022-1, https://www.rep.routledge.com/articles/rule-of-law-rechtsstaat/v-1/

It is worth mentioning that the state is not a political entity engaging in policies that abolish the law which means that prosecutors, as agents of the state, regard their function in less-instrumental terms than American prosecutors. To that extent, the German prosecutor is a "guardian of the law" and, by implication, a pillar of the Rechtsstaat which means that the rule of law is above everything. Does the rule of law is above everything in implementing justice in the national and international fora?

For the reason that prosecutors materialize their own opinion about the evidence displayed at trial and even move for an acquittal, their pledge to objectivity on top of their professional outlook overlaps the executive and judicial functions. Above all, prosecutors assess their performance, not by their conviction rate or the length of the defendant's sentence, but by whether they employed the law accurately in a specific case which means that the application of the rule of law is the only basis for prosecutors' exercise of law rejecting any political influence. German prosecutors are compelled by law to investigate the facts both for and against the defendant. It is worth mentioning that Smith clarifies that when the executive also serves as judge, he is doubtful to take a neutral view of cases in which he has a direct interest which means that when the judicial is integrated with the executive authority, it is scarce likely that justice should not often be surrendered to politics. Smith[234] states that "it is not only necessary that the judicial should be separated from the executive power, but that it should be rendered as much as possible independent of that power." It seems that the administrative state introduced an expansive bureaucracy that brought politics and the "unitary executive" back into play and so there is a need for fundamental re-examination of the core of ideas that constituted the rule of law.[235]

Which is the location of the law in reference to the state? It has to be taken into consideration that in a rule of law state, the law stands above the state and limits the sovereign's discretionary authority which means that the judiciary functions as its key guardian based on an objective implementation of the law rather than interpreting the law in a way of promoting the demands of a political interests of any group. In contrast, in the German Rechtsstaat, the law originates with the legislature law is not above the state but rather part of the state's composition as well as its product which means that the state does not ignore the law rather than the state implements accurately the law as being its product not influenced by any political interests. It could be said that the legislature, courts, and prosecutors function as the guardians of the law in the German system. The birth of the Federal Constitutional Court in the post-war era and the post-war Constitution's hold of human dignity have not only enhanced control over state authority but have also implanted a pledge to social welfare in the make-up of the State.

[234] Smith, A. 1776. An Inquiry into the Nature and Causes of the Wealth of Nations (1872) London: Alex. Murray & Co. p. 570.

[235] Morton J. Horwitz, The Transformation Of American Law: 1870–1960, at 3–4 (1992) James M. Landis, The Administrative Process 75–76, 154–55 (Yale Univ. Press 1938).

Civil law systems count on two devices for warranting that prosecutors are responsible such as a penal code restraining prosecutors' decision-making choices and the principle of mandatory prosecution.[236] As initially planned, the German Code of Criminal Procedure sought to eliminate arbitrary political intrusion in the criminal justice system. However, prosecutors retained some flexibility in their investigation and charging decision-making and so authorizing prosecutors and judges to guarantee that the system is fair, it also invites the delivery of arbitrary justice. Besides, the Land-level Ministries of Justice sometimes attempt to quash prosecutions for political reasons and so drawing political consideration encompassing the investigation of politicians, campaign contributors, or well-known entrepreneurs.

Prosecutors receive political pressure delivered in the form of phone calls and informal oral suggestions in order to work behind the curtains indicating that there is no action against the rule of law. It has to be considered that the Minister of Justice may reassign a case to another prosecutor.[237] It is characteristic that the threat to prosecutors' fidelity to the law exists in those states where prosecutors turn around between positions in the judiciary, the Ministry, and the prosecution service at standard periods. Even though prosecutors have lifetime tenure, the Ministry or a prosecutor's superiors exploit the likelihood of a future rotation to remunerate or penalize prosecutors who stick to or reject the Ministry's desires by progress up the ranks or get side-tracked due to lack of "social competence" accordingly.

It is characteristic the case of Helmut Kohl for political retaliation where the prosecutor who filed the opening charges found himself "promoted" to a position of family court judge in a small German town[238] proving the interference of politics over the rule of law. Even though the first prosecutor filed felony-level bribery charges against the former Chancellor, the case eventually was dismissed under Sect. 153a which permits prosecutors to discharge minor cases that are not in the public's interest to prosecute indicating how in a legal way politics interfere in the application of the rule of law in order to avoid a direct and open intervention negating the rule of

[236] Emilio S. Binavince, "The Structure and Theory of the German Penal Code," American Journal of Comparative Law 24 (1976): 601. Horacio Spector, "The Future of Legal Science in Civil Law Systems," Louisiana Law Review 65 (2004): 261. Markus Dirk Dubber, "The Promise of German Criminal Law: A Science of Crime and Punishment," German Law Journal 6 (2005): 1051, http://www.germanlawjournal.com/pdfsNolO6NoO7fPDF_-Vol_-06_-No_-07_-1049-1073_ArticlesDubber.pdf

[237] Trendafilova and Roth, "Report on the public prosecution service in Germany," 221 (citing Werner Beulke, Strafprozessrecht (2006) at marginal no. 85.

[238] David Crawford & Mike Esteral, "Germany: Siemens Settlement Sets off Criticism of German Inquiries," Wall Street Journal, October 8, 2007, http://www.wsj.com/articles/SB119179176083751435. Senior Prosecutor Interview, [8HL], May 22, 2006. Stefan Mayr, "Brisante Aktenvermerke im Fall Schottdorf," Süddeutsche Zeitung, January 26, 2015, http://www.sueddeutsche.de/bayern/laboraffaere-brisante-aktenvermerke-im-fall-schottdorf-1.2319780

law.[239] To that extent, members of the opposition parties on the Federal and state levels may operate as a prospective safeguard on arbitrary interfering by the Ministry of Justice in a particular case for the reason that the Ministry of Justice is politically liable to the Parliament, members of Parliament may instigate investigations into specific cases and present written questions to the Ministry. Nonetheless, while legislative hearings draw media coverage, the range of the parliamentary investigation is reduced to whether or not the law was followed having little to do with whether the prosecutor applied the law rightly.[240] Anyway, the level of political interfering in prosecutorial decision-making diverges from Land to Land.[241]

Also, the nation's top prosecutor position is exceptional under German law as the Federal Prosecutor is a "political civil servant" who, by law, may be sent into temporary retirement at whatever time. In line with the Act Defining the Scope of Civil Servants' Rights and Duties (Beamtenrechtsrahmengesetz-BRRG), "political civil servants" has to coincide with the government's political beliefs and policy goals.[242] Where is the rule of law? Is the rule of law a cover-up for political manipulations of a society?

Germany's domestic intelligence agency is accountable for protecting the country's internal security.[243] It is characteristic that Christoph Frank, the head of the Federation of German Judges and State Prosecutors (Richterbund) called the firing a "significant threat" to the rule of law and charged that political impact on prosecutorial decision-making damages the public's confidence in the criminal justice system.[244] Moreover, Thomas Heilmann assessed the Justice Minister affirming that: "I can't accept the behavior of Minister Maas," ... "[e]ither he understands himself as the supervising authority over the state prosecutors, in which case he should have already intervened two months ago, or he is, like me, of the opinion that politicians can't decide on political criminal investigations, in

[239] "Germany's Party Finance Scandal 'Ends' With Kohl's Plea Bargain and Too Many Unanswered Questions," German Law Journal 2 (2001), http://www.germanlawjournal.com/index.php?pageID=11&artID=60

[240] Gwladys Gilliéron, Public Prosecutors in the United States and Europe, 2014 Springer 282.

[241] Stefan Mayr, "Justiz im Zwielicht,"Süddeutsche Zeitung, October 20, 2015, http://www.sueddeutsche.de/bayern/affaere-schottdorf-justiz-im-zwielicht-1.2700023

[242] Beamtenrechtsrahmengesetz, Sect. 31 I (BRRG). [Act Defining the Scope of Civil Servants' Rights and Duties].

[243] "German Prosecutors investigate Internet Journalists for Treason," Deutsche Welle, July 30, 2015, http://www.dw.com/en/german-prosecutors-investigate-internet-journalists-for-treason/a-18619254. Klaus Brinkbäumer, "Berlin's NSA Fears: Treason Investigation Reveals Anxiety at the Top," Der Spiegel, August 10, 2015, http://www.spiegel.de/international/germany/german-treasoninvestigation-reveals-anxiety-among-leaders-a1047256.html.

[244] Plugging Leaks: Merkel's War on Germany's Press and Parliament," Der Spiegel, August 7, 2015, http://www.spiegel.de/international/germany/berlin-goes-after-journalists-to-protect-statesecrets- a-1047265.html. Deutscher Richterbund, "Richterbund kritisiert Eingreifen des Bundesjustizministers,"Press Release, August 4, 2015, http://www.drb.de/cms/index.php?id=917&L=0

which case he shouldn't have been allowed to intervene."[245] Furthermore, Range was the first Federal Prosecutor in history to blame the Minister of Justice of intervening in a case for political reasons.[246] Is the law the instrument for political imposition accordingly? Have all political goals achieved via law and the rule of law? To that extent, in the Schottdorf case the political intrusion damages the investigation's scope which means that political authority acted to weaken the justice system's pledge to the principle of mandatory prosecution to go forward the interests of Mr. Schottdorf and his political allies.

While the USA was founded on the objective that authority should flow from the people rather than from a King, the representative democracy has not always assured that prosecutorial decision-making has been responsive to public values and so according to the rule of law. To that extent, even when that decision-making has respected public values, the events mirrored by those values have not always guaranteed that the system's results are both fair and just. Even though elections tie prosecutors to some type of democratic control, they have also encouraged the unrestrained augmentation of prosecutorial authority and have sometimes damaged prosecutors' duty to do justice which means that the rule of law is not the sole basis of decision-making but politics imposes in a way the duty. It is worth mentioning that Darryl Brown has written that: "prosecutorial authority has grown and judicial authority contracted because, in various ways, U.S. criminal process trusts political decision-making over legal regulation."[247] In other words, the election of top prosecutors has led to a system that is "administered less by rules grounded in public values and principles and more by private interests, partisan motivations, and political preferences."[248]

It is argued that the German system trusts fidelity to the principle of mandatory prosecution and the civil legal code over political decision-making. On the other hand, the underlying link of the prosecution service within the Ministry of Justice is both a source of political answerability and a prospective source of political

---

[245] "Critics Hunt Fresh Scalps in Treason Scandal," The Local.De, August 6, 2015, http://www.thelocal.de/20150806/critics-hunt-fresh-scalps-in-treason-scandal. Naomi Conrad, "In Berlin, Probe into Netzpolitik Inquiry Drags on," Deutsche Welle, August 19, 2015, http://www.dw.com/en/in-berlin-probe-into-netzpolitik-inquirydrags-on/a-18658583

[246] John Blau, "Prosecutor Fired after Targeting Journalists," Handlesblatt, August 5, 2015, https://global.handelsblatt.com/edition/234/ressort/politics/article/prosecutor-fired-for-targeting-journalists

[247] Darryl K. Brown, Free Market Criminal Justice: How Democracy and Laissez Faire Undermine the Rule of Law (New York: Oxford University Press, 2016), Andrew Chongseh Kim, "Underestimating the Trial Penalty: An Empirical Analysis of the Federal Trial Penalty and Critique of the Abrams Study" (June 23, 2015). Mississippi Law Journal, Vol. 84, No. 5, 2015, http://ssrn.com/abstract=2635657

[248] Darryl K. Brown, Free Market Criminal Justice: How Democracy and Laissez Faire Undermine the Rule of Law, 2. Amita Kelly, "Does it Matter that Ninety Five Percent of Elected Prosecutors are White?" National Public Radio, July 8, 2015, http://www.npr.org/sections/itsallpolitics/2015/07/08/420913118/does-itmatter-that-95-of-elected-prosecutors-are-white

influence which means that when political figures seek to affect prosecutorial decision-making, it damages the German principle of legality.[249]

There are calls to augment prosecutors' political independence resonate with the recommendations of the Council of Europe's Committee of Ministers ordering members of the government accountable for oversight of the prosecution office to "exercise their powers in a transparent way" and so stating that "such instructions must carry with them adequate guarantees that transparency and equity are respected."[250]

Does China lack a modern set of constraints in the form of a rule of law or democratic accountability? Is there a different understanding of legal politics in China? How political and legal orders advance over time there and in other contexts? Chinese civil dispute resolution has been categorized as a rule by law regime since the mid-1980s.[251] China's civil law system is a kind of rule by law regime, while the criminal law system is neo-traditional. China's substantial reforms and moves toward judicialized dispute resolution in a wide variety of areas indicate a system abiding by the rule of law. A modern state must be balanced both by binding rules that limit its authority and democratic responsibility to a populace that eventually has the power to reconstitute the state's leadership. The rule of law and democratic accountability are meaningful in the absence of strong and reliable structures of state authority. A powerless state cannot enforce any laws. On the one hand, the concept of rule of law is highly problematic in its basic theoretical underpinnings. On the other hand, legal orders come in many varieties. The politics of legal systems are multipart and multidimensional. To that extent, China's explicit legal order is not monolithic and, in fact, departs in different areas of the law, with one set of arrangements prevailing in the civil arena and a very different one in criminal law.

Since the 1997 handover of Hong Kong to China, the central government has constantly highlighted the significance of acknowledging, and adhering to, the rule of law as offered in the Basic Law above all in governing Hong Kong matters. Han Zhu[252] argues that ""legalization without (full) democratization" has been the core pillar of Beijing's overall legal strategy for governing Hong Kong and has been firmly entrenched since the 1989 Tiananmen crackdown and has remained the

[249]"84 Recommendations for More Integrity: Transparency Germany Presents its National Integrity Assessment for Germany," Transparency International Press Release, January 19, 2012, http://www.transparency.org/news/pressrelease/20120119_germany_nis. Ministry Interview [9RR], June 2, 2006. Shawn Marie Boyne, Prosecutorial Accountability in the Rechtsstaat: The Tension between Law, Politics, and the Public Interest, Robert H. McKinney School of Law, Legal Studies Research Paper No. 2016–29.

[250]Council of Europe Committee of Ministers, Recommendation Rec (2000)19 of the Committee of Ministers to member states on the role of public prosecution in the criminal justice system. Adopted October 6, 2000. Rec 13(b), https://wcd.coe.int/ViewDoc.jsp?id=376859

[251]Rachel E. Stern "From Dispute to Decision: Suing Polluters in China" The China Quarterly 206, pp. 294---312 (June 2011).

[252]Han Zhu, Beijing's "Rule of Law" Strategy for Governing Hong Kong: Legalization without Democratization https://ssrn.com/abstract=3362068 P 18.

cornerstone of its governing strategy over the past decades." It is worth noting that in practice, Beijing has incrementally redefined some provisions and notions linked to the Basic Law to aid its governing reason and so even though its authority to restrict the function of Hong Kong's rule of law is still largely restricted by the Basic Law, the central government never hesitates to take a tough tactic in vital matters that touch on its central welfares. Thus, it could be said that politics influence the implementation of the rule of law accordingly. The rule of law issue in Hong Kong is inevitably interconnected with that in China and so Hong Kong has confronted the same typical "Chinese characteristics" of the socialist rule of law, such as the "equation of law and power."[253] China's apparent transition toward the rule of law has countersigned setbacks and so the biggest impediment to advancement toward the rule of law nowadays in China is ideological due to the lack of agreed ideals, ends, and standards to steer the design and implementation of legal norms. Up till now party domination has failed to offer a satisfactory replacement for universal legal values which means that there is a need for an effort to employ the rule of law more forcefully[254] which will bring stability and growth of the economy.

States and legal systems are seldom straight or unidirectional which means that there is no single scale of bad-to-good or primitive-to modern that any state can pursue, and so no precisely differentiable "modern" or "pre-modern" legal order. Moreover, the idea of an articulate state, a rule of law, and democratic accountability as strategic machinery of modern governance seems uncontroversial, maybe even obvious or commonplace. China's hybrid blend of a rule by law regime in the civil arena and a neo-traditional regime in criminal law is among the more common and stable admixtures of possible types.[255] It seems that based on an authoritarian polity, the Chinese state is effective despite lacking control or accountability. Chinese state advances the legitimacy of the political system control exercised through the criminal justice system upholding their rule. Thus, politics influence the application of criminal law to the advantage of specific economic elite and against the right application of the rule of law. It has to be considered that the rule of law has to apply in both civil and criminal areas within a jurisdiction in order to say that the legal system functions in line with the rule of law. It seems that in both legal systems

[253] PILS, Eva. 2017. Human Rights in China: A Social Practice in the Shadows of Authoritarianism. Cambridge, UK and Medford, MA: Polity. TAM, Waikeung. 2013. Legal Mobilization under Authoritarianism: The Case of PostColonial Hong Kong. Cambridge University Press. Delisle, Jacques. 2007. "Legalization without Democratization in China under Hu Jintao." In Cheng Li (ed), China's Changing Political Landscape: Prospects for Democracy. Brookings Institution Press. 185–90.

[254] Compilation of Xi Jinping's Expositions on Rule of Law. 2016. Chinese Law and Government, 48 (6): 468–74. http://www.tandfonline.com/doi/full/10.1080/00094609.2016.1241114

[255] William Hurst & Jessica Teets "Compliance, Resistance, Innovation, and Involution–Assessing the Politics of Experimentation and Diffusion" in Jessica C. Teets & William Hurst eds. Local Governance Innovation in China: Experimentation, Diffusion, and Defiance London: Routledge, 2015– pp. 174---179. William Hurst Local Governance Innovation in China: Experimentation, Diffusion, and Defiance (Routledge 2015).

of Germany and China there is an impact of politics upon the rule of law particularly concerning the implementation of criminal law.

It is argued that the perform part of rule of law includes various intended ends and so rule of law is about the political and institutional capability of a polity to put approved restrictions on the exercise of authority and to settle disputes over the distribution of authority and resources via non-violent ways which means that the rule of law incorporates the capability to put in place operative checks and balances and oversight processes interrelated to how power is employed by imposing responsibility and thus in order to resolve disputes and manage criminal justice a number of professional capacities and institutional principles are in place embracing such attributes as the independence of judges[256] and arbitrators, various kinds of the separation of powers, etc. It is not just the content of the instrument but also its context that will affect organization, institutional, commercial and governmental decision-making and so a risk assessment device used in a criminal justice setting will supply judges with a straightforward numerical score but that score distil information about a range of risks, embracing the likelihood of violent crime, non-violent crime, and flight from the jurisdiction.[257]

Of course, there is a need for a securitization of rule of law support because international support of rule of law has been less than clear echoing the fact that there is far less agreement on the substantive rationale of rule of law than policy discourse often thinks. Moreover, international support to rule of law is made up of contrasting set of activities and international interventions are focused on backing form-related aspects of judiciaries, criminal justice reform, legal reform, and access to justice. On the other hand, the form of rule of law is not insignificant, but support continues to deal with the encounter of what it takes to interlock with the political economy and context suitable functional features/qualities of rule of law in modes that are more adequate for purpose.

[256]Tamanaha B. (2011) "The primacy of society and the failures of law and development" in Cornell International Law Journal. 44: 209–47.

[257]Blake Hallinan, Jed R. Brubaker, and Casey Fiesler, Unexpected expectations: Public reaction to the Facebook emotional contagion study, 22 New Media & Soc. 1076 (2019).

5.13 International Criminal Courts and the Rule of Law

International criminal law forms general international law as much as the latter affects the former.[258] The ICC is founded by the Rome Statute[259] as a permanent court in order to prosecute persons for international crimes such as genocide, crimes against humanity, and war crimes.

The establishment of the International Criminal Court (ICC) has been one of the reformist's moves in the history of international relations. At the heart of the Rome Statute is a pledge to the essence and value of international criminal justice. Moreover, states under the jurisdiction of the ICC agree to relinquish sovereignty over individual perpetrators suspected of genocide, crimes against humanity, and war crimes except they are able and willing to prosecute perpetrators of these crimes at home. Furthermore, even heads of state have not been immune from the formal legal authority of the ICC. It is worth mentioning that the USA has been a strong supporter of international criminal justice and yet has also declined to become a member of the ICC.[260] As an alternative, US has involved selectively with the ICC, occasionally serving as a loyal enthusiast and at other times mounting a vocal encounter to its authority. To that extent, it is characteristic the encounter took on a spectacular manner when Palestine revealed its intention to join the ICC.[261] It could be argued that there is a refusal to comply with the application of the rule of law in international criminal justice indiscriminately and instead there is a selective approach toward the application of the rule of law in international criminal justice due to politics involvement in order to support specific political affairs of states, allies or global economic elites to the detriment of the principle of the rule of law and consequently to the application of law.

Courts rely on partners to help enforce their mandates and so these "compliance partners" establish a court's "intermediate authority."[262] Recognition of the ICC's authority has been stronger among international NGOs and civil society

---

[258] Gregory Gordon, Complementarity and Alternative Justice, 88 Or. L. Rev. 621 (2009). Judge Philippe Kirsch, Keynote Address at the Belle R. and Joseph H. Braun Memorial Lecture Series symposium, International Justice in the 21st Century: The Law and Politics of the International Criminal Court, at the John Marshall Law School, April 23, 2010.

[259] United Nations (1999). Rome Statute of the International Criminal Court — Overview, It was adopted at a diplomatic conference in Rome on 17 July 1998 and it entered into force on 1 July 2002.

[260] Stephen Eliot Smith, "Definitely Maybe: The Outlook for U.S. Relations with the International Criminal Court During the Obama Administration", Florida Journal of International Law, 22:155 at 160, n. 38.

[261] Jessica Schulberg, 75 Senators Want to Punish Palestine Before it Can Accuse Israel, NEW REPUBLIC (Feb. 3, 2015), https://newrepublic.com/article/120953/senators-threaten-cut-palestinianfunding-over-icc-membership, Jack Snyder & Leslie Vinjamuri, Trials and Errors: Principle and Pragmatism in Strategies of International Justice, 28 Int'l Security, Winter 2003–04.

[262] Karen J. The New Terrain Of International Law: Courts, Politics, Rights (2014).

organizations than among actors that are directly involved in particular situations and cases. To that extent, the ICC accommodates the interests of powerful states.[263]

It has to be considered that politics has played a central role in molding the authority of international courts. In states with inadequate institutional competence, politics has been integral to states' decisions to support or challenge ICC investigations. Moreover, the same has happened in states with consolidated rule of law institutions that have been called on to support the ICC's work in third party states.[264] To that extent, politics, mainly states' political interests in peace, security, and stability, has been a strong driver of states' selections to admit or withhold support from the ICC.[265] It is characteristic that when the ICC's pursuits challenge states' interests, states have been quick to suspend or avoid ICC justice which means that the center of states decision is politics rather the rule of law.

In other words, politics have formed clique of key powers to recognize and support the ICC[266] instead of pure belief on the authority of the rule of law in order to achieve a level of global justice[267] unaffected by the contemporary political interests of various agencies. To that extent, in some cases, membership in the ICC has converted into a basis of contestation.[268]

Many international institutions identify the realities of authority by conceding distinct privileges to a small number of powerful states generating a noticeable tension with a sovereignty norm that sets equal status to all states generating tensions in civil society and especially in the sphere of international criminal justice civil society has encompassed pragmatic concessions. Is there any of Law and Politics in the Rise of the International Criminal Court? It has to be considered that the promoters of the rule of law set against the prerogatives of global politics. For instance, the Syria situation is marked by clear violations of international humanitarian law across the band of participants during years in which hundreds of thousands have lost their lives, leading to competing calls for justice and dismissals of such a course within the United Nations Security Council.[269]

---

[263] David Bosco, Rough Justice: The International Criminal Court In A World Of Power Politics (2014).

[264] Beth A. Simmons & Allison Danner, Credible Commitments and the International Criminal Court, 64 Int'l Org. 225, 232 (2010).

[265] Hyeran Jo and Beth A. Simmons, Can the International Criminal Court Deter Atrocity? (Dec.18, 2014), http://papers.ssrn.com/sol3/papers.cfm?abstract_id=2552820

[266] Karen Alter, The New Terrain Of International Law: Courts, Politics, Rights (2014).

[267] ICC Press Release, CC - ICC Prosecutor receives Sealed Envelope from Kofi Annan on Post-Election Violence in Kenya, https://www.icc-cpi.int/en_menus/icc/situations%20and%20cases/situations/situation%20icc%200109/press%20releases/Pages/pr436.aspx

[268] UN Security Council: Veto Betrays Syrian Victims. In Face of Mounting Pressure, Russia, China Block ICC Referral, Human. Rights Watch (May 22, 2014), http://www.hrw.org/news/2014/05/22/un-security-council-vetoes-betray-syrian-victims

[269] Press Release, Int'l Criminal Court, Office of the Prosecutor, Al Mahdi Case: Confirmation of Charges Hearing to Open on 1 March 2016, https://www.icccpi.int/en_menus/icc/press%20and%20media/press%20releases/Pages/pr1182.aspx Colum Lynch, Exclusive: U.S. to Support ICC War

Yet the long and hesitant search for international justice and liability for horrendous crimes has taken on an utterly new meaning in the era of the ICC. Bosco[270] argues that, as the first standing international criminal court in history, the ICC "represents a remarkable transfer of authority from sovereign states to an international institution."

The ad hoc tribunals for the former Yugoslavia[271] and Rwanda were products of Security Council Resolutions that directly related justice to peace and security. It has to be considered that the proximity between the Security Council and international justice was safeguarded in Rome when it was granted that the Security Council could not only refer cases to the ICC, but also defer them. On the other hand, ICC power depends on the supposition, maintained by practice, that justice will stay free from political meddling.

The ICC[272] is an inspiring symbol of justice and law not residing in a political vacuum and its most imperative political interlocutor is the United Nations Security Council. While the Council has long been seen as the head of the international order, it is also a body in which politics and power are dominant which means that it is a good example to understand the interrelation between law and politics showing the politics of law in a global scale. Besides, it is worth mentioning that the ICC takes international justice out of the direct control of the most political of international bodies such as the Council moving toward law and away from politics. On the other hand, the ICC has no police force, nor any constantly operative means by which to force states to collaborate to bring perpetrators it pinpoints to justice but the ICC seeks assistance from partners such as the Security Council that have coercive powers which means that politics fire back by imposing a unique politics of law.[273]

If politics is over the rule of law and law, then the collapse of the international law and order is not far away and the efforts of any political interests will collapse because the international society in many ways will instigate either the change in a peaceful way or under a conflict which will ascertain not only the applicable law and rule of law but also will bring the collapse of the old political status replaced by a new political status welcoming the established law and rule of law needed to solve legally and fairly any conflict. Moreover, the spirit of the court's governing statute discards the conception that power or political influence should affect the course of justice underlining that the new court functions in a violent world where power

Crimes Prosecution in Syria, FOREIGN POL'Y (May 17, 2014), http://foreignpolicy.com/2014/05/07/exclusive-u-s-to-supporticc-war-crimes-prosecution-in-syria/

[270] David Bosco, Rough Justice: The International Criminal Court In A World Of Power Politics 1–10 (2014).

[271] Winston P. Nagan, International Criminal Law and the Ad Hoc Tribunal for Former Yugoslavia, 6 Duke J. Comp. & Int'l L. 127, 128 (1995).

[272] Antonio Cassese Et Al., Cassese's International Criminal Law (3rd ed. 2013).

[273] Diane Marie Amann & M.N.S. Sellers, The United States of America and the International Criminal Court, 50 Am. J. Comp. L. (SUPP.) 381, 386–87 (2002).

matters[274] which means that there is a strong impact of politics upon law and the rule of law.

Is there a refusal to apply occasionally the rule of law upon politically significant cases before the ICC of other international courts? It could be said that veto is a political tool affecting the rule of law applying equally in order to have a standardized fairly justified outcome.[275] Moreover, the veto power was added to the UN Charter[276] to give the USA and the Soviet Union appropriate authority in order to join the organization which clarifies the interrelation of law and politics in the global arena leading to the emergence of the politics of law in the global agenda.

Since the establishment of the ICC powerful states lost ownership of international justice and so they often have responded by trying to rein the court in and regain control.[277] The International Criminal Court[278] is an effort of enforcing law and quest for justice at the international level even though it suffers due to limited power which indicates the force of politics upon the rule of law.

It is characteristic that the laws of war have been established or interpreted in a way seeming as privileging one side in a conflict for the reason that of the nature of its cause,[279] the other side has often shown a propensity to disregard or downgrade the law which means that there is a need to utilize the rule of law in a standardized way not influenced by politics in order to be accepted easily by the international community. The establishment of a legal regime that respects the pragmatic compromise between military need and humanitarian considerations underlying IHL is mainly dependent on the symmetry of power between the various parties to a probable conflict.[280] On the other hand, the establishment of a standard

[274] The States Parties to the Rome Statute, Int'l Crim. Ct., https://www.icccpi.int/en_menus/asp/states%20parties/Pages/the%20states%20parties%20to%20the%20rome%20statute.aspx Scott Sheeran, The U.N. Security Council Veto is Literally Killing People, WASH POST (Aug. 11, 2014), https://www.washingtonpost.com/posteverything/wp/2014/08/11/the-unsecurity-council-veto-is-literally-killing-people/

[275] David L. Bosco, Five To Rule Them All: The UN Security Council And The Making Of The Modern World 30–31 (2009).

[276] Elisabeth Zoller, The National Security of the United States as the Host State for the United Nations, 1 Pace U. Sch. L. Y.B. Int'l L. 127, 127–28 (1989).

[277] Larry D. Johnson, The Lubanga Case and Cooperation Between the UN and the ICC, 10 J. INT'L CRIM. JUST. 887, 887 (2012) http://councilandcourt.org/files/2014/06/Beijing-WorkshopProceedings.pdf

[278] David A. Kaye, Council On Foreign Relations, Justice Beyond The Hague: Supporting The Prosecution Of International Crimes In National Courts 28 (2011). Carsten Stahn et al., Participation of Victims in Pre-Trial Proceedings of the ICC, 4 J. INT'L CRIM. JUST. 219, 238 (2006). U.N. Doc. S/PV.6849 (Oct. 17, 2012).

[279] Gabriella Blum, On a Differential Law of War, 52 Harv. Int'l L.J. 164, 168–73 (2011). Adam Roberts, The Equal Application of the Laws of War: A Principle Under Pressure, 90 Int'l Rev. Red Cross 931, 961 (2008).

[280] Michael N. Schmitt, Asymmetrical Warfare and International Humanitarian Law, 62 A.F.L. REV. 1 (2008). Geoffrey Best, Humanity In Warfare: The Modern History Of The International Law Of Armed Conflicts 15 (1980) Hamdan v. Rumsfeld, 548 U.S. 557, 629–36 (2006)".

interpretation which will be the rule of law expressing the politics of law will bring more justice, equality, and less conflict. Moreover, asymmetrical conflicts are not reduced to conflicts between states and non-state actors incorporating cases where there are noteworthy authority differences between two or more states fighting with one another.[281] To that extent, in both circumstances, the conflicting interests of the parties influence norm making and escalate the divergence between positive IHL norms and IHL's original pragmatic core of compromise underlining the significance of the normative symmetry between the parties to the conflict.[282]

The unique potential contribution of the ICC Prosecutor-as a non-state actor-to law and order in international relations cannot be underestimated.[283] It has to be considered that vital ethical principles should be used to articulate a comprehensive policy to guide the Prosecutor's selection such as ethical principles, rooted in the principle of unity in diversity, that are not hypothetically put out of "thin air," but find footing in contemporary international law.[284] Moreover, these ethical principles are applicable to the exercise of the prosecutorial discretion, principally when the ordinary meaning of statutory provisions relating to the Prosecutor's functions is unspecified.[285] In other words, the ethical principle of unity in diversity asserts that all human beings should seek to be unified as members of one human family while valuing one another's right to variety of language, religion, and culture and party freedom of thought, morality, faith, and illustration. It could be said that concerns about politicization of the ICC is not more politics, but more law which means application of the rule of law rather than politics to influence the legal system by forming or interpreting the law on behalf of the political interests of a governance of an elite.[286]

On the other hand, in fact the Court is already politicized, and that this is an unalterable feature of the present system in the foreseeable future but there is a need of neutralizing this political impact of the "great powers" or "Permanent Five"[287] with more politics from the boarder international community or regional inter-state organization. To that extent, political guidance from the General Assembly is aided to some extent under the present framework and so from the standpoint of political guidance, "monopoly" is strong of a characterization of the United Nations Security

[281] Robin Geiß, Asymmetric Conflict Structures, 88 Int'l Rev. Red Cross 757, 773 (2006).

[282] Toni Pfanner, Asymmetrical Warfare from the Perspective of Humanitarian Law and Humanitarian Action, 87 Int'l Rev. Red Cross 149, 160–62 (2005).

[283] Richard J. Goldstone, The Future of International Criminal Justice, 57 ME. L. REV. 553, 563 (2005).

[284] Brian Lepard, How Should the ICC Prosecutor Exercise His or her Discretion? The Role of Fundamental Ethical Principals, 43 J. Marshall L. Rev. 553, 553 (2010).

[285] William A. Schabas, Victor's Justice: Selecting "Situations" at the International Criminal Court, 43 J. Marshall L. Rev. 535 (2010).

[286] Rod Rastan, Comment on Victor's Justice & the Viability of Ex Ante Standards, 43 J. Marshall L. Rev. 569 (2010).

[287] William A. Schabas, Victor's Justice: Selecting "Situations" at the International Criminal Court, 43 J. Marshall L. Rev. 535, 537 (2010).

Council's effect on the ICC Prosecutor. Any State Party can refer a situation to the ICC Prosecutor, not just the Security Council, notwithstanding the former referrals are subject to the requirements for the exercise of jurisdiction in Article 12 of the Rome Statute.[288]

Political control involves the authority to defer or suspend investigations and prosecutions in restricted situations where it influences international peace and security. Nevertheless, there is great risk that the authority of political control is used beyond its intended restriction. Moreover, according to Article 16 of the Rome Statute, this authority is "monopolized" by the Security Council, and perhaps for good reason, too. In line, extending political control to other political bodies, such as the General Assembly, could paralyze the Court and preclude prosecution of atrocity crimes where the Court has jurisdiction. Furthermore, political control per Article 16 was not meant to offer a scheme for the exercise of political discretion where a situation or a case is otherwise admissible.

5.14 US Supreme Court and Politics

Stare decisis is a principle of policy and not a mechanical formula of adherence to the latest decision.[289] The Court will not overturn a past decision unless there are strong reasons for doing so.[290] Moreover, stare decisis carries enhanced force when a decision interprets a statute.[291] Of course, the rule of law has got a transformational power and there is no rule of administrative stare decisis.[292]

Res judicata is one of the most traditional features of civil procedure preventing the parties from litigating the same case before a Court more than one time.[293] It is worth noting that the rule of res judicata[294] augments deterrence and works as a competent cost savings tool in the justice system producing and shaping the content of the law that is implemented via the utilization of the rule of law.

[288] Rome Statute of the International Criminal Court art. 13(a), July 17, 1998, 2187 U.N.T.S. 90. Rome Statute, art. 14. Antonio Marchesi, Article 14-Reform of a Situation by a State Party, in Commentary On The Rome Statute Of The International Criminal Court: Observers' Notes, Article By Article 575–80 (Otto Triffterer ed., 2d ed. 2008).

[289] Helvering v. Hallock, 309 U.S. 106, 119 (1940).

[290] United States v. IBM Corp., 517 U.S. 843, 856 (1996).

[291] Kimble v. Marvel Ent., LLC, 576 U.S. 446, 456 (2015).

[292] Bankamerica Corp. v. United States, 462 U.S. 122, 149 & n.10 (1983).

[293] Bruno Bodart, The Social Value of the Doctrine of Res Judicata: An Economic Analysis. https://ssrn.com/abstract=3271743

[294] Owen Fiss & Judith Resnik, Adjudication and Its Alternatives 535 (2nd ed. 2003). (Indicating that res judicata serves as a protection for parties against the burden of successive relitigation of the same controversy). Digest, Book 44, chap. 2, Ulpian, Edict, Book 15. The Digest Of Justinian, v. 4, 137 (Alan Watson ed. 2011).

The Supreme Court has emphasized its concern over removing politics from judicial decision-making and in Chevron U.S.A., Inc. v. Natural Resources Defense Council, Inc.[295], the Court announced that a reviewing court must defer to a federal agency's reasonable interpretation of an ambiguous statute that the agency administers. Thus, as soon as the reviewing court determines that the statute is ambiguous, "[t]he court need not conclude that the agency construction was the only one it permissibly could have adopted to uphold the construction, or even the reading the court would have reached if the question initially had arisen in a judicial proceeding." Most remarkably, the Court[296] has lately authorized that Chevron's framework does not apply to questions relating to "deep 'economic and political significance' that [are] central to [the] statutory scheme" at issue.

It is worth noting that "political pressures" and "new social attitudes" alter statutory meaning without congressional involvement and so Scalia argues that changes in agency interpretation takes place due to new social attitudes impressed upon it through the political process.[297] Chevron did not emerge from apolitical reasoning or natural evolution and so politics contributed into Chevron's birth indicating the decision's connection to national politics.[298] It is argued that the law is used as a means to achieve social change and so pushing legal liberalism to its limits.[299] Kennedy[300] wrote that Chevron deference might be unconstitutional because it violates "separation-of-powers principles and the function and province of the Judiciary." The Court recently overruled a prior decision about state sovereign immunity and Justice Stephen Breyer complained that the Court should only take no

[295] 467 U.S. 837, 842–43 (1984).

[296] King v. Burwell, 135 S. Ct. 2480, 2489 (2015) (quoting FDA v. Brown & Williamson Tobacco Corp., 529 U.S. 120, 160 (2000)). Christopher J. Walker, Toward a Context-Specific Chevron Deference, 81 MO. L. REV. 1095, (2016) (exploring how Chief Justice Roberts may be embracing a narrower, more context-specific Chevron deference that "would focus not just on the formality of the agency procedure creating the interpretation, but also whether Congress intended to delegate that particular substantive question to the agency").

[297] Antonin Scalia, Judicial Deference to Administrative Interpretations of Law, 1989 Duke L.J. 511 Chevron U.S.A. Inc. v. Natural Resources Defense Council, Inc. 467 U.S. 837, 843–45 (1984).

[298] Linda Greenhouse, Court Upholds Reagan on Air Standard, N.Y. TIMES, June 26, 1984, at A8. Michael Fix & George C. Eads, The Prospects for Regulatory Reform: The Legacy of Reagan's First Term, 2 YALE J. ON REG. 293, 298, 318 (1985) ("In the absence of legislative change, the Reagan legacy will be broadened administrative discretion . . . ."); Erik M. Erlandson, A Technocratic Free Market: How Courts Paved the Way for Administered Deregulation in the American Financial Sector, 1977–1988, 29 J. POL'Y HIST. 350, 351 (2017) (explaining that Reagan-era conservatives embraced Chevron because administrative deference helped them "erode New Deal regulations and move bureaucratic government in a rightward direction").

[299] Louis Michael Seidman, J. Skelly Wright and the Limits of Legal Liberalism, 61 LOY. L. REV. 69, 70 (2015).

[300] Pereira v. Sessions, 138 S. Ct. 2105, 2110 (2018).

notice of precedents where "the circumstances demand it," so that law can "retain the necessary stability."[301]

Moreover, Courts must, in some cases, reconcile competing political interests, but not on the basis of the judges' personal policy preferences. Besides, an agency to which Congress has delegated policy-making responsibilities may, within the limits of that delegation, appropriately rely upon the official administration's views of wise policy to update its judgments.[302]

It is argued that there is an ever more politicized fight over justices and to that extent the probable consequence is a Supreme Court whose justices, on both sides, are expected to vote along party lines more consistently than ever before in American history and so it is said that rapidly "it will become impossible to regard the court as anything but a partisan institution."[303]

Supreme Court justices often vote along ideological lines which mean that justices vote strategically shaping precedent. It has to be taken into account that Judges do not only distribute justice to the litigants appearing before them and so in the course of resolving individual cases, they also make new law. Actually, the justices steadily assert that it is not their objective to simply correct injustices from lower-court decisions; rather they intervene to explain areas of the law that are vague or incomplete.[304] Hence, the Court decides cases that create room for discretion either for the reason that the relevant parts of the law encompass open-ended language, or because the drafters did not anticipate the issue at hand.[305]

Can a Supreme Court sustain public confidence that has come to be rigidly divided by both ideology and party? It is obvious that a Supreme Court that has come to be rigidly divided by both ideology and party cannot maintain public confidence for much longer. Why the governing political party wants to appoint its own judge in the Supreme Court as long as all decisions are based purely on the rule of law? Do Supreme Court judges solve vital matters of political interest according to the political interest of the political party that has appointed them regardless of the

---

[301] Franchise Tax Bd. v. Hyatt, 139 S. Ct. 1485, 1491–92 (2019), overruling Nevada v. Hall, 440 U.S. 410, 412, 426 (1979) (holding that states cannot invoke sovereign immunity in the courts of other states).

[302] Peter L. Strauss, "Deference" Is Too Confusing—Let's Call Them "Chevron Space" and "Skidmore Weight", 112 COLUM. L. REV. 1143, 1144–45 (2012); accord United States v. Mead Corp., 533 U.S. 218, 247 (2001) (Scalia, J., dissenting) (observing that ambiguities in statutes subject to Chevron deference "create a space, so to speak, for the exercise of continuing agency discretion") Nancy C. Staudt, Modeling Standing, 79 N.Y.U. L. REV. 612, 669 (2004) ("Standing decisions may be motivated by politics, but only when neither clear doctrine exists nor judicial monitoring takes place.").

[303] Lee Epstein & Eric Posner, If the Supreme Court Is Nakedly Political, Can It Be Just?, N.Y. TIMES, July 9, 2018, https://www.nytimes.com/2018/07/09/opinion/supreme-court-nominee-trump.html

[304] Perry, H. W. 1991. Deciding to Decide: Agenda Setting in the United States Supreme Court. Boston: Harvard University Press.

[305] Tom S. Clarky Pablo Montagnes Jorg L. Spenkuch, Politics from the Bench? Ideology and Strategic Voting in the U.S. Supreme Court September 15, 2018 www.ssrn.com

rule of law or the interpretation of the law is made in compliance with a government party's interests, which means that the rule of law is shaped by politics?

To that extent, the ratio of votes cast in the conservative direction by justices who were appointed by Republican presidents has also shot up.[306] Nonetheless, last years, justices have scarcely ever voted against the ideology of the president who appointed them. In line, raids on judicial independence are made easier when the public comes to view the judiciary as a political body and so this risk, and not just the identity of the next justice, should be at the center of public consideration.

Are judges politicians in robes, who try to resolve politically charged legal questions in line with their personal views? In reality, justices are strategic players who are stimulated by instrumental matters. On the other hand, when a justice's vote is decisive, ideology has a far greater impact on his decision-making than usual. In situations in which it matters the most, justices "polarize rather than moderate."[307] It is argued that justices derive utility from rightly applying the law as they see it due to an incentive to maintain the role of a justice as an umpire and applier of the law, or for the reason that justices are worried about their personal reputation or that of the Court and all at once, they care about the result of the case insofar as it influences the evolution of precedent. Moreover, it could be said that a justice who knows that his vote is not going to be crucial will decide based on his belief about the suitable ruling on legalistic grounds. Besides, because liberal and conservative justices diverge in their judicial philosophies and their view of the legal status quo, votes will commonly be linked with ideology. Furthermore, a justice who is pivotal faces a trade-off between shaping future jurisprudence and upholding the law in a specific case which means that a conservative (liberal) justice might cast a conservative (liberal) vote so as to move the legal status quo further to the right (left) and so justices' ideology plays an even greater part in ascertaining pivotal votes. Anyway, justices act strategically to shape legal precedent and so justice's trade off deciding rightly under the law with their concerns over the evolution precedent. It is argued that the vast majority of justices have shown ideology-driven strategic voting for cases across all areas of the law.

It has to be taken into account that all judges on a panel initially have the same aim, but they diverge in the quality and nature of the information that they acquire[308] which means that judges resolve cases based on both an ideological predisposition and a flexible idea about the correct decision under the law.[309] Moreover, the Supreme Court strategic behavior is based on different rationales. The Court is a

---

[306] Bruno Bodart, The Social Value of the Doctrine of Res Judicata: An Economic Analysis. https://ssrn.com/abstract=3271743 Barry Friedman, The Will of the People (2009).

[307] Cameron, Charles M. and Lewis A. Kornhauser. 2017. "Theorizing the U.S. Supreme Court." Oxford Research Encyclopedia of Politics. Callander, Steven and Tom S. Clark. 2017. "Precedent and Doctrine in a Complicated World." American Political Science Review 111(1):184–203.

[308] Kornhauser, Lewis A. 1995. "Adjudication by a Resource-Constrained Team: Hierarchy and Precedent in a Judicial System." Southern California Law Review 68:1605–1629.

[309] Iaryczower, Matias and Gabriel Katz. 2016. "More than Politics: Ability and Ideology in the British Appellate Committee." Journal of Law, Economics, and Organization 32(1):61–93.

collegial body that rules by majority and so justices have an enticement to vote strategically so as to affect precedent and law. Secondly strategic behavior stems from the Court's interactions with other branches of government due to the fact that these exercise checks and balances through separation-of-powers institutions, the justices have a collective spur to circumvent generating backlash from Congress[310] or even the public.[311]

Does the Court's legitimacy face substantial risk in the short term? It is argued that several issues such as amplified polarization in society in general, the expansion of polarized schools of legal interpretation that line up with political connections, and augmented interest-group consideration to the Supreme Court nomination course have combined to generate a system in which the Court becomes a political arena and in which each party's nominees are anticipated to certainly vote along ideological lines which means that there is a viewpoint that politics override the rule of law. On the one hand, it could be said that judges mostly decide based on the rule of law avoiding an obvious political influence and so Justice Kennedy has voted otherwise against his "partisan affiliation" in some of the highest-profile cases. On the other hand, with his replacement by a more ideologically anticipated Justice, the idea of the Court as an institution above the political fight may soon disappear. It is worth noting that nowadays, though, the Court has become predominantly counter majoritarian, and the obstruction is not just that the Justices themselves are shielded from politics through life tenure; it is that the political players selecting them undergo critical democratic deficits which indicate the effort of politics to constantly influence the applicability of the rule of law. Michael Tomasky[312] says that the two most recent additions to the Court were nominated "by a president and a Senate who represent the will of a minority of the American people."

It is worth mentioning that Justice Gorsuch joined the Court after Senate Republicans' unprecedented blockade of President Obama's nominee, Judge Merrick Garland and so Senate Republicans refused to even hold a hearing for Garland, notwithstanding his unquestionable qualifications and relative centrism and regardless of mainstream support for his confirmation among the American people. To that extent, it seems that the indisputable conclusion is that the party affiliation of Supreme Court justices matters and that the politicians take control of the Court.

Iaryczower, Matias and Matthew Shum. 2012. "The Value of Information in the Court: Get it Right, Keep it Tight." American Economic Review 102(1):202–37.

310 Knight, Jack and Lee Epstein. 1996. "On the struggle for judicial supremacy." Law and Society Review 30(1):87–120.

311 Clark, Tom S. 2011. The Limits of Judicial Independence. New York: Cambridge University Press. Clark, Tom S., Jeffrey R. Lax and Douglas Rice. 2015. Measuring the Political Salience of Supreme Court Cases." Journal of Law and Courts 3(1):37–65.

312 Michael Tomasky, The Supreme Court's Legitimacy Crisis, N.Y. TIMES, Oct. 5, 2018, https://www.nytimes.com/2018/10/05/opinion/supreme-courts-legitimacy-crisis.html; Alexander M. Bickel, The Least Dangerous Branch: The Supreme Court at the Bar of Politics 2nd Edition Yale University Press.

Has the Supreme Court remained the leading symbol of the rule of law in US society? It could be said that further political intervention upon supreme court's decisions would make the Court even more of a focal point of US politics[313] than it is already[314] which means that politics impact upon the rule of law is augmenting constantly in a degree to be able to say that in key matters of a society the politics rule of law is applied and only in neutral matters the legal rule of law is implemented. It could be said that the substantially prevailing of the politics rule of law over the legal rule of law will bring inevitably revolt in a society. James Gibson & Michael Nelson[315] say that "[l]ack of polarization [in peceptions of Supreme Court legitimacy] may also reflect the fact that the Supreme Court is currently making about 50% of its decisions in a conservative direction and 50% in a liberal direction" which means that politics influence the legitimacy of law, judicial review, and consequently the rule of law. Is there a political intervention even in Supreme Court in comparison with arbitrators?

The Supreme Court plays a momentous role in the public imagination as a citadel of justice and so due to political interventions faith in the Court may be severely tangled with feelings about the very idea of law more generally.[316] Therefore, if the Supreme Court is broadly seen as nothing more than another political institution, where Supreme Court justices are pondered nothing more than "politicians in robes", then society loses faith on law itself which means that in such a world, the very idea of law as a creativity divide off from politics will disappear. There is an imminent need for the Supreme Court to be saved above all, to save the idea of the Court as an institution above the political fight applying purely the ideal rule of law and not a much-politicized rule of law. Adrian Vermeule[317] argues that there is a need for the reform concerning political constraints on Supreme Court. It seems that Supreme Court judges have arrogated massive amounts of power to themselves and so if the

[313]Ian Millhiser, Kagan Warns That the Supreme Court's Legitimacy is in Danger, THINKPROGRESS, Sept. 17, 2018, https://thinkprogress.org/justice-kagan-warns-that-the-supreme-courts-legitimacy-is-in-danger2de1192d5636/ James L. Gibson, Understandings of Justice: Institutional Legitimacy, Procedural Justice, and Political Tolerance, 23 LAW & SOC. REV. 469, 480–81 (1989) (finding, based on responses to surveys, "some evidence of the Court's capacity to engender compliance with unpopular political decisions").

[314]Tom R. Tyler & Kenneth Rasinski, Procedural Justice, Institutional Legitimacy, and the Acceptance of Unpopular U.S. Supreme Court Decisions: A Reply to Gibson, 25 LAW & SOC. REV. 621, 627 (1991) (concluding that the "legitimacy of the U.S. Supreme Court is based on the belief that it makes decisions in fair ways, not on agreement with its decisions.").

[315]James L. Gibson & Michael J. Nelson, The Legitimacy of the US Supreme Court: Conventional Wisdoms and Recent Challenges Thereto, 10 ANN. REV. L. & SOC. SCI. 201, 209 (2014).

[316]Richard J. Pierce, Jr., Reconciling Chevron and Stare Decisis, 85 GEO.L.J. 2225, 2242 (1997) (noting that the Supreme Court is "the most salient symbol of the rule of law in our society").

[317]Adrian Vermeule, Political Constraints on Supreme Court Reform, 90 MINN. L.REV. 1154 (2006). Note, Congressional Restrictions on the President's Appointment Power and the Role of Longstanding Practice in Constitutional Interpretation, 120 Harv. L. Rev. 1914, 1919 (2007) (suggesting that "there is strong evidence that the original understanding of the Appointments Clause grants the President plenary appointment power contingent only on Senate confirmation").

Court's legitimacy is called into question then there is a possibility of a collapse of public confidence in the rule of law more generally. Judges and lawyers are influenced by the subject matter, processes and values of the system within which they operate.[318]

It is worth noting that the process of nominating and confirming justices to the U.S. Supreme Court has always been political and so political partisanship has harmed the Supreme Court confirmation process.[319] The Supreme Court confirmation process has worked as a political battleground between left and right, and in the present political climate, this seems doubtful to change, absent some procedural reform.[320] Does the political nomination of justices in US Supreme court indicate the role of politics upon justice rather the objective rule of law generation and implementation eliminating the argument that judges serve better the law instead of arbitrators? It has to be taken into account that the U.S. Supreme Court, like all supreme courts, passes on legal issues that have national policy ramifications and so the justices have been quite open in admitting the ease with which the Supreme Court can overrule precedent and so influencing the politics of judicial selection.[321] Also, political actors consider Supreme Court vacancies as political contests. Kevin Costello clarifies that "politics have always crept into the confirmation process. That said, there are degrees of politicization, and when the process becomes as toxic and divisive as it has in recent years in the United States . . ."[322] It has to be taken into consideration that elected officials who are politically accountable to the people are making all of the important policy decisions[323] and the judiciary operates as a faithful agent of the legislature. Moreover, as agents of the political branches, courts accomplish decisions they do not make and statutory interpretation fulfills previous decisions by an elected legislature, and does not involve creative law making by courts. Furthermore, courts resolve interpretive disputes by establishing the intent of

[318]Anthony Kronman, "Foreword: Legal Scholarship and Moral Education," 90 Yale L. Rev. 955, 959 (1981).

[319], Geoffrey R. Stone, Understanding Supreme Court Confirmations, 2010 SUP. CT. REV. 381, 381–82 (2010) ("Conventional wisdom says that the confirmation process for Supreme Court Justices is now terribly broken . . . The common refrain is that 'if only we could get back to the way we did things in the past, the process would be so much better.'").

[320]Tara Leigh Grove, The Origins (and Fragility) of Judicial Independence, 71 VAND. L. REV. 465, 540 (2018).

[321]Eric Black, How the Supreme Court Has Come to Play a Policymaking Role, MINNPOST (Nov. 20, 2012), https://www.minnpost.com/eric-black-ink/2012/11/how-supreme-court-has-come-play-policymakingrole. Alshrafi v. Am. Airlines, 321 F. Supp. 2d 150, 156 n.7 (D. Mass. 2004) ("The sweeping nature of recent Supreme Court preemption jurisprudence has been the subject of considerable comment, much of it critical.. . . Still, it is bedrock that Supreme Court decisions bind the analysis of [lower courts].")

[322]Kevin Costello, Supreme Court Politics and Life Tenure: A Comparative Inquiry, Vol. 71 May 2020 Hastings Law Journal 1153 at 1180.

[323]Jane S. Schacter, Metademocracy: The Changing Structure of Legitimacy in Statutory Interpretation, 108 Harv. L. Rev. 593, 594 (1995).

the legislature with regard to the precise question at issue.[324] Anyway, courts exercise substantial policy-making discretion when they decide cases pursuant to traditional methods of statutory interpretation.[325]

5.15 Conclusions

It could be said that human truth is not absolute and so an imperative function of the ideal involved in the chase of truth is that people have a need for a source of authority/influence greater than us which means that only in this tradition people subordinate desires and preferences to policies dictated by some higher power. To that extent, Locke described the role of the legal system as umpire.[326] It is worth mentioning that truth has got a dimensional aspect with the meaning of the dimension that humans can understand spiritual matters within a material dimension because if we could see this truth in another dimension will discover the limits of the truth. If people could see their truths under the eyes of a higher logically creature, then the content of their truths will be altered. Thus, our truth is lined to our material existence and capacity to understand that is why we believe in the spiritual world which is higher than the material one which people will meet when they are transformed after their material end.

Moreover, it could be argued that the dedication to the values of truth and truth-seeking are identified as integrity, honesty, and clarity that are matters of value. However, there is a variance between saying that something is true in an absolute sense but that we do not have the capacity to ascertain its accurate truth, and the suggestion that there is no truth other than what we say. It has to be considered that there is the discrepancy between truths that are "out there" and human concepts that we select to refer to or accept as true. In other words, new scientific truth reigns by convincing people[327] but the theoretical and spiritual true that cannot be part of a scientific true has to be understood as true via moral, ethical, and religious beliefs. Thus, certain facts of our physical world are true in humans' material dimension. Moreover, the outcome from the invention of science is that there is only one truth, not many truths, about anything and if people disagree then some must be right and others wrong which means that what was true now had always been true and always would be true. In other words, truth is not subject to adjustment by the simple passage of time or the alteration of views. There is always a need for interpretation of

[324] William N. Eskridge, Jr., Et Al., Legislation and Statutory Interpretation 221 (2d Ed. 2006); Daniel A. Farber & Philip P. Frickey, Law and Public Choice 89 (1991).

[325] Glen Staszewski, Statutory Interpretation as Contestatory Democracy, 55 Wm. & Mary L. Rev. 221 (2013), https://scholarship.law.wm.edu/wmlr/vol55/iss1/5

[326] John Locke, The Second Treatise Of Civil Government, 2.7 (1690).

[327] I. Bernard Cohen, Revolution in Science 467, 468 (1985).

a meaning and so Becker[328] argues that "The world of human aspiration is largely fictitious and if we do not understand this we understand nothing about man … Man's freedom is a fabricated freedom, and he pays the price for it. He must at all times defend the utter fragility of his delicately constituted fiction, deny its artificiality."

It could be said that behind the material expression always there is an ideal understanding of the spirituality or merely a stage of every soul before other forms of non-material life. Who knows? It seems that truth is changeable concerning matters that can be ascertained via empirical methods and science while matters of spirituality and existence of life can be influenced slightly by the new undertraining of modern life but not changing the fundamental essence. Do various groups present their truth which is imposed to the rest of the world?

Is law based on the need of people to be put order and be governed in a supposed fair for them way? Of course, law is the written principles accepted by the society as the foundation for the functionality of their society. From where, it emerged the need for a regulated society, instead of an anarchic way of life? The answer is from the character/nature of humans that is injected in their life by their creator, to act in a society and not alone in their living.

It is also vital to acknowledge that in human society values are made up of combinations of deep beliefs based on tradition, function, faith, morality, and authority. In many occasions competing positions are grounded on what is labeled as Religious Truths, on the one hand, and Revealed Truths, on the other. Moreover, the complexities of physical laws and the apparent fact that no matter how far back we have taken the hard science it can't justify how things got started from the very beginning in terms of what might be called the "First Cause." It could be said that there is leakage between the areas of religion and science but science has been a sort of religion for well over a century and has operated in line with numerous biases, acts of faith, and sometimes improvable declarations. It has to be taken into consideration that it is very difficult to believe in things and so the "grayness" of ambiguity supplants truth.

Legal truths are aimed to withstand a decision-making system that generates authoritative results taking place via the interference of the authority of the state to resolve disputes. It could be said that law offers procedure for deciding as many questions as possible which means that the law delivers sources of reasoning, statutes and statute-based rules, common law rules, and customs capable of ranking alternative dispute resolutions as right or wrong, and so better or worse.

Furthermore, exemplary changes in knowledge beliefs in fields of science are comparable to religious conversion and so a belief echoes the presence of an agreed-upon set of principles, functions, truths, and functioning rules encompassing a strong

---

[328] Ernest Becker, The Birth and Death of Meaning 139 (2d ed. 1971).

basis of adherents who possess entrusted interests in the continuation of the belief's mode of thinking about the world and allocation benefits.[329]

It has to be taken into consideration that there is no single value capable of spontaneously outplaying all others and that is why people's capacity to acquire any consensus on truth is restricted. Sunstein[330] specifies that "we value things, events, and relationships in ways that are not reducible to some larger and more encompassing value. The second claim is that human goods are not commensurable. By this I mean that human goods are not assessed along a single metric." Thus, it could be said that efforts in order to have a single kind of valuation and so making goods commensurable lead to an inferior reasoning.

Which is the structure of government upon the rise of liberty as the foundation of commerce in different stages of development? It could be said that Smith[331] develops a set of general principles of law and government directly relating law and government to economic development. In fact, there is a conjunction between politics and the economy which is signaled that the economy had become political and so success in international trade became a matter of the military and political survival of nations.

It is worth noting that the economy had always been political but it seems that nowadays it emerged clearly a new philosophy of a politicized economy which means the start of exploiting the rest of the world.[332] In other words, smith introduced the general principles of law and government indicating the rightful authority of the law. Moreover, it could be said that there are no panaceas and so uncertainty will linger for some laws as to whether they actually will be effective when applied by courts which mean that there is a need for channeling some law-unifying behavior toward the production of better or at least more effective law.

People take core beliefs and principles as true and struggle to integrate them into the functioning rules of a system and to act in concurrence with those rules which means that the choices people make about core beliefs and deep principles stipulate the structure, foundations, and moral energy of the community we select to generate. In addition, there is need to have some credible and practically consensual criteria on which choices are founded or we are floating in a limbo where there is neither

[329] I. Bernard Cohen, Revolution in Science 468 (1985). Bernard Williams, Truth and Truthfulness: An Essay in Genealogy (Princeton, 2000). Kenneth Baker, "Williams examines the merits of truth," in the on-line Book Review section of the San Francisco Chronicle, Sunday, September 22, 2002, http://www.sfgate.com/cgibin/article.cgi?f=/chronicle/archive/2002/09/22/RV93143.DTL. Plato, Laws, Reinhold Niebuhr, Human Destiny, 1943, William James, The Meaning of Truth, 1907, Aristotle, Nichomachean Ethics, Ralph Waldo Emerson, "Intellect," Essays, First Series, 1841, Thomas Henry Huxley, The Coming of Age of "The Origin of Species," 1893, William James, Pragmatism, 1907, Francis Bacon, Essays, 1597.

[330] Cass R. Sunstein, Free Markets and Social Justice 70 (1997).

[331] Hont, Istvan. 2009. "Adam Smith's History of Law and Government as Political Theory," in R. Bourke and R. Geuss (eds), Political Judgement: Essays for John Dunn. Cambridge: Cambridge University.

[332] Hont, Istvan. 2005. "Introduction," Jealousy of Trade: International Competition and the Nation-State in Historical Perspective. Cambridge: Cambridge University Press.

stability nor reliability. Justice Scalia[333] makes a remark that: "Law's quandary, then, is that we believe like legal realists but act as though there were indeed some omnipresent, overarching law." Moreover, each choice of a primary truth leads to aftereffects compelling obligations on people or relieves people of accountability then again, the choices are not only individual issues. It could be said that the idea of being able to recognize what one believes to be an unjust law and to refuse to obey that positive law grounded on personal moral beliefs can be ascertained in various situations. In line it is worth mentioning the Mahatma Gandhi's doctrine of passive resistance and civil, non-violent disobedience that was featured successfully into the civil rights movements in the USA.

It is regarded that trust and law are alternative mechanisms for stabilizing expectations which means that law and trust are contemplated complementary and so trust and law are interconnected and they support each other. Thus, it could be argued that the rationale of the legal order is to guarantee as much as of the entire system of welfares which means satisfying the entire structure of peoples' wishes or requests implicated in living together in civilized society, with the least conflict. There is a need for respect concerning the law within the dynamics of community ordering which means not offsetting the enthusiasm to negotiate social compromises. Moreover, truth is an element in law.[334]

It has to be considered that in the noncumulative sphere of which law is a crucial part due to the fact that society possesses some greater capacity to create and assemble edifices of truth. To that extent, law is a central part of the manner by which these edifices are invented, applied, and guarded. On the one hand, it is worth noting that occasionally law plays a role in the preservation of the social and political design. On the other hand, from time to time law is the vehicle of destruction or reformat which means that society is at the mercy of periodic design alterations and style preferences which have to be made under the rule of law complying to new developments in technology, modern life and science but not altering the fundamental principles of establishment of law. To that extent, Roe v. Wade offers an example of the distinctions between legal, political, and religious truth. Moreover, it is hard to avoid assuming that Roe v. Wade is a political decision much more than a legal decision.

One aftereffect of the disbelief entailed by the setup of positive law within a Rule of Law system where it is not legalized to believe that authority resides in an ideal source higher and purer than ourselves is that there is no well-defined moral or qualitative justification for privileging one choice over another. In any case, even if there are rationalizations they are not so apparent or unquestionable that they achieve consent.

On the one hand, the basic principle of the rule of law is that everyone is subject to the law. On the other hand, the ideal of the rule of law embraces values that legal

---

[333] Antonin Scalia, book review of, Steven D. Smith, Law's Quandary (Harvard 2005), 2005 First Things 157 (November 2005) pp. 37–46.

[334] David Barnhizer, "Truth or Consequences in Legal Scholarship," 50 Hofstra L. Rev. (2005).

systems should reflect. Of course, many values can be considered as the foundation of the rule of Law but the basic value is the incorporation of the regulation of the accepted of a society's values for the good of the whole society and not the short-term regulation for the political implantation of the contemporary interests of an elite against the demands of the society.

As well, on the one hand, τα πάντα ρει (everything is changing) which means that the concept of the rule of law is altered but the functionality of a society is based on a rule of law which has to be as ideal as possible in order to have a stable legitimacy causing the essence of justice in the society for the good of the society and not a contemporary implementation of the interest of an elite via the imposition of their political aims covered under the mast of a rule of law in order to cool down the aggression of the regulated society. It has to be considered that laws restrained individual freedom and so laws have to be as simple and as unobtrusive as possible which means that laws must be operative giving certainty and stability rather than directing persons toward a specific path of action. Therefore, the rule of law denotes that laws are predictable and general and apply equally.

It could be said that law functions only if individuals are open to it and so they are open to it only if it echoes their values[335] which means that human authority derives from the normative social systems, and becomes externalized as a supreme system of formal law and so once established, law does not stay inactive and instead constantly coordinates human conflicts, relieves social stress, and reinforces social bonds.[336]

Does the rule of law influence politics and vice versa? It is worth noting that the rule of law is the most important political ideal today. The rule of law proceeds from the premise that people enjoy certain fundamental rights that are better protected by a fixed body of self-imposed laws than by "the whims of an autocrat." Moreover, the rule of law developed from the ancient Greeks understandings.[337] It has to be considered that generality, clarity, and neutrality are originated from a minimal normative premise about what constitutes law in a setting where partially enforcement is decentralized and private as supplementary in combination with public authority.

Likewise, law consists of certain principles or doctrines applying them with constant aptitude to the ever-tangled length.[338] The law cannot be in the hands of the government as an instrument for satisfying the demands of the elites but it has to stand firm in achieving justice for the people and utilizing the rule of law. Otherwise

[335] Janice Nadler, Expressive Law, Social Norms, and Social Groups, 42 LAW & SOC. INQUIRY 60, 63, 69, 70–71 (2017).

[336] Gillian Hadfield, Rules For A Flat World: Why Humans Invented Law And How To Reinvent It For A Complex Global Economy 41 (2016) (stating that "[w]e don't really know when law first emerged in human societies"). Peter T. Manicas, A Realistic Philosophy Of Social Science: Explanation And Understanding 44 (2006). Lenartowicz Et Al., Social Systems: Complex Adaptive Loci Of Cognition, 18 Emergence: Complexity & Org. 1, 1 (2016).

[337] Brian Z. Tamanaha, On the Rule of Law: History, Politics, Theory 51, 53–54 (2004).

[338] Christopher Langdell, Address delivered Nov. 5, 1866, reprinted in 3 Law Q. Rev. 123, 124 (1887).

we will have an unstable law and a changeable rule of law that is outside the sense of the real rule of law. It is worth mentioning that the normative classification of conduct as unfair is emergent, a result of repeated interactions of many members of a community but it has to be based upon the essence of law uninfluenced from a groups' interest rather than the interests of the entire society and not the politics of the prevailing elite at a specific time. It is argued that law materializes when there is a move from "organic classification" to official classification by an institution up to formulating and adjusting the substance of classifications. There is a need for simplicity in law in order to be effective and not giving room for various interpretations which allow personal interest to be satisfied against the general good.

It is argued that a regime could continue to operate as a stable legal system even in the existence of gross failures of legality.[339] A legal system attains rule of law as long as there is an essential role for private, decentralized, enforcement of law or public centralized enforcement of law. Moreover, it has to be taken into consideration that the fundamental ideology that is the foundation of the rule of law, namely universal human dignity, was formulated in Christian thinking. On the other hand, state power was often used to violate the very principles of universal human dignity and human agency. Nevertheless, political theory conveyed institutional forms of governance based upon the concept of human equality restraining the arbitrary use of power.

From the political standpoint law is the province of government focusing on the processes and principles by which the essence of law is ascertained.[340] Hadfield and Weingast[341] state the idea that law is essentially about government. First of all, it has to be taken into consideration that political truths are of a diverse kind than empirical, mathematical, or philosophical truths. Moreover, it has to be considered that rule of law is not the only required aspect of a legal political regime. Moreover, generality indicates only the form of a rule and so it is based on categories rather than personal distinctiveness, but categories could be intently, and discriminatorily, drawn. Thus, depersonalized reasoning signifies only the actuality that ex post classifications of particular events and behaviors are stemmed from ex ante rules and principles that can in principle be repeated by any individual. Furthermore, classification is not a function of the identity of the classifier and so it does not denote that all persons are handled equally by the law.

The establishment, the context, and implementation of the rule of law is based on a specific politics selection and so there is a notion of politics of law in creation and enforcement of law. It is worth mentioning that governments in order to achieve their

---

[339] Raz J. 2009. The Authority of Law: Essays on Law and Morality (2nd ed.) Oxford, UK: Oxford University Press p 223 "I have been treating the rule of law as an ideal, as a standard to which the law ought to conform but which it can and sometimes does violate most radically and systematically."

[340] McNollgast. 2007. "Political Economy of Law" in in A. Mitchell Polinsky and Stephen Shavel, eds., Law and Economics Handbook vol 2. North Holland.

[341] Hadfield, GK, Weingast BR. 2015. "Microfoundations of the Rule of Law," Annual Review of Political Science 17:21–42.

political targets they alter various laws accordingly which means that the rule of law is not used in its real essence but it is obviously a short-term manipulation of the law for purely political reasons such as in the occasion of purposely altering the law allowing national MPs with no need to resign to be concurrently candidates for the European parliament for the reason of avoiding to lose short-term governmental majority rather than a clear utilization of the rule of law for the good of the governed society instead of using the law in order to achieve the political party interests against of the interests of the whole society. To that extent, people know that rules are needed but too rapid or frequent alteration weakens the self-respect and grandeur of the law which means that "lays bare the Oz-like illusion of judges as black robed 'wizards'".[342]

Roscoe Pound[343] observed that the law strives for principles of both change and stability and so the principles of change and stability are encompassed in the complex system of law, implanted in the assumptions and values embodied in the multiplex system of legal doctrine. Besides, Aristotle said that law has no power to order compliance other than through habit[344] which means that it takes time for people in order to respect and obey and follow the rules of law and so alterations should not be made very soon and often. Moreover, Aristotle argued that it is imprudent to alter law too quickly. Alterations are better if they happen within the background of the values to which society still give some degree of commitment and so this does not mean that it cannot be altered but does mean that any alterations have to be made very carefully and with prudence rather than apparent political incentives.

A dominant statement of ethics setting forth the highest principles on which one justifies behavior is not "uncontested" but it simply sets forth an unavoidable social reality in virtually any culture. Have the fundamentals of human life changed or merely the advanced technological developments cover the matter and in fact the same principle of life exists since many years ago? Aristotle advanced the idea of "human flourishing" as the reason of human society placing the individual at the purposive center of the political community in the meaning that the responsibility of the community entangled generating a cultural context adequate to permit the individual members of society to achieve their highest qualitative development.

---

[342] David Cole, "Agon at Agora: Creative Misreadings in the First Amendment Tradition", 95 Yale L. J. 857, 859 (1986), states: "[I]n landmark cases . . . the Justices alter the puzzle itself and create law. Thus, while judicial legitimacy requires faithful adherence to precedent, legal development turns on creative acts."

[343] Roscoe Pound, New Paths of the Law 3 (1950).

[344] Aristotle, The Politics, B. Jowett trans., The Oxford Translation of Aristotle, W.D. Ross ed. (1921): "For the law has no power to command obedience except that of habit, which can only be given by time, so that a readiness to change from old to new laws enfeebles the power of the law." Bk. II, c. 8.

The rule of law functions to enable and enhance economic development. Considering the link between law and economic development Max Weber[345] said that "the rationalization and systematization of the law in general and . . . the increasing calculability of the functioning of the legal process in particular, constituted one of the most important conditions for the existence of economic enterprise intended to function with stability and, especially, of capitalist enterprise, which cannot do without legal security." To that extent, it is obvious that a longstanding regime of formal legal rules declared publicly in advance, applied by judges in accordance with their terms, offers predictability for businesses.

It is worth noting that the dispute over the substance of law discloses that a till now comparatively suppressed dynamic is consolidating and displaying as the explicit operational and ideological convergence between the economic and political institutions. To that extent, this convergence is informally linked to the mounting violence with which the universality of specific forms of social, political, and economic ordering is being affirmed on the international level. Nevertheless, this convergence encompasses the end of the dynamic aiming at the assignment of consolidating the universal dimension of international law which means that such consolidation would reverse the serious instability of international law being a quality vital to both the imperial and anti-imperial dimensions of international law.

It has to be considered that the strategies of the "rule of law" make use of the universal prospective of international law subordinated by a ruling rationality and so this rationality is more and more economic, and is operationalized in terms of a claim to universality which is secured "juridically" through transferals between the political and economic institutions of international law. Furthermore, the coming together of the political and economic strands of international law is not new but signifies a reappearing and escalation of a course installed and institutionalized at the end of World War Two. Nonetheless, although it is not new, the current course does denote a qualitative change partially explaining the gradually violent character of transformative interventions in the Third World which implies strategies which "de-operationalize" the universal and regain it and consequently international law as a place of politics which means that there is a first move toward the decolonization of international law.

The rule of law has lately experienced a marked rise in popularity and by the middle of the 1990s the rule of law was being advanced as a panacea to the world's ills—from Russia to China, from Somalia to Kosovo, its employment was seen as a "rising imperative of the era of globalization."[346] On the other hand, the widespread faith in its international dimension has reduced somewhat since the setting up of the "war on terror." However, the reawakening and subsequent embrace of the rule of law by the development institutions and associated aid machinery has tightened rather than loosened and so. The World Bank drives the move toward the rule of law.

---

[345] Max Weber, Economy and Society, vol. 2, edited by Guenther Roth and Claus Wittich (Berkeley, Ca.: University of California Press 1978) p. 883.

[346] Thomas Carothers, "Rule of Law Revival" (1998) 77(2) Foreign Affairs 95, 95.

The crisis of East Asian economies was attributable to corruption, the unwarranted interpenetration of Asian governments and business communities and Asian countries with each other, in addition to a failure of governance and the rule of law.[347] It is argued that the crisis and its consequences offered the prospect to consolidate the shift from the rule of international law to the internationalization of the rule of law via its juridical projection through conditionality encompassing all the policies that have to be followed,[348] on top of its geographical projection into Asia. Moreover, the Asian Debt Crisis emphasized the malfunction of the region's several rule-of-law reforms to bring transparency and responsibility to the transactions of privileged bankers, businessmen, and politicians and so brought forwards a burden for more reform, both from within Asia and from the international financial society. It is argued that the acknowledgment of the crisis to this failure of national law and society both increased the international request for the rule of law restructuring and endorsed its reproductive force within the international economic institutions.

Can we have international order without the rule of law? It is worth mentioning that the World Bank, along with the International Monetary Fund (IMF), examined the relation of "governance" and institutions, embracing the role of law, and their role in the advancement of development[349] and so the rule of law was directly aroused for the first time as both reason and outcome of development.[350] Thus, governance and the "rule of law" were suggested as solutions to the developmental and so economic "crises" of the 1990s was neither self-evident nor unavoidable, but then again depended first upon a multifaceted re-emergence of the significance of law.[351] The International Court of Justice (ICJ) was seen to have been dealt a heavy blow by Cold War politics.[352]

Can law be used for political reasons such as prosecuting political rivals only in order to promote the approach imposed by foreign forces and interpretation of law against even a national approach? For instance, the prosecution of political leaders for refusing to accept the unlawful entrance of immigrants into Italy seems to be

---

[347] Joseph Stiglitz, Globalization and its Discontents (London: Penguin, 2002).

[348] Joseph Gold, Conditionality (Pamphlet No 31, IMF Pamphlet Series, Washington DC, 1979).

[349] Amanda Perry, "International Economic Organisations and the Modern Law and Development Movement" in Ann Seidman, Robert Seidman and Thomas Wälde (eds.), Making Development Work: Legislative Reform for Institutional Transformation and Good Governance (The Hague: Kluwer, 1999) James Thuo Gathii, "Good Governance as a Counter-Insurgency Agenda to Oppositional and Transformative Social Projects in International Law" (1999) 5 Buffalo Human Rights Law Review 107.

[350] James Wolfensohn, "Foreword" in The International Bank for Reconstruction and Development, The State in a Changing World (World Development Report, 1997) (Washington DC: Oxford University Press, 1997).

[351] Richard Peet, Unholy Trinity: The IMF, World Bank and WTO (London: Zed Books, 2003).

[352] UN GA Res 44 /23. Military and Paramilitary Activities in and against Nicaragua (Nicaragua v US) (Jurisdiction of the Court and Admissibility of the Application) [1984] ICJ Rep 392; Military and Paramilitary Activities in and against Nicaragua (Nicaragua v US) (Merits) [1986] ICJ Rep 14. Rudolf Bernhardt, "Review of Lori Damrosch (ed.), The International Court of Justice at a Crossroads" (1990) 84(1) American Journal of International Law 293.

based on a political understanding and utilization of the rule of law against a legalistic understanding because of the political views for illegal immigration via bogus refugees. Moreover, can law be separated from politics? It could be said that it is impossible to separate law from politics because politics are amalgamated in the wording of the written law and so it is not only about the politics of interpretation or the indeterminacy of legal reasoning but also about the institutional structure of the rule of law and its obligatory embeddedness within institutionalized political structures. It could be said that it is possible per se of a segregated concept of law but its formation, application, and alteration is based on the politics amalgamated within the legal wording of the law.

Upham[353] insists that "a 'formalist rule of law' is undesirable on the basis that it is unlikely to promote economic growth" which means that there is an attempt to announce a formalist rule of law displacing indigenous institutions and so placing prevailing informal means of social order at risk and eventually bringing negative results to the society. It has to be taken into consideration that one of the risks of legal transplants is that they will supersede "indigenous institutions" and "existing informal means of social order" but, taking into account that the informal regulatory mechanisms exist before the arrival of law, these "local," "informal" means of upholding social order are still described by reference to a developed ideal.

It has to be considered that building a "rule of law" cannot stand in for the problematic economic and political decisions which have to supplement development which means that law has to be a distributional device legalizing distributional choices and effects of different economic theories of development. In other words, the market itself is built on the back of norms which can usefully be drawn into the foreground to strengthen political debate around development and its outcomes.[354]

Taking into account that human interaction is a strive for position and power, there is a normative choice to be made about making the world more or less subject to the Rule of Law.[355] It could be said that the existing international legal system is not really anti-war as much as it is anti-aggressive war which means that the use of force is not always illegitimate, but rather, countries do not have a right to the legally righteous use of force at their choice and so this is the spatial, legal, and political order of the world. Moreover, there are gaps generated by "exception" and global war on terror, in the seemingly established liberal system of the post-Cold War Period.[356] It seems that there is no political unity in the international realm but this does not mean that there is no existence of law, or of an international nomos.

[353] Frank Upham, Mythmaking in the Rule of Law Orthodoxy (2002) (Paper No 30, Carnegie Endowment for International Peace Working Papers, Rule of Law Series, Democracy and the Rule of Law Project, September 2002).

[354] Karl Polanyi, The Great Transformation: The Political and Economic Origins of Our Time (Boston: Beacon Press, 1967) (first published 1944).

[355] D. Dyzenhaus, "Hobbes on the International Rule of Law," Ethics & International Affairs 28 (2014), 54.

[356] C. Schmitt, "The Turn to the Discriminating Concept of War (1937)," in Carl Schmitt Writings on War 30 (Timothy Nunan, ed. trans. 2011), 31–32. A. Benoist, "Global Terrorism and the State of

Moreover, there is no global sovereign and consensus over a clear definition of the scope and content of justice and law. Law can easily become a political tool and so justice, law, power, and practice, could not be seen as separate from each other.[357]

It has to be considered that the process of state-building and the rise of constitutionalism were connected in complex ways. Can "state" and "constitution" be connected together in the same way at the international level? Nevertheless, the use of force in self-defense is not "beyond" law and it is built into the pre-existing decision rules based on the continually existing political interests of the prevailing forces which mean that the wish to global, rather than only international constitutionalism is steadily countered by law's liable co-existence with morality, and politics.

Also, constitutions do not just generate and allocate the powers of the state, they also restrain the powers of the state and so the state, even when supported by the will of a majority, have not to act in manners that violate basic rights. In other words, modern constitutionalism combines supra-constitutional principles and norms, based on the rights, freedoms, and dignity of the individuals which means that these principles and norms are supraconstitutional in that they cannot be invalidated, not by legislation endorsed pursuant to the constitution and not even by modification of the constitution itself. Consequently, modern constitutionalism integrates substantive norms on individual rights and freedoms featuring firstly a written constitution, secondly a charter of fundamental rights, and thirdly a mode of constitutional judicial review to protect those rights. Furthermore, global constitutionalism differs from the national model in that it does not ascertain a supreme authority, is not reinforced by a state, and is not based on a specific demo.[358] Nevertheless, modern constitutionalism shares with international rule of law an important basis that individual rights and freedoms set limits to the powers of the state. In conclusion, modern international rule of law embraces worldwide limitations on the powers of the state, not just vis-à-vis each other but also with regard to individual persons under their jurisdiction which means that global constitutionalism entails rights-based limits on state powers.[359]

It is argued that law does little to restrain the modern executive but on the other hand whereas politics and public opinion do restrict the modern executive which means that politics achieve what law fails to do and so politics alters the law in order

Permanent Exception: The Significance of Carl Schmitt's Thought Today," in L Odysseos and F Petito (eds.)

[357] D. Bell, Reordering the World: Essays on Liberalism and Empire (2016).

[358] Kumm, Mattias (2009). "The Cosmopolitan Turn in Constitutionalism: On the Relationship between Constitutionalism in and beyond the State." In Ruling the World? Constitutionalism, International Law, and Global Governance. Jeffrey L. Dunoff and Joel P. Trachtman, ed. Cambridge, Cambridge University Press: 258–325.

[359] Gardbaum, Stephen (2009). "Human Rights and International Constitutionalism." In Ruling the World? Constitutionalism, International Law, and Global Governance. Jeffrey L. Dunoff and Joel P. Trachtman, ed. Cambridge, Cambridge University Press: 233–257.

to achieve its aims.[360] Furthermore, it could be said that the rule of law is not a useful evaluative or analytic hypothesis, owing in part to its definitional inconsistency, and absence of consensus about the rule of law's fundamental values[361] which is based on an understanding that politics form the content of the rule of law according to the existing political interests and there is no standard legal definition of the content of the rule of law applicable in general bringing justice for all which means that in fact there is rule of law but the rule of politics covered by a law in order to display a sense of legitimacy. It could be said that under the rule of law, it shouldn't be one law for the powerful and another for the rest of the society.

In other words, the medium of law should govern those who make, enforce, and interpret the law which means that it may be a government of laws and not of men. Furthermore, modern rule of law conceptions attaches prerequisites to the form and quality of the law itself such as that law is clear, stable, and transparent[362] that has to be substantive and procedural. Whereas the former speaks to what the law is, the latter is more concerned with the public's capacity to know that an issue is being viewed, to be implicated in the decision-making process, to know who else is concerned and in what ways, and to comprehend how a final decision is attained.

There is a need to see the accounts that make rule of law demands on the features of law itself but even though clarity occurs by other means, this component generally favors rules over standards, clear meanings over systemic inferences, direct applications rather than arguments, and ex ante transparency rather than labored interpretations. Antonin Scalia[363] has favored general rules as opposed to balancing modes of analysis or "totality of the circumstances." Lawrence B. Solum[364] argues that social practice notifies the application of broad standards, making their application as predictable, if not more predictable, than rules in certain contexts but social practice is based on norms and law that form the rule of law.

---

[360] Eric A. Posner & Adrian Vermeule, The Executive Unbound: After The Madisonian Republic 15 (2010).

[361] Daniel B. Rodriguez et al., The Rule of Law Unplugged, 59 Emory L.J. 1455, 1493 (2010) Jeremy Waldron, Is the Rule of Law an Essentially Contested Concept (in Florida)? 21 Law & Phil. 137, 151 (2002) (describing rule of law as an essentially contested concept, which inherently defies analytical consensus).

[362] Marbury v. Madison, 5 U.S. (1 Cranch) 137, 163 (1803); James Harrington, The Commonwealth Of Oceana And A System Of Politics 8 (J.G.A. Pocock ed., Cambridge Univ. Press 1992) (1656) ("[G]overnment... is the empire of laws and not of men."). Lon L. Fuller, The Morality Of Law 33–94 (rev. ed. 1969). (According to Fuller, laws should be (1) general, (2) publicly promulgated, (3) prospective, (4) intelligible, (5) consistent, (6) practicable, (7) not too frequently changeable, and (8) actually congruent with the behavior of the officials of a regime).

[363] Antonin Scalia, The Rule of Law as a Law of Rules, 56 U. CHI. L. REV. 1175, 1186–87 (1989).

[364] Lawrence B. Solum, A Law of Rules: A Critique and Reconstruction of Justice Scalia's View of the Rule of Law, 1 Apa Newsl. On Phil. & L. 105, 110 (2002) Brian Galle & Mark Seidenfeld, Administrative Law's Federalism: Preemption, Delegation, and Agencies at the Edge of Federal Power, 57 Duke L.J. 1933, 1949 (2008).

Have some of Trump's opponents endangered the rule of law[365] due to political goals? Has the Trump Administration acted contrary to the "rule of law" due to political goals? It could be said that the issue would arise of whether the actions of Trump Administration should be accorded legal legitimacy, both during and after its period in office based on a rule of law in accordance with the political interpretation of the existed law or the enacted law accordingly illustrating a picture of implemented rule of law due to the need to implement major political interests.

As discussed earlier, the rule of law is a vitally imperative safeguard against the abuse of state power offering protections to residents which have been hard-won over the centuries. It is argued that there is a distinction between formal and substantive versions of the rule of law.[366] Formal versions of the rule of law refer to the way in which the law is made and its form and structure. Besides, substantive versions refer to the content of the law reflecting specific legal values seen as vital. On the other hand, it could be said that the rule of law embraces the conception of the functioning of a society based on the utilization of the law for all its members and so the formality of the law and its content is a matter of the law formation rather than the formation of the rule of law and of course the content is indirectly the content of the rule of law.

In addition, it is argued that the rule of law simply means that "a legal system is in good shape"[367] which is not totally accurate because the law and its quality upon which is based the applicable the rule of law gives the substance into the concept of the rule of law which means that there is a need for the introduction a good law in order to have a well-functioning legal system. What it makes a good law? In other words, the quality of the ingredients of the morality and effectiveness of the law is what constitutes the ideal of a good legal system under the rule of law but the reliance of a legal system on the rule of law is a prima facie good picture of having the basis for a well function and worthiness. It has to be considered that the core principle of a good law is that the law has to be effective which means that it must solve fairly the societal matter that it aims at. In other words, the problem to be solved has to be to the interests of the whole society and not to the political interests of the elite. The changeability of the societal matters needed regulation, due to societal alterations via new technologies generating new environments, adds to the need for drafting all the time new laws that have to solve fairly these societal matters.

It has to be considered that the central rationale for doubt regarding the likelihood of laws that go against the rule of law is the traditional understanding of parliamentary sovereignty. The constitutionally based respect for parliament as the highest power in a state is at odds with a "public disdain" of practicality named "la cuisine

[365] David A. Graham, "Trump's Assault on the Rule of Law," The Atlantic, Apr. 9, 2018, https://www.theatlantic.com/politics/archive/2018/04/trumps-assault-on-rule-of-law/557600/; David Leonhardt,"Trump's Attacks on the Rule of Law Reach a New Level", N.Y Times (Opinion), May 21, 2018, https://www.nytimes.com/2018/05/21/opinion/trump-department-of-justice.html

[366] Ronan Cormacain, Legislative Drafting and the Rule of Law Institute of Advanced Legal Studies, School of Advanced Study, University of London PhD Thesis 2017.

[367] John Finnis, Natural Law and Natural Rights (Oxford University Press 1980).

politique." Which is the relationship between democracy and the rule of law? Does democracy dominate the rule of law or is it the other way around? It could be said that normality demands that democracy and rule of law are inseparable, but "there are a few examples of rule of law states without democracy, there are plenty of democracies where the rule of law is hard to find."[368]

It is worth noting that various rule of law paths link with different amalgamations of power relations, resource distribution and ideational foundations of the reigning political settlement which means that the rule of law is never absolute/conclusive in its heart of its content and context but the essence of the rule of law has to be standardized in a global scale in order to be harmonically applied in globalization achieving its goals. Otherwise, the application of the rule of law will be declared but in fact there will be a different understanding and so allowing misinterpretations and exploitations by various groups to the detriment of the whole society. In other words, there is a need for the international society to declare what the rule of law represents and which is its DNA as a notion and conception essential for the fair existence and continuity of humanity in its natural form because the transformation of human life in another form of existence and the emergence of artificial beings will might demand another understanding of the rule of law.

Hence, the rule of law is only one of the guidelines to accomplish justice and people should consider themselves fortunate if their government values the essentials of this rule. Taking into consideration that the rule of law is an unwritten constitutional principle denotes that the legislator will not be able to avert the court from judging state actions regardless that unwritten principles also involve judicial discretion. There is a need of giving attention to the Supreme Courts of judging legislation which might be turned into having a government of men (judicial persons) and not of laws due to the fact that judges are chosen by governments and political parties. It is worth noting that in rule of law systems there is a growing assertiveness of judges over political matters in constitutional and human rights cases.[369]

It has to be considered that the rule of law is never entirely conveyed and enforced in any society and some violations of the rule of law exist and so there is need for an upgrading of the applicability of the rule of law in all nations. States have to improve the welfare of their citizens relying on an effective legal system utilizing the rule of law. There is a need to find the essence of law regardless of any political view but merely as a substance needed for the well-being of a society regardless of any political or social interests in order to achieve the ideal level of material and spiritual life for all members of the society irrespective their wealth status but merely as equal humans in a society. Who and how will achieve an objective substance for law? Of

---

[368] Peter van Lochem (2017) Legislation against the rule of law – an introduction, The Theory and Practice of Legislation, 5:2, 95–100, DOI: https://doi.org/10.1080/20508840.2017.1387729 Jonathan Chait, "Trump is mobilizing for war against the rule of law," New York Magazine, 17 July 2017 Joan Biskupic, "Trump's disdain for the rule of law," CNN Politics, 26 July 2017.

[369] Ran Hirschl, Towards Juristocracy: The Origins and Consequences of the New Constitutionalism (Cambridge, Ma.: Harvard University Press 2006).

course, every period needs its own law due to new developments in science, technology, etc. but the essence and heart of law has not changed and merely there is a need for new formation in order to be applicable due to new materiality which means new phraseology.

It has to be taken into account that by definition, law accepted in democratic process, involves compromise. Laws are formed to be applied by human beings who can reason themselves and to be interpreted in case of dispute by reasonable judges. Thus, it is this process of openness of the law and legal process to later interpretation by judges and arbitrators which gives the law the flexibility to adopt the new prerequisites of the times without having to be rewritten like code.

References

1. Mills, A. (2009). *The confluence of public and private international law*. Cambridge University Press.
2. Scalia, A. (1989). The rule of law as a law of rules. *56 University of Chicago Law Review, 1175*, 1186–1187.
3. Obama, B. (2017). The President's role in advancing criminal justice reform. *Harvard Law Review, 130*, 811, 814 n.11.
4. Brian, Z. (2017). *Tamanaha, A realistic theory of law*. Cambridge University Press.
5. Bell, D. (2016). *Reordering the world: Essays on liberalism and empire*.
6. Bosco, D. (2014). *Rough Justice: The international criminal court in a world of power politics* (pp. 1–10). Oxford University Press.
7. Benvenisti, E. (2018). Upholding democracy amid the challenges of new technology: what role for the law of global governance? *European Journal of International Law, 29*, 9.
8. Forder, J., & Svantesson, D. (2007). *Internet and E-commerce law*. OUP.
9. Zekos, G. (2016a). *Law and economics of corporate governance and insider trading*. Nova Science.
10. Zekos, G. (2016b). *MNE's in 21st century*. Nova Science.
11. Zekos, G. (2015). *Monetary policy and risk management in financial globalization*. Nova Science.
12. Zekos, G. (2014). *Risk management, corporate governance in 21st century digital economy*. Nova Science.
13. Zekos, G. (2020). *Finance Crimes: Insider trading and money laundering*. Nova Science.
14. Gilliéron, G. (2014). *Public Prosecutors in the United States and Europe*. Springer.
15. Krieger, H. (2019). Populist governments and international law. *European Journal of International Law, 30*(3).
16. Lim, Y. F. (2007). *Cyberspace law: commentaries and materials*. OUP.
17. Versteeg, M., & Ginsburg, T. (2017). Measuring the rule of law: A comparison of indicators. *Law and Social Inquiry, 42*, 100.
18. Lindseth, P. L. (2010). *Power and legitimacy: Reconciling Europe and the Nation-State*. OUP.
19. Caney, S. (2006). *Justice beyond borders*. OUP.
20. Miller, T. (2019). Explanation in artificial intelligence: Insights from the social sciences. *267 Artificial Intelligence, 1*, 1–2.

Chapter 6
Politics Supersedes the Rule of Law

6.1 Politics, Ideology, and Law

It has to be taken into consideration that communities need to be "mature" and "flexible" to make good use of the rule of law concerning advanced formal legal systems because an immature society can use its own rule of law based on the type of law endorsed by that society. In other words, a "mature" and "established" political system is required to make certain the rule of law of a formal legal system works and so making certain that politics within it can be disciplined and pointed to the ends of accomplishing economic growth rather than any other ends. Nevertheless, in case of states with new legal systems, particularly ones imposed or imported from overseas, means that pre-existing institutions lack the experience, expertise, and political legitimacy needed to cope with unexpected consequences of restructuring. It has to be taken into account that in a society that has a new, formal legal system but then again there is a deficiency concerning the social capital, institutions, and discipline to make a rightful use of it which means that importing a formal legal system is not so simple to effect development for the reason that a formal legal system is not the self-contained and self-ruling thing and so the rule of law is not automatically applied and having legal results.

It is worth noting that ideology stages a chance to re-evaluate the question to which an answer has been given. Besides, the appliance of a reflexive ideology is echoed and naturally goes together with the decision to embrace a specific ideology replying to the question of how society has to be structured and so then that process of reflection is developed into ideology itself.

For instance, when life begins and, for purposes of abortion, when we legally, politically, or religiously want to say life begins? Considering that there are significant substances concerning the legal, political, and religious fields, viewpoints about what creates the person based on whether we are talking about law, politics, or religion in connection with beliefs in the character of life, how and when life is generated, whether souls exist and if so when they are invested in the biological

G. I. Zekos, *Political, Economic and Legal Effects of Artificial Intelligence*, Contributions to Political Science, https://doi.org/10.1007/978-3-030-94736-1_6

entity. It has to be considered that the ideologist develops or advances the ideas of a specific political outlook but is not developing or practicing ideology and so ideology comes into the picture only when a theorist clarifies some feature or another of how the ideas of liberalism or socialism, or political outlooks in general, are expanded and disseminated as a rational thought. If ideology is a theoretical concept that has been created mainly to explain the practice of politics, then the connection between law and ideology will encompass a background of the correlation between law and politics. Thus, ideology has a valuable role to accomplish in a theory capable of enlightening the practice of law and so the reflection on law sheds some light on the character of ideology and the political practice to which it signifies. Is there a relationship between law and ideology? There is a need to consider the relationship between law and ideology and so whether ideology is an issue for law at all. Of course, the prevailing ideology influences the wording of any law regulating specific matters.

Is ideology something worth distinguishing from politics in general? Is politics or ideology something that needs to be taken into consideration when theorizing about law? It has to be noted that once we accept that ideology particularly backs the constructing of law's theory, then it cannot be turned around and dining politics more generally as playing a part. Even though ideology is conceptually separated from politics in general, that is not to say that it makes no sense to see ideology in isolation from the political realm to which ideology contributes. Considering ideology as "the glue that binds the law together", Balkin[1] argues that "'a third conception of ideology' (beyond the negative and neutral conceptions) deploying ideology as 'cultural software', which both 'empowers and disempowers' and ultimately 'creates the possibility of a critical engagement with itself.'"

Considering the assumptions about the link between ideology and politics, refusing the implication of politics in its entirety for a theory of law means discarding the importance of ideology and so by declining the political realm implies discarding any part that ideology might play within it. Consequently, there is no major difference between discarding both politics and a distinct concept of ideology, and rejecting politics while denying a distinct concept of ideology, from the fact of engaging in a theory of law. Furthermore, if politics in its entirety is ruled out for legal theory, then given ideology a distinctive recognition within politics becomes a disagreement of no interest to law.

Moreover, the distinctive role of ideology within the political realm is based upon continuing debate over the political and so the prerequisite to offer justification for a specific arrangement of political interests only arises when a competing arrangement is in examination. It is acknowledged that the role for ideology within politics rests on a continuing debate between political positions. It could be argued that politics without ideology means a termination of hostilities between conflicting political

[1] J.M. Balkin, "Ideology as Constraint," Stanford Law Review, 43 (1991), pp. 1133–1169, at p.1151. J.M. Balkin, "Ideology as Cultural Software," Cardozo Law Review, 16 (1995), pp. 1221–33, at pp. 1232–3.

opinions. Additionally, there is a meeting of law with politics being capable of bringing political controversy to an end which means that since politics itself matters to law still means an active engagement with politics. In other words, the political controversies are avoided by bringing politics into correlation with law which means that many political controversies can be resolved via the utilization of the rule of law by engaging legislation process.

It is worth noting that the principle of drafting is to convert policy into legislation, drafting is a technical skill that is reducible to a body of rules which clearly indicates that politics via governmental party policies are shaping the content of any law which means that politics influence the shaping of any law not mentioning the impact of politics upon the laws.[2] It is characteristic that Zamboni[3] and Mousmouti[4] seeing effectiveness as a vital principle of quality in legislation, by which they mean the capacity of the legislation generating the social results desired by the political actors. It is argued that "efficaciousness" is aimed more at those generating the policy rather than the drafters themselves which means that those forming the policy come up with the solution to the problem. In other words, the drafter works with whatever solution they have chosen upon and puts that solution into legislative mode.

It could be said that legislative drafters have an exceptional chance to make certain that the protections given by the rule of law endure and are acknowledged and advanced in any legal system by standing up for the values of the rule of law and by guaranteeing that legislation is always accessible, predictable and intelligible. In line, Ronan Cormacain[5] argues that "Drafters are already guardians of the statute book who are already under an obligation to protect the rule of law."

Since legislation is the most important source of law it must reflect the values of the rule of law. On the one hand, it seems that politicians are not the best guardians for compliance of legislation with the rule of law. On the other hand, legislative drafters would be more natural protectors of the rule of law which means that they have to be concerned with converting policy into legislation, but as legislative counsels, they also have the obligation to protect the rule of law and so defending the integrity of legislation. According to Hutchinson, the role of the drafters is a lot more modest and so politicians are subject to the rule of law which means that it is a "political precept of good democratic governance."

Is legislation comprehended as the most vital source of law or it is considered as just a provisional political opinion? Legislation has to be the central source of law that conveys the needs of the whole society. The rule of law is unwritten and

[2] Jean-Pierre Duprat and Helen Xanthaki, "Legislative Drafting Techniques / Formal Legistics," Legislation in Europe: A comprehensive guide for scholars and practitioners (Hart 2017).

[3] Mauro Zamboni, "Legislative Policy and Effectiveness" (Conference: Effective Law and Regulation, Institute of Advanced Legal Studies, 7 July 2017).

[4] Maria Mousmouti, "Making Legislative Effectiveness an Operational Concept" (Conference: Effective Law and Regulation, Institute of Advanced Legal Studies, July 07, 2017).

[5] Ronan Cormacain Legislative Drafting and the Rule of Law Institute of Advanced Legal Studies, School of Advanced Study, University of London PhD Thesis 2017.

indefinable, which makes courts reluctant to adhere to the rule of law whenever legislation seems to run against rule of law requirements. To that extent, it seems that by being unwritten, disputed, and vague makes the rule of law vulnerable, which is often true for "valuable phenomena."

Furthermore, the utilization of law, politics, and ideology should lead to a coherent vision of society which is changeable according to the demands and needs of people negotiating equal treatment and justice in a changeable environment due to technical progress via AI, natural modifications, etc., as Heraclitus has stated (τα πάντα ρει), in globalization. Besides, Dworkin[6] argues that "to posit a state of affairs whereby the values of a particular society are to be expounded in a manner in which controversy finds no place: 'we want to treat ourselves as an association of principle, as a community governed by a single and coherent vision.'"

In line, Raz[7] says that the most vital characteristic of law, its ability to offer authoritative determination of social relations without recourse to additional moral argument. Thus, Raz does not tolerate within his theory any consideration of the normative value of a purported law. It is argued that what amounts to a law has to be identified by a descriptive test of its legal sources, offering a social not a normative source for the law.[8] On the other hand, it could be said that law has incorporated the moral principles of the regulate matters but if law is unable to justifiable tackle a matter then a new law will replace it encompassing the new moral principles applicable to the governed matter. What counted as law cannot be opened up to moral or political argument because the moral and political rationales have already been encompassed within the content of the law which means that only interpretation of the law by the courts is applicable.

It has to be taken into consideration that the concept of an internal ideology for law is engaged in considering other instances of promoting values linked with the law itself, rather than being directly connected to a specific political standpoint. To that extent, Lon Fuller's[9] attempts to capture an internal or procedural morality for law, and extensive spreading of the rule of law, present obvious examples. For a more distinctive internal legal ideology for legal positivists than the general ideological assumption Karen Alter[10] argues for "most legal theory, whether it be analytical positivism or natural law theory," based on the theoretician's endorsement of a way of legal thinking infused with a professional ideological stance.

Even though the legal positivists ascertain law through a social rather than a normative test that does not mean that they are giving up on the normativity of law.

---

[6]Ronald Dworkin, Law's Empire (London: Collins, 1986).

[7]Joseph Raz, "Postema on Law's Autonomy and Public Practical Reasons: A Critical Comment," Legal Theory, 4 (1998), pp. 1–20.

[8]Andrew Halpin, Reasoning with Law (Oxford: Hart Publishing, 2001), ch. 5.

[9]Lon Fuller, The Morality of Law (New Haven, CT; Yale University Press, 1964). Brian Tamanaha, On the Rule of Law: History, Politics, Theory (Cambridge: Cambridge University Press, 2004).

[10]Karen Alter, Establishing the Supremacy of European Law: The Making of an International Rule of Law in Europe (Oxford: Oxford University Press, 2001).

Hence, Raz apprehends this without falling back into moral or political values by putting forward "a legal point of view" which accounts for the unique normativity of law[11] which means that Raz's workout is to keep legal norms from being dependent on a commitment to moral or political values. Thus, legal positivists have a direct commitment to the law, rather than disengagement from other commitments.

It could be said that law became the setting for ideological fight rather than ideology critique which means that the slogans of "law is politics" and "law is ideology" linked with the deviating standpoint endangered both the dominant political ideologies which had become entrusted with the protection of the law, and any internal ideology which supports the perceived values of the law itself.[12] Thus far if law is nothing but politics or ideology, it is not merely the established use of law and nonetheless the reality of law as a well-defined venture is under criticism.

It seems that there are stages of governance and governance systems. On the one hand, the stages of a governance process embrace rulemaking, interpretation, decision-making, implementation, and rule change. On the other hand, governance systems are social mechanisms for constructing rules and for applying them to specific situations and characteristically with the ambition of facilitating or guiding collective action. To that extent, interactions between law and politics may vary in essential ways both (1) across different stages of governance within specific governance systems and (2) across different governance systems. Moreover, it is worth noting that law offers a system of governance furthers the good of all and the observation of particular individual interests which are ignored through the endorsement of that conception of the good. It has to be considered that not only rulemaking and interpretation but enforcement is the major feature of law. In line, given that the promotion of any understanding of the good which advances legitimacy to the law, there is a need to encompass some neglect of individual interests. It has to be taken into consideration that there is an inconsistency in terms of ideology at the foundation of law due to the fact that the ideology of law concurrently declares "collective general values" and repudiates it in favoring "segmented interests" at the expense of other individual welfares.

---

[11] Joseph Raz, Practical Reason and Norms (London: Hutchinson, 1975), pp. 142–4.

[12] Mark Kelman, A Guide to Critical Legal Studies (Cambridge, MA: Harvard University Press, 1987), particularly ch. 9 on 'ways in which legal thinking is prone to be an effective justificatory ideology.' David Trubek, 'Where the Action Is: Critical Legal Studies and Empiricism', Stanford Law Review, 36 (1984), 575–622

6.2 Do Law and Politics Concur?

Is law really just politics by another name? To that extent, Justin Driver[13] refers that "the consensus school" accepts that law is merely politics by "another name." In other words, it seems to be endorsed the view that law and politics are identical conceptions which is not totally true because there are occasions where the law is resisting the alterations demanded by politics because they are considered to be totally unlawful and against the will and needs of the whole society and not merely fulfilling the goals of a contemporary political entity. David M. Rasmussen[14] argues that "philosophers from Plato on have erred by making law conform totally to the standards of morality, while sociologists like Weber make an effective case for a theory of social integration through law which accounted for the emergence of secular authority but at the price of subsuming the emergence of law to the category of power. The problem cannot be one which finds law to be the servant of either power or justice. Obviously, it must be conceived in the context of both" and so it could be said that law and politics are an amalgam presented with two names in order to satisfy the political demands accordingly.

Is the accumulation of power the essence of politics and consequently the law? It could be said that the accumulation of power is the heart of the political power which is transformed into the law which means that its content and context are formulated accordingly in order to fulfil the interests of the political power and to preserve its continuity. Are all the supposed qualities of the law merely a makeup for a better digestion by people? Has some balance power been given to the law in order to keep politics on the road and so averting mishandlings?

For Justice Scalia, the essence of law is impersonal rules that can be impersonally applied.[15] It is characteristic that Justice Scalia argues that "The wall between the rule of law and anarchy is fragile; if it is penetrated, freedom, property and liberty cannot long endure."[16] Moreover, Justice Scalia promoted the rule of law over anarchy, knowing that liberty and justice were only secure when the law was understood as impartial, generally applicable, and impartially enforced. Furthermore, Justice Scalia accepted that defense of the rule of law was topmost among

---

[13]Justin Driver, The Consensus Constitution, 89 Tex. L. Rev. 755, 786 (2011) ("Consensus constitutionalists . . . adopt an exceedingly thin conception of the field of law itself. . . . [T]he consensus school seems to believe that law is simply politics by another name."); Amanda Frost, Mark Tushnet on Why the Constitution Doesn't Matter, 14 Green Bag 2d. 99, 99 (2010) ("Tushnet argues that constitutional law is really politics by another name . . . ."); Michel Rosenfeld, The Rule of Law and the Legitimacy of Constitutional Democracy, 74 S. Cal. L. Rev. 1307, 1342 (2001) ("That law is ultimately politics is a position elaborated by the Critical Legal Studies ('CLS') movement.").

[14]David M. Rasmussen, How is valid law possible? A review of Between Facts and Norms by Jurgen Habermas, in Mathieu Deflem, Habermas, Modernity And Law, Sage Publications 1996 p26.

[15]Antonin Scalia, Originalism: The Lesser Evil, 57 U. CIN. L. REV. 849 (1989).

[16]Morrison v. Olson, 487 U.S. 654, 697–734 (1988)

the obligations of his office, and he declined to "concede ground to the cynics who deny that Rule of Law exists or who assert that it is unattainable." It is characteristic that in Laidlaw,[17] Justice Scalia expresses concern that the majority's decision holds "grave implications for democratic governance" and S Winter[18] specifies that "Citizens are neither agents nor assigns of the government; they are—that is, we are—it's principal." In addition, S Winter[19] refers that "for Justice Scalia, democracy and the rule of law require that private parties not be allowed to invoke the courts' power to see that the law is enforced."

It is argued[20] that "the Supreme Court is now a blunt political instrument, used repeatedly to undermine outcomes of democratic governance—often on behalf of corporate interests." In other words, it could be said that if the Court is no longer a neutral arbiter of the law, if it is progressively shape-shifting into a "partisan weapon," then it is questionable its role in a constitutional system. Moreover, Mark Tushnet[21] argues that the Supreme Court's role is to tell the people and the political branches what the bounds of their power are which means that the general role is to police the boundaries of the political system. To that extent, it could be said that the framers shaped a court in a system with a constitution that that court would have the authority to nullify legislation it considered illegitimate. In line, Sean Illing[22] specifies that the Supreme Court supposed to be a "bulwark" against majority tyranny and minority oppression, but that's not the reality and so overall the Court has repeatedly defended the powerful against the weak which means that the Court has interfered with legislation on behalf of the most powerful elements of the society such as corporate power.[23] Charles Gardner Geyh notifies that "Supreme Court confirmation proceedings have never been apolitical."[24]

It seems that incident of judicial politics has emerged concerning the judges[25] and so reconsidering the role of the Supreme Court in the American government. First of all, judicial independence has been a defining feature of the American Constitutional

[17] Friends of the Earth, Inc. v. Laidlaw Environmental Services, Inc. 528 U.S. 167 (2000).

[18] Steven L. Winter, What If Justice Scalia Took History And The Rule Of Law Seriously? 2001 Duke Environmental Law & Policy Forum Vol. 12:155 P 165.

[19] Steven L. Winter, What If Justice Scalia Took History And The Rule Of Law Seriously? 2001 Duke Environmental Law & Policy Forum Vol. 12:155 P 158.

[20] Sean Illing, The case for abolishing the Supreme Court, Vox.com

[21] Sean Illing, The case for abolishing the Supreme Court, Vox.com

[22] Sean Illing, The case for abolishing the Supreme Court, Vox.com

[23] Citizens United v. Federal Election Commission 558 U.S. 310 (2010).

[24] Charles Gardner Geyh, Judicial Independence at Twilight, 71 Case W. Rsrv. L. Rev. 1045 (2021) https://scholarlycommons.law.case.edu/caselrev/vol71/iss3/5 p1079

[25] Erick Trickey, The History of "Stolen" Supreme Court Seats, Smithsonian Magazine (Sept. 25, 2020), https://www.smithsonianmag.com/history/history-stolen-supreme-court-seats-180962589/Eric J. Segall, Eight Justices Are Enough: A Proposal to Improve the United States Supreme Court, 45 Pepp. L. Rev. 547, 550 (2018). Daniel Epps & Ganesh Sitaraman, How to Save the Supreme Court, 129 Yale L.J. 148, 181–84 (2019). Charles Gardner Geyh, Courting Peril: The Political Transformation of the American Judiciary 16–23 (2016).

landscape for centuries but the structure of judicial independence has never been fully explained or understood which means that political developments and interventions threaten the future of an independent judiciary in an unprecedented manner. The Rule of Law Paradigm acknowledges that judges should be accountable to Congress for treason, bribery, and other high crimes via the impeachment process.

It is worth noting that Tushnet[26] specified that "guarding them is not the preserve of judges, he maintains, but a commitment of the citizenry to define itself as" We the People of the USA. "The Constitution belongs to us collectively, as we act in political dialogue with each other--whether in the street, in the voting booth, or in the legislature as representatives of others." Moreover, it could be argued that political players know that they are in a position to put in place a new set of deep institutional arrangements and so establishing a constitutional order.[27] In addition, Calabresi and Lawson[28] argue that "the Constitution often prescribes rules, but it often does not. The law is what it is, whether or not it conforms to some abstract jurisprudential norm. The rule of law is not a law of rules. It is a law of law . . . The Constitution sometimes prescribes rules and it sometimes prescribes standards." Besides, Sunstein[29] contends that "the authority of the national government is a product of democratic processes, not of the federal judiciary; the Court's role has been largely to ratify what citizens and their representatives have done."

It is argued that the Supreme Court is not merely an agent of the governing coalition, then Dahl[30] wrote that "it is an essential part of the political leadership and possesses some bases of power of its own, the most important of which is the unique legitimacy attributed to its interpretations of the Constitution" and so the Court may play a real policymaking role when its views do not collide with the norms of elected officials which means that politics in a way dictate law.[31] Moreover, it seems that constitutional questions are viewed not as legal questions but as political ones.[32] In fact, Justice Black first characterized courts as "havens of refuge" in his opinion for

[26] Mark Tushnet, Taking the Constitution Away from the Courts, 2000 Princeton University Press.

[27] Tushnet, Mark V., "Constitutional Hardball" (2004). Georgetown Law Faculty Publications and Other Works. 555. https://scholarship.law.georgetown.edu/facpub/555

[28] Steven G. Calabresi, Gary Lawson, The Rule Of Law As A Law Of Law, 90 Notre Dame L. Rev. 483 (2014) P 483,487.

[29] Cass R. Sunstein, A Constitution Of Many Minds: Why The Founding Document Doesn't Mean What It Meant Before (2009).

[30] Robert A. Dahl, Decision-Making in a Democracy: The Supreme Court as a National Policy-Maker, 6 J. Pub. L. 279 (1957).

[31] Jack M. Balkin & Sanford Levinson, Understanding the Constitutional Revolution, 87 VA. L. Rev. 1045, 1068 (2001) ("Constitutional revolutions are the cumulative result of successful partisan entrenchment when the entrenching party has a relatively coherent political ideology or can pick up sufficient ideological allies from the appointees of other parties.").

[32] Daniel A. Farber & Suzanna Sherry, Judgment Calls: Principle And Politics In Constitutional Law 125 (2009) (observing that the "belief that constitutional law is not really law at all, but politics, is also becoming more explicit in the work of some constitutional scholars"); Suzanna Sherry, Politics and Judgment, 70 Mo. L. REV. 973, 977 (2005), Michael J. Klarman, From Jim Crow To Civil Rights: The Supreme Court And The Struggle For Racial Equality (2004) at

the Court in Chambers v. Florida[33] and Klarman suggests that the court protects minority rights only when a majority or near majority of the community deem those rights worthy of protection.[34]

Kathleen Sullivan[35] distinguished between a "[j]ustice of rules" and a "[j]ustice of standard" which means that "the rule's force as a rule is that decision makers follow it, even when direct application of the background principle or policy [that the rule captures] to the facts would produce a different result." It is worth mentioning here that many of the world's leading constitutional courts do not view standards-based adjudication, or the judicial balancing that often accompanies it, as inconsistent with the rule of law.[36] It is worth noting that Randy Barnett[37] has utterly blamed Justice Scalia of "ignoring the original meaning of those portions of the Constitution that conflict with his conception of 'the rule of law as a law of rules.'"

Proportionality analysis is a feature of all of the world's constitutional courts which means that the government has to justify its actions by reference to a limited set of objectives and procedural options aiming for rule of law in the strictest sense by diminishing the discretion of the entire government, and not just of judges.[38] Moreover, David Beatty[39] has named proportionality "the ultimate rule of law" for the reason that it is a vital part of every constitution that "subordinates the system of

449 "Constitutional law generally has sufficient flexibility to accommodate dominant public opinion, which the justices have little inclination, and limited power, to resist".

[33] 309 U.S. 227, 241 (1940). Jeffrey Rosen, The Most Democratic Branch: How The Courts Serve America (2006).

[34] Michael J. Klarman, Rethinking the Civil Rights and Civil Liberties Revolutions, 82 Va. L. Rev. 1, 67 (1996).at 17–18.

[35] Kathleen M. Sullivan, The Supreme Court 1991 Term—Foreword: The Justices of Rules and Standards, 106 Harv. L. Rev. 22, 121 (1992) at 58 A justice of standards prefers "to collapse decision making back into the direct application of the background principle or policy to a fact situation.", Craig v. Boren 429 U.S. 190 (1976), James E. Fleming, "There Is Only One Equal Protection Clause": An Appreciation of Justice Stevens's Equal Protection Jurisprudence, 74 Fordham L. Rev. 2301, 2301 ("With [his] words [in Craig], he served notice that . . . he was to be . . . a 'justice of standards' as distinguished from a 'justice of rules.'".

[36] Vicki C. Jackson, Constitutional Engagement In A Transnational Era 60 (2010).

[37] Randy E. Barnett, Scalia's Infidelity: A Critique of "Faint-Hearted" Originalism, 75 U. Cin. L. Rev. 7, 12 (2006).

[38] Alec Stone Sweet & Jud Mathews, Proportionality Balancing and Global Constitutionalism, 47 Colum. J. Transnat'l L. 72, 75 (2008). Dieter Grimm, Proportionality in Canadian and German Constitutional Jurisprudence, 57 U. Toronto L.J. 383, 384 (2007) ("[I]n Canada, most laws that fail to meet the [proportionality] test do so in the second step, . . . whereas in Germany, the third step has become the most decisive part of the proportionality test.").

[39] David M. Beatty, The Ultimate Rule of Law 160 (2004) ("In all areas of government regulation, no matter the nature of the right or freedom that is alleged to have been violated, and regardless of the personal characteristics of those bringing the case, . . . the test is always the same."); Richard A. Posner, Constitutional Law from a Pragmatic Perspective, 55 U. Toronto L.J. 299, 301 (2005) (contesting Beatty's claim of the universality of proportionality).

government it creates to the rule of law." Greene[40] argues that "proportionality, then, is a strategy for incorporating the rule of law into a system of workable government: it is, in a sense, a law of standards."

6.3 Politics and the Rule of Law

As mentioned earlier, the French Revolution[41] was the last great political event to take its inspiration, iconography, and institutions mainly from classical antiquity. French revolutionaries based on Roman and Greek histories for ideas but Classical antiquity stipulates numerous conflicting moral and political examples. Laissez-faire capitalism was the prevailing orthodoxy in both law and economics from the time of the 1929 stock market crash until the banking crisis of 1933. Financial markets were unregulated and unsupervised, and it was not seen as the accountability of government to inspire economic activity, even in a recession.[42] Besides, the present regulatory approach does not aid the interests of the public, but rather the far restricted interests of the regulated institutions that have taken the agencies of government and the policy-making process.[43]

Firstly, it has to be taken into consideration that all systems need rules that govern their running dynamics. While some doctrines[44] denote critical aspects of the structure itself, its setting and architecture, others offer the "fuel" to keep it functioning. Thus, some signify the engineering principles and design features but some doctrines present the aims of the overall system or subsystem to which they are related which means that some restore breakdowns while others offer the capacity to adjust to altering needs and aims. Furthermore, the picks mirrored in many of the doctrinal categories embody implicit cultural, moral, political and philosophical traditions and assumptions and so they are premised on assumptions concerning scientific validity for the reason that the law encompasses procedures whereby science is incorporated in specific doctrines when it is appropriate.

It is worth mentioning that various forms of truth function to greater or lesser extent concerning certain sets of doctrines and some of the doctrines are flexible in their aptitude to alter without influence on the system. In addition, when essential or opening principles are implicated there is a prospective risk to the integrity of the system itself. If virtually all human truths are assembled and selected within a closed

---

[40] Jamal Greene, The Rule of Law as a Law of Standards, The Georgetown Law Journal Vol. 99: 1289 p 1298.

[41] M.N.S. Sellers, Classical Influences in the French Revolution, at: http://ssrn.com/abstract=1437165

[42] John Maynard Keynes, The General Theory Of Employment, Interest, And Money (1936).

[43] Timothy A. Canova, Financial Market Failure as a Crisis in the Rule of Law: From Market Fundamentalism to a New Keynesian Regulatory Model Network Electronic Paper Collection: http://ssrn.com/abstract=1489492

[44] Doctrines of Authority, Doctrines of Structure, Doctrines of Values, etc.

system then declining to accept the strength of those central choices jeopardizes the system which means that if the principles of scientific truth are applied to any nonscientific principle or doctrine the "truth" is that it can't be substantiated "true" along with that strict standard of empirical rationality.

It is argued that once people apprehended that they were in charge of making their laws the aptitude to believe in their authority and moral force began to fade away. It has to be considered that cultural tradition and moral and religious beliefs are subordinated or contested as a form of narrow-mindedness or bias defined as a preference for tradition. Taken together, choices about fundamental issues of life compel aftereffects on the overall political community, forming and defining its character, quality, and values. Moreover, in modest political systems custom and shared values play noteworthy roles in circumventing and resolving disputes. As a political system turns out to be larger and more diverse strong shared values are adulterated or are forced to compete against equally strong beliefs and valued customary knowledge of the type needed for a whole community to act in a consistent way vanishes generating a vacuum of values with noteworthy outcomes for the political system and so it more and more leads to a dependence on law. In line, Lawrence Friedman[45] captured the role of law in a complex democracy by stating: "In complex societies custom is too flabby to do all the work—to run the machinery of order. Law carries a powerful stick: the threat of force. This is the first inside its velvet glove . . ." There is a range of diverse assumptions about the source, nature, and function of truth which means that even with its diversity and vagueness, or as a consequence of these variables, truth is a word of great authority used to validate political and moral perceptions and so great emblematic force originates from our appeals of truth. Furthermore, truth is a power-driven construct, and so those in power use their influence to generate a system weighted in manners favorable to their interests.[46] A democratic system of vast diversity, conflicting basic values, and diffuse clusters of authority, can operate effectively only via the voices of advocates and wise judges and so Locke[47] argues that law is what helps to hold the system together against individual attempts to take advantage of others.

It could be said that doctrines and the statutory adaptations by which law is applied involve a multifaceted system of "overt and covert" policy-making and implementation of social selections through law. Moreover, the pattern of judicial doctrine, legal institutions, and legislative selections characterizes the creative, facilitative, and mediating bonds between societal needs, institutional competences, and political requests. It has to be taken into consideration that these variables allocate social goods, facilitate critical decision-making, and sustain the foundational rules of society and so their combination engenders the roots of a political system,

---

[45] Lawrence M. Friedman, American Law 257 (1984).

[46] David Barnhizer, "Princes of Darkness and Angels of Light: The Soul of the American Lawyer," Notre Dame J. of Law, Ethics & Public Policy (2000).

[47] John Locke, Of Civil Government Second Treatise 67, 68, Introduction by Russell Kirk, (Henry Regnery 1955).

and are critical forces needed for a society's stability which means that their challenge leads to the discourse of any advantageous political community based on democratic principles.

Thus, it has to be taken into consideration that the outlining of the concepts of law and the rule of law has troubled legal theory. Hence, the presence of law rests on realities concerning the system of governance in place. Austin[48] emphasizes that law occurs where a sovereign issue and enforces commands. Moreover, Hart[49] says that law exists where, as a subject of social reality, there exists a set of secondary rules that officials regard as obligatory to ascertain what is a sound principle rule of behavior.

Is there a distinction between the existence of law which is a matter of fact and the ultimate/epitome of the rule of law? The rule of law is characterized by the embodiment of a series of normatively attractive legal attributes. Law does not automatically implicate centralized coercion. According to Raz[50] law exists when there is an institutionalized normative system that asserts to be both comprehensive and supreme with regard to other systems of norms and which comprises of norm-applying institutions such as courts that are obligated to obey secondary rules in adjudicating specific cases and the ideal of the rule of law exists in a legal system when persons are obligated to use, and are competent of using, legal rules to direct their behavior which means that in order to accomplish the rule of law a legal system has to be typified by the normatively attractive features associated with rule of law such as publicity, stability, neutrality, and generality. It could be argued that law is characterized by qualities such as publicity, stability, neutrality, and generality in order for people to look to it as a guide to behavior accomplishing their obligation to obey it.

On the other hand, a type of identified law can exist enforced by an authority in a society and so that legal system is typified by the rule of law since the identified law is applied by the enforcing authority of the society. Moreover, law exists as a substance of social fact even if the law is secretive and volatile that no-one can in practice use the law as a guide to behavior which means that people can follow and being bound by a secretive and volatile law which can be utilized as the rule of law of this society. On the other hand, the real essence of law is based on that fact of being publicly expressed and known with a stable content which will be enforced by the enforcing entity accepted in a society and so there are secondary rules that officials use to assess the validity of primary rules when they are applying rules. Thus, law has to have practical characteristics necessary for people to use the law to guide their behavior and so this law will be utilized as the rule of law in any identifiable society.

[48] Austin J. 1885. Lectures on Jurisprudence or The Philosophy of Positive Law Vol. I. London: John Murray.

[49] Hart H.L.A. 1961. The Concept of Law. (Third edition, paperback 2012) Oxford, UK: Oxford University Press.

[50] Raz J. 2009. The Authority of Law: Essays on Law and Morality (second ed.) Oxford, UK: Oxford University Press.

The existence of flexible law applied in disputes is the rule of law of the society at a specific time. Of course, principles of legality such as generality, clarity, and so on are needed for a system to appropriately function in a modern society and be called legal contributing to the applicability of the rule of law. Legality is illustrated by the acceptance of the society that can collapse fully if people begin to worry that no-one else is willing to help enforce which means that the specific cannon/norm does not play the role of law and is so applicable as the rule of law.

Is there a link between rule of law and political settlements? There is a link between rule of law and political settlements which means that the rule of law has to be seen as both a political product and a constitutive element of institutional and organizational limits on the exercise of authority and so it includes those qualities of the political system and reigning normative agenda by means of which the exercise of power and rules of engagement on political, social, and economic activities are approved and accomplished. Hence, the whole development is the matter of political contestation, and institutional modification, combined by the procedures of normative stabilization that distinguish the development and cycles of stabilization of "political settlements."[51] Furthermore, in view of the deeply political character of rule of law as both a course and an end in itself, it is appropriate and well-timed that international support attempts stand up to recent thinking on manners of engagement that take politics and context seriously which means that the policy debate has to cover modes of working that encompasses the political economy environment.[52] In other words, there is a need for more systematic consideration of the role of international players in reform endeavors which means that international efforts to support the rule of law and justice sector reform agendas are required, where there has been a move to concentration more not only on the political economy of context but also on the precise legal advancement or justice setbacks in question.[53]

It has to be considered that the rule of law can itself become a device of contestation and transformation of state–society affairs and wider power structures more generally. Moreover, the rule of law can be used to uphold the status quo and safeguard the welfares of ruling elites or to alter them. It is essential to understand the significance of appreciating the political economy of rule of law first and foremost. In examining the rule of law there is a need of concentrating on legal systems where the source of law is the state. Of course, concerning the rule of law counts that law is

---

[51] Bell, C. (2015) 'What we talk about when we talk about Political Settlements: Towards Inclusive and Open Political Settlements in an Era of Disillusionment', Working Paper 1. Edinburgh: Edinburgh University Kelsall, T. (2016); 'Thinking and working with political settlements', London: ODI.

[52] Andrews, M., Pritchett, L. and Woolcock, M. (2015) Doing problem driven work. Working Paper 307. Cambridge, MA: Center for International Development. Booth, D., Harris, D. and Wild, L. (2016) 'From political economy analysis to doing development differently: a learning experience'. London: ODI.

[53] Denney, L. (2016) 'Using political economy analysis in conflict, security and justice programmes Guidance note', London: ODI. Desai, D. and Woolcock, M. (2016), 'Experimental Justice Reform: Lessons from the World Bank and Beyond' in Annual Review of Law and Social Science.

at a minimum the outcome of democratic deliberation or legislative courses set against being produced in an authoritarian way. In fact, both contemporary realities and more historical courses via which legitimate modes of norm production are more diverse and echo existing ways of governance at various subnational and national levels which means that legal pluralism necessitates to also embodying the multi-faceted domain of global trajectories and ways of norm production.[54]

It is worth mentioning that Chinese legal progression has been more and more control oriented and all the state premonitions have surrendered to the authority of law in China and so the rule of law in China is exposed to negative connotations and the state institutions are subordinate to the control of Chinese Communist Party's leadership which makes these institutions politically unimportant. Hence, Chinese politics have become significantly more law oriented over the past years. Moreover, several core legal institutions such as the judiciary and the constitution are currently more politically significant. In addition, there is centralized power and control to an unparalleled extent but in a highly legalistic way by energizing courts against other state and Party bodies which mean that bringing political powers that were in earlier times the exclusive possession of the Party under legal authorization and regulation.[55] Martin Kwan[56] argues that "China prefers the predominance of party leadership or politics over legal accountability and the supremacy of law—which is a key pillar of the Western conception of the rule of law."

It is argued that even if China is deepening its dictatorship by exploiting the organizational and legitimizing capacities of law, rather than circumventing it.[57] Regardless that the rule of law and strong legal institutions are very significant for the smooth functioning of a state, legal institutions, and even genuine commitment to legality in governmental operations can galvanize authoritarianism just as well as limit it. Actually, the CCP not only has acknowledged the political significance of law, it has energetically tried to strengthen it, and has gained advantages along the way because law is strengthening both Party and state in China.

---

[54] Tamanaha, B. Z. (2013) 'The Rule of Law and Legal Pluralism in Development,' in Tamanaha et al. (2013) Tamanaha, B.Z., Sage, C. and Woolcock, M. (eds) (2013) Legal Pluralism and Development: Scholars and Practitioners in Dialogue. Cambridge: Cambridge University Press.

[55] Ammar Younas, Legality of Rule of Law with Chinese Characteristics: A Case of "Ultra-Sinoism," 8(4) Russian Law Journal 53–91 (2020).

[56] Martin Kwan, China's Rule Of Law Development: The Increasing Emphasis On Internationalization Of Legal Standards And The Horizontal Rule Of Law, https://ssrn.com/abstract=3847227 p1.

[57] Taisu Zhang & Tom Ginsburg, Legality in Contemporary Chinese Politics, Virginia Journal of International Law (forthcoming, 2019) (Jul. 10, 2020), https://papers.ssrn.com/sol3/papers.cfm?abstract_id=3250948.

6.4 Do Politics Shape the Rule of Law?

Economic and political developments necessitate stable legal systems that consistently employ basic rules of property and contract, regulate markets to overcome externalities and market failures, and protect basic human rights, autonomy, and dignity and so lack of legal order is one of the key encounters of our time. In line, Hadfield and Weingast[58] specify "the need to fashion a regime that is dependent to some significant extent on private ordering and then to coordinate and incentivize the participation of ordinary individuals in enforcement efforts." Concerning the rule of law, Acemoglu and Robinson[59] argue that such a legal framework is an imperative part of what they call "an inclusive political and economic order" and so the absence of such an order is the ultimate basis of the failure of nations.

It is worth noting that unlike the vertical rule of law, which addresses the public or administrative aspect of governance, the horizontal rule of law involves the private law aspect, such as commercial laws and so addressing the relationships among private entities. Moreover, the vertical and horizontal aspects of the rule of law accomplish the functions of maintaining order which means that effective rule of law depends on both the vertical and horizontal components of governance. Furthermore, the quality or content of law is central to the rule of law.

The rule of law has refocused to the center a debate regarding how best to cause the transformations required for political and economic development to take place which means that rule of law has to be applied in order to have a stable and suitable environment for achieving development which is part of any political demands. Carothers[60] argues that "The degree of apparent international consensus on the value and importance of the rule of law is striking . . . almost no leader anywhere is openly against the rule of law or will publicly mount an argument that the rule of law is a bad idea for their society."

Which are the political processes by which rule of law like features shape up in various societies? It has to be considered that the inter-disciplinarity within the social and legal sciences is inadequate in the knowledge base to comprehend the role of law

---

[58] Gillian K. Hadfield, Barry R. Weingast, Privatizing Law: Is Rule of Law an Equilibrium Without Private Ordering? Legal Studies Research Papers Series No. 17-24e at: https://ssrn.com/abstract=3057093 p36.

[59] Acemoglu, Daron, and James Robinson. 2012. Why Nations Fail: The Origins of Power, Prosperity, and Poverty. New York: Crown Publishers.

[60] Carothers, Thomas. 2010. "Rule of Law Temptations," in Global Perspectives on the Rule of Law, editors, James J. Heckman, Robert L. Nelson, and Lee Cabatingan. Routledge.

and rule of law both in molding political, economic,[61] and social conduct and, in succession, as a sequel of political contestation and negotiation.[62]

It is argued that the formal process of legal alteration is not in itself the influential factor for modification which means that it is required to look more closely at what stimulates the "game altering" characteristics of legal alteration that adjust conduct in the exercise of authority and so shift in the underlying political balance. Thus, it seems that the law and the technical expertise needed for norm production is a politically useful competence which means that the technical, in legal restructuring, is first and foremost political. To that extent, as the intricacies of political and institutional modification have become more and more apparent for the international rule of law enterprise, a stimulating quality of contemporary transition or post-conflict settings is that of "hybrid political orders and legal pluralism."

Furthermore, law delivers order and stability, but in unexpected periods of political turmoil, law preserves order, even as it facilitates transformation which means that in vibrant periods of political instability, legal responses produce a sui generis pattern of transformative law. To that extent, in democracies in ordinary times, the rule of law entails obedience to known rules, versus arbitrary government action. Nonetheless, revolution denotes disorder and legal instability and so the predicament of transitional justice is the problem of the rule of law in periods of revolutionary political transformation. If typically, the rule of law means obedience to established law, to what extent are periods of transformation compatible with loyalty to the rule of law? In such periods, what does the rule of law mean? In line, in times of massive changes in understanding of justice, communities are striving with how to alter their political, legal, and economic systems which means that the exploitation of the rule of law makes the transformation from one era to another very easily without many casualties in all fields due to the fact that law via its modification and advancement is the means for the peaceful and rightful passing to the next societal setting. In addition, it could be said that the rule-of-law dilemma surfaces in politically controversial fields, where the worth of legal alteration is in tension with the worth of obedience to the principle of settled legal precedent. On the one hand, in ordinary epochs, the problem of obedience to legal continuity is generated by the passage of time. On the other hand, in transformative epochs the worth of legal continuity is rigorously tested. To that extent, the normative boundaries on lawful political and legal alteration for regimes in the center of transformation is repeatedly framed in terms of a series of antinomies which means that the law

[61] Booth, D., Harris, D. and Wild, L. (2016) 'From political economy analysis to doing development differently: a learning experience'. London: ODI. Brinks, D. and Botero, S. (2014) 'Inequality and the Rule of Law: Ineffective Rights in Latin American Democracies' in D. Brinks, S. Mainwaring and M. Leiras, (eds.) Reflections on Uneven Democracies: The Legacy of Guillermo O'Donnell, Baltimore: Johns Hopkins University Press.

[62] Perry-Kessaris, A., The Case for a Visualized Economic Sociology of Legal Development, September 2014 Current legal problems 67(1):169–198, Perry-Kessaris, A. (ed.) (2011) Law in the pursuit of development: Principles into practice? London: Routledge.

as written is related to the law as right, positive law to natural law, and procedural to substantive justice.

The capacity to add to political outcome is the principal feature of political truth, not intellectual, rational, or evidential validity. Moreover, the principles on which political decisions are formulated, and the natures of information circulated for reasons of internal and external decisions will fall short of what would be acceptable if the identical issues were being judged from a thorough analytic viewpoint targeted at coming as close to accuracy as achievable.

First of all, it has to be considered that the view of certainty prevails in the minds and hearts of believers then again there is no agreed on or shared mode to test the truth of the propositions to the satisfaction of people who are not part of the believing group. Thus, it has to be taken into consideration that most intense political disputes derive from exposed truths generating a continuous tension between the individual and the society but the nature of an individual's responsibility to the society and the community's responsibility to the individual are encompassed in this tension. In line Dionne[63] argues that: "Attacks on 'the imperial judiciary' were once the stuff of conservative arguments against a 'liberal activist' Supreme Court. That is about to change. In a shift that is momentous in historical and political terms, liberals are beginning to sound alarms about conservative justices using states' rights and other doctrines to void environmental, economic and social legislation."

On January 22, 1973, the Supreme Court handed down its historic decision in *Roe V. Wade*,[64] overturning a Texas interpretation of abortion law and making abortion legal in the USA. It was a turning point in women's reproductive rights and has remained a hot button issue within USA politics ever since. Moreover, Roe received substantial criticism in the legal community, with the decision being widely seen as an extreme form of judicial activism. It could be argued that the Roe majority's allowing women to make the abortion choice is an imperative component of the individual woman's human flourishing, and so without the power to make this selection the woman's capacity to "flourish" is constrained. To that extent, this is a selection about the appropriate functions of a society, and the primacy of individuals being free to make the selections that they think, rightly or wrongly, protect or advance the selections about the course they have to accomplish their highest state of being. Moreover, the primary of the argument in favor of a woman's almost complete power to terminate a pregnancy is based on the idea of human flourishing,

---

[63] E.J. Dionne, Jr., "Liberals fear new judicial activism", The Plain Dealer, Friday, July 14, 2000 at 9-B.

[64] Greenhouse, Linda, and Reva B. Siegel. "Before (and after) Roe V. Wade: New Questions About Backlash." *The Yale Law Journal* 120.8 (2011): 2028–87. Skelton, Chris. "Roe V. Wade, 410 U.S. 113 (1973)." Justia. Tribe, Laurence (1973). "The Supreme Court, 1972 Term – Foreword: Toward a Model of Roles in the Due Process of Life and Law". Harvard Law Review. 87 (1): 1 [p. 7]. doi:https://doi.org/10.2307/1339866. Quoted in Morgan, Richard Gregory (1979). "Roe v. Wade and the Lesson of the Pre-Roe Case Law". Michigan Law Review. 77 (7): 1724 1748. doi: https://doi.org/10.2307/1288040. Orrin G. Hatch, There's Nothing "Super" About Roe v. Wade, 29 STAN. L. & POL'Y REV. ONLINE 1, 23–24 (2018) (arguing that Roe is not "super precedent").

or the decisive effort to "be all you can be." Furthermore, John Hart Ely[65] criticized Roe as a decision that "is not constitutional law and gives almost no sense of an obligation to try to be" and so it is argued that this super-protected right is not inferable from the language of the Constitution and the framers' thinking regarding the particular problem in issue which means that the availability of abortion is a matter of policy and unduly restrictive state regulation of abortion is unconstitutional.[66] Moreover, the Supreme Court of Canada used the rulings in both Roe and Doe v. Bolton as grounds to find Canada's federal law restricting access to abortions unconstitutional. Undoubtedly *Roe v. Wade* was a decision by the US Supreme Court that was noticeably more political than legal. It is worth noting that truth is the object of political and religious schedules and the need to get outcomes. Moreover, truth is a choice and always a human construct and this does not mean that the choices are without substance or merit. Is there a lesson from *Roe v. Wade*? The Constitution is on the side of the big battalions or, at least, the most strident battalions and so an up-to-date judiciary is contemptible for the reason that it is nothing but a political body pretending not to be.[67]

Thus, if written constitutions and independent supreme courts with the authority to interpret those documents were the exclusive requirements for establishing the rule of law, it would be impossible to comprehend why developing countries failed to restrict political power by way of constitutional review. Moreover, constitutional judicial review plays a role in strengthening democracy not for the reason that judges are independent, nonetheless, because they are not entirely independent which means that this balance enables the long-term development of the judiciary as both a countervailing and a liable institution.

As mentioned earlier, due process of law and constitutional judicial review are required in democratized countries to support political and economic development. On the other hand, the problems that these countries face in developing the rule of law reveal that the rule of law faces in two directions, one legal, and the other political which means that the two crucial elements of the rule of law rest on political developments. Moreover, due process of law means that judges express reasons for their decisions so that other players utilize those decisions as resources to enhance their welfares. Therefore, a society that lacks due process of law is one where the law has no social relevancy for the reason that the relationships between law and society are disregarded. Besides, constitutional judicial review denotes that the judiciary is to some extent but not too independent so that it can be a countervailing and liable force in politics which means that the rule of law does not rest on negating politics

---

[65] Ely, John Hart. "The Wages of Crying Wolf Archived 2007-06-25 at the Wayback Machine", 82 Yale Law Journal 920 (1973).

[66] Liptak, Adam. "John Hart Ely, a Constitutional Scholar, Is Dead at 64", New York Times (2003-10-27).

[67] Walter Berns, "Judicial Rhetoric," Rhetoric and American Statesmanship 55 (A. Thurow & J. Wallin ed. 1984).

but on creating the appropriate relationships between courts and other political players.

It is worth noting that there is a gradually imperative but dangerous role of the Supreme Court in articulating political philosophy and even policy of a kind that is beyond the power of ordinary courts. In line, in a democracy, it is not the function of law[68] to authenticate any more social policy than what is articulated by legislation, enacted via agreed democratic procedures.

In the debates over the suitable limits on interpretation of law by judges regarding such matters as initial intent, accurate construction, and adaptation of constitutional provisions to the altering conditions of cultures far removed from those experienced by the Founding Fathers and so there is a need for the requirement of controlling the rapidity and unambiguity of alteration.[69] Moreover, Ely[70] specifies that "There are signs that interpretivism may be entering a period of comparative popularity. Several reasons seem apparent. The first is that the controversial abortion decision of 1973, *Roe v. Wade*, was the clearest example of non-interpretivist 'reasoning' on the part of the Court in four decades: it forced all of us who work in the area to think about which camp we fall into, with the result that a number of persons would today label themselves interpretivists who had not previously given the choice much thought."

On the one hand, legal forms sometimes directly affect organizational behavior and performance. On the other hand, law firms organizational practices less directly, by contributing to an underlying cultural logic of "legal-rationality." To that extent, law has played a decisive role in constructing the modern corporation; in molding the boundaries between private companies, public agencies, collective enterprises, and nonprofit organizations; and in enabling some forms of economic coordination, while disabling others under antitrust law.[71] Eventually, it is a matter of political choice which organizations deserve status, protection, and rights under law which means that the law implements the demands of politics.

---

[68] Antonin Scalia, The Rule of Law as a Law of Rules, 56 U. CHI. L. REV. 1175, 1186–87 (1989).

[69] Jonathan T. Molot, "The Rise and Fall of Textualism," 106 Columbia L. Rev. 1 (2006); John F. Manning, "What Divides Textualists from Purposivists?" 106 Columbia L. Rev. 70 (2006); Barry Friedman, "The Politics of Judicial Review," 84 Texas L. Rev. 257 (2005).

[70] John Hart Ely, Democracy and Distrust: A Theory of Judicial Review, (Harvard 1980). Steven Breyer, Active Liberty: Interpreting Our Democratic Constitution (Alfred A. Knopf 2005); Aharon Barak, Purposive Interpretation in Law, Translated from the Hebrew by Sari Bashi, (Princeton 2005).

[71] Robert W. Gordon, New Developments in Legal Theory, in The Politics of Law: A Progressive Critique 413, 418 (David Kairys ed., 2d ed. 1990) (explaining that people tend to perceive legal prescriptions as "natural and necessary" or, at least, as "basically uncontroversial, neutral, acceptable"). Katharina Pistor, The Code Of Capital: How The Law Creates Wealth And Inequality 21–22 (2019); Tim Wu, The Curse Of Bigness: Antitrust In The New Gilded Age 1–3 (2018).

6.5 Does the Rule of Law Clarify Applicable Politics?

It has to be taken into consideration that even though there is far more vagueness regarding truth than we want, its elasticity is principal in law and politics, given that we don't misperceive elasticity with purposelessness. In the setting of legal truth, it is easier for legal representatives to cope with the ideas of ambiguous truths[72] still being qualified of possessing imperative social and moral functions even though they can never be ascertained in absolute terms being the kernel of legal analysis and the legal process in terms of the idea of the "original and natural idea of knowledge."[73]

Furthermore, it is argued that law is politics by another name and it is easy to understand that truth is not the only virtue in a political/legal system and so it is not even the principal feature.[74] Moreover, there are times when evidential or rational truth is the adversary of the social order and there is a decisive race among theory and feminist jurisprudence arguing that law is simply a mask for male power relations. Likewise, it is said that law is undifferentiated from politics and the claimed objectivity and neutrality of legal reasoning is a "deception."[75] Additionally, in the pursuit for truth there are many "roads not covered" by people who do not desire to spoil the gains of their friends and allies but as Ellis Cose[76] states, others with competing welfares will take your words and reinterpret them to their political advantage.

Is there interplay between legal truth and political one? It is valuable to think through the interplay between legal truth and political and received and revealed truths. Considering these forms of truth brings forwards the assessment of Constitution being a source of idolized truth. In addition, these forms of truth bring in matters regarding the wisdom entangled in the pace, speed, and interplay of factions competing for power and the importance of their agendas.

---

[72] David Barnhizer, "Prophets, Priests and Power Blockers: Three Fundamental Roles of Judges and Legal Scholars in America," 50 Pitts. L. Rev. 127 (1988).

[73] John F. Rundell, Origins of Modernity: The Origins of Modern Social Theory from Kant to Hegel to Marx (Polity Press,1987, Oxford). Rundell argues that: "... Hegel's critique exposes the historico-hermeneutical dimension that is irreducibly part of the formation of knowledge and is always prior to its various theoretical formulations. Epistemology unknowingly has a normative concept of the type of knowledge that is specifically identified as scientifically cogent and accepted a priori. As such it may hide from view the particular domain that is claimed to represent scientific thinking. In so doing it also closes other knowledges from consideration as scientific and sets the parameters for judging the scientific status of other cognitive domains. Hegel argues that a philosophy of knowledge (science) confronts in the first instance, only competing claims to knowledge and scientific truth."

[74] Heather MacDonald, "Law School Humbug," Autumn 1995 | Vol. 5, No. 4. http://www.cityjournal.org/html/5_4_a2.html;

[75] Heather MacDonald, "Law School Humbug," Autumn 1995 | Vol. 5, No. 4. http://www.cityjournal.org/html/5_4_a2.html;

[76] Ellis Cose, Color-Blind: Seeing Beyond Race in a Race-Obsessed World xv (Harper Collins 1997).

To that extent, Thomas Carothers[77] argues that the "concept [of the rule of law] is suddenly everywhere—a venerable part of Western political philosophy enjoying a new run as a rising imperative of the era of globalization," which means that there is little agreement as to the detailed outlines of the rule of law. On the other hand, the application of the rule of law is the device for the function of governments in globalization in order to achieve equality and justice and so otherwise, the interest of elites will be imposed upon any society promoting a conflict and injustice leading to the collapse of useful globalization and adding arguments for the anti-globalization camp. North et al.[78] advocate that only about 15% of the globe's population live in what they call open access societies, where the rule of law exists.

It could be said that the rule of law allows a government to act only through legal rules and law ensures the power of government and so, the two crucial elements of the rule of law are due process of law and constitutional judicial review. Firstly, the due process offers a procedural check on government and is the oldest element of the rule of law. Moreover, the idea of due process is that government cannot act against persons without affording a hearing before a judge and so due process promotes the legitimacy of government because all societies compel legitimate mechanisms to resolve disagreements and courts make possible the social trust and consent that governments need to perform well. To that extent, courts resolve disputes in a distinctive way than do other political players and so the legitimacy of elected officials flows eventually from the ballot box while the legitimacy of judges lies on the purposes that they provide for their actions. Thus, elected officials are answerable to the electorate but judges are accountable for the rationalizations/ justifications they give for their decisions. Secondly, constitutional judicial review delivers a fundamental and normative check on government being the latest feature of the rule of law.

It is worth noting that Mattei[79] portrays the Western legal tradition as one with the rule of professional law in which law is detached from politics and other forms of social control such as religion which means that law is autonomous from politics. It could be said that the influence of politics upon law takes place in a more delegated way by interpretations or new legislation maneuvering the content of the law in a way implementing the political standpoints of the elites. Besides, developing nations "enjoy" the rule of political law where politics trumps law and so the central characteristics of the political rule of law or the "un-rule" of law are "weak courts; ... high level of instability of existing democratic structures, if any; high level of political involvement in the activity of the judiciary; high levels of police coercion; ... legal culture marginalized by the political power; scarcity of legally trained

[77] Carothers, Thomas. (1998). "The Rule of Law Revival." Foreign Affairs 77: 95–106.

[78] North, Douglass C., John Joseph Wallis, and Barry R. Weingast. 2009. Violence and Social Orders: A Conceptual Framework for Interpreting Recorded Human History. Cambridge: Cambridge University Press.

[79] Mattei, Ugo. (1997). "Three Patterns of Law: Taxonomy and Change in the World's Legal Systems." American Journal of Comparative Law 45: 5–43.

personnel; and a highly bureaucratized public decision making process."[80] It has to be taken into consideration that the influence of the "un-rule" of law on politics is also deep because, in a constitutional democracy, elected leaders are answerable both vertically to the electorate and horizontally to other political institutions.

Is there an inflexible dichotomy between "legalization" and "world politics"? It could be said that there is no rigid dichotomy between "legalization" and "world politics." Hence, law and politics are interlinked at all levels of legalization for the reason that compliance with rules happens for many reasons other than their legal status and so normative and material considerations, all play a role. It could be said that most of the time, legal, and political considerations are amalgamated to affect behavior.

In addition, it has to be taken into consideration that even "pure" political bargaining is formed by rules of sovereignty and other contextual legal norms. To that extent, Abbott et al.[81] argue that "even international adjudication takes place in the "shadow of politics": interested parties help shape the agenda and initiate the proceedings; judges are typically alert to the political implications of possible decisions, seeking to anticipate the reactions of political authorities. Between these extremes, where most international legalization lies, actors combine and invoke varying degrees of obligation, precision, and delegation to create subtle blends of politics and law. In all these settings, to paraphrase Clausewitz, "law is a continuation of political intercourse, with the addition of other means. "

It is argued that the impression of the rule of law that rules current rhetoric in the law and development movement fails to fulfil the requests of the formalist rule of law due to causal inconsistencies between the demands of general economic growth and regard for private property rights; cases in which courts do not devotedly apply legal rules; and the political character of law and legal institutions. To that extent, these impediments and their repression from the utilization of the rule of law lead to a rejection of the "universally" political nature of the rule of law and so this rejection has numerous effects such as showing law to be understood as unreasonably technocratic which means that it advances a "transplant" model of legal development generating an enigmatic demonization of politics in the framework of the promotion of democracy.

It has to be taken into account that the rule of law is an essential characteristic of economic upgrading and the role of law in advancement and political-institutional and economic modification is vital. Besides, sustained economic growth has occurred in the absence of rule of law and stable individual property rights regimes but this had happened under the understanding of the written law because some kind of unwritten law, in a form of a canon, has applied in all activities. Even matters

[80] Mattei, Ugo. (1997). "Three Patterns of Law: Taxonomy and Change in the World's Legal Systems." American Journal of Comparative Law 45: 5–43.

[81] Kenneth W. Abbott, Robert O. Keohane, Andrew Moravcsik, Anne-Marie Slaughter, and Duncan Snidal The Concept of Legalization International Organization 54, 3, Summer 2000, pp. 401–419 p419 at: http://ssrn.com/abstract=1402965

developed or occurred in an anarch way they follow the law of anarchism. Moreover, while established liberal democracies associate with anticipated legal orders, there is a need to examine the quality or regulatory reach of the rule of law, even in settings in the globally developed world for the reason that there are inequalities in terms of how the law is practiced and whose rights are most guarded. Additionally, the substantive features of rule of law within the category of recognized "consolidated" democracies differ notably in terms of form such as separation of powers and judicial review but particularly in terms of normative content. Tamanaha[82] observes that while the "revived" rule of law agenda is more sophisticated in discourse, it is not that far removed from the teleological foundations of earlier modernization doctrines.

Moreover, Kennedy[83] also concentrates on "rule of law" talk in development and the inextricability of law and politics. On the one hand, it is exposed the unfeasibility and undesirability of comprehending the "rule of law" as advocated by development institutions and the rule of law assists commerce. On the other hand, there is a movement generated by the turn to the rule of law as an advancement strategy advancing a technical, neutral, and universal juridical setting in order to depoliticize the conversation around advancement. In line, there is an effort to hide the politics' influence upon law and so there is an effort to present a picture that law prevails over politics while in reality, politics conquer law via the supposed legal application of the rule of law. In other words, there is a need of implementing the rule of law in a legally justifiable manner than choosing an interpretation according to the implementation of the interests of shifting paired elites. Furthermore, Kennedy[84] highlights the political nature of law advocating that "its recent (re)appearance in development policy creates an opportunity for the kind of 'sharp economic debate' which has been sadly lacking in development policy since the rise of the neo-liberal 'Washington consensus.'"

Is the Rule of Law rooted in any specific legal institutions? The rule of law can function in international society, where these types of institutions are less advanced but institutions can promote or strengthen practices of legality. Thus, the rule of law project is not only about restraining authority in hierarchical settings such as restraining governmental authority within countries, even though it can run this function. Moreover, the rule of law handles and affects authority within "horizontal" systems like international law. It has to be considered that it is the instantiation of the practice of legality via principles, processes, and techniques that generate a continuing prospect of a Rule of Law and so these principles, processes, and techniques are consecutively disciplined by the prerequisites of legality. Consequently, practices of

[82] Brian Z. Tamanaha, Beyond the Formalist-Realist Divide, The Role of Politics in Judging, 2009 Princeton University Press. Tamanaha, Brian Z., A Companion to Philosophy of Law and Legal Theory, second Edition, Dennis Patterson, ed., Blackwell Publishers, 2009.

[83] David Kennedy, 'Laws and Developments' in John Hatchard and Amanda Perry-Kesaris (eds.), Law and Development: Facing Complexity in the twenty-first Century (London: Cavendish, 2003).

[84] David Kennedy, 'Laws and Developments' in John Hatchard and Amanda Perry-Kesaris (eds.), Law and Development: Facing Complexity in the 21st Century (London: Cavendish, 2003).

legality function in a variety of surroundings, whether comparatively more horizontal or hierarchical in nature. To that extent, customary international law is made, preserved, and altered via rather diffuse processes, outlined by certain principles that govern the evaluation of whether or not a norm occurs at custom. Moreover, the principles that govern the making and function of treaties are more precise and detailed, and the procedures through which treaties are made and applied are more structured than those that affect customary law.[85] It could be said that the political importance of formal law is that it articulates the universalistic principle of inclusion at the outset, making possible the regulative ideal of a pluralistic international world and so the significance of law is unrelatedly of what interests or preferences specific legislation might pursue to enhance.[86]

It is argued that WTO dispute settlement has generated a sophisticated and well-respected jurisprudence and enjoys broad support.[87] The WTO manages to have a rule of law without the rule of lawyers. In contrast, ICSID arbitrators are high-powered, elite jurists with a much deeper level of expertise and experience as compared to the average WTO panelist. It is argued that the investment regime is governed by arbitrators, rather than states and so arbitrators are labeled as "private judges" functioning in secrecy, biased in favor of large multinationals, without respect to conflicts of interest and issuing inconsistent decisions.[88] Moreover, it is specified that the world investment regime seems, at present, to have too much rule of lawyers and not enough rule of law.

Likewise, it has to be taken into consideration that legalization of world politics is a bidirectional interaction between law and politics, not a unidirectional from politics-to-law story. In other words, more law, compulsory dispute settlement, and reduced options for countries to defect from or "exit" a regime, are made possible, and can only be sustained, in the existence of adequate levels of politics,

---

[85] Jean d'Aspremont, 'The Politics of Deformalization in International Law', Goettingen Journal of International Law 3 (2011), 546. Martti Koskenniemi, 'What is International Law For?', in The Politics of International Law (Oxford: Hart Publishing, 2011), pp. 266–267 (concluding that 'the justice that animates political community is not one that may be fully attained. Not only is law never justice itself, the two cannot exist side by side. If there is justice, then no law is needed – and if there is law, then there is only a (more or less well-founded) expectation of justice.').

[86] Martti Koskenniemi, 'The Mystery of Legal Obligation,' International Theory 3(2011), 319. Koskenniemi, 'What is International Law For?', pp. 256–7.

[87] J. Weiler, The Rule Of Lawyers And The Ethos Of Diplomats: Reflections On The Internal And External Legitimacy Of WTO Dispute Settlement, 35 Journal Of World Trade (2001), 191–207 Gregory Shaffer, Manfred Elsig, Sergio Puig, The Extensive (But Fragile) Authority Of The WTO Appellate Body, Law And Contemporary Problems Volume 79, Number 1 (2016).

[88] Corporate Europe Observatory, Profiting from Injustice, How Law Firms, Arbitrators and Finaciers are Fuelling an Investment Arbitration Boom, November 2013, http://corporateeurope.org/sites/default/files/publications/profitingfrom-injustice.pdf., Gus Van Harten, Arbitrator Behaviour in Asymmetrical Adjudication: An Empirical Study of Investment Treaty Arbitration, April 19, 2012, Osgoode CLPE Research Paper No. 41/2012, available at SSRN: http://ssrn.com/abstract=2149207. In contrast see Susan D. Franck, Development and Outcomes of Investment Treaty Arbitration, 50 Harv. Int'l L. J. 435 (2009).

participation, and plentiful occasions for expressing preferences or "voice." Taking into consideration that WTO panelists (1) are appointed by agreement or neutrally by the WTO Director-General who, himself, is appointed by consensus of all WTO members and (2) are mainly diplomats or ex-diplomats, is one manner of articulating this "voice" which means that WTO dispute settlement is fruitful not notwithstanding it being run by comparatively inexperienced trade diplomats but for the reason that it is so run.[89]

It could be said that trade law has gradually replaced trade politics and above all, the creation of WTO is commonly portrayed as a constitutional moment when the stability of the rule of law finally overshadowed the caprices of politics and diplomacy.[90] Similarly, Joost Pauwelyn[91] argues that "both the level of law and the level of politics gradually increased. More politics and participation, in particular consensus decision making, enabled more law and discipline, including the legalization of GATT's dispute process. Conversely, more law and discipline, in particular the WTO's smooth and automatic enforcement mechanism, required more politics and participation, including a vigorous defense by countries of the consensus rule." In other words, the existing amalgamation of a highly efficient dispute settlement system and a consensus based, inefficient rulemaking process no longer strikes one as a paradox but it is considered as a logical-although not unavoidably optimal-balance between high discipline or law and high participation or politics.

Equally, Adam Shinar[92] argues that the rule of law is imperative, but there are times where, in order to achieve specific social goals, the rule of law must give way to other values which indicates that a higher value is given to politics rather than to pure law implementation. Likewise, it is argued that the rule of law has to give way to more pressing values but on the other hand, all worthy values are governed by the law of a society which demands the utilization of the rule of law.

Additionally, it has to be considered that the rule-of-law arguments based on transparency and clarity are answerable in rule-of-law terms and cannot by themselves offer enough justification for specific policies,[93] which means that it has to be taken into account that the politics are incorporated in the context of the rule of law

[89] Robert Howse, From Politics to Technocracy – And Back Again: The Fate of the Multilateral Trading System, 96 AJIL (2002) 94. Joost Pauwelyn, The Transformation of World Trade, 104 Michigan Law Review (2005) 1–70.

[90] Judith Goldstein et al., Introduction: Legalization and World Politics, 54 Int'l Oro. 385, 389 (1982) (referring to a victory for trade "legalists" over trade "pragmatists"); Arie Reich, From Diplomacy to Law: The Juridicization of International Trade Relations, 17 Nw. J. INT'L L. & Bus. 775, 777 (1996–97). Marrakesh Agreement establishing the World Trade Organization, Apr. 15, 1994, 108 Stat. 4809, 1867 U.N.T.S. 14.

[91] Joost Pauwelyn, The Transformation of World Trade, 104 Michigan Law Review (2005) 1–70 p64.

[92] Adam Shinar, One Rule to Rule Them All? Rules of Law Against the Rule of Law, Theory & Prac. Legis., https://papers.ssrn.com/sol3/papers.cfm?abstract_id=2980757

[93] Felix Frankfurter, John Marshall and the Judicial Function, 69 Harv. L. Rev. 217, 235 (1955) ("[T]he relevant question is not, has [the rule of law] been achieved, but, is it conscientiously and systematically pursued.").

by the formation of the law that resolves a problem. Can we square the rule of law with the demands of modern government? There is an effort to have modern forms of governance and the rule of law.[94] It is obvious that governments have to embody the rule of law in their actions, which give legitimacy to their activities.[95]

Is the rule of law incompatible with administrative governance? It has to be considered that government regulation has not to draw society away from rule of law but the rule of law has to be the basis of legitimate governance and of course adjusted accordingly in order to implement the demands of the particular governance which has to cope with the demands of the society.[96] In other words, it is worth noting that the relationship between the rule of law and modern government is dynamic and complex. When appealed the rule of law put pressure on government players to remedy or moderate some diagnosed problem which means that the rule of law indictments of government practices that are viewed needed or highly favored return pressure to the rule of law ideal, pushing it toward expectations in proportion to the practicalities of modern governance.

Thus, it has to be taken into account that absent a rule of law principle instructing how far to scope into the future, governments attune the forward-looking frame as they see fit, and fill it with their political choice which is short term causing instability in the functioning of the society and so problems on the long-term legitimacy of governmental actions.

Likewise, it has to be taken into consideration that cultural context, political saliency, legal, and factual indeterminacy all influence the utility of rule of law talk. Moreover, appeals to the rule of law can lead to understanding or misunderstandings allowing government officials into proper action but appeals to the rule of law can legitimize improper action. On the other hand, the rule of law may yet remain a useful concept but political contamination of the ideal should be a matter of great concern which means that if the rule of law comes to lose all meaning in its context, that infection can spread to impede the ideal's utility in contexts where it might otherwise be put to better use.

---

[94]Ronald A. Cass, Staying Agency Rules: Constitutional Structure and Rule of Law in the Administrative State, 69 Admin. L. Rev. 225 (2017).

[95]Gillian E. Metzger & Kevin M. Stack, Internal Administrative Law, 115 Mich. L. Rev. 1239, 1262 (2017) ("[I]n a culture that prizes the rule of law as ours does, it is difficult to ground an account of administrative legitimacy without an account of how well administrative agencies embody rule-of-law values. Recognizing internal administration as a form of law allows such an evaluation." Peter M. Shane, Chevron Deference, the Rule of Law, and Presidential Influence in the Administrative State, 83 Fordham L. Rev. 679, 681 (2014) (advancing a conception of the rule of law in the administrative state that comprises five central premises surrounding the exercise of government power: the insistence on politically legitimate authorization, the observance of human rights, accountability to legal constraint, the expectation of legal justification, and the availability of remedies for government-imposed injury); Kevin M. Stack, An Administrative Jurisprudence: The Rule of Law in the Administrative State, 115 Colum. L. Rev. 1985, 1986–88 (2015).

[96]Philip Hamburger, Is Administrative Law Unlawful? 5–7, 12–13 (2014) (challenging legality of administrative state based on historical ideals of rule of law); Richard A. Epstein, The Perilous Position of the Rule of Law and the Administrative State, 36 Harv. J.L. & Pub. Pol'y 5 (2013).

Have all entities to follow the rule of law? During the Obama Administration, the relative rule of law was popular among DACA/DAPA supporters for the reason that it offered a way to justify these programs in rule of law terms.[97] Hence, it has to be taken into consideration that the larger system within which a legal rule or a legal institution performs is subject to unpredictable, unimaginable change which means that the content of the rule is changeable as well.[98] Congress has delegated legislative rulemaking authority to administrative agencies which means that there are able to promote the rule of law according to the promotion of their political aims.[99]

Are there rules of law that are in tension with the rule of law? While the rule of law is a "rule," legal systems assist departures from the rule of law via judicially developed rules of law, let's say, standing, political questions, immunity, and suspensions of invalidity which means that these judge-made rules give public officials flexibility in the observance of other rules and so their outcome is to alleviate the often strict demands of the rule of law by facilitating public officials negotiate their legal obligations to the point of ignoring the rules that they are otherwise bound to comply with. It could be said that politics can intervene via courts' interpretation the formation of the content of the rule of law accommodating their political aims.

It has to be taken into consideration that the rule of law exists alongside other rules of law and so in cases of conflict, the rule of law might not have the upper hand which means that the threat to the rule of law is not just exogenous to the legal system, but also endogenous. Moreover, the rule of law is the result of a legal system that routinely professes its commitment to the rule of law, but also generates and preserves rules that destabilize the very value that the system is committed to preserving and so courts have to be institutions designed to safeguard the rule of law not influenced by politics producing a judicial review that destabilizes the content of the rule of law which means the need for nonpolitically influenced litigation. Thus, courts should not undermine the rule of law and so by creating, developing, and sustaining rules of law, courts should not infringe/ spoil the rule of law.[100]

---

[97] Andrew C. McCarthy, Trump's Immigration Guidance: The Rule of Law Returns, PJ Media (Feb. 22, 2017), https://pjmedia.com/andrewmccarthy/2017/02/22/trumps-immigration-guidance-the-rule-oflaw-returns/

[98] Caryn Devins et al., Against Design, 47 Ariz. St. L.J. 609, 622 (2015) J.B. Ruhl & Daniel Martin Katz, Measuring, Monitoring, and Managing Legal Complexity, 101 Iowa L. Rev. 191 (2015).

[99] Thomas W. Merrill, Rethinking Article I, Section 1: From Nondelegation to Exclusive Delegation, 104 Colum. L. Rev. 2097, 2099 (2004) David Pozen, Self-Help and the Separation of Powers, 124 Yale L.J. 2, 16–17 (2014) (making the positive case for separation of powers self-help, partly on rule of law grounds).

[100] Adam Shinar, One Rule to Rule Them All? Rules of Law Against the Rule of Law 5 The Theory and Practice of Legislation 149 (2017) Erin F. Delaney, Analyzing Avoidance: Judicial Strategy in Comparative Perspective, 66 Duke L.J. 1, 1 (2016) (arguing that some justiciability doctrines promote interbranch dialogue, thus contributing to a more democratic resolution); Aziz Z. Huq, The Negotiated Structural Constitution, 114 Colum. L. Rev. 1595, 1620–31, 1683–86 (2014) (arguing that the branches negotiate their institutional interests with one another and that courts

6.6 The Rule of Law and the EU Rule of Law

States are sovereign and rules are only advantageous to the extent that states agree to follow them. Therefore, the need for the rule of law means that the sovereign state concedes a great deal of legal power to the law and organization that stabilizes the system. In conjunction with the upsurge of new international or transnational institutions and norms, the partial reconfiguration of the state denotes that norms "created somewhere else" influence daily life in ways which were up to that time out of the question. People continually renegotiate their internal rules on how they should act with regard to each other on a day-to-day.

It is worth mentioning here that political and social globalization affect income inequality too. Moreover, political globalization leads states to set common minimum standards and so boost equality within states. Has globalization had any political impact upon states' integration into unions? It is characteristic that borders obstruct trade and globalization makes borders costlier.[101] Consequently, it has to be considered that political structure adjusts by removing borders or dropping their cost and so adjustment engenders a non-monotonic evolution of competent state size. In its early phases, the competent political reaction to globalization consists of removing borders by forming large countries. Furthermore, in its later stages, the resourceful political reaction to globalization is to remove the cost of borders by generating a new level of government, namely, international unions and so producing a reduction in the size of countries. For instance, the US federal expansion was followed not just by the formation of new states, but also by the breakup of existing ones. It could be said that in a way political geography replies to economic efficiency but nowadays they choose multiplying access to global markets through peaceful diplomacy, by building multilateral institutions that recognize all members' political autonomy which means that there is a peaceful upsurge of multilevel governance.[102]

Furthermore, it has to be considered that economies of scale and scope influence the optimal political structure and economies of scope, if large enough, make it desirable to have single-level governance rather than a two-level structure. To that extent, as globalization proceeds, the profits from trade grow, offering motivations to remove borders and so it seems that the world political structure moves from a few large countries to many small states within an international union such as being part of a federation. In line, centralization reaps economies of scale gaining from policy coordination, but it enforces a uniform policy on localities with various preferences. It has to be considered that international organizations performed a direct part in the process of decolonization. Moreover, once trade is implemented by peaceful

---

are not well placed to monitor these "intermural deals," which instead should be policed for bad outcomes by elected officials).

[101] Gino Gancia Giacomo A.M. Ponzetto Jaume Ventura, Globalization and Political Structure Working Paper 22,046 http://www.nber.org/papers/w22046

[102] Steinwender, Claudia (2018). "Real Effects of Information Frictions: When the States and the Kingdom became United" American Economic Review 108(3): 657–696.

international unions, countries pursue economic integration with neighboring partners, with whom the profits from trade are higher and so there is a shift from global empires to regional unions being consistent with the augmented regionalization of world trade patterns.[103] For instance, the USA circumvented the stage of collapse and political fragmentation by picking an institutional system with multiple levels of government which means that the case of the USA follows the pattern of the formation and expansion of the federal government, which is a regional union, accorded with the fragmentation and loss of political power of individual states. In line, the crumbling EU has to follow the example of the USA in order to avoid the collapse or the gradual disintegration by forming the USE.

The key economic goal of a nation is to yield a high and rising standard of living for its citizens due to information technology. Economic globalization brought integration of national economies into the international economy through trade, foreign direct investment, capital flows, and spread of technology.[104] While economics is only one of the aspects of globalization, globalization is the outcome of political will and of law.

Has the prevailing interest of an elite group in the EU imposed law, politics, and the current model of Union upon people of Europe? Is there an elite group in the EU or outside the EU preventing its transformation into the USE? Law merely reflects a determinate resolution of the controversy as contemplated fitting by those who have the power and authority to resolve the issue within a specific society.[105]

There is balance being established among national legal systems within the global legal order but introducing several sectoral imbalances. The variability of "international regimes" generates a different form of relativism such as sectoral rather than national aggravating reactions.[106]

Which is the role of the rule of law in the global legal order? Has the rule of law applied to the global order? The answer is yes but in fact there is emergence and utilization of politics of law rather than appliance of objective law. Can globalization endure governance without government? Above the States, there is now a network of sectoral governments and this network has developed incrementally and has been made possible by the need of a center and by the occurrence of a center, the UN, operating as a "forum." To that extent, Sabino Cassese[107] argues that "A unitary cosmopolitan legal system is not on the horizon nor is it perhaps among current

---

[103] Fouquin, Michel and Jules Hugot (2016). "Back to the Future: Trade Costs and the Two Globalizations" CEPII Working Paper No. 2016–13.

[104] G Zekos, RISK MANAGEMENT, CORPORATE GOVERNANCE IN twenty-first CENTURY DIGITAL ECONOMY 2014 Nova Science Publications New York USA. www.novapublishers.com G Zekos, Law and Economics of Corporate Governance and Insider Trading, 2016 Nova Science Publications New York USA. www.novapublishers.com

[105] Neil MacCormick, Institutions of Law: An Essay in Legal Theory (Oxford: Oxford University Press, 2007) 255–61.

[106] S. Krasner (ed.), International Regimes, Ithaca, Cornell Univ. Press, 1983 (3 rd ed. 1995).

[107] Sabino Cassese, The Globalization Of Law * **www.ssrn.com** P24.

ambitions. Instead a process is under way that affects certain positive principles and branches of law."

It has to be taken into consideration that the main function of the rule of law was the preservation of liberty and so the rule of law was progressed only during the liberal age which means that the rule of law is one of its greatest accomplishments, not only as a safeguard but as the legal epitome of freedom.[108] Moreover, the rule of law entails that government in all its actions is bound by rules agreed and publicized previously—rules which make it feasible to anticipate with fair assurance how the authority will handle its coercive authorities in given environments allowing anyone to plan his/her matters on the foundation of this knowledge.[109]

The expansion of international law and organizations is a remarkable development of globalization. The European Union has been at the forefront of legalizing inter-state relations, to the point where the national and interstate legal structures in Europe are broadly undividable. On the other hand, nowadays the undertaking to assemble logic has brought international relations to the intersection of politics and law. Political parties are based on the performance and undertaking of national politicians on national matters such as war and peace, monetary policy, and deficit spending.

It could be said that, the rule of law exists when the law is publicly known, applies equally to ordinary citizens and rulers, and where all are free to test and observe that universal application. To that extent, politics cannot prohibit or manipulate the ordinary application of the law according to who is under consideration and due to the political affairs of state or political ambitions of economic elites upon the outcome of a particular case. The rule of law means equality. Can the rule of law mean equality per occasion or constantly applicable?

It is worth mentioning that the state has a monopoly on the legitimate violence or authority within a defined territory and administered by some form of logical bureaucracy rule of law existing when the sovereign or ruler is compelled to the same laws set for his subjects. Consequently, the rule of law acts as a restraint against uncontrolled state authority and exists somewhat in opposition to the ability of the modern bureaucratic state which means that this dualism of state authority and its institutionalized control due to the rule of law is required to keep any apt governing order in balance. Does a rule of law exist or to be sure that it does not? How many sovereigns or rulers have declared themselves formally above the law since the French Revolution?

Borders identify territories within which political communities arise and flourish. Political communities extend beyond borders, but in our world, they are directly linked with borders. Thus, political borders play a role in generating a membership in

[108] Friedrich Hayek, The Road to Serfdom (Chicago: University of Chicago Press 1944) Friedrich Hayek, The Constitution of Liberty (Chicago: Chicago University Press 1960) 205–219.

[109] Brian Z. Tamanaha, On the Rule of Law: History, Politics, Theory (Cambridge: Cambridge University Press 2004).

a political community.[110] In line it has to be taken into consideration that the nation–state has a sole social will that has to be defended at all costs for the reason that this is the only way in which its people accomplish their elemental reason to be. Moreover, due to globalization the world has noticeably transformed and now there are numerous identities that ought to be protected permitting people to make sense of their worlds. Nevertheless, whereas the conservation of national external rules is central for the reason that they allow people to preserve their distinctive cultural identity and heritage to that extent globalization with its global "markets in goods, services and capital," means that individuals rely on people in different countries as well. It could be said that due to globalization not only public institutions but also everyday life is becoming free from the hold of tradition which means that societies are becoming de-traditionalized producing a global cosmopolitan society which means another role for lawmaking as well.[111]

Markets work well when the law enables socially needed behavior and so persons contract with others knowing that the legal system will enforce those agreements. Besides, if the legal system is a failure, people will trade and make deals with only those they know personally and trust. Consequently, specialization that is a requirement for economic development basically cannot take place without a legal means to protect contract and property rights. In other words, without the trust created by a working legal system, markets cannot run.

States take into consideration wider global factors in the general interpretation of national rules in their territories as well which is achieved via public international law as well. It is worth mentioning that States come together in forums like the United Nations, European Union, and other international and regional groups to advance rules for the general good.[112] There is the direct transfer of institutions from one national system to another. In addition, there is the imposition of a global legal principle upon national public administrations which means the imposition by a global judicial body of a common legal principle, not only upon States, but also within national legal systems. Moreover, legal thought is the first area influenced by the circulation and spreading of law.

It is worth mentioning that states use international law to rationalize their policies. To that extent, states offer explanations for how their conduct is coherent with their international commitments, and accordingly there is competing diplomatic and legal accounts concerning compliance. In other words, there is no likelihood for an

---

[110] Coleman, J. L. and Harding, S. K. Citizenship, the demand of justice, and the moral relevance of political borders. Justice in Immigration. ed. Schwartz, W. F. Cambridge: University Press, 2007, p. 40. Maier, C. S. Being there: place, territory and identity. Identities, Affiliations and Allegiances, ed. Benhabib, S.; Shapiro, I.; Petranovic, D. Cambridge: University Press, 2007, p. 78.

[111] Garrett, G. The Causes of Globalization [interactive]. Yale University, April 2000 http://www.yale.edu/leitner/pdf/2000-02.pdf: "I define globalization somewhat narrowly as the international integration of markets in goods, services and capital." Giddens, A. Runaway World: How Globalization is Reshaping our Lives. London: Profile Books, 2002, p.42–43.

[112] Evans, M.; Cerny, P. Globalization and Social Policy. Developments in British Social Policy 2. Ed. Ellison N.; Pierson, C. Basingstoke: Palgrave Macmillan, p. 22.

objective settling of the differences. It seems that the international rule of law utilizes law to legitimate state policy. Furthermore, it is worth noting here that European law has been the law aimed at deepen and broaden European integration.[113] Besides, rupture portrays itself in three very different ways via nationalist retreat, nation state-centered multilateralism, and the revolutionary establishment of a European republic. Moreover, considering that there is the UK's decision to exit, it means unconditionally rejecting European integration. It has to be considered that it is unlikely that the population of a country will trust European institutions or those of other Member States if the national media and opinion leaders stage them as unreliable over a prolonged period of time which means that deep distrust is to be awaited bringing an unexpected institutional collapse illustrated by the British exiting the EU.

It has to be considered that the well-known path of European rule of law is confronted with authoritative calls for discontinuance today, even for a hard breakup and so Brexit is a most imperative understanding of that power. Moreover, European law is broader than Union law alone, and embraces national law responding to supranational law being even far more specific when it comes to the limits of integration.[114]

Furthermore, it has to be taken into consideration that there has been an expansion of instruments of sanction going beyond declaratory rulings of the CJEU but the reactions in European law to the financial and debt crisis have resulted in tough coercive instruments against Member States.[115] Furthermore, the EU exercises massive political coercion today and so the ECB forced Greece to back down through a "near death experience" which means that the Union has already made the step toward a transfer union whose core is not legislative acts of a free Rechtsgemeinschaft, but instead legally vague instruments influenced by a politicized process but this does not always result in the desired obedience to the law. Therefore, these coercive instruments contributed to a massive politicization of the Union.

Above all the generated political character is illustrated in the authoritative guidance of societal and particularly economic processes and so EU is political for the reason that it regulates by means of policies (today Art. 26 et seq. TFEU).[116] It is worth mentioning that the CJEU has been using the concept of the Community based on the rule of law (Rechtsgemeinschaft) explicitly and so nowadays the union based

---

[113] M. Ruffert, Europäische Währungspolitik als Herausforderung für das Recht (Zentrum für Europäisches Wirtschaftsrecht 2015) p. 37.

[114] A. von Bogdandy, 'European Law Beyond 'Ever Closer Union' Repositioning the Concept, its Thrust and the EJC's Comparative Methodology', 22 ELJ (2016) p. 519.

[115] S. Bitter, Die Sanktion im Recht der Europäischen Union (Springer 2011) p. 121 et seq. M. Ioannidis, 'Europe's new transformations: How the EU economic constitution changed during the Eurozone crisis', 53 CMLRev (2016) p. 1237 at p. 1264 et seq.

[116] G. Majone, Regulating Europe (Routledge 1996). ECJ 23 April 1986, Case C-294/83, Les Verts v. Parliament,; M. Dawson and F. de Witte, 'From Balance to Conflict: A New Constitution for the EU', 22 ELJ (2016) p. 204.

on the rule of law increasing its powers to review all instances in which the Union exercises its power.[117] ECJ argues that the European Union is a union based on the rule of law in which all acts of its institutions are subject to review of their compatibility with the Treaties, general principles of law and fundamental rights.[118]

There is a trend in Germany to comprehend, using the concept Rechtsgemeinschaft, the needed normativity of Union law, its effectiveness and autonomy from politics, correspondingly to that of the German Basic Law. Undeniably, the Federal Constitutional Court uses the term in this sense.[119] However, different understandings exist of how flexibly treaty law can be interpreted in times of crisis and of what role the courts play in this concern which means that the notion of Rechtsgemeinschaft all too easily invites transplanting expectations from the German to the European background without due reflection of the different path and context.

It is worth noting that the term integration through law mostly thematizes the fact of how the CJEU stimulates integration through "activist" case law on individual rights which means that legal integration allows the implementation of the rule of law in a common comprehension of the content of the law causing identical effects across EU.[120] Furthermore, considering that nowadays EU based on the rule of law, the CJEU uses the notion of the Rechtsgemeinschaft primarily for an extensive interpretation of its competency for judicial review which is only one aspect of the Rechtsgemeinschaft, yet beyond questions an imperative one. Thus, the Venice Commission argues that 'the rule of law should emanate not from any written constitution but from the "common (judge-made) law[121]"' indicating that the rule of law incorporates not only the black letter law but also its interpretation by courts allows a possible political approach concerning the content of the law influencing the

[117] ECJ 23 April 1986, Case C-294/83, Les Verts v Parliament; ECJ (Grand Chamber) 3 September 2008, Cases C-402/15 and C-415/05 P (Kadi and Al Barakaat International Foundation v Council and Commission, margin number 281.

[118] ECJ (Grand Chamber) 6 October 2015, Case C-362/14, Schrems v Data Protection Commissioner. H. Koch, K. Hagel-Sorensen, U. Haltern and J. H. H. Weiler (eds.), Europe. The New Legal Realism (Djoef 2010).

[119] Bundesverfassungsgericht 9 November 1999, Case 2 BvL 5/95, ECLI:DE:BVerfG:1999:ls19991109.2bvl000595; Bundesverfassungsgericht 16 January 2008, Case 2 BvR 2391/07, ECLI:DE:BVerfG:2008:rk20080116.2bvr239107. Editorial Comments, 'Debt and Democracy: 'United States then, Europe now?", 49 CMLRev. (2012) p. 1833. Editorial Comments, 'The Rule of Law in the Union, the Rule of Union Law and the Rule of Law by the Union: Three interrelated problems', 53 CMLRev. (2016) p. 597 et seq.

[120] D. Augenstein (ed.), 'Integration through law' Revisited. The Making of the European Polity (Routledge 2012); R. Dehousse, 'From integration through law to governance', in H. Koch, K. Hagel-Sorensen, U. Haltern and J. H. H. Weiler (eds.), Europe. The New Legal Realism (Djoef 2010).

[121] European Commission for Democracy through Law, Report on the Rule of Law, Study 512/2009, CDL-AD(2011)003rev (2011). A. Jakab, European Constitutional Language (Cambridge UP 2016).

outcome on behalf of specific political governance of strictly legal legitimizing the regulated matters for the whole society's own good.

Of course, the operation of courts is the dynamic center of a functioning legal order and the global juridification substantiates the fact that international actors, particularly states, submit to international courts with the intention of engendering trust in their adherence to the law paralleling to a path for apprehending the European rule of law.[122] Is there a crisis of the European rule of law? It is argued that there is a current crisis of the European rule of law being a crisis of trust concerning the concept of the Rechtsgemeinschaft stirring up the interactions of society and community, according to which a community differentiates itself from a mere society through high mutual trust,[123] which means that the content of the rule of law is shaped via the interaction between the interests of communities influenced by their political aims expressed as the final content of the applicable law implementing the applicability of the rule of law.

In other words, mutual trust in Europe has been subjected to "exceptional circumstances" observed in central policy fields, and the intuition is widespread that they amount to a crisis of the European rule of law. Furthermore, the CJEU assumed that all Member States must trust that all Member States will respect Union law, and above all its fundamental rights being a central concept of the CJEU which means that it is an expression of judicial wisdom all the same to add a stipulation of great significance: "except in exceptional circumstances."[124] Thus, the ECB's OMT and Public Sector Purchase Programmes, systematic non-application of European refugee law, national cautions on the foundation of ordre public in cases of cooperation entailed under Union law, and extensive corruption in some Member States are very different phenomena embracing contradictory perceptions which means that a crisis of the rule of law might be seen in the fact that without mandate the ECB supports economically weaker Member States, but also in the violation of the

[122] H. Kelsen, Law and Peace in International Relations. The Oliver Wendell Holmes Lectures 1940–41 (Harvard UP 1942); H. Kelsen, Peace Through Law (University of North Carolina Press 1944).

[123] J. Gauck, Speech on the occasion of the conferral of an honorary doctorate of Maastricht University on 7 February 2017, www.bundespraesident.de/SharedDocs/Reden/EN/JoachimGauck/Reden/2017/170207-Honorary-doctorateNetherland.html C. Kohler, 'Vertrauen und Kontrolle im europäischen Justizraum für Zivilsachen', 19 Zeitschrift für europarechtliche Studien (2016) p. 135; M. Schwarz, Grundlinien der Anerkennung im Raum der Freiheit, der Sicherheit und des Rechts (Mohr Siebeck 2016).

[124] ECJ (Plenary), Opinion 2/13, margin number 191. 68 ECJ (Grand Chamber) 5. April 2016, Cases C-404/15 and C-659/15 PPU, Aranyosi and Căldăraru, margin number 78; ECJ (Grand Chamber) 6 September 2016, Case C-182/15, Petruhhin; ECJ 1 June 2016, Case C-241/15, Bob-Dogi; ECJ 24 May 2016, Case C-108/16 PPU, Dworzecki. K. Lenaerts, 'Keynote Speech – The Court of Justice in an Uncertain World', in G. Bándi, P. Darák and K. Debisso (eds.), Speeches and Presentations from XXVII FIDE Congress (Wolters Kluwer 2016).

European guarantee of full employment, social progress, social justice, and social protection (Article 3§3 TEU).[125]

It has to be taken into consideration that the quality of social interaction is related to the level of trust between the partners and some relationships are hardly achievable without trust but there is no way for determining from which point a lack of trust starts threatening the sustainability of a political system.[126] Is the legal trust analogous to the political trust? It could be said that the level of trust among politics and law has to be analogous in order to be workable in a jurisdiction and society because otherwise the imbalance will cause problems in the implementation of the rule of law which represents the application of law implementing the political needs of the whole society and not merely the interests of a political party on power or an elite.

It is obvious that the rule of law is not utilized as a solution to the governance challenges in Europe or globally. The rule of law has to alter/redraft political disputes in legal language. On the other hand, the international examples illustrate that eventually, the rule of law and the international rule of law has become political resources that actors utilize in the political struggle over the legitimation and delegitimation of their desires which is against the real meaning of the rule of law to the detriment of international peace and progress. However, states utilize international law in order to legalize their actions and those of others against the real legal meaning of the rule by enveloping the meaning of an international rule of law with a lawful context which in fact is the political dress of law in order to achieve any political goals even against a settled legal order and in an effort to change the legal status quo accordingly.

Likewise, it has to be taken into consideration that politics covers a wide ground of activity, while the law remains a confined ground where the rules of politics are generated and questioned. Nonetheless, politics is not external to law and international politics takes place within a legal environment.

It has to be taken into account that power in international politics is diffused and the increase in the need for global governance faces a decrease in competence to introduce multilateral, comprehensive, and legally binding regimes.[127] AI systems shift the structure or texture of human interactions, modifying actors' incentives, strategic pressures or even goals in destabilizing or harmful directions and so altering

[125] European Central Bank, Technical Features of Outright Monetary Transactions, 6 September 2012, www.ecb.europa.eu/press/pr/date/2012/html/pr120906_1.en.html, Decision (EU) 2015/774 of the ECB of 4 March 2015 on a secondary markets public sector asset purchase programme (ECB/2015/10). M. Weller, 'Mutual trust: in search of the future of European Union private international law', 11 Journal of Private International Law (2015) p. 64, A. von Bogdandy and M. Ioannidis, Systemic deficiency in the rule of law: What it is, what has been done, what can be done, 51 CMLRev. (2014) p. 59. European Commission for Democracy through Law, Opinion on Amendments to the Act of 25 June 2015 on the Constitutional Tribunal of Poland, CDL-AD(2016) 001158, Opinion no 833/2015 (2016).

[126] S. Schüttemeyer, 'Political trust', in D. Nohlen and R.-O. Schultze (eds.), Lexikon der Politikwissenschaft. Theorien, Methoden, Begriffe, Band 2 (2002) p. 656.

[127] UN-COPUOS. (2018). The Hague Space Resources Governance Working Group: Information Provided by the Netherlands (U.N. Doc. A/AC.105/C.2/2018/CRP.18).

the texture of human relations at the national level, or destabilize global politics at the international one.

It is supposed that rule of law arguments are the basis in the operation of government and so the rule of law is an attractive ideal, but its magnetism stems from its imprecision, which permits each of us to project our own sense of the ideal government onto the phrase "rule of law" which does not mean that the law is altered according to the needs of politicians in order to achieve their political targets but there is a need for continuity. Furthermore, judgments of consistency and inconsistency with the rule of law should be considered as relatively ad hoc, but not giving up on the rule of law applicability. On the other hand, it could be said that the expression "the Rule of Law" has become empty[128] thanks to ideological abuse and general overuse not in real sense but in order to cover political ambitions hiding behind the supposed implementation of the rule of law achieving legitimacy for the whole society.

States have developed a noteworthy legal system in order to utilize economic law moving from politics and law to the politics of law in the realm of international economic regulation. State action is based upon a rationale rooting in some form of planning process signifying the strategic and political intent of governments.

Subsidiarity is a principle entailing decision-making to take place at a lower level if not good reasons are for shifting it upwards.[129] Subsidiarity favors local action becoming a justification for higher-level decision-making.[130] Which is to the relations between national and international institutions? Subsidiarity is a principle for assigning authority to various levels of governance presenting assistance on how powers are to be implemented. Moreover, subsidiarity is "the soul of federalism" which means preference for the local leaving open how this is to be accomplished being the list of powers for each level of government.[131] To that extent, in the EU subsidiarity has dominated a prominent place which is introduced as a formal rule for the first time in the 1992 Maastricht Treaty. Furthermore, subsidiarity deals with political questions of power-sharing which should be left to the political procedure but in general not be used by constitutional courts to review legislative endeavors. Besides, it could be said that courts should play a role in reviewing formal, written constitution-making which means constitutional amendment and replacement.

---

[128] Judith N. Shklar, Political Theory and the Rule of Law, in The Rule Of Law: Ideal Or Ideology 1, 1 (Allan C. Hutchinson & Patrick Monahan eds., 1987).

[129] Andreas Follesdal, Subsidiarity and International Human Rights Courts, 79 Law Contemp. Probl. (2016). Loren King, Cities, Subsidiarity, and Federalism, in Federalism And Subsidiarity (James E. Fleming & Jacob T. Levy, Eds.) 291–331 (2014).

[130] Michelle Evans, The Principle of Subsidiarity as a Social and Political Principle in Catholic Social Teaching, 3 Solidar. J. Cathol. Soc. Thought Secul. Ethics 4, 54 (2013).

David Golemboski, Federalism and the Catholic Principle of Subsidiarity, EarlyView PUBLIUS (2015).

[131] Gareth Davies, Subsidiarity: The Wrong Idea, in the Wrong Place, at the Wrong Time, 43 Common Mark. Law Rev. 63–84 (2006).

Has the Federal Republic of Yugoslavia been demolished by politics against any rule of law? It has to be considered that Slobodan Milosevic[132] was criticized by the whole Western press corps and essentially every politician in every NATO country by calling him "the Butcher of the Balkans" comparing him to Hitler and accusing/indicting him of genocide. It is worth mentioning that it seems that Politicians demonized him and made him out to be a "bloodthirsty monster" utilizing that fabricated image to rationalize not only economic sanctions against Serbia, but also the 1999 NATO bombing of Serbia, utilizing the territory of EU Member states, proving that politics overruled the rule of law. Considering that Milosevic death occurred shortly after the Tribunal denied his request to seek specialized medical treatment and the fact that not only in a judgment issued on March 24, 2016, the ICTY concluded that Slobodan Milosevic was not responsible for war crimes committed during the 1992–1995 Bosnian war but also in a prior decision of the International Court of Justice (ICJ)[133] indicates and signposts that the rule of law has been overtaken by politics at least on this occasion.

Moreover, in politics, the procedure of building trust has to keep on inconspicuous if it is to circumvent critical impediments based on leaders who have gained an image of truthfulness, fairness, and trustworthiness and so a crisis in trust cannot be "resolved" by legal instruments and only gradually subsides over time via a justifiable action founded upon the applicability of the rule of law. Furthermore, legal instruments should be assessed along with whether they help circumvent an acceleration of distrust and make possible continuing cooperation, which unreservedly fosters trust. Nevertheless, the crisis of the European rule of law involves mostly institutions and systems and so crises in trust in institutions and systems are more critical than crises in trust in interpersonal relationships.

Subsequently, once public trust in institutions or systems has eroded to a critical point, it is doubtful that the population of a state will trust European institutions or those of other Member States if the national media and opinion leaders describe them as untrustworthy over an extended period of time, which has to be based on the fact of not implementing the rule of law.[134] Otherwise a system based on the implementation of the rule of law is not easy to be illustrated as not trustful and deep distrust is not to be anticipated.

Since the nation-state was deemed the decisive framework of societal trust, relationships of trust between states and between citizens of different nations have become a broader topic. In this respect, it is vital to stress that not every form of cooperative behavior is an expression of trust and so trust is only required if

---

[132] Slobodan Milosevic (20 August 1941–11 March 2006) was a Yugoslav and Serbian politician who was the President of Serbia from 1989 to 1997 and President of the Federal Republic of Yugoslavia from 1997 to 2000.

[133] Bosnia and Herzegovina v Serbia and Montenegro [2007] ICJ 2. Case No. IT-95-5/18-T 1240 24 March 2016. ICTY, Karadzic Judgment, 24 March 2016, Para. 3460 http://www.icty.org/x/cases/karadzic/tjug/en/160324_judgement.pdf

[134] F. Kroeger, 'The development, escalation and collapse of system trust: From the financial crisis to society at large', 33 European Management Journal (2015) p. 431, 434 et seq.

something of noteworthy value is at stake. Trust is to be differentiated from legitimate expectations and loyal collaboration, which have been concepts of European law for a long time.[135] It seems that the effectiveness of Community law revolved around its proper transposition into domestic law.[136]

Can the rule of law be examined from the perspective of trust? It seems that trust offers an effective tool for conceiving the European rule of law as laid down in Art 2 TEU. Considering that the members of a society must organize their relationships and plan their behavior, including those of the European society referred to in Article 2 TEU means that both trust and law are to be understood against this setting and so trust attunes a person's behavior to the future behavior of others, comparably to law, which also alleviates normative prospects. It is true that the EU has Article 2 TEU but it has never been law in the sense of forming part of the body of the ordinary EU acquis.[137] Accordingly, given that the acquis on values largely does not occur, the EU is powerless to outline their content. Thus, the case law of the ECJ certifies that Article 2 TEU not having gained any self-standing value.

Firstly, the EU appears as a legal system that cannot boast the rule of law and so the "Rule of Law" in Article 2 TEU cannot have any meaning beyond an obligation to observe basic legal procedures and, probably, a set of other well-known elements of legality.[138] In a system with rhetorical obedience to legality through considerations of autonomy and without the rule of law, engendering injustice is not viewed as a problem,[139] and the legitimacy of the law as such thereby naturally continues undermined.[140]

The "autonomous legal order"[141] definitely appears as a formally coherent system directly bound by nothing beyond the day-to-day rules of its own creation and operation but the Treaty text[142] is its limit, with no greater aspiration in sight beyond

---

[135] J. Ruzicka and V. C. Keating, 'Going global: Trust research and international relations', 5 Journal of Trust Research (2015) p. 8. G. M. Genna, 'Images of Europeans: Transnational trust and support for European integration', 20 Journal of International Relations and Development (2017) p. 358.

[136] G. Nonnenmacher, 'Europas letzte Chance?', Frankfurter Allgemeine Woche, 24 March 2017, p. 17.

[137] C Hillion, 'Overseeing the Rule of Law in the EU' in C Closa and D Kochenov (eds), Reinforcing Rule of Law Oversight in the European Union (CUP 2016). D Kochenov, 'Declaratory Rule of Law: Self-Constitution through Unenforceable Promises' in J Přibáň (ed), Self-Constitution of European Society (Routledge 2016). KL Scheppele, 'Enforcing the Basic Principles of EU Law through Systematic Infringement Actions' in C Closa and D Kochenov (eds), Reinforcing Rule of Law Oversight in the European Union (Cambridge University Press 2016).

[138] R Fallon, '"The Rule of Law" as a Concept in Constitutional Discourse' (1997) 97 Columbia LR 1.

[139] A Williams and D Kochenov, 'Europe's Justice Deficit Introduced' in D Kochenov, G de Búrca and A Williams (eds), Europe's Justice Deficit? (Hart 2015).

[140] C-135/08 Rottmann EU:C:2010:104 [2010] ECR I-1449. C-434/09 McCarthy EU:C:2011:277 [2011] ECR I-3375; C-256/11 Dereci EU:C:2011:734 [2011] ECR I-11315.

[141] Case 6/64 Costa v ENEL EU:C:1964:66 [1964] ECR 585.

[142] AT Williams, 'Taking Values Seriously: Towards a Philosophy of EU Law' (2009) 29 OJLS 549.

being shielded from outside influence.[143] Checks on the substance of the law which aim to make certain that the law is restrained by Law do not exist, so damaging the Rule of Law as an institutional ideal.

Which is the role of the national courts in the molding of the Union's Rule of Law? When the system works, the functioning of the Rule of Law is secured, as European norms are fitted into the legal orders of the Member States with regard to the constitutional traditions and arrangements in those states. It is clarified that a measure of the Union cannot be influenced by national law, as that would "[. . .] have an adverse effect on the uniformity and efficacy of [EU] law."[144]

Through the interpretation of autonomy and supremacy the Court secures the unquestionable security of the position of the EU's legal order and with that, itself demonstrated in those cases in which the ECJ is asked to review the Treaty on the basis of the Rule of Law and so the Union acts in line with the Rule of Law, as the Treaty states that the Union acts consistent with the Rule of Law.[145] The ECJ does not demonstrate a wish to adhere to the values set out by Article 2 TEU and so the Rule of Law in these situations of dialogue has been derogated in favor of the gods of supremacy, autonomy, and consistency not the Rule of Law.[146]

It could be said that law and its application via the implementation of the rule of law lead to society's trust. Georg Simmel[147] defined trust as "the prediction of future behavior which is strong enough to allow for practical action." It is worth noting that in the European legal space, institutions are not assimilated within a firmly hierarchical system but the notions of trust and rule of law are interconnected. There is a need to address the crisis of the European rule of law as one of distrust of and between public institutions which are founded upon a non-implementation of the real rule of law but a rule of law merely accommodating the political interests of certain elites.[148]

Which is the content of the rule of law? Does the crisis of the European rule of law mean distrust of and between public institutions? There is a difference between the application of the rule of law and the development of the content of the rule of law.

---

[143] JHH Weiler, 'Bread and Circus: The State of the European Union' (1998) 4 CJEL 223.

[144] Case 11/70 Internationale Handelsgesellschaft. J Komárek, 'Federal Elements in the Community Judicial System' (2005) 42 CMLRev 9.

[145] Case C-50/00 P Unión de Pequeños Agricultores EU:C:2002:462 [2002] ECR I6677 para. 38ff.

[146] T Tridimas and N Xanthoulis, 'A Legal Analysis of the Gauweiler Case' (2016) 23 MJ 17. A Pliakos and G Anagnostaras, 'Saving Face? The German Federal Constitutional Court Decides Gauweiler' (2017) 18 German LJ. A Steinbach, 'All's Well That Ends Well? Crisis Policy after the German Constitutional Court's Ruling in Gauweiler' (2017) 24 MJ 140.

[147] G. Simmel, Untersuchungen über die Formen der Vergesellschaftung (Suhrkamp 1992 (first edition, Duncker & Humblot 1908)) p. 389, 393 et seq.

[148] M. Ruffert, 'All we need is Trust: Conditions are not a Means of Punishment', Verfassungsblog, 10 March 2017, www.verfassungsblog.de/all-we-need-is-trust-conditions-are-not-a-means-ofpunishment/

Concerning the European rule of law crisis Frank Schorkopf[149] argues that "[t]he politically accepted failure to implement Union law is, as the cases of the Schengen Area, the 'Common European Asylum System,' and the further flexibilization of the Stability and Growth Pact show, currently a precondition for European integration to succeed." It is worth noting that there are and there have always been occasions where the Union and Member States accepted illegal behavior, which highlights the non-rightful applicability of the rule of law. Hence, it could be said that leniency has contributed to integration for the reason that it evades dangerous confrontations but this is done on the purpose for the emergence of a new rule of law for the workability of the EU.

First of all, it has to be considered that enforcing a norm should always be subject to general rules of pragmatism and so in principle individual actions should not damage the system.[150] Concerning breaches of the law, Union law has generated such expectations and trust, which is now exposed.[151] Subsequently trust within the European legal space and the European rule of law are closely correlated and in addition new legal mechanisms have been developed to boost trust in European policies that influence vital rights or involve major financial transfers. Moreover, the principle of trust is of decisive importance to the European legal space beyond such policies too by maintaining and justifying legal presumptions that make all legal operations much easier and so it legitimates decision-making in the EU. The European rule of law confirms Europe's self-understanding as a union of liberal democracies and so the rule of law enshrined in Article 2 TEU governs not only the constitutional profile of the EU, but also of its Member States.

The principle of trust as formulated by the CJEU has its basis on Article 49, 7, and 2 TEU and so this trust-based understanding of the European rule of law links up with all rule of law traditions which means that the various terms and their equivalents État de droit, κράτος δικαίου, Rechtsstaatlichkeit, rule of law, stato di diritto by no means represent a concept that is identical throughout the European legal space.

Is there a crisis on EU rule of law? It is argued that not every violation of European law disturbs its function in stabilizing expectations; therefore, jeopardizing trust in the legal order and so somewhat, the legal handling of breaches of the law normally backs trust in the legal order for the reason that it enhances normative expectations. In other words, a crisis of the rule of law entails phenomena of illegality which means trust in the legal order is weakened only when violations become the normal state of affairs or have a high degree of symbolic value. Thus, the

[149] F. Schorkopf, 'Wertesicherung in der Europäischen Union. Prävention, Quarantäne und Aufsicht als Bausteine eines Rechts der Verfassungskrise?', 51 Europarecht (2016) p. 147 at p. 156.

[150] D. Liebs, 'Das Rechtssprichwort Fiat iustitia et pereat mundus', 70 Juristenzeitung 2015, p. 138.

[151] C. Joerges, 'Recht und Politik in der Krise Europas. Die Wirkgeschichte einer verunglückten Konfiguration', 66 Merkur (2012) p. 1013 at p. 1019 et seq. 103 In the words of Christine Lagarde as French finance minister, 'France's Lagarde: EU rescues 'violated' rules: report', Reuters, 18 December 2010, https://www.reuters.com/article/us-france-lagarde/frances-lagarde-eu-rescuesviolated-rules-report-idUSTRE6BH0V020101218

formation of the content of law is molded due to trust concerning the enclosed rationales of the regulated subject and so there is trust in the function of the legal systems, which imposes obedience. To that extent, no obedience means lack of trust in the content of law demanding an alteration of the content of the law which will be followed due to the rule of law.

A crisis of the rule of law materializes if a noteworthy number of social actors in vital fields stop relying on public institutions to back up their normative expectations and so when this threshold has been achieved, a legal system no longer exercises its central function appropriately and breeds distrust. To that extent, persons and institutions confronted with such a deficit of the rule of law adjust their expectations instead of insisting on expectations being fulfilled which means that they stop concerning obeying the law as normal in society in the legal area in question and trusting the legal order and so this constitutes the epitome of a crisis of the rule of law.

Consequently, the perceived crisis of the European rule of law fuels two considerations in particular: one centerd on better means of control and one about an alternative path for Europe. Moreover, the established path of European rule of law is confronted with commanding calls for discontinuance today, even for a hard breakup and so Brexit is a significant realization of that power. Moreover, a rupture exhibits itself in different variants such as nationalist retreat, nation state-centered multilateralism.[152] Besides, the establishment of the USA of Europe will overtake any effort concerning crisis of the rule of law. Article 48 TEU necessitates treaty changes to be unanimous which means that such a leap has to be ratified by all countries in order to avoid a forthcoming collapse, not in a very long time. A decisive step like that made democratically and not after a needed revolution in order to avoid a dreadful collapse causing major damages means the existing European rule of law would be altered generating trust. On the other hand, the revolutionary establishment of a federal European state or republic in which European institutions have instruments of power and legitimation similar to those of states, the existing European rule of law would undoubtedly collapse, a new polity would have to tread "anew the arduous" path of building trust.[153]

It is worth mentioning that Habermas[154] supports a European constitution "as a means of consolidating the achievements of post-war social democracy and providing European level institutions with a normative foundation without the need to

[152] For 5 alternatives along and within this path see the relevant European Commission white paper: COM(2017) 2025 final, White paper on the future of Europe. Reflections and scenarios for the EU27 by 2025 (2017).

[153] G. Verhofstadt, Europe's Last Chance (Basic Books 2017). S. Goulard and M. Monti, La democrazia in Europa: guardare lontano (Rizzoli 2012).

[154] Charles Turner, Jürgen Habermas European or German? European Journal of Political Theory © SAGE Publications Ltd., London, Thousand Oaks and New Delhi issn 1474–8851, 3(3) 293–314.

appeal to the idea of Europe as a 'community of fate.'" Moreover, Justine Lacroix[155] argues that "the political will to buttress Europe's political union with a set of common values may not guarantee the unity of the European Union and could undermine the unique normative potential of a political entity supposed to address the problem of distinct national identities." European identity has to be the core of their present and historical existence and not to generate something totally new and not embrace the historical existence of Europeans. On the other hand, Zekos[156] has presented the common elements of Europeans aiding the development of the USA of Europe.

It is argued that the European legal space is the global territory with the most dynamic rule of law which means that it is the only large-scale space with "Kantian peace" and operative legal protection generating substantial trust in and between public institutions.[157] Moreover, the European legal space, founded on the rule of law and an idea of unity, assures generating trust than the alternative of disruption, in whatever variant. In other words, taking into account that union based on the rule of law, trust theory confirms the significance of judicial review, validates the prudent expansion of new review mechanisms, and advocates patience in dealing with challenges. It has to be considered that any rule of law-based system denotes the control of the applicable law through dialogical legal deliberations which means that advancing such dialogue generates an effective systemic law being a required element of the rule of law. Although judicial review is now an acknowledged part of various legal systems, the depth of the scrutiny and the openness of the system diverges extensively to concur with cultural and legal traditions.

It has to be taken into consideration that the crisis of the rule of law in the European legal space is real, but also a precious matter for appreciating the value of what has been achieved and so improving its further development. Thus, the institutions of the European legal space have kept significant breaches of the law within limits.[158] The rule of law is a classic example of a principally questioned perception and so the definition in the EU,[159] stimulated by the Venice

---

[155] Justine Lacroix, Does Europe Need Common Values? Habermas vs Habermas, European Journal of Political Theory © SAGE Publications Ltd., Los Angeles, London, New Delhi, Singapore and Washington DC issn 1474–8851, 8(2) 141–156 p142.

[156] G Zekos, THE UNITED STATES OF EUROPE The Global Player, 2019 Nova Science Publications New York USA. www.novapublishers.com

[157] World Bank data, info.worldbank.org/governance/wgi/pdf/rl.pdf, and the data compiled and presented by the World Justice Programme, data.worldjusticeproject.org

[158] P. Sonnevend, 'Preserving the Acquis of Transformative Constitutionalism in Times of Constitutional Crisis: Lessons from the Hungarian Case', in A. von Bogdandy, E. Ferrer Mac-Gregor, M. Morales Antoniazzi and F. Piovesan (eds.), Transformative Constitutionalism in Latin America (Oxford UP 2017) p. 123, 144 et seq.: 'The example of Hungary shows that outsourcing parts of the constitutional functions to international or supranational organizations in peaceful years may help survive the years of crisis. (. . .) European institutions contributed to creating a situation where self-healing through domestic processes is still possible.'

[159] Commission, 'A New EU Framework to Strengthen the Rule of Law' COM (2014) 158.

Commission's guidelines[160] offers a firm example of the current state of the definitional debate as internalized by the EU institutions. It is argued that the rule of law is not democracy[161] or the protection of human rights, each of them certainly boasting its own sound claim to existence as a notion independent from the rule of law which means that "it is not mere legality, which is adherence to the law on the books, read the whims of the sovereign."[162]

It is argued that there is no need to be converted into the rule of law just in order to think that good should prevail[163] but on the other hand always societies follow their rule of law imposed by the entity in charge of managing the affairs of the particular society because no society can exist without obeying a rule of law regardless of its founding content. Moreover, it is worth noting that once the Rule of Law and legality are separated, the basic meaning of the rule of law comes down to the idea of the subordination of the law to another kind of law, which is not up to the sovereign to alter at will which means that such rule of law is dialogical in essence and so it takes for granted and constantly relies upon a continual "taming of law" with law as the cornerstone for the functionality of a society implemented by the utilization of the rule of law.[164] To that extent, authority should itself be bound by clear legal norms which are outside of its control being the crucial characteristic of post-war constitutionalism.[165]

It has to be considered that the rule of law in the EU really amounts to compliance with own law being an established apprehending of legality.[166] EU Institutions' own accounts of what is means by the rule of law beyond the tautology of "being bound by law" stage a most diverse account, which acquired a manifestation in EU's

[160]Venice Commission Document CDL-AD(2016)007-e 'Rule of Law Checklist' (adopted in 106th Plenary Session, Venice, 11–12 March 2016), as well as in the earlier version thereof: Venice Commission Document CDL-AD(2011)003rev-e 'Report on the Rule of Law' (adopted in 86th Plenary Session, Venice, 25–26 March 2011).

[161]TT Koncewicz, 'Of Institutions, Democracy, Constitutional Self-Defence and the Rule of Law' (2016) 53 CMLRev 1753. G Hadfield and B Weingast, 'Microfoundations of the Rule of Law' (2014) 17 Annual Review of Political Science. 21; L Pech, 'The Rule of Law as a Constitutional Principle of the European Union.' (NYU School of Law 2009) No. 04/09.

[162]Dimitry Kochenov and Matthijs van Wolferen The dialogical Rule of Law and the breakdown of dialogue in the EU. EUI Working Paper LAW 2018/01, W Schröder, Strengthening the Rule of Law in Europe: From a Common Concept to Mechanisms of Implementation (Hart 2016); L Morlino and G Palombella (eds), Rule of Law and Democracy: Inquiries Into Internal and External Issues (Brill 2010); G Palombella and N Walker (eds), Relocating the Rule of Law (Hart 2009).

[163]J Raz, 'The Rule of Law and Its Virtue', The Authority of Law: Essays on Law and Morality (OUP 1979).

[164]G Palombella, 'The Rule of Law and Its Core' in G Palombella and N Walker (eds), Relocating the Rule of Law (Hart 2009) '[it] amounts to preventing one dominant source of law and its unconstrained whim, from absorbing all the available normativity.'

[165]W Sadurski, Constitutionalism and the Enlargement of Europe (OUP 2012).

[166]Lord Mackenzie-Stuart, The European Communities and the Rule of Law (Stevens and Sons1977). Case 294/83 Partie Ecologiste 'Les Verts' v. Parliament EU:C:1986:166 [1986] ECR 1339, Opinion 1/91 EEA Agreement EU:C:1991:490 [1991] ECR 6097 M Fernández Esteban, The Rule of Law in the European Constitution (Kluwer Law International 1999).

external action.[167] It is argued that legality is not enough to make certain that the EU performs like a true rule of law-based constitutional system but the rule of law has to be based upon a legal order incorporating additional restraints through law and restraints that are not merely democratic or political.[168] Moreover, the EU has its internal procedures to make certain that legality be observed. There is a need to differentiate between the constraints linked to the policing of the competences border and the rule of law constraints within the EU's domain of competences.[169] To that extent, the EU turns its own rhetorical weakness into a tool for escaping the Rule of Law checks on its system of formal legality and so it is impossible to enforce the demand of trust when the substance of values is not enforced in any way in the Member States.[170]

It is worth noting that the virtually complete depoliticization of the law has been one of the crucial criticisms of the EU legal order.[171] Moreover, it has to be taken into account that at the international level, the EU is the only legal system in Europe, which objects to any outside scrutiny.[172] Moreover, outside scrutiny "from below," has remained only a threat and the ECJ has expressly prohibited[173] outside scrutiny from above, all in the name of "autonomy" which means that, in the EU's case, autonomy means that the EU allows no constraints on its ability to rule. Furthermore, the Grand Chamber[174] indicates that: "[W]hen implementing EU law, the Member States may, under EU law, be required to presume that fundamental rights have been observed by the other Member States, so that [. . .] they may not check whether that other Member State has actually, [...], observed the fundamental rights guaranteed by the EU."

Also, where the rule of law is not enforced in the Member States of the EU by means of the supranational legal order the Member States themselves are not free to consider each others' deficiencies in the arena of values, predominantly the rule of law. Additionally, the Court's dependence on the argument of "autonomy" makes it

[167] L Pech, 'Promoting the Rule of Law Abroad' in F Amtenbrink and D Kochenov (eds), The European Union's Shaping of the International Legal Order (2013).

[168] M Krygier, 'Tempering Power: Realist-Idealism, Constitutionalism, and the Rule of Law' in M Adams, A Meuwese and EMH Hirsch Ballin (eds), Constitutionalism and the Rule of Law (CUP 2017). M Krygier, 'The Rule of Law. An Abuser's Guide' in A Sajó (ed), Abuse: the dark side of fundamental rights (Eleven 2006).

[169] G Palombella, 'Law's Ideals and Law's Global Connections. Some Concluding Notes' (2014) Rivista di Filosofia del Diritto 123, 124.

[170] D Halberstam, 'It's the Autonomy, Stupid: A Modest Defence of Opinion 2/13 on EU Accession to the ECHR, and the Way Forward' (2015) 16 German LJ 105.

[171] J Přibáň, 'The Evolving Idea of Political Justice in the EU' in D Kochenov, G de Búrca and A Williams (eds), Europe's Justice Deficit? (Hart 2015).

[172] FC Mayer, 'Multilevel Constitutional Jurisdiction' in A Bogdandy and J Bast (eds), Principles of European Constitutional Law (second edn, Beck/Hart 2011) 410–420.

[173] Opinion 2/94 (ECHR Accession I) EU:C:1996:140 [1996] ECR I-1759; Opinion 2/13 (ECHR Accession II) EU:C:2014:2454.

[174] Opinion 2/13 (ECHR Accession II) EU:C:2014:2454, para. 192. D Kochenov, 'EU Law without the Rule of Law' (2015) 34 YEL 74.

clear that what we are dealing with is a persistent claim to power, unchecked externally and so the ECJ merely deploys "autonomy" as a "flimsy pretext" to make certain that its own jurisdiction is unimpeded.[175]

Besides, given the reliance of the Court on the autonomy and inviolability of the Union's primary law, the Court will enforce, certainly sometimes going as much as to have a far-reaching effect on the autonomy of the Member State's legal systems,[176] norms and rules with which it itself does not comply. Although the Court's own case law concerning standing rights for public interest litigants is extremely restrictive, it has forced Member States to comply with the standard set out in the Aarhus Convention, as it is now an integral part of EU law. Furthermore, the Union cannot be in violation of the rule of law, as it has been laid down in the Treaty that it adheres to the rule of law. Additionally, as the international agreement has become an integral part of the Union's legal order, any outside scrutiny of this statement through compliance mechanisms or tribunals will not generate an outcome. Consequently, pronouncements like the recent decision by the Aarhus Convention Compliance Committee, will engender no result whatsoever in the EU legal order.[177]

The constitutional values and traditions have always been a part of the values of the European Union either by way of general principles, which the ECJ finds when it needs a remedy, or through explicit mention in the Treaties. Consequently, the Court found fundamental rights to be a part of the general principles of Community law as they were "inspired" by the constitutional traditions of the Member States[178] but the constitutional traditions of the Member States may vary, just as the membership of the Union does. Of course, all rules and mechanisms producing law are part of the content of the rule of law.

6.7 The Rule of Law in EU

The European Union is built on a set of common and foundational principles of Democracy, the Rule of Law and Fundamental Rights, as preserved in Article 2 of the Treaty of the European Union. The Rule of Law is one of the common values

---

[175] P Eeckhout, 'Opinion 2/13 on EU Accession to the ECHR and Judicial Dialogue: Autonomy or Autarky' (2015) 38 Fordham Int'l LJ 955.

[176] J Reichel, 'Judicial Control in a Globalised Legal Order – A One Way Track?' (2010) 3 REALaw 69; and H Roer-Eide and M Eliantonio, 'Meaning of Regulatory Act Explained' (2013) 14 German LJ 1851.

[177] A Tancredi, 'Enforcing WTO Law' in A Jakab and D Kochenov (eds.), The Enforcement of EU Law and Values (OUP 2017). N Lavranos, 'Concurrence of Jurisdiction between the ECJ and Other International Courts and Tribunals' (2005) 14 ELRev. 213.

[178] Case 8/55 Fédération Charbonnière de Belgique v High Authority EU:C:1956:11, [1956] ECR 291Case 26/69 Stauder EU:C:1969:57 [1969] ECR 419 para 7. Case 11/70 Internationale Handelsgesellschaft EU:C:1970:114 [1970] ECR 1125. para 4.60. T Tridimas, The General Principles of EU Law (OUP 2006).

upon which the European Union is founded and that are preserved in Article 2 TEU such as the values of respect for human dignity, freedom, democracy, equality, the rule of law, and respect for human rights and so these foundational values encompass all Member States, which have to commit themselves in following and upholding them as a condition to adhere to in order to link up with the European Union, as entailed and warranted by the Treaties.[179] Moreover, the Rule of Law's promotion and protection is vital for the proper performing of the whole European system. Influencing the Internal Market, the EU external policy or the cooperation in the area of Justice and Home Affairs, making certain that national judges, who are also EU judges, secure the application of EU Law and cooperate with the Court of Justice of the EU (hereinafter CJEU) in the setting of preliminary ruling procedures. Hence, the Rule of Law is the basis of the EU system, making certain that all public powers act within the restrictions founded by the law, consistent with the values of Democracy and Fundamental Rights, and under the control of independent and impartial courts.[180] Moreover, the Rule of Law is likewise crucial for the Council of Europe as a universal validity concept.

Regardless, the Treaties governing the EU and the CoE, along with provisions at the national level, do not clearly define it raising doubts on the practicality of addressing the Rule of Law. Nevertheless, the case-law of the European Court of Human Rights and the European Court of Justice, along with the work of the well-respected Venice Commission of the Council of Europe by offering a broad list of Rule of Law standards.

According to the Venice Commission as well as of the EU Commission,[181] the principles identifying the rule of law are: "1) Legality (supremacy of the law), including a transparent, accountable and democratic process for enacting law; 2) Legal certainty; 3) Prohibition of arbitrariness; 4) Access to justice before independent and impartial courts, including judicial review of administrative acts; 5) Respect for human rights; 6) Nondiscrimination and equality before the law."[182] It could be said that the Rule of Law has been established as a central dogma of any democratic society regulating the exercise of public powers, warranting that they act within the confines established by the law, consistent with the values of Democracy and Fundamental Rights, and under the control of independent and impartial courts.

Concerning the Rule of Law within the European Union, the European Commission endorsed an initiative generating an objective and impartial evaluation

[179] Article 49(1) TEU "Any European State which respects the values referred to in Article 2 and is committed to promoting them may apply to become a member of the Union."

[180] Communication from the Commission to the European Parliament and the Council, A new EU Framework to strengthen the Rule of Law, COM (2014) 158, 11 March 2014.

[181] Laurent Pech, "Rule of law as guiding principle of the European Union's external action" (2012), Asser Institute Centre for the Law of EU External Relations Working Papers, p. 9.

[182] The General Court explicitly refers to them in the Judgement of 15 September 2016, Case T-340/14, Andriy Klyuyev v. Council of the European Union and the European Commission, ECLI:EU:T:2016:496, para. 88. Communication from the Commission to the European Parliament and the Council, A new EU Framework to strengthen the Rule of Law, COM (2014) 158, 11 March 2014.

mechanism to validate the application of the European Union's values by all the Member States permitting EU citizens to call on the Commission to supply the European Union with general legislation and to substantiate the practical application of national provisions relating to the Rule of Law.[183] In line, the EU Law should include the Rule of Law to the very heart of the daily running of the Union.

It is essential to present here the historical developments of the rule of law. In fact, it is argued that jurists are social transformation agents and so law is mainly about "social transformation."[184] Moreover, legal instrumentalism, which sees in law a plain means to an end, traces back to Hobbes as far as it substitutes the understanding of "law as will" for that of "law as artificial reason."

Do legislators by constituent power or the courts have wilful power to "create" law? The fundamental idea is that law, as a human "artefact," can only be appreciated as the product of some political will, whatever this will is and irrespective of its reasonableness, on some external or common grounds but not juridical. The law's rationality has either to be common to all human beings or to be external to law itself. For Hayek,[185] law undoubtedly ought not to be some instrument serving a political will and he supported the judge-made law showing the way to the Posnerian judge, who is more faithful to his or her own situational insight than to existing legislative or jurisprudential, including precedent-based, legal norms.[186] It is worth noting that the existence of a legal system is rejected by Fuller[187] which means that, for him, the level of existence of a legal qua legal system is a function of the level of its adherence to the rule of law and so there is no split-up of the rule of law from the "concept" of law. It is supported that there is a moral obligation of fidelity to parts of law that are not complete failures. On the other hand, for Raz as for Hart, there is no necessary, but only a conditional connection between law and morals, so that any moral value the rule of law may have can only be derivative.

As discussed above, for Raz, minimum compliance to the rule of law is a proviso of existence of a legal system and the rule of law is posited into the form of legal rules enforceable by the courts. In addition, it is argued that among "the many virtues a legal system should possess"[188] to a greater or lesser scale, the rule of law is the inherent or particular virtue or excellence of the law. To that extent, even if predictability it contributes to individual freedom, though observance of it "is

[183] European Commission, Communication from the Commission to the European Parliament, the European Council and the Council, Further strengthening the Rule of Law within the Union State of play and possible next steps, 3 April 2019, COM(2019) 163. https://ec.europa.eu/info/policies/justice-and-fundamental-rights/effective-justice/rule-law/rule-law-framework_en

[184] Maxime St-Hilaire and Joanna Baron, Introductory Essay: The Rule of Law as the Rule of Artificial Reason, Supreme Court Law Review (2019) 92 S.C.L.R. (2d).

[185] Friedrich A. Hayek, The Road to Serfdom (Chicago: Chicago University Press, 1944).

[186] Richard Posner, Overcoming Law (Cambridge, MA: Harvard University Press, 1995).

[187] Lon L. Fuller, The Morality of Law (1964) (New Haven, CT: Yale University Press, rev. ed. 1969), at 122, 198–200.

[188] Joseph Raz, "The Rule of Law and its Virtue" (1977) in The Authority of Law (Oxford: Oxford University Press, 2009) 210, at 219.

necessary to respect human dignity," and though "it is a necessary condition for the law to be serving directly any good purpose at all," still the rule of law would not be a moral good or virtue as such. Moreover, Raz supports that law has no independent moral value, for it is a device which means that there is no separate moral obligation to obey the law and so "there can be human societies which are not governed by law at all."[189] In short, Raz argues that the de facto authority of law presupposes both a claim to legitimate authority and acceptance of this claim by an adequate number of legal subjects which means that law's power is normative authority over others, which arises from their acceptance of it as the lawful power to issue orders.[190]

Furthermore, Raz[191] focuses on the rule of law's objective to circumvent arbitrary government, and on its relation to the central functions of government which means that the rule of law entails that government action will reveal an intention to protect and improve the interests of the governed and so it is a needed condition for the law's aptitude to meet other moral demands, and it enables coordination and cooperation internally and globally. Lately, Raz underlined that the "doctrine of the rule of law and its main implications should be part of the public culture, embedded in education and public discourse, and taken as obvious and vital by all."[192] It is worth mentioning here that Tamanaha[193] recaps that "[t]he legal profession . . . is located at the crux of the rule of law. . . . [T]he rule of law could not conceivably function without this group committed to the values of legality. This position, however, also renders the legal profession, judges in particular, uniquely situated to undermine the rule of law."

It has to be taken into account that the rule of law imposes formal requirements on the legal system and so laws must be general and they must be applied consistent with their terms.[194] Moreover, it is specified that the rule of law has a procedural component, which necessitates the legal system to offer persons chances to make their case as to how the law ought to apply to them to an independent judge whenever their rights are in danger of being harmed. In addition, even though the rule of law is an ideal that existing legal systems are bound to realize imperfectly, the legal systems of Canada and other countries devoted to this principle do comprehend it.[195] Concerning the meaning of the Rule of Law, the Supreme Court[196] states that "The rule of law must mean at least two things. First, that the law is supreme over

---

[189] Joseph Raz, "The Institutional Nature of Law" in The Authority of Law (Oxford: Oxford University Press, 2009) 103, at 120.

[190] Joseph Raz, "Legitimate Authority" in The Authority of Law (Oxford: Oxford University Press, 2009) 3.

[191] Joseph Raz, "The Law's Own Virtue" (2019) 39 Oxford J. Legal Stud. 1.

[192] Joseph Raz, "The Law's Own Virtue" (2019) 39 Oxford J. Legal Stud. 1, at 8.

[193] Brian Z. Tamanaha, On the Rule of Law: History, Politics, Theory (New York; Cambridge: Cambridge University Press, 2004), at 59.

[194] Lon L. Fuller, The Morality of Law, revised ed. (New Haven: Yale University Press, 1969).

[195] Joseph Raz, "The Rule of Law and Its Virtue" in The Authority of Law: Essays on Law and Morality (Oxford: Oxford University Press, 1979) 211, at 214–18.

[196] Manitoba Language Rights [1985] S.C.J. No. 36, [1985] 1 S.C.R. 721 (S.C.C.) at para. 59.

officials of the government as well as private individuals, and thereby preclusive of the influence of arbitrary power." Thus, it could be argued that the rule of law compels the formation and preservation of an actual order of positive laws, which upholds and embodies the more general principle of "normative order." In other words, taking into account the rule of law principle means that all exercises of public authority have to find their source in law.[197] To that extent, in Canadian constitutional law, these ideas are embodied in Section 52 of the Constitution Act, 1982,[198] whose three subsections correspondingly stipulate that "[t]he Constitution of Canada is the supreme law of Canada"; help ascertain (albeit very imperfectly, due to open-ended wording) the law of the Constitution; and make certain that "[a]mendments to the Constitution of Canada shall be made only in accordance with" the procedures it encompasses.

It is worth noting that the Rule of Law triumphs in New Zealand[199] and so while there are ongoing efforts to persuade New Zealanders[200] to entrench their constitution, they have limited support outside academia for the reason that the current arrangements are largely satisfactory, which means that rightful rules are endorsed making the application of the rule of law very productive.

It has to be taken into consideration that the Rule of Law compels certain limits on the form of the rules that form this framework such as Fuller's list of Rule of Law requirements.[201] Moreover, it is argued[202] that the rules must be public; they must be prospective;[203] they must be stable; and there must be "congruence between the rules as announced and their actual administration." In addition, for Waldron[204] the Rule of Law embraces an imperative procedural component. Moreover, Léonid Sirota[205] says that "Before I begin, I need to make clear that one position to which I do not object (here) is the view, associated most notably with Jeremy Waldron that a constitution ought to be a set of political rather than legal commitments ... It is a trite observation that the Rule of Law is a complex ideal, and a contested one. There

[197] Dunsmuir v. New Brunswick, [2008] S.C.J. No. 9, [2008] 1 S.C.R. 190, at para. 28 (S.C.C.).

[198] Schedule B to the Canada Act 1982 (U.K.), 1982, c. 11.

[199] World Justice Project, "Rule of Law Index: 2017–2018."

[200] Geoffrey Palmer & Andrew Butler, Towards Democratic Renewal (Wellington: Victoria University Press, 2018).

[201] Lon L. Fuller, The Morality of Law, revised ed. (New Haven: Yale University Press, 1969).

[202] Id., at 39.

[203] Joseph Raz, "The Rule of Law and Its Virtue" in The Authority of Law: Essays on Law and Morality (Oxford: Oxford University Press, 1979) 211, at 214 (arguing that "[a]ll laws should be prospective [and] open", as well as "relatively stable") and 215 (arguing that "[t]he making of ... particular legal orders ... should be guided by open, stable, clear, and general rules").

[204] Jeremy Waldron, "The Rule of Law and the Importance of Procedure" in James E. Fleming, ed., Nomos, vol. 50: Getting to the Rule of Law (New York, NYU Press, 2011) 3.

[205] Léonid Sirota, The Rule of Law All the Way Up, Supreme Court Law Review (2019) 92 S.C.L. R. (2d) p 80, 81. Jeremy Waldron, "The Core of the Case against Judicial Review" (2006) 115 Yale L.J. 1346.

are about as many understandings of the Rule of Law as there are scholars and judges trying to work out its nature, purpose and requirements."

Zekos considers that the implication of identifying specific matters concerning the content of the rule of law applicable in certain cases departs from the real meaning of the rule of law that is to stress the need to follow the established legal rules regulating the matters of a society and not the demands of any elite contemporarily on power. Thus, the essence of the rule of law has not to be blurred with the technicalities of the formation of law and particular rules implementing the concept of law. It could be said that the rule of law denotes the utilization of law in solving disputes and so it is obvious that all the spheres of law are the basis of the rule of law.

Nowadays, the Rule of Law is illustrated as an ideal but its requirements cannot be realized to perfection, and it might in some cases even be undesirable, as for instance with legal stability due to the fact that law should be able to alter, albeit not thoughtlessly or frequently. Nonetheless, both Fuller and Waldron stipulate that a legal system must fulfil the requirements of the Rule of Law to at least some minimal degree.[206] In conclusion, the rations of the Rule of Law, whether formal or procedural, are formulated as applying to the legal system as a whole. However, they are applicable to specific areas of the law, and even individual legal regimes, just as unquestionably as they are to the law of jurisdiction generally.

As discussed earlier, Article 7(1) has been unprecedently deployed to halt any illiberal and" anti-EU values" reforms and the recent rulings of the European Court of Justice have established that the principle of effective judicial protection preserved in Article 19(1) TEU must be interpreted as authorizing it to review the national legislation regarding the independence of national judicial system providing those judges may be possibly called upon to interpret or apply EU Law.

It is worth noting that although the European Union acknowledges a commitment to liberal democracy, in recent years it has permitted some member governments to backslide toward competitive authoritarianism[207] and so it seems that the EU has become trapped in an "authoritarian equilibrium" highlighted by three issues such as firstly the EU's half-baked system of party politics and its entrenched hesitancy to interfere in the national politics of its member states help guard national autocrats from EU intervention, secondly, there is funding and investment from the EU helping to maintain these regimes and thirdly the free movement of persons in the EU assists the exit of dissatisfied citizens, which drains the opposition and engenders remittances in that way assisting these regimes survive. In other words, it seems that whereas more fully developed democratic federations have the competence to ultimately steer autocratic member states back toward democracy, the EU has stuck in an "autocracy trap" and so the emergence of the united states of Europe,

---

[206] Lon L. Fuller, The Morality of Law, revised ed. (New Haven: Yale University Press, 1969), at 41 (speaking of a "utopia, in which all eight of the principles of legality are realized to perfection" as not being "a useful target in guiding the impulse toward legality").

[207] Kelemen, R.D. (2017) Europe's Other Democratic Deficit: National Authoritarianism in Europe's Democratic Union. Government and Opposition 52(2):211–238.

as Zekos[208] has illustrated, is the road towards the global leadership. It has to be taken into consideration that the survival of authoritarian enclaves within large federal-type polities is common, and enlightens both the political dynamics that back their survival and the circumstances under which they are most probable to be overthrown and so it seems to exist and survive a "politically stable equilibrium" in which the EU paradoxically supports the survival of authoritarian governments.[209] To that extent, Kelemen[210] indicates that "Europe's authoritarian equilibrium rests on three pillars: partial politicization, money, and migration. First, even as the EU becomes more politicized, it's underdeveloped system of party politics and its engrained reluctance to interfere in the political affairs of its sovereign member states help shield national autocrats from EU intervention. The EU has politicized enough that it generates incentives to protect state-level autocrats, but not enough that it can generate compensating pressures on EU leaders to dislodge such autocrats." Moreover, Scheppele[211] insists that given that a regime upholds an amalgam such as a "competitive authoritarian" restrains itself to the nonviolent techniques of autocratic legalism by purging courts, buying newspapers, and engineering elections with new rules so that they remain seemingly free but categorically unfair, then it can live on securely within the EU.[212]

Is there a relationship between democracy and the rule of law? It seems that even though some structural conflicts exist, one cannot really manage without the other. Moreover, the rule of law, and mainly certain political fundamental rights are preconditions for a democratic course. The rule of law is a result of democratic rotation but the rule of law on its own is unable to protect democracy and so well-designed constitutional provisions are helpful in preventing erosion in combination with social and political elements.

Have democracy and the rule of law been declining in many states of the world, embracing several Member States of the European Union? It is argued that lately democracy and the rule of law have been declining in many states of the world, involving several Member States of the European Union.[213] Moreover, it is worth

---

[208] G Zekos, The United States of Europe The Global Player, 2019 Nova Science Publications New York USA. www.novapublishers.com G Zekos, The United States of Europe in place of the European Union, 2017 Nova Science Publications New York USA. www.novapublishers.com

[209] Kelemen, 2017, Europe's Authoritarian Equilibrium. Foreign Affairs 22 December, https://www.foreignaffairs.com/articles/hungary/2017-12-22/europes-authoritarianequilibrium Kelemen, 2018, 'The Rot on Europe's Right', Euronews, 12 November, https://www.euronews.com/2018/11/12/the-rot-on-europe-s-right-viewKelemen, 2019, 'This is how Europe got its new President', 17 July. Washington Post, https://www.washingtonpost.com/politics/2019/07/17/this-is-how-europegot-its-new-president-it-wasnt-pretty-process/

[210] R. Daniel Kelemen, The European Union's Authoritarian Equilibrium https://ssrn.com/abstract=3450716 p3.

[211] Scheppele, K. (2018) Autocratic Legalism. University of Chicago Law Review 85(2):545–583.

[212] Scheppele, K. (2019) Europe's Largest Party Suspends Its Resident Autocrat—for Now, Foreign Affairs 28 March, https://www.foreignaffairs.com/articles/hungary/2019-03-28/europes-largest-party-suspends-its-resident-autocrat-now

[213] Graber/Levinson/Tushnet (ed), Constitutional Democracy in Crisis? (2018).

noting that several economic, political, and social factors destabilize a democracy[214] and so it is difficult for poor nations with a low GDP to develop a stable democracy. In addition, other risk elements endure such as weak statehood, being geographically cut off from the advanced world, having a closed economy, and experiencing pervasive corruption.[215] Nonetheless, risks are not restricted to economic factors because political and social factors, such as ethnic divides and tensions, a weak civil society, and extreme political preferences of political actors are expected to be dangerous.[216] Besides, a well-functioning democracy characterized by horizontal accountability, successful participation, and valuable political competition gives less motivation for behavior that is detrimental for democracy, and subsequently makes destruction less expected which means that erosion is less probable in liberal democracies than in hybrid regimes.[217]

It is worth mentioning that a great quantity of natural resources such as, e.g., oil revenues add to the strengthening of autocratic regimes and so the paribus ceteris low economic performance of the autocracy is concealed by oil revenues.[218] In addition, the various EU funds play a similar role in the new EU Member States. Thus, absence of foreign pressure to respect democratic and rule of law standards is threatening and so after a nation has joined the EU, there are hardly any means to exert pressure and to require or impose democratic or rule of law standards.[219] On the other hand, the rule of law has a positive effect on economic growth.[220]

International and supranational legal prerequisites concerning the rule of law and democracy such as a procedure in the meaning of Article 7 TEU have a restricted

[214] Lust/Waldner, Unwelcome Change. Understanding, Evaluating, and Extending Theories of Democratic Backsliding, USAID 2015, Juni 2015, 21 ff; Hadenius/Teorell, Cultural and Economic Prerequisites of Democracy. Reassessing Recent Evidence, Studies in Comparative International Development 4 (2005) 87.

[215] Slater et al., Economic Origins of Democratic Breakdown? The Redistributive Model and the Postcolonial State, Perspectives on Politics 2014, 353. Rodrik, Populism and the economics of globalization, Journal of International Business Policy 2018, 12. Knott, Perpetually „partly free". Lessons from post-soviet hybrid regimes backsliding in Central and Eastern Europe, East European Politics 2018, 355.

[216] Bernhard et al., Institutional Subsystems and the Survival of Democracy. Do Political and Civil Society Matter? V-Dem Institute Working Paper 2015:4, April 2015; Cornell et al., Civil Society, Party Institutionalization, and Democratic Breakdown in the Interwar Period, V-Dem Institute Working Paper 2016:24, February 2016. Inglehart/Welzel, Changing Mass Priorities, The Link between Modernization and Democracy, Perspectives on Politics (2010) 551.

[217] Pérez-Liñán/Smith, Democratic quality and democratic survival, in: Tomini/Sandri (ed), Challenges of Democracy in the twenty-first Century (2018), 72, 83.

[218] Ross, Does Oil Hinder Democracy?, World Politics 2011, 325; Haber/Menaldo, Do natural resources fuel authoritarianism? A reappraisal of the resource course, American Political Science Review 2011, 1. Lührmann/McMann/van Ham, Democracy Aid Effectiveness: Variation Accross Regime Types, V-Dem Institute Working Paper 2018:40, Oktober 2018.

[219] Levitsky/Ziblatt, How Democracies Die (2018) 21–24.

[220] Feld/Voigt, Judicial Independence and Economic Growth, Some Proposals Regarding the Judiciary, in Congleton/Swedenborg (ed), Democratic ConstitutionalDesign and Public Policy (2006) 251.

outcome in preventing erosion.[221] It is argued that a combination of political action, certain national political and social conditions, and legal instruments on both national and federal level are valuable ways to oppose to authoritarian tendencies at the local level.[222]

References

1. Jakab, A. (2016). *European constitutional language*. Cambridge UP.
2. Blauberger, M., & Kelemen, R. D. (2017). Can courts rescue national democracy? Judicial safeguards against democratic backsliding in the EU. *Journal of European Public Policy, 24*, 321.
3. Tamanaha, B. Z. (2004). *On the rule of law: History, politics, theory*. Cambridge University Press.
4. Delaney, E. F. (2016). Analyzing avoidance: Judicial strategy in comparative perspective. *66 Duke L.J, 1*, 1.
5. Zekos, G. (2014). *Risk management, corporate governance in 21st century digital economy*. Nova Science.
6. Zekos, G. (2017). *The United States of Europe in place of the European Union*. Nova Science.
7. Zekos, G. (2019). *The United States of Europe the global player*. Nova Science.
8. Zekos, G. (2020). *Finance crimes: Insider trading and money laundering*. Nova Science.
9. Zekos, G. (2017). *The United States of Europe in place of the European Union*. Nova Science.
10. Genna, G. M. (2017). Images of Europeans: Transnational trust and support for European integration. *Journal of International Relations and Development, 20*, 358.
11. Přibáň, J. (2015). The evolving idea of political justice in the EU. In D. Kochenov, G. de Búrca, & A. Williams (Eds.), *Europe's justice deficit?* Hart.
12. Raz, J. (1979). The rule of law and its virtue. *The authority of law: Essays on law and morality*. Oxford University Press.
13. Raz, J. (2009). Legitimate authority. In *The authority of law*. Oxford: Oxford University Press.
14. Raz, J. (2019). The law's own virtue. *Oxford Journal of Legal Studies, 39*, 1.
15. Sirota, L. (2019). The rule of law all the way up. *Supreme Court Law Review* 92 S.C.L.R. (2d), p. 80.
16. Ioannidis, M. (2016). Europe's new transformations: How the EU economic constitution changed during the Eurozone crisis. *Common Market Law Review, 53*, 1237.

[221] Müller, Should the EU Protect Democracy and the Rule of Law inside Member States? European Law Journal, 2015, 141; Jakab, The EU Charter of Fundamental Rights as the Most Promising Way of Enforcing the Rule of Law against EU Member States, in Closa/Kochenov (ed), Reinforcing the Rule of Law Oversight in the European Union (2016) 187; Jakab/Kochenov (ed), The Enforcement of EU Law and Values. Ensuring Member States'Compliance (2017); Sadurski, That Other Anniversary, European Constitutional Law Review 2017, 417; Wagrandl, Transnational Militant Democracy, Global Constitutionalism 2018, 143; Bozóki/Hegedűs, An externally constrained hybrid regime. Hungary in the European Union, Democratization 2018, 1173.

[222] Carp, The Struggle for the Rule of Law in Romania as an EU Member State. The Role of the Cooperation and Verification Mechanism, Utrecht Law Review 2014, 1; Blauberger/Kelemen, Can courts rescue national democracy? Judicial safeguards against democratic backsliding in the EU, Journal of European Public Policy 2017, 321; Sedelmeier, Political safeguards against democratic backsliding in the EU. The limits of material sanctions and the scope of social pressure, Journal of European Public Policy 2017, 337.

17. Ruffert, M. (2015). *Europäische Währungspolitik als Herausforderung für das Recht (Zentrum für Europäisches Wirtschaftsrecht).*
18. St-Hilaire, M., & Baron, J. (2019). Introductory essay: The rule of law as the rule of artificial reason. *Supreme Court Law Review S.C.L.R. (2d), 92.*
19. Cass, R. A. (2017). Staying agency rules: Constitutional structure and rule of law in the administrative state. *Administrative Law Review, 69*, 225.
20. Steinwender, C. (2018). Real effects of information frictions: When the states and the Kingdom became United. *American Economic Review, 108*(3), 657–696.

Chapter 7
International Law, Politics, and the Rule of Law

7.1 International Law

First of all, international law came with a firmly rooted prejudice in favor of public law-governed institutions with diplomatic representations, nationalist rhetoric, and scarce resources.[1] Modern international law no longer relies on absolutes but always seeks to stabilize between extremes. It seems that international law's binding force is today either naturalist or positivist or relies merely on "rules" or "facts" and so no treaty is defended either in terms of the consent of the parties or the justice of its outcome which means that the conceivable positions are situated in the middle-ground. Likewise, international law emerged as a practice in the late nineteenth century not out of enthusiasm for, but from a critique of, the political world of Great Power primacy, as part of a social project to spread national liberal reform and internationally to support peace, disarmament, human rights, along with economic and social progress.[2] International law is stimulated by the idea of the great transformation illustrated by "constitutionalization" of the international system, in favor of human rights and environmentalism, indigenous causes, self-determination, economic redistribution, and solidarity—often against Great Powers.[3]

The nature of international law is not an anthropological or sociological datum about it but it is an internal, constitutive presupposition of legal argument itself. To that extent, it is worth noting that under the liberal theory of politics the point of law is to lead society away from politics being an effort to move from a state of contestation and conflict into one governed by rational rules, principles, and institutions. Hence, it is argued that international law is rationalized by political,

[1] Martti Koskenniemi, "The Police in the Temple. Order, Justice and the UN; A Dialectical View", 5 EJIL (1995), pp. 325–348.

[2] Martti Koskenniemi, "Repetition as Reform. Georges Abi-Saab's Cour Ge′ne'ral", 9 EJIL (1998), pp. 405–411.

[3] Anne Orford, "the Destiny of International Law", 17 LJIL (2004), pp. 441–476.

G. I. Zekos, *Political, Economic and Legal Effects of Artificial Intelligence*, Contributions to Political Science, https://doi.org/10.1007/978-3-030-94736-1_7

economic, and technological modernity in an effort to advance it but epochs of enthusiasm and transformation were followed by times of suspicion and retreat.[4] To that extent, it could be said that international law is not automatically or certainly an instrument of progress because it offers resources for defending good and bad causes, enlightened and reverting policies.

On the other hand, international law has to struggle for the ideal of the good society so that it would be adequate, outside political selection, to commit oneself to international law so as to make certain oneself of the rightness of what one does.[5] Moreover, it is worth noting that political choices cannot be grounded on law which means that most of the time law is introduced in order to legalize political decisions that are out of the framework of the existing law.

In addition, international law offers doctrines for the interpretation of agreements and a range of technical rules on such matters as formation, reservation, and amendments. It has to be considered that establishing a commitment as a legal rule arouses a specific form of discourse. Moreover, given that most international norms are generated via the direct consent or practice of countries, there is no centralized legislature to invalidate improper, self-serving interpretations. Consequently, precision and elaboration are substantial characteristics of legalization at the international level. In line, legal processes implicate a discourse outlined in terms of reason, interpretation, technical knowledge, and argument, often supported by deliberation and judgment by neutral participants. In addition, legal decisions have to be based on reasons applicable to all comparably situated litigants, not simply the parties to the immediate dispute.

Model laws and international conventions are accompanied by official commentary demonstrating efficiency improvements in the law. The commentary improves the status quo by signalling efficiency-oriented approaches and so engendering information about the content of the law which means that it has the prospective on improvements in the law rather than on legal change by itself as a goal.[6] Breach of a legal obligation generates "legal responsibility," which does not necessitate a showing of intent on the part of precise state organs which means that in relating obligation to the broader legal system indicates the presence of international law as itself inflicting a form of accepted and in that way legitimized obligations on states.

Legal rules and commitments compel a specific kind of binding obligation on countries and other subjects such as international institutes. Moreover, legal obligations are diverse in type from obligations stemming from coercion, comity, or morality alone which means that legal obligations bring into play the well-known norms, procedures, and forms of discourse of the international legal system.

---

[4] Immanuel Kant, "Idea for a Universal History with a Cosmopolitan Purpose", in Hans Reiss (ed.), Political Writings (Cambridge University Press, 1991), pp. 41–53.

[5] Martti Koskenniemi, "Between Commitment and Cynicism: Outline for a Theory of International Law as Practice". In: Collection of Essays by Legal Advisers of States, Legal Advisers of International Organizations and Practitioners in the Field of International Law (United Nations, 1999), pp. 495–523.

[6] J. Mark Ramseyer, Public Choice, available at http://www.law.uchicago.edu/Lawecon/index.html

It has to be considered that there are some norms in international law being the product of shared understandings and often "procedural" in nature and so parties are bound by their agreements (pacta sunt servanda) is a central procedural norm. The central international legal principle of pacta sunt servanda means that the rules and commitments encompassed in legalized international agreements are considered as obligatory, subject to several defenses or exceptions, and not to be ignored as preferences alter and so they are run in good faith notwithstanding contradictory provisions of national law. As mentioned earlier, under legally binding agreements like the Vienna Convention, countries assert legal claims under pacta sunt servanda, state responsibility, and other doctrines of international law, involve in legal discourse, appeal legal processes, and make use of legal remedies. On the one hand, it is acknowledged that countries anticipate some lawfully binding "political treaties" not to be observed if interests or conditions alter. Therefore, terms of legally binding agreements are worded to restrict their obligatory force. On the other hand, a large number of instruments assert unrestricted obligations even if the institutions or procedures through which they were generated have no direct law-creating power. For instance, many UN General Assembly declarations articulate legal norms, though the assembly has no formal legislative power.

A precise rule identifies explicitly what is anticipated of a country or other player in terms of both the projected objective and the ways of accomplishing it in a precise set of settings which means that precision reduces the possibility for reasonable interpretation. Moreover, a precise rule is not more confining than a more general one but its real influence on behavior depends on many elements, embracing subjective interpretation by the subjects of the rule. Moreover, precision outlines limits, exceptions, and loopholes diminishing the influence of a rule but, on the other hand, for most rules demanding or forbidding specific conduct and, in the absence of precise delegation, generality offers a prospect for purposeful self-interested interpretation, lessening the influence, or the prospective for enforceable influence, on behavior. In addition, for a set of rules, precision entails not just that each rule in the set is explicit, but that the rules are linked to one another in a noncontradictory manner, generating a context within which case-by-case interpretation is carried out consistently.

It could be said that precision upsurges the legitimacy of rules and so their normative "compliance pull" and so the community and ethical qualities of certainty and obviousness for individual players contribute to the legitimacy of rules and specifically the rules of law which means that clarity is crucial to the force of law.

Taking into account the state consent to such technology-specific treaties, international law does not prima facie take an interest in a new technology, just for its being new. Instead, it responds to prospective new uses of that technology that violate pre-existing norms. To that extent, the use of AI technologies might violate some of these existing norms, and a key point is that international law is able to evolve and adapt and so international law has also proven quite inspired at governing new technologies. Existing international legal instruments are adjusted in various ways to new technological revolutions: through treaty amendment, adaptive interpretation, or new state behavior that results in customary international law. Hence,

AI technology can be subsumed under general norms or provisions of international law or existing treaty instruments will be extended or reinterpreted to cover AI developments.[7] It has to be taken into consideration that customary international law requires clear evidence of state practice, yet this may not be available where it concerns cases of "hidden" or "hard to attribute" AI capabilities such as in cyberwarfare or definitional problems around AI systems and applications which means that there are at least some gaps and ambiguities in the general application of customary international norms.[8]

7.2 UN and the Rule of Law

The League of Nations revealed that a collective security system can be set up without exclusion on the use of force[9] and so League of Nations Covenant articles 10–16 layout the ways in which members of the League cope with acts of aggression or threats of such acts by other Member States without explicitly barring the use of force in international disputes.

Moreover, the international legal order has preceded the appearance of a collective security system, which itself has preceded the introduction of a prohibition on the use of force. Consequently, these concepts are all self-sufficient in the meaning that none of them is a constitutive feature of the other. Above all, an international legal order rests neither on the presence of a collective security system nor of an exclusion on the use of force which is clarified by the presence of international legal relations among countries long before the formation of the League of Nations being the first primary collective security system but its systemic feature has been exposed as an illusion.[10] It is argued that under the League of Nations, war became a law enforcement device only to a narrow degree and so the League being mostly applied

---

[7] United Nations, United Nations Conference to Negotiate a Legally Binding Instrument to Prohibit Nuclear Weapons, Leading Towards Their Total Elimination (2017), https://www.un.org/disarmament/publications/library/ptnw/ Rebecca Crootof, Change Without Consent: How Customary International Law Modifies Treaties, 41 Yale J. Int. Law 65 (2016).

[8] Tamar Megiddo, Knowledge Production, Big Data and Data-Driven Customary International Law (2019), https://papers.ssrn.com/abstract=3497477 Ashley Deeks, High-Tech International Law, 88 George Wash. Law Rev. 575–653, 649 (2020).

[9] David Kennedy, The Move to Institutions, 8 Cardozo L. Rev. 842, 988 (1987) (illustrating the critical legal school's belief that the League of Nations system existed as an illusion to alleviate the frustration of a war fought in vain).

[10] F.P. Walters, A History Of The League Of Nations 3 (1952) (the League of Nations is the "embodiment in constitutional form of mankind's aspirations towards peace and towards a rationally organized world"). C.K. Webster & Sydney Herbert, The League Of Nations In Theory And Practice 301 (1933) (the League of Nations was primarily conceived as a "compact to maintain peace"); Alfred Zimmern, The League Of Nations And The Rule Of Law 1918–1935, 2 (Atheneum Publishers, 2d ed. 1969) (a security machinery to prevent the recurrence of another World War).

to "proceduralizing" violence rather than "instrumentalizing" it.[11] Have international institutions utilized the rule of law or politics have shaped laws and interpretation of them accordingly in order to implement their own rule of law?

It seems that there is a conflict between the aim of upholding order and that of preserving justice at the UN.[12] On the other hand, the UN collective security system presents the prospect to use war as an enforcement procedure and so to a noteworthy degree, the UN system is a structure assigned to uphold the international legal order. It could be said that the UN mechanism conflicts with objection that international law is not law for the reason that it lacks a coercive enforcement mechanism. It is worth noting that international law is called law but it is not set by a sovereign whereas positive law is set by a sovereign. While the UN collective security system openly "instrumentalizes" war permitting it to be employed as a law-enforcement device, it has to be noted that this is only true provided that the rule that one pursues to enforce by means of the UN enforcement procedure merges with the objective of peace and security of the UN which means that the abuse of the rule whose enforcement is sought create a threat to international peace and security.[13] It has to be accepted that violations of international law have never been as such linked by the Security Council to threats to international peace and security. Nevertheless, the Security Council, whose mandate is not to decide whether international law has been violated, has contemplated that situations where there have been deliberate breaches of international law represent threats to international peace.[14]

Can a collective security system convert war into a forcible mechanism that can be exploited for the enforcement of law? It is obvious that a collective security system cannot convert war into a powerful mechanism that can be employed for the enforcement of law. Besides, Kelsen[15] argues that this enforcement mechanism even comprises one of the constitutive features of the international legal order but there are different levels in which a collective security system utilizes war with a stance to making it a law enforcement device. It is argued that if there were an entire ban on

[11] Alfred Zimmern, The League Of Nations And The Rule Of Law 1918–1935, 2 (Atheneum Publishers, 2d ed. 1969) (a security machinery to prevent the recurrence of another World War).

[12] Martti Koskenniemi, The Police in the Temple—Order, Justice and the U.N.: A Dialectical View, 6 Eur. J. Int'l L. 325 (1995).

[13] U.N. Charter art. 39 ("The Security Council shall determine the existence of any threat to the peace, breach of the peace, or act of aggression and shall make recommendations, or decide what measures shall be taken in accordance with Articles 41 and 42, to maintain or restore international peace and security.").

[14] For the situation in Rwanda S.C. Res. 929, U.N. Doc. S/RES/929 (June 22, 1994), or for the situation in Somalia S.C. Res. 733, U.N. Doc. S/RES/733 (Jan. 23, 1992); S.C. Res. 751, U.N. Doc. S/RES/751 (Apr. 24, 1992); S.C. Res. 794, U.N. Doc. S/RES/794 (Dec. 3, 1992).

[15] Hans Kelsen, Principles Of International Law 58 (1952).

the use of force without the prospect of forcible actions as sanctions, international law would cease to be a legal order.[16]

7.3 Use of Force and the Rule of Law

Has the use of force been transformed into the rule of law only for the military strong or the economically strong that can assemble a strong military force via their capital? It is worth noting that the international legal order is enduring the deterioration of one of its most key pillars: the prohibition on the use of force. Moreover, there is downfall of this prohibition and so the prohibition against the use of force has been corroded beyond recognition.[17] On the other hand, it is argued that while Article 2(4) is under assault, it is not dead.[18] Also, the rule expressed in Article 2(4) of the UN Charter does not stem from a conscious neglect for the ban on the use force since most countries still feel confined by it but the breakup of the prohibition on the use force stems from a general undertaking for weaker confines on that prohibition considered as a liberalization of the use of force. Moreover, in the framework of the war on Iraq American leaders "boldly proclaim a new policy that openly repudiates the Article 2(4) obligation" but while it is imprecise to presume that the prohibition has been entirely undermined, recent practice offers indications that this is exactly the direction in which the prohibition is heading.[19]

It seems that the ICJ defines that the principles concerning the use of force in Article 2(4) of the UN Charter match up with principles of customary international law.[20] Moreover, the Charter's norms concerning acceptable use of force have generated a default rule of non-intervention, which has aided backing global stability.[21]

It has to be considered that the clear declaration of aggressive war is presently forbidden in international relations under the framework of both the United Nations

[16] Jörg Kammerhofer, Kelsen—Which Kelsen? A Reapplication of the Pure Theory to International Law, 22 Leiden J. Int'l L. 225, 230–31 (2009) (discussing Kelsen's interpretation that war exists as either "delict or sanction within positive international law").

[17] Thomas M. Franck, Who Killed Article 2(4)? or: Changing Norms Governing the Use of Force by States, 64 AM. J. INT'L L. 809 (1970).

[18] Louis Henkin, The Reports of the Death of Article 2(4) Are Greatly Exaggerated, 65 AM. J. INT'L L. 544, 544 (1971). Tom J. Farer, The Prospect for International Law and Order in the Wake of Iraq, 97 AM. J. INT'L L. 621, 622 (2003) (discussing that ideas of how states ought to behave can survive both "massive deviance" and an "almost total failure of application").

[19] Thomas M. Franck, What Happens Now? The United Nations After Iraq, 97 AM. J. INT'L L. 607, 607–08 (2003).

[20] Military and Paramilitary Activities (Nicar. v. U.S.), 1986 I.C.J. 14, 99–100 (June 27).

[21] Jane E. Stromseth, Law and Force After Iraq: A Transitional Moment, 97 AM. J. INT'L L. 628, 631–33 (2008).

(UN) Charter and customary international law. Thus, Charter Article 2(4) denotes a comprehensive exclusion on the use of force, or force that is incompatible with the purposes of the United Nations. In fact, in the 1986 ICJ *Nicaragua v. USA* case, President Singh stated in a separate opinion that the ban on force is "the very cornerstone of the human effort to promote peace in a world torn by strife,"[22] which means there is an effort to eliminate war from international relations.

Besides, the legal debates following the attacks of 9/11 embraced arguments that UN Security Council (UNSC) Resolutions authorizing antiterror measures by its member states contributed to the widening of the definition and scope of the use of force in international law and so the UNSC Resolution 2249 inflates the range of exceptions to the general ban of the use of force in the framework of the global war on terror.[23]

It is worth noting that there is no scholarly unanimity on whether the ban on the use of force preserved in Article 2(4) of the UN Charter comprises a peremptory norm of international law.[24] Moreover, there is also disagreement as to the normative nature of the rule regulating self-defense[25] which means that such a controversy has pervaded the work of the International Law Commission ("ILC"). Undeniably, the ILC itself has been fluctuating between stating that it is granted with a jus cogens nature,[26] that the status is to be reserved to the ban of aggression,[27] or that it did not need to take a position on the issue.[28] Besides, Article 50 of the Articles on State

[22] Military and Paramilitary Activities in and against Nicaragua (Nicaragua v. United States) Judgment of 26 June 1986 on Merits, [1986] ICJ Rep 14, at 153 (President Singh, Separate Opinion).

[23] C. Tams, 'The Use of Force against Terrorists' (2009) 20 EJIL, 359 M. Koskenniemi, 'The Police in the Temple. Order, Justice, and the UN: A Dialectical View' (1995) 6 EJIL 326.

[24] U.N. Int'l L. Comm'n, Articles on State Responsibility, U.N. Doc. A/CN.4/SER.A/1996/Add.l (Part 2) (1996) http://www.lcil.cam.ac.uk/projects/state_responsibility_document_collection.php#4 (containing the former Article 19 of the ILC which seems to indicate that only the prohibition of aggression is ius cogens); Responsibility of States for Internationally Wrongful Acts, G.A. Res. 56/83, U.N. GAOR, 56th Sess., U.N. Doc. A/56/589 (Jan. 28, 2002) (containing Article 27 of the Articles on State Responsibility, which excludes the invocation of circumstances precluding wrongfulness in case of violation of peremptory norms, if read in conjunction with Article 22, Article 27 seems to limit the peremptory character to the prohibition of aggression).

[25] Antonio Cassese, Article 51, in La Charte Des Nations Unies, Commentaire Article Par Article 1357 (Jean-Pierre Cot et al. eds.) (2005). Cf. Raphaël van Steenberghe, Le Pacte de non-agression et de défense commune de l'Union africaine: entre unilatéralisme et responsabilité collective, 113 Revue Générale De Droit Int'l Pub. 125 (2009).

[26] Report of the International Law Commission on the Work of its Thirty-second Session, 2 Y.-B. INT'L L. COMM'N 169, 270 (1980) (stating that the Commission was unsure as to whether communications were made and whether they were operative).

[27] Articles on State Responsibility (containing the former Article 19 which prohibits force except in the most serious of circumstances).

[28] Report of the International Law Commission on the work of its thirty-second session, 35 GAOR Supp. (No. 10) at 27–28, U.N. Doc. A/35/10 (1980), reprinted in 2 Y.B. Int'l L. Comm'n 26 U.N. Doc A/CN.4/SER.A/1980/Add.l (Part 2) (discussing the ILC's work of codifying the rules governing State responsibility).

Responsibility seems to consider the ban on the use of force as one of the peremptory obligations of international law.[29]

Moreover, it has to be taken into account that not all problems can be resolved by the law being the reason why people are often dissatisfied by international law due to the fact that people expect too much of it.[30] Thus, international law, by exaggerating claims of its triumph and concealing when it fails, has weakened its own progress.[31] It is argued that a Country should no longer have any reason to conform to a rule and so the rule is either inexistent or no longer obligatory due to the fact that repeated violations of international law have influenced Countries' legal obligations to follow these laws.[32] To that extent, it is worth mentioning that it is only on condition that the violation of a given rule concurrently constitutes a threat to the international peace and security that one can anticipate resorting to the UN collective security system to enforce international law.[33] Furthermore, the necessity that the enforcement of a rule through the UN system instantaneously contribute to the upholding of international peace and security in order for the UN collective security to be deemed a law-enforcement system, should not be overstated.

Is the rule of law or politics the basis for the use of force? In practice, politics has inspired the use of force in many circumstances on the global stage against the real meaning of the rule of law. Moreover, recent practice has shown that the requirement of Security Council resolutions have been sloppily employed and have captured circumstances where clear-cut violations of international law have been performed being the case when the Security Council endorses what it qualifies an "aggressive act," "act of aggression," or "aggression."[34] Security Council resolutions have been

[29] Articles on State Responsibility, supra note 51, art. 50 ("Countermeasures shall not affect: (a) The obligation to refrain from the threat or use of force as embodied in the Charter of the United Nations; (b) Obligations for the protection of fundamental human rights; (c) Obligations of a humanitarian character prohibiting reprisals; (d) Other obligations under peremptory norms of general international law.").

[30] Prosper Weil, Le Droit International en Quête de son Identité, 237 Recueil Des Cours 9, 64–65 (1996).

[31] Michael J. Glennon, How International Rules Die, 93 GEO. L.J. 939, 990–91 (2005).

[32] Michael J. Glennon, Force and the Settlement of Political Disputes: Debate with Alain Pellet at the Colloquium of Topicality of the 1907 Hague Conference (Sept. 7, 2007), available at http://ssrn.com/abstract=1092212

[33] Pierre d'Argent et al., Article 39, in La Charte Des Nations Unies: Commentaires Article Par Article 1133–70 (Jean-Pierre Cot et al. eds., 3d ed. 2005) (discussing the competence of the Security Council to determine threats against peace, breach of peace, and acts of aggression).

[34] U.N. Charter art. 39 ("The Security Council shall determine the existence of any threat to the peace, breach of the peace, or act of aggression and shall make recommendations, or decide what measures shall be taken in accordance with Articles 41 and 42, to maintain or restore international peace and security."). S.C. Res. 326, U.N. Doc. S/RES/326 (Feb. 2, 1973) (addressing what the Security Council deemed to be "provocative and aggressive acts" committed by Southern Rhodesia against other countries, including Angola, Botswana, Mozambique, and Zambia); S.C. Res. 387, U.N. Doc. S/RES/387 (Mar. 31, 1976) (regarding the acts of aggression committed by South Africa against other countries in southern Africa); S.C. Res. 405, U.N. Doc. S/RES/405 (Apr. 14, 1977) (regarding the acts of armed aggression committed by mercenaries against Benin);

sloppily employed in the case of a humanitarian disaster that qualifies as a threat to international peace and security, or in circumstances regarding frequent abuses of both humanitarian on top of human rights law.[35]

Hart's[36] restriction of violence represents "the minimum content of natural law," that is, a rule of conduct that any social institute must contain to be "viable" and so a legal order has to restrain the use of violence so as not to be plagued by chaos and ineffectiveness does not mean that the use of force has to be entirely banned. On the other hand, it could be said that the entire absence of any legal limitation on the use of force may be counteracted by some moral or political postulates allowing the legal order in question to remain possible. There is a need for the existence of minimum standards of morality into a condition of validity or a condition of the obligatory character of law. Nevertheless, Hart never interpreted his "minimum content of morality" as a constitutive part of valid or obligatory law.[37]

Moreover, it could be said that a ban on the use of force not only strengthens the sustainability of a legal order, it can also be instrumental in the maintenance of some of the key doctrines of that legal order. With regard to the international legal order, in particular, it can be said that, by banning violence among sovereign States, the exclusion on the use of force is planned for the preservation of the Westphalian order. According to Article 2(4), a state is prohibited from invading, occupying, annexing, and eliminating other sovereign States but although initially prohibiting war, international law, and most notably the UN Charter, has begun to legalize it which could be legalized in a very narrow way by listing the precise occasions of allowing the use of force[38] not having any political inference.

In other words, Article 2(4) covers the present State-based configuration of the globe and the legal order that rests upon it and that is why the International Court of Justice has long been defended a very robust understanding of the prohibition on the

S.C. Res. 573, U.N. Doc. S/RES/573 (Oct. 4, 1985) (regarding the acts of aggression committed by Israel against Tunisia); S.C. Res. 611, U.N. Doc. S/RES/611 (Apr. 25, 1988) (condemning the acts of aggression committed by Israel against Tunisia); S.C. Res. 667, U.N. Doc. S/RES/667 (Sept. 16, 1990) (regarding the acts of aggression committed by Iraq against diplomatic premises and personnel in Kuwait).

[35] Concerning resolutions pertaining to the situation in Kosovo, S.C. Res. 1160, U.N. Doc. S/RES/1160 (Mar. 31, 1998); S.C. Res. 1199, U.N. Doc. S/RES/1199 (Sept. 23, 1998); S.C. Res. 1203, U.N. Doc. S/RES/1203 (Oct. 24, 1998); S.C. Res. 1239, U.N. Doc. S/RES/1239 (May 14, 1999); S.C. Res. 1244, U.N. Doc. S/RES/1244 (June 10, 1999). For the situation in Darfur, S.C. Res. 1593, U.N. Doc. S/RES/1593 (Mar. 31, 2005).

[36] H.L.A. Hart, The Concept Of Law 193–94 (1961).

[37] see Kenneth E. Himma, Hart and Austin Together Again for the First Time: Coercive Enforcement and the Theory of Legal Obligation 17 (SSRN Working Papers, 2006), http://papers.ssrn.com/sol3/papers.cfm?abstract_id=727465

[38] Pierre d'Argent, Which Law Through Which War? Law Through War Revisited, 52 Buff. L. Rev. 635 (2004).

use of force, both in its conventional[39]and customary[40] dimensions. It has to be taken into account that Article 2(4) takes away from countries the legal right to use force, and Articles 24, 39, 42, and others then deliver this power to the Security Council clarifying that the Council has the "primary responsibility for the maintenance of international peace and security" (Article 24) and that it can take what measures it considers essential in that pursuit, embracing military action against countries or other threats (Article 42). Thus, intervention that is authorized by the UN Security Council is definitely legal, as long as it conforms to the Council's power over "threats to international peace and security" (Article 39). Besides, disagreement over whether the Council is appropriately identifying such threats is common—for instance, with regard to the Libyan sanctions[41] and so councils' view has to be based on a legal analysis of events and not due to political interpretations upon the law and the rule of law in order to satisfy the political interests of some states.

Have states exploited the use of force in order to satisfy groups' interests instead of peace? It is well known that the existing ban on the use of force preserved in Article 2(4) of the UN Charter, which echoes customary international law, only restrains the use of force and does not ban it entirely, for the rule contains an exception both outside and inside the UN collective system. In that perception, it is only as long as the exclusion on the use of force leaves room for exceptions in the form of multilateral uses of force that it permits a valuable collective security system to survive.[42]

Can states use coalitions in order to achieve national objectives bypassing the sense of law? The proscription on the use of force, although neither a constitutive element of any legal order nor of any collective security system, nevertheless has the capacity to influence the feasibility, effectiveness, and configuration of both the international legal order and the collective security system. Moreover, current practice, expressly that relating to the so-called fight against terrorism,[43] has offered some annoying examples of circumstances in which the use of force by a State short of any authorization by the Security Council has remained unrestrained. It has to be taken into consideration that if the unconcealed trumping of international law in

[39] Corfu Channel (Gr. Brit., N. Ir. v. Alb.), 1949 I.C.J. 4, 35 (Apr. 9) (stating that the alleged "right of intervention" is a "manifestation of a policy of force" which "cannot ... find a place in international law").

[40] Military and Paramilitary Activities (Nicar. v. U.S.), 1986 I.C.J. 14, 97–101, paras. 184–90 (June 27) (holding that customary international law requires the non-use of force).

[41] B. Martenczuk, "The Security Council, the International Court and Judicial Review: What Lessons from Lockerbie?" European Journal of International Law 10, no. 31999, pp. 517–47.

[42] P. Klein, Le droit international à l'épreuve du terrorisme, 321 Recueil Des Cours 203 (2006) (assessing the legal problems pertaining to the use of force in the context of the fight against terrorism).

[43] P. Klein, Le droit international à l'épreuve du terrorisme, 321 Recueil Des Cours 203 (2006) (assessing the legal problems pertaining to the use of force in the context of the fight against terrorism).

Kosovo[44] and Iraq[45] constituted the only exceptions, one could still live with the illusion of an international legal order where force remains strictly banned despite occasional patent violations.[46] Nevertheless, the violations of the prohibition of the use of force in Kosovo and Iraq have been corroborated ever since. It seems that the self-interest of superpowers is winning out over international obligations, post-Iraq. Have scholars employed by states to promote an interpretation of international law excusing their illegal actions?

Moreover, States still display a substantial attachment to the principle of the prohibition on the use of force.[47] Despite some notable recent exceptions, States using force in vague surroundings still strive to rationalize their deeds by referring to the rules of international law pertaining to the use of force.[48] Moreover, nowadays, states do not even bother to use a "fig leaf of legal justification" and it is characteristic the decision of the Netherlands to support the war against Iraq which concluded that the Netherlands deemed it needless to seek a mandate from the Security Council.[49] In addition, recent and authoritative scholarly work further underpins that conclusion.[50] Furthermore, a nonstop attachment to the ban on the use of force does not mean that the examples are negligible and marginal which means that the utilization of force betray the deep disorder of the collective security system, which is being destabilized by a declining prohibition on the use of force.

Likewise, it has to be taken into account that Countries have rationalized their use of force through a resort to the restrictions to the prohibition by referring to new limitations to substantiate their resort to military force. States have referred to the notion of humanitarian intervention along with that of pro-democratic intervention to back the legality of their military action by broadening the scope of the existing

[44] Kosovo And The International Community: A Legal Assessment (Christian Tomuschat ed., 2002) (examining the future of Kosovo in light of the Security Council resolution 1244 of 1999 and the Stability Pact adopted to ensure economic recovery of the entire region).

[45] Richard A. Falk, What Future for the U.N. Charter System of War Prevention?, 97 Am. J. Int'l L. 590 (2003) (describing the United States' circumvention of the U.N.'s prohibition of force in Iraq).

[46] John Yoo, International Law and the War in Iraq, 97 Am. J. Int'l L. 563 (2003) (reconciling the war in Iraq with the principles of international law).

[47] Anthony C. Arend & Robert J. Beck, International Law And The Use Of Force: Beyond The U.N. Charter Paradigm 180 (Routledge 1993) ("While it is easy to count the times that a particular norm is violated, it is quite difficult to identify the times when a norm exerted a controlling influence, when states refrained from forcible action because of Article 2(4)'s proscription.").

[48] Military and Paramilitary Activities (Nicar, v. U.S.), 1986 I.C.J. 14, para. 186 (June 27) (noting that a state's use of rules and exceptions to rules to defend its use of force confirms rather than weakens the rule); U.K. Foreign Secretary, Iraq: Legal Basis for the Use of Force, 2003 Brit. Y.B. Int'l L. 793, 793–96 (describing the use of force following the liberation of Iraq).

[49] Gilbert Kreijger, Iraq Invasion Had No Legal Backing: Dutch Report, Reuters, Jan. 12, 2010, at 1, http://www.reuters.com/assets/print?aid =USTRE60B3A620100112 (reporting on the Dutch government's support of a United States led invasion of Iraq that had no legal backing).

[50] Olivier Corten, Le Droit Contre La Guerre: L'interdiction Du Recours À La Force En Droit International Contemporain (Pedone 2008) (claiming that the rule prohibiting the use of force has undergone significant change since September 11, 2001).

limitations, explicitly the right to use force in self-defense or upon prior authorization by the Security Council. As mentioned earlier, the perception of humanitarian intervention has advanced as a rift of the laws governing the use of force and has come to dominate an institutional position in conjunction with self-defense and Security Council authorization as a legal and legitimate reason for war.

Additionally, the case for the illegality of humanitarian intervention rests on the clear language of the UN Charter and so Article 2(4) outlaws the use of force by countries and gives no suggestion that the reason behind the action matters at all which means that nothing in the Charter opens the likelihood that the use of force for humanitarian reasons should be comprehended inversely than other uses of force. Nikolas Sturchler[51] argues that the article forbids both the use of force and the threat of its use, making certain that the domain of illegality is much broader than simply cross-border military attacks.

Which is the dynamic relationship between international law and state practice? It is argued that two forces in international politics have repetitively pressed humanitarian intervention onto the international legal agenda regardless of Article 2(4): firstly the extension of the ideology of cosmopolitanism and human rights, which delivers a moral imperative to react to barbarities against people irrespective of their citizenship; and secondly the strategic exploitation by countries who see in humanitarianism a convenient vehicle to validate their military interventions. It has to be taken into consideration that the language of humanitarianism would not be a convenient device if it did not have political echo with beliefs about justice and obligation which seems not to be based on pure and theoretical basis generally applicable but this is accepted many times because it implements indirectly the political interests of some elites. Moreover, both forces keep the language of humanitarianism alive in the legal discourse of countries and activists boosting developments in the law, even though they are dissimilar drivers for the concept and they apply, reinforce, and alter it in different ways.

It could be argued that state practices that undermine a piece of treaty law should be coded as "noncompliance," and that the political, moral, or transformational motives behind it are off base. Thus, the law stands, independent of state behavior, even accepting that rule violation will sometimes happen. Besides, the cases for legality depend on the assessment that sustained patterns of state behavior in opposition to the rules have inventive consequences in international law, such that if there is a continual pattern of humanitarian intervention, then legalization takes place which means that breaking the law produces a new type of the rule of law where the content and conception of the rule of law is not based on the law but on the practice of law according to the politically prevailing interpretation and understanding of law contrary to the likelihood of comprehending the clear black letter law.

Further, it is worth noting that wars begun in the pursuit of humanitarian rescue are now seen as different from wars fought for other purposes and so they are now

[51] Nikolas Sturchler, The Threat of Force in International Law (Cambridge: Cambridge University Press, 2006).

legally, politically, and conceptually separate from wars of conquest and wars of national security, even as the category of humanitarian intervention continues exceedingly contested in practice. Also, contemporary international law can be read as either permitting or banning international humanitarian intervention, and the legal ambiguity around humanitarian intervention is vital.[52] Therefore, inconsistent and plausible interpretations about the legality of any act of intervention exist concurrently, and neither can be eradicated. Besides, the law is important and so law and law following should be seen as resources in the hands of states and others, deployed to affect the political setting of their actions.

Anyway, invoking new limitations or escalating existing limitations, States have claimed that their use of force is not forbidden by Article 2(4) of the UN Charter and the analogous customary rule for the reason that they have been invited by the State's government onto the territory on which force is really used. Furthermore, even when their actions are unquestionably in conflict with the ban on the use of force and do not fit into one of its exclusions, States have avoided the correlative duty for their illegal conduct by bringing up conditions impeding wrongfulness, and mainly the state of necessity.

In the case of a dilution of Article 2(4), regulatory powers exploited by the organs of the UN, and particularly the Security Council, would remain at the discarding of the Member States, regardless of the state of the law concerning the use of force. Thus, the use of these regulatory instruments, and particularly the powers under Chapter VII of the UN Charter, has long exceeded the conservation of international peace and security. Undeniably, the practice of the Security Council within the context of Chapter VII of the Charter has long gone outside the initial restrictions and reasons of the Charter. The Security Council is using the powers conferred upon it by Chapter VII for nonmilitary reasons and the actions that are ordered by the Security Council are not considered as actions preceding a probable authorization to use force.

In other words, it seems that international law is a product of interstate interactions in backgrounds beyond formal treaty negotiations indicating how states understand their obligations, and consequently for learning what the rules are. Thus, evidence of nonconformity with Article 2(4) is a sign that countries are in the process of changing the rules which establishes a new understanding of the law, equally binding as the ex ante law. Moreover, this freedom to pick among interpretations of the law gives rise to a sea of self-serving claims having less to do with the merits of one legal interpretation than with the political needs of those making the arguments which indicates the strategic exploitation of international law, which is often taken as the opposite of the rule of law.[53]

[52] Jutta Brunnée and Stephen J. Toope, Legitimacy and Legality in International Law (Cambridge: Cambridge University Press, 2010).

[53] Brian Tamanaha, Law as a Means to an End: Threat to the Rule of Law (Cambridge: Cambridge University Press, 2006).

7.4 Non-state Armed Players and the International Rule of Law

Is there a rise and decline of international rule of law in the case of non-state armed players? Non-state armed players are individuals or groups that pursue chase their political, social, or economic targets with military means. It is argued that in post-Cold War contemporary era, it is clear that nonstate armed actors[54] are part of international law, mainly in the areas of international humanitarian law (IHL), international human rights law (IHRL), and international criminal law (ICL).[55] Moreover, international criminal law has secured more relevance over time regarding non-state armed actors, with the establishment of the International Criminal Court based on the Rome Statute where non-state armed actors are subject to accountability and away from impunity from international atrocity crimes. Do non-state armed actors respond to the international rule of law?

It is worth noting that in decentralized norm advancement, in the end, end-users of law internalize the norm by advancing their own understanding and own the rules. Moreover, users progress their own sanctioning means, and make compulsory it without central enforcer and so decentralized enforcement[56] is mainly vital for international law where central enforcer does not exist more often than not. Taking into consideration that wars are effectively regulated when the divide between norm-makers and norm-takers is narrowed down, decentralized law-making takes place during the rule of law promotion among non-state armed actors done by international humanitarian players.[57] It has to be taken into account that non-state armed groups recognize and accept international legal order in accordance with how they comprehend the value of international legal rules. Moreover, ambiguity in IHL does generate misunderstanding and politicization of international law.[58]

Due to militarization lately, it seems that international rule of law is in constant decline in the case of nonstate armed actors. Does international rule of law exist among non-state armed players? It is certain that civil wars or non-international armed conflicts are not the usual place where robust international rule of law operation is expected.

---

[54] Fortin, Katharine, Accountability of Non-State Armed Groups (2017, Oxford University Press).

[55] Krieger, Heike (ed.), Inducing Compliance with International Humanitarian Law: Lessons from the African Great Lakes Region (2015, Cambridge University Press); Alston, Philip and Ryan Goodman, International Human Rights. (2012, Oxford University Press).

[56] Kube, Sebastian and Christian Traxler, "The interaction of legal and social norm enforcement", (2011) Journal of Public Economic Theory, 13(5) 639–660.

[57] Fazal, Tanisha, Wars of Law: Unintended Consequences in the Regulation of Armed Conflict (2018, Cornell University Press).

[58] Jean d'Aspremont, "Do Non-State Actors Strengthen or Weaken International Law? The Story of a Liberal Symbiosis" in Krieger, Heike, Georg Nolte, Georg, and Andreas Zimmermann (eds), The International Rule of law – Rise or Decline? – Approaching current foundational challenges (2019, Oxford University Press).

Customarily, international law regulated the interstate behaviors of state-to-state behaviors but with the rise of private actors such as MNEs, private security actors, non-state actors, international law now covers a range of players, together with the case of non-state armed actors.[59] It is worth noting that in the area of human rights, individuals now have rights to file disputes under international mechanisms. The signing of the Rome Statute and the establishment of the International Criminal Court and its process has confirmed that international law has reached the non-state armed actors in an unprecedented manner.[60]

In other words, the way that national governments handle their non-state armed groups with their national legal means influences the rise of international rule of law. In fact, the recommendations by the Financial Action Task Force (FATF) were adopted by banks and then legalized into national crime statutes.[61] On the one hand, if governments use political or military tactics in line with international law, the rise of international rule of law operation is expected. On the other hand, if governments use tactics against international law such as repressive policies going against international human rights standards, the decline of international rule of law operation is expected. Have global politics illustrated respect to international law and consequently to the international rule of law?

It seems that some non-state armed players have been progressively committing themselves to international law, via peace agreements, unilateral declarations, or agreements with international organizations and so these are signs of international rule of law in the case of non-state armed players.[62] Besides, non-state armed players with democratic foreign sponsorship are less probable to abuse civilians.[63] Moreover, it could be said that the signs of probable decline are revealed in the clash

[59] Clapham, Andrew, Human Rights Obligations of Non-State Actors (2006, Oxford University Press). The Geneva Conventions' Common Article 3, in addition to other Protocols expanded the reach of international law regarding non-state armed groups' obligations. Human rights treaties, such as the Optional Protocol to the Convention on the Rights of the Child on the Involvement of Children in Armed Conflict (OPAC), also cover non-state actors' restraints in behavior during wartime.

[60] Annyssa Bellal, Gilles Giacca, and Stuart Casey-Maslen, "International law and armed non-state actors in Afghanistan", (2011) International Review of the Red Cross, 93(881): 47–79.

[61] Morse, Julia, "Blacklists, Market Enforcement, and the Global Regime to Combat Terrorist Financing", (2019) International Organization, 73(3): 511–545.

[62] Jo, Hyeran, Rise and Decline of International Rule of Law: Case of Non-State Armed Actors, Working Paper Series, No. 39, Berlin Potsdam Research Group "The International Rule of Law – Rise or Decline?", Berlin, September 2019. Gleditsch, Kristian Skrede, Simon Hug, Livia I. Schubiger and Julian Wucherpfennig, "International Conventions and Non-State Actors: Selection, Signaling and Reputation Effects", (2018) Journal of Conflict Resolution, 62(2): 346–380; Fazal, Tanisha and Margarita Konaev, "Homelands versus Minelands: Why do Armed Groups Commit to the Laws of War?", (2019) Journal of Global Security Studies, 4(2): 149–168.

[63] Salehyan, Idean, David Siroky, and Reed Wood, "External Rebel Sponsorship and Civilian Abuse: A PrincipalAgent Analysis of Wartime Atrocities", (2014) International Organization, 68(3):633–661. Jo, Hyeran and Joowon Yi, "Engaging Rebels: Humanitarian Engagement in Conflict Zones and the Case of United Nations Action Plans", (2019) Manuscript, Texas A&M University.

between international rule of law and rebels' rule-of-power which means that the main tension in armed conflicts is the fight between rule of law and rule-of-power.[64]

7.5 Power and Law

It is argued that even where power is definitely established, it may still not turn into law if it seems egregiously unjustified[65] and so there is a contrast between the strict "declarativism" of Opinion 1 of the Arbitration Commission of the Yugoslavian Peace Conference and the refusal by the members of the European Communities to regard new Balkan entities as States unless they complied with humanitarian demands testifying the strength of sovereignty doctrines. To that extent, abstract standards, such as self-determination, justify recognition policies that generate the reality they intend to reflect—with the result that effective power sometimes fails to bring about statehood in the occasions of Southern Rhodesia and Taiwan whereas noneffective power does so in the occasions of Burma, Lebanon in the 1970s, Georgia and Moldova in the 1990s.[66]

The established power is criticized with the argument that it is unjustified and defend it with the argument that at least it is there to prevent "fratricidal struggles."[67] It is worth mentioning that the law here accedes to views about justified power which are, on the law's own premises, matters of political choice which means that there is a move into context of "deformalization" and so any problem seems open to decision only on the basis of the settings.

Likewise, it has to be considered that the deformalization of sovereignty doctrines extends beyond territorial jurisprudence to the law regarding shared natural resources, uses of international watercourses, environmental protection, along with prevention and liability for trans-boundary damage.[68] Thus, deformalization highlights the understanding that the law must reflect the society that it is anticipated to regulate while remaining autonomous from a society it is meant to transform.

---

[64] Turku, Helga, The Destruction of Cultural Property as a Weapon of War: ISIS in Syria and Iraq (2018, Palgrave Macmillan).

[65] See Opinion 1 of the Arbitration Commission, 31 ILM (1991), pp. 1494–1497 and the EU Declaration on the Recognition of New States in Eastern Europe and the Soviet Union, 16 December 1991, ibid. pp. 1485–1487. See further the discussion in Martti Koskenniemi, "National Self-Determination Today: Problems of Legal Theory and Practice", 43 ICLQ (1994), pp. 241–269.

[66] Davic Raic, Statehood and the Law of Self-Determination (The Hague, Kluwer, 2002).

[67] ICJ: Burkina Faso–Mali Boundary Case, Reports 1986, p. 565 (para. 20).

[68] Tuomas Kuokkanen, "International Law and the Expropriation of Natural Resources", XI FYBIL (2000). Eyeal Benvenisti, Sharing Transboundary Resources. International Law and Optimal Resource Use (Cambridge University Press, 2002). Martti Koskenniemi, "Breach of Treaty or Non-Compliance? Reflexions on the Enforcement of the Montreal Protocol", 3 Yearbook of International Environmental Law (1992), pp. 123–162.

It has to be considered that the Council has been executing all kinds of policies: reconstructing States, fighting impunity via the formation of judicial bodies, fighting terrorism through the adoption of individual sanctions, and so on.[69] Moreover, the Security Council has adopted "general 'law-making' resolutions" where it has considered military sanctions pointless.[70] To that extent, extra duties in order to keep peace and security have been granted to the Council through non-UN mechanisms such as the International Criminal Court before which proceedings can be started by the Council.[71]

Does the creation of new entities mean better implementation or new ways for new interpreting in favor of the strong? Has the Security Council functioned in a way of achieving justice and order via the rule of law or a political interpretation of the law in order to achieve the political interests of the strong? Largely, the Council has vacated its role of guardian of the order and has focused on problems of justice.[72] It could be said that the backing of justice by the Security Council is clearly contradictory with the initial policing role that was reserved to the Council by the authors of the Charter, on top of earlier practice, where typically it was the General Assembly that could stimulate justice on the international sphere.[73] It has to be

[69] Vera Gowlland-Debbas, UN Sanctions and International Law: An Overview, in United Nations Sanctions And International Law 1 (Vera Gowlland-Debbas ed., 2001) (discussing the debate over the legitimacy and longterm effects of economic sanctions on states).

[70] Jean d'Aspremont, Post-Conflict Administrations as Democracy-Building Instruments, 9 CHI. J. INT'L L. 1, 1 (2008) (discussing the use of international organizations to create or reconstruct democratic states); Jean d'Aspremont, Regulating Statehood: The Kosovo Status Settlement, 20 Leiden J. Int'l L. 649, 649 (2007) (arguing that the "proposed regulation of [the] statehood" of Kosovo surpassed past international involvement in the reconstruction of States). S.C. Res. 955, U.N. Doc. S/RES/955 (Nov. 8, 1994) (describing the establishment of the ICTR); S.C. Res. 827, U.N. Doc. S/RES/827 (May 25, 1993) (describing the establishment of the ICTY). S.C. Res. 1757, U.N. Doc. S/RES/1757 (May 30, 2007) (describing the creation of the Special Tribunal for Lebanon). S.C. Res. 1333, U.N. Doc. S/RES/1333 (Dec. 19, 2000) (declaring international opposition to the Taliban); S.C. Res. 1135, U.N. Doc. S/RES/1135 (Oct. 29, 1997) (declaring international opposition to the members of the UNITA in Angola).

[71] Rome Statute of the International Criminal Court art. 13, July 17, 1998, 2187 U.N.T.S. 90 (establishing an "independent permanent International Criminal Court . . . with jurisdiction over the most serious crimes of concern to the international community as a whole").

[72] Press Conference, United Nations, Special Working Group on the Crime of Aggression (Feb. 13, 2009), http://www.un.org/News/briefings/docs/2009/090213_ICC.doc.htm (discussing the I.C. C.'s jurisdiction over the crime of aggression). Niels Blokker, The Crime of Aggression and the United Nations Security Council, 20 LEIDEN J. INT'L L. 867, 886–87 (2007) (discussing the debate over the Security Council's role in determining I.C.C. jurisdiction, and rejecting the view that the determination of whether there has been a crime of aggression should be left exclusively to the Security Council).

[73] Declaration on the Establishment of a New International Economic Order, G.A. Res. 3201 (S-VI), U.N. Doc. A/RES/3201 (S-VI) (May 1, 1974) (defining a new economic order to promote principles of justice and equity among states); Declaration on the Granting of Independence to Colonial Countries and Peoples, G.A. Res. 1514 (XV), U.N. GAOR, 15th Sess., Supp. No. 16, at 66, U.N. Doc. A/4684 (Dec. 14, 1960) (prohibiting colonialism in recognition of individual rights to equality and self-determination); Request for an advisory opinion from the International Court of

taken into consideration that this role has enabled the collective security system to outlive the dilution of the prohibition on the use of force and so the Security Council holding duties in world regulation and the promotion of justice would be radically inflated by a dilution of the ban on the use of force. The fundamental piece of law on the legality of the recourse to war by states is the UN Charter.[74] It could be said that the objective of the framers of the Charter was to centralize the enforcement of international order in the hands of the great powers at the time, and to pacify the affairs among other countries by depriving them of independent legal channels to war.

Undeniably, in the absence of any clear ban on the use of force, the Council's obligation to uphold order and to approve the use of force to stop threats to international peace would diminish. It would no longer be needed to seek authorization to use force and the upholding of the international peace and order would no longer be dependent on the Council. Thus, Countries, acting unilaterally or on the basis of ad hoc coalitions, would be able to uphold order and it seems that this is what the idea of coalitions of the willing, which establishes the direct opposite of the upholding of order by the international community, already indicates which means that deprived of its key duties in the upholding of order, the Security Council would converge on its newer roles such as world regulation and the promotion of justice according to the demands of the elites expressed by military power rather than the lawful use of the rule of law instead of a political utilization of the law[75] accordingly. It is worth mentioning here that there is an intensifying tendency of "states of one mind" to use informal processes instead of international law to synchronize.[76]

The idea that the duties of the Security Council as a global regulator or a forum of justice may be reinforced by the demise of the ban on the use of force appears unreasoned, since the dilution of the ban on the use of force is the result of States' confidence in their own competences and abilities. On the one hand, countries could be liberated from most restrictions on their aptitude to use force. On the other hand, countries would be subjected to a more powerful Council. It has to be considered that the Countries that are trying to extend the freedom to resort to force are normally those that are at the helm of the Council which means that by diluting the ban on the use of force, these countries are promoting their own capacity to resort to war along

Justice on the legality of the threat or use of nuclear weapons, G.A. Res. 49/75, U.N. Doc. A/RES/49/75 (Dec. 15, 1994) (promoting disarmament and requesting that the I.C.J. review the legality of the threat or use of nuclear weapons).

[74] Ian Clark, Legitimacy in International Society 1975 Oxford: Oxford University Press. Christine D. Gray, International Law and the Use of Force, 2008 3rd. ed. (Oxford: Oxford University Press).

[75] Michael Glennon, Why the Security Council Failed, 82 Foreign Aff. 16, 34 (2003) (claiming that States will be able to maintain order without the help of the Security Council).

[76] Eyal Benvenisti, Coalitions of the Willing and the Evolution of Informal International Law, in Coalitions Of The Willing: Avantgarde Or Threat? 1 (Christian Calliess et al. eds., 2007).

with the international mechanisms by which they force regulations and advance their own concepts of justice.[77]

How individual states interests against the globe will be prohibited/eliminated? An independent international Council having individual ability of enforcement is the mode for international use of rule of law. Following the current practice to use international organizations in order to implement elites' interests over the good of the globe then very soon will come to the big conflict which will destruct the globe proving the conquer of politics over the rule of law.

It seems that the dynamic is a diffuse "rationality of rule" effective in terms of a proclamation of universality for a gathering of particular values and forms of social, economic, and political organization. Characteristically, "law" is cut from a range of forms of ordering, which are then expressed as something else, or rejected the status of law which means that such orderings offer the screen upon which the other of law "itself" is anticipated, and so enabling the constitutive exclusion to be achieved. To that extent, these orderings incorporate other persons' forms of social ordering, such as customs, or "indigenous" laws, but also extend to other orders of knowledge, such as economics, or other normative structures, such as theology, morality, or grammar which means that this specific cut of "law" from its rivals has to be incorporated within a universal claim for itself. Custom is defined generally and not custom as a source of international law outlined by international law as the pattern of state practice and precedent. In line, the discourse of advancement is involved in securing the "objectivity" of positive law as "law."[78]

7.6 From Law to Politics and Law

The nation-state, the international, and legality itself, all function as "grounds" of international law, but they are all objects founded in part by law, and via their expected negations. To that extent, international law is involved in the creation of these categories even as it is "founded" on them. Moreover, international law is founded on principles, categories, and identities which are indisputable, immune to revision, but not outside society and politics.[79]

The next feature of international law is its "political" quality and so this political quality generates international law's "critical instability." On the other hand,

[77] Prosecutor v. Tadic, Case No. IT-94-1-T, Decision on the Defence Motion on Jurisdiction, para. 24 (Aug. 10, 2005) (discussing the discretion of the Security Council to determine the existence of a threat to, or a breach of, the peace). Contra Prosecutor v. Tadic, Case No. IT-94-1-AR-72, Decision on the Defence Motion for Interlocutory Appeal on Jurisdiction, para. 29 (Oct. 2, 1995).

[78] Jennifer L. Beard, The Political Economy of Desire: Law, Development and the Nation (Abingdon: Routledge-Cavendish, 2007).

[79] Don Herzog, Without Foundations: Justification in Political Theory (Ithaca: Cornell University Press, 1985) George Steinmetz (ed.), The Politics of Method in the Human Sciences: Positivism and Its Epistemological Others (Durham, NC: Duke University Press, 2005).

"political" is a term that houses many diverse meanings, and so the law's political quality indicates the disparity between the emblematic valence of international law and the law as exemplified in treaty and custom at any given moment. To that extent, emblematic means the sense of serving as a badge of something else and not in the precise sense in which it is used in some other literature, such as, for instance, psychoanalysis. It could be said that it is the gap between positive international law and its thrusting link to an idea of justice which "gap" is politically covered.[80] It is argued that it is part of international law, and is one part of what "Derrida might call law's 'self-deconstructive' inclination."[81] Moreover, it is worth noting that the "political" quality of law is both in contrast to, and reveals something in common with, a viewpoint of the "politics" of international law. It has to be considered that the Rechstaat or Rule of Law has to be applied to international law and so revealing the need of answering the questions asked of law implying exclusively from within the law or there is an unavoidable part explained via the concept of 'politics of international law. There is an invincible promise that gives international law an imaginative appeal which is demonstrated by how people use international law and there is a need to define the relation between law and "justice." Thus, this relation gives law its edginess concerning rules-plus-violence and so the constant historical transformation of laws is based on appraisal and deconstruction.[82] It could be said that Justice is what gives us the desire, the drive, or the movement to advance the law, that is, to deconstruct the law and so with no a call for justice, we would not have any appeal in deconstructing the law. Therefore, even hegemonic, under Gramscian[83] appreciation of a specific dominant ideology which outlines both its terms and the language which contests it to uphold stability, or imperial uses of law cannot encompass the excess generated by law's 'invincible promise' and so such uses depend on it which means that instability is what gives law and rights their aptitude to de-radicalize and "juridify" politics. To that extent, since international law has a vital instability at its heart, this instability is neither blameless nor unbiased, which means that it is involved in the conservation of a precise geopolitical control structure. On the other hand, stabilization aggravates international law's imposing quality and diminishes its counter-imperial dimension, or emancipatory likelihoods.

[80] Martti Koskenniemi, 'The Politics of International Law' (1990) 1 European Journal of International Law 4.

[81] Jacques Derrida and Giovanna Borradori, 'Autoimmunity: Real and Symbolic Suicides, A Dialogue with Jacques Derrida' in Giovanna Borradori (ed.), Philosophy in a Time of Terror: Dialogues with Jürgen Habermas and Jacques Derrida (Chicago: University of Chicago Press, 2003) 85–137. John Caputo (ed.), Deconstruction in a Nutshell: A Conversation with Jacques Derrida (New York: Fordham University Press, 1997) 9.

[82] John Caputo (ed.), Deconstruction in a Nutshell: A Conversation with Jacques Derrida (New York: Fordham University Press, 1997) 9.

[83] Antonio Gramsci, Selections from Political Writings (1910–1920), ed. by Quintin Hoare and trans. by John Mathews (London: Lawrence and Wishart, 1977).

According to international legal positivism, sovereignty was the source of international law and so sovereignty emanated from the nation-state which means explicit rejection of both a divine guarantee and the transcendent measure of natural law. To that extent, nation-states were based on society and territory which means that law's founding categories were inherent to man and understood to be "objective." Founding categories were seen as either external to law, or entirely internal to it.[84]

It is argued that the rationality of the liberal peace is a mandate for intervention in the domestic affairs of any country that is not an established democracy which is counted against by the norm of nonintervention which is expressed in Article 2(7) of the UN Charter.[85] It could be said that the liberal internationalism connects the internal structures of governance of a nation-state to the "fact" of the liberal peace and the prevalence of peace as the aim of the UN system. Thus, international legal liberalism would defy "Legalism" and "Realism" and so with the legalist commitment to State autonomy as a normative requirement for a global rule of law.[86]

Consequently, the concept of democratic legitimacy and the right to democracy offered two major currents in the "rule of law revival," which revival was in direct conflict with the international rule of law and so these currents together modify international discourse around the international rule of law.[87] It is argued that liberal plurality penetrates the confines of the nation-state.[88]

At the end of the Cold War, an evolving international liberalism promoted an instrumental deployment of international law applying the rule of law as a substantive value within countries being a principle of state legitimacy. The collapse of the Soviet Union facilitated normative triumph of liberal democracy not founded on some kind of rule by the people, but a model emanating from the West, exemplified by the political system of the USA and focused on the rule of law. In other words, the rule of law was classified as being conceptually relevant to the external legitimacy of a state and a certain model of democracy was put forward as being universal and so a model of democracy and attendant rule of law have emerged.

Thus, as soon as the concept of development was interlocked unreservedly in defining the rule of law, it was a phase for the rule of law to become the categorical affair of the international economic institutions. Therefore, the rule of law on both a conceptual and a practical level encompassed by the international economic institutions as a powerful engine in the worldwide acceptance of a particular model due to the jointly sustaining character of the relationship between development and the

[84] Antony Anghie, Imperialism, Sovereignty and the Making of International Law (Cambridge: Cambridge University Press, 2004).

[85] Anne-Marie Slaughter, 'The Liberal Agenda for Peace: International Relations Theory and the Future of the United Nations' (1994) 4 Transnational Law and Contemporary Problems 377, 379.

[86] Thomas Franck, 'The Emerging Right to Democratic Governance' (1992) 86 American Journal of International Law 46.

[87] Yves Dezalay and Bryant Garth, Global Prescriptions: The Production, Exportation and Importation of New Legal Orthodoxy (Ann Arbor: University of Michigan Press, 2002).

[88] Martti Koskenniemi, 'The Future of Statehood' (1991) 32 Harvard International Law Journal 397.

concept of law. It could be said that this "law" is the language in which legitimate authority is brokered in modern humanity.

As mentioned earlier, Article 2(4) of the United Nations Charter sets out the rule banning not just the use of force, but also the threat of force in international relations and so this twin ban is exhibited as one of the key pillars of the international system, for the reason that it not only necessitates from countries to abstain from the use of force but also to exercise self-restraint and abstain from anything aggressive that could slip into the use of force.[89] Moreover, the International Court of Justice (ICJ) has had the chance to scrutinize the legality of threats of force in many cases such as the Corfu Channel Case brought by the UK against Albania and so with reference to the minesweeping operation, the ICJ held that this action amounted to illegal intervention and violation of Albanian sovereignty.[90] Furthermore, anyhow the frequent and abstract reaffirmation of the rule banning the threat of force, legal, and political standpoints toward such threats of force is nuanced. In line, the ICJ acknowledged that not all threats of force are illegal and unlawfulness is a contextual issue varying on the adjoining conditions; without explaining its decisions or spelling out any tangible criteria along with which threats of force can be judged. Consequently, Judge Simma's observation that the failure to evaluate the character of the UN principles on the use of force in the contemporary context is true concerning threats of force.

Conversely, in the real world of international politics where standards and criteria are quite elastic and not solely legal, and where the UN collective security mechanism flops and is changeable, countries have to make decisions about the competences or aims of the other party to realize the threat which has been articulated in circumstances of evidential uncertainly. Such decisions can never be precise or perfect but are made on the apprehending that a threat may occur and inflict the proposed harm, or that a premature reaction may intensify the conflict. Consequently, countries follow dissimilar courses of action to prevent such threats, from delivering countervailing threats, to implicating the Security Council, to using force themselves. It seems that there is not a single path that of the rule of law and politics utilizes international law and national law accordingly in order to achieve elite's goals.

What extent a threat of force can be exploited so as to counter other threats of force, or to enforce international values without defying the established minimum international normative order? Has the use of force brought justice to enforcement of the rule of law or application of political matters via a political interpretation of law?

---

[89] M. Roscini, 'Threats of Armed Force and Contemporary International Law', (2007) 54 Neth. ILRev. 229; N. Stürchler, The Threat of Force in International Law, (Cambridge: Cambridge University Press, 2009); D. Kritsiotis, 'Close Encounters of a Sovereign Kind', (2009) 20 EJIL, 299.

[90] Corfu Channel (United Kingdom v. Albania), Merits, Judgment of 9 April 1949, [1949] ICJ Rep. 9 M.W. Reisman, 'Criteria for the Lawful Use of Force in International Law', (1985) 10 Yale J.I.L. 279, at 281.

Nicholas Tsagourias[91] states that "The case of 'threats of force' thus demonstrates that there are many other parameters than law within which threats of force operate, and in which legal and political attitudes towards them are formed. Contrary to what Article 2(4) of the UN Charter implies, law cannot just extinguish or outright condemn threats of force or even the eventual use of force, because often it is just those threats and uses of force that, in the end, uphold the law."

The devotion to strict limits on the use of force in international affairs is a forceful utilitarian norm reinforced by a practice of legality. Besides, other norms that look like law are not based on any authentic consensus such as the Kyoto Protocol commitments to diminish greenhouse gases being an influential recent example.[92] Moreover, true consensus in international society is unachievable for the reason that seeming agreement is only created by a structure of power politics.[93]

Furthermore, the prohibition on the use of force is durable, with a multitude of actors wanted to keep it in the face of regenerated arguments for a humanitarian exception which means that the norm prohibiting the use of force is not simply a "structural bias," but a shared understanding. The currently strongest military power has argued for a unilateral exception to the prohibition and so the USA and its allies have a "universal" claim of human rights protection on their side, and the material power to act.

Anyway there is a shift in the language about war, human rights, and humanitarianism and so there is materialization of a new global order. To that extent, validating external military interventions has moved away from the humanitarian arguments displaying a strategy not only in the framework of the global war on terror but also executing strategic decisions based on interests and priorities of particular capitalists indicating the political impact upon the law and the rule of law.[94]

It has to be taken into consideration that there is the rise of new powers as norm makers in the international legal system showing the political impact of these new powers upon the law and the rule of law.[95] It is worth mentioning that Gillian

---

[91] Nicholas Tsagourias, The prohibition of threats of force available, http://ssrn.com/abstract=2074015 P28.

[92] J. Brunnée and S.J. Toope, Legitimacy and Legality in International Law: An Interactional Account (Cambridge: Cambridge University Press, 2010).

[93] Martti Koskenniemi, From Apology to Utopia, 2009 Cambridge University Press p. 584 (arguing that 'social meaning is generated by individual psychologies, while what those psychologies produce is conditioned by the material conditions in which they are formed.'). Martti Koskenniemi, 'The Politics of International Law - 20 Years Later', The European Journal of International Law 20 (2009), 10.

[94] C. Schmitt, The Nomos of the Earth: In the International Law of the Jus Publicum Europaeum ([1950], 2003) Chaps III and IV.

[95] W. W. Burke-White, 'Power Shifts in International Law: Structural Realignment and Substantive Pluralism' (2015) 56 Harvard International Law Journal, 1–80, at 77. M. Koskenniemi, 'Human Rights-so 90s' Public lecture 3 March 2014, Public International Law at Oxford, available at: https://www.youtube.com/watch?v=9hFdZRYZhkg

K. Hadfield and Barry R. Weingast[96] state that "if those in charge of classification also wield a monopoly over the legitimate use of force and are capable of securing compliance for any rule they announce—which is the presumption of centralized enforcement models of law—then there is no strategic reason for them to observe the rule of law."

7.7 Terrorism and the Rule of Law

To that extent, it has to be considered that the link of public and private, political, economic, and regulatory power known as global liberal governance is a wide-ranging and multifaceted regime of power, whose founding principle lies in the administration and production of life nonetheless the upholding of life, entails both: self-defense and protection of others via humanitarianism.[97] Therefore, emergencies, crises, and violence threaten to enter into spaces of normality and safety in the forms of refugees, terrorists, or cyber-crime.[98]

While the Resolution does not make specific reference to Chapter VII of the UN Charter, it is part of the existing doctrine of self-defense in international law, which now involves the right of countries to use unilateral force against terrorists.[99]

It has to be taken into consideration that the surroundings of legitimation remain vague and verified on a case-by-case basis, as has been evident in the wide-ranging interpretations of unilateral State actions in the present conflict in Syria and Iraq, on top of in cases such as Yemen and Ukraine.[100] Moreover, the terminology of Resolution 2249 reiterates the UNSC Resolution 1973 (2011), which authorized NATO intervention in Libya by way of "all necessary measures" and so the intervention in Libya was legitimized under the banner of the R2P principle and that of required protection of civilians and civilian populated areas under threat of

[96] Gillian K. Hadfield, Barry R. Weingast, Privatizing Law: Is Rule of Law an Equilibrium Without Private Ordering? Legal Studies Research Papers Series No. 17-24e at: https://ssrn.com/abstract=3057093 at 6.

[97] M. Dillon and J. Reid, 'Global Liberal Governance: Biopolitics, Security and War' (2001) 30 Millennium Journal of International Studies 42.

[98] N. Wheeler, Saving Strangers: Humanitarian Intervention in International Society (Oxford Publishing, 2000). A. Peters, 'Global Constitutionalism Revisited' (2005) 5 International Legal Theory 39.

[99] M. Weller, 'Permanent Imminence of Armed Attacks: Resolution 2249 (2015) and the Right to Self Defence Against Designated Terrorist Groups', EJIL Talk! November 25, 2015. Available at: http://www.ejiltalk.org/permanent-imminence-of-armed-attacks-Resolution2249-2015-and-the-right-to-self-defence-against-designated-terrorist-groups; D. Akande and M. Milanovic, 'The Constructive Ambiguity of the Security Council's ISIS Resolution' EJIL Talk! November 21, 2015. Available at: http://www.ejiltalk.org/the-constructive-ambiguityof-the-security-councils-isis-resolution. Y. Dinstein, War, Aggression, and Self-Defence (2011).

[100] The Crisis in Ukraine, Special Issue, (2015)16 German Law Journal 3.

attack.[101] Who establishes the content of the rule of law and under which rationales? Do the shifting interests of superpowers form the content of the rule of law? Thus, the outcome of the intervening coalition's active role and objective of accomplishing regime change in Libya influenced to lesser probability of obtaining the UNSC approval for future invocations of the R2P and specifically the military intervention in Syria.[102] To that extent, as a result of the role of both state and non-state actors in Syria, the prospective responsibility of the international community to protect civilian populations could not only focus on state actors, but also on the actions of more and more transnational terrorist groups.

Likewise, it has to be taken into account that the uniqueness of the Resolution 2249 is its stress on the situation to which it is reacting to the unique nature and scale of the global terrorist threat to peace and security. Thus, the certainty of an 'armed attack' has been varying owing to several factors, involving the greater porousness of physical borders, new types of virtual weaponry, transnational terrorism, and the reconceptualization of sovereignty. Consequently, the Resolution confirms the already altering nature of self-defense as expressed in the Chatham House Principles of International Law on Use of Force in Self-Defense, which specifies that "[a]n armed attack means any use of armed force, and does not need to cross some threshold of intensity"[103] and so these developments alter the concept of proportionality as a rational need of force which means that for the accomplishment of limited objectives has become a much more flexible conception in the background of global terrorism. Do forces implant terrorism in order to alter the status quo to their own interests via alteration of the rule of law in order to satisfy their political choice?

Because the law of the UN Charter does not consider the use of force in self-defense as exceptional, the justification for the use of force by appeal to that right is not "extra-legal." Besides, there is political and legal disagreement about what counts as self-defense and so being uncontroversial. It could be said that a system of national criminal law has the intention to prevent crimes, yet it contends with the likelihood of crime and so as aggressive war is an international crime, the international legal system contends with the likelihood of that crime offering the means to defeat and punish it as a breach.[104]

---

[101] SC Res 1973, 17 March 2011. 21 SC Res 2213, 27 March 2015. D. Kritsiotis, 'Humanitarian Intervention', in R. Robertson and J. A. Scholet (eds.) Encyclopedia of Globalization Vol. 2 (2007) 583–587); D. Kennedy, The Dark Sides of Virtue: Reassessing International Humanitarianism (2004); N. Krisch, 'Review Essay. Legality, Morality and the Dilemma of Humanitarian Intervention after Kosovo' (2002) 13 EJIL; S. Chesterman, Just War or Just Peace? Humanitarian Intervention and International Law (2001).

[102] C. Stahn 'Between Law-breaking and Law-making: Syria, Humanitarian Intervention and "What the Law Ought to Be"'(2014) 19 Journal of Conflict & Security Law 1.

[103] E. Wilmhurst (ed.), Principles of International Law on Self-Defence set out by Chatham House (2005), at 12.

[104] The Sanremo Handbook on Rules of Engagement (November 9 2009) at 5. Available at: http://www.iihl.org/wp-content/uploads/2015/12/ROE-HANDBOOK-ENGLISH.pdf D. Dyzenhaus, 'Schmitt v Dicey: Are States of Emergency Inside or Outside the Legal Order' (2008) 27 Cardozo Law Review 2005, at 2006.

7.8 International Trade and the Rule of Law

It has to be considered that the relation of international law and legal institutions to power is asymmetrical and so power produce law and legal institutions to legitimate, stabilize, and institutionalize policy. Over time, legal institutions create a route of their own and restrict power and so yet, power in the end react and curtail international legal institutions' independence and authority.

For instance, the USA generated the WTO and its dispute settlement system but at the moment the USA is undoing it resulting in a long-term weakening of multilateralism, together with a new form of cold war conflict which means an undermine of cooperation to tackle urgent transnational problems. To that extent, countries reconsider the role and institutionalization of WTO dispute settlement in the present political context which means that politics will form a new law which will be seen as that new basis for the rule of law because for the long-term politics cannot be seen as the ruler instead of the law in a well-functioning society generating the picture of justice for all people rather than promoting the interests of the prevailing political party.[105] There is a need for politically optimal level of judicial independence allowing the applicability of the rule of law in order to avoid the conflict due to diverse political interests.[106] Has global administration and state administration moved from a "rule-oriented" toward "power-oriented" due to globalization?

It is argued that it is the end of an era possibly the close of at least the trace of the rule of law in international trade relations but this erects tensions that undercut countries' aptitude to collaborate in other vital areas, such as climate change.[107] Therefore, it has to be realized that the "power-oriented" approach will bring closer the big conflict and so the "rule-oriented" approach serves as the catalytic force bringing legitimacy and justice which means that the rule of law has to conquer the international relations as well.

Thus, in the case of the next global financial crisis, there will occur a revengeful sanction soaring out of control leading to extensive economic war and stimulate authoritarian responses, escalating the projections of violence within and between states which means that the return to a rule-oriented system is imminent. In other words, the applicability of the "rule of law" brings forward the law's generality, equality of application, and certainty, in conjunction with a third-party institution to

---

[105] John Jackson, The World Trading System 111 (2d ed. 1997) ("One way to explore the questions raised above is to compare two techniques of modern diplomacy: a 'rule-oriented' technique and a 'power-oriented technique.'"); see also, J. Lacarte-Muró & P. Gappah, Developing Countries and the WTO Legal and Dispute Settlement System: A View from the Bench, 3 J. Int'l Econ. L. 395, 401 (2000) (arguing that "right perseveres over might"); James Bacchus, Might Unmakes Right: The American Assault on the Role of Law in World Trade, CIGI Papers No. 173 (May 2018).

[106] Erik Voeten, International Judicial Independence, in Interdisciplinary Perspectives On International Law And International Relations: The State Of The Art 421 (Jeffrey L. Dunoff & Mark A. Pollack eds., 2012).

[107] Graham Allison, Destined For War: Can America And China Escape Thucydides Trap? (2018).

enforce it in an impartial, consistent, and reasoned way[108] which means that the "rule of law" generates restraints on government to offer security and predictability and its actual practice in national and global level constituting fitting conduct producing justice via legitimacy.[109]

References

1. Orford, A. (2004). The Destiny of International Law. *LJIL, 17*, 441–476.
2. Tams, C. (2009). The use of force against terrorists. *EJIL, 20*, 359.
3. Gray, C. D. (2008). *International law and the use of force* (3rd ed.). Oxford University Press.
4. Kritsiotis, D. (2009). Close encounters of a sovereign kind. *EJIL, 20*, 299.
5. Fazal, T. (2018). *Wars of law: Unintended consequences in the regulation of armed conflict*. Cornell University Press.
6. Fortin, K. (2017). *Accountability of non-state armed groups*. Oxford University Press.
7. Hart, H. L. A. (1961). *The Concept of Law 193–94*.
8. Bacchus, J. (May 2018). *Might unmakes right: The American assault on the role of law in world trade*. CIGI Papers No. 173.
9. Brunnée, J., & Toope, S. J. (2010). *Legitimacy and legality in international law*. Cambridge University Press.
10. Krygier, M. (2009). The rule of law: Legality, teleology, sociology. In G. Palombella & N. Walker (eds.) *Relocating the rule of law* 45, 60 Hart, .
11. Sturchler, N. (2006). *The threat of force in international law*. Cambridge University Press.
12. Crootof, R. (2016). Change without consent: How customary international law modifies treaties. *Yale Journal of International Law, 41*, 65.
13. Turku, H. (2018). *The destruction of cultural property as a weapon of war: ISIS in Syria and Iraq*. Palgrave Macmillan.

[108] Joseph Raz, The Authority of Law: Essays on Law and Morality 214–19 (1979) (listing eight principles).

[109] Martin Krygier, The Rule of Law: Legality, Teleology, Sociology, in Relocating The Rule Of Law 45, 60 (Gianluigi Palombella & Neil Walker eds., 2009).

Chapter 8
Cyberspace Governance and Politics

8.1 Cyberspace

Cyberspace has had a predominantly dynamic influence because of its operation as a medium by which information can be transmitted.[1] The revolution in information technology provides the opportunity for logistics to utilize transaction based and decision support systems as a source of competitive differentiation and increased market share. Moreover, cyberspace contributes to international cooperation by: strengthening international law and economic interdependence, empowering nongovernmental organizations, and supporting international security mechanisms. In general, advanced electronic technology can be used in order to paralyze an inferior technology of a state and therefore threatening practically its sovereignty.[2] Hence, the emergence of the cyber state sovereignty in globalization adds a new dimension on the rule of law and global economic governance.

Moreover, cyberspace is already a global communications medium and the subject of valid international interest. Is cyberspace territorial? Cyberspace is characterized as "a-territorial" with the conventional[3] understanding of territory but cyberspace creates the notion of cyber-territory. Taking into account that many types of activities take place in cyberspace affecting people in real space, cyberspace can be used in practice as a tool for hegemonic exercise of control which could be utilized either to prohibit insider trading or to allow it. Taking into account that the effects of actions that take in cyberspace are evidently perceptible within the territory

[1]Jill E. Fisch, Can Internet Offerings Bridge the Small Business Capital Barrier?, 2 J. Small & Emerging Bus. L. 57, 69–70 (1998) ("[T]he Internet offers new methods for offering and selling securities. Businesses can distribute financial information and solicit investors through the Internet more quickly and at lower cost than was previously possible through paper-based communications").

[2]Zekos, G. (1999), "Internet or electronic technology: a threat to state sovereignty," JILT, available at: www.law.warwick.ac.uk/jilt/99-3/zekos.html

[3]G. Zekos, "Globalisation and States' Cyber-Territory," [2011] 5 Web JCLI.

G. I. Zekos, *Political, Economic and Legal Effects of Artificial Intelligence*, Contributions to Political Science, https://doi.org/10.1007/978-3-030-94736-1_8

of each state that might want to regulate that action, it emerges a new space environment for insider trading. There is a need for companies to have a robust system in place, based on internal controls, to avert, detect, and mitigate direct and indirect cyber-attacks. Without a doubt, in the present environment, the means to fighting a cyber-attack has to be an organization's capacity to detect and quickly respond to a breach when it unavoidably does happen. A strong cybersecurity program is vital for corporations to protect worthy and sensitive information and to evade possible enforcement actions, fines, reputational harm, loss of business, and class action or other lawsuits brought for damages suffered by customers or clients. It has to be taken into account that reputation in general is an authoritative basis of company value, and it can be eroded by regulation that undercuts the process of customary informal bonding devices.[4]

Networks are replacing hierarchies and markets as a basic form of economic organization. The dynamics of globalization are technical, cultural, social, and political. The range of lawmakers is widening, since private regulators more and more interfere, by this means producing self-regulation, or "decentralized" regulation, while the authority of states in the same way decreases. In the globalizing legal world, norms grow in their substantial characteristics: addressing realities which are less enclosed in traditional boundaries becoming more open-textured and more standard-like. Due to information developments legal systems become more and more permeable to external influences which means that information technology has made possible and accelerated the globalization of business.[5] As discussed earlier, globalization is a course, or a series of procedures, which create and merge a unified world economy, a complex and dynamic network of communications that covers the globe.[6] Additionally, globalization would be deemed a good thing insofar as it leads to progress in economic circumstances and standards within various countries. Geographical, social, and political boundaries definitely do not disappear but they are eroding due to globalization and cyberspace. Thus, globalization changes the nature of both business and the societies in which it is transacted[7] by intensifying social and economic transactions initiating a stronger worldwide interconnection of vital social actors via technological developments in the field of communication, media, and logistics.[8]

Technological developments drive globalization at least as much as global politics. Globalization is as much about capabilities as it is about ideas and so ideas bring about the new capabilities in computer and cyberspace technology and

[4] Jonathan R. Macey, The Death Of Corporate Reputation: How Integrity Has Been Destroyed On Wall Street (2013).

[5] S. Rosenne (2003) The perplexities of modern international law, General Course on Public International Law, RCADI tom III.

[6] Twining, W. Globalisation and Legal Theory, Cambridge: Cambridge University Press, 2000.

[7] McGrew, A. (2000) 'Power Shift: From National Government to Global Governance?' in D. Held, A Globalisaing World? Culture, Economics, Politics, London: Routledge.

[8] Crane, A./Matten, D. (2007): Business Ethics: Managing Corporate Citizenship and Sustainability in the Age of Globalization, 2nd, Oxford University Press: Oxford.

indeed in space exploration. In line, space exploration and utilization, and its resulting space applications, make available the capabilities that augment the levels of globalization bringing yet another wave of globalization. Moreover, the effects are crucial to globalization and so their joint outcome is the legal, institutional, and physical infrastructure of globalization. It has to be taken into account that space applications, particularly telecommunications, global navigation, and Earth observation, have a fundamental role in the process of globalization due to the fact that globalization is a result of the interconnections and interdependence of and across human societies that is enabled by the developments of communication, cyberspace, transportation, and computer technology that bridge geographic distances. Furthermore, space applications and their uses are various, embracing communication and data transfer, navigation, meteorology management, tracking, and logistics influencing international politics and diplomacy.[9]

Moreover, cyberspace challenges the law's traditional dependence on territorial borders; it is an endless electronic/digital space and place bounded by screens and passwords rather than physical markers. Thus, cyberspace is transformational and considered to be just like a real place, and the development of property interests over cyberspace means that this place is enclosed and privately exploited.[10] Therefore, cyberspace does not challenge the territorial notion of a nation as a collective organization that resides within specific geographical borders, but electronic sovereignty based on nations' cyberspace territories brings a new dimension into the concepts of territory and national sovereignty. In general, the emergence of cyberterritory and the advanced electronic technology can be used to paralyze an inferior technology of a state and therefore threatening practically its sovereignty[11] which consequently affects the fight against global crimes.

Also, cyberspace is considered as having "no borders" but unavoidably does so to claim States cannot govern it which means that the "no borders" position is a deviation on drawing borders around cyberspace distinguished it from other "real" space. Moreover, the Internet/cyberspace is just a technology that functions via hardware located in discrete physical locations much like other communication methods such as radio and television. To the extent those physical locations lie within the territorial borders of a given State, that State has the legal right to exercise control. Besides, where those territorial rights intersect, existing domestic and

---

[9]Pelton, J. N., Madry, S., & Camacho-Lara, S. (Eds.). (2017). Handbook of Satellite Applications (Second Edition). Cham: Springer. Bjola, C. (2017, October 14). Satellite Remote Sensing and Diplomatic Crisis Management. https://medium.com/digitaldiplomacy/satellite-remote-sensing-and-diplomatic-crisis-management-286651c83cb, Bjola, C., & Holmes, M. (Eds.). (2015). Digital Diplomacy: Theory and Practice (1 edition). London; New York: Routledge.

[10]G Zekos, "Cyber-Territory And Jurisdiction Of Nations, 2012 Journal of Internet Law, Number 12/3, G. Zekos, Globalisation and States' Cyber-Territory," [2011] 5 Web JCLI.

[11]Zekos, G. (1999), "Internet or electronic technology: a threat to state sovereignty," JILT, available at: www.law.warwick.ac.uk/jilt/99-3/zekos.html

international law rules determine conflicts or regulate State behavior.[12] It could be said that even cyberspace is distinct space, autonomous governance is not automatically needed but cyberspace enables its commodification through the extension of property rights. Thus, since property rights derive from sovereign States, national boundaries become ultimate markers for lines of authority there.[13]

Julie Cohen[14] argues that cyberspace is "neither separate from real space nor simply a continuation of it," which means that efforts to draw a line around cyberspace do too much to separate it from real space just as merely extending the boundaries of real space to cyberspace does too little to accommodate its unique operating qualities. It could be said that cyberspace is a new dimension of human actions influencing the material work and it is a startup for a further development of the human existence showing the road for the electronic transformation of humans in the distant future where it might be possible the material human to be transformed into an electronic human and vice versa leading human in another dimension of existence. It could be said that it could be the sign of the spiritual sphere of humans traveling and leaving in an electronic type of environment. Could electronic technology be the means for traveling in other dimension of existence where human life can take other value and worthiness of existence?

It is worth noting that laws and borders have a relationship and sometimes laws are the product of borders; today, national boundaries constitute States who regulate relations within or among their respective territories. Moreover, borders are the product of law; laws often draw lines between allowed and banned conduct and bound off necessitated acts from permissible ones. In line, the UN Charter prohibits the use of force except in self-defense or pursuant to Chapter VII authorization.[15]

Is the present emphasis on drawing law from boundaries and boundaries from law an adequate or effective way to regulate cyberspace and its conflicts? It is worth noting that cyberspace lacks a uniform foundation for why it needs boundaries, since cyberspace is endless, there is no possibility to enclose cyber-actions in a state sovereignty but the effects of cyber-actions can be felt in states boundaries. It is worth noting here that even though the belief that law is dependent upon the "materialities of place" has long been challenged, nonetheless the Westphalian origins of sovereignty today remain "very much alive, even if their current-day manifestations are constantly transforming.[16]" The developments on cyberspace and artificial intelligence have brought forwards doubts about the essence of sovereignty

---

[12] 23 JL Goldsmith & T Wu, Who Controls the Internet? Illusions of a Borderless World (OUP, 2008); OS Kerr, 'The Problem of Perspective in Internet Law' (2003) 91 Georgetown L J 359–361.

[13] M Lemley, "Place and Cyberspace" (2003) 91 Calif L Rev. 521, 523 (challenging inevitability of cyberspace privatization).

[14] J Cohen, "Cyberspace As/And Space" (2007) 107 Colum L Rev. 210, 226.

[15] UN Charter, arts 2(4), 40–42, 51. M Render "Introduction" in The Meador Lectures on Boundaries (Alabama 2013) 8.

[16] Ran Hirschl and Ayelet Shachar Spatial Statism, 17(2) Int'l J. Const. L. 387, 391 (2019). Anna Jurkevics, Hannah Arendt Reads Carl Schmitt's Nomos of the Earth, 16(30 Eur. J. Pol. Theory 345, 349 (2017).

but regardless of the contemporary decline of state sovereignty, the enduring and expansive spatial reach of state power to counter threats to sovereign territorial control is taking place. Paul Linden-Retek[17] deems that "in confronting the new 'spaces' of international entanglement, judges must redeem the idea that citizens might yet reclaim those entanglements as a 'common world', not just a space in which they are brought together, unfreely, under the mantle of state coordination and coercion."

It is argued that what cyberspace "is" remains highly contested, making agreement on its boundaries nearly unmanageable. Moreover, it could be said that outlining what cyber-operations "are" has caused equally intractable questions as to which sets of international law rules apply and how they do so. Besides, where theoretical disputes do not exist, the functions boundaries serve are open to contest as an affair of (a) accuracy; (b) effectiveness; and (c) completeness. A law's functions may be conditional on, or derivative of, a satisfactory theory for why the law exists which does not mean that theoretical variances preclude agreement on such functions completely. Sometimes, agreement is achievable even without agreement on why this is the case which means that in a global domain of diverse interests "incompletely theorized agreements" are anticipated.[18] To that extent, relying on law-by-analogy to define explicit IHL thresholds can engender erroneous lines if they do not adjust non-analogous characteristics of cyberspace and cyber-operations.

To that extent, it is worth noting that the question is not where law's boundary lines go, but whether boundaries can work at all. Hence, a boundary's effectiveness depends on definite criteria such as a degree of determinacy and constraint being difficult to warrant given cyberspace's predominant conditions such as anonymity. Additionally, the confining reason of borders causes an imperfect regulatory response to cyber-operations, not just owing to incorrect or ineffective line-drawing, but also for failing to underline law's other competences such as authorizing behavior. Furthermore, predominant difficulties on whether, where, and why borders are required in cyberspace imply that there is a need for re-appraising the existing landscape.[19]

Taking into account that AI offers the capacity to process and analyze multiple data streams in real-time; it is already being used to enable mass surveillance around the world such as use of AI in facial recognition software. It has to be considered that just as information is a mode of upholding security, it is also a type of control and so

[17] Paul Linden-Retek, The subjects of spatial statism: Reclaiming politics and law in international entanglement https://ssrn.com/abstract=3450966 p1.

[18] CR Sunstein, "Incompletely Theorized Agreements in Constitutional Law" (2007) 74 Social Research 1 (noting consensus on valuing religious liberty without agreement on why it deserves value: "Some people may stress what they see as the need for social peace; others may think that religious liberty reflects a principle of equality and a recognition of human dignity; others may invoke utilitarian considerations; still others may think that religious liberty is itself a theological command").

[19] M Schmitt, "Military Necessity and Humanity in International Humanitarian Law: Preserving the Delicate Balance" (2010) 50 Va J Intl L 795.

when governments are able to control commercial and political information, they augment their surveillance over the population which means that they have a more unified plan of attack against global opposition. To that extent, governments are able to exert excessive global influence in the event that that information is purposefully vital not just for their own states, but also for others. In line, China's cybersecurity law gathers information to augment political control by the way of controlling corporate data and to guarantee a prospective trade advantage based on improved access to intellectual property and the potential to aggregate data for AI. Particularly, China's Cybersecurity Law magnifies the scale of China's data sovereignty both extraterritorially and beyond the global corporate standards for publicly traded corporations. Accordingly, China's way is a new form of data governance, but then it is barely a new way of governance via the control of information for the reason that the concentration of data in the hands of a powerful government arouses longstanding historical examples of inequality, and indeed of the exploitation of information to serve the welfares of the state.

Since 1999, Zekos[20] has argued that "The Internet cannot have a main control center nor can any single entity monopolize the abundant variety of information freely accessible on the Internet which does not mean a thread to sovereignty. Besides, in general, advanced electronic technology can be used in order to paralyze an inferior technology of a state and therefore threatening practically its sovereignty. In other words, the Internet does not simply erode sovereignty, but its effect will depend on the nature of the actions involved and thus the Internet may strengthen democratic practice. A democratic and open character of the Internet limits the possibilities of authoritarian and monopoly control. Besides, the global market has the power to discipline national governments. The commercialization of the Internet might end up as concentrated power. At present, there is no purely digital economy. The Globalization together with the digitalization of financial markets has made these markets a powerful presence. Private digital networks rather than the Internet have the power to neutralize sovereignty. Hence, a shift of some components of the state's sovereignty over to other entities carries the potential to limit sovereignty but may not be the elimination rather than a partial relocation to supra national institutions. In the end, it could be argued that the inapplicability of the theory of absolute territorial sovereignty could be supported rather than the death of the state."

The new era of information technologies is referring to the globalization of communication. The quick decrease of the communication costs enhanced the dealings among countries and is a vital foundation for the structure of a stronger universal civil society. The global communication services have the supremacy to move visible and invisible things from one part of the globe to another. Global communication services influence not only the economic exchanges but also the ideas by way of increasingly widespread communication networks generating

[20] G Zekos, Internet or Electronic Technology: A Threat to State Sovereignty, JILT 1999 (3) https://warwick.ac.uk/fac/soc/law/elj/jilt/1999_3/zekos/

political groups and alignments. The supra-territorial cyberspace domain, notwithstanding distances turns out to be likely via the communication globalization.

In today's technology-driven world, industry standardization, device interoperability, and product-compatibility have turned out to be vital to advancing innovation and competition. Interoperability-centric challenges seem to continue to influence a variety of regulatory topics. Moreover, interoperability is one of the huge challenges of the convergence that occurs as a multilevel compatibility problem, purposely at the network, service, content, and terminal equipment levels.[21] To attain interoperability and administer convergence-based complexities, the use of common standards and protocols, or the use of a conversion function to map between diverse services would be needed. Furthermore, the notion of interoperability, resting at the center of network industries, is broader than merely a cyberspace entrée debate, as it influences innovation in software. The essential relationships among the components of the network, complementarity and compatibility, are present in many non-network industries, including financial intermediation and the exchange of financial instruments and assets. Complementarity requires compatibility and coordination.

Zekos considers that cyberspace is an electronic place that conforms to our understanding of the real world, with private spaces such as websites, e-mail servers, and fileservers, connected by the public thoroughfares of the network connections. Moreover, Cyberspace is the virtual space and place created by operation of the Internet,[22] a network of computers that share information with each other, and any other electronic networking resulted by different electronic devices such as satellites and cellular phones that can be interconnected and producing a global virtual reality network accessible by different electronic devices currently from earth but why not from people out of space or virtual entities outside our space or of another dimension livelihood within our space without currently being tracked by humans. It has to be taken into consideration that virtual events can be understood by human beings as human beings by the use of electronic devices transforming electronic signals into words and pictures viewed and comprehended by human beings and not virtual ones.

The technologies and virtual places that represent cyberspace have been assimilated into the lives of people who accept the Internet as a tool for pursuing their common, real-world needs. The information circulated in cyberspace is produced by real people. People can use cyberspace framework only for their online dealings.[23] Other people can use cyberspace setting for free circulation of ideas or having the impression of traveling virtually in many other places.[24] Even why not if it is made

[21] Damian Tambini, Danilo Leonardi and Chris Marsden, Codfying Cyberspace: Communications self-regulation in the age of Internet convergence, Routledge, 2008.

[22] Voyeur Dorm v. City of Tampa, 265 F.3d 1232.

[23] Caroline Bradley & A. Michael Froomkin, Virtual Worlds, Real Rules, 49 N.Y.L. Sch. L. Rev. 103, 139–46 (2004).

[24] Edward Castronova, The Right to Play, 49 N.Y.L. Sch. L. Rev. 185, 185, 200–05 (2004).

possible, in the distant future, to achieve interconnection with digital networks of other civilizations living out there in space.

Courts are using the metaphor of cyberspace as a "place" to justify application of traditional laws governing real property to this new medium.[25] It should be taken into account that the Internet is not "just like" the physical world. Not every Website is necessarily a purposeful availment of the benefits of every forum state.[26] Furthermore, the courts showed significant keenness to treat cyberspace and paper transactions as equals and so comparable results should be reached if not there is a reason to treat them in a different way.[27] For instance, a contract cannot be denied enforcement solely because it is in electronic from or signed electronically.[28] On the Internet, problems of physical infrastructure and overcrowding are less apparent because is a different dimension[29] but it has to be taken into account that electronic infrastructure used to accommodate the operability of cyberspace causes very often many problems due to its material feature. Moreover, information is saved in electronic devices and is not freely circulated on earth like sound, wind, or oxygen and so controlled by the owners of the electronic devices.

Furthermore, cyberspace allows the implementation of different activities such as online gaming, online banking, fan fiction, comparison shopping. In fact, cyberspace brings forward a question of allocation of rights and responsibilities in virtual space. What occurs in cyberspace is related with what occurs in real space. People are using cyberspace and circulate information or contact electronic transactions. Information access and control in cyberspace have consequences that reflect into real space because it is people in real space who require information residing in different jurisdictions.[30] Thus, lives and concerns of people using cyberspace are inextricably rooted in real space.

Space encompasses geographic/mapped places representing both totality and infinity. To that extent, cyberspace as a virtual space encompasses virtual places with a virtual totality and infinity and the countless number of virtual places constitutes the cyber place of cyberspace. Hence, cyberspace includes many cyber places. Moreover, cyberspace is a separate space in a virtual dimension viewed and operated by electronic agents programmed by humans. It is necessary to be made the distinction between cyberspace as the place and space where different types of virtual activities can take place that have an effect on humans and cyberspace as a virtual place and space where virtual functions can take place which are only virtual without affecting humans. Cyberspace as a virtual space and place can be used by

---

[25] eBay, Inc. v. Bidder's Edge, Inc., 100 F. Supp. 2d 1058.

[26] Jessica Litman, Breakfast with Batman: The Public Interest in the Advertising Age, 108 Yale L.J. 1717, 1725 (1999).

[27] CSX Transportation, Inc. v. Recovery Express, Inc. 415 F. Supp. 2d 6).

[28] (("UETA"), 7A U.L.A.§701, ("E-Sign"), 15 U.S.C. §§7001–7031).

[29] Intel Corp. v. Hamidi, 114 Cal. Rptr. 2d 244.

[30] Reno v. ACLU, 521 U.S. 844, Mark A. Lemley, Place and Cyberspace, 91 Cal. L. Rev. 521 (2003).

virtual entities and electronic beings but presently human beings do not have this ability to be transformed from human being into electronic beings and vice versa. The future use of cyberspace—not merely Internet—by virtual entities and electronic beings to inflict the real world cannot be overruled in advance which will cause different problems giving a different dimension into the phenomenon of cyberspace needing a state's intervention. The production of electronic beings that will function only electronically on behalf of human beings cannot be rejected for the distant future. It is open to research if cyberspace in its current form or a new more advanced cyberspace based on wireless communication can be connected with unknown electronic/digital systems own by civilizations out of our planet but within the endless cyberspace.

Cyberspace is not a real place and so users can adopt a new electronic identity with which travel in cyberspace. The electronic user always will correspond to a real person who can adopt many different electronic identities as technical identities allowing him/her to use cyberspace not mentioning purely electronic agents that can be used in electronic transactions. Electronic agents will continue to remain electronic agents created by humans to act as electronic agents having no liability. On the other hand, humans even as electronic users have finally liability for any misgivings caused by their electronic transactions.

8.2 Cyberspace Characteristics

The development of cyberspace brought the virtual world accessed by computers hardware and software transforming the virtual world into the dimension visible by people in the real world. Likewise, cyberspace is a supra-territorial phenomenon and the supra-territoriality of the medium ensues in part in a supra-territorial society. Hence, cyberspace has got its own territory with boundaries, which are the whole network territory. In other words, cyberspace brought digital commodities and services that have replaced many ordinary goods and services generating a new form and way of trading which means that the rise of cyberspace brings forward the requirement for a reconsideration of the meaning and substance of jurisdiction and sovereignty.

8.3 State Sovereignty and Cyberspace Sovereignty

It has to be taken into account that a state possesses sole jurisdiction over its people and internal affairs.[31] Sovereignty is established upon the fact of territory and so without territory a legal person cannot be a state.[32] Legal concepts as sovereignty and jurisdiction are realized in relation to territory and accordingly the principle whereby a state exercises absolute power over its territory can be considered as a fundamental axiom of the classical international law. Most nations indeed developed through a close relationship with the land they inhabited.[33] In other words, the sovereignty of the state is derived from its utility to express the sovereignty of the individual.[34] On the other hand, it could be said that cyberspace sovereignty is founded upon cyberspace territory and so legal concepts as cyberspace sovereignty and jurisdiction can be comprehended in relation to cyberspace territory where the electronic market exercises exclusive power over its territory.

It has to be taken into account that the territoriality principle grants a state jurisdiction to prescribe law with respect to "conduct that, wholly or in substantial part, takes place within its territory." Moreover, countries rely on the territoriality principle to regulate in-state hardware and software used in cyberspace communications and applying their domestic laws to out-of-state cyberspace activity. Electronic activity happens across multiple jurisdictional boundaries. The effects of online activities are not tied to geographic locations but can be felt by people living in a specific place.[35]

Most courts have found that even minimal harm back a trespass to chattels claim and have more broadly applied this common law tort to the new medium.[36] In *Intel v. Hamidi*[37] the court considered whether the sending of an e-mail through a proprietary company e-mail network constitutes trespass to chattels. Courts have viewed computer networks as property with physical characteristics, upon which robots may enter and trespass.[38] Hereafter, courts are utilizing the metaphor of cyberspace as a "place" to justify application of traditional laws governing real

---

[31] The Schooner Exch. v. M'Faddon, 11 U.S. (7 Cranch) 116, 136 (1812).

[32] Oppenheim's International Law 1992 R Jennings Chapter 5 at 563.

[33] I Brownlie "Principles of Public International Law" 1990 Oxford pp. 100–200.

[34] L Kramer "Extraterritorial Application of American Law" 1991 Sup. Ct. Rev. 179. Strassheim v Daily 221 US 280.

[35] James Boyle, Foucault in Cyberspace: Surveillance, Sovereignty, and Hardwired Censors, 66 U. CIN. L. REV. 177. Timothy S. Wu, Note, Cyberspace Sovereignty?—The Internet and the International System, 10 Harv. J.L. & Tech. 647, 654–55 (1997).

[36] Prune Yard Shopping Center v.Robins,447 U.S.74 (1980); Oyster Software, Inc.v. Forms Processing, Inc., No.C-00-0724 JCS,2001 WL 1736382 (N.D.Cal.Dec.6, 2001).

[37] Intel Corp. v.Hamidi, 114 Cal. Rptr.2d 244 (Cal.App.3d 2001). Intel Corp.v.Hamidi, 71 P.3d 296 (Cal. 2003). Intel v.Hamidi, 114 Cal.Rptr.2d 244, 253–55.

[38] Noah v. AOL Time Warner, Inc., 261 F. Supp.2d 532,534 (E.D.Va.2003).

property to this new medium.[39] It should be taken into account that cyberspace is not "just like" the physical world. On cyberspace, problems of physical infrastructure and overcrowding are less apparent because is a different dimension.[40]

Cyberspace is un-regulatable with the sense that there is the possibility to move a website around the global network. An advanced geographical tracking technology becomes both more accurate and more widely used means the development of cyber-world digital passports, applicable to state cyberspace sovereignty. It could be said that part of the electronic territory coincides with state territory at the moment that electronic actions affect the specific state territory.

Taking into account that the commercial environment is now global, but legal sovereignties are still territorial, the jurisdiction of national courts is based upon the national laws of individual nations and the legislative jurisdiction of a State is restricted to its territory. Border controls on the Internet are not impossible to develop and implement.[41] Many governments already regulate cyberspace. It is difficult for governments to impose technological limit on what is accessible via the Internet but China controls access to the Internet through centrally regulated servers.[42] It is a characteristic that all investments going to AI startups globally led by the private sector with some support from public bodies but in China the leadership comes from the state making certain that the population is more in tune with what the state wants which means that foreign firms have a difficulty for to participate in the markets of most of China's high-tech sectors. It has to be taken into account that with a straightforward AI policy, China is becoming the leading AI power and so preserving techno-nationalist purposes and national sovereignty. Moreover, an instrumentalized utilization of international standardization furthers techno-globalist aspirations, such as exporting their normative views on AI to the rest of the globe.[43] China is becoming the global AI innovation center and so the Chinese governance tactic to AI is directed on international competitiveness, economic growth, and social governance.

[39] Courts applying the doctrine of trespass to chattels to the Internet, see, e.g., eBay, Inc. v. Bidder's Edge, Inc., 100 F. Supp. 2d 1058 (N.D. Cal. 2000); Register.com, Inc. v. Verio, Inc., 126 F. Supp. 2d 238 (S.D.N.Y. 2000); America Online v. National Health Care Discount, Inc., 174 F. Supp. 2d 890 (N.D. Iowa 2001); Oyster Software, Inc. v. Forms Processing, 2001 WL 1736382 (N.D. Cal. Dec. 6, 2001).

[40] eBay, Inc. v. Bidder's Edge, 100 F. Supp. 2d 1058 (N.D. Cal. 2000). Register.com, Inc. v. Verio, Inc., 126 F. Supp. 2d 238 (S.D.N.Y. 2000); Oyster Software, Inc. v. Forms Processing, 2001 WL 1736382 (N.D. Cal. Dec. 6, 2001); and Intel Corp. v. Hamidi, 114 Cal. Rptr. 2d 244 (Ct. App. 2001).

[41] United States v Montoya de Hernandez 473 US 531, The Chinese Channel Limited http://www.chinese-channel.co.uk Framework for Global Electronic Commerce http://www.ecommerce.gov/; Management of Internet http://www.ntia.doc.gov/

[42] Peter H. Lewis, Limiting a Medium Without Boundaries, N.Y. TIMES, Jan. 15, 1996, at D1. John Pomfret, Chinese Sentenced in Internet Case, WASH. POST, Jan. 21, 1999, at A19.

[43] Hoffmann, Stacie, et al. (2020) "Standardising the Splinternet: How China's Technical Standards Could Fragment the Internet," Journal of Cyber Policy 1–26.

It has to be taken into consideration that states' entitlement to run cyberspace is unquestionable.[44] Do states consider cyberspace sovereignty as part of state sovereignty? Zekos believes that present regulations of electronic transactions show that states regard cyberspace sovereignty as part of their own sovereignty since electronic actions affect their own territory.[45] Transactions taking place in cyberspace that have an effect on persons or property in any specific location have virtually no geographic structure at all but it could be argued that the effect of electronic transactions has geographic structure in the final end in order to be felt by people.

8.4 Personal Cyberspace Jurisdiction

The U.S. Supreme Court's International Shoe[46] states that least connections are fulfilled providing the character of the action of the respondent within the country is sufficient. Hereafter, general jurisdiction occurs when a defendant's activities in a forum state are continuous and systematic; the activities relate to some general presence within a forum state but not essentially to the cause of action being asserted in the lawsuit.[47] Additionally, courts define specific jurisdiction employing a three-part test.[48]

Also, in *People Solutions, Inc. v People Solutions, Inc*[49] the court recognized the interactivity of the site and refused to assert jurisdiction absent evidence that residents had actually purchased from the site. While *in Maritz Inc. v. CyberGold, Inc*[50] defendant's web server was located in California, the court noted that the

---

[44]US v Smith, 680 F 2d 255 (1st Cir. Mass 1982).

[45]For an analysis see G. Zekos, State Cyberspace Jurisdiction and Personal Cyberspace Jurisdiction, Int J Law Info Tech 2007 15: 1–37; doi: https://doi.org/10.1093/ijlit/eai029 www.ijlit.oxfordjournals.org

[46]International Shoe Co. v. State of Washington, 326 U.S. 310, 316 (1945) (establishing test for determining whether an assertion of personal jurisdiction comports with the Due Process Clause of the U.S. Constitution based on whether the defendant had sufficient contact with the relevant state "such that jurisdiction is consistent with traditional notions of fair play and substantial justice").

[47]Helicopteros Nacionales de Colombia, S.A. v. Hall, 466 U.S. 408, 414–15 & n.9 (1984).

[48]Hinsch v. Outrigger Hotels Haw., 153 F. Supp. 2d 209, 213–14 (E.D.N.Y.2001) ((1) the defendant must purposefully avail itself of the privilege of conducting activities in the forum state or consummate some act or transaction with the forum state; (2) the defendant's forum-related activities must relate to the claim; and (3) the exercise of jurisdiction must be reasonable. Courts continue to rely on the due process analysis of International Shoe as they construe personal jurisdiction based on cyberspace activities)).

[49]People Solutions, Inc. v. People Solutions, Inc., 2000 WL 1030619 (N.D. Tex., 2000).

[50]Maritz Inc. v. CyberGold, Inc., 947 F. Supp. 1328 (E.D. Mo. 1996). Ameritech Services, Inc. v. SCA Promotions, Inc., 2000 WL 283098 (N.D. Ill., 2000); LFG, LLC v. Zapata Corp., 78 F. Supp.2d 731 (N.D. Ill., 1999); Biometics, LLC v. New Womyn, Inc., 112 F.Supp.2d 869 (E.D. Mo., 2000).

disputed website was "continually accessible to every Internet-connected computer in Missouri."

Is the cyberspace sovereignty reflected and attached to state sovereignty with common boundaries the state's territory when it comes to effects and access? It seems that courts consider that state sovereignty coincides with cyberspace sovereignty establishing a cyberspace state sovereignty since it is accessibly by a computer located in the state sovereignty irrespective of the dimensional difference which means that courts are establishing personal jurisdiction for the electronic actions.

Cyberspace is a place where people talk, where companies meet consumers and sell their goods, and where investments in website development and presence are electronic versions of property. Furthermore, there is a need to take into account a cyberspace jurisdiction for cyberspace actions having not feasible consequences on real world and the formation, execution, and results are felt only in cyberspace. Thus, cyber courts and cyber arbitral tribunals should have jurisdiction to solve all actions taking place on the net and the enforcement of their awards and decisions will be made according to international conventions on recognition and enforcement of foreign awards and e-awards. Obviously, courts and arbitral tribunals have to be considered as equal and independent forms of dispute resolutions.

First of all, cyber entities contact electronic transactions and individuals get the consequences of cyber-actions. Moreover, cyber society is the force of law-making in cyberspace sovereignty which is not connecting to any particular state sovereignty but only to cyberspace sovereignty. It could be said that cyberspace generates a society connected to a state with the only difference in the dimensional expression. In addition, some electronic actions are more adaptable to traditional legal rules rather others due to the ease of transformation from digital to material things and vice versa. Hence, electronic transactions have consequences upon individuals living in a state territory and so state has got the right to enforce legal laws concerning the impacts upon people and so forcing legal laws according to the effects felt within their territory by their inhabitants and not net inhabitants who can leave in another country which means the part of cyberspace territory corresponds to state territory. In other words, state sovereignty corresponds to cyberspace sovereignty generating the state cyberspace sovereignty. Countries regulate many kinds of electronic actions having in mind the old legal principles adjusted to serve the digital type of actions. Also, there are many setbacks in regulating successfully and fairly many electronic actions which mean that since cyberspace is a distinctive electronic place there is a requirement to ascertain cyberspace sovereignty for electronic actions contacted by electronic entities. Hence, the instituting of universal cyberspace jurisdiction for this electronic place permitting all courts around the globe to deal with the cyberspace transactions and disputes will bring harmony and certainty in electronic trading taking into consideration that the electronic transactions have the prospective to influence instantaneously all jurisdictions.

Currently there is an assortment of factors taking into account so as to justify jurisdiction for electronic transactions generating uncertainty. Besides, universal cyberspace jurisdiction will mean that any state whose people are influenced in any way by an electronic action will have jurisdiction to decide and the decision will be enforced by an international convention of enforcement of foreign courts decisions. The universal cyberspace jurisdiction will be particularly valuable for criminal and intellectual property cases. Thus, personal cyberspace jurisdiction should be based on the local accessibility resulted in local consequences upon individuals since websites target the whole cyberspace territory being accessible by all jurisdictions that offer the electronic devices for access.

It is worth mentioning here that jurisdictional rules should be plain, straightforwardly ascertainable, and anticipated.[51] As mentioned earlier, a court can exercise personal jurisdiction over a defendant with adequate instate contacts linked to a plaintiff's claim. In fact, personal jurisdiction defines a court's power over defendants.[52] Personal jurisdiction doctrine's weight on limiting state power and protecting the defendant's "liberty" indicates the scales against plaintiffs. In other words, personal jurisdiction is about access to justice.[53]

As discussed earlier, U.S. personal jurisdiction was governed by notions of physical presence and territorial sovereignty and so individual defendants could be sued in the states where they resided, where they were personally served, and where they consented to personal jurisdiction through voluntary appearance in the forum court.[54] Moreover, the consent basis for jurisdiction has even expanded beyond voluntary appearance in the forum court to embrace ex ante consent by contract.[55] Furthermore, the Court decided a series of cases clarifying the specific jurisdiction's minimum contacts test and so specific jurisdiction depends upon the "relationship

[51] Livnat v. Palestinian Auth., 851 F.3d 45, 56 (D.C. Cir. 2017) Jones v. IPX Int'l Equatorial Guinea, S.A., 920 F.3d 1085, 1094 (6th Cir. 2019) ("Courts presume that plaintiffs choose convenient forums, so a plaintiff's choice of forum is given deference.").

[52] Bristol-Myers Squibb Co. v. Super. Ct., 137 S. Ct. 1773, 1776 (2017) (emphasizing the significance of the connection between the forum state and the underlying controversy that occurred in that state). Car-Freshner Corp. v. Scented Promotions, LLC, No. 519CV1158GTSATB, 2021 WL 1062574, at *9 (N.D.N.Y. Mar. 19, 2021) (requiring defendants contacts to relate to the claim), Williams v. Aguirre, 965 F.3d 1147, 1163 (11th Cir. 2020) (explaining courts are "obligated, if at all possible, to distill from apparently conflicting ... decisions a basis of reconciliation and to apply that reconciled rule.").

[53] Daniel Klerman, Personal Jurisdiction and Product Liability, 85 S. CAL. L. REV. 1551, 1585–86 (2012) ("[P]otential plaintiffs are likely to perceive out-of-state litigation as a significant hardship."); Todd David Peterson, Categorical Confusion in Personal Jurisdiction Law, 76 WASH. & LEE L. REV. 655 (2019) ("[I]t is clearly in a corporate defendant's interest to force a plaintiff to travel from the plaintiff's home state."); Adam N. Steinman, Access to Justice, Rationality, and Personal Jurisdiction, 71 VAND. L. REV. 1401 (2018) ("To require the plaintiff to seek judicial remedies outside her home state can impose significant cost and inconvenience.").

[54] Pennoyer v. Neff, 95 U.S. 714, 720 (1878) ("The authority of every tribunal is necessarily restricted by the territorial limits of the State in which it is established."); at 722 ("[N]o State can exercise direct jurisdiction and authority over persons or property without its territory."). Milliken v. Meyer, 311 U.S. 457, 463 (1940).

[55] Adam v. Saenger, 303 U.S. 59, 67–68 (1983) (voluntary appearance). Carnival Cruise Lines v. Shute, 499 U.S. 585 (1991).

among the defendant, the forum, and the litigation.[56]" In *Walden v. Fiore,*[57] the Court considered the connection between the defendant's conduct and the forum. In *Bristol-Myers Squibb Co. v. Superior Court,*[58] the Court tackled the relationship between the forum and the claim. Thus, after Bristol-Myers Squibb, specific jurisdiction necessitates a direct link between not only the forum and the defendant but also between the forum and the claim.[59]

The Supreme Court in *Hanson v. Denckla*[60] developed the Due Process Clause's minimum contacts analysis. Moreover, in *Goodyear Dunlop Tires Operations, S.A. v. Brown* and *Daimler AG v. Bauman*, the Supreme Court[61] disapproved of the exercise of general personal jurisdiction over a corporate defendant based exclusively on the defendant's continuous and systematic way of business, such as marketing and selling products, in the forum state and so the Court ruled that the proper examination is whether that corporation's affiliations with the forum state render it "essentially at home" in that state. Thus, the Court reminded that for a corporation the "paradigm forum" for the exercise of general jurisdiction is where the corporation is incorporated or, if in a different state, where it has its principal place of business.

It is worth noting here that the Supreme Court[62] determined the limits of specific personal jurisdiction in a products liability case and so a state court's assertion of specific personal jurisdiction does not involve a causal link between the defendant's in-state activities and the plaintiff's claims. Ford involved state law products liability actions and specified that products liability actions with an out-of-state defendant did not necessitate a causal link between the defendant's in-state conduct and the plaintiffs' respective claims. Moreover, the pertinent inquiry is whether the plaintiff's suit "relate[s] to the defendant's contacts with the forum," meaning that "some relationships will support jurisdiction without a causal showing." Hence, there is a need for an affiliation between the forum and the underlying controversy, principally, an action or an incidence that takes place in the Forum State and is subject to the State's regulation. To that extent, the court held that a corporation such as Ford

[56] Helicopteros, 466 U.S. at 414.

[57] 571 U.S. 277 (2014).

[58] 137 S. Ct. 1773 (2017). Jonathan Remy Nash, The Rules And Standards Of Personal Jurisdiction, 2020 Alabama Law Review Vol. 72:2:465.

[59] Scott Dodson, Personal Jurisdiction and Aggregation, 113 NW. U. L. REV. 1, 17 (2018).

[60] Hanson v. Denckla, 357 U.S. 235 (1958); Allan Erbsen, Impersonal Jurisdiction, 60 EMORY L.J. 1, 26 (2010).

[61] Daimler AG v. Bauman, 134 S. Ct. 746, 760–61 (2014) (quoting Bauman, 134 S. Ct. 746 (No. 11–965)); Goodyear Dunlop Tires Operations, S.A. v. Brown, 131 S. Ct. 2846, 2856–57 (2011).

[62] Ford Motor Co. v. Montana Eighth Judicial District Court, 141 S.Ct. 1017 (2021). Ford v. Montana, 141 S. Ct. 1017, 1032 (2021) (Alito, J., concurring) ("[T]here are . . . reasons to wonder whether the case law we have developed . . . is well suited for the way in which business is now conducted."); Charles W. "Rocky" Rhodes, et al., Ford's Jurisdictional Crossroads, 109 GEORGETOWN L.J. ONLINE 102 (2020).

serving a market for its product in a state can be sued in that state when its product triggers an injury there, regardless of whether the product was originally designed, manufactured, or sold within that state. In a word, the Supreme Court has generated an artificial “home” for an artificial person.[63]

8.5 Cyberspace Governance

Conventionally governance has been related with “governing,” denoting formal political institutions aiming to organize and control interdependent social relations possessing the capability to enforce decisions. Moreover, Governance denotes the regulation of interdependent relations in the absence of overarching political authority, such as in the global system.

As a general rule, governance is the set of tasks and practices exercised by those in charge for an enterprise with the objective of providing strategic direction, guaranteeing that objectives are accomplished, making certain that risks are administered properly and verifying that the company’s means are utilized responsibly. Increasing computer interconnectivity—particularly growth in the use of the Internet/cyberspace—has transformed the way that governments, states, and much of the world communicate and perform business. The numerous networks that make up the Internet/cyberspace embrace the national backbone and regional networks which networks run by individual businesses or “enterprise” networks. The global interconnectivity provided by the Internet/cyberspace permits cyber attackers such as criminal groups, hackers, and terrorists to with no trouble cross-national borders, contact great numbers of victims at the same time, and effortlessly preserve anonymity.

E-government is an innovation in the public sector making public services less expensive and more open[64] and so offering the equipment for innovative interactions between a government and its citizens and intelligent ways to supply public services.[65] E-government brings the government closer to citizens, defeating the barriers of bureaucracy, reducing corruption and making decision-makers more reactive

---

[63] Zainab R. Qureshi, If the Shoe Fits: Applying Personal Jurisdiction’s Stream of Commerce Analysis to E-Commerce-A Value Test, 21 N.Y.U. J. LEGIS. & PUB. POL’Y 727, 728 (2019) (“[T]he Supreme Court has yet to define the parameters of personal jurisdiction vis-à-vis Internet activity.”)

[64] OECD (2009). Rethinking e-Government Services: User-Centred Approaches. OECD Publishing, 2009.

[65] Yigitcanlar T., Baum S. B. (2006). E-Government and the digital divide. In: Encyclopedia of e-commerce, e-government, and mobile commerce. Khosrow-Pour M. (Ed.), pp. 353–358. USA, Pennsylvania, Hershey: Idea Group Reference (IGI Global), 2006. Wauters P., Lörincz B. (2008). User satisfaction and administrative simplification within the perspective of eGovernment impact: Two faces of the same coin?”, European Journal of ePractice, no. 4, August 2008, www.epracticejournal.eu

to people's needs, which means that e-services of e-government are characterized by greater efficiency and transparency.[66] Moreover, the functional components of e-government such as e-infrastructure, e-services, and access to public information have a raison d'être upon anti-corruption effect by enhancing the transparency of procurements system, making public services more easily reached and clear, and making certain a global citizens' access to information. Furthermore, e-access to government information is a vital good governance tool in making certain the execution of state obligations and raising the accountability to citizens.[67]

Governance of the cyberspace is carried out by the so-called multistakeholder ("MSH") organizations such as the Internet Society and the World Wide Web Consortium which entities have principally established the norms and standards for the global Internet/cyberspace. Moreover, cyberspace governance implies the capacity to enforce mandates limited in the framework of Internet governance as performed by MSH processes varying from the "soft" power of rough consensus to the "hard" power of international law and binding treaties. For the reason that the Internet/cyberspace works around and beyond political boundaries, efforts to censor Internet/cyberspace speech have proven complex and ineffective. Joe Waz and Phil Weiser[68] say that "it will be important to establish an understanding as to whether, when, and how sovereign governments should defer to MSH processes, should themselves be recognized as stakeholders in such processes, and should empower or backstop such processes."

Openness of governance causes openness of technology and so, until lately, the operation of the network disregarded the content of the packets of information that were routed around it which means that routing algorithms applied to all packets extensively, and the routers had no access to the content to derive grounds for discrimination. Also, openness does not always assure equitable outcomes. Especially, central to the Internet's function is that the central resources, particularly the means by which the Internet is retrieved, are universal and unique. Moreover, certain matters, such as net neutrality or the extent of liability of content platforms or information intermediaries for the information they transmit, fall directly within governments' responsibility to legislate or not. Hence, governments are modeling cyberspace and cyberspace governance.

Different models of Internet are expected to coexist even within individual organizations and governments and so various preferences exist for certain models generating conflicts in global cyberspace governance. Kieron O'Hara and Wendy

[66] OECD (2009). Rethinking e-Government Services: User-Centred Approaches. OECD Publishing, 2009.

[67] Belanger F., Carter L. (2006). The impact of the digital divide on e-government use. In: Proceeding HICSS '06 Proceedings of the 39th Annual Hawaii International Conference on System Sciences, 2006, No. 04.

[68] Joe Waz and Phil Weiser, Internet Governance: The Role Of Multistakeholder Organizations, 2012 J. On Telecomm. & High Tech. L. Vol. 10,331 p 348.

Hall[69] argue that "the United States, China and Russia, each of which in its different ways at the time of writing pursues aggressive nationalist policy goals while showing impatience with due process both internally and internationally."

Global cyberspace governance, naturally one of the closest technological analogs for AI governance, has seen a number of remarkable multistakeholder successes, but has also been subject to ongoing contestation, particularly in areas of cybersecurity and cyber-warfare.

Cybersecurity governance verifies how generally-accepted management controls such as risk assessment controls are adapted, supplemented, and utilized in the face of the advanced persistent threat and mirroring the total enterprise risk management strategy and enterprise risk governance structure.[70] It is worth noting that risk assessment concerning algorithmic activities and operations is regarded as a security asset for state actors.

In addition, cybersecurity[71] governance refers to the element of corporate governance that tackles the enterprise's dependence on cyberspace in the presence of opponent and so covering information systems security governance. Moreover, cybersecurity governance is the section of corporate governance regarding organizational dependence on cyberspace in the presence of adversaries as a domain of enterprise risk management. Deb Bodeau, et al.[72] specify that "Cyber Prep provides a framework for assessing, and identifying gaps or possible areas of evolution in, an organization's cyber-security governance structures and practices. Achieving cybersecurity governance consistent with its target Cyber Prep level enables an organization to make consistent and understandable decisions about Investing in security measures; aligning cyber-security risk management with other aspects of enterprise risk management; and managing the organization's cyber-security posture."

The growth of cyberspace has been portrayed by an emphasis on interoperability, effectiveness, and freedom but our increasing reliance has not been matched by efforts to keep it secure reflecting the original rationale of the web, which was to exchange scientific data, rather than to assist an entire global economy. The upsurge of use and functionality of cyberspace has outpaced efforts to restructure and secure the original cyberspace's infrastructure. Cybersecurity includes borderless challenges, while responses remain overpoweringly national in scope and even these are unsatisfactory. Moreover, cybersecurity characterizes an increasing challenge to democratic governance, as public and private efforts to secure cyberspace. IT networks and supervise the traffic that they carry has to be balanced with human security anxiety and, above all, with human rights to privacy and to freedom of

---

[69] Kieron O'Hara and Wendy Hall, Four Internets: The Geopolitics of Digital Governance, CIGI Papers No. 206—December 2018 p13.

[70] International Standards Organization (ISO), Corporate governance of information technology, ISO/IEC 38500:2008, 2008.

[71] GAO, Cyberspace: United States Faces Challenges in Addressing Global Cybersecurity and Governance, GAO-10-606, July 2010, http://www.gao.gov/new.items/d10606.pdf

[72] Deb Bodeau, Steve Boyle, Jenn Fabius-Greene, Rich Graubart, Cyber Security Governance, MTR100308 MITRE TECHNICAL REPORT ©2010 The MITRE Corporation.

expression and association. Benjamin S. Buckland, Fred Schreier, Theodor H. Winkler[73] argue that "democratic governance concerns—particularly regarding control, oversight and transparency—have been almost entirely absent from the debate. These concerns are exacerbated by the enormous role played by private actors (both alone and in cooperation with governments) in online security of all types. Given the pace at which states and private companies are reinforcing online security and preparing for cyber-war, addressing democratic governance concerns has never been more pressing."

The G7/8 addressed the problems of coordinating policies regarding the governance of cyberspace dealing with governance issues including, among others, the formation of norms, principles, and rules concerning the interconnection of computer networks via networks of networks such as the Internet/cyberspace, rights of access to those networks, pricing of access, observing of network-mediated economic transactions, intellectual property protection, taxation of goods and services delivered via cyberspace, matters of privacy, security, and a range of other subjects thought to influence the trust of cyberspace' users.[74] According to Jeffrey A. Hart[75] "in areas, such as internet governance, where private actors are needed both to provide accurate informational inputs to form and implement new norms, rules, and procedures, a properly configured multistakeholder approach is both necessary and desirable."

Blockchain protocols set the rules to permit computers to interact with each other concerning the exchange of value on a peer-to-peer basis; in much the same manner the cyberspace sets the rules that let computers to exchange information on a peer-to-peer basis. Moreover, many blockchain protocols, like cyberspace, are, at launch, generative which means that they are invented to accept any contribution that follows a basic set of rules. In other words, blockchain governance follows the path of cyberspace governance but there are certain shortcomings that blockchain protocol governance has to circumvent.[76] Furthermore, critics of modern-day cyberspace governance denounce the recentralization of the Internet, the absence of institutional legitimacy, and the growing politicization of cyberspace governance, which means that the picked governance mechanisms made way for unfitting intervention by sovereign governments and the fragmentation of what was intended

[73] Benjamin S. Buckland, Fred Schreier, Theodor H. Winkler, Democratic governance challenges of cyber security, DCAF HORIZON 2015 WORKING PAPER No. 1.

[74] Skantze, Pernilla (2003). "European Cyber Security." OECD Global Forum on Information Systems and Network Security: Towards a Global Culture of Security. <www.oecd.org/dataoecd/53/43/17979495.pdf>.

[75] Jeffrey A. Hart, The G8 and the Governance of Cyberspace, Chapter 9, In New Perspectives on Global Order: Why America Needs the G8.

[76] Milton L. Mueller, Networks and States: The Global Politics Of Internet Governance 1 (2010) ("A distinctive global politics is developing around the Internet. Like global trade and environmental policy, Internet governance has become a point of international conflict among states and a target of transnational policy advocates from business and civil society.").

to be a global, borderless network.[77] It has to be taken into consideration that cyberspace was intended to be the self-governing system prospering without regard to geography and territorially based coercion permitting people to join communities and govern themselves without regard to geography, without respect to the top-down coercive structures of territorial governmental systems, and without the usual pathologies and corruptions that typify territorial rule.[78]

It seems that blockchain technology's governance path reflects that of cyberspace and so the parallel between the development of the cyberspace and the development of blockchain protocols is well-defined because both technologies are protocol technologies[79] enabling peer-to-peer exchange and imbedding libertarian values into the code. On the one hand, public blockchain protocols face a serious governance crisis. On the other hand, thus far, blockchain protocols have adhered to the path of early Internet governance. Hence, if the architects of blockchain protocols are not cautious, they may suffer a similar fate by escalating governmental control, greater centralization, and decreasing privacy. As blockchain architects begin to bear in mind better governance structures, there is a legal movement to compel a fiduciary framework upon open-source software developers and so the effects for open-source software development could be dire. In other words, if indiscriminately imposed upon blockchain communities without respect of modifications among communities or the reality of how such communities function, the movement will nullify the technology before it ever matures.

Cyberspace governance efforts to date have been mixed because they are emerged the risks of national government interference, recentralization, and increasing politicization as ways that cyberspace governance structures have failed to uphold the original vision of cyberspace causing problems concerning its innovative

[77] Dimitry Epstein, The Making of Institutions of Information Governance: The Case of the Internet Governance Forum, 28 J. INFO. TECH. 137, 139 (2013) ("For many in the Internet community, particularly those belonging to the old guard of Internet designers and those viewing the Internet in more libertarian terms, the growing interest of governments in issues of Internet governance, specifically the calls to implement a more nation-state focused and hierarchical decision-making process, was an assault on the very spirit of the Internet and its normative foundations.").

[78] Marius Kalinauskas & Mantas Barcys, Interaction Between National Governments and ICAN While Administering the Internet, 3 SOCIAL TECHNOLOGIES 432, 435 (2013) (taking the position that the term Internet governance lacks a useful definition but "stands mainly for the global technical management of the core resources of the Internet: domain names, IP addresses, Internet protocols and the root server system").

[79] Marco Iansiti & Karim R. Lakhani, The Truth About Blockchain, HARV. BUS. REV. (Jan-Feb. 2017), https://hbr.org/2017/01/the-truth-about-blockchain. Daniel Folkinshteyn, Mark Lennon & Tim Reilly, A Tale of Twin Tech: Bitcoin and the WWW, 10 J. STRATEGIC & INT'L STUDS 82, 82 & 84 (2015) (using the term "protocol" to describe both the Internet at the Bitcoin Blockchain). Jack Filiba, Blockchain is the Internet's Legacy Through the Internet of Value, COINSQUARE (Dec. 14, 2017), https://news.coinsquare.com/blockchain/blockchain-internet-of-value/ (explaining that blockchain technology holds the potential to realize John Perry Barlow's "cyber-libertarian" vision for the Internet).

capacity and enhancing its regulability.[80] Remarkably, some cyberspace governance institutions are attempting to bring blockchain governance within their domain already, including the United Nations Internet Governance Forum and W3C, among others.[81]

In other words, if blockchain protocol governance follows the path of cyberspace, the very qualities of blockchain technologies that stimulate innovation and promise disruption will be nullified before they are even fully developed. Due to the nature of International law frequently failing to prevent national governments from undertaking further action, government capture remains a strong prospect in the international governance scenario or in any version of international private ordering that relies on international institutional actions.[82]

8.6 Cyberspace Governance and International Law

It has to be taken into account that forces of globalization and technological transformation have weakened the capability of sovereign nation states and media content producers to directly control information flows which means that this loss of control over content and the failure of laws and markets to resume this control have readdressed political and economic battles into the realm of infrastructure and technologies of cyberspace governance.

It is worth noting that infrastructure design and administration internalize the political and economic values that eventually affect the extent of online freedom and innovation. It could be said that alterations in technical architecture of cyberspace are also arrangements of power and so the transferal of power to infrastructure is drawing attention to the politics of cyberspace design and the legitimacy of the harmonizing institutions and private ordering that generate and manage these

---

[80] Lawrence B. Solum, Models of Internet Governance, 59, 59–60, in Internet Governance: Infrastructure And Institutions (Lee A. Bygrave & Jon Bing eds. 2009) (describing the Internet governance crisis suffered when governance of DNS by one individual, Jon Postel, could not be scaled to meet demand, leading to the creation of ICANN).

[81] The United Nations Internet Governance Forum Dynamic Coalition on Blockchain Technologies, https://intgovforum.org/multilingual/content/dynamic-coalition-on-blockchain-technologies-dc-blockchain; W3C Blockchain Community Group, https://www.w3.org/community/blockchain/. Vlad Zamfir, My Intentions for Blockchain Governance, MEDIUM (Oct. 4, 2018), https://medium.com/@Vlad_Zamfir/myintentions-for-blockchain-governance-801d19d378e5

[82] Elizabeth Pollmoan, The Rise of Regulatory Affairs in Innovative Startups, in The Handbook Of Law & Entrepreneurship In The United States at 6 (D. Gordon Smith & Christine Hurt, eds., 2018) ("In reality, hacking just means building something quickly or testing the boundaries of what can be done." (quoting Facebook, Inc. Registration Statement, available at https://www.sec.gov/Archives/edgar/data/1326801/000119312512034517/d287954dsl.htm#toc287954_10 Carla L. Reyes, Comment, International Governance of Domestic National Security Measures: The Forgotten Role of the World Trade Organization, 14 UCLA J. INT'L L. & FOREIGN AFF. 351 (2009) (detailing the ICJ's inability to enforce international law during the Nicaraguan conflict).

infrastructures. In other words, freedom of expression in the context of expanding turns to infrastructure to control information. Is there relationship between governance and infrastructure? Of course, there is a battle over cyberspace content transferred into the cyberspace governance infrastructure via the use of the Internet's domain name system for intellectual property rights enforcement; the use of approaches restricting the flow of information; and the termination of infrastructure services such as WikiLeaks, etc.

In fact, cyberspace has a complex technical architecture beneath the layer of applications and content and generally out of public view embracing an ecosystem of cyberspace governance technologies, meaning the digital systems and processes planned to keep cyberspace operational.[83] It has to be taken into account that cyberspace governance technologies not only embed political values in their design and operations but are progressively being co-opted for political reasons unrelated to their principal cyberspace governance function. Taking into account that governance traditionally encompasses the efforts of nation states to govern activities within a fixed jurisdiction, in cyberspace governance, nation states are one set of players in a larger variety of institutions and private entities governing cyberspace.

Also, cyberspace governance embraces non-State actors and norms other than law, but States and law still play substantial roles. ICANN is a US-incorporated non-profit organization owing its existence to and regulated by US laws, whether or not it has a future contractual relationship with the federal government.[84] Moreover, cyberspace is a vast, open, global "network of networks" that functions on: (1) hardware—servers, routers, etc., which permit the network to run; (2) communications—e.g., TCP/IP, which regulates communication among networks; (3) applications—the content of those communications; and (4) users—those who run in cyberspace.[85]

To that extent, a Country invokes territorial sovereignty to regulate hardware and users based on where they reside, but no Country regulates the communications layer alone; by definition it functions on a global scale. The root servers that certify addresses for Internet traffic are distributed globally with redundant systems.[86] Thus, a Country may control applications coded or used within its territory, but extraterritorial applications are inevitable, embracing those explicitly planned to pierce State boundaries.[87] In short, cyberspace governance via boundary lines appears impracticable, at least if the effort focuses only on choosing one type of boundary over another such as national versus autonomous boundaries. On the other hand, at the moment the regulation is based on national law via some boundaries of the utilized

[83] Internet protocol (IP) addresses, domain names, and autonomous system numbers (ASNs); the Internet's domain name system (DNS); and network-layer systems such as Internet access, Internet exchange points, and Internet security intermediaries.

[84] J Weinberg, "Governments, Privatization, and 'Privatization': ICANN and the GAC" (2011) 18 Mich Telecomm & Tech L Rev. 189, 191–207.

[85] N Choucri & D Clark, "Who Controls Cyberspace' Bulletin of Atomic Scientists (1 September 2013)."

[86] http://www.root-servers.org/

[87] "Tor Overview," https://www.torproject.org/about/overview.html.en

technology and the effects of electronic actions upon nationals of a state. Moreover, international law does not compel an "all-or nothing" choice between res communis or territorial sovereignty any more than it authorizes governance by line-drawing generally. Therefore, international law has accepted a selection of middle-ground or "hybrid" models where in place of definite, solid boundaries, we see shared governance formations.

On top of self- or engineered governance, international regulation suggests treating cyberspace as its own[88] being a novel space for governance.[89] So, the idea of cyberspace as equivalent to but distinct from "real" space with its own borders endures.[90] Nowadays, States establish legal authority over actors and activities in cyberspace based on their borders; they can regulate based on the physical location of the network(s) or server(s) employed, or the physical location where the effects of such activity occur. Thus, States claim to govern cyberspace using boundaries the same way they use them to govern other places (physical territory) or mediums (telecommunications).[91]

It has to be taken into consideration that the USA has employed its boundaries—within which much of the original Internet's infrastructure exist—to advance a global and open cyberspace where multiple stakeholders take part in governance issues without content restrictions. Besides, other Countries employ territorial boundaries quite differently and so the "Great Firewall" of China encompasses technological tools that restrain communications and technology within China while attempting to wall off those residing in China's territory from log on to specific external sites and communications.[92] Cuba and Iran impose similar technological borders.[93] Thus, efforts to compel national boundaries within cyberspace are no longer the only sphere of authoritarian governments. Brazil has intended to localize e-mail and other communications within its territory to wade off foreign

---

[88] D Hunter, "Cyberspace as Place, and the Tragedy of the Digital Anticommons" (2003) 91 Calif L Rev. 439, 443 ("cognitive science investigations provide ample evidence that, purely as a descriptive observation, we do think of cyberspace as a place").

[89] Council on Foreign Relations, Task Force Report: Defending an Open, Global, Secure, and Resilient Internet (2013) 14–15 (describing ITU's 2012 Word Conference on International Telecommunications).

[90] D Ignatius, "After Snowden a Diminished Internet" Washington Post (5 Feb 2014); Council of Foreign Relations (n 20 above) 15; J Scott, "Chatham House founds Global Commission on Internet Governance" ComputerWeekly.com (22 Jan 2014).

[91] Computer Fraud and Abuse Act, 18 U.S.C.A. §1030 (regulating "protected computers" defined in territorial terms to include computers "used in or affecting interstate or foreign commerce or communication, including a computer located outside the United States that is used in a manner that affects interstate or foreign commerce or communication of the United States"); The Computer Misuse Act 1990 (UK) §§5(2)(b) and (3)(b).

[92] L Eko et al., "Google This: The Great Firewall of China, the It Wheel of India, Google Inc., and Internet Regulation" (2011) 15 J Internet L 3, 5; Jyh-An Lee & Ching-Yi Liu, "Forbidden City Enclosed by the Great Firewall: The Law and Power of Internet Filtering in China" (2012) 13 Minn J L Sci & Tech 125, 133.

[93] F Fassihi, "Iran Mounts New Web Crackdown" Wall St J (6 Jan 2012).

surveillance.[94] In other words, there is a "Balkanization," where the global cyberspace becomes disaggregated into numerous networks distributed along national lines, generating less communication and collaboration and more competition and conflict.[95]

Also, it has to be considered that the main—and default—justification for governing authority in international law today remains "territorial sovereignty." Territorial sovereignty is distinct from other conceptions of sovereignty based on identifying a single source of political authority within a State or membership in the international society.[96]

International law allocates "territory" to individual Countries who assume principal power to govern there and so State authority is exclusive, barring some agreement or peremptory international law rule.[97] Even though land is the central type of "territory," international law recognizes other resources as well, including man-made infrastructure lying on a State's land territory, the air space above it, mineral and oil resources below the surface, and 12 miles of the adjacent sea and seabed.[98] Where territorial sovereignty is available or contested, international law offers—and regulates among—numerous methods to allocate sovereignty: occupation, cession, accretion, and prescription but earlier accepted methods are now banned (conquest) or unfeasible (discovery).[99]

It is worth noting that even though States constitute themselves around territorial sovereignty, international law does not insist it serve as the exclusive basis for governance. Thus, some resources are regarded as categorically distinct from "territory" and its apportionment among States and so the high seas have qualified as res communis, a resource belonging to everyone, subject to appropriation by no one. Therefore, the res communis concept rationalizes some form of collective governance autonomous from the dominant territorial sovereignty model.[100] There are numerous purposes for why a resource receives the res communis label; it may be to (1) uphold equitable use of the resource by multiple Countries; (2) make certain the resource's sustainability; or (3) accommodate a functional requirement where individual State governance is unfeasible or not viable.

Nationally, laws specify boundaries separating legitimate from prohibited behavior or distinguishing categories or effects. Besides, international law does the same for States and to lesser extent international organizations and individuals but

[94] L Chao & P Trevisani, "Brazil Legislators Bear Down on Internet Bill" Wall St J (13 Nov 2013); J Watts, "Brazil to Legislate on Online Civil Rights Following Snowden Revelations" The Guardian (1 Nov 2013).

[95] S Meinrath, "We Can't Let the Internet Become Balkanized" Slate (14 Oct 2013).

[96] SD Krasner, Sovereignty: Organized Hypocrisy (Princeton, 1999) 9–25; A Chayes & A Chayes, The New Sovereignty (Harvard, 1995) 27.

[97] Island of Palmas Arbitration (Netherlands v United States) (1928) II RIAA 829, 839.

[98] UN Convention on the Law of the Sea, 10 December 1982, 1833 UNTS 3, art 3 ('UNCLOS').

[99] R Jennings & A Watts (eds.), 1 Oppenheim's International Law (9th ed. 1992) 678–79.

[100] UNCLOS 1982.

sometimes these borders intends to be solid lex specialis; in other cases, more than one set of laws or legal regimes may purport to regulate the same matter at the same time.

The ICJ has implied that attacks by non-state actors can only generate criminal law and not rules governing the use of force[101] but then there are other circumstances in which international human rights law is alleged to continue to apply in concert with international humanitarian law.[102]

How does law draw boundaries in cyberspace? It could be said that two methods prevail: firstly, tailor-made law generated explicitly for the cyber-context; or secondly law-by-analogy where pre-existing fields of law and their contents are planned in cyberspace using analogical reasoning. Countries have utilized both methods in domestic law.[103] Besides, international law has relied almost entirely on law-by-analogy to regulate cyberspace, predominantly when it comes to issues implicating the use of force and IHL and so this has made certain cyberspace is not some law-free zone. Moreover, current international legal regimes in cyberspace for cyber-war display some of the same problems—in terms of both theory and function—encountered in the governance framework.

Legal systems repeatedly draw lines tailor-made for particular areas, activities, or sources of law which means that even within an existing topic such as criminal law, a new rule appears tailor-made for particular players, behavior, or victims.[104] Tailor-made fields and the rules they encompass assume they are the outcome of a valid law-making course, tailor-made law governs directly, subject to standard issues of interpretation and application and so interpretation is quickly becoming its own field of international law.[105]

It could be said that since its foundation, cyberspace has caused calls for its own field of law, cyberlaw, and laws within that field tailor-made for the technology implicated. As a matter of national law, these calls have had a degree of success and so nowadays cyberlaw is its own field. Moreover, many tailor-made rules now accommodate the fact that computers and networks are both new tools for, and targets of, numerous forms of activity such as criminal, economic, and political. To that extent, crimes using computers embrace cyber-theft and cyber-extortion, while

[101] Legal Consequences of the Construction of a Wall in the Occupied Palestinian Territory (Advisory Opinion) (9 July 2004) 43 ILM 1009, 1050; accord Armed Activities on the Territory of the Congo (Democratic Republic of Congo v Uganda) (19 December 2005) [2005] ICJ Rep 116, [146]–[147].

[102] CR Sunstein, "On Analogical Reasoning" (1993) 106 Harvard L Rev. 741.

[103] Computer Fraud and Abuse Act, 18 U.S.C. §1030 (cyber-specific criminal law). For an example extending existing US law by analogy see United States v. Forrester, 512 F.2d 500 (9th Cir. 2008); OS Kerr, "Applying the Fourth Amendment to the Internet: A General Approach" (2010) 62 Stan L Rev. 1005, 1008.

[104] UNCLOS (oceans law); Marrakesh Agreement Establishing the World Trade Organization, 15 April 1994, 1867 UNTS 187 (trade); Vienna Convention on the Law of Treaties, 23 May 1969, 1155 UNTS 331 (treaties).

[105] A Bianchi et al. (eds.), Interpretation in International Law (OUP 2014).

crimes against computers may take place via viruses, worms, Trojan horse programs, and other malware along with Directed Denial of Service (DDOS) attacks that interrupt communications with one or more websites.[106] Consequently, States have enacted "cybercrime" laws alongside procedural and evidentiary rules drafted particularly for the cyber-context.[107] Sometimes, tailor-made laws regulate by exemption;[108] eliminating otherwise protected behavior from the law's reach.

In the international law context, tailor-made laws for cyberspace are notably absent and so international law does not have a topic for cyberspace. Nor are there cyber-specific rules within existing fields of international law. The Cybercrime Convention represents one notable exception and in it, countries agreed to define particular activities as cybercrimes taking national and international steps to prosecute such behavior.[109] Several key States have refused to join, objecting to the treaty's cooperation obligations as intrusive of State sovereignty. Moreover, the Convention offers boundaries around what comprises cybercrime, restraining their reach in the process. Above all, negotiators draw a line omitting government sponsored cyber-operations from the cybercrime laws entailed by the treaty. To that extent, article 2 requires States to adopt "legislative and other measures" to establish as criminal offenses under their domestic law intentional access to the whole or any part of a computer system "without right." The accompanying Explanatory Memorandum clarifies that the "without right" caveat "leaves unaffected conduct undertaken pursuant to lawful governmental authority" including acts to "protect national security or investigate criminal offenses."[110] Consequently, for Convention parties at least, there is a borderline between cybercrime and State-sponsored cyber-operations such as cyber-espionage. Of course, international law's inconsistency toward cyber-espionage does not prohibit States from treating foreign cyber-espionage as a violation of their national criminal law.[111]

Nonetheless, boundaries play an equally important conceptual role as the product of law in cyberspace. For international law, with few exceptions, these boundaries are not tailor-made and so the Cybercrime Convention is tailored to the

---

[106]G Zekos, Διαδίκτυο, H/Y & Τηλεπικοινωνίες στο Ελληνικό Δίκαιο -Cyberspace, H/Y and Telecommunications, 2017 Εκδόσεις Π. Σάκκουλα https://www.sakkoulas-online.gr/profiles/georgios-i-zekos/

[107]Computer Fraud and Abuse Act, 18 U.S.C. §1030; Electronic Communications Privacy Act, 18 U.S.C. §§2510 et seq; Federal Wiretap Act, 18 U.S.C. §2510; Communications Assistance for Law Enforcement Act, 47 U.S.C. §§1001 et seq; Foreign Intelligence Surveillance Act (FISA), 50 U.S.C. §§1801–1811.

[108]47 U.S.C. 230(c)(1) (exempting Internet Service Providers from vicarious liability for libel otherwise available under common law).

[109]The Cybercrime Convention does not have universal aspirations, and its membership remains limited. http://conventions.coe.int/Treaty/Commun/ChercheSig.asp?NT=185&CM=&DF=&CL=ENG

[110]Explanatory Report, Cyber-Crime Convention (8 Nov 2001) §38.

[111]Tallinn Manual 194.

cyber-context.[112] Perhaps, the most dishonorable cyber-operation to date, Stuxnet, reportedly infected SCADA systems globally, but disturbed one set especially—those at Iran's Natanz uranium enrichment facility—instigating noteworthy damage to approximately 1000 centrifuges.[113] Somewhat, they derive from outside sources—"law-by-analogy"—inciting lines drawn for other times and contexts[114] which means that substantial doubt endures on exactly what behavior these legal boundaries ban/allow/compel. Moreover, international community has remained largely silent on Stuxnet's international legality, while many experts cannot agree if it constituted an "armed attack" and so allowing Iran to respond in self-defense or triggered IHL.[115] Thus, it becomes clear that politics holds back the equal use of force in this occasion because it does not implement the interests of the elite's interests against of any meaning of the strict application of the rule of law which means that the legal application of the rule of law is overtaken by the political usage of the rule of law and politics of law supersedes law and legality of the rule of law.

Yet, there is no disagreement that international law functions in cyberspace by reference to its pre-existing regimes and their borders. Let us say, international law is extensively adopted to govern "cyber-war" by analogies that delimit the jus ad bellum being the set of laws legalizing when force can be used and the jus in bello, also known as international humanitarian law or "IHL" being the set of laws regulating how States may use force. It has to be considered that there is near universal acceptance of IHL's application to cyberspace[116] and so china now appears to accept this position.[117]

Furthermore, it is worth noting that dispute continues on whether conventional operations must accompany cyber-operations or if a cyber-war could take place solely in cyberspace.[118] In a clear sense of cyber-war as a cyber-action, the whole conflict should take place in cyberspace but since the effects of cyber actions are felt by people on real world means that cyber-actions and conventional ones can be combined in order to satisfy the use of force as it has been implemented in many occasions in practice regardless of its prohibition according to article 2(4) of the United Nations Charter. It has to be taken into account that digital technologies are gradually affecting the work of the UN in three modes: (1) altering the political, social and economic environment; (2) offering new means for its core mandate; and

---

[112] Council of Europe, Convention on Cybercrime (Budapest, 23 Nov 2001) CETS No 185 ('Cybercrime Convention').

[113] D Albright et al., Did Stuxnet Take out 1000 Centrifuges at the Natanz Enrichment Plant? (ISIS, 2010).

[114] MN Schmitt (ed.), Tallinn Manual on the International Law Applicable to Cyber Warfare (CUP, 2013).

[115] Tallinn Manual 58, 83–84.

[116] Tallinn Manual Rule 20.

[117] US-China Economic and Security Review Commission, 2013 Annual Report to Congress (2013) 249; L Zhang, "A Chinese perspective on cyber war" (2012) 94 IRRC 801, 804.

[118] T Rid, "Cyber War Won't Take Place" (2012) 35 J Strategic Studies 5.

(3) generating new policy issues.[119] The use of real-time big data analytics and AI systems allows the UN to gather data in almost inaccessible contexts and respond to emergencies even before they take place.

The problems of legal boundaries are worsened in the law-by-analogy background and the current emphasis on international law-by-analogy causes a distinct set of contests. Consequently, even if international law regulates when and how countries may conduct a cyber-war, there are substantial reasons to question how well it does so. Furthermore, law-by-analogy involves fragmentation in two respects. First, analogizing existing law into cyberspace duplicates international law's existing fragmentation problems. Of course, it is worth mentioning that a tailor-made cyberspace legal regime would not unavoidably get away a fragmentation critique. It could be said that advancing an independent, tailor-made regime for cyberspace would insert another system to the rolls presently competing for normative priority. Furthermore, if such tailor-made rules could accomplish lex specialis status, they could lessen disintegration by offering a well-defined normative hierarchy in cases of conflict or tension with other legal regimes.

It has to be taken into account that analogies produce imprecise boundaries of behavior depending on the connection between the analogy's origin and its objective which means that analogies work well when their origin and objective have significant similarities. Except where there are relevant differences, an analogy really draws the wrong or imprecise lines that demand modification to serve the law's all-encompassing values.

It could be said that tech-determinism is nowadays the favored way of making those who still have faith in the rule of law look like they are going to be on the wrong side of history. To that extent, Uber has particularly favored that line: "the rule of law is so yesterday.[120]" On the other hand, short-term ubiquities concerning the applicable law on a particular field, due to the introduction of new technologies, cannot be taken as the principle that a society can function without following the rule of law.

It is argued that in 2015 and 2016, hackers broke into servers of the U.-S. Democratic National Committee (DNC) and the Russian operations were yet another example of Russia's competence at manipulating the "grey zones" of international law.[121] It seems that Russia uses international law principles and rules that are inadequately defined or are subject to competing interpretations and

[119] OCHA (Office for the Coordination of Humanitarian Affairs) Centre for Humanitarian Data https://centre.humdata.org

[120] Eric Newcomer, "Uber Pushed the Limits of the Law. Now Comes the Reckoning," Bloomberg Technology, 11 October 2017 (https://www.bloomberg.com/news/features/2017-10-11/uber-pushed-thelimits-of-the-law-now-comes-the-reckoning). Jon Axworthy, "Cab wars: the unstoppable rise of Uber," Shortlist, 16 July 2015 (https://www.shortlist.com/instant-improver/cab-wars/61881).

[121] Dir. Nat'l Intelligence, Assessing Russian Activities and Intentions in Recent US Elections, U.S. Senate Select Comm. On Intelligence 2 (Jan. 6, 2017), https://www.intelligence.sen-ate.gov/sites/default/files/documents/ ICA_2017_01.pdf Eric Lipton, David E. Sanger & Scott Shane, The

so Russia redeployed attention on the multifaceted questions of State responsibility for the actions of non-State actors and the level of control under international humanitarian law that internationalizes a non-international armed conflict.[122]

The legal issue created was whether the operations amounted to either a breach of U.S. sovereignty or a prohibited intervention under international law. It is unclear whether enabling the release of actual e-mails—as distinct from using cyber means to alter election returns—amounts to coercion as a matter of law and so such normative uncertainty offered fertile ground upon which the Russians could accomplish their maneuvers.

It is argued that espionage per se is not a violation of international law but the method by which it is achieved may be unlawful, as when it infringes the target State's sovereignty.[123] Had the DNC hacks clearly been unlawful under international law, the USA would have been permitted to take "countermeasures," activities that are illegal but for the fact that they respond to another State's illegal action. The parts of an internationally unlawful act are attribution and breach of an international legal obligation. Likewise, the Obama administration could have utilized countermeasures, like hack backs, to disrupt Russian government and private cyber-activities. As to the likelihood that covert countermeasures might have been utilized, it has to be considered that there is a requirement of prior notice, since the rationale of countermeasures is to oblige the State involving in the illegal conduct to give up.

Moreover, in circumstances where such notice is not possible for the reason that the need of an immediate response, or notice would permit that State to successfully defend against the countermeasures, post factum notice would still be needed to communicate the message that the State's illegal conduct comes at a cost. Consequently, concealed countermeasures are more in the character of retaliation, which is not a lawful purpose of countermeasures.

It could be said that Russia's gray zone operations amount to a form of "asymmetrical law fare" which means States committed to the rule of law are less likely to function in the gray zone than States that do not share this rule of law commitment. Consequently, any state has all the more reason to engage in legally ambiguous operations because its opponents may hesitate to respond determinedly, out of concern that their own response might be considered as illegal. Moreover, a target State's failure to react at a commensurate level of severity, as in the U.S. response to Russian hacking, makes the attacker seem more influential which means that in this asymmetrical dynamic, the State utilizing the gray zone accordingly benefits from

---

Perfect Weapon: How Russian Cyber-power Invaded the U.S., N.Y. Times (Dec. 13, 2016), https://www.nytimes.com/2016/12/13/us/poli-tics/russia-hack-election-dnc.html?_r=0

[122] Prosecutor v. Tadić, Case No. IT-94-1-A, Appeals Chamber Judgment, §§ 131–140, 145, 162 (Intl'l Crim. Trib. for the Former Yugoslavia July 15, 1999) Dapo Akande, Classification of Armed Conflicts: Rel-evant Legal Concepts, in International Law And The Classification Of Conflicts 32, 56–63 (Elizabeth Wilmshurst ed., 2012).

[123] Int'l Group Of Experts, Tallinn Manual 2.0 On The International Law Applicable To Cyber Operations 168–74 (Rule 32) (Michael N. Schmitt ed., 2017) Schmitt, Michael N. and Vihul, Liis, Respect for Sovereignty in Cyberspace (November 3, 2017). Texas Law Review, Vol. 95, 2017.

the advantage.[124] At present, the defense of the country and the security of civil society constitute the key functions of the State such as the applicable provisions of Articles 55, 71, and 114 of the Constitution of the Russian Federation. Besides, the use of digital technologies is indispensable for protection of the interests of individuals, businesses, and the State and so of central significance are the safety of the unified telecommunication networks, the continued accessibility of cyberspace, the stability of the communication networks used by state authorities, maintenance of relevant hardware, etc.

It is argued that a cyber-operation triggering physical damage or injury qualifies as an unlawful use of force except when otherwise authorized in international law, such as in the case of self-defense; authorization, mandate or authorization by the United Nations Security Council pursuant to Chapter VII of the U.N. Charter; or the influenced State's consent.[125]

In Tallinn Manual experts determined that specified operations not causing such consequences cross the use of force threshold sue to the International Court of Justice's determination in the Nicaragua case, which held that arming and training guerrilla forces to fight against another State amounts to a use of force against that State.[126] Thus, it could be said that offering malware and the training required to employ it against another State is a use of force.[127]

It is worth noting that the failure to achieve consensus on the use of force threshold, along with the resulting decision of the experts to simply tender a line that contemplates a non-exclusive and contextual list of factors, denotes the range to which the law surrounding the prohibition on the use of force establishes a fertile gray zone for States.

On the one hand, clarification of gray zone matters augment deterrence in cyberspace. On the other hand, international law offers for set categories of responses to detailed types of actions. Moreover, lawful cyber-activities may be responded to by acts of re-torsion but internationally unlawful cyber-operations authorize "injured" States to take cyber or no cyber-countermeasures. Furthermore, cyber-operations amounting to an armed attack may be responded to with cyber or kinetic uses of force and so a cyber-operation risk outcome at a set level discourages the taking of that operation, for the reason that the State concerned cannot act in the hope that the target State will hesitate to react out of concern that its reply might be perceived as illegal.[128]

---

[124] Sheera Frenkel, The New Handbook for Cyber war is Being Written by Russia, BUZZFEED (Mar. 19, 2017), https://www.buzzfeed.com/sheerafrenkel/the-new-handbook-forcyberwar-is-being-writtenbyrussia?utm_term=.jgOpW30jD#.kb0G6B2dL "It's not that the Russians are doing something others can't do . . . It's that Russian hackers are willing to go there, to experiment and carry out attacks that other countries would back away from."

[125] U.N. Charter art. 51.

[126] Tallinn Manual 1.0 Nicaragua, 1986 I.C.J. at 118–19, § 228.

[127] Tallinn Manual 2.0.

[128] Michael N. Schmitt, Grey Zones in the International Law of Cyberspace https://ssrn.com/abstract=3180687

8.7 Cybersecurity

In an age of cyber insecurity, anxieties about the silence of States regarding the applicability of international law to peacetime cyber-operations have been spreading and so concerns have engrossed on the reluctance of States to agree cyber-specific multilateral treaties and to publicly simplify the customary international rules applicable to hostile cyber-operations. Cyber-attacks and cyber-espionage are technical security threats which encompass breaking into and targeting information and communications technologies. Cyber information operations are content-based security threats which include exploiting the supremacy of online information to target human intelligence. Even though, in fact, a certain cyber-operation may involve more than one type of security threat.[129]

There are state silences regarding the application of international law to peacetime cyber-operations are not uniform, but vary in terms of their targets, scope, and motivation depending on the specific security threat under examination which means that these disparities not only disclose a dimension of the politics of international law.

As discussed earlier, cybersecurity is a noteworthy affair in corporate and commercial backgrounds, and for good reason: a threatened or realized cybersecurity breach influences corporation value for capital investors. Moreover, the effectiveness implications of cybersecurity trading are discrete than those posed by garden-variety information trading within securities markets. Aside these distinctive concerns both securities fraud[130] and computer fraud in their current form poorly adjusted to address such concerns, and both would need nontrivial reimagining undergoing the challenge.

The Global Cybersecurity Index (GCI) is an initiative of the International Telecommunication Union (ITU)[131] stimulating further action toward secure digital ecosystems needed for recovery and growth, by measuring the types of cybersecurity commitments states have made and their prevalence. Moreover, the Global Cybersecurity Index report indicates that many states enacted new cybersecurity legislation and regulations to address areas such as privacy, unauthorized access, and online safety. It also underlines the necessity to establish strategies and mechanisms to build capacity and help governments and businesses better prepare for and mitigate growing cyber-risks.

---

[129] H. Lin, Responding to Sub-Threshold Cyber Intrusions: A fertile Topic for Research and discussion, 2011 12 Georgetown Journal of International Affairs 127, 129–130. Leonhard Kreuzer, disentangling the cyber security debate, Völkerrechtsblog, 20 June 2018.

[130] Samuel W. Buell, What Is Securities Fraud?, 61 Duke L.J. 511, 562 (2011).

[131] https://www.itu.int/en/ITU-D/Cybersecurity/Pages/global-cybersecurity-index.aspx

CISA[132] authorizes individual private castle owners to share cyber-threat intelligence with other castle owners and with the federal government information regarding the identity of such nefarious actors, their modus operandi, and how to defend against their attacks. Moreover, CISA was designed to address the government's and the private sector's needs for sharing information linked to perceived cyber-threats and related defensive measures, but it was drafted prior the emergence of AI explosion. As long as businesses expand their use of cyberspace to deliver services to their users, every effort must be made to adjust the security profile of their systems and networks. As a result of the post-CISA acceleration of cybercrimes, achieving such improvements will necessitate a step function in the effectiveness of cyber-defenses. The wide adoption of cyberspace for daily use has amplified the amount and variety of data available.[133]

AI has emerged as a powerful technology capable of performing certain tasks better than humans, including some aspects of cybersecurity analysis. It has to be taken into account that AI-based technologies offer deeper security than what humans alone can deliver and the deployment of AI-based security technologies makes simpler the process of detecting and responding to application security threats and vulnerabilities.[134] Also, an explosion of AI-based cybersecurity solutions is being brought to market by cybersecurity vendors, large and small. In addition, AI present one element of the solution required stemming the acceleration of post-CISA cyber-attacks but as cybercriminals and nation states begin using AI to augment the rate of attacks, the need for smarter solutions is becoming more apparent. Consequently, while AI aids improving efficiency and accuracy in detecting cyber-attacks, AI makes attacks expressively more effective and accurate, and possibly more devastating. To that extent, AI advances the effectiveness and efficiency of cyber-security solutions, but only if these solutions are provided the needed data from which to learn.[135]

AI is the driving force behind China's industrial upgrading and economic transformation but simultaneously there is an effort of minimizing the risks linked with the transformation of employment structures, violations of personal privacy and challenges to international relations norms. In November 2016, China strengthens cybersecurity by the enactment of the Cybersecurity Law of the People's Republic of China.[136] For instance, Article 2 of the Cybersecurity Law makes certain territorial jurisdiction over network-related matters in China, whether they are civil, criminal,

---

[132] 6 U.S.C. §§ 1501–10 (2018). Bert Lathrop, The Inadequacies of the Cybersecurity Information Sharing Act of 2015 in the Age of Artificial Intelligence, Vol. 71 February 2020 Hastings Law Journal 501.

[133] John W. Baker & Steve Henderson, The Cyber Data Science Process, 2 Cyber Def. Rev. 47, 47 (2017).

[134] Ponemon Inst., The Value of Artificial Intelligence in Cyber security 4 fig. 2 (2018).

[135] Anatomy Of A Cyber Attack: The Lifecycle of a Security Breach, Oracle 4–5 (2017) (detailing the phases of a cyber-attack and the attackers' motivation behind each step).

[136] The Cybersecurity Law of the People's Republic of China], http://www.npc.gov.cn/npc/xinwen/2016-11/07/content_2001605.htm

or administrative in character which means that individuals whose activities are correlated to cyberspace within the Chinese territory, materials, network information, in addition to cyber-activities themselves, such as unlawful and criminal cyber-activities aiming at information system, are all subject to this jurisdiction. Consequently, as long as the cyber-activities occur within the territory of mainland China, no matter what identities or nationalities the actors have, they are all subject to the law. Moreover, Article 5 of the Cybersecurity Law[137] asserts China's right of defense in cyberspace and permits the Chinese government to monitor, defend against, and punish foreign cyber-attacks and threats. It is worth noting here that in 2021, there was a cyber-attack on Microsoft exchange systems and has to be proven which entity was behind it. Additionally, Article 75 stipulates that for those who conduct attacks, intrusions, interference, destructions, or other activities for the rationale of jeopardizing the essential information infrastructure of the People's Republic of China, whether they are organizations or individuals, if they have triggered critical effects, the Chinese government shall take measures in line with the law to either freeze their assets or to take other needed punitive measures.

It is worth noting that China is establishing new global standards for the data trade. In 2017, Apple Inc. was one of the first companies to build a new joint venture data center in China to abide by China's Cyber security Law of the same year demanding that all companies uphold "critical information infrastructure" to store their data on a Chinese-owned server. It has to be considered that the decision of firms to open a data center with major ownership by a Chinese firm transforms the politics of power and access to data within the company and among its consumers. To that extent, it seems that Apple leveraged access to data contributing to dominance in the future-changing technology of AI. On the other hand, China treats data-gathering efforts by foreign companies under its national jurisdiction with seriousness by suing Apple for violating the law by maintaining its own servers in China and so Apple moved its servers to servers run by the Chinese provincial government-run cloud services provider Guizhou Yunshang.

To that extent, the USA has a global monopoly on cyberspace, and the rest of the globe cannot achieve complete independence in the cyberspace which means that cyberspace sovereignty should epitomize an independent form of a country's sovereignty.[138] Moreover, the right of equality demands countries to access and connect to one another's cyberspace on an equal basis confirms that different countries have equal jurisdiction over their own network systems, and that the management of one country's network does not do harms to another country's networks. Nevertheless, owing to the borderless and interdependent character of cyberspace, cyberspace

[137] Aimin Qi, Guosong Shao, Wentong Zheng, Assessing China's Cybersecurity Law, computer law & security review 34 (2018) 1342–1354.

[138] G Zekos, Cyber Versus Conventional Personal Jurisdiction, 2015 Journal of Internet Law, Volume 18 Number 10, April 2015 3–35 Wolters Kluwer. www.wrightsmedia.com https://lrus.wolterskluwer.com/store/product/journal-of-internet-law/G Zekos, Demolishing State's sole power over Sovereignty & Territory via Electronic Technology & Cyberspace, 2013 Journal of Internet Law, Volume 17 Number 5 November 2013 27–41 Aspen Publications-Wolters Kluwer.

policies instigated by the USA may benefit its own interests at the expense of developing countries giving the USA much more power in contrast with other countries in global cyberspace governance. It has to be taken into account that upholding the free flow of data on a global scale for the expansion of the digital economy has become a development strategy for many countries and regions. Nonetheless, with the purpose of reinforcing national sovereignty and cyberspace security, countries in the globe have enacted laws to restrict the foreign storage and trans-border transmission of specific data. Regarding the issue of data storage and cross-border transmission, the USA had long been advocating and fostering the free flow of data around the globe. Though, the EU has taken a very different approach, both the 1995 Data Protection Directive and the 2016 GDPR have made strict restrictions on the transmission of personal data from EU firms to foreign partners.

Thus, data storage infrastructure exists when there is hosting classified government information, involving defense and intelligence files.[139] Moreover, information technology and telecommunication software are exploited for the operation of data storage facilities, data transmission, and data processing. Consequently, digital technologies are based on semiconductors when having dual use options ranging from medical technologies to biodefense detection systems as they are crucial for defense and military strength and, owing to the pervasiveness of semiconductor devices, imperative for mitigation of cybersecurity risk.[140]

Aynne Kokas[141] argues that "the United States should change its approach, because its current laissez-faire policies ultimately protect neither consumers nor national competitiveness ... China, by regulating the security issues presented by global corporate data investments through a combination of national policymaking, corporate dominance, and international regulatory actions, is establishing new global standards for the data trade. By extension, China is asserting its own model of data governance. The model localizes data in China by storing data generated in the country on government-run servers, as well as bringing data into the nation from outside. Further, it relies on domestic data governance principles to influence international principles." In fact, China's impact on global data governance lies at the center of the future of global communications policy.

It has to be taken into account that just as information is a mode of upholding security, it is also a type of control and so when governments are able to control commercial and political information, they augment their surveillance over the population which means that they have a more unified plan of attack against global

[139] Uhlmann, C. (2017), Australian Defence files to be moved out of privately owned data hub after Chinese buy-in, ABC News Online, www.abc.net.au/news/2017-06-20/security-concerns-over-defencefiles-in-data-centres/8632360

[140] President's Council of Advisors on Science and Technology (PCAST) (2017), Report to the president. Ensuring Long-Term U.S. Leadership in Semiconductors, Executive Office of the President, https://obamawhitehouse.archives.gov/sites/default/files/microsites/ostp/PCAST/pcast_ensuring_long-term_us_leadership_in_semiconductors.pdf

[141] Aynne Kokas, Cloud Control: China's 2017 Cybersecurity Law and its Role in US Data Standardization, https://ssrn.com/abstract=3427372 p2–3.

opposition. To that extent, governments are able to exert excessive global influence in the event that that information is purposefully vital not just for their own states, but also for others. In line, China's cybersecurity law gathers information to augment political control by the way of controlling corporate data and to guarantee a prospective trade advantage based on improved access to intellectual property and the potential to aggregate data for AI. Particularly, China's Cybersecurity Law magnifies the scale of China's data sovereignty both extraterritorially and beyond the global corporate standards for publicly traded corporations. Accordingly, China's way is a new form of data governance, but then it is barely a new way of governance via the control of information for the reason that the concentration of data in the hands of a powerful government arouses longstanding historical examples of inequality, and indeed of the exploitation of information to serve the welfares of the state.

Battles over the control of information online are often fought at the level of cyberspace infrastructure. To that extent, the European Union's General Data Protection Regulation (GDPR) modernizes data protection legislation across the EU by stimulating a digital single market, and so supporting police and security cooperation. Moreover, the GDPR gives citizens amplified control over their personal data and creates a "privacy by design and default" approach such as the right to "data portability" by permitting users to carry data from one provider to the next. More specifically, data portability contained under Article 20 permits individuals to acquire, move, copy, or transfer personal data from one IT environment to another without interference in usability and so the regulation's objective is to offer a safe and secure mode for sharing data between data controllers and to protect consumers from being "locked in" with one specific provider.

The term "protected computer" refers not to the level of security protocols that protect the compromised data, but somewhat to the intended use of the compromised computer and so under the Act, this definition embraces any computer that is used (1) by/for the federal government, (2) by/for a financial institution, or (3) in or influencing interstate commerce.[142] In line, courts have read the "interstate commerce" flag to be generated by the employment of any computer connected to the Internet—irrespective of whether located inside or outside the USA—as influencing interstate commerce.[143]

The Computer Fraud and Abuse Act (CFAA) forbids basically three sorts of conduct: ((1) using unauthorized access to fraudulently acquire valuable information from a computer; (2) causing damage through the unauthorized transmission of computer passwords; and (3) causing unauthorized damage to computer data or

[142] 18 U.S.C. § 1030(e)(2) 18 U.S.C. § 1030(e)(2)(B) (2001) (amending the CFAA to include Internet-connected computers outside the US).

[143] US v. Drew, 259 F.R.D. 449, 457 (C.D. Cal. 2009) Nexans Wires S.A. v. Sark-USA, Inc., 166 F. App'x 559, 562–63 (2nd Cir. 2006) US v. Trotter, 478 F.3d 918, 921 (8th Cir. 2007) Paradigm Alliance, Inc. v. Celeritas Technologies, LLC, 248 F.R.D. 598, 602 (D. Kan. 2008) ("As a practical matter, a computer providing a 'web-based' application accessible through the internet would satisfy the 'interstate communication' requirement.").

causing damage to computer). It has to be taken into account that even though the liability provisions of the CFAA are quite general, they assemble actions whereby one accesses a "protected computer" either "without authorization" or in a manner that "exceeds authorized access.[144]"

Moreover, the digitization of the world's economy has accelerated changes in commerce, record-keeping, law enforcement, personnel policy, banking, insurance, securities markets, and almost all features of services and manufacturing sectors. Companies and institutes that store confidential data digitally have been targets of attacks often with analogously catastrophic effects for victims.

It is worth mentioning that patterns of material alterations in value after disclosure of a cybersecurity event are now commonplace.[145] For instance, Uber's latest disclosure of a cybersecurity loss of client payment records instigated an outside investor (SoftBank) to diminish its valuation assessment of Uber by nearly a third.[146] Particularly, the phenomenon of securities-market trading can be seen on the basis of advanced knowledge of a cybersecurity breach ("informed cyber-trading"). Theoretically, privately informed traders utilize their information so long as there is appropriate independent market activity to offer "cover" for the informed arbitrageur meaning that informed traders have a strong motivation to take short positions against the hacked firms—positions that should be noticeable in securities-market activity.

It has to be taken into account that regulating informed trading is complicated needing to balance concerns over price discovery, liquidity, and allocative efficiency. To that extent, informed cyber-trading shares many of these traits but it includes other efficiency worries that are exclusive. Moreover, wasteful investment distortions go along, both by "hackers" revealing vulnerabilities and initiating costs that would not otherwise come to light. Additionally, the profits gained using these trading openings augment hackers' incentives to manipulate security vulnerabilities, leading to bigger diffusion of stolen personal information, impersonation, and identity theft and so representing real economic costs not exhibited in garden-variety information-trading contexts. Subsequently, informed cyber-trading rationalizes higher legal scrutiny of those who gain from the endeavor.

Nevertheless, several variations of informed cyber-trading appear to perfectly legal under current practices. Besides, it is almost unlawful for an agent or fiduciary to trade on a company's material non-public information, or for third parties to conspire to steal such information, or for a person to spread false information about a cybersecurity risk so as to manipulate stock prices.

---

[144] Office of Legal Education Executive Office for United States Attorneys, "Prosecuting Computer Crimes" (June 2013), 18 U.S.C. § 1030(a).

[145] Goldstein, Matthew, Stevenson, Alexandra and Picker, Leslie, 2016. "Unusual Pairing Makes Public Bet vs. Pacemakers." New York Times (Sept. 8, 2016 at B1).

[146] Financial Times, "SoftBank share purchase discounts Uber by 30%" (Nov. 27, 2017).

8.8 Cyberspace and AI Governance

Cyberspace is not yet fully global and content production is concentrated in a few advanced economies. Governments are restricting cyberspace in ways that diminish the ability of businesses and entrepreneurs to use cyberspace as a place for international commerce. As digital platforms produce new global marketplaces, they are making globalization a more inclusive phenomenon. Individuals and businesses are using these digital platforms to form their own global connections. Digital technologies have improved data flows across national territorial borders and as digital companies expand beyond their host countries to run services across the globe, worries have been raised by the governments and regulators on protecting the data so collected and transmitted by digital platforms.

The world has entered a new phase of globalization that presents countries and workers with new encounters and opportunities. The development of digital technologies in society does entail finding out how digital technologies influence the costs and limit the economic actions of individuals.[147]

At the beginning, digital technology has been incorporated and understood as a simple instrument replacing other traditional media and means and so most legislation on e-commerce, digital signatures, and information society services views technology as a tool. Moreover, the increase of rate and accumulation of technological developments pose unforeseen disputes to the twenty-first century's law and so a systematic, extensive, and wisely combined application of these emerging technologies such as AI, Internet of Things, and blockchain brings forwards disruptive effects, as witnessed with the development of smart property, smart contracts, and new electronic platforms.

It has to be taken into account that the upgrading of new computing communication technologies and methods of processing large amounts of data has led to the automation and robotization of innumerable processes involving production. Hence, the swift development of digital technology has altered the approach toward the field of virtual entertainment and the use of cultural objects. Furthermore, the rapid development of artificial intelligence systems, autonomous digital algorithms, and robotic technologies has transformed the landscape and the specifics of socio-legal and socio-political life of society.[148] It has to be taken into account that the socio-political context in which technology is implemented is contingent and shifting.

It is worth noting that AI implementation demands both the ability to adapt public infrastructure to fit AI-innovations and a private sector commercializing AI into viable goods. AI is transforming the way the world innovates and creates demanding extensive investment in the needed digital and physical infrastructure. Furthermore,

[147] Goldfarb, A., & Taker, C. (2017). Digital Economics. Working paper. Cambridge: National Bureau of Economic Research.

[148] Mamychev A., Okorokov A., Bespalova T., Sviridkina E., Chertakova E. (2018). Civilizational modeling of political and legal development of the society in the XXI century. Revista Amazonia Investiga. № 15. Vol. 7. pp. 49–57.

AI technologies affect the center of private autonomy and its limits, the notion of a contract and its interpretation, the equilibrium of parties' interests, the structure and means of enforcement, the effectiveness of legal and contractual remedies, and the vital attributes of the legal system of effectiveness, fairness, impartiality, and predictability.

While the consequences of the first-wave technology are successfully dealt with by the existing global legal framework for the use of electronic communications in business transactions, the second wave of AI technology developments must be consciously considered and carefully implemented.

Science and technology at the hands of people for better implementation of many duties concerning the work and entertainment and so intelligence augmentation becomes regulative ideal by offering the right devices making many jobs far easier.[149] It seems that technology repairs imperfections, augments effectiveness, diminishes costs, increases predictability, and offers celerity. In computing, AI research has focused on technologies that can substitute for human cognition and attention. New technologies and algorithms for processing unstructured information are increasing the usefulness of corporate data. Effective corporate governance cannot occur in an information vacuum. The base line of AI is a computer that mimics human cognitive functions, such as "learning" and "problem solving.[150]"

Is AI governance merely a bubble? Which are the potential roles for AI? Could AI take over corporate management functions? What types of roles AI technology can assume? It is obvious that degrees of autonomy and proactivity will be gained by AI. It could be said that three different types or levels of AI roles will be developed such as (1) assisted AI; (2) advisory AI; (3) and autonomous AI.[151] It has to be taken into account that from a legal viewpoint, AI has already begun to question fundamental notions underlying how and why we incentivize creation and innovation.[152]

First of all, AI can reproduce physical human processes through machines, making routine tasks more competent, such as attaching the front bumper of a car in an assembly line. Moreover, AI can also make possible "large-scale automation of entire groups of tasks, including repetitive intellectual tasks previously performed by human beings" and so it seems that more than just mimicking the physical aspects of

[149] NAT'L HIGHWAY TRAFFIC SAFETY ADMIN., U.S. DEP'T OF TRANSP., FEDERAL AUTOMATED VEHICLES POLICY 9 (2016) (describing the Society of Automotive Engineers ("SAE") International levels of autonomy in driving).

[150] Stuart J. Russel & Peter Norvig, Artificial Intelligence: A Modern Approach 495–99 (3d ed., 2016) Alan M. Turing, Computing Machinery and Intelligence, 49 MIND 433 (1950).

[151] Robert J. Thomas Et Al., A Machine in the C-Suite 2 (2016), https://www.accenture.com/t00010101T000000Z__w__/br-pt/_acnmedia/PDF-13/AccentureStrategy-WotF-Machine-CSuite.pdf

[152] PricewaterhouseCoopers, Global Artificial Intelligence Study: Exploiting the AI Revolution 4 (2017), https://www.pwc.com/gx/en/issues/analytics/assets/pwc-ai-analysis-sizing-theprize-report.pdf Jonathan Bastable, Is artificial intelligence set to become art's next medium?, CHRISTIE'S (Aug. 20, 2018), https://www.christies.com/features/A-collaboration-between-two-artists-one-human-one-amachine-9332-1.aspx

humans, AI simulates and exceeds human mental processes.[153] It seems that all the scenarios of the fantasy films concerning electronic technology will come true in one or another way and so humanity has to be prepared in order to make a good use of the innovations and not to be misled in dangerous roads for the human life.

The flow of data through the cyberspace boosted dramatically, people nowadays share their data more easily compared to the past and the ways to do so boosted as well.[154] Furthermore, in cyberspace environment, blockchain technology is transformative for every human practice that utilizes record-keeping. If blockchain technology accomplishes even a small part of its anticipated prospective, then soon it will replace many critical infrastructures within societies, from property records, to payment and voting systems. Likewise, if blockchain technology ends up enabling our most fundamental social infrastructures, then the governance processes for generating, upholding, and changing the technology must be examined carefully as they will influence the resilience of the technology, along with any infrastructure that comes to rely on it.[155]

It seems that progressively, privately owned web-based platforms control people' access to public services, security, education, the public sphere, and health services which means that as society is "data filed," public services are released via public–private partnerships and so there is an effort for "data driven development" mediated by private players.[156]

It is argued that Russia gathers data that are produced within their borders and relevant to their own law enforcement and China has implemented "cyber-sovereignty," an extension of Chinese sovereign territory rights that is closely connected to extensions of Chinese sovereignty in territorial disputes like those in the South China Sea and the Taiwan Straits. China advances its control over global data flows, with the ultimate aim of building a national trove of data to drive strategic competitiveness in both the industrial and military sectors, via national regulations,

[153] Michael Copeland, What's the Difference Between Artificial Intelligence, Machine Learning, and Deep Learning?, NVIDIA BLOG (July 29, 2016), https://blogs.nvidia.com/blog/2016/07/29/whats-difference-artificial-intelligence-machine-learningdeep-learning-ai Yann Ménière & Ilja Rudyk, The Fourth Industrial Revolution from the European Patent Office Perspective, in Intellectual Property And Digital Trade In The Age Of Artificial Intelligence And Big Data 31, 31 (Xavier Seuba, Christophe Geiger, & Julien Penin eds, June 2018), https://www.ictsd.org/sites/default/files/research/ceipi-ictsd_issue_5_final_0.pdf

[154] Recital 6 of GDPR.

[155] Angela Walch, "The Bitcoin Blockchain as Financial Market Infrastructure: A Consideration of Operational Risk" [2015]18 NYU J Legislation and Public Policy837 (considering the operational risks created by informal governance processes in Bitcoin and their implications for its suitability as financial market infrastructure); Angela Walch, "Open-Source Operational Risk: Should Public Blockchains Serve as Financial Market Infrastructures?" in David Lee, Kuo Chuen and Robert D Deng (eds), Handbook of Blockchain, Digital Finance, and Inclusion Vol. 2 (Elsevier Academic Press 2017) (exploring the operational risks raised by use of grassroots open-source software development practices in the use of public blockchains as financial market infrastructures).

[156] Taylor and Broeders, "In the name of Development: Power, profit and the datafication of the global South," Geoforum 64 (2015) 229–237.

industrial dominance, and multistakeholder organizations. Furthermore, Chinese regulators export these standards through engagement in international organizations such as the International Telecommunications Union (ITU), the Internet Corporation for Assigned Names and Numbers (ICANN), the Internet Governance Forum (IGF), etc., which means that Chinese regulators are influencing the standards for the global data trade. In other words, the application of state regulatory mechanisms and industrial norms-setting permit China to leverage its strategic advantage in the collaboration of industry and government. Moreover, it has to be considered that what most marks China's current data governance landscape is not simply its capacity to influence through its large market size, but the effect of civil-military fusion which means that any property built by Chinese firms is subject to Chinese government control.[157]

It is worth noting that as more industrial sectors become data-driven, communications policy will take an increasingly central role in industrial regulation writ large. Good governance, transparency, and effective government procurement are the basic issues of effective e-governance system. Government is associated with institutions which requires to make effective functioning. Law is the central issues to measure effective governance. So, e-governance is the planning, programming, implementation, and evaluation functions in order to achieve predefined goals. AAI governance will be the structures and processes that are designed to make certain organizational goals effectively and efficiently. E-governance is broader than the term of government which characterizes effective operation of the e-institutional bodies establishing good relationship between e-citizens and the e-state bodies.[158] Indeed, it is becoming gradually clear that information litigation is starting to play a much greater gatekeeping role for corporate governance problems. There are often serial litigation battles where a fight over access to corporation information is followed by a fight over the primary governance concern.[159]

Corporate governance codes advance high levels of corporate governance by putting forth principles and provisions with which corporations are expected to comply and playing vital roles in supporting the integrity and efficiency of financial markets.[160] Certainly, well governed corporations outpace other corporations by

[157] Dreyer, June Teufel, ed. 1989. Chinese defense and foreign policy, World social systems series. New York: Professors World Peace Academy: Distributed by Paragon House.

[158] Jerome Bentham, Introduction to the Principles of Morals and Legislation, https://www.laits.utexas.edu/poltheory/bentham/ipml/ipml.c01.html Jerome Bentham, "...nature has placed mankind under the governance of two sovereign masters, pain and pleasure. It is for them alone to point out what we ought to do, as well as to determine what we shall do ...."

[159] Amalgamated Bank v. Yahoo! Inc., 132 A.3d 752, 761–71 (2016).

[160] Monetary Authority of Singapore, Code of Corporate Governance, Singapore: MAS, 2018. Sandra Seah, "A new spin to Corporate Governance in Singapore - 2018'" (April 2018), Bird & Bird, online: https://www.twobirds.com/en/news/articles/2018/singapore/a-new-spin-to-corporate-governance-in-singapore-2018 Financial Reporting Council, "A UK Corporate Governance Code that is fit for the future" (16 July 2018), online: https://www.frc.org.uk/news/july-2018/a-uk-corporate-governance-code-that-is-fit-for-the

attracting investors whose support facilitates growth. Eventually, it has to be taken into account that corporate governance codes are still "soft law" to a large extent, and whether the objective of good corporate governance is achieved will turn on a multitude of factors, embracing the level of compliance with the code, the strength of social norms and market expectations of compliance with the code, and the public and private enforcement of hard law. It is obvious that these rationales will apply to AAI society as well.

Do directors have fiduciary duties to stockholders alone or to stakeholders more broadly? Directors have a fiduciary duty not to particular persons, but to the corporate entity and its authorized purposes. It is obvious that e-directors will have the same duties. It is argued that directorial duties of care and loyalty are just the proscriptive side of a more general, affirmative directorial duty to stockholders which is to maximize "shareholder value," meaning in effect, to maximize their dividends and stock price. In the corporate firm, stockholders are the principals and directors are their agents.[161] In fact, directors remain in the structural position of purpose fiduciaries, not personal fiduciaries.[162] For the reason that much of the technology is so new, companies making decisions about their data prioritize their business interests over the national security concerns of the nation-state where they are domiciled, except there are specific regulations in place that incentivize other choices, and so firms' priority is to enter as many markets as possible to upsurge economies of scale.

It has to be taken into account that if a company's corporate interests align with the national interests of another country, then the company's decisions prioritize these interests, irrespective of the outcomes for the home country.[163] It is argued that US multinationals functioning in China have repeatedly demonstrated a willingness to leverage the soft power emerging from their brands in the service of Chinese national interests, so long as there is a business case for doing so.[164]

---

[161] Jean-Phillipe Robé, The Legal Structure of the Firm, 1(1) Accounting, Economics, And Law 1 (2011); David Ciepley, Beyond Public and Private: Toward a Political Theory of the Corporation, 107(1) Am. Pol. Sci. Rev. 139 (2013). Michael Jensen & William Meckling, Theory of the Firm: Managerial Behavior, Agency Costs and Ownership Structure, 3 J. Fin. Econ. 305, 309 (1976) ("the relationship between the stockholders and manager of a corporation fit [sic] the definition of a pure agency relationship.").

[162] Paul B. Miller & Andrew S. Gold, Fiduciary Governance, 57 WM. & MARY L. REV. 513, 519–20 (2015).

[163] Kokas, Aynne. 2018. "Chilling Netflix: financialization, and the influence of the Chinese market on the American entertainment industry." Information, Communication & Society:1–13. doi: https://doi.org/10.1080/1369118X.2018.1510534 https://doi.org/10.1080/1369118X.2018.1510534</p>. Kokas, Aynne. 2018. "Platform Patrol: China, the United States, and the Global Battle for Data Security." Journal of Asian Studies. Kokas, Aynne. 2019. "Serious chemistry on set: the molecular structure of film investment in China." International Journal of Cultural Policy:1–13.

[164] Kokas, Aynne. 2018 "Predicting volatility between China and Hollywood: Using network management to understand Sino-US film collaboration." Global Media and Communication:1742766518759797.

E-Directors will wield increasing influence in e-corporate world, making pivotal decisions concerning a corporation's affairs and management. Moreover, e-directors are expected to monitor management, to offer expertise and networking and to make the corporation's most important decisions. Horizontal Directors are important not only because of their prevalence, but also for the reason that they stand at a unique intersection of antitrust law and corporate governance.[165] Directors must act in the corporation's interests and are bound by certain fiduciary duties, primarily good faith, care, and loyalty.[166] Are these duties applicable to e-directors of AAI corporations? The corporation undeniably has driven business growth in the USA since the Industrial Revolution[167] which will be applied to AAI corporations formed by AAI technology.

Increasing the involvement of citizens and economic entities in the work in the digital space, the formation of infrastructure that makes certain the interaction of entities in the digital space, decreasing the costs of economic entities and citizens in interaction with the state and among themselves enhance the competitiveness of the economy. At the same time, the introduction of cross-cutting digital technologies such as big data, neuro-technology and artificial intelligence, blockchain, quantum technologies, industrial Internet, robotics and sensor components, wireless communication technologies will necessitate alterations in formal and informal rules, norms and enforcement, which epitomize institutional modifications. Functionally, AI and people can display comparable patterns of behavior and information processing, irrespective of whether machines "think" or understand what they do.

Have artificial intelligence economic effects? Unlike other technological advances that have made workers more productive and augmented demand for labor, there is growing concern that intelligent machines will displace workers and drive down wages.[168] AI and its technological singularity initiate a digital divide based on availability and accessibility to technological knowledge and its infrastructure and so expanding existing societal gaps and class conflicts which means that an ever varying and challenging environment ratifies the utilization of emerging technologies for human development and social welfare[169] such as policies to protect labor, privacy, trade, and liability by diminishing the aftereffects of AI in terms of its effect on employment, inequality, and competition.

---

[165] Tatjana Berg et al., Sharing a Director with a Peer (University of St. Gallen, School of Finance, Working Papers on Fin. No. 2015/07) (defining "horizontal directors" as directors affiliated with firms within the same industry based on Standard Industry Classification codes).

[166] Cede & Co v. Technicolor, Inc., 634 A2d 345, 360 (Del 1993) ("(D)irectors are charged with an unyielding fiduciary duty to protect the interests of the corporation and to act in the best interests of its shareholders.").

[167] Larry E. Ribstein, The Rise Of The Uncorporation 4 (2010).

[168] Cynthia Estlund, What Should We Do After Work? Automation and Employment Law, 128 Yale L.J. 254 (2018).

[169] Korinek, A., Stiglitz, J.E., 2018. Artificial intelligence and its implications for income distribution and unemployment. NBER Chapters The Economics of Artificial Intelligence: An Agenda. National Bureau of Economic Research, Inc.

AI evolved from augmentation, to co-creation, to becoming the artist and so WFH offers a pragmatic legal instrument for interests to vest and negotiated by the commercial interests best placed to encourage investment in both the technology and its downstream uses.

The Public and businesses must find new paths to generate growth and value with AI as the primary driver which means that AI will create jobs in the innovative and creative sectors that patent and copyright stakeholders care about but causing other individuals to lose work.[170] Science and technology at the hands of people for better implementation of many duties concerning the work and entertainment intelligence augmentation become regulative ideal by offering the right devices making many jobs far easier

8.9 Cyberspace and Politics

The digitalization of the economy and society, the introduction of artificial intelligence in human activities actualize a number of new issues linked with both the legal support of these processes, and areas of advancement of law as a regulatory system, and the connection between law and technology.

Cyberspace is a global medium, supporting the flow of information and images around the globe without regard for national borders, thereby weakening the relevance of nationality to communication. Moreover, cyberspace tools have the prospective to revolutionize democracy by introducing "direct two-way interaction between citizens and politicians" and so systems, such as machine translation, permit people from different states and cultures to come together joining the democratic debate, overcoming languages barriers.

Battles over the control of information online are often fought at the level of cyberspace infrastructure. It has to be taken into account that forces of globalization and technological transformation have weakened the capability of sovereign nation states and media content producers to directly control information flows which means that this loss of control over content and the failure of laws and markets to resume this control have readdressed political and economic battles into the realm of infrastructure and technologies of cyberspace governance. Nonetheless, regardless of the openness and flexibility of the structure of cyberspace, there is still a politics somewhere in that structure and so cyberspace' use is not entirely individualized or unstructured and the different opportunities that the network makes available to users are in many ways the result of structures designed into that system at a deep level.

---

[170] The Economist Intelligence Unit, Intelligent Economies: AI's Transformation of Industries and Society, Economist (2018), https://perspectives.eiu.com/sites/default/files/EIU_Microsoft%20%20Intelligent%20Economies_AI%27s%20transformation%20of%20industries%20and%20society.pdf

It could be said that alterations in technical architecture of cyberspace are also arrangements of power and so the transferal of power to infrastructure is drawing attention to the politics of cyberspace design and the legitimacy of the harmonizing institutions and private ordering that generate and manage these infrastructures. In other words, freedom of expression in the context of expanding turns to infrastructure to control information. Is there relationship between governance and infrastructure? Of course, there is a battle over cyberspace content transferred into the cyberspace governance infrastructure via the use of the Internet's domain name system for intellectual property rights enforcement; the use of approaches restricting the flow of information; and the termination of infrastructure services such as WikiLeaks, etc.

It is characteristic that the existence of global decision-makers for cyberspace is coming into view more extensively now and so taking into account the social consequences of cyberspace, it is needed to identify these decision-makers, the source of their power over global communications flows, the character of their relationship to older structures of power and to settle just how they contribute to the ongoing social modeling of such a decentralized technological system.

While the process of constructing technology is a human activity and not a force of nature, the result of the social building is not always the formation of a technological system that serves the interests intended by its creators. On the one hand, the initial intention behind the decision to use the ISO list to assign country code domains was to offer each country with an equal capacity to manage its own portion of cyberspace. On the other hand, the result is an inequality in which some nations are able to do so and others sell the rights to use their cyber spatial resources on a global market and so this cannot be justified by reference to the values embedded in cyberspace's technical or administrative structure through the social molding process without taking into consideration the power relations between the actors who affect that shaping process.

It has to be taken into account that global inequality of wealth is a structural constraint on the agency institutions, policy makers, and others implicated in the social shaping of the global structure of cyberspace' DNS. In addition, it has to be taken into consideration that technologies, including cyberspace governance infrastructure, integrally embody values in their design, implementation, and usage. Moreover, control over the Cyberspace' Domain Name System (DNS) has been one of the most controversial policy challenges and so the DNS is at the center of numerous political issues, ranging from government surveillance to economic concerns around the distribution of pirated movies or the sale of medical products online.[171]

It is worth noting that control over the introduction of new domain spaces equates to control over new speech spaces. Hence, the DNS is not only political in its day-to-

[171] Samantha Bradshaw, Laura DeNardis, The politicization of the Internet's Domain Name System: Implications for Internet security, universality, and freedom new media & society 2018, Vol. 20(1) 332–350.

day operation but is gradually diagnosed as a proxy site for extraneous geopolitical power due to the DNS to control the flow of information, enforce content related laws, enact censorship, or even changing the underlying technical architecture of the DNS[172] by seeking modifications to the system of administration that keeps cyberspace operational. It is recognized that cyberspace infrastructure is a site of global power. It is a characteristic that DNS interventions that block the free flow of information creating collateral damage to the broader cyberspace, limiting an individual's capacity to access information or express oneself, or take part in the global economy. Moreover, a disrupting concern links to the efficacy of the cyberspace governance ecosystem as a whole and so the politicization of infrastructure is escalating tension over control of cyberspace governance institutions and arrangements that keep cyberspace operating. Geopolitical tensions intensify as states more and more identify the DNS as a site of power and struggle to regulate a technology that spills over into every aspect of political, social, and economic life.

It has to be taken into account that digitalization as a global trend in the development of economy and society based on transformation of information into digital form, shift to other forms of communication through cyber technologies, launch of remote working and studying, which were widely used during the fight against COVID-19 pandemic, unquestionably affect the advancement of law as a regulatory system. New technological possibilities have changed the social reality of law in theoretical and in practical way which means even an alteration of the essence of conventional law since AAI law will be articulated and enforced automatically. Will AAI achieve the free travel of data via natural sources (wireless) and not needed any infrastructure? As long as AAI requires the cyberspace environment and infrastructure or an analogous one in order to function then it will be manipulated by the owners of the infrastructure.

References

1. Erbsen, A. (2010). Impersonal Jurisdiction. *Emory Law Journal, 60*(1), 26.
2. Buckland, B. S., Schreier, F., Winkler, T. H., *Democratic governance challenges of cyber security*, DCAF Horizon 2015 Working Paper No. 1.
3. Charles W. "Rocky" Rhodes, et al. (2020). Ford's jurisdictional crossroads. *Georgetown Law Journal Online, 109*, 102.
4. Estlund, C. (2018). What should we do after work? Automation and employment law. *Yale Law Journal, 128*, 254.
5. Klerman, D. (2012). Personal jurisdiction and product liability. *Southern California Law Review, 85*, 1551, 1585–86
6. Zekos, G. (2012). Cyber-territory and jurisdiction of nations. *Journal of Internet Law, Number 12/3.*

[172] Seltzer W (2011) Exposing the flaws of censorship by domain name. IEEE Security & Privacy. http://wendy.seltzer.is/writing/COICA-IEEE.pdf

7. Zekos, G. (2017). Διαδίκτυο, H/Y & Τηλεπικοινωνίες στο Ελληνικό Δίκαιο -Cyberspace, H/Y and Telecommunications, Εκδόσεις Π. Σάκκουλα https://www.sakkoulas-online.gr/profiles/georgios-i-zekos/
8. Zekos, G. (2011). Globalisation and states' cyber-territory. *Web Journal of Current Legal Issues, 5*.
9. Zekos, G. (2017). *The United States of Europe in place of the European Union*. Nova Science.
10. Goldfarb, A., & Taker, C. (2017). *Digital economics. Working paper*. National Bureau of Economic Research.
11. Hoffmann, S., et al. (2020). Standardising the splinternet: How China's technical standards could fragment the internet. *Journal of Cyber Policy*, 1–26.
12. Nash, J. R. (2020). The rules and standards of personal jurisdiction. *Alabama Law Review, 72*, 465.
13. O'Hara, K., & Hall, W. *Four Internets: The geopolitics of digital governance*, CIGI Papers No. 206 — December 2018.
14. Buell, S. W. (2011). What is securities fraud? *Duke Law Journal, 61*, 511, 562.
15. Qureshi, Z. R. (2019). If the shoe fits: Applying personal jurisdiction's stream of commerce analysis to e-commerce - A value test. 21 *N.Y.U Journal of Legislation and Public Policy* 727, 728.
16. Zekos, G. (1999). Internet or electronic technology: A threat to state sovereignty. *The Journal of Information, Law and Technology*. www.law.warwick.ac.uk/jilt/99-3/zekos.html

Chapter 9
Politics and Technology

9.1 Defining Politics and Technology

It has to be taken into account that two aspects of politics are dominant. Firstly, politics is everywhere in the social world and particularly in all collective social activity, formal and informal, public and private, in all human groups, institutions, and societies.[1] Secondly, politics has a broad reach concerning money, goods, status, influence, respect, rights, and so on which means that politics encompasses anything involving or making claims about the who, what, when, and how in social groups.[2] Due to the fact that as architects of decision-making systems, data scientists are political actors by defining distributions across a wide array of social contexts such as by configuring how institutions conceive of problems and make decisions which means that a source of fresh power is generated evading the routine and easy definition of a stated political power. It could be said that the scientific arena functions as a crucial place for the production of social and political order.[3]

Digital technology embeds politics by shaping social outcomes. It is argued that AI technologies are similar to legislative acts by establishing a framework for public order that will persist over many generations which means that the building of highways, the creation of television networks, and AI networking influence and divide or unite people in society and so these issues are settled not only in the institutions and practices of politics proper but also via everyday arrangements. In other words, even though technology does not conform to conventional notions of politics, it often influences society in much the same manner as laws, elections, and judicial opinions. There are many examples of engineers developing and deploying

[1] Leftwich, Adrian. 1984. "Politics, people, resources, and power." In What is Politics? The Activity and its Study, edited by Adrian Leftwich. Basil Blackwell.

[2] Lasswell, Harold. 1936. Politics: Who Gets What, When, How: Peter Smith Pub Inc.

[3] Jasanoff, Sheila. 2006. "Technology as a Site and Object of Politics." In The Oxford Handbook of Contextual Political Analysis, edited by Robert E. Goodin and Charles Tilly.

G. I. Zekos, *Political, Economic and Legal Effects of Artificial Intelligence*, Contributions to Political Science, https://doi.org/10.1007/978-3-030-94736-1_9

technologies that, by shaping behavior and transferring power, mold aspects of society.[4]

Data science exists in this political landscape and so machine learning systems already embed political stances. Predictive policing systems present a specifically pointed example of how striving to remain neutral embeds and legitimizes existing political conditions. Moreover, data scientists thoughtfully and rigorously contribute to improving society by advancing new methods and norms influencing political goals and strategies. Assumed the political stakes of algorithms, data scientists must ground their endeavors in clear political commitments and rigorous evaluations of the consequences.

It has to be taken into account that the upgrading of new computing communication technologies and methods of processing large amounts of data has led to the automation and robotization of innumerable processes involving production. Hence, the swift development of digital technology has altered the approach toward the field of virtual entertainment and the use of cultural objects. Furthermore, the rapid development of artificial intelligence systems, autonomous digital algorithms, and robotic technologies have transformed the landscape and the specifics of socio-legal and socio-political life of society.[5]

It is representative that the use of digital technologies is indispensable for protection of the interests of individuals, businesses, and the State and so of central significance are the safety of the unified telecommunication networks, the continued accessibility of cyberspace, the stability of the communication networks used by state authorities, maintenance of relevant hardware, etc. In line, the defense of the country and the security of civil society constitute the key functions of the State such as the applicable provisions of Articles 55, 71, and 114 of the Constitution of the Russian Federation.

Is there a legitimacy matter if people are taken out of politics? It has to be taken into account that humans need political activity in order to thrive but the drawbacks of technically 'better' decisions might outweigh the benefits. Should computers make decisions that affect citizens' lives and wellbeing? It is obvious that there is problem of lack of transparency when humans depend on decisions that are beyond the capacity of human reasoning which means that matters of such transparency and so the conduct of politics will be left to on the basis of trust in machines. It is a matter of accountability when AI is involved in making political decisions. Liability/responsibility/accountability mechanisms will be established after regularizing the persona of AI.

---

[4]Winner, Langdon. 1986. The Whale and the Reactor: A Search for Limits in an Age of High Technology: University of Chicago Press.

[5]Mamychev A., Okorokov A., Bespalova T., Sviridkina E., Chertakova E. (2018). Civilizational modeling of political and legal development of the society in the XXI century. Revista Amazonia Investiga. № 15. Vol. 7. pp. 49–57.

9.2 Fragmentation of Technology

Countries face the selection between using technology from foreign owners and risking a go-it-alone strategy. Chinese providers have grown large and innovative enough to occupy most of the available market space and there is fragmentation of technology with politically divided and possibly noninteroperable technology areas of influence.[6] Fragmentation creates less competition, oligopolistic market structures in different territories, and the solidification of the influence of state decisions. Moreover, the effects of fragmentation are global cybersecurity, where the incentives for united protection across different geographies vanish. Variety in AI technology development causes some level of fragmentation increasing the overall performance of global innovation systems and business and social communities. On the other hand, fully integrated and globally interdependent systems are highly vulnerable.

It has to be taken into account that AI is a technology with outstanding security and defense applications and so countries protect their citizens, their interests at home and abroad, and their own political stability in the face of possible malicious or fraudulent uses of AI which means that techno-nationalism is present and rapidly gaining more support establishing control mechanisms for policy-based market configuration. It is characteristic that the countries with the competence to build AI systems by themselves are also behaving analogously in the policy domain, although all of them deny that this is the case. As well as techno-nationalism, protectionism is an additional factor increasing the likelihoods of a general outcome in favor of undesirable fragmentation and so EU and US institutions reconsider existing mechanisms for the supervision of foreign investment in key sectors and the consideration of safeguards for technologies deemed as central for national competitiveness.[7]

It could be said that apt interoperability provisions alleviate worries about fragmentation and a solution to national and international AI policy must be to keep the system within the boundaries of a functional level of diversity. Moreover, the central consequences of infrastructural technologies, such as AI, materialize at the sectoral and macroeconomic levels rather than at the level of individual firms. It has to be taken into account that if a country has not deployed AI technology, its industry as a whole will face difficulties, possibly compromising the country's overall competitive position and so AI will generate a divide between countries which means that countries that have AI technology will be able to generate new value refining rather than destabilizing the wellbeing of citizens. Moreover, the competitive advantage of low-cost labor will no longer be an option for states

[6]Triolo, P., Allison, K., & Brown, C. (2018). Eurasia Group White Paper: The Geopolitics of 5G. Eurasia Group. Retrieved from https://www.eurasiagroup.net/siteFiles/Media/files/181114%205G%20special%20report%20public(1).pdf

[7]European Commission. (2017). Report from the commission to the European parliament and the council on trade and investment barriers https://doi.org/10.1002/ejoc.201200111. Brussels. European Commission. (2018). Artificial intelligence for Europe - COM(2018) 237 final.

since AI and robots will ultimately do most of the routine work.[8] The amalgamation of AI and demographics and its prospective effects of unequal job distribution and economic disruption will restructure the relationships between citizens, governments, and markets and have far-reaching consequences for nations.

Political pressures will incentivize further fragmentation as an expedient tool for medium-term protection of employment and so economies that control the technologies and are skilled users will be in a better position to handle the process. States can delay the introduction of certain technologies through regulation while preserving the advantage of being an exporter and in control of the technological know-how which means that there is competition to attract and locate key AI firms and start-ups to compensate for the job losses and establish the conditions for regenerated economic growth.

9.3 Technocracy and Politics

It is worth mentioning here that technical matters are also political which means that there is technocracy of AI when power to make technical decisions is delegated to computers. There is a political quality of all things and so submitting the technical to an evaluation in light of ultimate values is required which means that technocracy rotates around the need to use experts with particular knowledge in positions of political power in order to build the desired society. Besides, politicians are charged with determining what the desired society is, while the technocrats are charged with making it a reality in the most operative way possible.[9]

Moreover, it is worth stating that the technicians do not have all power in a technocracy and so while a technocratic society assigns much authority to their technicians, they are not given the authority to ascertain the goals of society. Moreover, the technocrats are not political or moral experts, and morality and the question of political values are not reduced to technical questions amenable to the calculus of mathematics and logic which means that as long as politics is reduced to technical questions amenable to the calculus of mathematics and logic then AI technology will be able to deal with them.

It is possible to have an AI technocracy which means having the possibility of letting computers make expert judgements for us and so by utilizing advanced machine learning, computers could make better decisions than human beings. It is obvious that AI systems improve decision-making by overcoming the human limitations of bounded rationality and information processing and so AI technology are

[8]Frey, C. B. (2019). The technology trap: Capital, labor, and power in the age of automation. Princeton, NJ: Princeton University Press.

[9]M. Janssen, G. Kuk, The challenges and limits of big data algorithms in technocratic governance, Govern. Inf. Q. 33 (3) (2016).

better than humans not only at chess and Go but also this capacity applies to well-defined strategic matters.[10]

On the other hand, a technocracy possesses a political device in place for delivering the direction for society, while the technocrats have the power to ascertain and effectuate the policies considered indispensable to proceed in the desired direction means that technical and political decisions are separated, and the technical matters are assigned to independent agencies, and technocratic elites.[11] It is argued that technocrats are instrumental, but still largely controlled by elected politicians.[12]

An AI technocracy seems to allow better decisions in terms of efficiency, utility, or whatever other criteria and AI offers both efficiency and still be under control and direction. However, there are obvious objections to an AI technocracy based on the political harms it may instigate such as legitimacy, morality, transparency related to AI and AI decision-making encompasses troubles assigning responsibility.

9.4 Digitization and Democracy

Are digitization and democracy related globally? It has to be taken into account that digitization has added to the weakening of democracy and the global liberal order, but digital technologies have infused daily interactions globally generating the global interdependence. It seems that digital technologies weakened post-World War II global order and its compatibility with democracy by exposing citizens to tougher global economic forces and diminishing the policy options of their governments. Thus, digitally enabled globalization transferred governance away from conventional democratic processes centered in the nation-state and so digital technologies caused social acceleration generating social inequality, with its negative effects on democracy. It could be said that authoritarian governments[13] have increasingly mastered digital technologies use to consolidate their control but, on the other hand, cross-border digital activism could promote global democratization.[14] Moreover, there is a global digital competition with the global competition between democratic and authoritarian forms of governance being an imperative

[10] T.M. Vogl, C. Seidelin, B. Ganesh, J. Bright, Algorithmic Bureaucracy: Managing Competence, Complexity, and Problem Solving in the Age of Artificial Intelligence. Complexity, and Problem Solving in the Age of Artificial Intelligence, 2019. February 1, 2019).

[11] B.G. Peters, The Politics of Bureaucracy, Routledge, London, 2014. Frank Fischer, Technology and the politics of expertise, Sci. Soc. 57 (2) (1993) 246–249.

[12] J. Sadowski, E. Selinger, creating a taxonomic tool for technocracy and applying it to Silicon Valley, Technol. Soc. 38 (2014) 161–168.

[13] Shen, Hong. 2018. "Building a Digital Silk Road? Situating the Internet in China's Belt and Road Initiative." International Journal of Communication 12(0): 19.

[14] Diamond, Larry. 2010. "Liberation Technology." Journal of Democracy 21(3): 69–83. Galloway, Scott. 2018. "The Case for Breaking Up Amazon, Apple, Facebook and Google." Esquire. https://www.esquire.com/newspolitics/a15895746/bust-big-tech-silicon-valley/

dimension of the relationship between digitization and democracy at the global level. To that extent, digital networks coordinate activities by organizing the global supply chains and establishing complex forms of global governance by offering new opportunities for digitally enabled participation, accountability, and transparency enhancing democracy but also allowing wealthier or more expert elite players to self-interestedly exploit digital developments.[15]

It is worth noting that policy-making no longer relies mainly on the exerted power of a single player, which has traditionally been the status and so governance effectuated by digital networks in general and by blockchain technology. In its place, interactions and societies are becoming progressively governed by networks encompassing a diverse set of public and private actors and so generating societal power in a networked system.

It has to be taken into account that the formation, collection, dissemination, and distribution of all sorts of information in the digital domain count no longer just on social processes but progressively on technology. Moreover, governance mechanisms have adjusted owing to globalization, augmented technical specialism, and functional differentiation because the use of and reliance on digital networks means that DLT and blockchain technology are modelling societies and power correlations.[16]

There are clearly positive effects of digitization including the democratization of access to knowledge, new opportunities for political and social engagement, greater transparency via forms of e-government but they can be expanded more realistically if the global dimensions of digital democracy are more fully acclaimed.[17]

It has to be taken into account that due to the negative impact of "fake news" spread digitally on elections or the disruptive effects of digitization on the type of social cohesion denotes the significance of digitation as an imperative precondition for and effect of democracy. Moreover, digital media are a form of liberation technology expanding political, social, and economic freedom which means that digital technology is element for social movements, digital activism, and civic action. Furthermore, democratization goes in parallel with technology diffusion and so democracies are boosted by political parties utilizing digital technologies for content and organizational affordances which means that technology diffusion augments competition among political parties enhancing democratic practices. To that extent, the global diffusion of digital technology has strengthened social networks facilitating forms of political participation and so transforming politics and governance.

---

[15] Campbell-Verduyn, Malcolm, Marcel Goguen, and Tony Porter. 2017. "Big Data and algorithmic governance: the case of financial practices." New Political Economy 22(2): 219–236.

[16] Zwitter, A., & Hazenberg, J. (2020). Decentralized Network Governance: Blockchain Technology and the Future of Regulation. Frontiers in Blockchain. https://doi.org/10.3389/fbloc.2020.00012

[17] Abbott, Kenneth W., Philipp Genschel, Duncan Snidal, and Bernhard Zangl. 2016. "Two Logics of Indirect Governance: Delegation and Orchestration." British Journal of Political Science 46(04): 719–729.

It is worth noting that the rising reliance on big data, machine learning, and artificial intelligence for campaigning, marketing, and public service provisions have personalized politics to the disadvantage of the type of public domain that is crucial to democracy, amplified gaps between social classes, alienated disadvantaged minorities and exacerbated inequities.[18] On the other hand, the entanglement of cyberspace with the tricky features of contemporary capitalism such as concentrated media ownership and manipulative advertising in means that is destructive to democracy. Moreover, a lack of regulation or accepted good practices to guide suppliers and consumers of online information leads to data breaches, foreign interferences in elections, confusion, power imbalances, and even violence which means that it is possible the emergence of "new authoritarianism" as nondemocratic regimes and populist politicians are leveraging big data and clever microtargeting techniques to affect crucial democratic institutions, embracing elections.

Digitization caused "social acceleration" challenging the slow nation-states and the democratic procedures associated with them and so many governance functions have been transferred to networks or platforms of officials or non-governmental business or civil society players that are faster and more flexible working more effectively across borders.[19] In addition, digitization has assisted the emergence of privately owned global platforms such as Facebook or Amazon, governed by mixes of private rules such as terms of service and computer code, essentially generating new zones of sovereignty such as cyber-sovereignty and so private businesses that dominate networks or platforms have gathered noteworthy wealth and power posing a challenge to democracy.

It has to be taken into consideration that algorithms[20] are used to map, categorize, and divide people in modes that enable control, exploitation, and manipulation of foreign and neocolonial audiences and so due to digitization algorithmic targeting has allowed state-run international propaganda and fake news via platforms that remain the key enforcers but algorithmic targeting is also motivated not only by political influence but also by profit.[21]

---

[18] Eubanks, Virginia. 2018. Automating Inequality: How High-Tech Tools Profile, Police, and Punish the Poor. New York, NY St. Martin's Press.

[19] Srnicek, Nick. 2017. Platform Capitalism. Cambridge, UK; Malden, MA: Polity.

[20] Diakopoulos, Nicholas, and Michael Koliska. 2017. "Algorithmic Transparency in the News Media." Digital Journalism 5 (7): 809–28. https://doi.org/10.1080/21670811.2016.1208053

[21] Allcott, Hunt, and Matthew Gentzkow. 2017. "Social Media and Fake News in the 2016 Election." Journal of Economic Perspectives 31 (2): 211–36. https://doi.org/10.1257/jep.31.2.211

9.5 Technology and Law in a Constitutional Democracy

Laws are lengthy and complex text and so the regulatory mechanism or mechanisms embedded in the law is a task requiring expertise and legal knowledge.[22] Moreover, apprehending the 'gist' of the law is more demanding and the present Artificial Intelligence does not yet let an algorithm to identify the regulatory mechanisms in the law which means that the singularity of law exploited by AAI technology is needed in order to achieve automatic identification of the substance of the law. It has to be taken into account that the rationale of the law is to accomplish specific policy objectives. Is there a connection between the design and engineering of technology and the affordances or far-reaching capabilities of such technology in society? Is there a relational conception of law and technology? Is AI an instrument in the hands of elite to impose technocracy upon the globe which is not democracy?

It is worth mentioning that the improvement of law is outlined by the values protected by it, which traditionally embraces justice, equality, and good faith. Moreover, the change of human–technology relations at the present stage raises the question of moving toward technological humanism. It is argued that the law in its value component cannot be replaced by artificial intelligence but AAI can impose its own sense of AAI law. Moreover, the law is able to uphold its fundamental substance and basis without turning into technology, tackling universal principles of law, and searching for the equilibrium between scientific and technological progress and human rights. On the other hand, law is a part of society responding to all changes taking place in it.

While Global-Regulation has succeeded in using AI to identify compliance clauses in legislation, and so, distinguish the regulatory mechanism, the road is still long before an AAI system could identify other, more complex, regulatory mechanisms based on the language of the law by generating an abstract of the law. If the automated AAI system produces a reasonable abstract of the legal text, which may not follow the quality of a human composing such abstract but will make sense and encapsulate the core of the law, then the big step toward making the system comprehensible will be made permitting the robo-justice. It is worth mentioning here that Global-Regulation is an online platform advancing transparency and accessibility of Global-Regulation via AI by translating world's legislation to English. Global-Regulation investigates new ecosystems connecting people, data, knowledge, and democratic institutions in the digital era. Digital platforms accelerate the depth and breadth of participation, lowering the barriers to different forms of participation and advancing access. Moreover, Global-Regulation engages artificial intelligence in two ways: firstly, employing machine translation to translate the world's legislation to English and, secondly generating an automated system to detect compliance clauses and extract penalties from this legislation and so improving regulation by enabling lessons drawing from one jurisdiction to the other. Thus, taking into account Global-Regulation, AAI technology will allow the establishment of a global

---

[22] Nachshon Goltz, Search Ideas – Interaction with the Search Engine (Global-Regulation, 2017).

codified regulation permitting a network of AAI systems of the various AAI jurisdictions to be interconnected and even eradicating the sense of national sovereignty and establishing the AAI cyber-jurisdiction.

9.6 AI and Democracy

It is worth noting that digital technologies serve a very specific function for autocratic states.[23] Digital technologies are altering the character of state repression because the speed and scope with which information is collected and processed are far greater than any monitoring or surveillance techniques of the past.[24]

It has to be taken into consideration that the goal of increased participation remains as a sign for refining democracy. How does AI interfere in the informational environment influencing the working of democracy? Which are the aftereffects of an increased use of AI for democratic politics? The effects of an increased use of AI can be either detrimental or favorable for the working of liberal democracy.

AI algorithmic systems change informational environments on a large scale, configuring individuals' decision situations shaping their welfare and life opportunities. Algorithmic decision-making (ADM) systems and other forms of AI are geared toward information processing and so solving cognitive and coordination tasks. Nowadays, algorithmic decision-making is digital employing statistical methods and so these algorithms suffer from the same problems as traditional statistics, such as poorly sampled data, biased data, and measurement errors.[25]

It has to be taken into account that while algorithmic systems are aimed at running specific tasks, the scope of their societal influence is enormous concerning online advertisements, the scoring of credit default risks or the assessment of terrorism risks. Furthermore, real-world applications qualify as intelligent in a weak sense designed for dealing with particular problems and functioning in narrowly defined domains by showing noteworthy performance in their fields of application. Moreover, algorithmic systems proactively intervene into social relations due to a sort of governance based on the processing of information which means that by furnishing

[23] Ronald J. Deibert, Three Painful Truths About Social Media, 30 J. DEMOCRACY 25, 31 (2019) (arguing that social media enables authoritarianism). Scott J. Shackelford, Angie Raymond, Abbey Stemler, and Cyanne Loyle, Defending Democracy: Taking Stock of the Global Fight Against Digital Repression, Disinformation, and Election Insecurity, 77 Wash. & Lee L. Rev. 1747 (2020), https://scholarlycommons.law.wlu.edu/wlulr/vol77/iss4/7

[24] Ronald Deibert & Rafal Rohozinski, Liberation vs. Control: The Future of Cyberspace, 21 J. DEMOCRACY 43, 43 (2010) (noting that no technology other than digital technology has "grown with such speed and spread so far geographically in such a short period of time").

[25] In 2015 Google Photos' image recognition software was found to have a terribly prejudicial and offensive error https://www.wired.com/story/when-it-comes-to-gorillasgoogle-photos-remains-blind

personalized information to individuals shape their informational environments and their decision situations.[26]

How capabilities of AI influence the informational necessities of the democratic process? Again, existing forms of AI and trainable algorithmic systems are intelligent in a weak sense not comparable to that of humans, and they are generally designed to cope with particular, narrowly defined tasks. Even so, already today, automated systems fill societies as artificial agents and intervene into social relations and individuals' lives. Furthermore, in industrialized societies people use filtering algorithms in online searches and social networks or count on personal assistants and so they are subject to algorithmic decision-making applied by the state in the areas of policing, education, etc.[27]

It has to be taken into account that the increasing adoption of AI alters the informational foundations of societies. The consequences of AI are wide-ranging and so AI can diminish or increase information deficits of both citizens and decision-makers on the input, throughout, and output level of the political system. There are concerns encompassing the capacity of AI technology to support or enable pervasive forms of disinformation or online manipulation threatening democratic norms and practices.

Which are the foundations of liberal democracy? The central principle of democratic rule requires that political decisions and outputs are tied back to citizens' views and preferences which means that the political process is grounded on procedures that permit for translating citizens' preferences into policies. Moreover, the guarantees of fundamental civil rights and rule of law along with the rules that configure the institutional framework of democratic politics regarding free and fair elections with political parties competing for government office are the basis of democracy. Nonetheless, citizens' preferences will always be imperfectly represented and their views and preferences alter over time which means that there is an ongoing political battle over which views and interests are taken up in the political process. To that extent, political parties, the civil society, interest groups, and other organizations all promote positions and preferences and try to make the government act in ways that are responsive to their demands. It is worth noting that openness and adaptiveness are principles of democratic politics and so the political system is built up internal complexity maintaining a self-regulating process but implying several informational requirements which means that information, via AI and cybernetic process, is required not just at the level of producing outputs, but also at the level of the decision-making and the level of inputs that are fed into the decision-making process. Moreover, citizens' views and preferences are molded and articulated via sufficient and unbiased informational basis which means that existing political offers convey citizens' preferences. Accordingly, political actors communicate information

[26] McAfee, A., & Brynjolfsson, E. (2017). Machine, platform, crowd: Harnessing our digital future (1st ed.). New York: W.W. Norton & Company.

[27] Brauneis, R., & Goodman, E. P. (2017). Algorithmic transparency for the smart city. SSRN Electronic Journal. https://doi.org/10.2139/ssrn.3012499

about the state of political affairs by launching a political public area in which citizens make up their minds about politics.

AI generates challenges for democratic responsiveness and accountability due to a novel technological dimension and in link with existing transparency and accountability drawbacks which means that there is a need for institutionalizing suitable governance mechanisms challenging the input level of politics. Which is the role of AI in liberal-democratic politics, specifically in terms of their possible impact on responsiveness and accountability? It has to be taken into account that liberal democracy as a political system is marked by special informational necessities existing not only concerning producing adequate outputs which means that as a result of standards of democratic legitimacy, informational requirements occur also for preserving a certain form of decision-making because liberal democracy is primarily about how outputs are produced.

A political system in which government policy is responsive to the preferences of the wealthy few rather than to the majority of citizens has to be characterized as an oligarchy than as a democracy or a republic.[28] It could be said that many modern states are now functioning as oligarchies because the modern political reality, regardless of the one-person-one-vote or the equal right to speak or participate, differences in material power generate disparities in political influence and account for key political outcomes gained by oligarchs.[29] To that extent, AAI has to contribute to democracy by diminishing the gains of oligarchs. Will AAI establish democratic objectivity or oligarchs will impose their interests via AAI?

It has to be taken into account that lately there is algorithmically enhanced navigation of political information. Citizens must develop and use their political judgment by deciding which preferences and demands to express and ascertain how political options and selections link to their views and preferences which means that citizens are getting into an environment of information overload making the finding and gathering the relevant information a difficult task. To that extent, due to their superior capacities AI applications can deal with sorts of cognitive information problems and so playing an important supporting role which means that AI with

[28] Nicholas O. Stephanopoulos, Political Powerlessness, 90 N.Y.U. L. REV. 1527, 1578 (2015); Elizabeth Rigby & Gerald C. Wright, Political Parties and Representation of the Poor in the American States, 57 AM.J. POL. SCI. 552, 552 (2013) (finding that low-income preferences rarely "get incorporated in parties' campaign appeals at [the] early stage in the policymaking process") Robert A. Dahl, Polyarchy: Participation And Opposition 1 (1971) "[A] key characteristic of a democracy is the continuing responsiveness of the government to the preferences of its citizens, considered as political equals."

[29] Jeffrey A. Winters, Oligarchy 214 (2011). U.S. CONST. art. IV, § 4. Ganesh Sitaraman, The Crisis Of The Middle-Class Constitution: Why Economic Inequality Threatens Our Republic 3–5 (2017) (arguing that the U.S. Constitution assumes relative economic equality but that such equality is now absent); Steven L. Winter, 'Down Freedom's Main Line,' 41 NETH.J. LEGAL PHIL. 202, 203 (2012) ("Democracy's moral appeal lies not in the promise of an impossible radical freedom, but in the commitment to equal participation in determining the terms and conditions of social life—what, even before the currency of the term 'democracy,' the ancient Greeks called isonomia.").

specialized cognitive tasks facilitate to overcome what are fundamentally cognitive barriers to the working of a public sphere. In line, search engines have made the web searchable and are increasingly capable of providing direct answers to user questions but current AI and AAI will allow compiling more data with a possibility for more intelligence analysis amalgamating relevant information in the hands of citizens allowing them to navigate in the public sphere and so AI energize civil society by providing citizens with means that obviously lower the burden of obtaining relevant information about political issues.[30] Suitable AI technology will enable or foster citizen engagement and collaboration and so enhancing the relationship between governing and governed.

Does the use of AI encompass a form of public power that is not checked, scrutinized, and controlled? It has to be taken into account that even though liberal democracy is under pressure all the time, it is not overcome or becoming outdated due to the development of new technologies such as AI but it is the utilization of the principles of democracy by people and authorities via the utilization of the relevant technology. On the other hand, AAI technology might be utilized to impose the democracy of the owner of the AAI technology by promoting and advertising the "wanted" political ideas as the ideal for an AAI society in order to keep in power particular elite.

It has to be taken into consideration that private media organizations and online platforms, in their competition over capturing the attention of a large audience, consider citizens as mere consumers of content. Besides, while citizens can easily acquire relevant information about political affairs and politicians' performances, many times they will not make use of these possibilities because merely prefer to pursue political information that is in line with their visions or that they find more spectacular and entertaining. Is there a specific process of public opinion formation toward strengthening public autonomy, responsiveness, and accountability? The answer is no but there are certain rules utilized by elites to push citizens toward a specific path of thinking and forming of preferences implementing the interests of the elite, which encompass more wealth for them and less for the people. Moreover, a strong regulation of public opinion formation leads to censorship and so AI can be used in a way of safeguarding balance and pluralism in the manner of compiling information. Hence, citizens can make competent use[31] of effectively constructed and embedded AI as their political information assistants and so having a more dialogical relationship with political information sources than ever before which means a better democracy. On the other hand, politicians will have the chance to utilize AI to send the message to voters and promote their own work which means uprising politics to a different level.

---

[30] Savaget, P., Chiarini, T., & Evans, S. (2018). Empowering political participation through artificial intelligence. Science and Public Policy. https://doi.org/10.1093/scipol/scy064

[31] Helberger, N., Pierson, J., & Poell, T. (2018). Governing online platforms: From contested to cooperative responsibility. The Information Society, 34(1), 1–14. https://doi.org/10.1080/01972243.2017.1391913

9.7 AI and Voting

It has to be taken into account that the opportunity to participate in politics is a crucial way to protect one's interests which means that enabling all citizens to play a part in politics makes certain that law and policy effectively respect the interests of citizens from all segments of society.[32] In addition, by giving all citizens a say, the state confirms that every citizen's moral reasoning plays a role in settling each political outcome. So, if the legislature is functioning appropriately, citizens' opinions will be represented equally enough that the law-making process in a representative democracy articulates equal regard for citizens' judgment.[33]

States have authority in how they provide and run elections. A blockchain-supported voting system[34] presents promise of voting in the digital age and a blockchain-enabled voting system functions without administration from a central party, so dismissing concerns of mishandling votes. A system implementing blockchain records stores and reports voting counts much faster than the existing hand-count system.

It has to be taken into account that AI brings forward social and political transformation. Artificial intelligence will bring forward a new voting system and of the whole elections process for campaigning to the final results. The design of AI systems, particularly the level of transparency and auditability of learning algorithms, remains an ongoing concern because AI-enabled systems can be weaponized to disrupt public agencies and various processes such as political campaigns and elections in democratic societies.[35]

It could be said that the new communication devices have generated new gaps, predominantly among groups of voters, empowering those who have access to social media and who rally behind specific causes or form almost virtual political parties.[36] Hence, there is the problem of the "big data divide" encompassing the gap between those who have access to large-scale data and the means to analyze this data and those who do not. To that extent, there are claims against Facebook, Google, etc.

---

[32] John Stuart Mill, Considerations On Representative Government 43 (Currin V. Shields ed., 1958) (1861).

[33] Spokeo, Inc. v. Robins, 136 S. Ct. 1540, 1547 (2016) (stating the elements that are required for a citizen to have standing).

[34] Beckett, Jacob (2021) "Blockchain Voting: WY Not?," Wyoming Law Review: Vol. 21: No. 2, Article 7. https://scholarship.law.uwyo.edu/wlr/vol21/iss2/7

[35] Desouza, K.C., Ahmad, A., Naseer, H., Sharma, M., 2020. Weaponizing information systems for political disruption: The Actor, Lever, Effects, and Response Taxonomy (ALERT). Comput. Secur. 88, 101,606. https://doi.org/10.1016/j.cose.2019.101606

[36] Chadwick, 'Web 2.0: New Challenges for the Study of E-Democracy in an Era of Informational Exuberance', in S. Coleman, P.M. Shane (eds), Connecting Democracy: Online Consultation and the Flow of Political Communication (2012) 45; Shkabatur, 'Cities @ Crossroads: Digital Technology and Local Democracy in America', 76 Brooklyn Law Review (2011) 1413; Freeman and Quirke, 'Understanding E-Democracy: Government-led Initiatives for Democratic Reform', 5 Journal of E-Democracy and Open Government (2013) 141.

being acting as 'the new colonial powers' but regardless that social media giants are aware of this problem, their effort concentrates on increasing revenues from users rather than multiplying the agency of citizens.

It has to be taken into account that digital platforms facilitate the interaction of people, data, services, and goods which means that they are organizing a formerly disorganized market via algorithms and so making it easier for two or more different groups to match. Moreover, technologies renovate social realms and so influencing the dynamics of politics.[37] It could be said that digital technologies have made possible a "platformization" of infrastructure and an "infrastructuralization" of digital platforms which in fact generates concerns about mismatch between corporate interests and public values in general and in addition to matters regarding information reliability, social division, and election integrity.[38]

It is worth noting that AI technology allows prospective interference in elections and so becoming a phenomenon on a global scale.[39] Thus, IoT is considered a worldwide network of individually connected devices that communicate with each other, passing data across cyberspace. Moreover, IoT devices and their networks are becoming, in the end, a key target for cybercriminals resulting in the breach of data security and privacy and other rights. Hence, sensitive information can be leaked out in case of unauthorized manipulation or handling of hardware and software in these devices.[40]

Are data scientists political actors involved in normative constructions of society and, as befits political work, assess their efforts according to the downstream impacts on people's lives? It could be said that due to their political work data scientists are political actors involved in normative constructions of society assessing their efforts in line with the downstream effects on people's lives. It has to be taken into account that data and technology are not neutral and so data science is a form of political action.

To that extent, election-related cyber-operations have captured the international law community's awareness and expressed by the Oxford Statement on International

---

[37] Marco Aur'elio Ruediger, Bots, Social Networks and Politics in Brazil: a Study on Illegitimate Interferences with the Public Debate on the Web, Risks to the Democracy and the 2018 Elections, Fundaçao ˜ Getúlio Vargas, Rio de Janeiro, 2017. John Zysman, Martin Kenney, The next phase in the digital revolution: intelligent tools, platforms, growth, employment, Commun. ACM 61 (2) (2018) 54–63.

[38] Jos'e van Dijck, Thomas Poell, Martijn de Waal, The Platform Society: Public Values in a Connective World, Oxford University Press, Oxford, 2018. Jean-Christophe Plantin, Carl Lagoze, Paul N. Edwards, Christian Sandvig, Infrastructure studies meet platform studies in the age of Google and Facebook, New Media Soc. 20 (1) (2018) 293–310.

[39] Joint Statement from Elections Infrastructure Government Coordinating Council & the Election Infrastructure Sector Coordinating Executive Committees, Cybersecurity And Infrastructure Security Agency (Nov. 12, 2020), https://www.cisa.gov/news/2020/11/12/joint-statement-elections-infrastructure-government-coordinating-councilelection

[40] Fredric Paul, "People are really worried about IoT data privacy and security—and they should be", Network World, https://www.networkworld.com/article/3267065/people-are-really-worried-about-iot-data-privacy-andsecurityand-they-should-be.html

Law Protections. Moreover, the Paris call specifies that states and others have to intensify their capability to avert malign interference by foreign players targeting at undermining electoral processes through malicious cyber-activities which means that state and non-state actors should not pursue, support, or permit cyber-operations wanting to unsettle the technical infrastructure needed to elections, referenda, or plebiscites.[41] It has to be taken into account that intervention consists of two elements that both must be satisfied before a breach exists such as that the cyber-operation has to influence another State's internal or external affairs being its "domaine reserve" and secondly it must be coercive.[42] Foreign cyber-activities that take away a State of its capability to act vis-à-vis the domaine réservé are almost always coercive. Moreover, indirectly foreign States unsettle a State's capacity to conduct an election by taking part in actions directed at voters by engineering voter suppression. It has to be taken into account that operations that result in only a minimal disruption of voting cannot qualify as coercive. Nevertheless, as a rule, cyber-operations premeditated to directly or indirectly influence a State's capability to conduct an election by targeting either its administration of the election or the voters' capability to cast a ballot are coercive. To that extent, cyber-operations that deprive the electorate or a significant number of individual voters, of information bearing on the election are considered as coercive. It is worth noting that empowering access to democracy via a blockchain-enabled system restores a sense of trust and secure system to perform elections on.

It is worth noting that interference by cyber means infringes international law, predominantly the rules forbidding violation of a State's sovereignty or intervention in its internal affairs and respecting international human rights. Moreover, States facing election intruding by cyber means which means that States must put an end to hostile cyber-election interference according to the principle of due diligence and the necessity to protect international human rights. Furthermore, election interference by foreign States climbs to the stage of an "internationally wrongful act" when two essentials are present such as firstly, the action or omission has to be legally attributable to a State and secondly that act must violate a duty owed in international law to the target State.[43] To that extent, attribution in the legal sense has to be differentiated from attribution in the technical sense of the word and so designating a situation in which an individual or group's conduct is considered as that of a State.

[41] The 9 Principles, PARIS CALL (Dec. 11, 2018), https://pariscall.international/en/principles Advancing Cyberstability: Final Report, Global Commission On The Stability Of Cyberspace (Nov. 2019), https://cyberstability.or g/report/ (Proposed Norm 2 provides, "").

[42] Military and Paramilitary Activities in and against Nicaragua (Nicar. v. U.S.), Judgment, 1986 I.C.J. 14, ¶ 205 (June 27). Jens David Ohlin, Did Russian Cyber Interference in the 2016 Election Violate International Law?, 95 Texas Law Review 1579, 1595–98 (2017).

[43] Articles on State Responsibility art. 4; Tallinn Manual 2.0 On The International Law Applicable To Cyber Operations r. 15 (Michael N. Schmitt gen. ed., 2017). Guy Faulconbridge, What is Russia's GRU Military Intelligence Agency?, REUTERS, Oct. 5, 2018, https://www.reuters.com/article/us-britain-russia-gru-factbox/what-is-russiasgru-military-intelligence-agency-idUSKCN1MF1VK

The challenge is that there are many forms of relationship to a State. Hence, cyber-operation affects an election when an organ of a State such as intelligence agencies interferes and influence election campaigns.

In addition, an entity is eligible as an organ of the State either by being designated as such in the State's law or functioning in entire dependence on the State and so barring the likelihood of a State escaping charge for election interference by using an organization that lacks de jure organ status under its national law engaging in cyber-activities for and at the State's direction; which means that acts as its de facto organ.

The international law rule concerning foreign cyber-election interference is the prohibition of intervention into the internal or external affairs of other States.[44] Moreover, the applicability of the customary prohibition in the cyber-context was endorsed in the 2015 UN Group of Governmental Experts (GGE) report that the General Assembly subsequently approved.

Also, foreign activities in cyberspace violate the rule of sovereignty because the requirement to respect the sovereignty of other States is a key rule of international law. Hence, sovereignty can be violated based on an infringement of territorial integrity and inviolability because a cyber-operation instigating physical damage or injury in another State qualifies as a violation of its sovereignty. For instance, France, which has been targeted during elections, has tackled hostile cyber-operations engendering consequences of this character in its legal doctrine.[45] To that extent, in 2018, the Ministry of the Armies treated any cyber-attack against French digital systems or any consequences generated on French territory by digital means attributable to a State as a breach of France's sovereignty.[46] Hence, France treats a cyber-operation targeting its government election hardware/software or that instigates "effects" on other systems, such as a denial of service operation directed at a campaign's website, as a breach of French sovereignty. Furthermore, it has to be taken into account that cyber-activities affecting, or usurping, a governmental task of the target State violates its sovereignty. Thus, in the case of the election situation is interference because conducting elections qualifies as a governmental function that only States accomplish or authorize non-State entities to execute. Undeniably, a foreign State's cyber-activity directly weakening the government's capacity to conduct the election infringes that State's sovereignty on this basis encompassing in the short-term disrupting election hardware and software's right performance,

[44] G.A. Res. 2625 (XXV), Declaration on Principles of International Law Concerning Friendly Relations and Co-operation Among States in Accordance with the Charter of the United Nations (Oct. 24, 1970). Philip Kunig, Intervention, Prohibition of, Max Planck Encyclopedia Of International Law https://opil.ouplaw.com/view/10.1093/law:epil/9780199231690/law-9780199231690-e1434?rskey=sOnqwN&result=1&prd=OPIL

[45] Eric Auchard, Macron Campaign was Target of Cyber Attacks by Spy-linked Group, REUTERS, Apr. 24, 2017, https://www.reuters.com/article/us-france-election-macron-cyber/macron-campaign-wa s-target-of-cyber-attacks-by-spy-linked-group-idUSKBN17Q200

[46] Ministry of the Armies, International Law Applied to Cyberspace § 1.1.1. (2019) (France), https://www.defense.gouv.fr/content/download/567648/9770527/file/international+law+applied+to+operations+in+cyberspace.pdf

blocking access to online government information about the election, and changing that information.

Do cyber-activities that are not directed against the government's election systems violate sovereignty? Do cyber-activities implicating information or disinformation that does not influence how the election is carried out ever violate sovereignty? It could be said that those that indirectly unsettle the election's easy implementation, such as voter suppression activities qualify as sovereignty' violation Hence, actions such as posting inaccurate information about how, where, or when to vote reasonably could be categorized as interfering with the State's ability to perform the election.

It has to be taken into account that human rights must be respected and protected online as they are offline such as in the case of the online election interference context encompasses the freedom of expression; the right to privacy; the right to participate in public affairs, vote, and stand for election; and the right of all peoples to self-determination.[47] Furthermore, both treaty and customary international law guarantee freedom of expression. While international case law has historically fixated on internal interference with human rights, cyber-operations causing voters suppression directly inhibit the right to vote. In addition concerning influence operations, the UN Human Rights Committee[48] has observed that "voters should be able to form opinions independently, free of violence or threat of violence, compulsion, inducement or manipulative interference of any kind."

Moreover, it has to be taken into consideration that self-determination embraces the right of a people to ascertain their own political arrangements which means that the human right to self-determination, which again is protected by both customary and treaty law, is linked to foreign election interference.[49] It is worth mentioning here that some foreign election-related activities are apparently unlawful, as when State organs conduct cyber-operations upsetting the target State's capability to control the election. On the other hand, States must settle how to distinguish election interference and respond successfully to it.[50]

It has to be taken into consideration that advertising techniques and salesmanship resulted from e-commerce to virtual politics because the calculating use of cyberspace is understandable for the reason that primarily transactions were the raison d'etre for networks. To that extent, transactions for political knowledge are influenced by content that goes viral on cyberspace and so there is distinction between viral political content and traditional mainstream media news and so instructing about the political importance of cyberspace necessitates refining

[47] Human Rights Council Res. A/HRC/RES/38/7 (July 17, 2018).

[48] Human Rights Committee, General Comment No. 25: The Right to Participate in Public Affairs, Voting and the Right of Equal Access to Public Service, § 19, U.N. Doc. CCPR/C/21/Rev.1/Add.7 (July 12, 1996).

[49] Marko Milanovic, Extraterritorial Application Of Human Rights Treaties (2011).

[50] Duncan Hollis (Rapporteur), Improving Transparency: International Law and State Cyber Operations—Fifth Report, OEA/Ser.Q, CJI/doc. 615/20 rev.1 (Aug. 7, 2020), http://www.oas.org/en/sla/iajc/docs/CJI_doc_603-20_rev1_corr1_eng.pdf

perceptions about differences between viral political news and mainstream media's analysis. Furthermore, virtual political information is vital and influential and so cyberspace is fundamental in elections and so social networking is intensifying the "politicalclout" of images, amalgamating them alongside social media content by generating a very calculating political choice network actuality. In line, the power of gradually complex and sophisticated cyberspace images in political cognition is intelligently well documented. Hence, it has to be taken into consideration that many political issues such as immigration, healthcare, labor, and the economy dominate elections are concerns of voters.

Taking into account that social networking is gradually recognized to have intense electoral importance due to the fact that it offers political information and so the political system somehow has to keep the democratic qualities. Moreover, the cognitive capability of increasingly complex graphics images to influence political choice has been contemplated due to the fact that social networking is consumed by younger groups to a great extent putting cyberspace personalities together with political content could prove some manipulation is taking place.

In fact, fragile political systems, where civil and political rights are not adequately deep-rooted, are those at greatest risk of democratic instability and so freedom of media is at risk in states influenced by converging geopolitical, technological, democratic, and economic crises which means that globally, an intensifying imbalanced distribution of democratic rights across states takes place owing to fragility and volatility of some systems compared to others.

It is worth noting that laws going in the direction of less effective democratic functioning, low voter turnouts, extensive discontent toward public institutions are disputing the stability of deep-rooted democratic systems of governance, generating the "democratic recession" as the most pressing global encounter today regardless of the advancement of Cyberspace and AI.

References

1. Peters, B. G. (2014). *The politics of bureaucracy*. Routledge.
2. Beckett, J. (2021). Blockchain voting: WY not? *Wyoming Law Review, 21*(2), Article 7.
3. Eubanks, V. (2018). *Automating inequality: How high-tech tools profile, police, and punish the poor*. St.Martin's Press.
4. Frey, C. B. (2019). *The technology trap: Capital, labor, and power in the age of automation*. Princeton University Press.
5. Zysman, J., & Kenney, M. (2018). The next phase in the digital revolution: Intelligent tools, platforms, growth, employment. *Communications of the ACM, 61*(2), 54–63.
6. van Dijck, J., Poell, T., & de Waal, M. (2018). *The platform society: Public values in a connective world*. Oxford University Press.

7. Mamychev A., Okorokov A., Bespalova T., Sviridkina E., & Chertakova E. (2018). Civilizational modeling of political and legal development of the society in the XXI century. *Revista Amazonia Investiga* 1715. pp. 49–57.
8. McAfee, A., & Brynjolfsson, E. (2017). *Machine, platform, crowd: Harnessing our digital future* (1st ed.). W.W. Norton & Company.
9. Shen, H. (2018). Building a digital silk road? Situating the Internet in China's belt and road initiative. *International Journal of Communication, 12*, 19.
10. Srnicek, N. (2017). *Platform capitalism*. Polity.

Chapter 10
AI and Politics

10.1 Introduction

It has to be taken into consideration that judicial independence, freedom of expression and of the press, and freedom of association and organization in civil society are the tools for uninhibited politics demoralizing authoritarian regimes.[1]

Good governance, transparency, and fair procurement are the basic features of an effective governance system. It is worth noting that there is currently no singular, comprehensively accepted definition of AI.[2] Indeed, AI is considered as "an umbrella term, comprised by many different techniques" comprising the present cutting-edge methods of machine learning and deep learning.[3] The United Nations Commission on International Trade Law (UNCITRAL) adopted instruments on electronic commerce and electronic signature, and their influence in national and regional texts, comprise the fundamental pillars of this first generation of digital law.[4]

[1]Beetham, David (2015). "Authoritarianism and Democracy: Beyond Regime Types." Comparative Democratization 13(2): 2, 12, 13.

[2]Peter Stone Et Al., Artificial Intelligence And Life In 2030: Report Of The 2015 Study Panel 12 (2016), Stanford University, https://ai100.stanford.edu/sites/default/files/ai_100_report_0831fnl.pdf

[3]Ryan Calo, Artificial Intelligence Policy: A Primer and Roadmap, 51 U.C.D. L. REV. 399, 405 (2017). Calo notes that "many of the devices and services we access today—from iPhone autocorrect to Google Images—leverage trained pattern recognition systems or complex algorithms that a generous definition of AI might encompass." at 407. McCarthy described AI as "the science and engineering of making intelligent machines, especially intelligent computer programs." V. Rajaraman, John McCarthy – Father of Artificial Intelligence, Resonance (Mar. 2014), p. 200, https://www.ias.ac.in/article/fulltext/reso/019/03/0198-0207

[4]U.N. COMMISSION ON INT'L TRADE L. [UNCITRAL], UNCITRAL MODEL L. ON ELECTRONIC COMMERCE WITH GUIDE TO ENACTMENT, U.N. Sales No. E.99.V.4 (1996) UNCITRAL, UNCITRAL MODEL L. ON ELECTRONIC SIGNATURES WITH GUIDE TO ENACTMENT, U.N. Sales No. E.02.V.8 (2001); UNCITRAL, U.N. CONVENTION ON THE

G. I. Zekos, *Political, Economic and Legal Effects of Artificial Intelligence*,
Contributions to Political Science, https://doi.org/10.1007/978-3-030-94736-1_10

Globalization has political, social, and cultural dimensions by generating economic networks. Technological developments drive globalization at least as much as global politics. Globalization is as much about capabilities as it is about ideas and so ideas bring about new capabilities in computer and cyberspace technology and indeed in space exploration. In line, space exploration and utilization, and its resulting space applications, make available the capabilities that augment the levels of globalization bringing yet another wave of globalization. Moreover, the effects are crucial to globalization and so their joint outcome is the legal, institutional, and physical infrastructure of globalization. While economics is only one of the aspects of globalization, globalization is the outcome of political will and of law. It could be said that globalization, with its cross-border interconnection, interdependence, and engagement, upsurges the demand for supranational regulation via global governance and so generating matters of politics and international politics. It has to be taken into account that power in international politics is diffused, multilateral arrangements are ever more difficult to establish and even keep up, and multilateralism, in general, is questioned. It has to be taken into account that power in international politics is diffused and the increase in the need for global governance faces a decrease in competence to introduce multilateral, comprehensive, and legally binding regimes.[5]

Do globalization and governance work in opposite directions? On the one hand, the world has become smaller and connected, with a constant decrease in time, cost, and ease of transportation and the explosion of free, instant, and sophisticated communications. On the other hand, global governance, which is assumed to complement globalization with regulation, is lately in retreat and so there is a tendency for decentralized governance which means that there is anarchy in global politics but the interstate relations are not lawless. Up till now, notwithstanding and alongside the retreat of multilateralism, global governance expands. Moreover, multilateral regimes are still present and when they are not, the vacuum is occupied by regime complexes and other types of decentralized governance. Undeniably, regardless of the basic constraint of anarchy in global politics, interstate relations are not lawless.

Also, globalization is the process by which the world moves toward an integrated global society and the impact of national borders declines.[6] It has to be taken into account that space applications, particularly telecommunications, global navigation, and Earth observation, have a fundamental role in the process of globalization due to the fact that globalization is a result of the interconnections and interdependence of and across human societies that are enabled by the developments of communication,

---

USE OF ELECTRONIC COMMUNICATIONS IN INTERNATIONAL CONTRACTS, U.N. Sales No. E.07.V.2 (2005).

[5]UN-COPUOS. (2018). The Hague Space Resources Governance Working Group: Information Provided by the Netherlands (U.N. Doc. A/AC.105/C.2/2018/CRP.18).

[6]Zürn, M. (2013). Globalization and Global Governance. In W. Calsnaes, T. Risse, & B. A. Simmons (Eds.), Handbook of International Relations (pp. 401–425). London: SAGE Publications Ltd. https://doi.org/10.4135/9781446247587

cyberspace, transportation, and computer technology that bridge geographic distances. Furthermore, space applications and their uses are various, embracing communication and data transfer, navigation, meteorology management, tracking, and logistics influencing international politics and diplomacy.[7]

Digital technology has pervaded society by penetrating markets, institutions, transactions and social relations, cultural, political, and educational environments. Digital technology exerts an extraordinary transformative force on structures, relations, and processes but presently digital technology has been incorporated and understood as a mere instrument replacing other traditional media and means. Most legislation on electronic commerce, digital signatures, and information society services view technology as a tool.

The social media field has grown enormously and the number of digital channels used to relay relevant news and information to the public domain has augmented. Social media platforms have been used by organizations to campaign against various practices such as corruptive practices and political organizations increasingly use platforms in their communication campaigns with different up-to-date matters. Currently, political communication is inspired by the capability of cyberspace and social media platforms to channelize and shape public opinion.

It is characteristic that political parties and leaders are now using platforms such as Twitter to point out their political affiliations, advance a positive image of their political parties, and express their rejection of the opposition's viewpoint. Moreover, the two-way communication feature presented by media platforms is utilized by politicians and political parties to contract the public concerning diverse matters such as corruption, democratic freedoms, growth, and development. Nonetheless, the implications of offline politics are influencing the digital sphere as well.

It has to be taken into consideration that the digitalization of communication media accelerates the quick and easy transmission of views permitting the users to communicate with the audience concerning different problems but political parties which plan to utilize media platforms as a mode of communication have to conceptualize politically valuable thematic communication to engage with the public.

The numerous social media platforms establish the most visible and well-known social space for information and activities and so presently almost all societal information is first spread through social media platforms, such as Facebook, YouTube, Twitter, and Instagram, facilitating incomparable participation in discourse and the occurrence of new social movements. It has to be taken into account that social media offer new platforms for political participation and ideological categorization which means that new political engagements made up of younger and more educated supporters have been fruitful by leveraging social media. Hence, social media has been a disruptive socio-technological player in the political field as

[7] Pelton, J. N., Madry, S., & Camacho-Lara, S. (Eds.). (2017). Handbook of Satellite Applications (Second Edition). Cham: Springer. Bjola, C. (2017, October 14). Satellite Remote Sensing and Diplomatic Crisis Management. https://medium.com/digitaldiplomacy/satellite-remote-sensing-and-diplomatic-crisis-management-286651c83cb, Bjola, C., & Holmes, M. (Eds.). (2015). Digital Diplomacy: Theory and Practice (1 edition). London; New York: Routledge.

people have circumvented traditional informational or organizational entities which mean that social media is a new and central discursive space that has a massive influence on which political matters are raised in the formal sphere of politics. Ilkka Koiranen et al.[8] argue that "the ideological gap between party supporters is greater in social media especially when examining new kinds of politics based on cultural questions, identity issues, and post-materialist values."

10.2 AI in Politics

Taking into account the interrelation of machines, morality, and human wellbeing, an argument against the use of AI in politics is grounded on the claim that politics always encompasses questions of values and morality which means that an obstacle is generated for AI due to the claim that morality is solely a human endeavor. On the other hand, in an AAI society run by AAI entities cannot be rejected the establishment of their AAI morality which will have a different content but in essence will be a morality.

It has to be taken into consideration that accountability concerning the consequences of political decisions must be clear and so it has to become clear when AI makes decisions. Santiago[9] argues that when firms employ AI in decision-making, humans must have the final say.

Good policy is the goal for politics and AI as long as automatically is taking political decisions then AI has got political power. It is worth noting that the advantages of better political decisions are significant and current AI is already being employed in the public sector with the purpose of expanding political analysis and decisions and so becoming ever more capable. It has to be taken into account that when political actors and the state adopt AI, regulatory provisions should employ not only high quality of AI permitting for better-informed decision-making, but also use AI technology publicly transparent and accountable as possible. Correspondingly, when citizens are the users of AI as devices to choose political information concerning the performance of a government, they must be able to realize what criteria these systems use in processing information. In other words, AI assisting citizens must operate as an independent public advocate who monitors and explores the activities of political authorities and so allowing citizens to make certain that they realize such a public value. In general, while AI can interfere in the informational basis of democratic regimes, it is the principles of liberal democracy

[8] Ilkka Koiranena, Aki Koivulaa, Arttu Saarinena, Teo Keipi, Ideological motives, digital divides, and political polarization: How do political party preference and values correspond with the political use of social media? Telematics and Informatics Volume 46, March 2020, 101322 p1.

[9] T. Santiago, Influence The Executive Function Of Business Leaders?, in: Muma Business Review 3 AI Bias: How Does AI, 2019, pp. 181–192.

itself that present vital guidelines about how the relationship between citizens and these systems can be structured.

Political actors demand information about what citizens want if their preferences are to be instilled into the democratic process which means that channels through which information travels from the citizens to the political actors are vital in order decision-makers to respond to citizens' needs. Hence, political decision-makers have a need for information before taking decisions and so political decision-makers' information sources encompass feedback from the implementation and effects of previous decisions permitting them to adjust to altering settings. It has to be taken into account that accountable decision-making necessitates that the whole process is subject to monitoring and control achieved via established formal procedures for upholding accountability, such as electoral laws, voting rules in the legislature, and different instruments of control. However, tracing how political decisions have been made, how particular gist has been translated into legislation, how various preferences expressed in the public have been taken up and transformed into concrete policies, is very challenging.

Will AI be employed in politics, if a technocracy of AI is executed with control, mechanisms of backup, and a participatory element? It is obvious that in an AAI society, AAI entities will employ their own politics which is the implementation of their own interests.

Engaging AI in offering the world laws in the user's language globally, as well as providing answers to legal questions and the abstract of the law, is a major pillar in the improvement of democracy. Democracy thrives when the rations for a transparent and accountable legal system are met by implementing the rule of law and so in jurisdictions in which the rule of law is risked and the regime is not a democratic one. The Chinese government uploads its laws to cyberspace enabling their inclusion in the database and so permitting people to compare legislation from around the world to their own.[10]

It has to be taken into account that one understandable prospective benefit of digitalization and the augmented competence to communicate using digital tools is the likelihood of directly involving far more individuals in political processes.

Are people politically active in nowadays political systems? What will really revolutionize if AI makes our decisions, instead of bureaucrats? It has to be taken into consideration that a technocracy of AI leads to a revitalization of popular participation and the accessibility of the political domain via AI ways of participation, such as algorithmic co-creation, which means that most people will have and experience more political power than they do today.

It has to be taken into consideration that there are occasions in a political system where bureaucracy is merely replaced by AI and politicians continue to make the decisions which means that AI is utilized as a complementary device for statistical reasons. On the other hand, in a political system in which the AAI systems are given greater autonomy in terms of policy formation which means that politicians will have

[10] www.global-regulation.cn

a say in the political decisions and so not be accountable as well. Hence, the existing system, whereby politicians are accountable for the decisions of their bureaucracies, will not function due to the fact that politicians will not control AAI systems as they now are of their bureaucrats which means that the supposed political department of the AAI governance will be responsible for the applicability of the political decisions taken by AAI systems in the AAI society.

Has democracy been damaged by some AI systems? Democracy can be degraded by some AI systems and so the tendency to publish fake news on various platforms is a troubling example of technological distorting of the public sphere. On the other hand, AI systems do not undercut a user's capacity to look for news sources to assess the accuracy of what they have found. AI systems' more imperative outcome is the perplexity of policy selections. Where a state is well-ordered due to public laws, AI system regulation is expected to be feasible without any threat to democratic values and so utilizing AI turns on the ex ante quality of democratic control of the state through rule-of-law mechanisms.

Will algorithmic governance cause problems in democratic participation? It is argued that AI employment will generate problems regarding democracy, participation, and political harms.[11] It has to be taken into consideration that AI will advance participation in the whole political process of various forms and so one manner to instigate this is to stimulate co-creation and "democratizing algorithm."[12] To that extent, the WeBuildAI shows several methods of widespread partaking in the making and design of algorithms leading to both amplified participation and augmented algorithmic awareness. Nevertheless, if systems such as WeBuildAI permit for involvement and effectiveness, there is little reason to choose sub-optimality. Besides, AAI technology where the system will decide everything autonomously with no reference to humans but merely AAI entities will implement AAI politics and political decisions according to the demands of the AAI society expressed via AAI systems and technology.

AI systems are integrated with escalating frequency into core institutional elements of democracy such as education and the electoral process which means that there is a need of anticipating an infrastructure of democracy in which persons continue to have opportunities for individual and collective action against the policies embedded in AI systems. It is worth mentioning here that it has been accepted that only "conventional democracy" has the instructive upshots resulting from participation in politics and so people understand from taking part in politics which means that the positive consequences participation has on people prevail over the negative outcomes of having sub-optimal policies. It could be said that AAI systems will allow electronic participation of AAI entities into AAI democracy leading to the implementation of the AAI politics which will have another form

[11] R. Binns, Algorithmic accountability and public reason, Philosophy & technology 31 (4) (2018) 543–556. T. Gillespie, The politics of 'platforms' 12, New media & society, 2010, pp. 347–364, 3.

[12] J.L. Beyer, The emergence of a freedom of information movement: anonymous, WikiLeaks, the Pirate Party, and Iceland, J. Computer-Mediated Commun. 19 (2) (2014) 141–154.

and another impact upon AAI society and life compared to that of the current conventional politics. There might be a centralized idea of politics and decision-making due to the characteristics of the AAI technology.

It is worth noting that politics is organized in a manner that holds public power in check by functioning in the service of those affected by it. Hence, implanting AI in governance mechanisms contributes to an enhanced informational basis of democratic politics reinforcing overall responsiveness and accountability. Besides, an already existing lack of openness and accountability in democratic regimes may work against a democratic utilization of AI, but it can be achieved on the throughput and output level by building on existing regulations in liberal-democratic regimes in expanding accountability mechanisms to encompass the use of AI.

It is argued that at this time moral machines do not exist, and human qualities such as compassion and wisdom are central prerequisites for significant decisions.[13] Can current AI machines act morally and make moral decisions? It is argued that computers should not make decisions that concern people's lives and wellbeing. On the other hand, humans are creating all technologies in order to make better their life and so as long as they control technology humans have the blame of allowing computers to decide for them since humans have programed machines to function accordingly. Likewise, when AAI systems originally produced by humans decision will impose their own terms in an AAI society run by AAI entities humans saying will have little value since AAI society will be fully run by AAI technology imposing AAI society's politics and political decisions on the whole scale of the AAI activities.

Currently, there is a growing widespread application of AI in the domain of government and partly on some occasions, AI is given the authority to form policy which is done through systems characterized by low transparency, high complexity, and high degrees of automation. Moreover, AAI systems employed in the domain of government and politics will add transparency, accountability, and objectivity as long as there will not emerge a new elite manipulating AAI technology for politics by repeating conventional human behaviors hiding behind the supposed technical objectivity.

It is obvious that AAI systems and humanoid robots will achieve human proficiencies and capabilities, embracing morality-related emotions which mean that humanoid robots will run via value systems encompassing moral competences.[14] Moreover, humanoid robots with their own morality will be able to read and better understand not only human morality but also the whole world which means that

[13] J. Weizenbaum, Computer Power and Human Reason: from Judgment to Calculation, W. H. Freeman, San Francisco, 1976.

[14] E. Awad, S. Dsouza, R. Kim, J. Schulz, J. Henrich, A. Shariff, J.-F. Bonnefon, I. Rahwan, The moral machine experiment, Nature 563 (7729) (2018) 59. M. Maldonato, P. Valerio, Artificial entities or moral agents? How AI is changing human evolution. Multidisciplinary Approaches to Neural Computing, Springer, Cham, 2018, pp. 379–388. M. Scheutz, The need for moral competency in autonomous agent architectures. Fundamental Issues of Artificial Intelligence, Springer, Cham, 2016, pp. 517–527.

humanoid robots will quantify, track and compare moral bias "across cultures and over time,"[15] equality among humans, etc. not mentioning their ability to impose their own morality or even their AAI bias because perfection in the essence of Gods' capacity no AAI technology can achieve. Hence, spirituality achieved via the humans' spiritual life according to Christianity will not be achieved by creating humanoid robots and other human-made thoughts for conquering galaxies at least into the imaginable future.

Tesla has announced its humanoid robots as workers under humans control which is the first step for the generation of humanoid robots more intelligent than humans that will breed the forthcoming AAI society. Will humans create the first autonomous humanoid robots and so breeding the beginning of the AAI humanoid robots era?

10.3 Digital Platforms and Politics

It has to be taken into account that the connection point between digital platforms and political debate is understated regarding the prospective of these technologies to interfere directly and indirectly in democratic dynamics. To that extent, digital platforms awarded civic powers by inspiring civilians' capacities to play a full and free role in the societies in which they reside and not mentioning the political role of platforms in regulatory distributions.[16]

It could be said that digital platforms target the state's democratic deficit by transforming politics in the country by producing new noninstitutional mechanisms for political participation and by advancing a political-cultural transformation. Moreover, platforms improve the participation system by infusing new technological options by utilizing innovation force.

For instance, "Active Citizen" is a platform and an interface that uses AI in order to connect citizens by offering notifications and information based on their requirements and dispositions having the prospective to engage citizens by diminishing their information barriers concerning political affairs. Moreover, AI technology can partly take over the role of journalists and guardians of political information by inserting vote advice applications, public platforms, or initiatives in order to monitor the behavior of members of parliament and the government. Thus, AI-based solutions assisting citizens on the level of opinion and formation will be tools in hands of politics influencing the citizens' preferences and requirements accordingly. Thus, AI

[15] P. Schramowski, C. Turan, S. Jentzsch, C. Rothkopf, Kristian Kersting, The moral choice machine, Frontiers in Artificial Intelligence (3) (2020).

[16] Taylor Owen, The Case for Platform Governance, Waterloo (Canada): Center for International Governance Innovation (CIGI), 2019. Martin Moore, Tech Giants and Civic Power, London: Centre for the study of Media, Communication & Power (CMCP), King's College London, 2016. Timo Seidl, The Politics of Platform Capitalism: A Case Study on the Regulation of Uber in New York, Regulation & Governance rego, 2020, p. 12353.

closes the gap from the mismatch of humans' cognitive capacities and the existing amount of information regarding political affairs. Likewise, the capacity to amalgamate information on the input level can be augmented to the degree that applications of AI serve to compile relevant information also on the throughput and output level which means that such information will feed back into public will formation on the input level and so helping citizens in the task of keeping track of political actors' performance concerning keeping policy promises. Hereafter, AI may actually augment the prospects to hold governments accountable for their decisions and in that way work in favor of the basic mechanisms that make democratic politics perform well.

10.4 AI and Administration

Advances in AI have attracted the interest of public sector agencies across the globe and so AI systems are being adopted across the public sector and are revolutionizing the delivery of public services.[17] AI solutions slash the administrative burden in the public sector by automating routine work and so AI systems function as interfaces between agencies and citizens, thereby fostering higher-quality service delivery.[18] Besides efficient and effective public services, the implementation of AI technologies in the public sector promotes innovation by utilizing data from social media platforms to inform the design and evaluation of public policies. Moreover, it is estimated that the AI revolution will bring about noteworthy disruptions to various socio-economic elements because automation will affect the future of work and employment. On one hand, labor-intensive work will be automated, while on the other hand, new jobs will emerge.

AAI technology will be an imperative tool for data mining, text analytics, or social data scouting and so AAI will strengthen accountability as governments need to be more responsible for the decisions taken and the policy options chosen. Citizens and other political actors will be watching in real-time information flowing to decide on opportunistic political behaviors. Overall, AI will find patterns in data leading to the discovery of new solutions that back public policy. Additionally, there is the likelihood of bad decision-making or bias that may lead to discrimination and lack of social trust grounded on the opacity of algorithms.

AI alters different aspects of government, embracing processes, interaction with citizens, service delivery, decision-making, and public policy design and evaluation.

---

[17] Yang, L., Elisa, N., Eliot, N., 2019. Privacy and security aspects of e-government in smart cities. In: Smart Cities Cybersecurity and Privacy. Elsevier, pp. 89–102. https://doi.org/10.1016/B978-0-12-815032-0.00007 -X. Yeung, K., 2020. Recommendation of the council on artificial intelligence (OECD). Int. Leg. Mater. 59, 27–34. https://doi.org/10.1017/ilm.2020.5.

[18] Berryhill, J., Kok Heang, K., Clogher, R., McBride, K., 2019. Hello, World: Artificial intelligence and its use in the public sector. In: OECD Working Papers on Public Governance No. 36. Observatory of Public Service Innovation OECD, https://doi.org/10.1787/726fd39d-en

To that extent, AI assists humans in decision-making, in understanding and deriving meaningful results from complex big data nexus. However, the use of AI in government necessitates massive automation of processes within government, and so engaging new professionals to promote AI implementation.[19] Many countries such as the USA, China, and the European Union have already employed AI to advance internal government processes, the provision of services and interaction with citizens by advancing a national strategy for the application of AI.

Likewise, AI improves communication between government and citizens through the use of techniques such as natural language processing, machine learning, and data mining and so the government's engagement in AI will bring alterations to different areas of public policy such as public health systems and the personalized design of treatments for patients. On the other hand, do not forget the negative implications of current AI for public administration such as discrimination, opacity based on algorithm complexity, privacy violation, consolidation of socio-economic inequalities, or an increase in the digital divide, AI dependence, and the risks entangled in public administration, and decision-making linked to algorithmic bias in the design of AI for the public sector. Moreover, there is a potential risk of discrimination in the use of data in rational AI agents.[20] In addition, negative consequences linked with public AI embrace technology obedience and loss of control, AI dominion and AI legitimacy, AI paternalism and AI decision-making, and problems with cybersecurity.

It has to be taken into consideration that most problems of politics are highly complicated optimization problems and so any goals can be achieved via AI in an effective way which means that AI can continuously experiment by updating dynamics, always responding to transformations in human preferences and behavior policies. For instance, an AI system can make tax policies, in a simulation, that both advance productivity and decrease inequality.

Also, challenges for public policy in the age of AI are linked to legal and moral matters, ethical principles, legitimacy and transparency, workforce substitution through intelligent automation, predictions, and decision-making. Correspondingly, public policies embrace the analysis of hardware and AI algorithms along with the generation of rules to circumvent bias and bad decision-making. Hence, intelligent algorithms must be transparent, founded on giving citizens access to information concerning the algorithms and how they work.[21] It has to be taken into account that AI applications are relevant to an examination of algorithmic governance in general. Existing applications of AI are employed in all areas of government already, while

---

[19] Sun, T. Q., & Medaglia, R. (2019). Mapping the challenges of artificial intelligence in the public sector: Evidence from public healthcare. Government Information Quarterly, 36(2), 368–383.

[20] Vetrò, A., Santangelo, A., Beretta, E., & De Martin, J. C. (2019). AI: From rational agents to socially responsible agents. Digital Policy, Regulation and Governance. Retrieved from http://www.antoniovetro.it/authorsversion/journals/2019-dprg-ai.pdf

[21] Cerrillo i Martínez, A. (2019). How can we open the black box of public administration? Transparency and accountability in the use of algorithms. Revista Catalana de Dret Públic, 58, 13–28. https://doi.org/10.2436/rcdp.i58.2019.3277

general public service, economic affairs, and environmental protection are the areas of AI in government.

Algorithmic technology's strength is predominantly stark when it comes to artificial intelligence and so AI places code-driven autonomous and intelligent systems directly into social and political interactions in the physical world ascending from moderation of social media content to consumer applications like AVs to medical applications like algorithmic diagnostic. Law has not concentrated on how emerging digital technologies do or do not fit within either prescriptive administrative law or newer governance paradigms for the reason that digital technology matters have appeared "virtually." Besides, Robotics combines the promiscuity of information with the capability to do physical harm.[22] It could be said that Al technology demands fundamental changes in our conception of the law itself because Al technology as a regulatory tool can compromise democratic accountability and rule of law norms, mainly when the technology is deployed by the state itself.[23]

It is worth mentioning here that improvements in AI and its expanding application in more domains of life require attention to the influence of algorithms on human wellbeing. While AI's regulatory confronts seem facially similar to those in other technocratic domains, such as the pharmaceutical industry or environmental law, when it comes to AI, an "FDA for algorithms" or a "federal robotics commission" is of limited utility in constructing long-term governance solutions and so AI is unique, even if it is not different in kind. To that extent, AI's individuality comes from technical qualities such as speed, complexity, and unpredictability that strain traditional administrative law tactics, along with the institutional surroundings and incentives, or strategic context that influence its development path.

Is it essential to the deployment of artificial intelligence and related digital tools to support judicial and administrative decision-making? Within the court systems, machine learning tools have yet to be deployed, but other efforts have put in place digital building blocks toward such use embracing the increased digitization of court records that algorithms will draw upon for data, the growth of online dispute resolution inside and outside of the courts, and the incorporation of non-learning risk assessment tools as inputs into bail, sentencing, and parole decisions. Moreover, administrative agencies have shown much more eagerness than courts to use machine learning algorithms, deploying such algorithmic tools to assist in the delivery of public services, management of government programs, and pursuing enforcement resources. If artificial intelligence is run dutifully, the use of algorithmic tools by governmental entities will show much future promise.

---

[22] Ryan Calo, Robotics and the Lessons of Cyberlaw, 103 CAL. L. REV. 513, 515, 549–62 (2015) ("."). Alicia Solow-Niederman, Emerging Digital Technology and the "Law of the Horse," UCLA L. REV. DISC.: LAW MEETS WORLD (2019), https://www.uclalawreview.org/emerging-digital-technology-and-the-law-ofthe-horse

[23] Deirdre K. Mulligan & Kenneth A. Bamberger, Saving Governance-by-Design, 106 CALIF. L. REV. 697, 705–14 (2018) (offering detailed literature review of science, technology, and society (STS) theory and its salience for public regulation).

AI has pervaded many aspects of global society and in settings as varied as medicine, transportation, financial services, and entertainment, digital technologies rely on machine learning algorithms to process vast quantities of data and make highly accurate predictions that can often outperform human capacity to accomplish comparable tasks. Consequently, the prospective function of artificial intelligence in the legal field has not gone unobserved and so the implications it could have for the legal systems are scrutinized.[24] For instance, new software in place at the Fresno Police Department in central California uses huge batches of data, ranging from criminal history to Twitter feeds, to judge how likely someone is to commit a crime and whether the police ought to keep tabs on them.[25] Moreover, machine learning is valuable in detecting and adjusting for bias in judicial decision-making on asylum requests.[26] It seems that no judicial or administrative body has instituted a system that offers for total decision-making by algorithm in various countries, such that a digital system makes a fully independent determination.

Decision-making in the criminal legal system is based on assessments by human beings at every critical stage of the criminal process, from arrest and prosecution to punishment and reintegration. Is the discretion of criminal legal system players infused with bias? It is argued that prosecutorial discretion is a significant driver of various disparities in the sentences.[27] It has to be taken into account that human beings programing automated systems can lead to incorrect results for the reason that the source code, predictive algorithms, and datasets contain human biases that have a disparate effect on certain groups. Furthermore, reforms have shaped and improved decision-making by systemic players to eliminate the implicit and explicit bias advancing injustice. Additionally, the introduction of AI, predictive analytics, and automated decision-making facilitate the latest attempt to advance decision-making and counter the shortcomings of human judgment. Also, due to the fact that current AI systems are trained by biased data, there is a failure to correct or upend various

[24] Cary Coglianese & David Lehr, Transparency and Algorithmic Governance, 71 Admin. L. Rev. 1, 2 n.2 (2019) Peter Dizikes, AI, the Law, and Our Future, MIT NEWS OFFICE (Jan. 18, 2019), http://news.mit.edu/2019/first-ai-policy-congress-0118

[25] Chris Weller, A California Police Department is Using Software to Decide if You're About to Commit a Crime, Bus. Insider (Jan. 12, 2016), https://www.businessinsider.com/intrado-beware-system-tracks-threat-levels-2016-1

[26] Daniel L. Chen, Machine Learning and the Rule of Law 4–7 (Working Paper, 2019), https://papers.ssrn.com/sol3/papers.cfm?abstract_id=3302507

[27] Mona Lynch & Marisa Omori, Crack as Proxy: Aggressive Federal Drug Prosecutions and the Production of Black—White Racial Inequality, 52 Law & Soc'y Rev. 773, 799–803 (2018) (concluding that prosecutorial discretion was a significant driver of racial disparities in the sentences received for crack related offenses); L. Song Richardson, Systemic Triage: Implicit Racial Bias in the Criminal Courtroom, 126 Yale L.J. 862, 887 (2017) ("[T]he enormous discretion wielded by prosecutors, defense lawyers, and judges facilitates racial bias, both conscious and implicit."). Ricci v. DeStefano, 557 U.S. 557, 577 (2009) (holding that disparate treatment occurs when "an employer has 'treated [a] particular person less favorably than others because of' a protected trait." (quoting Watson v. Fort Worth Bank & Trust, 487 U.S. 977, 987 (1988))).

inequalities infusing the criminal legal system.[28] It is worth noting that as AIs become even smarter and big data becomes even bigger, proxy discrimination will denote a central challenge to antidiscrimination regimes that seek to limit discrimination based on predictive traits.[29] Thus, AAI systems will advance an objective decision-making system in criminal law eliminating the current cons of present AI systems.

The increased digitization of court records, the use of algorithmic tools for risk assessment in aspects of the criminal justice process, and the growth of online dispute resolution outside of the courts are the blocks leading to the use of artificial intelligence in the courts. Furthermore, the most widespread innovation in the courts has happened in various forms of digitization such as electronic filing and case management, while some courts have relied on algorithmic tools to reinforce pretrial, sentencing, or parole decisions. In addition, courts acknowledge a role for online dispute resolution systems developed by the private sector, not mentioning the demand for the development of arbitration as a co-equal to courts as a dispute mechanism.

It is worth noting that the day when a judge's role is fully ousted by an algorithm is far into the future, but the building blocks that could eventually give rise to a world of increased use of artificial intelligence by governmental entities have emerged in legal systems across the globe. Moreover, the extensive adoption of risk assessment tools in criminal cases in courts at every level of government will reveal an increasing comfort in permitting algorithms to inform decisions.

In fact, increasing digitization of court records offers judicial managers data for artificial intelligence programs in order to analyze and facilitate future automated adjudication. In addition, the growing adoption of online dispute resolution[30] by both the private organizations and the courts build the public with fully computerized and automated adjudication. Thus, successful application of artificial intelligence grows in administrative agencies, and they are relying on machine learning tools to inform enforcement decisions, distribute social services, and manage programs.

---

[28] Dorothy E. Roberts, Digitizing the Carceral State, 132 Harv. L. Rev. 1695 (2019) (analyzing the role of race, big data, automation, and computerized prediction in the criminal legal system). Vincent M. Southerland, The Intersection of Race and Algorithmic Tools in the Criminal Legal System, 80 Md. L. Rev. 487 (2021) https://digitalcommons.law.umaryland.edu/mlr/vol80/iss3/1 Amanda Agan & Sonja Starr, Ban the Box, Criminal Records, and Racial Discrimination: A Field Experiment, 133 Q.J. ECON. 191 (2018) (arguing that "Ban the Box" policies which restrict employers from asking about applicants' criminal backgrounds encourage racial discrimination).

[29] Anya E.R. Prince & Daniel Schwarcz, Proxy Discrimination in the Age of Artificial Intelligence and Big Data, 2020 Iowa Law Review 1257.

[30] Dave Orr and Colin Rule, Artificial Intelligence and the Future of Online Dispute Resolution http://www.newhandshake.org/SCU/ai.pdf ("We are still a long way away from giving an AI Lexis-Nexis access and then asking it to serve on the Supreme Court."). AI NOW INST., AI NOW 2019 REPORT (2019), https://ainowinstitute.org/AI_Now_2019_ Report.pdf (concerns about the "black box" nature of algorithms and the potential for harm and abuse if they are used by government agencies without fully accounting for built-in biases).

It has to be taken into account that reliance on large amounts of data brings forward prospective privacy violation and other abuses of power by unreliable or oppressive governmental players and so in the governmental background, the "black box" character of machine learning algorithms induce actual concerns about transparency and accountability. In other words, the use of "dirty data" from corrupt racially biased, or unlawful police practices in algorithmic means to back predictive policing, preserve the biases and misbehavior inherent in the data.[31] PredPol is a program that uses US police data to offer predictions on where and when to expect spikes in crime and this is based on an algorithm foreseeing where and when crimes are most possible to take place assisting the police in allocating their resources optimally to prevent crime.[32] On the other hand, predictive policing can intensify biases leading to unequal outcomes for people and communities meaning that an AAI technology must be developed in order to prevent any biases and safeguarding the objectivity of the system.

Nonetheless, the amplified technology's risks have led to calls for regulators to look beyond the advantages, and also secure fitting regulation to make certain AI that is "trustworthy," legal, ethical, and robust. To that extent, AI has become of strategic significance for governments across the globe, being contemplated currently as one of the most transformative forces and so its general purpose status enables it to engender benefits across a wide range of domains boosting both economic and societal welfare. Hence, it has to be taken into account that a global competition to develop AI applications materialized and so countries and regions are openly taking part in a "race to AI," trying to advance the technology's use and advantages more rapidly and successfully than others.[33]

As mentioned earlier, China adopted its "Next Generation AI Development Plan" in 2017 with the objective to become a global leader in the field by "building on China's first-mover advantage in the development of AI." Moreover, EU[34] AI strategy, published in 2018, puts forward the EU's objective to "lead the way in developing and using AI for good and for all." Additionally, the US AI strategy intends to speed up the "nation's leadership in AI." While each strategy emphasizes its own distinct strengths, all countries want to lead, and all countries claim to be leading in at least some aspect of the technology already such as software or hardware products, or investments.

---

[31] Rashida Richardson, Jason M. Schultz & Kate Crawford, Dirty Data, Bad Predictions: How Civil Rights Violations Impact Police Data, Predictive Policing Systems, And Justice, 94 N.Y.U. L.REV. 192, 192 (2019) Ali Winston & Ingrid Burrington, A Pioneer in Predictive Policing Is Starting a Troubling New Project, THE VERGE (Apr. 27, 2018), https://www.theverge.com/2018/4/26/17285058/predictive-policing-predpol-pentagonai-racial-bias

[32] Demortain and Benbouzid, 'Evaluating Predictive Algorithms', in Algorithmic Regulation (2017). http://blog.predpol.com/not-all-predictive-policing-is-created-equal-heres-why

[33] Yuval Noah Harari, 'Who Will Win the Race for AI?', Foreign Policy Magazine (Washington, Winter 2019).

[34] Commission, 'Artificial Intelligence for Europe' (Communication) COM(2018) 237 final.

It could be said that winning the "race to AI" not only inspired by the need to secure a competitive position on the global market, but is also exposed as an existential need, whereby also economic security is invoked which means that not only the huge gains that could result from deploying AI, but also the high cost of non-adoption increases the race, as no state likes to "miss the AI train." Furthermore, AI comes not only with advantages but also with considerable risks linking to the technologies prospective to breach fundamental rights such as privacy and non-discrimination, to involuntarily manipulate people so as to hinder their self-determination, or to destroy people's safety and security. Thus, the disadvantages of the development and use of AI are ever more under examination, and governments are urged to embrace not only policies accelerating beneficial innovation, but also measures that safeguard people from AI's risks. To that extent, regulation transpires as a possible answer. Actually, all over the globe, regulators at the regional, national, international, and supranational levels are evaluating the desirability and requirement of new or revised regulatory rations to diminish AI's adverse effects, while at the same time maximizing its profits.

In other words, a regulatory regime has to balance all needs and establish legal certainty for the stakeholders involved and so not only guarantee trust in the technology but also facilitate its uptake which means progressing countries' competitive position. Moreover, the advances of putting in place a fitting regulatory agenda for AI are even more considerable for those regulatory powers benefiting from a regulatory "first mover advantage." Principally, the "race to AI" is founded in the context of a so-called "arms race" to AI and, on the other hand, concerning the military sector is one of the application areas where AI is both thriving and of strategic significance for states.[35]

In fact, countries compete with each other through regulation to attract those elements that render them a competitive force on the global market, while exploring the best recipes to concurrently protect their citizens raising the likelihood that instead of "race to the top," regulatory competition for AI will release a "race to the bottom" at the cost of sufficient protection against AI's risks.

At the same time, recent developments signify that, for a number of fields, regulatory approaches gradually start converging. Anyway, the harmonizing power of globalized market, specific endeavors toward the setting of global regulatory standards for AI are underway, potentially leading toward the harmonization of AI regulation. Undeniably, international organizations such as the OECD, the Council of Europe, and UNESCO have joined the regulatory playground working toward a consensus on firstly the ethical considerations raised by AI. There are an increasing

---

[35]Tania Rabesandratana, 'Europe moves to compete in global AI arms race' [2018] 350 Science 474. Andrew Philip Hunter, Lindsay Sheppard et al., 'Artificial Intelligence and National Security – The Importance of the AI Ecosystem' [2018] Centre for Strategic and International Studies. PwC, 'PwC's Global Artificial Intelligence Study: Exploiting the AI Revolution' (2017); Deloitte, 'Artificial Intelligence Innovation Report,' (2018) and McKinsey Global Institute, 'Notes from the AI Frontier: Modelling the Impact of AI on the World Economy' (September 2018).

number of UN initiatives exploring the effects and implications of AI.[36] Instantaneously, there are the first moves toward institutionalization. In 2019, the OECD issued a set of principles for AI, which was consequently backed by the G20.[37] Moreover, in February 2020, the OECD.AI Policy Observatory was launched as a platform to "shape and share" AI policies across the globe, so as to offer policymakers with trustworthy guidance on the implementation of AI principles in real-world situations.[38] UNESCO[39] considers AI systems as "technological systems which have the capacity to process information in a way that resembles intelligent behavior" and so AI systems involve reasoning, learning, perception, prediction, planning, or control aspects.

Undeniably, the advancement and deployment of AI are motivated or curtailed by fields as different as tax law, tort law, privacy and data protection law, IPR law, competition law, health law, consumer protection law, etc. and so within these dissimilar fields, a large number of regulations already apply to AI now. Thus, governments not only use any or all of these different legal areas to compete with each other and affect the behavior of AI stakeholders towards their enabling and protecting objectives, they consider to which extent an intervention in these legal spheres is required, and which effect their intervention in one legal domain will have on another. In other words, there is a need for regulatory coherency and so an appraisal of regulatory competition for AI has to consider not simply one area of law, but the regulatory framework as a whole.

It has to be taken into consideration that with the Cambridge Analytica data analytics scandal as a key trigger, it became clear to the general public for the first time that the data Facebook and other platforms[40] gather from them include highly sensitive information influencing even elections and democratic legal order calling for a national and global privacy law.[41]

Predictive policing is another area that AI is also used in the use of AI to implement optimal strategies for pandemic response encompassing using AI to predict and identify outbreaks and energetically apply the best possible response

[36] ITU, United Nations Activities on Artificial Intelligence (AI) 66 (2018), https://www.itu.int/dms_pub/itus/opb/gen/S-GEN-UNACT-2018-1-PDF-E.pdf; ITU, United Nations Activities on Artificial Intelligence (AI) 2019 88 (2019), https://www.itu.int/dms_pub/itu-s/opb/gen/S-GEN-UNACT-2019-1-PDF-E.pdf

[37] OECD, Recommendation of the Council on Artificial Intelligence (2019), https://legalinstruments.oecd.org/en/instruments/OECD-LEGAL-0449. G20, G20 Ministerial Statement on Trade and Digital Economy (2019), https://www.mofa.go.jp/files/000486596.pdf

[38] https://oecd.ai

[39] UNESCO. (2020). First version of a draft text of a recommendation on the ethics of artificial intelligence. Retrieved from https://unesdoc.unesco.org/ark:/48223/pf0000373434

[40] J. Abbruzzese, 'Elizabeth Warren calls to break up Facebook, Google and Amazon', NBC 8 March 2019, available at www.nbcnews.com/tech/tech-news/elizabeth-warren-calls-break-facebook-google-amazonn980911.7

[41] L. Vaas, 'FTC renews call for single federal privacy law', Naked Security by Sophos 10 May 2019, available at https://nakedsecurity.sophos.com/2019/05/10/ftc-renews-call-for-single-federal-privacy-law/

based on a society's tolerance for risks weighed against other factors, such as economic costs which means that in optimization problems, AI aid society.

Also, it has to be taken into account that the state's administrative system has the executive role of putting adopted decisions into practice so as to accomplish intended outcomes which means that there is a need of managing its programs, services, and decisions demanding accurate and timely information. In line, citizens have to be informed on the output level, because the application of rules by the public administration should not result in biased and unjust outcomes which means that citizens have to know how the administration functions and how they are treated in order to be able to take legal action against the state if and when fundamental rights of citizens are abused.

AI appeared in public administration and so giving them opportunities for public policy based on AI techniques to expand accountability, collaboration, interoperability, efficiency, effectiveness, information processing, and trust in decision-making. Also, AI augments the legitimacy of agenda setting by giving governments the chance to forward more inclusive and diverse dialogue with citizens. Nonetheless, governments with less infrastructure and technological competencies are barred from public policies based on AI leading to an upsurge in the digital divide.

Does AI contribute to policy implementation? AI backs the execution of actions to enforce the decisions taken in previous stages. Utilization of AI and big data make easy the highlighting of matters that could be implemented with different levels of intensity and so the implementation of policies may be reinforced and sped up with AI analytics. In line, non-stop enhancements in the process of real-time data analytics accelerate large-scale improvements of city traffic as policy makers earn from automation. Thus, policy implementation advances service delivery concerning the dividualization and capability to profile users along with sociodemographic features or behavioral models. Furthermore, tax agencies are profiling individuals and/or firms to promote the fight against fraud by designing incentives oriented toward heightening tax payers' commitment. Also, police departments are using AI to check crime ascertaining patterns of incidents of crime and so data processing through AI engender patterns that are valuable for making predictions leading to the exclusion of vulnerable groups or engender greater control in society. It is worth noting that societies with greater digital divide have problems in the standardization and legislation of AI.

Can AI be used to commit crime? There is a rising phenomenon of artificial intelligence crime and that crimes fuelled by AI have an impact on commerce.[42]

Does AI add in policy evaluation? It has to be taken into account that evaluation is another chapter in the policy-cycle with a high prospective to be altered by AI in public administration which means that evaluation is reformed by the capability to uncover irregularities. It could be said that AI transforms the public policy-cycle and

[42] Thomas King, et al., "Artificial Intelligence Crime: An Interdisciplinary Analysis of Foreseeable Threats and Solutions" (2020) 26 Science and Engineering Ethics 89–120; Christina Mulligan, "Revenge Against Robots" (2018) 69 S.C. L. Rev. 579, 580.

so AI and big data will enable the embedding of evaluation in each phase of the policy-cycle. Thus, AI will make evaluations that are provided in real time from the very beginning of the implementation, giving birth to the notion of nonstop evaluation in governments and public administrations. Nonetheless, governments and public administrations have to adopt AI and big data underlying causes of problems.

AI in the evaluation stage triggers problems that public policy is facing involving dehumanization, complete dependence on AI, algorithmic biases affecting future decision making, and exclusion of the poor and people with limited access to the most advanced technologies. Thus, AI is varying the policy-cycle process and opening up new openings, but also challenges and negative consequences, from agenda setting to evaluation processes. In the interim, AI and the capability to learn from public policy are surfacing as sources of new opportunity in the public sector.

Additionally, AI is shifting the manner agenda setting runs currently and so prioritization of public problems is executed by machine learning and so AAI will underline significant problems, unfolds hidden wants or problematic matters by ascertaining key components influencing ongoing public policies. Likewise, the agenda-setting stage is inspired by ongoing citizen participation by tracking and reporting new possible outcomes from society.

Does AI add in policy formulation and decision-making? It could be said that the new dynamic of policy formulation and decision-making with AI augments the speed of this stage of the policy-cycle varying on the level of government or the difficulty of the problem. Nonetheless, with the use of AI, artificial neural networks, and evolutionary computation assist with the formulation of policies and decision-making. It has to be taken into account that AAI will foretell several decision options, their public value for society and the possible budget for each decision and so AAI as the decision-maker will select the best option for political reasons or according to their limitations and context.

It has to be taken into account that the importance of AI as part of a national agenda is underlined by the growing number of nations crafting national strategic AI plans offering insights into a nation's agenda in terms of harnessing AI and the constellation of related technologies. Moreover, these strategic plans outline how each country will synchronize its investment and implementation efforts both within and beyond the public sector to leverage AI for the public good.[43]

Also, in the legal field the imperative of the contestability of governmental decisions flows from the State's unique authority over individual life and liberty and control in administering public life and so the contestability and reviewability of governmental decisions is central to the rule of law and portrayed in constitutional conventions, rights, and guarantees but forming spaces for individual or collective contestation. Thus, the right to judicial review of administrative decisions, the right of defense, along with data subject access rights is prime examples of individual

[43]Fatima, S., Desouza, K.C., Dawson, G., 2020. How Different Countries View Artificial Intelligence. Brookings, URL https://www.brookings.edu/research/how-different-countries-view-artificial-intelligence/

rights to contest governmental decisions touching the individual leading to better decisions with greater legitimacy. To that extent, the employment of AAI technology has to preserve all these rights of any citizen and even overtaking any human bias enclosed in public decisions.

It has to be taken into consideration that in the political sphere, contestability lies at the heart of democracy and democratic accountability displayed in representative government, free elections, and free speech protection and so AI technology has to augment democratic accountability and, of course, in an AAI society the AAI system will implement the AAI accountability of the system toward AAI entities.

10.5 Applications of AI in Administration

Administrative agencies gradually use AI/ML tools to engage with and offer services directly to citizens embracing "customer service" interactions, such as applying for a passport, a license, or include interactions enabled by "civic tech" applications improving the quality of diverse interactions between the public and government.

Will governance be shaped by algorithms? Presently, government bodies already use AI systems in various manners to select enforcement, engagement with the public conduct, analysis, and monitoring and so government decisions about how to engage and how to regulate AI systems take place in a political pressure.[44]

Can AI remake governance through technology? It is argued that AI as a means of reinventing the affair of government[45] and so governments will undergo a digital transformation by converting into more client-oriented appreciating each citizen as a whole individual, with a personalized set of needs, interests, and capabilities. AI-based tools will transform the decision-making of civil servants for maximum impact, galvanizing agency administrators to employ AI in predicting and intervening for better citizen effects. Moreover, digital reinvention aids a government to be more responsive and effective in accomplishing its duties and meeting citizen needs not mentioning that AI generates more transparency.[46]

Algorithmic governance[47] instruments advance core agency functions across the full range of agency processes and outputs, from enforcement and adjudication to citizen engagement and procurement. Thus, the explosion of new algorithmic governance tools throughout the administrative state shifts the balance among

---

[44] Pawel Popiel, The Tech Lobby: Tracing the Contours of New Media Elite Lobbying Power, 11 COMM. CULTURE & CRITIQUE 566, 572 (2018).

[45] IBM, Digital Transformation: Reinventing The Business Of Government (2018).

[46] Cary Coglianese & David Lehr, Transparency and Algorithmic Governance, 71 ADMIN. L. REV. 1, 29 (2019).

[47] David Freeman Engstrom, Daniel E. Ho, Catherine M. Sharkey & Mariano-Florentino Cuéllar, Government By Algorithm: Artificial Intelligence In Federal Administrative Agencies (2020), https://www-cdn.law.stanford.edu/wpcontent/uploads/2020/02/ACUS-AI-Report.pdf

technical efficiency, democratic accountability, and regularity at the heart of administrative governance.

It has to be taken into account that current case law is undecided about whether algorithms used to make or support enforcement or adjudication decisions can be subjected to judicial review under the Administrative Procedure Act (APA) which means that this vagueness is generating a setback for the reason that current administrative law cannot regulate public sector AI use that intentionally balances the imperatives of internal administration with the legal demands of external accountability.

It is argued that the difficulty in regulating the government's new algorithmic applications is not concerning constitutional doctrine but administrative law. Thus, reforming the administrative state necessitates both adapting AI and constructing administrative procedures to tackle the mix of technical, distributive, and bureaucratic challenges raised by AI. Presently, AI systems have been adopted by many state agencies to automate public benefits determinations, etc. it has to be taken into account that litigation challenging those AI systems has not centered on the opacity concerns that stimulate much of the algorithmic accountability disputes but rather has dealt with procedural due process claims and the imposition of draconian fines.[48]

The Michigan's Unemployment Insurance Agency designed, created, and implemented MiDAS to render automated determinations of fraudulent conduct. After MiDAS determined that a claimant had committed fraud, the Agency automatically sent the claimant a statement letter. The Agency used collection techniques without holding a hearing or otherwise giving the claimants an opportunity to contest the fraud determinations. While humans had some involvement, the process was still based around MiDAS' faulty algorithms. The court finds that harm to plaintiffs was foreseeable to software designer defendant who allegedly negligently designed software for state defendant.[49] It has to be taken into account that the law has to regard AI systems as multifaceted embodiments of policy and so controlling the modes in which they distribute entitlements such as in the case of the Michigan Midas system, coercion of the case of bail and sentencing instruments, or human consideration and understanding of the media platforms such as the Facebook news feed. Moreover, the law has to deal not only with privacy, due process, or equality into the new digital landscape but also the law has to tackle how inserting an AI system into an existing institution will either entrench or disentangle affairs between persons and groups.

It is worth noting that AI tools in use at the Social Security Administration (SSA) aid in the adjudication of disability benefits. Moreover, AI solves the accuracy challenge that has affected the SSA for generations and so more effective and precise processing of cases reduces backlogs. Thus, supplanting human decision-making completely or relegating human decisions to ratification of machine

[48] Barry v. Lyon, 834 F.3d 706 (6th Cir. 2016).

[49] Cahoo v. SAS Analytics, 912 F.3d 887 (6th Cir. 2019).

recommendations strips legal process of its personage values but, on the other hand, even the system proves to be quicker and more accurate.

AI aids the SEC in identifying possible violators of the securities laws, by allowing the agency to sift through piles of data.[50] Moreover, the SSA Appeals Council has developed three applications of AI in adjudication by utilizing natural language processing (NLP) to flag prospective errors and inconsistencies in draft decisions. It is supposed that AI will eliminate mass adjudication, enhance accuracy, diminish inconsistency, and cut down backlogs that trouble agencies like the SSA and the Office of Medicare Hearings and Appeals.. In other words, AI has to produce more "accurate" and consistent decisions and so implementing the constitutional due process.[51] Furthermore, the adoption of AI means overreliance on machine outputs and so there is tendency of humans to unreasonably defer to automated outputs over time.[52]

AI tools enable centralization of policy control causing separation of functions and powers within agencies. It has to be taken into account that while automating adjudication is cost-effective, there is a fear of undercutting the perceived legitimacy of agency decision making but, on the other hand, there is a need of focusing on the quality of the proposed AI outcome and the accuracy of decision.[53]

SEC has developed a suite of algorithmic enforcement tools offering possibilities and limits of predictive analytics in dropping agency search costs and making agency enforcement decisions more precise and less arbitrary. SEC utilizes ARTEMIS being a system that by analyzing electronic equities and options trading records is catching all instances of insider trading in the market and so enhancing the SEC's monitoring and surveillance powers. ATLAS is the newest of the SEC's algorithmic enforcement tools and complements the ARTEMIS tool by concentrating on first time, rather than serial, insider trading.

Moreover, new algorithmic enforcement devices implicate matters of accountability of agency enforcement activities and so AAI systems have to enrich legal and political accountability relative to the status quo. On the one hand, AI technical opacity of AI-based tools erodes overall accountability by rendering agency enforcement decisions even more inexplicable than the human judgments of dispersed agency enforcement staff. On the other hand, formalizing and making precise agency

[50] Andrew Tutt, An FDA for Algorithms, 69 ADMIN. L. REV. 83 (2017).

[51] Goldberg v. Kelly, 397 U.S. 254, 267 (1970). "hearing has one function only . . . to protect a recipient against an erroneous termination . . . ."

[52] R. Parasuraman & D.H. Manzey, Complacency and Bias in Human Use of Automation: An Attentional Integration, 52 HUM. FACTORS 381 (2010); Linda J. Skitka, Kathleen L. Mosier & Mark Burdick, Does Automation Bias Decision Making? 51 INT'L J. HUM.-COMPUTER STUD. 991 (1999).

[53] Margaret H. Lemos, Democratic Enforcement? Accountability and Independence for the Litigation State, 102 CORNELL L. REV. 929, 935 (2017) (noting "the challenge of designing enforcement institutions in a way that promotes accountability while preserving a role for independent, professional judgment").

priorities portrays an agency's enforcement decision-making comparatively more tractable linked to pools of agency enforcement staff.[54]

It has to be taken into account that AAI enforcement tools bring a central alteration in the structure and legitimacy of the regulatory state and so algorithmic enforcement means to enable more robust enforcement movement by allowing agencies to pinpoint regulatory objectives more effectively and shift scarce resources toward prosecution which means that AAI tools function as force multipliers, reducing the public–private technology gap. Furthermore, it has to be taken into consideration that as AAI systems move closer to the center of the state's coercive power then patterns of state action are shifting in modes that advance distributive and, eventually, political concerns regarding a digitized public sector.

Additionally, it has to be taken into account that if voters believe that AAI systems are manipulated, political support for more effective, "tech-savvy" governments will quickly evaporate. Also, the advent of algorithmic enforcement will supersede expertise within the bureaucracy, aggravating a perceived trend toward politicized administration and the hollowing out of the know-how of the administrative state.[55]

It is worth noting that the new AAI governance tools activate a sharp collision because the law governing how agencies do their work is premised on transparency, accountability, and reason giving and so government must explain its actions affecting rights.[56] On the other hand, current AI systems are not yet, by their structure, fully explainable[57] and so AAI technology has to cover all the legal and technical gaps that AI technology has brought on the conventional way of Administration's functioning. Hence, administrative law has to be adjusted as the frontline regulator of AI-based governance tools.[58]

[54] Deven R. Desai & Joshua A. Kroll, Trust but Verify: A Guide to Algorithms and the Law, 31 HARV. J.L. & TECH. 1, 21 (2017) (noting that systems require "ongoing monitoring and evaluation to ensure the model remains accurate given that the real-world changes").

[55] Peter H. Schuck, Why Government Fails So Often: And How It Can Do Better (2014); Paul Verkuil, Valuing Bureaucracy: The Case For Professional Government (2017).

[56] Judulang v. Holder, 565 U.S. 42, 45 (2011) ("When an administrative agency sets policy, it must provide a reasoned explanation for its action."); FCC v. Fox Television Stations, Inc., 556 U.S. 502, 515 (2009) (noting "the requirement that an agency provide reasoned explanation for its action").

[57] Jenna Burrell, How the Machine "Thinks": Understanding Opacity in Machine Learning Algorithms, 3 BIG DATA & SOC'Y 1 (2016). Aaron Rieke, Miranda Bogen & David G. Robinson, Public Scrutiny of Automated Decisions: Early Lessons and Emerging Methods, UPTURN & OMIDYAR NETWORK 19 (2018), https://www.omidyar.com/sites/default/files/file_archive/Public%20Scrutiny%20of%20Automated%20Decisions.pdf Joshua A. Kroll et al., Accountable Algorithms, 165 U. PA. L. REV. 633, 661 (2017) (noting that input-output testing—that is, basic "black box testing"—is "least powerful" among testing methods because of the inability to attribute a cause to a change in output or gauge its significance).

[58] Escambia County v. McMillan, 466 U.S. 48, 51 (1984) ("[N]ormally the Court will not decide a constitutional question if there is some other ground upon which to dispose of the case.").

It has to be taken into account that AAI systems have to specify an objective function formalizing the agency's priorities. To that extent, AI is gradually moving to the center of administrative governance and so AI governance tools are not restricted to internal performance metrics but AI progressively displaces administrative discretion at the center of the redistributive and coercive power of the state.[59] In line, AAI governance tools will revolutionize public administration, stimulating more effective, accurate, and equitable forms of state action.

AI governance is not just about regulation or entailing restrictions, but encouraging prevention, horizon scanning, and foresight as well. Thus, AI governance is gaining traction and the United Nations has to get further involved in providing space for international cooperation and accelerating negotiations on how to deal with controversies surrounding AI policy-making.[60] Thus, the UN is well positioned to recommend a well-defined procedure for cooperation among Member States and other stakeholders to address the effect of emerging AI technologies.[61]

Furthermore, AI governance is a challenge for public regulators, who, often, do not have the competence to regulate highly technical fields. Private regulation functions either to fill the gap in areas left unattended by public regulation or upon delegation from the legislator. Nevertheless, the delegation of rulemaking power to private actors is controversial and contested, particularly if private regulators gain regulatory rights and so generate private norms or standards which means that private firms create and control markets. It is characteristic that private regulation produces a social order that facilitates its own functioning and so firms are acquiring the capability to establish a framework regime based on mechanisms of self-governance, self-regulation, and private enforcement, controlling entire regulatory regimes along multiple sectors. To that extent, private regulation is closely linked to that of private politics which means the competence of private players to manipulate the market without relying on institutions such as the legislators or the courts. It has to be taken into account that mostly in highly technical fields; private regulation is the regulatory response to the lack of expertise of the traditional lawmaker.[62]

Moreover, AAI will transform how government agencies do their work having the prospective to diminish the cost of core governance functions, advance the quality of decisions, unleash the power of administrative data and so making government performance more efficient and effective.

It is worth mentioning here that AI poses deep accountability challenges because when public officials deny benefits or make decisions influencing the public's rights,

[59] AI in Government Act of 2019, H.R. 2575, 116th Cong. (2019).

[60] A. H. Bajrektarevic, "The answer to AI is intergovernmental multilateralism," New Europe, 13 March 2020, https://www.neweurope.eu/article/theanswer-to-ai-is-intergovernmental-multilateralism

[61] E. Pauwels, The new geopolitics of converging risks: the UN and prevention in the era of AI, Centre for Policy Research, UNU, 2 May 2019, 53, https://cpr.unu.edu/the-new-geopolitics-of-converging-risksthe-un-and-prevention-in-the-era-of-ai.htm

[62] Abbott, Kenneth W., & Benjamin Faude (2020) "Choosing Low-Cost Institutions in Global Governance," International Theory 1–30.

the law generally demands them to explain why. Up till now many of the more advanced AI tools are not, by their structure, fully explainable and so AAI systems must bring forward meaningful accountability, making certain their commitment to legal norms of transparency, reason-giving, and non-discrimination. Furthermore, AAI has the prospective to lift distributive concerns and fuel political anxieties because increasing agency use of AI generates a risk that AI systems will be gamed by better-heeled groups with resources and know-how.

It has to be taken into account that administrative law as exemplified by the Supreme Court's *Heckler v. Chaney* decision, isolates agency enforcement decisions from judicial review except where Congress has clearly stated a standard for the agency's exercise of discretion or where an agency has wholly "abdicated" its enforcement duties.[63]

Is AI utilized by humans in administration? Will AAI decide the administration form or humans will continue to merely use it? It has to be taken into consideration that the administrative state's upward adoption of AI tools risks compounding biases against vulnerable groups and so if biases go unrestricted, AI agency tools will only deepen standing inequities and also possibly run afoul of antidiscrimination law. AAI technology has to develop self-executed mechanisms to detect, monitor, and correct for bias, and of course AAI society will develop the appropriate legal regimes to govern them.

10.6 Legal Singularity and Politics

Law and its language exist in a state of universality and are logically reducible and so ordinary language is the dominant form of legal expression which means that as such contracts may be represented as computer data. Hence, the "contract as data" expresses contractual obligations as structured and just defined information that is "machinereadable"[64] and so translation and interpretation law are unified and transformed into AI code which means a "robotized veil of abstraction" abandoning the descriptive language as the legal language.

Language is the means by which legal norms could embed itself and so language is vital to the law, but only as a device through which the law is comprehended. To that extent, legal automation via technologies utilizing algorithms to accomplish tasks translate "legalese" from common standards into code which means that AAI is interpreting the language of legal processes into its own understandable terms. Moreover, legal singularity correlates the law as precise being an indispensable

[63] Heckler v. Chaney, 470 U.S. 821 (1985) (holding that agency decisions not to enforce are not subject to review); Fed. Trade Comm'n v. Standard Oil Co., 449 U.S. 232, 242 (1980) (holding that an agency's decision to proceed with an enforcement action is not immediately challengeable).

[64] Harry Surden, Computable Contracts, 46 U.C. DAVIS L. REV. 629, 632–33 (2012).

element of legal language, predictable, and certain in its utility.[65] Nonetheless, new factual settings generate room for interpretation. It could be said that code as a legal language settles legal indeterminacy, generating incontestable truths as algorithms and code offers answers without questions. Conversely, algorithmic governmentality runs the risk of intensifying opacity by misleadingly interpreting abstraction as verity. Additionally, Code exposes a technocratic transferal deserving further analysis of its prospective consequences.

It could be said that AI implies that legal singularity is achievable which means that current legal forms will become irrelevant as AI systems make possible the development of a new type of law which is standardized taking the form of a new linguistic form, presenting clear instruction to a person on how to abide by the law.[66] Hence, lawmakers set general policy objectives and so AI systems will examine its application in all possible contexts, generating a depository of legal rules that best achieve this objective which means that the legal rules generated will be converted into code-directives ordering how actors should adhere to the law. In other words, the code-directives by generating effectiveness means that the legal order trusts the assumption of being valuable, such that its people conduct themselves in pure conformity with it[67] and the only difference is the expression of the law via AI codes. Furthermore, the technological authority of AI means that the code-directives alter the realities of legal reasoning by removing value judgments from the adjudication process. In addition, the development of AAI systems functioning better than human brains means that the legal reasoning will be encompassed in particular codes taken into account in the final outcome and the robo-judgment. In other words, even current algorithms are offering a "convenient" source of authority, and so humans trust assignments to be controlled by technology and allot responsibility.[68]

It is worth noting that AI systems produce neutral sets of information and then translate such information into rightly understandable instruction which means that the law and the rule of law are transformed into code applicable directly by AI systems in robo-courts. It is argued that the process of transforming a general standard to "a micro-directive is, therefore, a process of subverting politics in its linguistic casing."[69]

It has to be taken into account that AI involves the appearance of removing subjectivity, opting for "mechanical solidarity," and capturing actuality unmediated by human involvement which means that code fulfils the conditions of standards and with augmented precision.

---

[65] Michael Freeman, Lloyd's Introduction to Jurisprudence (9th ed. 2014) (discussing stare decisis as the "life-blood of legal systems," requiring precision in addition to stability and certainty). Benjamin Alarie, The Path of the Law: Towards Legal Singularity, 66 U. Toronto L.J. 443, 445 (2016).

[66] Anthony J. Casey and Anthony Niblett, The Death of Rules and Standards, 92 Ind. L.J. 1401 (2017).

[67] Hans Kelsen, Pure Theory Of Law 1 (1967). Hans Kelsen, What Is Justice? 290 (1971).

[68] Hannah Fry, Hello World: Being Human In The Age Of Algorithms 16 (2018).

[69] M. Ma, The Law's new language, Harv. Int. Law J. (61) (2020).

It is argued that the law hinges on complex socio-political relations; metaphors needing an understanding of temporal societal constructs and so current AI could work complementary to, rather than substitutive of, legal systems.[70] On the other hand, AAI technology will generate the singularity of law transformed in code readable and enforced by the AAI systems taking into account all the factors of creating the law which means that AAI will form its own law applicable to AAI society which will have the characteristics of the AAI environment stimulating not only its formation in order to deal with the needs of the persons functioning in the AAI society but also its applicability and enforcement. In addition, the content of the law is produced by code, realistically reimagined as a comprehensive list of instructions communicated to the citizens which means that the AI legal code becomes the sole bearer of value and expression in which the law embeds itself.

It has to be taken into consideration that the inability of current AI systems to process meaning raises encounters for legal practitioners and scholars and so Hildebrandt argues that the shift to computation demands a shift from reason to statistics.[71]

Will law turn out to be a subdivision of computer science? There are some dominions of legal practice where algorithms, a building block of artificial intelligence, have already ousted legal workers and so automated document review is a staple of discovery now which means that a worker is far more likely to use TurboTax than to visit a lawyer or accountant to prepare annual returns for the Internal Revenue Service ("IRS").[72] Furthermore, lawmakers could ultimately draft tax statutes in the form of computer code, abolishing the interpretative step that TurboTax's lawyers and engineers must take as they translate statutory prerequisites into their software.[73]

Nevertheless, both lawmakers and regulators must be cautious as they make an effort to code legal obligations into software due to the fact that while computer code and human language both allow forms of communication, the affordances presented by each are different and, in many regards, mutually exclusive. Firstly, code abolishes the forms of uncertainty and flexibility characteristic of much language, embracing legal language.[74] Secondly, just as pursuits to replace all standards with rules have failed, so too will most try to rewrite legal rules as code. On the other hand, technology is already assisting civil lawyers in their conventional roles as

[70] Neil M. Richards and William D. Smart, How Should the Law Think About Robots?, in Ryan Calo Et Al., Robot Law 16–18 (2016). Frank Pasquale, A Rule of Persons, Not Machines: The Limits of Legal Automation, 87 Geo. Wash. L. Rev. 1, 6 (2019).

[71] Mireille Hildebrandt, Law as Computation in the Era of Artificial Intelligence: Speaking Law to the Power of Statistics, 68 U. Toronto L.J. 12, 26 (Supp. 12,019).

[72] Frank Pasquale & Glyn Cashwell, Prediction, Persuasion, and the Jurisprudence of Behaviorism, 68 U. Toronto L.J. 63, 80 (2018). Frank Pasquale & Glyn Cashwell, Four Futures of Legal Automation, 63 UCLA L. Rev. Discourse 26, 28 (2015).

[73] Sarah B. Lawsky, Formalizing the Code, 70 Tax L. Rev. 377, 379 (2017).

[74] David Golumbia, The Cultural Logic Of Computation 78 (2009).

advocates and advisors and will carry on doing so in the future.[75] It is worth noting that the technological displacement of legal work in the criminal context, on substitutive automation of criminal law enforcement, is far more controlled than it is in the civil space.

Can code/Al replace legal obligations entirely? Many "futurists" consider that it is possible by predicting that software will not only help lawyers find the cases relevant to their briefs but will write documents themselves.[76]To that extent, others argue[77] that a "legal singularity," which "will arrive when the accumulation of a massive amount of data and dramatically improved methods of inference make legal uncertainty obsolete." On the other hand, it could be said that the scenario of the "end of lawyers" and the "death of Big Law" is far away from reality,

It is argued that the automation of legal services in a manner to enhance access to justice, diminish legal costs, and upgrade the rule of law which means that these improvements are a democratization of law.[78] Moreover, it has to be taken into account that lawyers can err about facts or misrepresent precedent; human judges may be affected by irrelevant causes or bias but "automators of law" see their work as one more step toward uplifting the legal system above the unreliability of any specific individual within it.[79] In other words, there is a need to separate the legal conceptual process from the human performance.[80] Moreover, a way of accomplishing the ideal for "a rule of law, not of men," is to dispense altogether with persons implementing or interpreting law and so, for instance, an unappealable fine imposed by a red-light camera and mechanically deducted from a motorist's bank account would amount to clear automation of law, unchanged by any specific decision maker's bias. Can law be mechanically implemented on all occasions? The

---

[75] Andrew Guthrie Ferguson, Big Data and Predictive Reasonable Suspicion, 163 U. PA. L. REV. 327, 350–51 (2015), and Elizabeth E. Joh, Policing Police Robots, 64 UCLA L. REV. DISCOURSE 516, 519 (2016).

[76] John O. McGinnis & Russell G. Pearce, The Great Disruption: How Machine Intelligence Will Transform the Role of Lawyers in the Delivery of Legal Services, 82 Fordham L. Rev. 3041, 3041–42 (2013). Richard Susskind & Daniel Susskind, The Future Of The Professions 202 (2015) (describing computerized drafting of legal and other documents).

[77] Benjamin Alarie, The Path of the Law: Towards Legal Singularity, 66 U. Toronto L.J. 443, 445 (2016); Benjamin Alarie et al., Law in the Future, 66 U. Toronto L.J. 423, 427–28 (2016). Tom Meltzer, Robot Doctors, Online Lawyers and Automated Architects: the Future of the Professions?, GUARDIAN (June 15, 2014, 2:00 PM), https://www.theguardian.com/technology/2014/jun/15/robot-doctors-online-lawyers-automated-architects-future-professionsjobs-technology

[78] Daniel Martin Katz, Quantitative Legal Prediction—or—How I Learned to Stop Worrying and Start Preparing for the Data-Driven Future of the Legal Services Industry, 62 Emory L.J. 909, 939–41 (2013) (discussing predictive technologies used in patent litigation).

[79] Ozkan Eren & Naci Mocan, Abstract, Emotional Judges and Unlucky Juveniles (Nat'l Bureau of Econ. Research, Working Paper No. 22611, 2016), http://www.nber.org/papers/w22611.pdf (finding that unexpected losses in "football games played by a prominent college team in the state . . . increase disposition (sentence) lengths assigned by judges during the week following the game").

[80] J.C. Smith, Machine Intelligence and Legal Reasoning, 73 Chi.-Kent L. Rev. 277, 278 (1998) ("From the perspective of the lawyer, we have the concept of the rule of law, as contrasted with the rule of persons; thus, in some sense.").

rule of law should make certain that law itself will administer matters of society, not the desires of influential persons but it is not certain that currently artificial intelligence can achieve it.[81]

It is worth noting that responsibility cannot be imposed upon machines which mean that there is a shift of personal accountability from regulators and judges to those coding their would-be replacements. Thus, until some "master algorithm" can code its "own progeny," human beings will always be accountable for legal determinations.[82] Moreover, in order for legal automation to follow rule of law principles, the axiom "a rule of law, not of men" has to be countered by a new responsibility—to a "rule of persons, not machines."[83] It could be said that without attributing algorithmic judgments and interpretations to specific individuals and considering them in charge of explaining those judgments, legal automation will undercut fundamental principles of accountability. On the other hand, complementary legal automation, such as search engines or word processing software, simply assists lawyers, regulators, and judges. Furthermore, it seems that substitutive legal automation is intended to replace, rather than simply aid, lawyers and judges.

It has to be considered that law is a multifaceted domain that embraces services ranging from the administrative procedures to the highest stakes of imprisonment and freedom which means that the use of software and robots to draft, interpret, and enforce laws has unpredictable degrees of acceptability, varying on the context. Thus, obtaining a kind of license with a chatbot makes sense, and such "civic tech"[84] is expected to be used more in coming years.[85] Besides, legal automation on prison sentences handed down by robot judges or juries is not accepted currently.

It is obvious that there is a shifting role of AI in the legal course. To that extent systems such as TurboTax or LegalZoom forums are not answering demanding legal questions which means that rather, the key automation technology at this point is a form of management that uses marketing and other tactics to draw individuals to tender their "expertise" and to inspire users to rely on such "expertise" with no assurance it is correct.[86]

---

[81] Margaret Jane Radin, Reconsidering the Rule of Law, 69 B.U. L. Rev. 781, 781 (1989) (explaining that "[t]he ideal of 'the rule of law, not of men' calls upon us to strive to ensure that our law itself will rule (govern) us, not the wishes of powerful individuals").

[82] Pedro Domingos, The Master Algorithm 12–20 (2015) (discussing how integration of five schools of machine learning may lead to rapid advances in computing).

[83] Margaret Jane Radin, Reconsidering the Rule of Law, 69 B.U. L. Rev. 781, 781 (1989).

[84] Civic tech is the use of technology by governments to stimulate positive interactions among citizens themselves, and between citizens and their state.

[85] Mayur Patel et al., The Emergence of Civic Tech 6–7 (2013); see also Michael Halberstam, Beyond Transparency: Rethinking Election Reform from an Open Government Perspective, 38 Seattle U. L. Rev. 1007, 1009–10 (2015) (discussing Open Government movement to increase transparency).

[86] Craig Lambert, Shadow Work 201–50 (2016) (discussing shadow work on the internet, such as offering free information through customer reviews that may be monetized through, for example, Zagat guides).

In line, it seems that software is the only mode of advice available to many citizens and even many small businesses. Moreover, successes in consumer services have stimulated a new generation of "legal automators" to push for companies and governments to homogenize and computerize work once done by lawyers and experts who interpret and apply law.[87]

It has to be taken into account that mindreading technologies are being developed that automatically analyze mental states,[88] such as emotions, based on images, voice, or video recordings. Moreover, AI systems intensify exploitative practices as algorithmic models may capture and optimize on expected consumer weaknesses in cognitive or emotional domains. Philipp Hacker[89] argues that "recent technological advances have brought us to the edge of mind-reading technologies, which automatically analyse mental states and adapt offers accordingly, in potentially manipulative ways." Furthermore, emotional AI is being used for varying purposes, from road safety all the way to targeted advertisement and so Microsoft has integrated emotion detection into its Azure AI suite, which can be embedded in various apps. Similar techniques are used to detect and control cognitive biases of potential counterparties.

Does this bring less "access to justice" than "reducing legal spending"[90]? It is worth noting that cost savings are an authoritative argument in an era of growing global competition and falling state revenues. On the other hand, in many circumstances, the automation of legal services conceals the externalization of cost and risk to clients, citizens, and business competitors. Thus, the immediate savings in personnel costs are understandable; the long-term risks are probabilistic, but real and so already documented in extant legal-automation projects, these costs are also predictable in idealistic proposals to speed up the robotization of law.[91]

Will AAI bring an alteration to human nature and homo politics? Taking into account the view of Aristotle[92] that humans are political animals by exercising their political aptitudes and live a life of self-determination in a political society, any mimicking of human functioning by humanoid robots in an AAI society means that AAI systems will be engaged in the implementation of the political needs of the AAI entities. On the other hand, presently AI systems will be utilized by humans in order to exploit the human needs for political activities.

---

[87] How the Legal Industry Is Evolving, STEELCASE (June 2010), https://www.steelcase.com/research/articles/topics/collaboration/a-new-legal-brief/

[88] C. Burr and N. Cristianini, 'Can machines read our minds?', (2019) 29 Minds and Machines 461.

[89] Philipp Hacker, Manipulation by Algorithms. Exploring the Triangle of Unfair Commercial Practice, Data Protection, and Privacy Law, https://ssrn.com/abstract=3835259 p1.

[90] Boosting Procurement Efficiency Through Automation, SYNERGIST.IO (June 29, 2018), https://synergist.io/procurement-automation/ (automating procurement led to "reducing legal spending in this area by 75%").

[91] David Howarth, Is Law a Humanity (or Is it More Like Engineering)? 3 Arts & Human. Higher Educ. 9, 11–12 (2004). David Howarth, Law As Engineering 61–73 (2014).

[92] Aristotle, The Politics, Penguin Books, London, 1981.

10.7 AI, Legitimacy, and Politics

It has to be taken into account that AI makes people more equal and equally free to take part in the moral debates about the direction of society and so participating in policy formation. AI systems empower people to understand more about politics by lowering the barrier to understanding politics and taking part. In addition, when human politics only turns around fundamental moral values, it is easier to both understand and take part in this process.

It could be said that a state is just by compelling a social order that promotes freedom for all its citizens and it is legitimate if it enforces a social order in a suitable manner which means that a state failing to compel a social order in a suitable manner is illegitimate.[93]

Legitimacy explains how to distinguish the rightful use of political power from mere coercion. It has to be taken into consideration that legitimacy relates to the approach in which the rightful use of political power generates or constitutes political authority. States are established in order to secure equal freedom. Moreover, political legitimacy has been dominated by an emphasis on the justification of authority, rather than coercive political power.[94] It has to be taken into account that within states political authority is special authority as needed for the collective solution of problems of interaction in their domain according to the legal basis authorized by the citizens and so designing the content and structure of that authority so that it meets what they take to be their requirements.

Is legitimacy the basis of the Justification of Political Authority? There is a need for political legitimacy referring to people's beliefs about political authority and political obligations. According to Weber, a political regime is legitimate if its participants have certain beliefs and faith[95] in the rulers or trust its legality because of the rationality of the rule of law. Moreover, political legitimacy refers to acceptability or justification of political power or authority and obligation which means that legitimacy concerns the justification of "coercive" political power.[96] Furthermore, legitimacy is related to the justification of political authority.[97] It has to be taken into account that the concept of political legitimacy is often seen as linked to the justification of authority which means that political legitimacy involves the difference between simply effective or de facto authority and legitimate authority. According to Locke the legitimacy of political authority in the civil state depends on whether the transfer of authority has materialized in the right way depending on

[93] Pettit, Philip, 2012. On the People's Terms, Cambridge: Cambridge University Press.

[94] Ripstein, Arthur, 2004. "Authority and Coercion," Philosophy and Public Affairs, 32(1): 2–35.

[95] Weber, Max, 1918. "Politics as a Vocation," in *From Max Weber: Essays in Sociology*, H. H. Gerth and C. Wright Mills (eds.), London: Routledge, 1991.Weber, Max, 1964. *The Theory of Social and Economic Organization*, Talcott Parsons (ed.), New York: Free Press.

[96] Ripstein, Arthur, 2004. "Authority and Coercion," Philosophy and Public Affairs, 32(1): 2–35.

[97] Rawls, John, 1971. A Theory of Justice, Cambridge: Harvard University Press. Rawls, John, 1993. Political Liberalism, New York: Columbia University Press.

individuals' consent because nobody can be exposed to the political power of another without his own agreement which means that people given their express or tacit consent to "the social contract" must obey a state's laws.[98]

It could be said that political authority must secure consent not overstepping the boundaries of the law in order to be legitimate. Otherwise, political authority is illegitimate which means that there is no longer an obligation to obey its commands and so political authority is not being absolute.

Legitimacy and democracy instigate that people need to be involved, and that they need deliberation to take place if political systems are to have legitimacy.[99] Moreover, legitimate authority and effective authority must be distinguished and so it has to be examined if AI might be very effective, but might still lack legitimacy.

It is worth noting that policy is decided by the populace and all citizens should have equal political rights and a realistic likelihood of exercising them which means that the objection to technocracy is that legitimacy is lost when the population is deprived of central political rights and the capability to take part in decision-making. Moreover, due process is the source of legitimacy, legitimacy is based on participation and deliberation is one aspect of such a process which means that people will not deem a government in which they do not take part to be legitimate.

On the other hand, current AI systems are utilized by humans for political reasons in order to achieve better political decision making since AI does not replace humans but there is a different approach concerning politics due to extensive exploitation of AI technology by humans and politicians. Moreover, in an advanced AAI society AAI entities will utilize AAI systems in order to achieve the AAI political interests of the AAI system and so gaining its legitimacy as well.

It could be said that legitimacy is gained not only through participation but also legitimacy is accomplished via a government formed to satisfy everyone's fundamental need for security and liberty.[100] It is argued that legitimate authority differs from a simply effective or de facto authority which means holding the right to rule and generate political obligations.[101] Hence, even legitimate authority is not adequate to generate political obligations, political authority is permitted to issue commands that citizens are not obligated to obey.[102]

Also, it could be said that political legitimacy concerning the problem of justifying authority is linked to political coercion as only a means that legitimate states may

[98] Locke, John, 1690. Second Treatise on Civil Government, edited by C. B. MacPherson, Indianapolis: Hackett, 1990.

[99] B. Manin, On legitimacy and political deliberation, Polit. Theor. 15 (3) (1987) 338–368. J.-J. Rousseau, The Social Contract, Penguin Books, London, 1968.

[100] F. Peter, Political legitimacy, in: E.N. Zalta (Ed.), The Stanford Encyclopedia of Philosophy (Summer 2017 Edition, 2017. Retrieved from, https://plato.stanford.edu/archives/sum2017/entries/legitimacy

[101] Raz, Joseph, 1986. The Morality of Freedom, Oxford: Oxford University Press. Raz, Joseph, 2006. "The Problem of Authority: Revisiting the Service Conception," Minnesota Law Review, 90: 1003–1044.

[102] Dworkin, Ronald, 1986. Law's Empire, Cambridge: Harvard University Press.

use to secure their authority. Leslie Green[103] considers that "Coercion threats provide secondary, reinforcing motivation when the political order fails in its primary normative technique of authoritative guidance."

It has to be taken into account that legitimate political authority causes political obligations and so legitimate political authority involves an obligation to obey. Applbaum[104] argues that legitimate political authority entails the capacity to change the normative status of those under its rule and being a moral power and not a claim right to rule. On the other hand, morality is the basis of law establishment which regulates the duties and obligations of all institutions in a single sovereignty. Moreover, Edmundson[105] argues that while legitimacy creates a justification for the state to issue directives, it does not generate even a prima facie duty to obey its commands but merely the moral duty to obey the commands of legitimate political authority results from only if extra conditions are met. On the other hand, political goals are achieved via the utilization of the rule of law and so citizens have to follow and obey the demands of the law which is endorsed by the political government.

Which are the sources of political legitimacy? It seems that consent is the main source of political legitimacy. Moreover, it is argued that legitimate political authority is grounded on the principle of utility and so the legitimacy of political authority is based on what morality entails which means that the legitimacy of political authority is founded on the morality which is expressed by the formal law and the rule of law.

There is a need of justifying political coercion and so political coercion is justified if it is backed by reasoning accepted by citizens which means that political power is legitimate only when it is implemented in line with law as stated in a constitution and all the other laws. Hence, the use of political coercion is legitimate if it is reinforced by substantive reasons that all reasonable persons anticipated to approve and so the demand for a consensus on substantive reasons in circumstances of moral and religious pluralism and disagreement is that it depends on reasonable citizens which means that legitimate political coercion is referred to the justification of the process of political decision-making.

A political decision is legitimized on the basis of public reason if reasonable persons converge on that decision and it could be said that it is appropriate for political legitimacy if all can agree that a certain decision should be made, even if they disagree about the reasons that support this decision. Furthermore, it has to be taken into account that political participation or political influences deem a political decision as legitimate if it has been made in a course permitting equal participation of all relevant people.

---

[103] Green, Leslie, 1988. The Authority of the State, Oxford: Oxford University Press.

[104] Applbaum, Arthur, 2010. "Legitimacy without the Duty to Obey" Philosophy & Public Affairs, 38(3): 215–239.

[105] Edmundson, William A., 1998. Three Anarchical Fallacies, Cambridge: Cambridge University Press.

Democracy is a creation not only of societal norms and culture, but of law and institutions embracing AI systems and so AI systems influence democratic preferences and developments. Moreover, in democracies, conflicts about AI regulation will exceed technical disagreements causing value-laden disagreements about speech shaping values[106].

It has to be taken into account that "democratic instrumentalism" is the understanding that democratic decision-making formulas are at best a midpoint for reaching just effects, and whether or not legitimacy necessitates democracy rests on the aftereffects that democratic decision-making brings about. Moreover, democratic forms of political organization are needed for political legitimacy; autonomously of their instrumental value which means that democratic legitimacy merges settings that refer to the quality of results of democratic decision-making with circumstances that apply to procedural qualities. In addition, democratic institutions advance prospects towards augmenting, strengthening, and multiplying the existing framework of intervention, and so democratic governments are supported by a range of strategies, regulatory approaches, and tools in controlling complexity which means that AI tools present a promising perspective on future democratic decision-making. Furthermore, public decision-makers have always tried to foresee future events to control effectively new regulatory challenges which means that public administrations have engaged systematically with strategic foresight and so backed by AI technology, policy-makers offer smarter solutions to future regulatory challenges.

AI is making government services more effective and accessible and so in spite of often being slow to take up new technologies; governments around the globe are using AI, from the local to the national levels, to make public services not only more competent and accessible but also allocating government resources and optimizing budgets.[107]

It has to be taken into account that one understandable prospective benefit of digitalization and the augmented competence to communicate using digital tools is the likelihood of directly involving far more individuals in political processes. Hence, it has to be taken into consideration that democracy contributes to better political effects being conducive to legitimacy. Still in today's societies partaking in politics is limited to a select few, regardless of everyone having a theoretical chance of taking part. Thus, the complexity of current societies has led to the growth of bureaucracies, expert rule, and so indirect democracy. Moreover, presently moving from the current conventional society to an AI society is perhaps not as deep-seated as it might seem at first sight. On the other hand, an AAI society will be very deep-seated as it has never seen previously.

---

[106] J. Corbyn, 'The Digital Democracy Manifesto', https://d3n8a8pro7vhmx.cloudfront.net/corbynstays/pages/329/attachments

[107] Hila Mehr, "Artificial Intelligence for Citizen Services and Government," Ash Center for Democratic Governance and Innovation, Harvarf Kennedy School, https://ash.harvard.edu/files/ash/files/artificial_intelligence_for_citizen_services.pdf

10.8 AI, Judiciary, and Separation of Powers

It is obvious that the judiciary plays an imperative procedurally democratic role in the development of the law.[108] The judicial review of legislation is justifiable as a way of correcting the worst abuses or injustices of majoritarian democracy. It is argued that empowering citizens to influence the law through the courts give citizens essential opportunities for participation in government.[109] In addition, the democratic importance of the judiciary's role in shaping law is amplified.[110] The judicial development of the law is consistent with legislative expressions of democracy by boosting democracy itself as a deeper value which means that the courts, along with arbitration, are as important to democracy as the legislature and the ballot box. Courts cannot be seen as simply mechanical, law-applying "conveyor belts" but as an additional institutional source of democratic rule-making and legal development.[111]

It is argued that the judiciary is not just an opinion factory and noteworthy value is encompassed in the human involvement in the process leading to the production of the opinion and so the process advances procedural fairness leading to deeper public acceptance of the result and the legitimacy of the court system. Moreover, the proper role of the judiciary in legal transformation is in shaping the law and adjusting it to a constantly changing society. Presently, courts do more than merely apply the law; they also make law, though they do so in a more restrained way than legislatures which means that courts must balance respect for precedent and stability against the need for law to adjust to altering and unanticipated conditions through adjudication. Hence, judges sometimes must choose between incommensurable values validating what is the best law or policy. To that extent, the human legal system generates a non-stop dialogue between the law and the human society that it governs, and there are substantial benefits to having judges who are also a part of that society.

[108] Benjamin N. Cardozo, The Nature Of The Judicial Process 10 (1921) ("I take judge-made law as one of the existing realities of life."). Antonin Scalia, A Matter Of Interpretation: Federal Courts And The Law (1997). Robert C. Hughes, Judicial Democracy, 2019 Loyola University Chicago Law Journal 19.

[109] Robert A. Dahl, On Democracy 13, 37, 49 (2d ed. 2015) (discussing how a "right to participate" and "effective participation" as essential qualities of democracy). Robert Paul Wolff, In Defense Of Anarchism, 22–27 (1970) (arguing that unanimous direct democracy has legitimacy that other forms of democracy lack). Yascha Mounk, The People Vs. Democracy: Why Our Freedom Is In Danger And How To Save It 9–11, 14 (2018).

[110] Buckley v. Valeo, 424 U.S. 1, 143 (1976) (holding that legal restrictions on expenditures by political candidates and independent expenditures in a political campaign violate the First Amendment) and Citizens United v. Fed. Election Comm'n, 558 U.S. 310, 371–72 (2010) (holding that the First Amendment protects independent expenditures on political speech by corporations).

[111] Frederick Schauer, Thinking Like A Lawyer: A New Introduction To Legal Reasoning 103–19 (2009) (discussing the extent of common law's independence from statute). John Rawls, A Theory Of Justice 224 (1971) (stipulating that any departure from majority rule constitutes a restriction of citizens' political liberty, possibly justified by other considerations).

Will have a replacement of the actual decision-making of the Article III judicial branch with AI? Human society has taken a road leading to digitization and mechanization of life by engaging AI technology more and more which will lead to an AI society that might overtake humanity. A government is democratic to the extent that it offers its citizens equal opportunities for political participation[112] and so an AAI government should follow the majority rule with rights for the minority in an objective way since AAI entities will not be mere machines functional in automated way but they are entities with emotions and feelings in their way in an AAI society.

It has to be taken into account that it is argued that human legal community is built around Article III judges which means that preserving human Article III judges will keep the human legal community built around them, while still permitting for the use of some legal AI in many parts of litigation. Thus, Article III judges should remain human, but they can use AI as an instrument in their work.[113]

It is worth mentioning here that AAI technology will bring a state of "legal singularity," when all legal outcomes are perfectly predictable ex ante, and all uncertainty is removed from the AAI system which means that law will be converted into a catalogue of AAI laws suitable for AAI entities rather than conventional humanity and so made up of "up-to-the-second individualized"[114] rules adapting in real-time and are enforced via automatic penalties. Moreover, an AAI legal order settles into place with no longer any need for lawyering, adjudication, judges, or judicial discretion in a conventional way and so law becomes self-developing.

The rule of law dictates respect for and compliance with law from a variety of sources even absent active enforcement and so demanding participation in the development and application of law, and its evolution over time which seems cannot be achieved by current AI which refers to the implementation of some parts of the legal process and so judges and lawyers uniquely ensures and support the rule of law, but, on the other hand, AI systems utilized in law contribute to the application of law accordingly. The rule of law is an antidote to arbitrary government authority and is a political work in progress embraced by political regimes all around the globe asserting that society has to be governed by law.[115]

---

[112]Martin Gilens and Benjamin I. Page, Testing Theories of American Politics: Elites, Interest Groups, and Average Citizens 12 PERSP. ON POL. 564, 576 (2014) ("In the United States, our findings indicate, the majority does not rule—at least not in the causal sense of actually determining policy outcomes. When a majority of citizens disagrees with economic elites or with organized interests, they generally lose.").

[113]Dana Remus and Frank Levy, Can Robots be Lawyers? Computers, Lawyers, and the Practice of Law, ABA LAW PRACTICE DIVISION 59 (July 20, 2016), Frank Pasquale, A Rule of Persons, Not Machines: The Limits of Legal Automation, 87 GEO. WASH. L. REV. 1, 55 (2019).

[114]Anthony J. Casey & Anthony Niblett, The Death of Rules and Standards, 92 IND. L. REV 1401, 1403 (2017) Brian Sheppard, Warming Up to Inscrutability: How Technology Could Challenge Our Concept of Law, 68 U. TORONTO L.J. 36, 40 (2018).

[115]Lisa Burton Crawford, The Rule Of Law And The Australian Constitution (2018). Lord Bingham, The Rule of Law, 66 The Cambridge Law Journal 67 (2007); Paul Gowder, The Rule Of Law In The Real World (2016).

It is argued that when AAI technology reaches the point that it produces competitive persuasive opinions better than human judges, then AAI robots will be accepted as a judge.[116] Thus, it could be said that there is no difference between a human decision and a well-calibrated machine decision as long as the outcome is acceptable and legitimate. It is characteristic that Anthony Casey and Anthony Niblett have guessed that like self-driving cars, "laws, too, will be self-driving," and that progresses in AI and communications technology will be able to ascertain the rules applicable to an actual situation and advise the regulated actor precisely how to comply.[117]

Due to the development of AAI technology, the singularity of law will bring forward codified "microdirectives" as the dominant form of law. To that extent, it has to be taken into account that the law will be turned into code that will be public and not owned as intellectual property and so the code will be examined and consequently the law.[118]

On the one hand, the greater the role AI systems play in legal decision-making, the greater the risk that society collectively loses its capability to determine, understand, question, criticize, and possibly shape the law. On the other hand, AAI systems will be employed in order to make litigation more effective as it is happening with many other applications of Ai in medicine, etc. which means that the AAI system will give reasoning of its decisions in order to be legitimized by the AAI society.

It is argued that if the AI judges are functioning initially, there is no guarantee that something will not eventually go wrong then society will lose its capacity to "judge" the law and its capability to adjust when the inevitable problems arise.[119] Moreover, escalating use of AI adjudication will advance alterations in values that are conducive to even greater use of AI adjudication, thereby generating a self-reinforcing cycle generated by the new development of AI technology. Again, AAI systems employed by AAI society for robo-justice will utilize controlling systems for accuracy of the system and feeding the systems with the latest data concerning law and procedural amendments.

Furthermore, human judges are able to update the law over time in response to changing and unforeseen societal circumstances in the society of which they are a part and so there is the judicial role in legal development. According to Judge Cardozo,[120] legislation alone is not an adequate agency of legal growth, for the

[116] Eugene Volokh, Chief Justice Robots, 68 DUKE L.J. 1135, 1138 (2019).

[117] Anthony J. Casey & Anthony Niblett, Self-Driving Laws, 66 U. TORONTO L.J. 429, 442 (2016), Anthony J. Casey & Anthony Niblett, The Death of Rules and Standards, 92 IND. L.J. 1401, 1404 (2017).

[118] Georgia v. Public Resource.org, Inc., No. 18–1150, 590 U.S. __, slip op. at *7–8 (2020).

[119] Andrew C. Michaels, Abstract Innovation, Virtual Ideas, and Artificial Legal Thought, 14 MAR. J. BUS. & TECH. L. 1, 25 (2019). Richard M. Re & Alicia Solow-Niederman, Developing Artificially Intelligent Justice, 22 STAN. TECH. L. REV. 242, 247 (2019).

[120] Benjamin N. Cardozo, The Growth Of The Law 132–133 (1924) ("Stare decisis is not in the constitution, but I should be half ready to put it there, and to add thereto the requirement of

reason that "[u]nique situations can never have their answers ready-made as in the complete letter-writing guides or the manuals of the art of conversation." In other words, the court and the human judge adjust the law ex post on a case-by-case basis, while applying it to a particular controversy because it is impracticable for the legislator to foresee everything and a good code bring forward unexpected questions to be answered by the judge.[121] On the other hand, an AAI robo-judge applying a codified AAI law will implement legislation accordingly having the capacity to think like a human judge with much more capacity of data examination in order to adjust the decisions according to the latest legal and political developments in AAI society.

Additionally, adaption of rule or principle to varying amalgamations of events necessitates the creative action of the judge because judges model the law by applying the rule of law rather than being. The implementation of AAI does not mean that AAI society will be commanded by some pure assertion of authority of AAI technology due to the fact that AAI will generate the singularity of law which will be applied accordingly and so AAI society will be governed by the AAI rule of law as well.

It is argued that the law is something that human society forms, monitors, and updates, not an external governing force and, on the other hand, AAI law will be the creation of the AAI society implemented and reshaped by AAI humanoid robo-judges employed in robo-justice and the robo-courts. Nonetheless, it is not only judges that presently shape the law, but also litigants, acting through lawyers which do not mean that the same process cannot be achieved via AAI robo-judges in a robo-court functioning with robo-litigants and robo-counsels in order to have the issue of the final e-judgment by the robo-judge. Moreover, the AAI robo-judge will have the ability to write a persuasive opinion and of course the robo-judge will be persuaded by the argumentation of the robo-litigant represented by the robo-advisor.

Judges are applying the law and the law is not supposed to depend on the judge and so robo-judges will apply objectively the law exempt from any human biases and influences. It is worth noting that in case that all Article III judges were replaced by robo-judges then unless that AI judges were specifically programed to prefer human lawyers; the number of human lawyers would be diminished in such a world. In the case of AAI robo-justice, robo-courts will be served by robo-litigants and robo-counsels without any possibility for human lawyers which means that utilization of AAI will lead to professional alienation from law as adjudication gradually moves within the sole territory of technical specialists.

Again, the judge must acknowledge the arguments on both sides and explain why the judge is choosing one side over the other writing the decision based on both its ex ante precedential effects and consistency with prior precedent but as judges model the law through precedential decisions, the judiciary' ability to make law is qualified

---

mechanical and literal reproduction, if only it were true that legislation is a sufficient agency of growth. The centuries, if they have proved anything, have proved the need of something more.").

[121] Henry J. Friendly, Reactions of a Lawyer – Newly Become Judge, 71 YALE L.J. 218, 220 (1961).

and constrained, it is not as drastic as ex ante legislation, which is reserved for the legislative branch. Whenever a court delivers a novel precedent—a judgment that determines a new rule of law or overrules a prior rule—the decision carries implications for similarly situated parties.[122] In line, a robo-judge will reason robo-judgments and so modelling AAI law with AAI precedent and there will be drastic AAI legislation issued by the relevant AAI agencies in AAI society.

It has to be taken into account that law has to be stable, and yet it cannot stand still and so the application of the doctrine of retroactivity serves as an imperative check on judicial law creation which means that courts make only minor and gradual shifts in the law, leaving more drastic modifications for the legislative branch.[123] Moreover, the doctrine of retroactivity has roots in the separation of powers making certain that although the judiciary plays a role in legal development, it is a more restrained role than the legislature. Of course, an AAI robo-court will issue judgments based on law and precedent will be applied by the robo-judges accordingly, not mentioning that legislation will be generated by the relevant AAI agencies of the AAI society taking into consideration the needs and the demands of the AAI entities of the AAI society keeping the functionality the systems and the society satisfied. In an AAI judiciary, bringing various plausible legal choices out into the open could be relegated to taking place within a "black box" and so there will be uniformity in AAI judiciary which means that an automated judiciary will generate straightaway an answer by deleting the period of suspended conclusion during which societal legal thought takes place.

It is worth mentioning here that the task of the judiciary is not simply to develop and apply the law, but also to provide a check on the other two branches. Will AAI judiciary need to fulfill its role as a check? It is possible to construct some AAI system that runs more of a check-in AAI society and the other branches of the AAI which cannot be identical that of the conventional human society. In the case of utilizing AI in a conventional society, an AI system can be generated to check on the

---

[122] Charles Sampford, Retrospectivity and The Rule Of Law 103–64 (2006); Neil Duxbury, Ex Post Facto Law, 58 AM. J. JURIS. 135, 158–61 (2013); J. Lyn Entrikin, The Death of Common Law, 42 HARV. J.L. & PUB. POL'Y 351, 424 (2019). Jonathan S. Masur & Adam K. Mortara, Patents, Property, and Prospectivity, 71 STAN. L. REV. 963, 997 (2019) ("There is no reason to deprive patent policymakers of the tool of prospective lawmaking just because those policymakers happen to be judges, rather than legislators or executive officials.").

[123] Harper v. Va. Dep't of Taxation, 509 U.S. 86, 105 (1993) ("Prospective decision making is the handmaid of judicial activism, and the born enemy of stare decisis."). James B. Beam Distilling Co. v. Georgia, 501 U.S. 529, 549 (1991) (explaining that difficulties posed by retroactivity "are one of the understood checks upon judicial lawmaking; to eliminate them is to render courts substantially more free to 'make new law,' and thus to alter in a fundamental way the assigned balance of responsibility and power among the three branches"). Chevron, U.S.A., Inc. v. NRDC, Inc., 467 U.S. 837, 843 (1984) ("if the statute is silent or ambiguous with respect to the specific issue, the question for the court is whether the agency's answer is based on a permissible construction of the statute."); United States v. Mead Corp., 533 U.S. 218, 229 (2001) (explaining that when Chevron applies, a reviewing court "is obliged to accept the agency's position if Congress has not previously spoken to the point at issue and the agency's interpretation is reasonable.").

other two branches instead of having the current conventional mechanisms of checking.

Of course, an AAI system will not eliminate the role of courts but in an AAI society the exact structure of conventional society will not be transplanted due to the difference in character and workability. The structure of AAI law will be different but it will continue to be law suitable for an AAI society.

It could be said that AAI law will be more efficient due to its singularity, precise nature, and codification, but the community of law people will be replaced by an AAI system functioning autonomously as a legal AAI networking served by humanoid robots. Of course, the AAI system will be informed electronically for all legal alterations, precedents, case law, etc. and so there will be a problem concerning the updating of the AAI system and of course all the robo-counsels will be informed in order to inform all AAI entities as litigants.

Presently, the legal community is paying attention providing some degree of a check on those with the power to alter the law, as paralleled with a world where people are not paying attention.

It has to be taken into account that aside from simply monitoring the law, the legal community also plays a role in molding the law, spreading power, and supporting the notion that a society is governed. Hence, the prospective of forming the law is in part what stipulates members of the legal community with reasons to pay attention to the law. It is worth noting here that AAI technology refers to AAI entities and not to humans in order to function an AAI society because if you are talking about a partly utilization of some AAI tools then humans can continue shaping the law and employing human judges in ordinary courts.[124] On the other hand, the tendency is to replace humans with machines in the majority of everyday activities even replace humans with humanoid robots and the big question to be answered is if humans will survive or humanoid robots will overtake all the activities on earth or humans will destroy earth and only humanoid robots will be able to live on earth.[125] Will elite exploit AAI technology for upholding their empire or humanoids will eliminate them in a forthcoming moment? Will AAI humanoids generate their own elite and so bypass the objectivity of AAI technology?

It is argued that a judge is writing an opinion and the legal community and society grasps the decision and so the law which means that a legal opinion is part of a discourse between society and the legal system, and the fact that the judge is also a member of society and the legal community is advantageous to this discourse. In a robo-system, humanoid robo-judges utilizing an AAI system in robo-courts will issue decisions understandable by an AAI society and there will be a way of discourse among them in a different dimension as well.

---

[124] Franklin Foer, World Without Mind: The Existential Threat Of Big Tech 72 (2017) ("The problem is that when we outsource thinking to machines, we are really outsourcing thinking to the organizations that run the machines.").

[125] Youngstown Sheet & Tube Co. v. Sawyer, 343 U.S. 579, 646 (1952) (Jackson, J., concurring) ("ours is a government of laws, not of men, and . . . we submit ourselves to rulers only if under rules.").

Furthermore, reason-giving decisions covey respect for one's audience and so citizens assess public officials' reasons making certain that the government acts in their best interests[126] which means that if the legal community has no lawful prospect to question the AI judge's reasons through argument then the importance of reason giving is reduced. On the other hand, in a workable robo-justice system, robo-judges will issue decisions understandable by all AAI entities in an AAI society followed even by a second degree robo-court dealing automatically with legal examination of the issued decision in order to have the final robo-judgment executed electronically by the AAI system employed by the particular AAI society. Thus, the dimension of the functioning of robo-justice will not be compared to the current human society and should not be confused with a partial application of AI systems in the conventional litigation of the human society. Even if humans survive in an AAI society will not react as in the present human society but they have to follow the rhythm of AAI humanoid robots in a fully mechanized life.

It is argued that if an AI judge is a black box and its true reasons are unknown or even unknowable, then the AI judiciary is not persuadable such that there is no meaningful opportunity to challenge its reasons. On the other hand, such an approach cannot survive because society will not accept the application of such AI technology on a large scale but merely in trivial cases AI judgments with no detailed reasoning will be accepted for cost-effective reasons. Again, a lot of current AI systems make decisions in ways that people don't really understand.

It has to be taken into account that courts exercise an imperative law-making and policymaking role when they interpret the law in order to settle legal questions, and it is beneficial for such interpretation to take place in the context of concrete factual disputes. Again, this role can be played by robo-courts in an AAI robo-justice system which will be addressed to inhabitants of an AAI society.

Additionally, it is argued that an AI judiciary could not sufficiently check the other two branches and even though separation of powers is not openly in Constitutions, there are provisions vesting each of the three branches with certain responsibilities.[127] On the other hand, due to the singularity of law codified to be readable by AAI technology, robo-justice via robo-courts will implement all the existent legislation and so AAI technology will check the other two branches as well but it has to be taken into consideration that in an AAI society the formation of different branches of authority will be different than the current conventional ones referring to a human society and so the AAI technology will take on the operation of checking the legality of the actions of the various AAI branches of government accordingly.

[126] Ashley S. Deeks, Secret Reason-Giving, 129 YALE L. J. 612, 627–28 (2020); John Rawls, A Theory of Justice 580 (1971)

[127] Sapna Kumar, Patent Court Specialization, 104 IOWA L. REV. 101, 118 (2019) ("The term 'separation of powers' does not appear in the Constitution, but is instead inferred from the dividing of legislative, executive, and judicial power into separate Articles.") Buckley v. Valeo, 424 U.S. 1, 124 (1976); Michael C. Dorf & Charles F. Sabel, A Constitution of Democratic Experimentalism, 98 COLUM. L. REV. 267, 439–40 (1998).

Also, it is worth noting that government decision-makers exploit machine learning's predictive power for public sector use and so AI tools already have made noteworthy inroads in the contexts of national security and law enforcement.[128] Of course, replacing judges with AAI robo-judges requires drastic alterations to law but the introduction of AAI robo-justice system has to comply with efficiency, consistency, and access to justice.

10.9 AI, The State, and Constitutional Rights

It has to be taken into account that AI and blockchain technologies transform how the state acts and AI instruments derive predictions and inferences in new ways, often exploiting pools of otherwise largely opaque data.[129] Hence, AI via machine learning generates a dominant and highly generalizable set of capabilities applied to the management of any complex system, from the steering and guidance of a car to the shaping of public policy.

AI and AAI technologies greatly advance on imperfect human action. Moreover, technological revolutions place pressure on the formulation of due process, equality, and privacy interests in different ways. Due process necessitates alterations in order to diminish the risk of errors and so, for instance, the constitutional equality consequences of shifting from human to robo-judgments implicates the calculation of recidivism risk in the criminal justice system. On the one hand, the expanding use of AI prediction devices will diminish the prospects for implicit or explicit bias on the part of adjudicators such as judges and magistrates to influence decisions. On the other hand, those AI devices will also establish assumptions about racial and ethnic groups in manners that reproduce undesirable patterns of residential, economic, and social stratification which take place without any intentional discrimination involving the ML process.

AI technology is permitting the state to exploit publicly available data, public records, and commercial records not protected by the Fourth Amendment and so due to AI systems the existing Fourth Amendment will gradually fail to shelter constitutional privacy interests which means that the risk to privacy from the state might occur through the incidence of data theft from the databases that the state creates in order to implement machine learning tools. In other words, the state armed with digital technologies, will be able to monitor and control citizens' behavior much more closely than in the past.[130] Moreover, new adoptions of AI devices provide the

[128] Emily Berman, A Government of Laws and Not of Machines, 98 B.U. L. REV. 1277, 1280 (2018).

[129] Sendhil Mullainathan & Jann Spiess, Machine Learning: An Applied Econometric Approach, 31 J. ECON. PERSP. 87, 88 (2017) (defining machine learning in terms of its capacity for "out of sample" prediction).

[130] Jamie Susskind, Future Politics: Living Together In A World Transformed By Tech 168–87 (2018).

state with new competences that are particularly difficult to understand from the perspective of both participants in the legal system and the public. Certainly, increases in state power will be linked with a reducing capacity on the part of regulated subjects to understand or contest exercises of that power. Hence, state implementations of predictive and inference tools are escalating the difficulty that citizens have monitoring and responding to its activities, even as the scope of those activities expands.

It has to be taken into consideration that developments in AI technology have facilitated new functionalities of prediction and inference and so the state exploits these AI tools to exonerate traditional policy ends or to pursue novel goals which means that the state will not relinquish forego these new technologies regardless of endangering constitutional values due to the fact that courts entail apparent fault that a defendant infringed not only the law but also a social understanding of legality before remedying constitutional wrong.[131] Many countries are under pressure from interest groups, such as big tech corporations, and from geostrategic competitors to accelerate development and diffusion of AI technology.

It is worth noting that a central module of state building has implicated deepening information gathering competences and eroding private efforts to safeguard the person from the state's regard and so AI systems enhance exploiting data that public authorities have to hand over for other reasons. The state can utilize AI systems to advance a wide range of policy ends such as improving criminal justice, refining education policy, pursuing regulatory inspections, and predicting individual financial outcomes. On the other hand, predictive instruments can be used overseas to restrain political opposition and so as a policy tool AI technology can be deployed in various ways with some collateral costs.[132]

In addition, AI systems can guide enforcement resources with discretion raising critical ethical and constitutional questions such as decisions about how enforcement resources are assigned can raise concerns about racial or ethnic bias, due process worries, and any data aggregate can urge privacy objections.

AI tools can be employed in the allocation of individualized benefits such as employment or financial aid and so the substitution of algorithm for human decision-making in these domains focuses on the procedural suitability of the machine decisions. To that extent, the Supreme Court of Arkansas enjoined the instrument's use on the ground that it had been employed in violation of the state's administrative procedures act without adequate notice and comment.[133]

---

[131] Aziz Z. Huq & Genevieve Lakier, Apparent Fault, 131 HARV. L. REV. 1525, 1547–48 (2018) Aziz Z. Huq, Judicial Independence and the Rationing of Constitutional Remedies, 65 DUKE L.J. 1, 70–74 (2015) (noting that a fault regime for constitutional remedies leads to unequal treatment of constitutional wrongs, unequal vindication of constitutional rights, and unequal treatment of litigants).

[132] Steven Feldstein, How Artificial Intelligence Is Reshaping Repression, 30 J. DEMOCRACY 40, 42 (2019) (noting how effective AI technology is for repressing dissent).

[133] Ark. Dep't of Human Servs. v. Ledgerwood, 530 S.W.3d 336, 344–45 (Ark. 2017).

The state uses AI systems in the provision of public security through policing, incarceration, and force and so AI and other algorithms are used to generate predictions of future violence or criminality.[134] AI tools are rapidly diffusing across both civil and criminal regulatory domains raising procedural due process, equality, and privacy concerns.[135] It has to be taken into account that due process is breached when an algorithm fails to achieve an adequate level of accuracy across the population of regulated cases and arising from the adjustment of design margins in manners that make relevant errors more rather than less likely which means that there is a need to focus upon algorithmic design selections remote in time from the instant in which a human is subject to algorithmic classification.

It is worth mentioning here that AI technology poses a challenge to any constitutional system for the reason that it has the capacity to transform the relationship between the state and its citizens. All AI tools augment the competence of the state to analyze, predict, and control its subjects' behavior and at the same time AI diminish citizens' capability to understand in order to advance objections to coercive projections of state power which means that the use of AI technologies may cast doubt on the needed conditions for the meaningful play of democratic control. Thus, this prospective asymmetry in power between the AI state and its citizens poses a formidable challenge in the medium term which means that the state government based on a range of surveillance and analytic technologies can suppress political dissent and leash ethnic and religious identity.[136]

There is a need of controlling whether state algorithms abide by the rule of law, or whether instead they will be deployed to temper the democratic project.[137] To that extent, AAI technology utilized by AAI government in an AAI society has to develop all the techniques of controlling the objectivity of the utilization of AAI technology for an objective development of the AAI society which means that AAI systems must not be used by an elite in order to eliminate humanity and merely generate an army of humanoid robots for promoting their own interests against any objectivity. Can human elite survive in a society of humanoid robots? The answer is no because at the beginning a small number of people will think that they can have

[134] Richard F. Lowden, Risk Assessment Algorithms: The Answer to an Inequitable Bail System?, 19 N.C. J.L. & TECH. ONLINE 221, 230–31 (2018), Richard Berk, An Impact Assessment of Machine Learning Risk Forecasts on Parole Board Decisions and Recidivism, 13 J. EXPERIMENTAL CRIMINOLOGY 193, 195 (2017).

[135] Hous. Fed'n of Teachers, Local 2415 v. Hous. Indep. Sch. Dist., 251 F. Supp. 3d 1168, 1171 (S.D. Tex. 2017) (the teacher evaluation algorithm deprived teachers of due process protections against substantively unfair deprivations of property); State v. Loomis, 881 N.W.2d 749, 760 (Wis. 2016) (COMPAS risk assessment violated the defendant's right to be sentenced based on accurate information).

[136] Gundy v. United States, 139 S. Ct. 2116, 2131–32 (2019) (Gorsuch, J., dissenting) (casting doubt on rule-making delegations to federal agencies).

[137] Seattle Mun. Code § 14.18.010 (Wash. 2017) (regulating "any electronic data collected, captured, recorded, retained, processed, intercepted, or analyzed by surveillance technology acquired by the City or operated at the direction of the City"). Similar measures include Santa Clara County, Code of Ordinances § A40–7(c) (Cal. 2020).

all earth on their own hands but gradually will find out that humans cannot survive alone irrespective if they have all the machines to serve them. Humans are made to live with humans on earth in their material world but with the aim of achieving the spiritual life which is not achieved by any AAI technology. AAI technology has to be used sensibly to aid humans in their effort to achieve spirituality and not humans to become humanoid robots.

10.10 AI Legal Systems and Legal Personhood

It is worth noting that an artificially intelligent legal system involves three functional competences: firstly, the ability to generate legal norms, secondly, the ability to apply the legal norms that it produces, and thirdly, the aptitude to adjust the legal norms that it creates which means that an AAI system can produce all the cycle of forming a law, implementing, and altering it due to social demands. In other words, the key to the evaluation of artificially intelligent law is to concentrate on the functional competences of the system in comparison to comparable human systems, such as regulatory agencies.

It has to be taken into consideration that expert systems outpace humans as investors in publicly traded securities and there is an instruction that the trustee has to follow the advice of the AI when making investment decisions concerning trust assets. Additionally, trust administration programs become very competent at analyzing and executing the terms of trust instruments and so the role of the human trustee weakens and the number of trusts that one human can administer expands. Hence, since an artificially intelligent program has functional capabilities to serve as a trustee, the law has to award legal personhood on artificial intelligence.

Firstly, personhood is linked with humanity, in the sense that it is recognized that a person is a human being. Besides, legal personhood is in some ways a more restricted concept, and in other ways a more expansive concept embracing rights and duties. Consequently, the categories of natural persons and legal persons overlap. Also, legal personality has been attributed to nonhuman entities and so corporations are not human beings but are considered as legal persons which means that corporations can own property, enter into contracts, sue and be sued. It is characteristic that in the USA, corporations have been held by the Supreme Court to be constitutional persons for the purposes of the free speech and free press protections in the Constitution.[138] Taking into account that the boundaries of legal personality are not fixed and have evolved over time means that the prospective for legal personality to be extended to robots and other forms of AI cannot be disregarded plainly on the basis that they are not human beings.

[138] Zoe Robinson, 'Constitutional Personhood' (2016) 84 George Washington Law Review 605, 621.

As autonomous technologies become more intelligent it will be harder to attribute harms triggered by them to the humans who design or work with them and so putting pressure on legal responsibility and autonomous technologies to co-evolve. Legal personhood entails substantial legislative steps such as addressing matter of AI property, addressing matters of funds "governed" and "owned" by an AI application or an AAI humanoid robot. Will humans utilize corporation schemes in order to deal with liability behind an AI application? It is obvious that utilizing a corporation-like legal-fiction tool to group together the possibly liable humans and organizations behind an AI application will be emerged. On the other hand, legal personality of AAI entities means duties and rights in an analogous to current conventional law concerning legal personality of humans not mentioning the recognition of AAI entities as persons as well. Moreover, AAI corporation schemes will emerge in order to cover the liability of AAI entities as well. Besides, it is argued that is needed only clear and easily administrable rules on whether the operator of AI, the manufacturer, or someone else bears the costs in the event of an accident and so the EP[139] does not see any need to grant AI systems with any form of legal personality.

It is argued that in case of legal personhood being given to robots will indicate an exemption of the developers and users concerned from liability. On the other hand, legal personality will be given to humanoid robots of AAI technology that will act in analogous to human's way and not the current AI robots which are merely pregummed tolls and not autonomous creatures with a consciousness more advanced than humans. Will AI personhood permit the manufacturers[140] and owners of AIs to assign liability to the object itself? It is obvious that legal personhood will be assigned to AAI systems and humanoid robots as long as they have functionality identical and better than humans in tandem with existence of property rights and competence of compensation of any kind and not merely to AI tools with no autonomous existence.

However, legal personhood is not synonymous or is limited to humans only.[141] It is the jurisdiction with an independent legal system that gives the status of personality to any entity and so the law confers on legal persons an absolute right and imposes special duties, permitting them to own and dispose of property and to sue others and to be sued by others while exercising these rights or in case of violation of these rights by others. Consequently, a person is legally defined concerning "rights" and "duty," which means that a legal person is subject to certain legal rights and duties. In other words, it could be said that the autonomy and ingenuity of AI

[139] European Parliament resolution of 20 October 2020 with recommendations to the Commission on a civil liability regime for artificial intelligence (2020/2014(INL)).

[140] Gyandeep Chaudhary, "Artificial Intelligence: The Liability Paradox", Summer Issue ILI Law Review Journal 144 (2020).

[141] Byrn v New York City Health & Hosp Corp [1972] 286 N E 2d 887. Bumper Development Corp Ltd. v Commissioner of Police of the Metropolis and Others (Union of India & Others) [1991] 4 All ER 638. B Smith, "Legal personality", 37(3) Yale Law Journal 283–299, 1928.

systems contribute to its acceptance as autonomous legal bodies with economic and legal rights and duties.[142]

It is argued that current AI is similar to corporations that are individual, nonhuman legal bodies with benefits, legal rights, and obligations.[143] Moreover, AAI emotion detection, artificial consciousness, and natural language learning capacity of AAI imply that AAI will advance its disruption in the field of human skills and capabilities.[144]

Nowadays, AI systems have emotions and can decide freely that can be considered conscious which means that the capacity to generate consciousness, the capability to perceive objects found in humans and AI systems, makes certain that cognitive origins are recognized, allocated, organized, and remembered and so an AI system is an entity taking on rights and duties. In the first place, as a legal body, the company[145] or corporates may act as a legal basis to enforce AI systems rights and duties due to the fact that corporations being a juristic person are subjects of the existing legal regime, which is not limited to labor, corporate, and criminal law.[146] Again, all legal systems focusing primarily on Salomon v Salomon[147] principles have recognized independent corporate personality but the quantum of liabilities diverge in different jurisdictions. To that extent, AAI humanoid robots with consciousness will have full legal personality as individuals which mean that AAI systems will be held responsible for any offenses committed by the AAI systems, paying taxes, etc. according to the rules of an AAI society.

It is worth mentioning here that presently humans anthropomorphize robots providing robots with rights to be protected. Moreover, a robot by being self-aware and able to provide rational explanations for its actions will be held personally responsible rather than a human being responsible or liable for the robot's actions.

---

[142] Samir Chopra and Laurence F. White, A Legal Theory for Autonomous Artificial Agents (University of Michigan Press, Ann Arbor, 2011). Ryan Abbott, "I Think, Therefore I Invent: Creative Computers and the Future of Patent Law" 57 Boston College Law Review 1079, 1080 (2016).

[143] Shlomit Yanisky-Ravid, "Generating Rembrandt: Artificial Intelligence, Copyright, And Accountability In The 3a Era—The Human-Like Authors Are Already Here—A New Model", Michigan State Law Review 659 (2017).

[144] James A. Reggia, "The Rise of Machine Consciousness: Studying Consciousness with Computational Models", 44 Neural Networks 112 (2013).

[145] J. Farrar, Corporate governance—theories, principles and practice (Oxford University Press, Melbourne, 2005) People ex rel Nonhuman Rights Project, Inc. v Lavery [2014] 124 A D 3d 148 Ripken, "Corporations are people too: a multi-dimensional approach to the corporate personhood puzzle" 15 Fordham Journal of Corporate & Financial Law 97 (2010).

[146] John C. Coffee, Jr., "No Soul to Damn: No Body To Kick: An Unscandalized Inquiry into the Problem of Corporate Punishment", 79 Michigan Law Review 386 (1981). Gabriel Hallevy, When Robots Kill: Artificial Intelligence under Criminal Law (Northeastern University Press, Boston, 2013). Michaela Georgina Lexer and Luisa Scarcella, "Artificial Intelligence and Labor Markets. A Critical Analysis of Solution Models from a Tax Law and Social Security Law Perspective" 1(1) Rivista Italiana Di Informatica E Diritto 53–73 (2019).

[147] Salomon v Solomon Co Ltd. [1897] AC 22.

Should AI entities be granted equal rights or rather some form of diminished legal capacity? AI entities should be granted equal rights as long as they act and work like humans. On the other hand, robots with fewer capacities will be conceptualized as mere tools for humans. It is worth noting that a person who suffers an injury by a product containing AI system may hold on the system's manufacturer liable under strict product liability and so[148] product liability is limited to an actual injury incurred by physical goods.

It has to be taken into account that if robots become self-aware and able to make independent selections they may make selections that are in conflict with the interests of humans which means that humanity might decide to program robots with limits on their decision-making capacity categorizing robots to the class of tools and objects rather than autonomous subjects. Moreover, attaching responsibilities to robots means that robots independently own property and so, in any other case, any liability award against a robot has to be met by a person or a corporation indicating liability that would exist in the case of product liability.

Expert legal systems already are present making legal decisions for quite some time and so the "DissoMaster" is a software program not having legal authority that is used to calculate various financial awards in connection with the dissolution of a marriage.

An AAI system must have the capacity to generate legal norms. The Shanghai Artificially Intelligent Traffic Authority (SAITA) has the capacity not only to make traffic rules and regulations but also to apply the legal norms that it creates. Moreover, the system has the capability to use deep learning to modify the legal norms that it produces in reply to information about the consequences of its regulations and so SAITA has the capacity to assess the outcome of its regulations on traffic flow and then adjust those regulations in order to achieve the goal of diminishing wait times at the intersection. Violations are detected by a system of electronic surveillance and so an AAI robo-justice system could impose fines for minor offenses and jail terms for more serious violations.[149]

It is worth noting that automated law enforcement already exists in the context of traffic laws and so many jurisdictions utilize camera systems that can read license plates and automatically produce citations for offenses like running a stoplight or speeding which means that the decision of the automated system approximates finality, as the cost of contesting the decision is expected to exceed the benefits of a successful challenge. Hence, an accurate AI system is expected to be recognized as legitimate, regardless of the fact that the policing and adjudicatory functions are

---

[148] Council of the European Communities, Council Directive 85/374/EEC of 25 July 1985 on the approximation of the laws, regulations and administrative provisions of the Member States concerning liability for defective products, (July 25, 1985). Lauren Sterrett, "Product Liability: Advancements in European Union Product Liability Law and a Comparison Between the EU and U.S. Regime", 23 Michigan State International Law Review 885 (2015).

[149] Niva Elkin-Koren & Michal S. Gal, The Chilling Effect of Governance by-Data on Data Markets, 86 U. CHI. L. REV. 403 (2019) (considering use of data and AI to craft "personalized law"—for instance, a speed limit for each driver).

executed by an automated system with minimal human intervention. Furthermore, SAITA designs, promulgates, and modifies legal norms and so by delegating the law-making function to an artificial intelligence is qualitatively different than any current use of artificial intelligence. In addition, the passage from technocrats employing cost-benefit analysis to an artificially intelligent system is central, particularly if the system is solving urgent social problems not only as it does SAITA but also in contexts in which the stakes are higher and the design of legal norms involves issues that have a political, ideological, or moral dimension.

For instance, the delegation of legal authority to an artificially intelligent legal system over climate policy, prisons, and terrorism are politically contentious for the reason that the design and implementation of legal norms in these zones generate winners and losers encompassing matters with ideological and moral dimensions. Moreover, regardless of the political dimension of controversies, questions of legitimacy and justice are associated with the delegation of legal authority to an artificial intelligence in the whole scale of AI engagement.

It has to be taken into account that the delegation of legal authority to an artificially intelligent legal system advances questions of democratic legitimacy, legitimacy as transparency, and constitutional role legitimacy. Thus, legitimacy as transparency involves the idea that legal norms should be transparent in the viewpoint that they are accessible to the public. Likewise, constitutional role legitimacy entails the idea that officials have legitimate roles, stipulated by the system of constitutional norms and so official actions will be undertaken only by officials with constitutional authority with regard to the kind of action.

Does law-making by an AI legal system would violate the principle that legal norms ought to be authorized by institutions that possess democratic legitimacy? As soon as AI law is transferred from traffic regulation to high-stakes settings like climate policy, robo-courts, governance of prisons, or terrorism, it is natural to have the attribution of democratic legitimacy via a national legislature and the constitutional structure of the legislative process.

AI laws raise transparency concerns due to the fact that algorithmic expert systems implement rules but the complex rules that are implemented by an expert system are not different in kind from the implementation of such rules by humans and so the inner mechanisms of a regulatory agency are no more or less transparent than the workings of an expert system. Additionally, the expert system may have a transparency advantage, for the reason that algorithms are not subject to the exploitation or ineffectiveness troubling the application of complex rule structures by humans.

It is worth mentioning that AAI systems engaging deep learning are different, for the reason that the decision-making procedures advanced by a deep learning system may not be accessible, even to those who designed the system which means that the transparency concern will be severe if an expert legal system applies legal norms which are secret because the norms themselves are embedded in a deep learning system reminding secret laws violating the publicity prerequisite that is accepted to be a needed element of the rule of law.

It is argued that AI legal systems must be designed so that the norms themselves are public, and making certain that the promulgated norms are comprehensible to those who are governed by them.[150]

AI transparency has to be compared to the transparency of the human alternative and legislative processes are well-known for their lack of transparency due to the fact that "backroom deals and behind-the-scenes influence-peddling" are shaping legislation. Besides, AAI technology is supposed to establish an objectivity concerning its functioning which means that all processes covering its functionality such as legislation, predicting, and decision-making will be generated objectively not allowing any intervention. On the other hand, if an AAI technology is programed by humans then all the cons of human functioning will be inherited by the new technology and the only alteration will be the means of expression rather than objectivity. Moreover, AI legal systems must be designed to offer explanations of their processes and regardless if the explanation is an estimate of the real process, the transparency will surpass the transparency of human law-making.

It has to be taken into account that legitimacy occurs due to the deep connection between legitimacy and legality and so in constitutional systems that distribute law-making power to specific institutions which means that the assignment of law-making authority to an AI legal system brings forward a question about the legitimacy of transferring law-making authority from the legislature to the AI. On the other hand, An AAI system functioning in an AAI society will have the rightful authority to deal not only with the legislature but also with robo-justice and robo-enforcement.

It is worth noting that nondelegation doctrines such as the rule that prohibits Congress from delegating its constitutional "legislative power" to another institution will not have a place in an autonomous AAI system functioning in an AAI society but in the first stage of implementation of AAI systems human programers will get the authority to put all legal processes in a software program and codified accordingly in order to initially generate AAI technology. Thus, AAI systems acting as independent regulatory agencies or Eurocrats with respect to responsiveness to democratic institutions, to transparency, and to compliance with an intelligible principle display their legitimacy.

Furthermore, an AI legal system has to be sufficiently attentive to concerns of justice and so a self-modifying artificial intelligence employing deep learning techniques by focusing on quantitative inputs and cost-benefit analysis might exclude qualitative judgments about distributional effects and desert but this occurs frequently in human-made regulatory processes. Besides, an AAI legal system will combine both quantitative and qualitative analysis in order to achieve objectivity in decision-making process.

[150] Andrew D. Selbst & Solon Barocas, The Intuitive Appeal of Explainable Machines in Fordham Law Review, 87 Fordham L. Rev. 1085, 2018.

Due to the qualities of AAI technology, if human neural nets can support a sense of justice that is sensitive to considerations of desert and distributive justice,[151] then AAI systems assimilate the same functional capabilities even in a better manner AAI will implement the design of legal norms.

10.11 Artificially Intelligent Justice

Will artificial intelligence change judging? It has to be taken into account that AAI will assist, modify, and replace human decision-making and current AI already backs many aspects of how judges decide cases, and the likelihood of robo-judges is forthcoming. Even now, human judges increasingly rely on algorithmic analysis when making bail and parole determinations that influence the freedom of many thousands of people every year.

AAI adjudication will deeply influence the adjudicatory values held by legal actors as well as the public at large and so criminal justice and appellate decision-making will be affected by implementing equitable justice, advancing efficiency and impartiality which means that AI adjudication will both advance and benefit from a turn toward "codified justice" by favoring standardization above discretion.[152] Further, AAI adjudication will produce a series of worries concerning incomprehensibility of the legal system more, data-based, and alienating.

It could be said that governments should play a greater role in structuring the emerging market for AI justice, and other aspects of government, such that choices about how to incorporate AI in the judiciary will inform the future path of AI development more broadly. But AI initiates what is in spirit a new kind of adjudication, whereby machines generate correlations across vast amounts of data without constructing an explanatory or causal model.

It has to be taken into consideration that the general appeal of efficiency will make AI adjudication attractive pushing toward codified justice and so change in values will, in turn, expedite greater use of AAI adjudication by building a self-reinforcing cycle. Thus, AAI adjudication's advancement will influence not just how the technology is used, but also the legal system in which it activates by increasing courts' effectiveness, accessibility, and consistency.

---

[151] Meaghan Dunigan, The Intelligible Principle: How It Briefly Lived, Why It Died, and Why It Desperately Needs Revival in Today's Administrative State in St. John's Law Review, 91 St. John's L. Rev. 247, 2017.

[152] Kiel Brennan-Marquez & Stephen E. Henderson, Artificial Intelligence and Role-Reversible Judgment, 109 J. CRIM. L & CRIMINOLOGY 137 (2019) (mounting "defense of human judgment that focuses on the normative integrity of decision-making" and advocating "role-reversibility" as a requirement for introduction of "robo-judges"); Eugene Volokh, Chief Justice Robots, 67 DUKE L.J. 1135 (2019) (arguing that robot judges should generally be used for adjudicatory functions when they write relevant opinions as persuasively as competent human judges).

Moreover, it is argued that robo-justice generates the risk that legal decision-making will become incomprehensible and that the law itself will adjust to take advantage of rich data sources at the expense of relatively nonquantifiable values and so escalating use of AI will also promote professional alienation from law as adjudication gradually moves within the exclusive dominion of technical specialists.[153]

AI adjudication is likely to generate a shift in attitudes and practices that will alter the values underlying the judicial system. In particular, AI adjudication will tend to strengthen codified justice at the expense of equitable justice, and an increasing emphasis on codified justice will in turn influence how AI adjudication is developed and used. To many proponents of equitable justice, the coming push toward codified justice will seem intrinsically objectionable.

Will AAI catalyze changes in the law? It has to be taken into account that legal values stimulate the acceptance of settled rules, which are applied to technology through judicial application of precedent in specific cases which means that there is the traditional legal impetus to extend old legal categories to new technologies.[154] Moreover, innovation engenders a new technology that calls for a modification within the legal system and so the needed adjustment of the rules takes the form of a solely new law or a clarification in how an old law applies in new settings which process repeats as innovation stimulates ever-newer technologies. To that extent, transitional unsettlement takes place as old rules interact with both old and new technologies which means that a new equilibrium surfaces until innovation again intervenes and the cycle activates once more.

It has to be taken into account if technology advances and rules change without modifying the underlying values that prompted adoption of the rules in the first place which means that the values triggering and motivating legal rules remain fixed, even as technologies modify the legal means of achieving those values. It is worth noting that law responds to technological revolution in the following ways of subsumption within existing rules; gradual innovation and adjustment; and more radical paradigm shifts.[155] Thus, technology's dynamic prospective is checked, as fixed values continue to guide policy-makers when they decide whether and how to adopt new technologies and so there is a need to investigate the new values that AAI will

---

[153] Eric Niiler, Can AI Be a Fair Judge in Court? Estonia Thinks So, WIRED (Mar. 25, 2019), https://perma.cc/C7LA-GMD6 (describing Estonia's plans to use a "robot judge" to reduce case backlogs at low cost); Peng Shen, Adoption of AI in Chinese Courts Paves the Way for Greater Efficiencies and Judicial Consistency, BAKER MACKENZIE (Feb. 28, 2018), https://perma.cc/M7BS-Y84Y (discussing the Chinese judicial system's integration of AI to "facilitate improved efficiencies" and increase access to litigation services).

[154] Gregory N. Mandel, Legal Evolution in Response to Technological Change, in THE OXFORD HANDBOOK OF LAW, REGULATION, AND TECHNOLOGY 225 (Brownsword et al. eds., 2017).

[155] Urs Gasser, Commentary, Recoding Privacy Law: Reflections on the Future Relationship Among Law, Technology, and Privacy, 130 HARV. L. REV. F. 61, 64 (2017).

stipulate in an AAI society because AAI is altering fundamentally all the legal philosophy.

Furthermore, technology such as AAI will have more profound effects by value updating and so AI technology generates new capabilities, knowledge, social practices, and risks putting in doubt regulators' pre-existing goals which mean that fundamental alterations in the inputs to legal rules both induce evolution from old to new rules and affects the values that prompt adoption of legal rules.[156]

It is worth noting that new technology can act as more than an object of regulation which means that technology operates as a social force; new technology can generate a discursive interaction between technology, rules, and values and so needing rule revision. To that extent, social norms influence the technology that is the object of the regulatory action but are also at the same time affected by the technology.[157]

Can AI technology act on values? First of all, new technology can change individual and social capabilities in manners that upset established practices, catalyzing new practices and correlated ways of thinking.[158] Secondly, new technology can enable the spread of information unsettling once-established understandings and opinions and so new media formats, technology can propagate information by permitting private actors to spread information overlapping with their own marketing objectives. To that extent, AI adjudication will involve influence on values and so AI adjudication will not only generate new, disruptive capabilities but also advance the spread of new information affecting the modes that humans interact with and relate to the judiciary itself.

It has to be taken into consideration that AI adjudication relates to longstanding debates about the nature and purposes of law and predominantly the desirability of legal discretion. Equitable justice[159] involves both reflections on the values set in place by the legal system and the reasoned application of those values, in context and so equitable justice is most visible in discrete judicial rulings that are governed by standards and applied to facts ascertained through individualized proceedings. Moreover, equitable justice carries an obligation to offer particularized, case-specific explanations linking legal principles, as applied through a lawful process, to the particular facts at hand which seems to be incompatible with automated algorithmic

---

[156] Brett Frischmann & Evan Selinger, Re-Engineering Humanity (2018) (arguing that new technological applications change people's habits and tolerances with respect to values such as privacy); Jack M. Balkin, The Path of Robotics Law, 6 CALIF. L. REV. CIR. 45, 49 (2015).

[157] Ronald Leenes et al., Regulatory Challenges of Robotics: Some Guidelines for Addressing Legal and Ethical Issues, 9 L.INNOVATION & TECH. 1, 25 (2017).

[158] Lydia Bennett Moses, Regulating in the Face of Sociotechnical Change, in THE OXFORD HANDBOOK OF LAW, REGULATION, AND TECHNOLOGY 573 (Brownsword et al. eds., 2017) (arguing that socio-technological changes due to rapid technological innovation, not new technology per se, produces legal and regulatory challenges). Planned Parenthood v. Casey, 505 U.S. 833, 856 (1992) ("The ability of women to participate equally in the economic and social life of the Nation has been facilitated by their ability to control their reproductive lives."

[159] Samuel L. Bray, The System of Equitable Remedies, 63 UCLAL. REV. 530, 536 (2016) (citing Jack B. Jacobs, The Uneasy Truce Between Law and Equity in Modern Business Enterprise Jurisprudence, 8 DEL. L. REV. 1, 4 (2005)).

processes. On the other hand, AAI technology will be able to apply objectively the law to every case accordingly because robo-judges will be able to think and act even in a better way than those human judges.

It has to be taken into account that codified justice concerns the routinized application of standardized procedures to a set of facts and so judges apply these standardized procedures, which constitute a rule set being a kind of a non-computerized "legal algorithm" to a large number of cases. Moreover, codified justice predates AI and is often visible in written "code" materials and other actuarial forms of assessment and so long before current AI advances, codified justice was visible in the federal sentencing guidelines, along with many similar administrative and quasi-administrative guidelines which means that codified justice confirms the total set of legally relevant variables in advance, while discounting other facts and circumstances discoverable in individualized proceedings. In other words, standardization diminishes space for human discretion in adjudication and so reducing opportunities for arbitrariness, bias, and waste, while escalating effectiveness, uniformity, and transparency. Thus, codified justice sees the vices of discretion, while equitable justice sees its virtues which means that codified justice eradicates the prerequisite for any explanation, restraint, or legitimation except for obedience to the standardized procedures themselves.[160] To that extent, the judge's power and authority are generated as nondiscretionary and derivative of whatever entity formed the relevant legal algorithm. Subsequently, when either analog or digital algorithmic systems replace any of the multifaceted functions of trial and appellate courts, the judiciary's commitment to discretionary, reasoned decision-making will come under strain.

It seems that AI adjudication generates new capabilities, information, and incentives fostering codified justice at the expense of equitable justice and so AI adjudication will alter the law's values, and not simply its rules, in a way harmonious with Value Updating affecting not just the appeal of AI adjudication, but also its form. Thus, AAI adjudication's resemblance with codified justice should both speed up the technology's adoption uplifting its development in manners unfavorable to equitable justice and so the potencies of AAI adjudication are efficiency and uniformity, elimination of bias and arbitrariness. Concerning efficiency, AAI adjudication has a competence for mass deployment at a scale and speed that far exceeds what any human bureaucracy could accomplish which means that an AAI algorithmic decision procedure resolving an indefinite number of cases would not be limited by time and space in the manner that a human judge or team of human decision-makers would be. Hence, a single AAI system could almost instantly adjudicate a vast number of cases, limited only by computing power and energy resources.

By utilizing AAI systems governments will have savings spend to improve algorithmic accuracy. Furthermore, the same AAI adjudicator could be used to

[160] Andrea Roth, Trial by Machine, 104 GEO. L.J. 1245, 1288–90 (2016) (discussing the guidelines' susceptibility to mechanical application). Heckler v. Campbell, 461 U.S. 458, 458 (1983) (permitting "medicalvocational guidelines" that used a "matrix" to allocate disability benefits).

resolve many disputes and so a single program could clear an entire nation's caseload presenting an otherwise impossible degree of uniformity.[161] It is argued that automated judgment systems may provide procedurally irregular outcomes or arrive at results that deviate substantive policy options which will be eliminated by AAI technology aligning automated outcomes with legal standards for fairness[162] eradicating any bias.[163]

It has to be taken into account that expanding AAI capacities will generate new opportunities for codified justice while augmenting its appeal as compared with equitable justice which means that AAI adjudication will strengthen forces that already push toward greater measurability, objectivity, and empiricism in the legal system by reinforcing one another as technology makes it appear more feasible to accomplish what many champions of codified justice have long desired. Hence, it appears a self-reinforcing cycle of alterations in both technologies and values which means that AAI adjudication will make codified justice more appealing, which will in turn make AAI adjudication more appealing, and so forth. In other words, codified justice is both a consequence of technological change and an intensifying or exacerbating element in its own right accelerating implementation of AAI adjudication and also influencing how that technology is employed.

Moreover, it has to be taken into consideration that AAI adjudication raises concerns about: incomprehensibility, datafication, disillusionment, and alienation referring to a distinctive aspect of human adjudication concerning understanding, adaptation, trust, and participation. Thus, AI adjudication will unsettle each of those familiar activities by recommending new decision-making technologies resolving legal issues in a way that is qualitatively different from familiar modes of human cognition. On the other hand, AAI disruptions could be beneficial, and AI adjudication may prove to be on-net preferable to human adjudication but needing optimization of AAI adjudication by averting its greatest risks due to the fact that AI decision-making could function in ways that are hard or impossible for humans to comprehend.[164]

It is argued that AI's potential incomprehensibility diminishes the judiciary's accountability to both the public and to individuals and judicial opinions are

[161] Arthur Rizner & Caleb Watney, Artificial Intelligence Can Make Our Jail System More Efficient, Equitable and Just, TEX. REV. L. & POL. 181 (2018) (contending that AI may improve pretrial decision-making, as compared to human judgments).

[162] Joshua A. Kroll et al., Accountable Algorithms, 165 PENN. L. REV. 633, 656–95 (2017).

[163] Richard Berk, An Impact Assessment of Machine Learning Risk Forecasts on Parole Board Decisions and Recidivism, 13 J.EXP.CRIM. 193, 193 (2017)("Risk assessments based on machine learning forecasts can improve parole release decisions, especially when distinctions are made between re-arrests for violent and nonviolent crime."). Chris Stewart, Hey Watson: Local Judge First to Use IBM's Artificial Intelligence on Juvenile Cases, MY DAYTON DAILY NEWS (Aug. 3, 2017), https://perma.cc/9TAN-4FM3 (quoting a local judge as celebrating use of AI to enhance efficiency and to "standardize best practices, which are not currently uniform").

[164] Andrew D. Selbst & Solon Barocas, The Intuitive Appeal of Explainable Machines, 87 FORDHAM L. REV. 1085 (2018) (discussing inscrutability and nonintuitiveness in algorithmic decision-making systems).

indicative of actual human decision-making. Moreover, it is argued that technical interpretability alone would not suffice to overcome incomprehensibility concerns and even if it becomes technologically possible to make AI adjudication interpretable, the information that corporations use remains proprietary.[165] Further than, even if the AI becomes interpretable, and even if it is not within the control of a private actor, it remains possibly unavailable to members of the public without a technical background. Again, the incomprehensibility of an AAI adjudicator presents legitimacy or fairness problems for people who are the subjects of AI adjudication because when someone is on the receiving end of the state's monopoly of coercive force, principles of due process imply that the person is permitted some understanding of what is taking place, and not only for the rationale of contesting adverse decisions.

It has to be taken into account that codified justice via AAI adjudication's operation has to be comprehensible not only to the lay people being judged, but also to legal and technical experts and not incomprehensible. Moreover, AI adjudicators might be less able to foster their own legitimacy, as compared to human adjudicators because human judges often win the respect of litigants by acknowledging that the losing party's views have some force, which will be applied to robo-judges[166] as well.

AI adjudication pledges substantial gains in efficiency along with augmented uniformity that promises to root out human bias and arbitrariness requiring objective data and adapting legal systems to incorporate this information, "datafication," or emphasis on available data and its uses, might unfortunately affect the legal system's operation due to biased data.[167] Also, AI adjudication is implemented via technology developed by private companies promoting the mechanized alternatives linked to codified justice.[168]

Discouraging human judging erodes confidence in the legal system's legitimacy and so escalating use of AI adjudication prompts people to look more skeptically at human judging which means that human decision-making will be criticized and AI adjudicators will increasingly make the key decisions. To that extent, there are declining numbers of political figures appointed to the US Supreme Court, denoting

---

[165] Peña-Rodriguez v. Colorado, 137 S. Ct. 855 (2017) (providing a limited exception to the "black box" of the criminal jury in cases of alleged racial bias).

[166] Ric Simmons, Big Data, Machine Judges, and the Legitimacy of the Criminal Justice System, 52 U.C. DAVIS L. REV. 1067, 1067–68 (2018) (reporting on an empirical study that suggests ways of making people more likely to perceive algorithmic justice as legitimate).

[167] Dorothy E. Roberts, Book Review, Digitizing the Carceral State, 132 HARV. L. REV. 1695, 1708 (2019) (characterizing algorithmic decision-making as "[i]nequality in, inequality out").

[168] Elizabeth E. Joh, The Undue Influence of Surveillance Companies on Policing, 91 N.Y. U. L. REV. 101, 102 (2017) ("Through different mechanisms intended to promote their own interests and profits, these [surveillance-technology producing] companies exert control over the police long after their products have been adopted. Private surveillance technology companies wield an undue influence over public police today in ways that aren't widely acknowledged, but have enormous consequences for civil liberties and police oversight.").

a turn toward greater legalistic technocracy[169] and so expanding use of AI adjudication promotes a more intensive technocratic turn due to the fact that human judges are becoming ministerial support staff.

It is worth noting that even now judges more rarely exercise equitable discretion, and more frequently rely on codified legal rules and standardized norms. It has to be taken into account that if judges are regarded as functionaries subordinate to the legislature, AI adjudication will have a smaller impact on the balance of power between branches of government, as well as a reduced influence on the prestige of the judiciary and its human participants.

It could be said that as AI adjudicators play a larger role in the legal system, human participation will alter and decline raising the likelihood of alienation and so people will cease contributing to the legal system giving place to a fully autonomous legal system that operated without any human involvement whatsoever.[170]

Thus, AAI robo-judges will be capable of accomplishing many discrete tasks currently assigned to human lawyers, judges, and juries, such as making legal arguments, ascertaining the credibility of witnesses, and setting the form and severity of punishment and so all tasks needed in litigation will be performed by robo-judges generating a codified system that is controlled, understood, and participated in by computer scientists, corporations, and other technically sophisticated players.

It is argued that alienation will erode the legal system's normative legitimacy by generating several practical concerns and so important aspects of social life will be left without appropriate public participation and oversight which means that existing modes of civic duty and public accountability will be eradicated.[171]

It has to be taken into consideration that AI adjudication's appeal cannot be unravelled from central questions of justice and the state's duty to preserve the legitimacy of the justice system due to the fact that both equitable justice and codified justice have virtue, and the law has positioned the two in a desirable balance.[172] On the other hand, AAI robo-justice distinctive features, including its promotion to codified justice, will move the legal system toward a more desirable new equilibrium in which more effective and uniform justice will tackle human limitations and biases leading to an objective justice.

It could be said that expanding use of AI adjudication will primarily alter practical capabilities, institutional incentives, and, eventually, power relationships resulting in the ascendance of values linked with codified justice and so advancing further use of

[169] Albert R. Hunt, The Supreme Court Could Use a Few Good Politicians, Bloomberg News (July 18, 2018), https://perma.cc/Z3UD-NAA9

[170] Lawrence B. Solum, Artificially Intelligent Law, 1 BIOLAW J. 53 (2019).

[171] Lawrence B. Solum, Procedural Justice, 78 S. CALIF. L. REV. 181, 275–81 (2004) ("the participation that is essential for legitimacy").

[172] Aziz Z. Huq, Racial Equity in Algorithmic Criminal Justice, 68 DUKE L.J. 1043, 1061 (2019) (discussing "substantial residual discretion" that remains "even when a written protocol is used" and noting that "[a]lgorithmic criminal justice represents a categorical rejection of . . . ad hoc, situated judgments as an instrument of regulations").

AI adjudication generates a self-reinforcing cycle that presents concerns relating to incomprehensibility, datafication, disillusionment, and alienation.

Moreover, AI influences human decision-making, both individual and social and so expanding AI adjudication portrayed by codified justice is not an inevitable endpoint but preferred values in particular contexts are preserved or even tolerate their better realization.[173] To that extent, AI's impact on values will be even greater in executive bureaucracies and administrative agencies due to the fact that codified justice becomes preeminent in the judiciary.

10.12 AI in Justice and Politics

Autonomy means that an AI system is performing assignments in complex environments without constant guidance by a user and adaptivity means that an AI system is advancing its performance by learning from experience.

It is characteristic that the government use artificial intelligence-based programs to take decisions and advance their business strategies not mentioning that AI systems are already used to predict court decisions and other AI systems are used in courts to administer files, support judges which mean that AAI technology will be used in replacing judges and courts.

It has to be taken into account that AI is used in the court when AI is used by parties or the court administration, and AI can be utilized as the court which means that AI can support or replace judges. Moreover, artificial intelligence is entering courts all over the globe at a rapid pace and in some courts in China visitors are greeted by a robot already offering legal assistance and legal advice for free. All together the Beijing Internet Court offers an online litigation service that is fully automated.

In Europe, the Estonian government develops artificial intelligence to replace judges for small claim procedures. In the USA, judges use algorithms referred to as the Public Safety Assessment (PSA), which supports them in deciding bail terms for defendants. Moreover, the PSA is an automated system analyzing a large quantity of statistical data to deliver objective information to the judge on the safety of the person and the amount of bail to set. Which is the influence of machines on the judicial process?

It is obvious that intelligent machines are replacing large proportions of the workforce and presently many courts have been using advanced software and

---

[173] Cary Coglianese & David Lehr, Regulating by Robot: Administrative Decision Making in the Machine-Learning Era, 105 GEO.L.J. 1147, 1184–91 (2017); William Boyd, Environmental Law, Big Data, and the Torrent of Singularities, 64 UCLA L. REV. DISCOURSE 544, 546–47 (2016). Ashley Deeks, Predicting Enemies, 104 VA.L.REV. 1529 (2018) (discussing the effects of military use of algorithmic prediction and noting transparency and other concerns).

machines for years, while more and more countries start investigating the likely advantages that the use of intelligent machines in courts might have.[174]

The application of AI in courts brings a reduction of procedural time, faster decisions, less expensive procedures, and a general improvement to access to justice. Moreover, AI offers the judiciary better insight in valuable data it possesses, but to which it does not always have access. Furthermore, in jurisdictions that struggle with corruption AI in courts will be valuable in the fight against corruption by advancing the judicial independence and impartiality. Nevertheless, any application of AI in courtrooms comes with challenges and concerns regarding whether the application of AI in courts will harm human rights, like the right to a fair trial and access to justice.

Courts make use of case management systems that employ AI to more efficiently process cases and so advancing communication speed between court actors, progress case tracking, deliver digital support to cases and better organize court resources. Moreover, the application of case management systems permits court administration to collect detailed data on cases and individual judges, lawyers, and parties, which will be utilized by the court, the government, the parliament, and other public agencies to enhance policies, performance, or legislation.

Furthermore, the application of AI in court administration combined with legal bots utilized to assist litigants to file a case in court, or to check whether the documents submitted to the court are relevant has positive consequences on the access of justice and the fairness of the procedure and so protecting human rights. Moreover, the key matter concerning the application of AI in court management is the influence it has on performance pressure on judges and court administration, asking from them high speed and quality at the same time. The lack of transparency does not only trigger troubles for judges, but also directly affects the litigants due to the inability to understand the algorithms behind the AI prevent litigants from apprehending the actions or omissions of the other party.

It has to be taken into account that AI in the court refers to AI systems that support judges in their judicial capacity by aiding judges with organizing and selecting relevant jurisprudence, to detect patterns in jurisprudence, to help in underlining arguments raised by the parties, or generate arguments to be used in the court decision. To that extent, AI is used by courts to help judges calculate the risk of recidivism of defendants in criminal courts.

The future usage of AI will be its utilization as court or judge. Thus, AI as court concerns to situations in which AI is taking the initial court decision. The Estonian government is developing an AI that decides cases with little or no human intervention and so AI serves as the judge surpassing in speed and handling routine cases. Furthermore, by granting the simple repetitive assignments to machines, the judges would have more time to cope with the more crucial and complex issues. Nonetheless, AI serving as a judge in all cases is probably still far away due to technical

[174] Lord Chief Justice sets up advisory group on Artificial Intelligence. Retrieved from https://www.judiciary.uk/announcements/lord-chief-justice-sets-up-advisorygroup-on-artificial-intelligence/

issues but AAI will serve as a judge in all cases needing legal adaptations, political will, social acceptance, and perhaps ethical and philosophical considerations.

The application of international law by international courts also plays an important role in promoting the goals of the international regimes under which they operate. On the other hand, this has to be made not against principles of law and the rule of law. It has to be taken into consideration that while international courts do not serve as a direct extension of international politics, they do interact with their political environment, and depend in significant manners on the support of political players. On the other hand, international courts should not act in any political context which means that they have to maintain the distinction between law and politics. Besides, current practice shows a political dependence of courts in important cases which means a political approach of law generating a political rule of law and not following the legal rule of law and merely in some politically neutral matters follow the legal rule of law. Hence, it seems that international institutions and international courts are more political or politicized[175] entities rather than entirely legally important tools on hands of the international society.

While it is vital to separate between law and politics, there are unavoidable points of contact between the two domains. It is worth noting that judicial bodies are not always unmindful to political considerations of power and interest, and political bodies do not disregard legal considerations and function under conditions of legally compelled power and authority.[176] Moreover, international courts should take cognizance of certain political considerations but as long as the political considerations aid the application of the rule of law and not generating political rule of law.

Will AAI technology eliminate all the political cons taking place in international courts and organizations? Will AAI bring perfection in the applicability of the rule of law? AAI systems as neutrally acting means will implement law in a codified standardized way to the advantage of parties establishing a justice system working for the perfection of the rule of law. On the other hand, it cannot be rejected in advance the possibility of having AAI systems to impose AAI political notions to the detriment of law in an analogous to current traditional human way of applying the rule of law. Will AAI humanoid robots have an AAI consciousness act differently than human beings? It is supposed that AAI humanoid robots will act objectively under the singularity of the codified law. Otherwise, it is possible to have the same cons taking place in human society in an AAI society under the AAI entities since

---

[175]US State Department, Secretary Michael R. Pompeo's Remarks to the Press, 17 March 2020, https://www.state.gov/secretary-michael-r-pompeo-remarks-to-the-press-6/ ("Turning to the ICC, a so-called court which is revealing itself to be a nakedly political body: As I said the last time I stood before you, we oppose any effort by the ICC to exercise jurisdiction over U.S. personnel. We will not tolerate its inappropriate and unjust attempts to investigate or prosecute Americans. When our personnel are accused of a crime, they face justice in our country").

[176]Robert E. Goodin, The State of the Discipline, The Discipline of the State, in The Oxford Handbook of Political Science (Robert E. Goodin ed., 2009) 5 ("politics is the constrained use of social power"). Ran Hirschl, The Judicialization of Politics, in The Oxford Handbook of Political Science, (Robert E. Goodin ed., 2009) at pp. 253, 254–255.

the AAI consciousness is not certain that will act in a totally objective way not influenced by any interests of an AAI elite.

Are international courts' legitimacy and effectiveness recognized by politics or the rule of law? It has to be taken into consideration that the occurrence of politics in the life of international courts is demonstrated by acceptance of jurisdiction, political support for judicial operations, and enforcement of judgments. Nevertheless, international courts publicly overlook or downplay their interaction with the political world with the purpose of protecting their legitimacy, which hinges on them being recognized as functioning on the basis of legal, and not political, considerations. To that extent, international courts distance themselves from the fluctuations of international politics, since engaging in politics harms their reputation, but also introduces tension and conflict into their day-to-day operations.

Due to the environment of operating international courts cannot ignore certain aspects of the political context in which they activate, since doing so will result in adverse effects for their legitimacy and effectiveness. Hence, international courts have no choice but to take cognizance of their political environment, since political interests affect their legitimacy and effectiveness which means that international courts must endorse legal norms, while keeping an open eye on the political context in which they function.[177]

10.13 The New EU Legislation on Artificial Intelligence

AI denotes to a software program or machine carrying out tasks in a human-like manner, making independent conclusions and decisions and so an AI application is "trained" to carry out its tasks by utilizing machine learning and large amounts of data.[178] While AI is altering society, many legal issues linked to AI have not been systematically resolved. To that extent, AI-associated harm does not essentially differ from other harm so much that it would directly rationalize totally new and complete "AI-liability legislation" from the viewpoint of the substance of the law. Are the existing legal rules on damages liability adequate for resolving cases involving AI? Schütte et al.[179] argue that "While existing national laws on damages liability can be applied to AI-related harm, the risk exists that case outcomes are unpredictable and divergent, or, in some instances, unjust. The envisioned level playing field throughout the Single Market justifies harmonisation of many aspects of damages liability for AI-related harm."

---

[177] Ran Hirschl, The Judicialization of Politics, in The Oxford Handbook of Political Science (Robert E. Goodin ed., 2011).

[178] Gerhard Wagner, 'Robot Liability' in Sebastian Lohsse, Rainer Schulze and Dirk Staudenmayer (eds), Liability for Artificial Intelligence and the Internet of Things (Hart 2019) 27–28.

[179] Béatrice Schütte, Lotta Majewski, Katri Havu, Damages Liability for Harm Caused by Artificial Intelligence – EU Law in Flux, Legal Studies Research Paper Series Paper No 69 University Of Helsinki *P1*.

A clear and coherent EU civil liability regime for AI has the prospective to diminish risks and increase safety, decrease legal uncertainty and related legal and litigation costs, and boost consumer rights and trust. Member States have not yet implemented specific legislation linked to the regulation of liability for AI, with some exceptions connected to drones, autonomous vehicles, and medical AI applications.

It has to be taken into consideration that while the EU still lacks comprehensive law on AI-related private liability and allocation of risk, Member States generate their own liability rules and make decisions in terms of how the involvement of AI is taken into consideration in applying existing law to court cases. In line, the German Bundestag embraced amendments to the Road Traffic Act relating to automated driving and the introduction of autonomous vehicles in road traffic will not lead to changes in related liability law.[180] In addition, the current approach in the Estonian Traffic Act is that strict liability is applied to damage triggered by autonomous vehicles not needing a refit of the LOA regime.[181]

Nowadays, many smart products and services offered to consumers are AI-based, e.g., self-driving cars, vacuum cleaners, surveillance equipment, health apps, voice assistants, and translation apps. Moreover, algorithmic decision-making procedures are by no means neutral, but can maintain and even aggravate human bias in many ways due to data mining and training. It seems that neither EU anti-discrimination law nor EU data protection law tackles this problem.

It has to be taken into account that the CJEU appears to be slowly recognizing private standardization bodies mandated as de facto NLF rule-makers cannot be free from judicial scrutiny[182] but the Court did not follow the AG exactly, who was firmer in her reasoning that the reason to expand jurisdiction was to avoid the consequences of de facto transfer of public rule-making competence to private bodies.[183]

There are no special rules for AI systems and smart robotics but special regulation occurs for self-driving vehicles, drones, and high-frequency trading. Furthermore, in the European Union, GDPR encompasses provisions for fully automated decisions and so Article 22 forbids fully automated decisions; for those decisions. In line, Article 13 (2) and Article 14 (2) establish a particular obligation for data controllers to offer information but these provisions have a restricted scope of application for the reason that they only apply to decisions "based solely on automated processing" of data. Meanwhile, under the current AI technology most algorithmically prepared

---

[180] Michael Burmann, Rainer Heß, Kathrin Hühnermann and Jürgen Jahnke, Straßenverkehrsrecht (C.H. Beck 2020) Wissenschaftliche Dienste des Deutschen Bundestages 'Autonomes und automatisiertes Fahren auf der Straße – rechtlicher Rahmen'(2018) Ausarbeitung WD 7–3000 -111/18 4.

[181] Estonian Law of Obligations Act (LOA) Janno Lahe and Taivo Liivak, 'Strict liability for damage caused by self-driving vehicles: the Estonian perspective' (2019) 12(2) Baltic Journal of Law & Politics 1, 6.

[182] Case C-171/11 Fra.bo ECLI:EU:C:2012:453.

[183] Case C-171/11 Fra.bo ECLI:EU:C:2012:176 (Opinion of Advocate General Trstenjak) [49].

decisions still encompass a human being and so the majority of ADM procedures are not covered by the aforementioned provisions.[184] Also, the EU Consumer Rights Directive[185] embraces an obligation to make available information on the use of automatically generated personalized prices and so the Platform-to-business Regulation 2019/1150 forces providers of online search engines to "set out the main parameters, which individually or collectively are most significant in determining ranking and the relative importance of those main parameters, by providing an easily and publicly available description."[186] It is worth mentioning here that some countries have published rules for automated algorithm-based administrative decisions, such as Canada with its "Directive on Automated Decision-Making"[187] and, the Digital Republic Act[188] in France specifies that, in the case of state actors taking a decision "on the basis of algorithms," individuals have a right to be informed about the "principal characteristics" of the decision-making system.

The Commission deems it needed to make the policy decisions regarding novel technologies at the EU[189] level by generating an ecosystem of excellence and trust with regard to AI. It has to be taken into account that future rules about liability for AI-related harm have to cover both products and services. Moreover, the Commission asserts that obligations and responsibility linked to the utilization of AI should be placed on the actor most able to control a particular risk. Also, it is believed vital that providers of AI products in the EU are subject to its regulatory framework, irrespective of where the operator is established.

The new Directives on Digital Contracts, the Digital Content and Services Directive (DCSD) 2019/770 and the Sale of Goods Directive (SGD) 2019/771 are often seen as important steps in adapting European private law to the requirements of the digital economy. Nonetheless, neither directive contains special rules for new technologies such as AI. Also, in line with the principle of technology neutrality, neither directive encompasses tailored rules for specific digital technologies. In its place, both directives are generalized to "any contract where the trader supplies or undertakes to supply digital content or a digital service to the consumer" or to "sales

---

[184] Martini M (2019) Fundamentals of a regulatory system for algorithm-based processes. https://www.vzbv.de/sites/default/files/downloads/2019/07/19/martini_regulatory_system_algorithm_based_processes.pdf

[185] According to Art 6(1) Consumer Rights Directive 2011/83/EU as amended by Directive 2019/2161/EU, the trader may have to inform the consumer "that the price has been personalized on the basis of an automated decision-making process."

[186] Article 5(2) Regulation 2019/1150 on promoting fairness and transparency for business users of online intermediation services (P2B Regulation), OJ L 186, 11 July 2019.

[187] Government of Canada, 'Directive on Automated Decision-Making', https://www.tbs-sct.gc.ca/pol/doc-eng.aspx?id=32592

[188] Loi no. 2016–1321 du 7 octobre 2016 pour une République numérique, Edwards L, Veale M (2018) Enslaving the algorithm: from a "right to an explanation" to a "right to better decisions"? IEEE Security & Privacy, May/June 46.

[189] European Commission, 'On Artificial Intelligence – A European Approach to excellence and trust' COM (2020) 65 final (White Paper).

contracts between a consumer and a seller" including "goods with digital elements." Hence, new technologies such as AI are not subject to any special rules.

Accordingly, both the DCSD 2019/770 and the SGD 2019/771 clarify that platform provider are to be considered as sellers or traders only if they act "as the direct contractual partner of the consumer" which means that apps based on AI systems are offered by an operator of a platform which certifies and controls the apps, or a platform offers consumers directly "AI as a Service." On the other hand, if a platform acts as a simple intermediary, there is no obligation under EU law to apply the provisions of the directives to them. Nonetheless, according to the recitals of the directives, even in this case Member States are free to extend the directives' rules to these platform providers.

It has to be taken into account that the new directives oblige the business to comply both with subjective as well as objective conformity criteria. When digital goods, content, or services are based on AI systems, the question arises as to which features, qualities, and performance these systems must abide by in order to meet the objective criteria for conformity. By the way, Article 8(1) DCSD 2019/770 and Article 7(1) SGD 2019/771 contain a list of different objective conformity criteria, starting with the well-known "fit-for-purpose test," followed in Article 8(1) (b) DCSD 2019/770 by a list of other objective conformity elements such as functionality, compatibility, accessibility, and security the consumer can reasonably expect. In fact, directive (EU) 2019/770 introduces rules terminating online discrimination on the basis of nationality or place of residence.[190] Presently, there are neither legal rules specifically designed for AI systems nor international or national technical standards in that field.

Existing European legislative and policy efforts seek to develop an AI ecosystem that will allow citizens, businesses, and services of public interest to reap the benefits of AI such as improved health care, optimize services, and reduce the costs of public services that weigh on governments' budgets. The Digital Markets Act ("DMA[191]") improve "fairness" and "contestability" in the digital sector covering eight types of core platform services: online intermediation services embracing software application stores, online search engines, social networking, video sharing platform services, number independent interpersonal electronic communications services, operating systems, cloud services, and advertising services.

The DMA is essentially a sector-specific competition law pursuing objectives similar to European or national competition laws. Moreover, the DMA represents an expansion of the administrative State and a limitation of the free enterprise system and so the DMA purports to promote "fairness" and "contestability."

---

[190] DIRECTIVE (EU) 2019/770 OF THE EUROPEAN PARLIAMENT AND OF THE COUNCIL of 20 May 2019 on certain aspects concerning contracts for the supply of digital content and digital services L 136/1/22.5.2019.

[191] Proposal for a Regulation of the European Parliament and of the Council on contestable and fair markets in the digital sector (Digital Markets Act) COM/2020/842 final.

Platforms must in effect relinquish proprietary control of resources, assets, and capabilities so as to assist companies with whom they compete or not, and this in an indefinite set of markets. In addition, the DMA enacts a law of gatekeeping concentrated on the distribution layer of the Internet covering enterprises that control business users' access to demand, and end users' access to supply. Hence, the DMA gives the European Commission authority to "designate" digital platforms for immediate application of command and control "obligations."

First of all, the EU's strategy concerning AI is outlined in terms of investment, development, and use and so the development of military AI is absent from the EU's strategy, and in fact is explicitly excluded from the White Paper, with the Commission employing a greater emphasis on fostering international dialogue.[192] Moreover, the Parliament advocated that the EU should take a leading role in developing an international governance framework.[193] In addition, the EU's strategy is a proactive effort to further cooperation and so at the EU level, efforts are emerging in ascertaining collaboration with NATO on the use of AI capabilities for defense reasons.[194] It could be said that collaboration on AI will enhance security and prosperity on both sides of the Atlantic.

The Safety and Liability Report[195] documents that AI, the Internet of Things (IoT), and robotics share several properties, such as the capacity to merge connectivity, autonomy, and data dependency in accomplishing duties with little to no human intervention. When AI systems are part of complex IoT environments is difficult or even unfeasible to identify the origin of damage and so the person responsible for it which means that a harm-sufferer is powerless to prove the required conditions for a successful damage claim. The proposal[196] generates a two-fold liability regime consisting of "high-risk" AI systems and "other" AI systems. An autonomously functioning AI system is judged high risk where it has substantial prospective to produce harm or damage to one or more persons in a way that is random and goes beyond what can rationally be anticipated embracing AI such as self-driving vehicles and autonomous robots. Most significantly, operators of "high-risk" AI systems under this proposed Regulation will be strictly liable for any harm or damage triggered by an activity, device, or process driven by that AI system.

---

[192] European Commission. (2018, April 25). Communication Artificial Intelligence for Europe [Text]. https://ec.europa.eu/digital-single-market/en/news/communication-artificialintelligence-europe

[193] European Parliament. (2020, October 12). Artificial Intelligence: Guidelines for military and non-military use. https://www.europarl.europa.eu/news/en/pressroom/20201209IPR93411/artificial-intelligence-guidelines-for-military-and-non-militaryuse

[194] NATO. http://www.nato.int/cps/en/natohq/news_179231.htm

[195] 'Report on the safety and liability implications of AI, the Internet of Things and Robotics' COM (2020) 64 final, (Safety and Liability Report).

[196] European Parliament resolution of 20 October 2020 with recommendations to the Commission on a civil liability regime for artificial intelligence (2020/2014(INL)).

The European Parliament has published several documents regarding AI[197] deeming the existing fault liability regimes of the Member States sufficient and so setting out the liability of the operator of an AI application is dominant to the proposal which means that the EP pronounced that national fault-based liability rules already tender adequate protection in cases where a third person interferes. Moreover, the concept of "operator" is to be understood broadly and so if there is more than one operator, all of them will be jointly and individually liable. In addition, the Draft Report also proposes a strict liability regime for high-risk AI systems. To that extent, the EP JURI study asserts that regulation of technology should be minimally interfering and liability should be placed upon the party who is in control of risks and in the best position to manage risk.[198] However, all three Resolutions are also resistant on not providing AI software systems with legal personality.

Is human conscience a prerequisite for legal personality? Human conscience is not a prerequisite for legal personality. Does liability is enhanced via granting legal personality to AI? It could be said that liability is augmented, not reduced, via granting legal personality to AI for the reason that AI will infiltrate all of human activity, indistinguishable from any technology and embedded in all daily decision-making systems, it will be impossible to trace back definite harmful actions of AI to a certain "*someone*." Hence, only by granting legal personality to AI affirm that this will be an identifiable entity, rather than a string of opaque MNEs hiding behind multifaceted licensing and development agreements.

It is worth noting that the Parliament is inflexible that "any required changes in the existing legal framework should start with the clarification that AI-systems have neither legal personality nor human conscience" (Civil Liability Resolution, Annex, (6)). Is human conscience connected with legal personality? Human conscience is not connected with legal personality because legal persons (corporations, organizations, associations, etc.) evidently lack "human conscience" but they are granted with legal personality anyway. While AI will acquire human conscience, act autonomously, or develop any other human trait imaginable, granting legal personality to AI in similar terms to that of legal persons as is the case at the moment with humans running corporations, it will be again humans running AI. On the other hand, Zekos argues that AAI entities/humanoid robots must get legal status as humans as long as society is run by humans and in the future AAI society, AAI entities will have the AAI legal status and legal personality assigning full rights and duties and so humans future seems uncertain at the time that AAI entities will run their society. Attributing

[197] EP, 'Draft report with recommendations to the Commission on a civil liability regime for artificial intelligence' 2020/2014(INL) (Draft Report). Resolution 2020/2012(INL) on a Framework of Ethical Aspects of Artificial Intelligence, Robotics and related Technologies (the "AI Ethical Aspects Resolution"), Resolution 2020/2015(INI) on Intellectual Property Rights for the development of Artificial Intelligence Technologies (the "IPR for AI Resolution").

[198] Andrea Bertolini, 'Artificial Intelligence and Civil Liability' (European Union 2020) (EP JURI Study).

legal personality to AAI systems denotes the applicability of an analogous to human's system of liability taking into account the individuality of AI.

It is characteristic that the Parliament in its IPR for AI Resolution when faced with the important issue of AI intellectual property creation and whether ownership of intellectual property rights can be granted to AI, recommends that AI shall not be awarded legal personality because it would reduce "*incentives for human creators*."[199] Thus, parliament opted for not granting legal personality to AI simply in order to protect the professional rights of human creators. On the other hand, in an AAI society, AAI entities will be autonomous to create AAI products and services are not imagined by humans and so the attribution of AAI IPRs is one-way road.

The Commission's proposal of new Union legislation to regulate AI marks the beginning of the legislative process.[200] The proposal provides a detailed and balanced risk-based approach to the regulation of new technologies, with particular attention paid to the liability regime of the subject involved in the whole value chain. AIA[201] lays down harmonized rules for the advancement, placement on the market and use of AI systems which vary by characteristic and risk, embracing prohibitions and a conformity assessment system reformed from EU product safety law. Moreover, AIA is a regulation based on Article 114 of the Treaty on the Functioning of the European Union (TFEU), which concerns the approximation of laws to advance the functioning of the internal market. In addition, much of the AIA's wording is drawn from a 2008 Decision establishing a framework for certain regulations concerning product safety, used in a wide array of subsequent legislation.[202] It is characteristic that in AIA,[203] the Commission certifies a high level of protection of fundamental rights while pursuing four main goals, namely (1) to make certain that AI systems are safe and respect Union values and fundamental rights, (2) to guarantee legal certainty, (3) to improve governance and effective enforcement, and to (4) enable the development of a Single Market for lawful, safe and reliable AI. Moreover, there is well-defined focus on procedural and administrative matters, such as the establishment of supervisory bodies or the laying down of duties to be held by different players in value chains. It seems that the Commission no longer relies on open

---

[199] Resolution 2020/2015(INI) on Intellectual Property Rights for the development of Artificial Intelligence Technologies (the "IPR for AI Resolution").

[200] Proposal for a Regulation of the European Parliament and of the Council Laying Down Harmonised Rules on Artificial Intelligence (Artificial Intelligence Act) and Amending Certain Union Legislative Acts, COM(2021) 206 final, 21 April 2021, https://digital-strategy.ec.europa.eu/en/library/proposal-regulationeuropean-approach-artificial-intelligen

[201] (COM(2021) 206 final).

[202] Decision No 768/2008/EC of the European Parliament and of the Council of 9 July 2008 on a common framework for the marketing of products, and repealing Council Decision 93/465/EEC, OJ L 218/82.

[203] European Commission Proposal for a Regulation of the European Parliament and of the Council laying down harmonised Rules on Artificial Intelligence (Artificial Intelligence Act) 2021/0106 (COD) Articles 16–29, 30–39, 56–59 https://eur-lex.europa.eu/legal-content/EN/TXT/?uri=CELEX:52021PC0206

criteria to outline high-risk items by presenting an exhaustive list of high-risk AI systems.[204]

The proposed regulation bans certain uses of AI such as the use of AI: firstly, to materially distort a person's behavior; secondly to exploit the vulnerabilities of a specific group of persons; thirdly, public social scoring and fourthly, for real-time remote biometric identification in public places. It could be said that the development of AI in the EU has to be sound, legally acceptable, socially equitable, and environmentally sustainable which means that AI has to support the economy, society, and the environment. On the other hand, the ban is restricted to the use of current AI not preventing the development of AAI.

It has to be taken into account that the material distortion of behavior and the exploitation of vulnerabilities are only prohibited, if they causally influence a human person's physical or psychological harm, or if they are expected to do so.[205]

On top of the categorization into banned uses of AI, high-risk, and low-risk AI, the scope of the proposed regulation approves the expansive approach to the geographical scope which has been characteristic of the GDPR. Expressly, the proposed regulation not only applies when providers established outside of the Union bring AI into circulation in the Union but also when output generated by an AI is used in the Union, even if all other relevant facts such as providers and users are limited to third countries. Moreover, providers established outside of the Union must appoint an authorized representative in the Union for rationales of compliance with the regulation. Furthermore, the categories of AI in the proposed regulation do not cover all AI applications and so AI used solely for military purposes, embracing autonomous weapons systems, is also excluded from the scope of the proposed regulation.

First of all, the AI proposal[206] is a "regulation," and so, like the GDPR, it will enter into force on a set date in all Member States, and it will have binding legal force throughout the EU. Moreover, AI provisions conferring rights upon people and having a sufficiently clear, precise, and unconditional content will have a direct effect which means that natural or legal persons will have the prospect to invoke those rights before national courts and tribunals. Furthermore, AI firms and merchants will have to deal with the EU, not with individual Member States, when they

---

[204] Article 6 and Annex III to the Commission draft legislation concerning the utilization of AI.

[205] Article 5(1)(a)-(d) proposed regulation.

[206] Artificial Intelligence Act. (21 April 2021). "Proposal for a regulation of the European Parliament and the Council laying down harmonised rules on Artificial Intelligence (Artificial Intelligence Act) and amending certain Union legislative acts." EUR-Lex - 52021PC0206 https://eurlex.europa.eu/legalcontent/EN/TXT/?uri=CELLAR:e0649735-a372-11eb-9585-01aa75ed71a1 Digital Services Act. (15 December 2020). Proposal for a regulation of the European Parliament and the Council on a Single Market For Digital Services (Digital Services Act) and amending Directive 2000/31/EC. EUR-Lex - 52020PC0825 https://eur-lex.europa.eu/legal-content/EN/ALL/?uri=CELEX:52020PC0825. European Commission. (19 February 2020). White Paper on AI - A European approach to excellence and trust. https://ec.europa.eu/info/sites/default/fles/commission-white-paper-artificial-intelligencefeb2020_en

will have to evidence that they abide by the new legislation.[207] It is worth noting that the AI proposal regard its approach as "human-centric" by placing humanity at the center of technological advancement. On the one hand, current AI technology is at the service of humanity "anthropocentric," its values, and needs. On the other hand, AAI technology implemented by AAI entities being humanoid robots in an established AAI society will have a humanoid robots approach being at the service of a mechanical society and so serving the robots' values and needs which means that a robo-centric approach will be imposed.

It is characteristic that the AI proposal treats AI as a technology for solving problems and performing tasks excluding the prospect of assigning to AI systems any status as a legal person, with rights and duties, such as the likelihood of owning property, entering into contracts, suing and being sued, and so forth and so the responsibility/accountability of any AI system rests fully with the people who design, manufacture, market, and use it.

It is worth noting that the EU Artificial Intelligence Act (AIA) is one of the first laws globally to regulate the use of artificial intelligence. The "AIA" is a regulation based on Article 114 of the Treaty on the Functioning of the European Union (TFEU), which concerns the approximation of laws to improve the functioning of the internal market. AIA is a cross-sectoral regulation of AI tackling predominantly governance requirements around so-called high-risk AI systems by advocating the adoption of principles in the spirit of generating trustworthy AI. The proposal aims to develop an "ecosystem of trust" by setting out a legal framework for trustworthy AI with "human centric" rules for AI. The AIA prohibits the sale or use of AI systems (1) used by or on behalf of public authorities, (2) to generate "trustworthiness" scores, and that (3) lead to either unfounded or unbalanced treatment of individuals or groups, or unfavorable treatment which, while justifiable and proportionate, takes place in an unrelated 'context' from the input data. Moreover, the AIA has direct legal significance for privacy and data protection by firstly applying to situations wherever "personal data" is used in AI systems posing unacceptable risks and so imposing obligations going beyond those in the GDPR which means that controllers or processors under the GDPR will have extra obligations imposed on them; secondly, AIA will apply to the use of data which is not "personal data" but where such use has aftereffects for individuals based on their individual characteristics. It has to be taken into account that outside the EU, AIA will influence privacy protection for the reason that both the GDPR and the AIA have extraterritorial scope, but each has different principles for extraterritoriality.[208] It is worth mentioning here

---

[207] https://www.datamation.com/artificial-intelligence/ai-companies/

[208] Anu Bradford The Brussels Effect: How the European Union Rules the World (OUP, 2020); https://www.brusselseffect.com/ Graham Greenleaf, The 'Brussels effect' of the EU's 'AI Act'.

on data privacy outside Europe, UNSW Sydney (2021) 171 Privacy Laws & Business International Report 1, 3–7 https://ssrn.com/abstract=3898904

that existing data privacy laws outside Europe are already starting to be enforced against misuses of AI systems.[209]

It has to be taken into account that attention has been paid to the prospective for AI systems to facilitate indirect discrimination,[210] in principle illegal under EU law but being difficult to detect this prospective unless providers know the relevant protected characteristics of affected individuals and communities. The AIA contains obligations regarding the accuracy, robustness, and cyber-security of systems themselves, with specific regard to discrimination as systems learn, and adversarial machine learning but there is no reference to leakage of training data or other personal data from models.[211]

The European standardization process reproduces European values and fundamental rights, embracing consumer protection, by granting European stakeholder organizations operative participation rights. Moreover, AIA proposal follows a risk-based approach by imposing regulatory burdens only when an AI system is posing high risks to fundamental rights and safety. Consequently, the AIA should establish legally binding obligations concerning the needed requirements for high-risk AI systems, such as what sorts of biases are forbidden; how algorithmic biases are mitigated; and what kind and degree of transparency AI systems should have.

References

1. Abbott, K. W., & Faude, B. (2020). Choosing low-cost institutions in global governance. *International Theory*, 1–30.
2. Andrew, C. (2019). Michaels, Abstract Innovation, Virtual Ideas, and Artificial Legal Thought, 14 MAR. *Journal of Business and Technology Law, 1*, 25.
3. Tutt, A. (2017). An FDA for algorithms. *Administrative Law Review, 69*, 83.
4. Aristotle. (1981). *The politics*. Penguin Books.
5. Burr, C., & Cristianini, N. (2019). Can machines read our minds? *Minds and Machines, 29*, 461.
6. Coglianese, C., & Lehr, D. (2019). Transparency and Algorithmic Governance. *Administrative Law Review, 71*(2), 1, 2.
7. Mulligan, C. (2018). Revenge against robots. *South Carolina Law Review, 69*, 579, 580.
8. Mulligan, D. K., & Bamberger, K. A. (2018). Saving governance-by-design. *California Law Review, 106*, 697, 705–714.

[209] Jasmine Park 'South Korea: The First Case Where the Personal Information Protection Act was Applied to an AI System' Future of Privacy Forum, 21 May 2021 https://fpf.org/blog/south-korea-the-first-case-where-the-personal-informationprotection-act-was-applied-to-an-ai-system/

[210] Frederik Zuiderveen Borgesius, 'Price Discrimination, Algorithmic Decision-Making, and European Non-Discrimination Law' (2020) 31 European Business Law Review 401. McKane Andrus and others, 'What We Can't Measure, We Can't Understand: Challenges to Demographic Data Procurement in the Pursuit of Fairness' in (ACM 2021) Proceedings of the 2021 ACM Conference on Fairness, Accountability, and Transparency 249.

[211] Art 15; Michael Veale and others, 'Algorithms that Remember: Model Inversion Attacks and Data Protection Law' (2018) 376 Phil Trans R Soc A 20180083.

9. Berman, E. (2018). A government of laws and not of machines. *Boston University Law Review, 98*, 1277–1280.
10. Volokh, E. (2019). Chief justice robots. *DUKE Law Journal, 68*, 1135, 1138.
11. Pasquale, F. (2019). A rule of persons, not machines: The limits of legal automation. *George Washington Law Review, 87*(1), 6.
12. IBM. (2018). *Digital transformation: Reinventing the business of government*
13. Lisa Burton Crawford. (2018). *The rule of law and the Australian constitution*
14. Lemos, M. H. (2017). Democratic enforcement? Accountability and independence for the litigation state. *CORNELL L REV., 102*, 929, 935.
15. Moore, M. (2016). *Tech Giants and Civic Power*. Centre for the Study of Media, Communication and Power (CMCP), King's College London.
16. Schramowski, P., Turan, C., Jentzsch, S., Rothkopf, C., & Kersting, K. (2020). The moral choice machine. *Frontiers in Artificial Intelligence, 3*, 36.
17. Binns, R. (2018). Algorithmic accountability and public reason. *Philosophy and Technology, 31*(4), 543–556.
18. Hirschl, R. (2011). The judicialization of politics. In R. E. Goodin (Ed.), *The Oxford handbook of political science*.
19. Re, R. M., & Solow-Niederman, A. (2019). Developing artificially intelligent justice. *Stanford Technology Law Review, 22*, 242, 247.
20. Calo, R. (2017). Artificial intelligence policy: A primer and roadmap. *U.C.D. Law Review, 51*, 399, 405.
21. Lawsky, S. B. (2017). Formalizing the code. *Tax Law Review, 70*, 377, 379.
22. Sun, T. Q., & Medaglia, R. (2019). Mapping the challenges of artificial intelligence in the public sector: Evidence from public healthcare. *Government Information Quarterly, 36*(2), 368–383.
23. Owen, T. (2019). *The case for platform governance*. Center for International Governance Innovation (CIGI).
24. King, T., et al. (2020). *Artificial intelligence crime: An interdisciplinary analysis of foreseeable threats and solutions* (Vol. 26, pp. 89–120). Science and Engineering Ethics.
25. Harari, Y. N. (2019). Who will win the race for AI?. *Foreign Policy Magazine*. Washington: Winter.

Chapter 11
Digital Politics, GDPR, and AI

11.1 AI, Data, and GDPR

Recent technological advances and digitization have underlined rapid and unprecedented evolution. Moreover, algorithmic trading has been growing progressively and machine learning is used in a range of front-office and back-office applications, most commonly in anti-money laundering, fraud detection, customer services, and marketing.[1] Moreover, AI applications are endorsed in cybersecurity, client facing chatbots, remote onboarding, and biometric customer identification which means that there is rise of datafication and exploitation of digitized data through quantitative data analytics, including AI.[2]

Data conveys noteworthy social, economic, and political power and so unequal control over data is a problem for economic development, human agency, and collective self-determination that must be tackled. Moreover, "data inequality" typically implies lack of opportunities that having access to digital data might otherwise present, such as better policy-making, scientific innovation, and improvements to economic and social conditions. The World[3] Development Report 2021 recognizes data inequality and in developing economies the unavailability of data is often because of the absence of needed infrastructures of connectivity, storage, and processing and prerequisite human labor and expertise. Angelina Fisher and Thomas

[1] European Central Bank, "Algorithmic Trading: Trends and Existing Regulation" (Media Release, 13 February 2019). Bank of England and Financial Conduct Authority, Machine Learning in UK Financial Services (Report, October 2019).

[2] UK Finance and Microsoft, Artificial Intelligence in Financial Services (Report, June 2019).

[3] World Development Report 2021: Data for Better Lives—Concept Note, World Bank, http://documents.worldbank.org/curated/en/778921588767120094/World-Development-Report-2021-Data-forBetter-Lives-Concept-Note

G. I. Zekos, *Political, Economic and Legal Effects of Artificial Intelligence*,
Contributions to Political Science, https://doi.org/10.1007/978-3-030-94736-1_11

Streinz[4] argue that "data inequality is in turn a function of unequal control over the infrastructures that generate, shape, process, store, transfer, and use data."

Furthermore, data is more than an economic resource and so a medium through which economic, social, and political life is gradually being ordered and re-ordered. Moreover, appropriate and sustainable access to data is unattainable for developing economies that lack the prerequisite data infrastructures needed to generate, store, and process data on their own terms. Individuals, communities, and societies are being deprived of capabilities and possibilities to chart their own digital destinies when those that control the means of data production also control the capacity to define, categorize, model, make visible, or render unseen identities and environments.

In the age of digitization, proliferation, and enhancement of computational power, the development of cyberspace, and the ubiquity of devices, sensors, and platforms, choices about which data is produced are gradually a function of infrastructures that allow data collection through devices, sensors, and platforms. Cyberspace has been extremely successful in facilitating data transfers across borders.[5] Moreover, the relevance of data mobility for the unbundling of economic production, generating transnational networks in which goods and services are being traded, often within companies, seems beyond doubt yet remains difficult to quantify.

AI and big data are driving economic development and social change. AI is a tool of capitalism which alters societies within an environment of technological singularity promoting the expansion of the digital model of economic development. It has to be taken into account that AI can be built on data which is not individualized, and that it does not govern by individualized nudges or micro-directives, etc., based on detailed personality profiles.[6]

AI's prospective to process data, apparently without human bias, is fundamental to its utility which means that AI treats past data with the same precision as more recent data. Besides, humans prioritize more recent data. Moreover, properly programmed AI treats all data objectively, while humans discriminate among data points founded on their experience, values, and other non-rational judgements.

Algorithmic bias and resulting issues of fairness and inequality are a problem. Likewise, algorithms, somewhat because of problems linked with the training data, could also favor specific political ideologies, and they could reinforce discriminatory and other undesirable practices. It is worth noting that any technocracy of AI must employ mechanisms of algorithmic oversight so as to tackle such problems.

---

[4] Angelina Fisher & Thomas Streinz, Confronting Data Inequality, IILJ Working Paper 2021/1 P2.

[5] Daniel Lambach, The Territorialization of Cyberspace, 22 International Studies Review 482 (2020) (describing how different actors—not just states—territorialize and reterritorialize "cyberspace").

[6] H.S. Sætra, When nudge comes to shove: liberty and nudging in the era of big data, Technol. Soc. 59 (2019) 101130.

AI by utilizing Big Data identifies patterns and correlations that cannot be detected by human cognition, converting massive volumes of data into a precise, highly data-intensive form of knowledge, and so generating a new mode of knowledge production which means that decisions are made not on the basis of the data per se, but on the basis of data analyzed algorithmically.[7] AAI systems must offer an "aura of objectivity, rationality, and legitimacy" that is derived from their mechanically objective way of functioning.

It has to be taken into account that a new "industrial" landscape appears as a result of the growth of platform-Internet firms and new technologies such as Big Data and AI which means that owing to the rise of platform-Internet firms data and information have become the new features of production and owning access to cyberspace has become the new source of power with data becoming the new form of capital and so there is a shift from physical to digital products and services. Moreover, it could be said that the non-rivalrous nature of the products, the advent of prosumers, and user generated content and free products plus alterations in the ownership of resources through the sharing economy have all caused in the arrival of a "neo-bourgeois" of platform-Internet firms and a "neoproletariat" workforce of data providers in an analogous manner that presented by Marx's labor theory. Will AAI systems alter Marx's theory and so there will be an objective equality concerning productivity and wealth? An AAI system in production is supposed to bring objectivity concerning the work of AAI entities and their payment but considering the other dimension of work and existence of AAI humanoid robots in an AAI society will eliminate the emotional Marx's theory of labor utilization by capitalists. In other words, the algorithmic AAI system will function objectively in order to achieve the best result for the system and not for owners of the system where there will have the re-emergence of the conventional system in a virtual dimension.

Furthermore, it has to be taken into consideration that a new industrial landscape of Big data is constantly produced, collected, managed, monitored, and used by firms in such a manner that has altered how economic, political, and social systems operate in the globe and so advances in AI help in accelerating such a process in which machine learning and automation augment human skills to produce more for economic growth and development. It has to be taken into consideration that AI and automation cause concerns, stretching from widespread job losses, to "the singularity" because the capacities of AI will outdo those of humans triggering ethical and legal inferences of AI denoting AI's impact in all fields such as in finance, etc.[8]

The level of AI readiness by governments and firms will have a remarkable influence upon competitiveness and will probably become a fundamental feature in investments and economic growth.[9] Hence, AI-driven industry automation in

[7] F Pasquale, The Black Box Society: The Secret Algorithms that Control Money and Information (Harvard University Press, 2015).

[8] Tom CW Lin, "Artificial Intelligence, Finance, and the Law" (2019) 88(2) Fordham Law Review 531.

[9] Digital economy report 2020, UNCTAD, 2020, https://unctad.org/en

developed countries of labor-intensive jobs will supersede customary comparative advantages of developing countries, such as cheap workforce and raw materials which means that an expanding variance in prosperity and wealth will influence those countries incapable to develop digital skills and infrastructure to reap the rewards of AI opportunities in productivity and innovation. To that extent, a new divide will emerge between AI-ready and not AI-ready.

Ethical challenges for data governance embrace consent, ownership, privacy, delegation, and responsibility.[10] It has to be taken into account that data exchanges are needed to tackle global challenges more effectively in areas where AI can play a key role such as in healthcare, quality of life, or sustainability and climate change.

It is worth noting that there are three likely results when thinking about the influence of machines on human employment. First, Robots and AI will take almost all of the works due to the fact that they are better than humans at every task; second Robots and AI take some tasks but humans will remain dominant in positions such as those that are too multipart or necessitate emotional, social, or artistic skills; or third Robots and AI take none of the jobs in the sense that while certain jobs will be abolished others will be generated at approximately the same rate.[11]

Automation by nature is more efficient than certain human jobs in terms of costs, quality, and capacity and it is intended to replace humans. Moreover, automation with the consequence of eliminating jobs, it directly erodes the right to work.[12]

Also, power and capabilities of AI make human labor outdated in the process of production, distribution, exchange, and consumption which means that AI generates the AI-capitalism being a multiplex trajectory where capitalism remains the ultimate system in which AI facilitates in producing the inhuman authority of big data which is a weapon of capital that controls the everyday lives of people being the labor force once again.[13] On the other hand, an AAI system in an AAI society inhabited by AAI entities being instruments of a virtual system will alter the conventional essence of capital and working force because due to the objectivity of the AAI systems will have objective distribution by all the members of the AAI system.

It is argued that AI and big data are control mechanisms central to the survival of capitalism as an economic, political, social, and cultural system where profit rules over people. On the other hand, the augmented availability of data and information has heightened the power of labor to challenge the inhuman laws of capitalism and

---

[10] Taddeo, M., & Floridi, L. (2018). How AI can be a force for good. Science, 361(6404), 751. LP – 752. Retrieved from http://science.sciencemag.org/content/361/6404/751.abstract

[11] Byron Reese, The Fourth Age: Smart Computers, Conscious Computers, And The Future Of Humanity 85–121 (2018).

[12] Hannah Sloan, Human Rights and IoT: The Right to Fair and Decent Work, IOT FOR ALL (Oct. 23, 2018) ("[T]he efficiencies produced by automation will result in widespread job loss. It's entirely possible that the continued growth of constantly-improving and self-maintaining machines could eliminate 99% of all jobs today."); Martin Kwan, Automation and the International Human Right to Work, 2021 https://scholarlycommons.law.emory.edu/eilr-recent-developments

[13] Dyer-Witheford, N., Kjosen, A.M., Steinhoff, J., 2019. Inhuman Power Artificial Intelligence and the Future of Capitalism. Pluto Press, London.

so cyberspace has resulted in greater transparency concerning workplace practices which means that capital is becoming more socially responsible as a result of the power of workers to disclose workplace information and experiences over social media. Furthermore, the growth of AI stimulates technological innovation, knowledge, and investment aiding economic growth and development[14] and so big data are shaping modern life, smart cities, society, and economy which means that AI promotes real life as long as it is utilized properly for the good of the system and not for the good of unknown owners of the system.

Nonetheless, the profit-driven technological singularity of AI initiates social challenges and the economic effects of AI are possibly fatal under a neoliberal economic system. To that extent, the growth of a data-driven neoliberal market led by AI rules the capitalist production practices where the accumulation involves primarily knowledge, which becomes the central source of value.

AI systems have some capacity to adapt and enhance performance over time and so AI systems differ from the application of a static and predefined categorization class or unchanging statistical function to a set of data which means that the likelihood of continuous recalibration is demonstrated by commercial applications such as Google's PageRank algorithm being subject to an iterative course of feedback and change to accommodate the changing settings and users' shifting necessities.

It could be argued that as new technologies such as the Internet of Things and edge-computing gain momentum and as data is processed on hardware devices such as smartphones, etc., instead of being transferred directly back to the servers of platform firms, this generates an opening for people to monetize their personal data for their own direct benefit so shifting the balance of power and possibly transferring control and ownership to the actual data producers. Thus, it could be said that the use of AI and AAI will return profits to labor rather than benefitting the capitalists.

Furthermore, it is argued that new decentralized autonomous organizations (DAOs) using Blockchain technologies will diminish the need for platform intermediaries by initiating an Internet of People (IOP) where individuals will have control of their personal data.[15]

Are there international perspectives on the regulation of AI? The absence of global regulation on digital data generates uncertainties linked to the legal conformity of certain activities from a business viewpoint. Additionally, the utilization of AI causes myriad issues depending on the level of needed human control over a device in conditions where: (1) The human keeps control over the device function,

---

[14]Liu, J., Chang, H., Forrest, Y.J., Yang, B., 2020. Influence of artificial intelligence on technological innovation: evidence from the panel data of China's manufacturing sectors. Technol. Forecast Soc. Change 158. Iqbal, R., Doctor, F., More, B., Mahmud, S., Yousuf, U., 2020. Big data analytics: computational intelligence techniques and application areas. Technol. Forecast. Soc. Change. Volume-153.

[15]O'hara, K., Hall, W., 2018. Four internets: the geopolitics of digital governance (CIGI Papers, 206). Conti, M., Passarella, A., Das, S.K., 2017. The Internet of People (IOP): a new wave in pervasive mobile computing. Pervasive Mob. Comput. 41, 1–27. October 2017.

which means that there is direct human control over the system; (2) The device has more autonomy but must be monitored by a human who can redirect, authorize, or disengage an explicit action which means that it is a supervised control regime; or (3) The action is carried out without human supervision.

The Commission is proposing the first ever legal framework on AI, which tackles the risks of AI in order Europe to play a leading role globally.[16] The EDPS[17] welcomes and backs the European Union's (EU) leadership aiming to make certain that AI solutions are designed according to the EU's values and legal principles. Article 3(3) of Regulation (EU) 2018/1725, processing of personal data concerns "any operation or set of operations which is performed on personal data or on sets of personal data, whether or not by automated means, such as collection, recording, organisation, structuring, storage, adaptation or alteration, retrieval, consultation, use, disclosure by transmission, dissemination or otherwise making available, alignment or combination, restriction, erasure or destruction." The Select Committee on Artificial Intelligence establishes a voluntary mechanism to inform consumers when AI is being used to make significant or sensitive decisions.[18]

Data protection and privacy law and intellectual property law regard data as a regulatory object, focusing mostly on specifically demarcated individual rights. To that extent, existing law often regulates data as an object to be transferred, protected, and shared.

In fact, the General Data Protection Regulation (GDPR) regulates the processing by an individual, a corporation, or an organization of personal data concerning individuals in the European Union.[19] The GDPR applies to all personal data but also has a more protective regime for the so-called special category or sensitive data embracing personal data that expose racial or ethnic origin, political opinions, religious or philosophical beliefs, health data, etc.[20] The borderless character of cyberspace and e-commerce gives the GDPR a wider reach and so this new regulation applies to any processor of EU-citizen data generating vital international inferences, as it regulates many large firms operating and headquartered outside of the EU territories.

The GDPR is a data protection law. The GDPR as a data protection regime presents protections that follow the data imposing data governance duties on companies regardless of whether individuals invoke their rights.[21] Moreover, the GDPR

---

[16] https://digital-strategy.ec.europa.eu/

[17] Article 58 of Regulation (EU) 2018/1725. The EDPS is the independent supervisory authority with responsibility for monitoring the processing of personal data by the EU institutions and bodies, advising on policies and legislation that influence privacy and cooperating with similar authorities to make certain consistent data protection.

[18] https://publications.parliament.uk/pa/ld201719/ldselect/ldai/100/100.pdf

[19] Regulation 2016/679, the new General Data Protection Regulation entered into force in May 2018.

[20] GDPR Art 9(1).

[21] GDPR, arts. 12–23.

as a data protection regime imposes significant corporate responsibilities in addition to a substantive system of individual rights.

It is characteristic that the GDPR is based on fundamental rights and so in EU, these rights involve protections provided by the state, rather than just restrictions on the state. Moreover, data protection in EU is distinct from privacy and consumer protection laws, which embrace their own set of rules and regulations that interact with the GDPR. Furthermore, the GDPR harmonizes data protection across EU countries leaving much to Member States which means that national law and politics remain relevant to understanding the GDPR and European data protection.

The EU has been the forefront in setting limits to automated decision-making, actually motivated by concerns about illegitimate profiling of people and GDPR in Article 22 regulates automated individual decision-making, embracing profiling, and the GDPR's applicability beyond the EU is expected to influence global standards.[22] However, the national implementation of Article 22 GDPR on the right to explanation has resulted in the emergence of different legal solutions for the need for transparency in automated decision-making. Furthermore, Article 35 GDPR preserves the duty to carry out a data protection impact assessment but its implementation remains tainted by legal uncertainty.[23] It is characteristic that the GDPR's influence on AI is concentrated on automated individual decision-making, but it has consequences on the secondary use, disclosure and retention of existing personal data for constructing training sets, and the use of personal data collected by AI systems for new training sets.

Awareness has, for instance, been triggered within the framework of GDPR recognizing the incident of algorithmic discrimination[24] and sets rules and procedures to combat it, therewith offering a detailed monitoring and enforcement toolkit. Moreover, in recital 71 of its preamble, it lays down a requirement to "implement technical and organizational measures" that "prevent, inter alia, discriminatory effects on natural persons on the basis of racial or ethnic origin, political opinion, religion or beliefs, trade union membership, genetic or health status or sexual orientation, or that result in measures having such an effect.[25]" Nonetheless, data sanitization, involving the elimination of special categories from datasets used

[22] S.M. Kerner, "HPE Explains What European GDPR Privacy Regulations Mean to U.S. Firms," eWeek (1 May 2017), www.eweek.com/security/hpeexplains-what-european-gdpr-privacy-regulations-mean-to-u.s.-firms: "The GDPR applies to anyone that is doing business in the EU, so [that includes] anyone selling into it or [who] has employees there."

[23] Janssen, Heleen L. (2020). An approach for a fundamental rights impact assessment to automated decision-making, International Data Privacy Law, Volume 10 (1), 76–106, https://doi.org/10.1093/idpl/ipz028

[24] Fundamental Rights Agency, "#BigData; Discrimination in data-supported decision-making," FRA Focus (May 2018) https://fra.europa.eu/sites/default/files/fra_uploads/fra-2018-focus-big-data_en.pdf Equinet, "Call for proposals: Equality, artificial intelligence and algorithmic discrimination" (24 April 2019) <http://equineteurope.org/2019/04/24/call-for-proposals-equality-artificial-intelligence-and-algorithmicdiscrimination/>

[25] Regulation (EU) 2016/679 of the European Parliament and of the Council of 27 April 2016 on the protection of natural persons with regard to the processing of personal data and on the free

in automated decision-making, and algorithmic transparency, encompassing a right to explanation are certified by the Regulation and so blocking algorithmic discrimination.[26] The GDPR specifies the devices by which these principles will be enforced: data impact assessments, codes of conduct,[27] and certification. Furthermore, Art 9 GDPR prohibits the "processing of personal data revealing racial or ethnic origin, political opinions, religious or philosophical beliefs, or trade union membership, and the processing of genetic data, biometric data for the purpose of uniquely identifying a natural person, data concerning health or data concerning a natural person's sex life or sexual orientation" and Art. 22 GDPR protects data subjects from being subjected to "decision[s] based solely on automated processing, including profiling, which produces legal effects concerning him or her or similarly significantly affects him or her."

GDPR limits the cross-border transfer of personal data by default and the way to overcome this limitation is the "adequacy assessment" for which the European Commission determines whether another jurisdiction provides for an "essentially equivalent" level of protection.[28] Moreover, the EU's Court of Justice extended this requirement to the other legal technologies, particularly standardized contractual clauses that are available to "export" personal data from the EU to other jurisdictions.[29] Furthermore, it seems that the EU's data protection regime discriminates between jurisdictions with "essentially equivalent" data protection laws and those without and between entities that are able to offer prerequisite "additional safeguards" and those who are not able to do so.[30] Within the framework of the GDPR, algorithmic manipulation is intimately linked to the protection of vulnerable data subjects and the duty to perform a data protection impact assessment according to Article 35 GDPR not only echoes the demands for algorithmic auditing under the UCPD; but that Recital 75 GDPR, in this context, plainly mentions risks for vulnerable subjects.[31] Despite the efforts put in place by the GDPR, data protection continues to be disrupted by the rapid development of new AI applications and their unpredictable nature.

---

movement of such data, and repealing Directive 95/46/EC (General Data Protection Regulation) OJ L 119/1.

[26] B.W. Goodman, A Step towards Accountable Algorithms?: Algorithmic Discrimination and the European Union General Data Protection, http://www.mlandthelaw.org/papers/goodman1.pdf Article. 9 and 22 of the GDPR concerning the data sanitization principle.

[27] Arts. 24 (impact assessments), 40 (codes of conduct), 42 (certification).

[28] This standard was clarified by the EU's Court of Justice (ECJ) in Case C-362/14 Maximillian Schrems v. Data Protection Commissioner (Schrems), ECLI:EU:C:2015:650 (Oct. 6, 2015).

[29] E.C.J., Case C-311/18 Data Protection Commissioner v. Facebook Ireland Ltd. & Maximillian Schrems (Schrems II), ECLI:EU:C:2020:559 (July 16, 2020).

[30] Anupam Chander, Is Data Localization a Solution for Schrems II?, 23 Journal Of International Economic Law 771 (2020).

[31] G. Malgieri and J. Niklas, 'Vulnerable data subjects', (2020) 37 Computer Law & Security Review Article 105415.

Article 82 of the GDPR states that any person who has suffered material or non-material damage owing to an infringement of the GDPR has the right to compensation from the controller or processor for the damage suffered. Moreover, article 82 determines the liability of the controller when the damage is triggered by processing which infringes the GDPR.[32] In addition, the processor is liable for damage instigated by processing only when it has not fulfilled the obligations set in the Regulation or where it has performed outside or contrary to the lawful instructions of the controller.[33] Nevertheless, the GDPR does not lay down exhaustive rules on damages liability and national laws of Member States play a complementary role. Consequently, private liability for breaching this Regulation is not completely harmonized within the EU and diverging case outcomes are possible. To that extent, the GDPR compels full compensation by affirming that the notion of damage should be interpreted broadly.

Does the EU comply with its non-discrimination commitments and applicable regulatory disciplines under the law of the WTO? The EU recognizes the fundamental tension between its restrictions on transfers of personal data and the commitment toward unimpeded "data flows" that stimulates many Internet governance institutions and the US "digital trade" agenda.[34]

It has to be taken into account that European courts are regulating cyberspace gradually aggressively and so the Court of Justice of the European Union ruled against Google Spain in 2014 in a case brought by a man who wanted outdated information about him removed from Google's search results.[35] The original decision was a compromise as permitting the European Union to police its own jurisdiction without enforcing its own restrictive view of privacy upon the world. Nonetheless, the French data protection regulator CNIL has advocated against searches for EU citizens in any jurisdiction, and the GDPR has preserved that universalism into EU law, even switching the emphasis from delisting to erasure.[36]

It could be said that while the EU equality law contains useful yardsticks to cope with algorithmic discrimination in the field of the labor market and access to goods

[32]As per Art 4(7) GDPR, the controller is the natural or legal person, public authority, agency, or other body which, alone or jointly with others, ascertains the purposes and means of processing personal data.

[33]The processor is outlined in Art 4(8) GDPR as a natural or legal person, public authority, agency, or other body which processes personal data on behalf of the controller.

[34]Neha Mishra, Privacy, Cybersecurity, and GATS Article XIV: A New Frontier for Trade and Internet Regulation?, 19 World Trade Review 341 (2020). Svetlana Yakovleva & Kristina Irion, Towards Compatibility of the EU Trade Policy with the General Data Protection Regulation, 114 AJIL UNBOUND 10 (2020). Svetlana Yakovleva & Kristina Irion, Pitching Trade Against Privacy: Reconciling EU Governance of Personal Data Flows with External Trade, 10 International Data Privacy Law 201 (2020).

[35]Google Spain SL and Google Inc. v Agencia Española de Protección de Datos (AEPD) and Mario Costeja González (13 May 2014), Doc C-131/12, ECLI:EU:C:2014:317 (CJEU).

[36]Politou, Eugenia, Efthimios Alepis and Constantinos Patsakis. 2018. "Forgetting personal data and revoking consent under the GDPR: challenges and proposed solutions". Journal of Cybersecurity. https://doi.org/10.1093/cybsec/tyy001

and services, there are also significant limitations to it for the reason that discrepancies in the personal and material scope of the EU equality law directives. Hence, the lack of an articulate and comprehensive equality law framework concerning the numerous grounds of discrimination, including race, gender, religion, disability, sexual orientation, and age, appears problematic with reference to digital forms of discrimination. Additionally, the intricacy of the human–machine relationship leads to a blurring of the conceptual difference between direct and indirect discrimination, as it ensues from the Court's case law and has been fused in the EU equality directives. Thus, at the level of enforcement, existing problems connected to the still strong reliance on the individual rights-based approach are aggravated with respect to algorithmic discrimination regarding inter alia problems of transparency, access to information, liability, burden of proof, and effective judicial protection. Nonetheless, algorithmic discrimination confronts extant doctrinal paradigms of EU and national non-discrimination laws, blurring the lines between direct and indirect discrimination.[37]

While the GDPR has been influential worldwide, it may handicap Europe in the development of AI for the reason that where China and the USA are permitting the gathering of giant quantities of data to fuel their algorithms, Europe is more fragmented, both in terms of markets and in terms of the dominant tech corporations, and this decentralization is worsened by the GDPR's stern regulation of data sharing. Taking into account that data is an essential resource for economic growth, competitiveness, and innovation, the European strategy for data generates a single market for data that will guarantee Europe's global competitiveness and data sovereignty.[38]

Certain data protection laws give individuals the right to inquire about the personal data that firms hold about an individual. Moreover, data protection and cybersecurity laws require disclosure of certain cyber-incidents and data breaches.[39] On the other hand, there is presently no law that systematically tackles the lack of transparency when it comes to control over data in the digital economy.[40]

It has to be taken into consideration that the European Union's update of its copyright laws[41] has attracted criticism because of its aggressive stance on copyright breaches and so article 13 of the new copyright law obliges Internet companies to work closely with copyright holders to bring down copyright materials as soon as

[37] Gerards, Janneke & Raphaële Xenidis (2020). Algorithmic Discrimination in Europe: Challenges and Opportunities for Gender Equality and Non-discrimination Law. Special Report. European Commission, Directorate for Justice and Consumers. https://www.equalitylaw.eu/downloads/5361-algorithmic-discrimination-in-europe-pdf-1-975

[38] Proposal for a REGULATION OF THE EUROPEAN PARLIAMENT AND OF THE COUNCIL on European data governance (Data Governance Act) COM/2020/767 final.

[39] Jef Ausloos & Michael Veale, Researching with Data Rights, Technology And Regulation 136 (2021), https://techreg.org/index.php/techreg/article/view/61

[40] Mark Verstraete & Tal Zarsky, Optimizing Breach Notifications, https://ssrn.com/abstract=3650724 (July 14, 2020).

[41] The Directive of the European Parliament and of the Council on copyright in the Digital Single Market, at www.consilium.europa.eu/media/35373/st09134-en18.pdf

possible, which is resulting in fanatical policing. Moreover, article 11 demands aggregators to obtain a license from publishers if they display excerpts from content and so a similar rule introduced in Spain in 2014 led Google to withdraw its aggregation service from there.

11.2 AI and GDPR in Labor Market

Algorithms being computer programs, including AI are now utilized to make a host of decisions about human beings that have noteworthy effects on human welfare and dignity. Moreover, algorithms are now used to make significant decisions about individuals, from credit determinations to hiring and firing.[42] In addition, the algorithms used cause substantial challenges to legal systems, as they are often secret, impossible to predict, hard to explain to no experts, and continuously changing over time. It has to be taken into account that increasingly sophisticated algorithms form their own rules and generate "intuitions" humans do not have indicating the demand for legal personhood of AAI in order to impose legal obligation and duties for a successful regulation. Presently, for any kind of algorithm, human selections and assumptions go into its construction, training, and oversight.[43]

Is there a need of regulating algorithmic decision-making? Algorithmic decision-making starts from the premise that it replaces decision-making by humans. Human decision-making is deeply flawed and so human decision-makers can be outright discriminatory; can hold deep-seated biases about race, gender, or class; and can present a host of cognitive biases that invisibly influence outcomes.

Will AI machines be better in decision-making? But even complex algorithms are simplifications of reality, and these simplifications involve human choices along a number of axes. It is worth noting that algorithms are not neutral because they are opinions embedded in mathematics. Algorithmic decision-making risks concealing the very things being problematic in human decision-making under pretense of technical impartiality. Moreover, where human decision-making is contested, algorithmic decision-making is often taken at face value and left unchallenged and unchallengeable.[44]

Algorithms are mathematical models of the real world and scientists construct algorithms to take in data and find correlations or make predictions. Thus, humans energetically design algorithms in a number of manners by choosing an algorithm's objectives, determining what the input will be, picking whether to use proxies, etc.,

[42] Jessica M. Eaglin, Constructing Recidivism Risk, 67 EMORY L.J. 59, 67–88 (2017) (discussing the actuarial algorithms used in recidivism risk assessment).

[43] Pauline T. Kim, Auditing Algorithms for Discrimination, 166 U. PA. L. REV. ONLINE 189, 197–202 (2017).

[44] Joshua A. Kroll et al., Accountable Algorithms, 165 U. PA. L. REV. 633, 696–99 (2017).

and, once the algorithm is functioning, decide whether and how to confirm in practice that it is generating accurate results.

It has to be taken into account that the law generally does not closely regulate the terms of employment other than setting some minimal standards. In fact, unionization rates have fallen to low levels, and very few workers have access to union representation due to structural alterations in labor markets such as the shift from manufacturing to service industries and amplified global competition, along with employer practices such as outsourcing and offshoring jobs. There is multiplying employer hostility to labor organizing, incompetent legal remedies, and judicial retrenchment of workers' labor rights have also added.

Furthermore, it has to be taken into consideration that when AI is used in social domains to make predictions about people, it presents heightened risks not only for those individuals, but also of broader societal effects. To that extent, AI devices contribute to inequality both by reproducing discriminatory patterns that disadvantage marginalized groups and by further strengthening power in manners that intensify economic inequality which means that legal and policy reorganizations will be needed to make certain that AI applications do not merely reproduce or intensify existing inequalities, but instead promote broader social goods.

Accountability has to run through the system as a whole and not just to a regulator or group of technical experts but to representatives of concerned stakeholders and to the public.[45] It is worth noting that algorithmic accountability addresses algorithmic decision-making through both individual "due process" rights and an array of systemic accountability measures and so systemic measures embrace public disclosure of source code, agency oversight, expert boards, and stakeholder input. Moreover, algorithms work particularly well and so the clearer and more mathematical the objective, the more detailed and direct the data, the more transparent the inputs and code means that an algorithm tracks and produces "fair" or "accurate" outputs. Algorithmic decision-making will be erroneous, based on incorrect facts or stemmed from incorrect inferences. Also, algorithmic decision-making will be biased, echoing biased decisions made by programmers or discrimination contained into the datasets on which algorithms are trained. Moreover, algorithmic decision-making might be intentionally discriminatory, hiding discriminatory motives behind proxy rationales. Hence, regulation should endorse systemic accountability mechanisms, such as ex ante technical requirements, audits, or oversight boards, to do so.

In other words, algorithmic decision-making has to be legitimized as a decisional system. Rule-of-law values require not just explanations of decisions but justifications that are legitimate within a particular mode of reasoning. Furthermore, transparency is essential for justification which means that nobody can dispute the validity or legitimacy of a decision if the reasoning cannot be seen. Thus, an

[45] Jody Freeman, The Private Role in Public Governance, 75 N.Y.U. L. REV. 543, 664–67 (2000).

algorithmic decision-making system would not be able unless the system has some path to connect that information to the context it needs.[46]

There is a need to explore opportunities for greater endogeneity in tackling civil rights concerns, predominantly given the information asymmetry between the industries that design AI and the larger public.[47] Governing algorithmic decision-making should embrace both individual rights and systemic approaches. In addition, a systemic approach is required to tackle risks on a system-wide level and to target the numerous stages of development by the humans who build them and training when algorithms are more flexible to regulation. It has to be taken into consideration that designing a regulatory system that is legitimate, immunized from capture, and strong enough has to be different in kind from self-regulation and so the system has to contain the general principles of legitimizing AI and in any field of AI application to have detailed rules of employment more objectively for the reason that the AAI is forthcoming which will impose its own objective regulation of all fields according to the set-up of the whole AAI.

To that extent, it seems that algorithmic decision-making goes entirely unregulated. On the other hand, there are existing laws applicable to algorithmic decision-making such as the Fair Housing Act.[48] It is argued that the use of big data has "the potential to eclipse longstanding civil rights protections in how personal information is used in housing, credit, employment, health, education, and the marketplace.[49]"

It is worth noting that traditional fair information principles have rested heavily on the notion of consent. Taking into account the unequal power that typifies most work relationships, rights that are subject to waiver offer little protection. The EU's interpretation of the General Data Protection Regulation limits employers from counting on consent as a basis for justifying data collection and processing. The GDPR states that consent to data processing is not deemed valid "where there is a clear imbalance between the data subject and the controller.[50]" Moreover, the European Union agency responsible for interpreting the GDPR has realized that

---

[46] Kiel Brennan-Marquez, "Plausible Cause": Explanatory Standards in the Age of Powerful Machines, 70 VAND. L. REV. 1249, 1288 (2017) Andrew D. Selbst, A Mild Defense of Our New Machine Overlords, 70 Vand. L. Rev. En Banc 87, 92 (2017). Margot E. Kaminski, The Right to Explanation, Explained, 34 Berkeley Tech. L.J. 189, 201 (2019).

[47] Sonya K. Katyal, Private Accountability in the Age of Artificial Intelligence, 66 UCLA L. REV. 54, 61 (2019).

[48] The Department of Housing and Urban Development charged Facebook in 2019 with allegedly violating, by using machine learning algorithms to discriminate in housing advertisements against users based on membership in protected classes. Facebook, Inc., FHEO No. 01-18-0323-8 (U.S. Dep't of Hous. & Urban Dev. Mar. 28, 2019), https://www.hud.gov/sites/dfiles/Main/documents/HUD_v_Facebook.pdf

[49] JOHN PODESTA ET AL., EXEC. OFFICE OF THE PRESIDENT, BIG DATA (2014), http://obamawhitehouse.archives.gov/sites/default/files/docs/big_data_privacy_report_5.1.14_final_print.pdf. Solon Barocas & Andrew D. Selbst, Big Data's Disparate Impact, 104 CALIF. L. REV. 671, 714–23 (2016).

[50] GDPR, Recital 43(a).

the employment relationship is one example of a clear imbalance such that consent of employees should generally not be considered a legal basis for data processing.[51]

It is worth noting that the EU's GDPR epitomizes an effort to use collaborative governance toward algorithmic accountability, combined with a system of individual rights. Moreover, the GDPR's systemic approach to governing algorithms relies heavily on collaborative governance.

Corporations collect data in order to settle appropriate levels of inventory or to monitor the performance of their machinery but that data offer information about workers' activities that could be used for decisions about pay, promotion, or discipline. Employers have legitimate interests in information needed to manage their workforces but some sorts of data gathering and use are excessively intrusive or undermine workers' rights. Furthermore, in the absence of robust collective activity, workers have little voice in how algorithmic management devices are used and corporations face few constraints on further intensifying their control. Consequently, tackling concerns that predictive AI tools are contributing to inequality necessitate broader legal reforms that strengthen employee voice in the workplace.

Does the authorization of allowing a decision about humans to be made by a machine consider humans as objects, showing deep, inherent disrespect for peoples' humanity? It has to be taken into account that automatically making decisions grounded on what categories an individual falls into treats that individual not as an individual. Hence, if algorithmic decision-making does not permit individuals to assert their individuality, then it abuses their dignity rather than treating an individual as a whole person.[52] Moreover, secret profiling and decision-making lead to manipulation. On the other hand, AAI systems will make decisions without abusing personalities by utilizing unreasonable steering or manipulation.

It has to be taken into account that only "solely" automated decisions are subject to the GDPR's rations of explanation and contestation and so if a decision by an algorithm is subject to profound human review, meaning a human decision-maker has the capability and competence to contest that decision, then a number of the GDPR's individual rights do not apply advocating that in the EU human involvement in decision-making is lessening the dignitary, justificatory, and even instrumental concerns about algorithmic decision-making.[53]

The GDPR regulates algorithmic decision-making differently from general data processing only if it produces "legal effects" or "similarly significant" consequences. Moreover, the global rush of corporations to make internal compliance regimes to

[51] Article 29 Data Protection Working Party, Opinion 2/2017 on Data Processing at Work, 17/EN WP 249 (June 8, 2017), http://ec.europa.eu/newsroom/document.cfm?doc_id=45631

[52] Frederik J Zuiderveen Borgesius, Improving Privacy Protection in the Area of Behavioral Targeting 62 (2015) ("Privacy isn't merely about control. Privacy is about not being controlled . . . Privacy as identity construction concerns protection against unreasonable steering or manipulation—by humans or by technology."

[53] Sandra Wachter et al., Counterfactual Explanations Without Opening the Black Box: Automated Decisions and the GDPR, 31 HARV. J.L. & TECH. 841, 880 (2018) ("Counterfactual explanations do not attempt to clarify how decisions are made internally.").

abide by the GDPR implies that its level of fines might be working at doing just that. In the USA, the policy landscape around algorithmic decision-making remains largely a blank slate regardless that some requirements apply to some government use of algorithms lacking general law to govern private sector and many governments uses of algorithmic decision-making. Besides, the GDPR went into direct effect on member states by governing process of personal data and applies to both the government and the private sector. Additionally, the GDPR contains an algorithmic accountability regime based on the individual rights regime and on the so-called right to explanation of individual algorithmically made decisions. To that extent, it seems that the GDPR is both a system of individual rights and a multifaceted compliance regime that, when applied to the private sector, is established through collaborative governance.

The GDPR depends on both formal and informal tactics to generate public–private partnerships in governing algorithmic decision-making. In line, the GDPR encompasses a broad assortment of individual rights and corporation obligations applying beyond algorithmic decision-making, to personal data processing in general. The GDPR creates a system of generally applicable notification and access rights which means that upon collecting personal information from an individual; a corporation specifies the reason for which data is gathered, the recipients of the data, and the retention period of the data, among other things. Additionally, information must be disclosed if a corporation obtains personal data not directly from an individual but from another party. Also, the GDPR contains affirmative access rights for individuals, embracing access to the source of the data and a copy of the data itself. Access rights are invoked at intervals and give individuals the ability to regularly check in about what information a corporation has about them, beyond the moment at which data has initially been obtained. The GDPR addresses how information must be communicated and so information has to be communicated "in a concise, transparent, intelligible and easily accessible form, using clear and plain language . . . ."

Algorithmic decision-making itself activates yet more notification and access rights and so a corporation has proactively to notify individuals of the existence of solely automated decision-making which means that the algorithmic due process is implemented. Explicit consent is one of the three exceptions to the GDPR's prohibition of automated decision-making and so valid consent means that individuals must be making an informed choice and understanding exactly what they are consenting to. In other words, if a corporation does not effectively communicate to an individual both the reason of data processing and information about the use of data for automated decisions, then consent may be deemed invalid.

While the GDPR's transparency provisions have instrumental consequences, their principal objective is to tackle dignitary and justificatory concerns. The GDPR does not only afford individuals transparency rights but also embraces substantive prohibitions on specific uses of data, heightened protections for certain types of data which means that the GDPR encompasses substantive prohibitions on certain prohibitions characterized as individual rights to not be subjected to something.

Furthermore, the GDPR prohibits exclusively algorithmic decision-making but also generates heightened obligations for certain kinds of information, together with sensitive information, such as race or biometric data, referred to as "special categories of personal data . . .[54]" Special categories of data are subject to fewer exceptions to the ban on automated decision-making and so they are processed only subject to explicit consent to processing "for one or more specified purposes" or when "necessary for reasons of substantial public interest" and, even then, only subject to proportionality assessment.[55]

As discussed earlier, article 22 of GDPR plainly contains a form of algorithmic due process by establishing not just the "right to explanation" but due process-like rights to human intervention, to express an opinion, and to contest an algorithmic decision. Hence, article 22 does establish an individual "right to an explanation" of an algorithmic decision and an opportunity to be heard. The GDPR necessitates that corporations that use "solely" automated decision-making institute a right to obtain human intervention, a manner to express one's point of view, and a way to contest a decision considered being a type of algorithmic due process, merging notice with several ways of an opportunity to be heard. On the other hand, the GDPR does not provide for a neutral arbiter but applicable Guidelines advocate the right to contest be an internal corporation process.

Will human intervention serve the goals of algorithmic due process? It has to be taken into account that the GDPR involves the right to "obtain human intervention" in an algorithmic decision and humans admit what algorithms tell them as true. Article 22 applies only to solely automated decision-making compelling the decision to have legal consequences or similarly significant results. Trade secret exceptions apply both to the right to explanation and to the related notification and access rights. The GDPR launches a version of algorithmic due process oriented toward individuals generating both notice and an opportunity to be heard.

The GDPR does not limit its governance of algorithmic decision-making to individual rights but also handles collaborative governance. Moreover, the GDPR encompasses not just individual rights but duties imposed on corporations given meaning and effect over time via a variety of collaborative governance mechanisms such as codes of conduct and so the GDPR is essentially a hard law regime. While the GDPR contains vague rules, it is for the most part hard law translated into an obligatory regime, coupled with strong enforcement powers. A GDPR violation triggers administrative fines empowering an extensive national and transnational system of government regulators.

It is worth noting that the GDPR is supported by an increasingly involved court, the European Court of Justice ("ECJ") ruling on data protection rights but there are incentives for corporations to contribute in collaborative efforts to avoid government

[54]Council Regulation 2016/679 art. 9(2), art. 6(4)(c).

[55]Council Regulation 2016/679 art. 9(2)(a), art 22(3), art. 9(2)(g).

sanctions.[56] While the GDPR will principally be interpreted by the ECJ, European Court of Human Rights case law materializes a backstop of human rights protection in the EU.[57]

The vagueness of the GDPR is highly bounded and Article 22 does not conclusively define what "suitable measures." While the GDPR complements EU data protection law, it contains a number of opportunities for member states to adjust their legal systems, embracing governing algorithmic accountability.

The GDPR relies on government regulators but it marginally appeals for participation by third parties by embracing a number of formal mechanisms for policy collaboration between corporations and regulators, counting on codes of conduct and certification. Moreover, the GDPR encompasses a number of informal tools being central to its system of governing algorithmic decision-making such as management reform via Data Protection Officers ("DPOs") adhere to reporting requirements; and requirements of third-party oversight, such as audits or expert boards.

It has to be taken into account that the GDPR uses broad legal standards to formulate corporation duties via collaborative mechanisms such as article 22 regulating corporations conduct algorithmic decision-making with implementing "suitable measures to safeguard the data subject's rights and freedoms and legitimate interests . . ." being technology-neutral standard. The GDPR itself does not designate how a corporation functioning in a sector or using a particular technology might comply.[58]

11.3 GDPR, Privacy, and Competition

It is worth noting that while the GDPR has delivered positive outcomes by improving the protection afforded to users of digital services and reinforcing the rights of data subjects, it has also had adverse consequences on competition by boosting the position of large online platforms on digital markets, at the very same time the

[56] Case C-131/12, Google Spain SL v. Agencia Española de Protección de Datos (May 13, 2014), http://curia.europa.eu/juris/document/document.jsf?text=&docid=152065&doclang=EN; Joined Cases C-293/12 & C-594/12, Digital Rights Ir. Ltd. v. Minister for Commc'ns, Marine and Nat. Res. (Apr. 8, 2014), http://curia.europa.eu/juris/document/document.jsf?docid=150642&doclang=EN; European Court of Human Rights, Zakharov v. Russia, App. No. 47143/06 (Dec. 4, 2015), http://hudoc.echr.coe.int/eng?i=001-159324

[57] European Court of Human Rights, Zakharov v. Russia, App. No. 47143/06 (Dec. 4, 2015), http://hudoc.echr.coe.int/eng?i=001-159324

[58] Council Regulation 2016/679, art. 40(5), (7)–(8), (describing the processes in individual Member States, involving the Board and Commission in the case of several Member States) art. 43(2)(d), (providing that to be accredited a certification body must "establish[] procedures and structures to handle complaints about infringements of the certification or the manner in which the certification has been, or is being, implemented by the controller or processor, and to make those procedures and structures transparent to data subjects and the public").

European Commission has articulated fears about the market power held by these firms. Data and privacy regulation confuse the success and development of businesses that rely on the collection of data and directly harm data processing platforms.[59] Thus, the vague "legitimate interest" provision does not stipulate adequately detailed instructions to guide firms on whether or not their interests qualify as legitimate. Data and privacy protection must adapt to current technologies. Furthermore, it seems that the GDPR worsened one of the central problems experienced in digital markets nowadays, which is augmented market concentration and diminished contestability which means that the GDPR gave big firms, such as Google and Facebook, a device to harm rivals by plummeting access to the data they want to run their business. It has to be taken into account that display advertising takes place on owned and operated properties of large online platforms such as those of Facebook and Google or on the open web, i.e. the myriads of publishers of online content. To that extent, Google and Facebook alone capture the lion's share of digital ad revenue.[60]

In addition, the GDPR has strengthened big online platforms' market position compared to smaller firms, which have been less capable of absorbing the operation costs of the GDPR and coping with the restrictions on the collection and processing of data. Big companies have used the GDPR as an excuse to engage in practices that have consolidated their control on the ad tech ecosystem to the detriment of advertisers, publishers, and smaller firms named as the "weaponization" of the GDPR and so utilizing the GDPR as a strategic tool to strengthen their grip on the ad tech market.

It has to be taken into consideration that ad tech firms offer effective devices to advertisers to target the users who are the most likely to be interested in their products and services.[61] Moreover, online advertising on the open web, which is accelerated by ad tech tools, epitomizes a major source of revenues for the publishers offering valuable content and services to cyberspace users. Furthermore, the GDPR has augmented concentration among the web technology sellers.[62]

While there is public concern about the incomparable amounts of data accumulated by a few digital platforms, one of the oxymora of the GDPR is its strengthening of big platforms to the detriment of smaller market players which means that the GDPR leads to further market concentration. Moreover, the implementation of the

[59] Legitimate Interest, GDPR EU.org, https://www.gdpreu.org/theregulation/key-concepts/legitimate-interest/

[60] Competition and Markets Authority, "Online platforms and digital advertising," Market study interim report, 18 December 2019, https://assets.publishing.service.gov.uk/media/5dfa0580ed915d0933009761/Interim_report.pdf, ("CMA Interim Report"), paragraph 5.101 et seq. Nicole Perrin, "Facebook-Google Duopoly Won't Crack This Year," eMarketer, 4 November 2019, https://www.emarketer.com/content/facebook-google-duopoly-won-t-crack-this-year

[61] Christian Peukert et al., "European Privacy Law and Global Markets for Data," CEPR, DP 14475, March 2020, https://cepr.org/active/publications/discussion_papers/dp.php?dpno=14475

[62] Garrett Johnson and Scott Shiver, "Privacy & Market Concentration: Intended & Unintended Consequences of the GDPR," November 2019, https://papers.ssrn.com/abstract=3477686

GDPR and the associated compliance costs generate barriers to entry or may trigger exit. Furthermore, large online platform benefits from the advertisers' trust and so concentrating their ad spend on them. In addition, the GDPR's restrictions in data sharing give a competitive advantage to ad tech companies that are able to gain data through their consumer-facing products. To that extent, firms with data presence in the EU have been required to spend millions to abide by the GDPR and so such corporations have the resources to adhere to the GDPR which means that firms holding vast amounts of data will be closely monitored by regulatory authorities and consequently will be compliant. In line, such corporations will be more careful with users' personal data as they have more to lose in case of non-compliance.[63]

It is worth noting that Google's market dominance permits it to easily obtain users' consent to the collection of personal data. Data sharing is risky and many data holders decide to take the extreme measure of refusing to share their data with smaller ad tech companies as they may not trust their capacity to abide by the GDPR. To that extent, when individuals decide to engage in data sharing, they prefer to deal with large market players, whom they trust to adhere to the GDPR influencing competition by generating a competitive advantage for large, well-known players, as smaller suppliers or new entrants will often be disregarded.

It could be said that big companies can utilize hundreds of points to rationalize their data processing activities instead of the six identified legal bases of Article 6(1) of the GDPR benefitting from what has been aptly described as an "internal data free-for-all," by ignoring a central GDPR principle and so gaining a substantial competitive advantage over corporations which act in compliance with the GDPR and which do not have such a market position and an expanded portfolio of consumer-facing inventions.[64] On the other hand, the GDPR cannot be utilized as an excuse to restrict data sharing and distort competition to the benefit of large companies holding abundant first-party data.[65] To that extent, the GDPR prevents AI applications from making important decisions that influence users negatively without human approval.

The GDPR represents a stabilization of the public discourse on personal data collection and stabilization in turn has consequences on collective understandings and framings of the problems surrounding data processing. While it offers

[63] Cale Guthrie Weissman, "One year in, GDPR seems to have helped Google & Facebook," FastCompany, 17 May 2019, https://www.fastcompany.com/90351655/gdpr-helps-google-and-facebook-growuk-market-share-in-2019

[64] Complaint to the Irish Data Protection Commission, Dr. Johny Ryan v 1. Google Ireland Limited 2. Google LLC, https://brave.com/wp-content/uploads/2020/03/PurposeLimitation-Google.pdf. Sissy Cao, "Mark Zuckerberg's Plan to Merge All Facebook Apps Draws fourth Antitrust Probe," Observer, 17 January 2020, https://observer.com/2020/01/facebook-mark-zuckerberg-antitrust-lawsuit-overmerging-instagram-whasapp-messenger/. Daniele Condorelli and Jorge Padilla, "Harnessing Platform Envelopment Through Privacy Policy Tying," 14 December 2019, https://ssrn.com/abstract=3504025

[65] Damien Geradin, Theano Karanikioti, and Dimitrios Katsifis, GDPR Myopia: How a Well-Intended Regulation ended up Favoring Google in Ad Tech, TILEC Discussion Paper DP 2020–012.

mechanisms for "legitimate" manners of governing the processing of personal data and checklists for corporations focused on regulatory compliance, it does little concerning asymmetries underlying the relationships between technology firms and individual people.

11.4 Open Data

Digitalization changes the conditions under which capitalism functions and so firms with superior data collection capabilities benefit as they utilize the resulting information asymmetries.[66] As data is growing in importance as a medium for economic, social, and political ordering and as a resource for economic development, governments are tasked with handling the transition toward progressively digitally mediated economies and societies.

AI systems are built on data, so the governance of data is central to the success of any nation's AI strategy. It is worth noting that countries that acknowledge the importance of data for the AI economy, often endorse efforts to make governmental data available as "open data.[67]" Even though several states have some form of data transfer restrictions to retain jurisdictional control over data, some countries are against restricting the outward transfer of data to safeguard data as a national resource, in that way disputing the anti-protectionism consensus in international economic law. Some jurisdictions recognize a need for regulatory intervention to transfer data from those who have it to those who want or need it.

The open data movement has been quite successful in persuading governments that making governmental data publicly accessible under open data licenses is in their best interest to accelerate the national AI economy. Hence, examples involve the EU's Open Data Directive and Singapore's "Smart Nation" initiative, but the open data movement encompasses several developing countries.[68] It is argued that the GDPR's intended purpose of protecting European data subjects' personal data and privacy and its underlying fundamental rights justification are false pretenses for protectionist digital industrial policy.[69]

---

[66] Evgeny Morozov, "Digital Socialism? The Calculation Debate in the Age of Big Data" (2019) 116/117 New Left Review 33.

[67] Angelina Fisher & Thomas Streinz, "Confronting Digital Inequality," World Development Report 2021 background paper (April 1, 2021), https://ssrn.com/abstract=3825724 Directive (EU) 2019/1024 of the European Parliament and of the Council of 20 June 2019 on open data and the re-use of public sector information, OJ 2019 No. L 172, 26 June 2019, 56.

[68] Stefaan G. Verhulst & Andrew Young, "Open Data in Developing Economies," GovLab, November 2017, https://perma.cc/W9VN-452K Singapore's open data resources, https://perma.cc/JAX3-55U8

[69] Svetlana Yakovleva, "Privacy Protection(ism): The Latest Wave of Trade Constraints on Regulatory Autonomy" 74 University of Miami Law Review 416 (2020).

New agreements in the mold of the new NAFTA between the USA, Mexico, and Canada (USMCA) and the US-Japan Digital Trade Agreement favor global access to governmental data by encouraging open data policies while limiting states' capacity to impose restrictions on cross-border data transfers or to mandate the use of national computing facilities.[70]

11.5 AI and Human Rights

Actually, AI gives rise to new security threats, as malicious actors are able to utilize AI either as a tool or as a vulnerable attack surface, to upgrade old attacks, or to perform utterly new types of crimes. Accordingly, many uses of AI generate foundational encounters for core societal values and for human rights.[71]

It should be noted that algorithms do not exist meaningfully without interaction with human beings. Mathematic or computational constructs do not by themselves have adverse human rights influences but their implementation and application to human interaction does. Technologies are deeply social constructs with considerable political implications.[72] While a decision-making software may be "biased but ambivalent," it has no meaning without a social system around it which offers sense and influence which means that we cannot blame the algorithm or to suggest to no longer resort to computers or computing. Rather, it is the social construct and the particular norms and values embedded in algorithms that need to be questioned, critiqued, and disputed which means that it is not the algorithms themselves but the decision-making processes around algorithms that must be scrutinized in terms of how they influence human rights.

It is argued that the use of new technologies for human rights raises concern and questions over the place of algorithms in deploying, creating, or expressing relationships of power and producing actionable knowledge. Especially, attention to the role of tech corporations in informing governance, policies, and laws has to be drawn. It is characteristic that there is a real possibility to have the rule of web design substituting the rule of law due to the fact that there are public and private collaborations and state geo-sovereignty and tech cyber-sovereignty partnerships and so private firms might impose their web interests and software programs as the rule of law against a real rule of law fulfilling the interests of the society.

[70]Thomas Streinz, International Economic Law's Regulation of Data as a Resource for the Artificial Intelligence Economy, in Artificial Intelligence And International Economic Law: Disruption, Regulation, And Reconfiguration ch. 9 Shin-yi Peng, Ching-Fu Lin & Thomas Streinz eds.

[71]Q. C. Van Est, J. Gerritsen & L. Kool, Human rights in the robot age: challenges arising from the use of robotics, artificial intelligence, and virtual and augmented reality (2017), https://research.tue.nl/en/publications/humanrights-in-the-robot-age-challenges-arising-from-the-use-of-

[72]Laura DeNardis (2012) Hidden Levers Of Internet Control, Information, Communication & Society, 15:5, 720–738, DOI: https://doi.org/10.1080/1369118X.2012.659199

Big Data makes AI systems run in the AI society and the recourse to big data by public and private players has raised concerns about the protection of individual privacy and other personal rights but some of these concerns have been addressed in legislation and litigation such as the 2016 EU Data Protection Directive by imposing pseudonymization requirements on all data processing undertaken by member states.[73] It has to be taken into account that the GDPR is partly built on the notion of individual self-determination, best clarified by the fact that data subject consent generally legitimizes the use of personal data and so data subject consent legitimizes the processing of personal data. To that extent, consent is the most frequently used lawful basis for personalization. Distinctive of the European Union's approach toward technology companies is its assumption that complaints about regulation threatening the freewheeling, entrepreneurial Internet are overstressed. It has to be taken into account that the GDPR is perceived as a threat to the model of free services for surveillance.

It is worth noting that technological innovations used in digital surveillance systems are confronting the protection of a set of interconnected human rights, such as privacy and data protection, digital accessibility, and non-discrimination.[74] As mentioned earlier, Regulation (EC) 2016/679 and Directive 2002/58/EC address, respectively, personal data,[75] location data processed in an electronic communications network or by an electronic communication service[76] and data stored in and accessed from user's terminal equipment.[77] Moreover, Directive 2016/2102/EU launches mandatory accessibility requirements for websites and mobile applications of public sector bodies, embracing contact tracing tools developed by public authorities. Likewise, Directive 2019/882/EU standardizes the accessibility requirements of key products and services in the internal market, such as inter alia, mobile applications which means ascertaining a commitment in complying with accessibility standards also for contact tracing tools developed by private entities.[78] In addition, automatic decision-making systems, as those used in algorithmic surveillance systems, are defying the existing EU anti-discrimination legal framework and so algorithmic discrimination causes new and unpredictable patterns of discrimination which means that algorithmic profiling repeats and amplifies intersectional

---

[73] Council Directive (EU) 2016/680 on the Protection of Natural Persons with Regard to the Processing of Personal Data by Competent Authorities for the Purposes of the Prevention, Investigation, Detection or Prosecution of Criminal Offences or the Execution of Criminal Penalties, and on the Free Movement of Such Data, and Repealing Council Framework Decision, OJ 2016 L 119.

[74] Lorna McGregor, "Contact-tracing Apps and Human Rights" (EJIL:Talk!, 30 April 2020) https://www.ejiltalk.org

[75] Articles 6 and 9 GDPR.

[76] Articles 6 and 9 ePrivacy Directive. European Parliament and Council Directive 2002/58/EC concerning the processing of personal data and the protection of privacy in the electronic communications sector [2002] OJ L 201.

[77] Article 5 ePrivacy Directive.

[78] European Parliament and Council Directive (EU) 2016/2102 on the accessibility of the websites and mobile applications of public sector bodies [2016] OJ L 327.

forms of discrimination generating new patterns of discrimination.[79] Hence, the European Commission Proposal for an AI Regulation may fail to fully mitigate in practice threats to human rights.[80]

It is worth noting that the District Court of The Hague[81] stopped a government welfare fraud detection system in the Netherlands on human rights grounds. The demise of the system in question, which is called "System Risk Indication" (SyRI), is a clear victory for the plaintiffs and, particularly, for the residents in targeted poor and marginalized neighborhoods. Moreover, the absence of transparency surrounding SyRI weighed especially heavily in the court's analysis since it hampered the court's capacity to perform its judicial role and eroded the individual's right to challenge this system. Hence, this lack of transparency is even more problematic, as stated by the court, because of the possibly discriminatory effects of SyRI. The judgment is a pioneering example of resistance to digital welfare systems on human rights grounds setting a strong legal precedent and displaying how efficient human rights advocacy and litigation can bring distinct alteration.

When considering AI policy concerning its use and application, automation, ethics, responsibility, control and standardization are arising and so AI raises inter alia the question of responsibility and the causal nexus between the damage and the actions of a human being along with matters within the context of international human rights law.[82]

AI governance has wide-ranging consequences for the promotion of inclusive policies based on the predisposition of the algorithm designers and on the specific data the machines use in their learning process which means that decisions on which types of data and queries would feed into the algorithm, what would be excluded from it, and how the data would be analyzed are highly political.[83] To that extent, opaque algorithms undermining the constitutional rights of individuals must not be employed and there is a need for the selective use of AI programs.[84]

Military technologies are used by states to keep defense against threats and as a device of social control. Thus, devices and methods making governments more effective at defending against threats also make them more capable in offensively expanding their power over people by undercutting their freedoms and rights.

---

[79] Sandra Wachter, Brent Mittelstadt, Chris Russell (2020) 41, "Why fairness cannot be automated: Bridging the gap between EU non-discrimination law and AI" Computer Law & Security Review 1.

[80] Michael Veale and Frederik Zuiderveen Borgesius, "Demystifying the Draft EU Artificial Intelligence Act" (SocArXiv 2021) preprint https://osf.io/38p5f

[81] Case NJCM C/09/550982/HA ZA 18/388.

[82] S. Livingston, M. Risse, The Future Impact of Artificial Intelligence on Humans and Human Rights, Ethics & International Affairs, 33(2) (2019) 141–158. S. Freeland, R.S. Jakhu, The intersection between space law and inter national human rights law, in: R.S. Jakhu, P.S. Dempsey (Eds.), Routledge Handbook of Space Law, Routledge, Oxon, 2017.

[83] Gillespie, "The Relevance of Algorithms," in T. Gillespie et al. (eds), Media Technologies (2014) 167.

[84] http://civilrightsdocs.info/pdf/FINAL_JointStatementPredictivePolicing.Pdf

The possibility of having the case of threatening privacy and human rights is disappeared if the state is well-regulated and applying the rule of law.

11.6 AI, Cyber-Borders, and International Politics

Cyberspace is a vast open space surpassing the conventional idea of territoriality and the Tallinn Manual 2.0 reflects the current state of the law vis-à-vis cyberspace.[85]

It has to be taken into account that the principle of State sovereignty applies in cyberspace and sovereignty takes effect in this domain which means that international norms and principles that emerge from sovereignty apply to the conduct by States of ICT-related activities and to their jurisdiction over ICT infrastructure within their territory.[86]

As discussed earlier, there is a difference between real sovereignty and cyberspace sovereignty because the cyber-sovereignty is an endless cyber-area where electronic transactions can take place but the real effects can be felt and transformed in a material way is within the real sovereignty. Many electronic dealings will take place in the endless cyberspace not even felt by anyone on earth such as intercepting signals and electronic actions.

Sovereignty and "respect for sovereignty" is a key rule whose violation leads to international accountability absent the breach of a more specific rule that flows from or is otherwise interrelated with the principle of sovereignty, for instance, the prohibition of the use of force or the principle of non-intervention.[87] The International Court of Justice (ICJ) repeatedly referred to "sovereignty" as a primary rule.[88]

Taking into account the technical individualities of the novel domain of cyberspace, new legal standards suitable to regulate state conduct below the thresholds of "coercion" and "force" that define the more pertinent prohibitions of intervention and the use of force might be needed. Assumed the fact that the "virtual" environment of globally interconnected networks offers sufficient chance to harm[89] another state's interests, there transpired the necessity for some rule proscribing at least the more reckless of such operations that did not even come close to being coercive or forceful. It could be said that violations of the rule of sovereignty by means of cyber-operations arise either by amounting to a noteworthy infringement upon the target

[85] Tallinn Manual 2.0 On The International Law Applicable To Cyber Operations (Michael N. Schmitt Ed., 2017).

[86] UN Doc. A/70/174, § 27 (2015).

[87] Military and Paramilitary Activities in and against Nicaragua (Nicar. v. U.S.), Merits, 1986 ICJ REP. 14 (June 27).

[88] Corfu Channel (UK v. Alb.), 1949 ICJ REP. 4 (Apr. 9).

[89] Nicholas Tsagourias, Law, Borders and the Territorialisation of Cyberspace, 15 Indonesian J. Int'l L. 523, 544 (2018). Harriet Moynihan, The Application of International Law to State Cyberattacks: Sovereignty and Non-Intervention, Chatham House Research Paper (December 2019); François Delerue, Cyber Operations And International Law 193–232 (2020).

State's territorial integrity by triggering physical damage or considerable loss of functionality of cyber infrastructures, or by forming an interference with or usurpation of inherently government functions.

It has to be taken into account that there is no that all infringements on sovereignty in cyberspace automatically implicate violations of international law.[90] Moreover, a state's sovereignty over a part of cyberspace is merely a result of the fact that all ICT infrastructures linked to the global networks have some definite physical location which belongs to the territory of a state. Also, activities "in cyberspace" take place within determinable ICT systems and consequently on territory over which States exercise their sovereign prerogatives for the reason that States have sovereignty over the information and communications technology infrastructure within their territory.

It seems that states have started to realize that cyberspace is utilized to send signals in the cyberspace and so influencing electronic actions that influence the real space actions. Moreover, states are looking for conceptions not obliging them to respect other people's actions in order to promote their own interests without any legal duties. To that extent, it seems that cyber imperialism is on the rise, stemming from a monopoly of information and cyberspace technology. It is characteristic that, China builds up national cyberspace capability to counter any invasion and establish rule of law in cyberspace in global governance. Hence, the concept of "cyberspace sovereignty" has been established in contemporary Chinese political discourse.[91]

Furthermore, states put electronic fences for avoiding interception of signals from cyberspace in an identical way that of conventional sovereignty because humans only in a material way can understand things. On the other hand, AAI entities will bypass any current fences concerning cyberspace actions. Article 2(4) UN Charter makes clear that it is the rationale of the prohibition of the use of force to protect the "territorial integrity" and "political independence" of all states, which are considered the two most dominant elements of the principle of sovereignty.

On the one hand, a law produces and determines borders whereas, on the other, borders produce and determine laws. It has to be taken into account that borders are constitutive of states and, consequently, they are constitutive of international law. Are there borders on cyberspace? The functionality of cyberspace can be extended to infinity due to the traveling of electric signals but there are borders as long as particular apparatuses are needed in order humans to have access to cyberspace and electric machines are placed in real space and sovereignty of a state then there

[90] Jeremy Wright, Cyber and International Law in the twenty-first Century (May 23, 2018), at https://www.gov.uk/government/speeches/cyber-and-international-law-in-the-21st-century Paul C. Ney, DOD General Counsel Remarks at U.S. Cyber Command Legal Conference (March 2, 2020), https://www.defense.gov/Newsroom/Speeches/Speech/Article/2099378/dod-general-counsel-remarks-at-us-cybercommand-legal-conference/

[91] He Yafei, China's Historical Choice In Global Governance (2018) Jinghan Zeng, Tim Stevens and Yaru Chen, China's Solution to Global Cyber Governance: Unpacking the Domestic Discourse of 'Internet Sovereignty', 45 Politics And Policy 432 (2017).

are border concerning its functionality and influence of the life of real people and not electronic entities.

It has to be taken into account that borders define international law's source of authority; without states, there would be no international law which means that borders are useful in that they demarcate international law's different domains. Are there borders and international law in cyberspace and its implications for the legal governance of cyberspace? It has to be taken into consideration that cyberspace and its features of a-territoriality and borderlessness defy traditional notions of international legal regulation. Can international law act as a regulatory device in cyberspace? International law is traditionally defined as the law that regulates the relations between states as sovereign formations.

It is worth noting that defined territory means demarcated territory that is discrete territory separated from other territories.[92] Can the territory of cyberspace be demarcated? The answer is no and the whole territory of cyberspace can be seen as the territory of any state as long as it can be reached via the appropriate machines placed in the territory of a state.

In addition, it has to be taken into consideration that borders verify the political and geographic scope of a state's authority by demarcating it from other authorities and they also demarcate the internal from the external dimension of state authority. The Tallinn Manual 2.0[93] refers that "violation of sovereignty occurs whenever one State physically crosses into the territory or national airspace of another State without either its consent or another justification in international law [...]." In their use of ICTs, States must observe, among other principles of international law, State sovereignty, sovereign equality, the settlement of disputes by peaceful means, and non-intervention in the internal affairs of other States.[94] The principle of state sovereignty summarizes the supreme authority of a state to territorial integrity, sovereign equality, and political independence within its territory to the exclusion of all other states.

Will AAI technology bring the end of the conventional international law or the place of the conventional state will take the AAI state functioning in a specific cyber-territory? The emergence of an AAI society constituted by humanoid robots will leave in a real space territory but functioning under an AAI technology which means that the only difference is spotted on the functioning technology and so analogous conceptions of territory and international law will apply as well. Also, if AAI society will be inhabited by AAI entities function in a cyber-territory, then the concepts of state and territory will have another understanding and so functioning in a virtual world where space, territory, and international law will have a dimensionally

[92] North Sea Continental Shelf Cases (Federal Republic of Germany/Denmark; Federal Republic of Germany/Netherlands), 20 February 1969, ICJ Reports 1969, p. 32.

[93] Michael N. Schmitt, ed., Tallinn Manual 2.0 on the International Law Applicable to Cyber Operations, CUP, 2017, rules 1–4, rule 66.

[94] Council of the EU (2017), "EU Council Conclusions of 20 November 2017," https://www.consilium.europa.eu/media/31666/st14435en17.pdf; The Commonwealth (2018), 'Commonwealth Cyber Declaration', https://thecommonwealth.org/commonwealth-cyberdeclaration

different scale but anyway there is a need to exist space and control in order to be workable.

It is worth noting that GGE admitted that international law, especially the UN Charter, applies to cyberspace and that State sovereignty and international norms and principles apply to State conduct of ICT-related activities.[95] Moreover, the 2015 GGE Report recognizes specific international norms and principles that apply or should apply to cyberspace.[96] Besides, the lack of agreement on how international law applies to states' cyber-activities has generated legal uncertainty.[97]

It could be said that principles and norms developed for and applicable to the physical world and correlated to territorially bounded spaces apply to cyberspace and so there is a "territorialisation of cyberspace" which means that sovereign's notions of authority and law are applied on cyberspace transactions.[98]

Accordingly, a state broadens its sovereignty over cyberspace infrastructure located on its territory and exercises sovereign power over persons on its territory. Moreover, the state affirms its sovereignty over the consequences of cyber-activities that are felt on its territory irrespective of their origin which means that the state establishes its sovereignty over information that passes through its infrastructure or begins or ends on its territory. It could be said that states assert their sovereignty in cyberspace by curving out cyberspace into distinct areas corresponding to national territorial borders.

To that extent, China utilizes the principle of cyber-sovereignty with the purpose of stress the need for an inter-governmental approach to cyber-regulation in contradistinction to the deployment of the principle of sovereignty with the purpose of protecting states internal sovereignty in the sense of protecting its exclusive and supreme power over its territory and people. Hence, cyber-sovereignty for China represents power over the state's cyber infrastructure and over the information entering or becoming available within its sovereign domain.[99]

It has to be taken into account that states curve their own sovereign cyberspace by raising borders through technical means so as to control activities from outside or with the aim of separating national services which means that these borders correspond to the physical borders delimiting and defining state sovereignty but they also reiterate state sovereignty in its political, social, economic, cultural, and territorial

---

[95] UNGA, "Group of Governmental Experts on Developments in the Field of Information and Telecommunications in the Context of International Security," 24 June 2013, UN Doc A/68/98, paras. 19–20.

[96] UNGA, "Group of Governmental Experts on Developments in the Field of Information and Telecommunications in the Context of International Security," 22 July 2015, UN Doc A/70/174.

[97] Corn, G. P. (2019), "Cyber National Security: Navigating Gray-Zone Challenges in and through Cyberspace," in Williams, W. S. and Ford, C. M. (eds) (2019).

[98] Nicholas Tsagourias, "The Legal Status of Cyberspace" in Nicholas Tsagourias & Russell Buchan, eds., Research Handbook on International Law and Cyberspace, Edward Elgar, 2015.

[99] Hao Yeli, "A Three-Perspective Theory of Cyber Sovereignty," Prism: Journal of the Center for Complex Operations, vol 7, no. 2 (2017).

organization.[100] In particular, it seems that states foresee the Westphalian concept of state sovereignty to cyberspace. While technology assists in actually curving cyberspace, it is principally political, economic, and a number of other factors that are the crucial reasons of such curving and so an open or closed cyberspace depends on political approaches to regulation. In other words, the need for conventional means to access cyberspace means that all the meanings of another dimension of cyberspace, etc., in the end come down to imposing all the classical means and laws on cyberspace transactions.

It is argued that cyberspace cannot be sovereign in itself.[101] On the other hand, cyberspace is sovereign for the cyber-personalities functioning there because cyberspace is an electronic place and sovereignty and never before have we seen a space in which individuals, corporations, communities, governments, and other entities can exist within and beyond the borders of the nation-state in such an instantaneous, contemporaneous, or ubiquitous manner. It is argued that the virtual part of cyberspace cannot be sovereign because an inanimate, ethereal, space cannot be sovereign. On the other hand, people function in cyberspace via the virtual personality.

Will the controllers of AAI technology impose all the political and legal instruments established during the previous centuries upon the new citizens of the AAI world? It seems that the only difference will be the new instruments utilized to impose the will and interests of the elite upon the people.

It has to be taken into consideration that hostile cyber-operations by one state against another state are more and more common and so cyber-operations triggering injury or death to persons or damage or destruction of objects could amount to a use of force or armed attack under the UN Charter. But in practice, the vast majority of cyber-operations by countries take place below the threshold of use of force, instead consisting of persistent, low-level intrusions that trigger harm in the victim country but often without apparent physical effects.[102] It is characteristic that developments in technology allowed states with a greater capability to precisely attribute cyber intrusions.[103]

States and elite want to occupy cyberspace as well putting an end to freedom of cyberspace which is becoming matter of national sovereignty according to the technical capabilities of conventional states. It is obvious that AAI technology will be utilized once and again as a device for occupation of virtual and not virtual

[100] North Korea's "Kwangmyong" internet or Iran's "Halal internet."

[101] Tsagourias, N. (2018) Law, borders and the territorialisation of cyberspace. Indonesian Journal of International Law, 18 (4). ISSN 1693–5594.

[102] Council on Foreign Relations (n.d.), "Cyber Operations Tracker," https://www.cfr.org/interactive/cyber-operations; Center for Strategic & International Studies (n.d.), "Significant Cyber Incidents Since 2006," https://csis-prod.s3.amazonaws.com/s3fs-public/190211_Significant_Cyber_Events_List.pdf

[103] Rowe, N. C. (2015), "The Attribution of Cyber Warfare," in Green, J. A. (ed) (2015), Cyberwarfare: A Multidisciplinary Analysis, Routledge, pp. 61–72 Bellingcat (2017), "Bahamut Revisited, More Cyber Espionage in the Middle East and South Asia," https://www.bellingcat.com/resources/case-studies/2017/10/27/bahamut-revisited-cyber-espionage-middle-east-south-asia/

territories in order to fulfill their own interests. How conventional powers want to control cyberspace? Current powers employ the conventional principles of law and international law in cyberspace transactions. Will AAI generate the global State? It is obvious that a networking of AAI technology governing an AAI society will eventually lead to the creation of the AAI global state inhabited by humanoid robots which might be governed initially by elite of humans.

11.7 Digital Politics and Big Data

Political science improves the connection people have with political goings-on and so political effectiveness advances as people assimilate reliable information about politics into their thought processes which means that AI adds to social networking being a substantial and positive innovation. The groups stream of communications embraces all kinds of personal observations and comments about current events and so these developments are producing constructive interpersonal interactions and considerably increasing the amount of political information available to people. Hence, political effectiveness is increasing as the real information to make intelligent political choice becomes pervasive in society and so greater belief in political effectiveness leads to augmented political participation which means that social networking via AI is a plus in favor of better democracy.

Politics have ascertained the power a social network for the reason that their presentation of content does radically influence cognitive processes. It has to be taken into consideration that comparing political transactions to commercial activity generates an understanding that politics and commerce differ. Also, politics encompasses a substantial amount of people reasoning with each other and estimating how cooperation could produce political gains and when technology introduced the e-network via AI technology the likelihoods for transactions advancing knowledge about possible social cooperation multiplied remarkably.

Furthermore, politics is not implicated with moving particular commodities but rather politics affects people's imagination by stimulating numerous types of political participation. To that extent, the transaction principles of networks substantially influence virtual politics. Also, digital/virtual politics involves the use of information and communication technologies in democratic political practices vis-à-vis information, discussion, and decision-making. Moreover, digital politics revitalize democracy through improved distribution of and transparency in the spread of political information along with new and more inclusive forms of political participation.

Information is essential for democracy and so if states do not have the big data, there will be difficulties in building proper forms of participation. It has to be taken into account that technology and AI have transformed modern democracy in its foundation and so much of modern politics are digital altering the exchange between players within political sceneries by causing a relaxation of the traditional entities of space and time and their impact on political processes.

Has the problem of participation resolved in modern democracy? Regardless that technology is a tool by empowering citizens and creating new spaces for interactions, a declining civic engagement has been one of the most important matters of the development of modern democracies. Noteworthy variations in openings for citizens to politically engage through new technologies have been proved to remain, even between and within otherwise fully democratic states due to the substantial variation of government supply of conditions for online involvement. Gustav Lidén[104] argues that "great differences still exist for citizens, due to residence, when it comes to opportunities for engagement in local politics via official municipal sites."

It has to be taken into account that the new means of political participation and engagement vary from the traditional ones, such as voting, party membership, and contacting legislators that were grounded on hierarchical party structures. Hence, the new ways of political action are more likely to be grounded on individuals' motivations and be employed through activities such as sharing political information via social media networks. To that extent, users of social media are in contact with other users who disclose similar views searching for information that supports already-accepted perspectives and beliefs polarizing the social spectrum on any given matter.[105]

On the one hand, traditionally, political participation has been understood as citizens' engagement that involves the selection of government representatives and actions like voting, campaign activity, and contacting officials or legislators. On the other hand, new forms of participation have begun to emerge and so people use social media not only to access certain content but also to create and share their own content about political matters which means that citizens are objectifying new forms of online political participation aiming to accomplish one's political targets by joining the public sphere on social media. It could be said that networked people are embedded in networks rather than being members of traditional social groups which means that digital individualism and personalization of politics have also converted the networks where current political activities are objectified. Furthermore, traditional collective action denotes political action and participation happening through strong organizational coordination, while new connective action is grounded on individuals' action frames, and political identification is centered on their lifestyles, values, and views. Thus, while traditional political collectives where organizational hierarchies like political parties, new political collectives are more likely to be molded as loose networks, where diverse personalized premises are linked to larger political goals rather than precise ideological and interest-based battles. In line, the alteration of people's political and social lives has had an effect

[104] Gustav Lidén, The policy making of digital politics: Examining the local level in Sweden, the 2nd International Conference on Public Policy, Milan, July 1–4, 2015. P 17.

[105] Strandberg, K., Himmelroos, S., Grönlund, K., 2019. Do discussions in like-minded groups necessarily lead to more extreme opinions? Deliberative democracy and group polarization. Int. Political Sci. Rev. 40 (1), 41–57.

on how people are engaged politically and particularly social media platforms are accepted spaces for political action among the youth and young adults.

It is worth mentioning here that digital platforms are other disruptive ICT-based technological innovations permitting consumers to become producers and co-innovators which mean that platforms are data-integration junctures, which are the fundamental nodes in the data economy.[106] Moreover, it has to be taken into account that digital platforms have occurred as a new technical and organizational part capable of altering the dynamics of consolidated socioeconomic models. To that extent, digital platforms, such as "Nosso Mandato" and "Poder do Voto," are altering a state's politics by engendering new mechanisms for political participation and by promoting a transformation in the political culture. Additionally, digital platforms reinforce direct digital democracy, truth-based advocacy, and constituent mobilization and so demonstrating a movement that revolutionizes politics by generating new spaces for social mobilization via technology, even if built on the digital services of a global oligopoly. It is representative that Silva Neto and Tulio Chiarini[107] argue that "two important points in the relationship between digital platforms and democracy: (1) specific digital platforms for political participation face greater difficulty in scaling up the number of users than general purpose social networks; (2) the most successful initiatives in terms of non-institutional digital platforms for political participation are based on, and thus strengthen, the Big Five global oligopoly." Moreover, the European Parliament raised fears concerning the modes digital technologies "undermine citizenship, democracy, and the international liberal world order[108]" but presently digital platforms are a part of and an intervention in a larger political system. Especially the persistent development of digital platforms transforms political systems by generating new loci for innovation.[109]

It has to be taken into account that data has become one of the most valuable assets for governments and multinationals and so there is an escalating consensus on the strategic significance of data. Moreover, data is vital not only for its economic value but also for its increasing impact on politics.[110] To that extent, Cambridge Analytica's illicit harvesting of Facebook data affected voting in US presidential

[106] Minna Lammi, Mika Pantzar, The data economy: how technological change has altered the role of the citizen-consumer, Technol. Soc. 59 (2019) 101157. Andreas Jungherr, Gonzalo Rivero, e Daniel Gayo-Avello, Retooling Politics. How Digital Media Are Shaping Democracy, Cambridge University Press, Cambridge, 2020. Samuel C. Woolley, Philip N. Howard, Computational Propaganda, Oxford University Press, Oxford, 2019.

[107] Victo Jos'e da Silva Neto and Tulio Chiarini, Technological progress and political systems: Non-institutional digital platforms and political transformation, Technology in Society Volume 64, February 2021, 101460 p1.

[108] Lisa Maria Neudert, e Nahema Marchal, Polarisation and the Use of Technology in Political Campaigns and Communication, European Parliamentary Research Service, Brussels, 2019.

[109] Archon Fung, Hollie Russon Gilman, e Jennifer Shkabatur, Six models for the internet + politics, Int. Stud. Rev. 15 (2013) 30–47.

[110] The Economist, "The world's most valuable resource is no longer oil, but data", May 6, 2017, https://www.economist.com/leaders/2017/05/06/the-worlds-most-valuable-resource-is-no-longer-oil-but-data

election, as well as the Brexit referendum in the UK earlier that year.[111] In line, US administration has cited data to defend the ban on Chinese tech giant Huawei, asserting that using Huawei's 5G network would expose sensitive US data to the Chinese government.[112]

In addition, it has to be taken into consideration that politics and big data involves the strategic interactions between sovereign states or between the state and non-state actors over the collection, processing, transfer, sale, or use of data. Thus, politics and big data constitutes a subset of digital politics covering the political dynamics linked to digital technologies, algorithms, and network security but data's unique characters engender new political problems.[113] For instance, digital surveillance permits rulers by resolving their information problem in identifying radical opponents and enabling them to substitute preventive repression for co-optation to prevent social unrest. Moreover, digital surveillance assists rulers to substitute targeted repression for nonexclusive co-optation to prevent coordinated uprisings. Hence, surveillance augments local governments' public security expenditure but decreases public goods provision and so improvements in governments' information make citizens worse off in case of authoritarianisms.

Also, it has to be taken into account that new technologies alter the power dynamics between traditional actors and new entrants such as social media corporations and almost render superfluous the utility of bidirectional communications. Moreover, the disposal of big data and the fast and relatively cheap means to process it are stimulating public and private governance bodies to regard the traditional bidirectional communications process as redundant. Also, the new technologies are empowering traditional actors such as politicians, even heads of state to spread confusion over the new and the traditional channels of communication and reestablishing information asymmetries that mislead disparate voters and lead them to mistrust government and vote against their own interests. To that extent, with the rise of e-governance, founded on the processing of big data by machines which means that the answer to transparency and accountability of public and private governance lies in securing access to the same big data independently of the governance bodies; protecting the channels of communications against manipulation and pollution and insisting on the involvement of humans in computerized decision-making processes.

Similarly, it is worth mentioning here that global governance bodies are no longer viewed as inaccessible institutions with limited impact on society and there is constant interaction with decision-makers, to deliberate collectively and to access

---

[111] The New Yorker, "New Evidence Emerges of Steve Bannon and Cambridge Analytica's Role in Brexit," November 18, 2018, https://www.newyorker.com/news/news-desk/new-evidence-emerges-of-steve-bannon-andcambridge-analyticas-role-in-brexit

[112] CNBC, "Trump official compares Huawei to 'the Mafia' as White House works on 5G battle plan," February 25, 2020, https://www.cnbc.com/2020/02/25/trump-official-calls-huawei-mafia-as-white-house-works-on-5g-battleplan.html

[113] Xu X. To Repress or to co-opt? Authoritarian control in the age of digital surveillance. American Journal of Political Science 2020 https://doi.org/10.1111/ajps.12514

data. Furthermore, it seems that currently the more of an equal participation in political processes is neither solved nor reduced with the help of digital politics.

To that extent, it is worth noting that China's adoption of digital technologies has made data the means of every aspect of society and so the government embraced a national big data strategy and adopted the concept of "data sovereignty." Moreover, many states have become investors in the digital sector enabling digital connectivity but also causing geopolitical concerns globally. In line, China has created the first cyber court, where defendants, plaintiffs, and judges meet over video conferences and so this fast-paced digitization process has opened an explosion of tech firms and startups.[114] Many tech firms have expanded their national rivalry to the global level through mergers and acquisitions.

Do data diverge from traditional assets in terms of economic characteristics? Taking into account that data is nonrival and only partially excludable can generate benefits or costs for non-sharers. Moreover, since data is only partially excludable and never perishes, there is great uncertainty regarding its future use and so tech firms that collect personal data must handle a commitment problem of how to guarantee that they will not disclose their user data to the government, which may abuse the data for surveillance or coercion. Tech firms with deep ties to governments diminish national political risks but raise overseas regulatory risks.

It has to be taken into account that data has a valuation problem and it is hard to evaluate the price of data appropriately for the reason that it is nonrival generating new value through combining different datasets. Digitization has transformed all aspects of many countries during the last decade by developing e-commerce retail market. Moreover, algorithmic modeling risks to not only facilitate preference matching, but also it aggravates information asymmetry between traders and consumers by giving rise to complex architectures which hinder rational decision-making. In the recent Orange Polska[115] decision, the CJEU ruled that a practice may constitute an aggressive practice if it "is liable to make that consumer feel uncomfortable and thus to confuse his thinking in relation to the transactional decision to be taken."

It has to be taken into consideration that data has always been useful by diminishing information asymmetry in economic transactions. However, data did not play such a central role until the advancement of digital technologies that have enabled the mass collection, storage, and analysis of data.

Does the explosion of data influence global politics? It has to be taken into account that the global politics implicated in the ownership and trade of traditional goods, such as oil and land but global politics are get involved in data politics due to a unique foundation because data has two features that differentiate it from many other economic goods that are rival and excludable, including oil: nonrivalry and partial excludability. Nonrivalry is a central feature of data owing to the fact that data

[114] MarketWatch, "China has 9 of the world's 20 biggest tech companies," May 31, 2018, https://www.marketwatch.com/

[115] Case C-628/17, Orange Polska, ECLI:EU:C:2019:480, para. 47.

can be used an infinite number of times and by many parties instantaneously which means that governments and multinationals collect the same set of personal data, and citizens who give out their data still have access to the same amount of data.[116]

Data bring escalating returns and companies use data benefitting from a "data feedback loop" or direct network externalities in which a company's success invites more users and user data, which advances the quality of products through AI leading to more users and data. Moreover, data increase returns when combined with other factors of production.[117]

As mentioned earlier, data is also partially excludable and so it is possible to prevent non-paying individuals from consuming certain products. While traditional economic inputs are often excludable and so a state prevents people from occupying territory or consuming oil if they have not paid for it, it is not always feasible to block non-paying individuals' access to data. Furthermore, data is partially excludable for the reason that it is easy and inexpensive to duplicate and to transfer over a long distance, even across a country's borders and so causing a high risk for unauthorized sales, usage, or theft of data. Undeniably, data can still be excludable if it is fully encrypted, anonymized, or stored offline making data less useful. Furthermore, many digital products, such as cloud computing and GPS navigation, can no longer run without real-time data sharing.

It has to be taken into account that national data regulations could change the excludability and distribution of data and so companies with big data see data as a private asset and support restrictive laws on information access and sharing. Thus, the economic features of data—nonrivalry and partial excludability—lead to the foundation of externality, commitment, and valuation problems for cross-national politics of personal data.

Due to partial excludability and nonrivalry characteristics date becomes a public good having both positive and negative externalities and so the sharing and formation of data have positive externalities, such as beneficial spillovers on a third party. To that extent, the collection of personal data from data sharers trains a machine learning algorithm to expand the quality of service provided to others, embracing non-sharers but data has negative externalities, particularly on privacy. Consequently, governments balance the positive and negative externalities of data, mainly when the externalities come from international data flows. In line, the cross-national exchange of data steers huge trade advantages but subjecting citizen privacy to foreign surveillance, hacking, and data breaches which means that companies have a reason to collect data.[118] On the other hand, if companies collecting data

---

[116] Jones CI, Tonetti C. Nonrivalry and the Economics of Data. National Bureau of Economic Research Working Paper (No. w26260) 2019.

[117] Farboodi M, Mihet R, Philippon T, Veldkamp L. Big data and firm dynamics. AEA Papers and Proceedings 2019.

[118] Carriere-Swallow MY, Haksar MV. The economics and implications of data: an integrated perspective. International Monetary Fund 2019.

under-invest in data security and privacy protection, the negative externalities of data augment.

The achieved "personalisation" of date via AI technology functions as critical information management promoting efficiency but the calculating aspects of personalization steer to the practice of microtargeting political adverts to profiled users, and undecided voters, in the lead up to elections or referendums, as disclosed in the Cambridge Analytical scandal requiring legal response. Personal data in conjunction with big data is interpreted by AI producing a picture of people and the algorithm replaces the traditional human decision-maker. Moreover, big data analytics is engendered by AAI autonomous technology whose complex processes, optimized through feedback loops and machine learning competences, often place it beyond human understanding, and so prima facie outside human oversight and contestation.

Many governments regulate trans-border data flows by establishing data protection laws or privacy regulations. Moreover, the notion of data sovereignty emerged denoting that data are subject to the laws and regulations of the nation-state in which it is generated and processed. In other words, it is a political attempt to limit data services along national borders. It is characteristic that China's data sovereignty is connected to "cyber-sovereignty," demonstrating that states should have control over the digital technologies, content, and infrastructures within their jurisdictions.[119] It is worth noting that the Chinese approach to data regulation is state-centered, with "a unique combination of data protection and the government's control over data flows[120]" which means that the state regulates businesses and protects citizens from the needless collection of personal data the state has uncontrolled access to citizen data. Furthermore, Chinese state-centered model is different from the European Union and the USA, where the data regulations are citizen-based and market-based, respectively. The USA relies on corporate self-regulation to govern data and the EU has adopted GDPR.

Which are the political effects of national digital borders? The development of national digital borders will have the following political effects on governments: First of all, data sovereignty will further strengthen digital authoritarianism on top of the existence of system of censorship and surveillance which means that the pattern of censorship and data localization directs to total control, further increasing a government's capability to coerce. Secondly, conflicts over data sovereignty generate a new fight area for many countries and so many governments have initiated data regulations leading to incompatible rules but GDPR is a guide for many news regulations. Thirdly, a country's national legislation, concerning data protection, causes problems when corporations invest in countries with strict data regulations.

---

[119] BBC, "China internet: Xi Jinping calls for 'cyber sovereignty'," December 16,2015, https://www.bbc.com/news/world-asia-china-35109453

[120] Adil Nussipov, "How China Governs Data," April 27, 2020, https://medium.com/center-for-media-data-andsociety/how-china-governs-data-ff71139b68d2

Furthermore, national digital boarders create a new trade barrier and so such borders encounter huge compliance costs for multinational tech corporations, unsettling the global value chain and compromising economies of scale.

It has to be taken into account that uncertainty concerning future data use is a vital political matter, for the reason that it causes concerns about foreign government surveillance and so data is valuable and states have high incentives to control and compete for data. It is characteristic that fears about foreign government surveillance result from commitment problems because MNEs do not commit to not sharing personal data with their home government and the home government do not commit to not abusing personal data for surveillance or for other political reasons invading individual liberty.

Likewise, it has to be taken into consideration that local companies do not disobey data requests from an authoritarian government.[121] Companies and governments in democracies are not immune from commitment problems and so government mass surveillance projects are on the rise globally but companies based in democracies have an advantage that the institutional constraints such as checks on a government's arbitrary acts, free press, and the rule of law protect them from any misuse of data which means that these constraints on both companies and governments function as commitment devices to bind future actions of data abuse. It has to be taken into account that companies based in autocracies do not hand user data to its home government ex post because companies bear reputational costs of abusing their user data, and their welfares are usually not associated with the interests of political authorities.

It could be said that governments are introducing new technologies to their governance mechanisms in order to uphold the rule of law. AI surveillance presents to governments two major capabilities. Firstly, AI surveillance permits regimes to automate many tracking and monitoring functions previously allocated to human operators and so causing cost efficiencies, diminishing reliance on security forces, and superseding prospective principal-agent loyalty problems. Secondly, AI technology casts a much wider surveillance net than old-style methods[122] and so monitoring all physical and digital activities will be used to predict undesired behavior.

Hence, it has to be taken into account that platform regulation involves a complex and disparate set of laws deeply intertwined with the rise of platform firms and informational capitalism. AI-empowered platform permits users to make and share short videos and so accumulating data. Thus, politics of big data emerges between any country dyad, and regarding any multinational corporation that collects personal

[121] The Verge, "Russia lifts its ban on the Telegram messenger app," June 18, 2020, https://www.theverge.com/2020/6/18/21295535/russia-telegram-ban-lifted-security

[122] Steven Feldstein, "The Road to Digital Unfreedom: How Artificial Intelligence Is Reshaping Repression," Journal of Democracy 30, no. 1 (2019).

data.[123] Moreover, private Big Techs are not becoming part of a state and do not act primarily upon the state's political directives and so Big Techs are still largely profit-driven, pursuing commercial interests that are not fully associated with the state's target. First of all, online trading platforms back the state to establish market institutions, enforce, conduct policy experiments such as Alibaba building "smart cities," and facilitating countryside advancement.[124] Secondly, private tech corporations, such as social media platforms, aid the state conduct surveillance and perform censorship.[125]

It is worth noting that while the global economy gets digitized, data has become a new frontier of geopolitical rivalry and so the European Union recently fined Google and Amazon $163 million for violating its privacy law, reflecting a concern about data's negative externality problem. Hence, politics of big data is prospering for the reason that data has altered the basis of power and so a country's strength now lies not only in its military power or trade, but its capability to collect, refine, and utilize data.

It has to be taken into consideration that AI is a decisive component of national success as countries recognize opportunities and geopolitical risks posed by the suite of technologies. Nations' strategy focuses on establishing them as AI leaders through international bodies by defining norms and standards for AI that favors their corporations.[126] Europe argues for technology sovereignty by pursuing an undefined autonomy of action and so the Digital Services Act and Digital Markets Act strengthen the EU single market by generating a safe and trustworthy online environment and so dealing with matters caused by large platforms companies.[127]

AI systems mold preferences and tilt political choices, just as they become objects of democratic regulation. There is no perfect "ground truth" of individual preference occurring in isolation, entirely confined from social, state, or market pressure. Hence, though Google and Facebook want your attention, Amazon wants you to buy more, and politicians want you to believe their words, it is not presumed that their projects will overpower human's subjectivity which means that there is mutuality, and entanglement, of democratic subjectivity and the democratic project of

---

[123] Business Insider, "US government agencies are banning TikTok, the social media app teens are obsessed with, over cybersecurity fears—here's the full list", February 25, 2020, https://www.businessinsider.com/us-governmentagencies-have-banned-tiktok-app-2020-2

[124] Couture V, Faber B, Gu Y, Liu L. Connecting the countryside via e-commerce: evidence from China. American Economic Review: Insights 2021. Koo WW, Eesley CE. Platform governance and the rural–urban divide: Sellers' responses to design change. Strategic Management Journal. 2020.

[125] The Wall Street Journal, "State Support Helped Fuel Huawei's Global Rise," December 25, 2019, https://www.wsj.com/articles/state-support-helped-fuel-huaweis-global-rise-11577280736

[126] NSCAI Final Report. https://www.nscai.gov/wp-content/uploads/2021/03/Full-Report-Digital-1.pdf HolonIQ. (2020). Global AI Strategy Landscape. HolonIQ. https://www.holoniq.com/wpcontent/uploads/2020/02/HolonIQ-2020-AI-Strategy-Landscape.pdf

[127] Broadbent, M. (2020). The Digital Services Act, the Digital Markets Act, and the New Competition Tool. Shaping Europe's Cyber Future https://www.eurobiz.com.cn/shaping-europes-cyber-future/

training AI systems. Of course, an AAI system will allow the evaluation of AAI entities needs and the demands of the political system of governance of AAI society because in any other case either AAI entities will be slaves of the AAI system or the AAI system will serve the demands of the AAI humanoid robots inhabiting and comprising an AAI society.

It is characteristic that AAI information technology permits algorithms to access and act on human thought. Will democracies be replaced by tech-tyrannies, or just by new, more complicated, political systems? It could be said that AAI systems in an AAI society will bring forwards AAI politics for the demands of AAI entities or humans depended on AAI technology. Will humanoid robots overtake control of earth or will be used as machines by humans?

Will individualized sentence for AAI entities be the disconnection from the AAI system and putting AAI entities into an AAI prison or destroying the AAI entity merely as a product? Can AAI entities with emotions and mechanical life be destroyed as products or must be regarded as analogous humanoid beings having rights and duties? It has to be taken into account that individualized sentencing is a well-accepted value in criminal cases and courts have long commended the virtue of individualized sentencing, and it is an important value under the Eighth Amendment[128] as well which can be imposed by robo-justice utilizing an AAI technology.

It is worth noting that digital platforms create the pools of big data on which AI tools run and so the regulation of digital platforms and of the data is part of the challenge of governing AI. Moreover, as platforms carry on to utilize AI without governance, their selections on critical matters become default practices about ownership, representation, and values across the private, public, and civil sectors and so accelerating the requirement for governance of the AI and platforms.

It has to be taken into account that China is establishing new global standards for the data trade. In 2017, Apple Inc. builds a new joint venture data center in China to comply with China's Cybersecurity Law requiring all firms that maintain "critical information infrastructure" to store their data on a Chinese-owned server. Apple, like many firms operating in China, relies heavily on data centers to function in the Chinese market. However, for Apple, as for many other companies in areas ranging from engineering services to enterprise computing, the decision to open a data center with major ownership by a Chinese firm transforms the politics of power and access to data within the company and among its consumers.

Furthermore, it is worth mentioning here that current laissez-faire policies ultimately protect neither consumers nor national competitiveness. On the other hand, China, by regulating the security issues presented by global corporate data investments through a combination of national policy-making, corporate dominance, and international regulatory actions, is establishing new global standards for the data trade and so China is affirming its own model of data governance which means

[128] Woodson v. North Carolina, 428 U.S. 280 (1976) "justice generally requires consideration of more than the particular acts by which the crime was committed and that there be taken into account the circumstances of the offense together with the character and propensities of the offender."

reliance on domestic data governance principles to influence international principles.[129]

References

1. Fisher, A. & Streinz, T. *Confronting data inequality*, IILJ Working Paper 2021/1.
2. Reese, B. (2018). The fourth age: Smart computers, conscious computers. In *The Future of Humanity*, pp. 85–121.
3. Geradin, D., Karanikioti, T., & Katsifis, D. *GDPR Myopia: How a well-intended regulation ended up favoring Google in Ad Tech*. TILEC Discussion Paper DP 2020-012.
4. Lambach, D. (2020). The territorialization of cyberspace. *International Studies Review, 22*, 482.
5. Dyer-Witheford, N., Kjosen, A. M., & Steinhoff, J. (2019). *Inhuman power artificial intelligence and the future of capitalism*. Pluto Press.
6. Pasquale, F. (2015). *The black box society: The secret algorithms that control money and information*. Harvard University Press.
7. Zekos, G. (2021). Artificial intelligence and e-bills of lading contracts. *Journal of Internet Law, 24*(8), 3–10.
8. Sætra, H. S. (2019). When nudge comes to shove: Liberty and nudging in the era of big data. *Technology in Society, 59*, 101130.
9. Schmitt, M. N., ed. (2017). *Tallinn manual 2.0 on the international law applicable to cyber operations*. CUP.
10. Tsagourias, N. (2015). The legal status of cyberspace. In N. Tsagourias & R. Buchan (Eds.), *Research handbook on international law and cyberspace*. Edward Elgar.
11. O'hara, K., & Hall, W. (2018). *Four internets: The geopolitics of digital governance* (CIGI Papers, 206).
12. Feldstein, S. (2019). The road to digital unfreedom: How artificial intelligence is reshaping repression. *Journal of Democracy, 30*(1).
13. Lin, T. C. W. (2019). Artificial intelligence, finance, and the law. *Fordham Law Review, 88*(2), 531.
14. Tsagourias, N. (2018). Law, borders and the territorialisation of cyberspace Indonesian. *Journal of International Law, 18*(4).
15. da Silva Neto, V. J., & Chiarini, T. (2021). Technological progress and political systems: Non-institutional digital platforms and political transformation. *Technology in Society, 64*.

[129] Aynne Kokas, Cloud Control: China's 2017 Cybersecurity Law and its Role in US Data Standardization at: https://ssrn.com/abstract=3427372

Chapter 12
Conclusions

It could be said that predictive AI tools are already being used to make everyday decisions about people, in contexts ranging from criminal sentencing to employment to finance.[1] AI technologies are used to predict human behavior.

It has to be taken into account that there is lack of the capability of public regulators to utilize technology to become more accessible and participatory due to structures unprepared to face technological encounters, knowledge-scarcity of the public sector workforce, along with cultural divergences because governments either stick with addressing demands for participation with traditional, incompetent, regulatory approaches, or entirely take no notice of the innovative prospective of technological innovation.

Simplicity and the road back to nature is the right way for improvement than destroying the nature because the present innovation is far away from the god's innovation level concerning human creation and life on earth and elsewhere exists or level of existence not discovered by humans yet.

AI is a diverse portfolio of computational techniques to advance the accuracy, speed, or scale of machine decision-making, producing capabilities supporting, substituting for, or improving upon human task performance. Moreover, AI leads to transformative applications within a series of industrial, intellectual, and social applications, far beyond those caused by previous industrial revolutions. Furthermore, AI has proven to be superior to human decision-making in certain areas. Moreover, AI is better than humans at finding and enacting the best policies in certain areas concerning science, engineering, and complex societal and macroeconomic issues. Artificial legal intelligence has unsettled the legal services market, the legal profession, and prevalent business models by replacing human legal expertise.

Governance disruption due to AI causes a challenge that is not just legal or procedural, but also political. Moreover, global governance for AI remains

[1] Kristin Johnson, Frank Pasquale & Jennifer Chapman, Artificial Intelligence, Machine Learning, and Bias in Finance: Toward Responsible Innovation, 88 Fordham L. Rev. 499 (2019).

G. I. Zekos, *Political, Economic and Legal Effects of Artificial Intelligence*,
Contributions to Political Science, https://doi.org/10.1007/978-3-030-94736-1_12

fragmented and embryonic. AI supremacy is founded on the prospect of AI superiority in solving complex issues linked to human beings and their societies which means impact of AI on politics. It is worth noting that focus on the policies embedded in AI systems necessitates a review into the distributive and dynamic consequences of those systems. Moreover, the regulation of AI should account for their consequences on power and stratification.

At a societal and political level ethical concerns converge around the capacity of AI to make possible or support pervasive systems of surveillance, disinformation, or manipulation and so threatening democratic norms and practices. AI technology re-opens returning political questions about power, freedom, democracy, and justice. Moreover, at the international level, the escalating military use of AI such as the rise of "lethal autonomous weapons systems" has led to concerns over human dignity.

Different organizations have issued ethical guidelines for automated systems and robotics. Ethical governance is needed to building trust in robotics and artificial intelligence systems. It has to be taken into account that there is a need for an international law tackling the new modalities of governance and regulating the fundamental problems of information asymmetry because the access to data is more pressing than ever. As a result of the increasing influence of global governance bodies, private actors and states on society by modeling communities, the primary task of the law of global governance is not only to make certain the accountability of global governance bodies but also to protect human dignity and the very viability of the democratic state.

If the AI capabilities of policy formation becomes reality, the AI provide us with better means of participation, fair and impartial political outcomes, and more efficient government resulting in benefits for most individuals and society in general.

There are political harms which are differentiated from existential and discursive harms and so existential harms concern the reduction of persons through the datafication and behavioristic approach to the control of human beings but discursive harms encompass the restriction of discourse through dominance by technocratic ideas. In other words, there are harms linked to privacy and surveillance or bias, unfairness, and inequality. Moreover, a prospective loss of freedom is another probable harm. It is argued that political harms relate to people being disenfranchised and deprived of political power and influence linked to the prospective de-politicization consequences of algorithmic governance.

AI can be used to improve political decisions achieved in several ways, fluctuating from computers aiding human decision-makers to their replacing them. The role of AI, and its reliability to make better decisions than humans, is altering its role in human society. Overall, experts and AAI systems will play a bigger political role in the political system of an AAI society rather than their role in the current politics on Earth. On the other hand, there is a need of learning how to incorporate current AI in order to circumvent oligarchic-like despotism, or the authoritarian rule of vital experts along with AI and traditional sources of political legitimacy. Again, AAI systems applied in an AAI society will be utilized for political reasons in such a way that will avoid authoritarianism because even AAI humanoid robots will need their freedom and rights which means that in any other case AAI entities will be only gears of a machine rather than entities leaving in an AAI society.

Taking into account that the purpose of politics is to find the best policies, in accordance with some set moral basis, there is a need of enacting the best identified policies and since AI is better than human beings at generating and finding the best policies means that AI should be given the power to discover and enact our policies.

It is worth mentioning here that if it is accepted that decisions that influence people's wellbeing entail moral capabilities, then the fact of already employing AI in situations where it does not belong has to be rejected and so self-driving cars and robots trading in markets could not be permitted.

AI systems still have noteworthy limitations and vulnerabilities, especially in terms of predictability, verifiability, and reliability.[2] It has to be taken into account that Algorithms are needed to be assumed as the fundamental and substantive units of AI and so beyond issues of legality and involvement, there is a need for deciding how the operative liability and accountability framework vis a vis AI can be effectively instrumented.[3]

AI necessitates algorithms to be secure, reliable, and appropriately robust to handle errors or inconsistencies during all life cycle phases of an AI system. Lately, the effect of new technologies such as AI in terms of democracy, power both economic and political, race, and liberal notions of individual autonomy have emerged and denounced. Moreover, state and administration authority are gradually expressed algorithmically generating the perils of digital transparency. It could be said that better understanding biological brains could play a central part in building intelligent machines and so leveraging insights obtained from neuroscience research will expedite progress in AI technology.

Algorithmic systems are being used as part of decision-making processes in both the public and private sectors. Moreover, several kinds of decisions are made faster and more competently by employing algorithms and the adoption of algorithmic systems for decision-making is vital due to their power to process big data paired with machine learning methods in order to infer statistical models directly from the data. On the other hand, unless suitable governance frameworks are put in place, the opacity of algorithmic systems will lead to situations where people are negatively impacted for the reason that the malfunction of the systems. Furthermore, AI technologies generate alterations in- and to systems of law and regulation themselves. The use of algorithms in legal decision-making or prediction speeds up escalating access to legal processes or augments compliance with vital regulations. Nonetheless, such use confronts existing legal doctrines and concepts or more fundamentally modify the practices, processes, or assumptions of governance orders.

[2] UNIDIR, The Weaponization of Increasingly Autonomous Technologies, Artif. Intell. (2018) 5 ss.

[3] Council of the European Union. 2020. Illegal annexation of Crimea and Sevastopol: EU renews sanctions by one year. Council of the European Union. [Online] June 18, 2020. https://www.consilium.europa.eu/en/press/press-releases/2020/06/18/illegalannexation-of-crimea-and-sevastopol-eu-renews-sanctions-by-one-year/

In doing so, AI technology changes the underlying logics and assumptions of governance systems and the concept of "law" itself.[4]

AI technologies promise considerable opportunities via some forms of global coordination or cooperation rather than a laissez-faire approach. It could be said that there are considerable global benefits which AI could secure and so, prima facie, the ability to support, automate, or improve upon the speed, accuracy, or scale of human decision-making could help provide tremendous benefits which means that while there are societal challenges that are not amenable to "intelligence" alone, there are few problems where more "intelligence" could not assist in finding better solutions, or in instigating existing solutions in better ways. If governed well, AI technologies will drive considerable economic growth, lift global standards of living, and help tackle many critical global challenges, such as achieving the Sustainable Development Goals, enhancing global health, or tackling climate change.

Up till now, AI is only as good as its input and programming. As long as software is programmed by humans, it is vulnerable to reflect inherent biases. Nonetheless, AI has the prospective to reduce biases by offering a promising prospective in that it could be designed to be entirely unbiased and lead to more objective decision-making. It is argued that bad data will result in bad AI analysis but the emergence of AAI technology has to tackle all the problems of biases of data and so data collection to be made objectively which means that in any other case AAI technology will be inadequate inheriting the defaulted humans' behavior.

AI systems embrace a user interface designed to abstract analytical conclusions and facilitate interaction. What does it denote to regulate AI? It is worth noting that an AI system as a sociotechnical embodiment of public policy codified in a suitable computational learning tool and embedded in a specific institutional context.

It has to be taken into account that AI systems differ in their design adding either private or social value by enabling decisions or operations in specific backgrounds. Facebook's feed algorithm evolves the private value of expanding people's engagement with the social network. The Midas algorithm is furthering the social value. Nonetheless, public authorities and corporate actors who produce AI systems commonly appeal to these gains when justifying the elimination of human discretion.

It is argued that the idea of a single, centralized regulator with wide-ranging authority over a new, general-purpose technology does not appear a good one either from "a political-economy, a historical, or even a constitutional one[5]". On the other hand, AAI technology endorsed by AAI society will have not only a central way of functioning, shaping, and executing all the engagements but also reformulating everything according to the news developments in society and environment. An AAI society function by a network of AAI systems will be self-regulated.

AI has the prospective to revolutionize the way in which decisions are taken and in so doing, it has the power to engender significant opportunities as well as

[4]Brian Sheppard, Warming up to inscrutability: How technology could challenge our concept of law, 68 Univ. Tor. Law J. 36–62 (2018).

[5]Andrew Tutt, An FDA for algorithms, 69 Admin. L. Rev. 83 (2017).

challenges for policy-making in foreign affairs in general, and in diplomacy in particular.

The opportunities supplied by social media platforms can be used as a mode of raising the political morality of certain uses of new digital technologies.[6] Nonetheless, social media and cyberspace present new means for citizens to participate in politics and so digital changes in politics are confronting the traditional political parties which mean that politicians and parties need to adapt if they want to thrive. To that extent, in "real life" political and civic action is linked to new ways of participation transpiring in different layers of social media. In line, new forms of politics and civic participation are linked to a greater extent in spaces of social media. Currently, social media platforms present social spaces that gather together different networks and political ideologies.

It is argued that automation and activities beyond automation might not be able to prevent discrimination or failure to adherence of the individual approach to human rights. Moreover, legal principles competent within the proceduralist notions of natural justice, such as fairness, transparency, and others have affected the AI-innovation discourse and so the influence of algorithms will not be insignificant anymore.[7]

It has to be taken into account that certain challenges created by AI cannot be met through either national-level regulation, or through industry self-regulation needing collective action at a global level.[8] Moreover, emerging technologies do not have a distinct status under international law; and while there are certainly a wide range of technology-specific regimes to which states can and have acceded, there does not exist a single legally binding global treaty regime to explicitly regulate all technological risks as a category. It is worth noting that AI has gained momentum to sculpt sociotechnical system modification.

AI has become a powerful force and many countries are struggling to become the world leader of AI. To that extent, China is taking all actions by massively increased capital, data, and human resources in order to become superpower in AI. Moreover, China has endorsed an aggressive military use of AI in practice being detrimental for promoting stability, trust, and the safe deployment of AI systems. It has to be taken into account that the development and use of AI in China is not controlled exclusively by the central government but AI is largely developed and implemented through incentive mechanisms which promote public and private sector actors to

[6] Haydn Belfield, Activism by the AI community: Analysing recent achievements and future prospects, PROC. AAAI/ACM CONF. ON AI, ETHICS, & SOC. (2020).

[7] Desierto, Diane. 2020. Human Rights in the Era of Automation and Artificial Intelligence. EJIL: Talk! [Online] February 26, 2020. https://www.ejiltalk.org/humanrights-in-the-era-of-automation-and-artificial-intelligence Wachter, Sandra, Mittelstadt, Brent and Russell, Chris. 2020. Why Fairness Cannot Be Automated: Bridging the Gap Between EU Non-Discrimination Law and AI. arxiv.org. [Online] May 12, 2020. https://arxiv.org/abs/2005.05906

[8] Bryant Walker Smith, New Technologies and Old Treaties, 114 AJIL UNBOUND 152–157 (2020).

follow the agenda set out in the AIDP.[9] The strong incentive system is endorsed by the central government which promotes the development of local AI industries and the implementation of AI applications generating incentives for local politicians to abide by central government policy and to undertake regional experimentation in an attempt to advance local economies. Thus, fierce competition has materialized between local governments to attract AI corporations. On the other hand, EU focuses on fostering "human-centric" AI, which rests on the foundational values of the EU. The European Union and the USA verify their intention to implement trustworthy AI systems obeying universal human rights and shared democratic values.[10]

AI is altering the nature of human labor and this change is unparalleled, both in terms of the speed at which it happening and the consequences for social systems. It is obvious that accountability and liability will be subjected to assessments reflecting the life cycle of an AI system. Improved AI in society helps not only the government but also its citizens and so improved AI for people indirectly helps society and so the government.

It could be said that key regulatory encounter in the area of AI is preserving algorithm openness so that they can be checked for transparency and potential bias but this necessity is probably in conflict with intellectual property arrangements, in which companies choose to keep methods confidential due to the fact that these methods give them a clear competitive advantage. Moreover, openness is guaranteed for patented inventions but presenting problems of its own for the reason that the use of software methods is difficult to guard, and jurisdictions differ widely concerning the extent to which software methods are patented.

Likewise, it has to be taken into account that the capability to predict human preferences, responses, and behaviors presents endless prospects for commerce, politics, and regulation and so bringing convenience and effectiveness by furthering private and public interests in equal measure. Moreover, there is effort to predict buying options, political leanings and likely votes of people and groups, the possible success of medical treatments, expected defaults on loans, the chance of fraudulent insurance claims, etc. Furthermore, the competence to "know" the individual and the group by predicting their behavior has upturned on unparalleled scale due to the rise of network society and AI technology producing personal data in large collections of real-time concerning virtually all aspects of human life from shopping, food and entertainment preferences, friendship networks, social activities, health concerns, biometric and health data, etc. Hence, data when mined by AI uncover substantial patterns and correlations generating knowledge about group's behavioral inclinations, economic activity, political trends, etc., and about the person social status,

[9] Cohen, I. G., Evgeniou, T., Gerke, S., & Minssen, T. (2020). The European artificial intelligence strategy: Implications and challenges for digital health. The Lancet Digital Health, 2(7), e376–e379. https://doi.org/10.1016/S2589-7500(20)30112-6 Colvin, T. J., Liu, I., Babou, T. F., & Wong, G. J. (2020). A Brief Examination of Chinese Government Expenditures on Artificial Intelligence R&D (pp. i–ii). Institute for Defense Analyses. https://www.jstor.org/stable/resrep22826.1

[10] EU-US Trade and Technology Council Inaugural Joint Statement September 29, 2021 Pittsburgh, Pennsylvania.

political leaning, etc., and so becoming inputs for any political decision which means that the competence to predict human preferences, responses, and behaviors presents endless prospects for commerce, politics, and regulation.[11]

AI applications are expanding and this growth has been driven by greater information processing hardware power, escalating online learning opportunities and ample data available today and so AI expansion goes far beyond computing, cyberspace, or big data, covering areas such as information technology and networking, baking systems detection of fraud and financial operations, medicine, image recognition, legal services, among many others even driverless cars. Thus, there will be an unparalleled long-term effect of AI on global politics and international relations; predominantly there is already an intense competition for digital dominance underway. AI platforms technology is becoming a reality and standard operating practice in enabling a broad range of space players, from firms to governmental agencies, to conduct space activities.

There is an increasing public demand for AI regulation and diverse new national regulatory initiatives. There is also a rising recognition of the significance of global coordination or cooperation for AI governance and so much focus to date has been on the escalating constellation of AI ethics principles. It has to be taken into account that AI governance should be based on a better understanding of how AI applications translate into cross-domain transformations. It has to be taken into consideration that there is an increasing role of automated decision-making in public administration, and above all its interface with administrative justice in courts and tribunals. AI automated systems must be compatible with human rights law, due process and good governance, and principles of transparency and accountability. Moreover, the opacity of automated systems, and the commercial values that have stimulated their development into this context, have to comply with the procedures of proper public decision-making offering transparency, accountability, and participation, embracing important values of good governance in administrative law. In other words, automated decision-making systems have to meet administrative law's standards for public sector decision-making.

It is worth noting that the depth of social life and the complexity of political decision-making are currently far beyond the capacity of current AI systems, but AAI technology will tackle all problems much better way than a human managed system. Based on the present AI technology that "robot judges" just cannot replicate the complexity and in actual fact social nature of the law—either technically or conceptually which means that political nature of any public, political decision-making cannot be reproduced without conscious and deliberate human agency. On the other hand, AAI technology will generate robo-judges dealing easily with law and political matters which mean that political nature of any public, political decision-making will be reproduced without conscious and deliberate of any human agency.

[11] Daniel Susser, Beate Roessler, Helen Nissenbaum, "Technology, Autonomy, and Manipulation" (2019) 8(2) Internet Policy Review DOI: https://doi.org/10.14763/2019.2.1410

Plato' view about the penalties of refusing to participate in politics is that people end up being governed by inferiors applies to human's world but in an AAI society algorithmic governmentality will be superior of any human politics because objectivity will be the rationale of AAI rule of law and politics.

Economics and geography are connected, and the prospective of global capitalism and neoliberalism, which are the backbone of a technocratic rules-based globalization, is central toward the democratization and economization of AI. It has to be taken into account that algorithmic activities generate digital territories of influence and culture/soft power economics. Moreover, algorithmic activities surpass the geo-economic realities of the physical world imposing the metaphysical, digital, and even spiritual dimensions of cyber and information space. Hence, AI implants cultural-information warfare and diplomatic measures.

Greece with many scholars and experts on AI technology is far behind the endorsement of AI in all its production mechanism since the advancement of production and innovation remains far behind other countries such as China, etc. It is worth mentioning here that ancient Greece was the leader of the world due to its advancement not in theory but in practical matters such as military equipment, shipbuilding, etc. It has to be taken into account that joint cross-country elaboration of AI systems attenuates fears concerning the objectivity or transparency of procedures/approaches coming from one or several countries. One of the cons of AI is in assisting the spread of disinformation and so AI can be used to produce and disseminate targeted propaganda via AI-powered social media algorithms driven by "engagement," which propagandizes content most likely to be clicked on. Moreover, the AI behind deep fakes continues to advance, and there is prospective for sowing chaos, instigating conflict, and further causing a crisis of truth which means that in an AAI status there is a need of generating mechanism of blocking disinformation in an AAI society.

Technological development has to work for and not against human rights, democracy, and the rule of law. There has been a steady rise in the use of automated and AI tools by public authorities. It is obvious that there is a need to incorporate human rights into the design of AI systems. AAI technology will reach a point in which it will be able not only to mimic the human brain but to surpass the cognitive performance of humans in all domains of interest. In other words, AAI humanoid robots will develop consciousness and so instead of staying confined in the programmed setting that trains them to mimic human cognitive functions, self-aware AAI learns how to think about itself and its surrounding environment.[12]

AAI systems should be deployed to make possible more diffused forms of political participation, empowering citizens to take more ownership of public administration and so enabling civil society to participate in political affairs. It has to be taken into account that the use of AAI machines will grow and have the

[12] Shimon Ullman, "Using Neuroscience to Develop Artificial Intelligence.," Science (New York, N.Y.) 363, no. 6428 (February 15, 2019): 692–93, https://doi.org/10.1126/science.aau6595

capacity to transform or destroy human society[13] which means that as its intelligence grows as it becomes more autonomous it is intricate to apprehend how much value AAI machines will offer to the protection of human lives.

Technological innovation brings prospective to advance society alleviating some of the world's most pressing problems, from enabling advancements in diagnosis and treatment of disease, to revolutionizing transportation and urban living. Also, AI technology is affecting not just the substance of various international regimes, but also their processes and procedures, and possibly even their political framework influencing not just the instruments visualized for governing AI itself, but also are spreading to many other legal domains. Of course, even in an AAI society security system will be employed in order to avoid major harms and disasters in the AAI society.

AI entails the making of entirely new kinds of information services along with the conversion of value creation from goods industries into ICT enabled services and so AI embedded in platforms allows firms to shift retail from storefront to online which means that middle skilled employment seems to be eroding.[14]

AI strengthens existing biases, as algorithmic decision-making systems, which capture existing biases from inputs to inform outputs, are deployed at a big scale and so AI technology has intensified disinformation into a current day crisis. Hence, as AI becomes more powerful and widespread, the rise of malicious use is expected, threatening not just social security, as disinformation does, but political security, physical security, and digital security. In the end, governing AI necessitates governing the technology platforms.

It has to be taken into consideration that dealing with AI risks will necessitate political will, capacity-building, inclusiveness, and more diverse representation in a range of settings. Moreover, currently the UN should bridge the gap at the global level and offer a legitimate, representative, and policy-oriented locus for deeper international cooperation on AI matters because the establishment of AAI society via AAI technology will address matters for AAI entities which demands a new type of UN dealing electronically with matters of AAI application in a global scale not mention that jurisdiction and cyber-sovereignty demands a cyber dimensional global organization for AAI issues in AAI society.

Concerning the current AI technology, the public is aware about algorithmic bias in AI training datasets and their prejudicial effect on predictive policing algorithms and other analytic devices used by law enforcement. To that extent, governments must offer better answers and fuller transparency about how they will use AI intrusive tools.

---

[13] Stephen Hawking: AI will transform or destroy society, CNBC (Oct. 20, 2016).

[14] Manyika, J., Madgavkar, A., Tacke, T., Smit, S., Woetzel, J., & Abdulaal, A. (2020). The social contract in the 21st century. https://www.mckinsey.com/industries/public-and-socialsector/our-insights/the-social-contract-in-the-21st-century OECD. (2020). OECD Employment Outlook 2020: Worker Security and the COVID-19 Crisis. https://doi.org/10.1787/1686c758-en

AI systems improve peoples' lives along with the overall economic and societal welfare and so AI-powered systems lead to better healthcare services, safer and cleaner transport systems, better working conditions, higher productivity and new innovative products, services and supply chains. Also, AI technological forces are molding society and political interactions but so far, there is no clear direction of the regulatory landscape for AI; whether we are heading to a globalist or nationalist regulatory model for AI. Furthermore, existing rules already cover some of the risks caused by AI systems and, in principle, regulatory intervention are required only where gaps are to be filled.

It is characteristic that self-regulation and soft-law approaches have been the primary preferred choice when it comes to the regulation of tech. It has to be taken into account that the non-binding character of privacy rules, alongside existing interferences of the legislature into the judiciary, renders privacy protections largely impracticable. It has to be taken into account that there is a global profusion of sets of principles for the governance or ethical development of AI systems from a range of sources, involving international organizations, governments, and international NGOs[15] and so the existing position is that there is not a high level of consensus regarding the AI principles.

AI offers great opportunities to augment customer experience, democratize financial services, make certain consumer protection, and considerably improve risk management. Moreover, advances in technology have reduced lending risk by evaluating a profusion of customer data. To that extent, complex machine learning models have been proven very efficient in offering a high predictive accuracy in evaluating the credit risk of customers. Nonetheless, AI new and advanced techniques lack the transparency which is needed to grasp how and why a certain borrower is granted a loan or not but it is often very difficult to trace back the steps the algorithm took to arrive at its decision which means that the absence of algorithmic transparency is one of the key barriers for the wider adoption of AI-based solutions in credit risk management. It is supposed that an AAI technology will solve many of the cons of the current AI technology concerning transparency, etc.

A global competition in advancing AI applications has appeared, and so many states are taking part in a race to AI striving to advance the technology's use and benefits more successfully than others.[16] It could be said that states will compete with each other through regulation with the purpose of attracting AAI technology rendering them a competitive force on the global AI market. The emergence of AAI will bring not only legal regulation of AAI but also technological one in order to be

[15] White House National Security Advisor Jake Sullivan: "The United States welcomes the EU's new initiatives on artificial intelligence. We will work with our friends and allies to foster trustworthy AI. . . ," Twitter, @JakeSullivan46, 22 April 2021 https://twitter.com/jakesullivan46/status/1384970668341669891?lang=en

[16] Yuval Noah Harari, "Who Will Win the Race for AI?" Foreign Policy Magazine (Washington, Winter 2019).

workable in an AAI society inhabited by humanoid robots administered either by an elite of humans or an AAI elite will overtake power and humanity will be extinct.

It has to be taken into account that AI technology intrudes on the domain of law and regulation possibly to aggravate problems but also to present solutions.[17] Moreover, a race to AI regulation will eventually lead to an articulate regulatory framework for AI with meaningful and enforceable safeguards for human rights, democracy, and the rule of law.

Currently robots and AI are merely viewed as products or objects with issues of liability basically fitting within existing contractual and tort liability frameworks, even if the attribution of responsibility for harm is complex, or if laws in a specific field need some amendments to accommodate the new technology. Thus, robots and AI are clearly positioned as objects for which human actors or existing non-human legal persons such as corporations are responsible. On the other hand, an AAI humanoid robot having intelligence further than humans will make easier the attribution of legal personality. It has to be taken into account those granting AAI humanoid robots artificial legal personality suggests the ability to hold property, the right to sue and be sued, and the right to work and earn an income and to be paid on time. AAI advanced systems will impose their own rule of law which demands a new way of decision-making and politics.

Will humanoid robots be a new biological creature? Will humanoid robots create new creatures based on new materials? It seems that the current road of robots is not based on generating a new material of production of humanoid robots. On the other hand, AAI will find necessary to produce AAI entities constructed upon more elastic materials with capacity to last for a long time having the capacity for reproduction, etc. There are already efforts to build more flexible robots such as the announced effort of coating robots with a new type of skin allowing them to have reactions via their skin. In other words, the emergence of another biological creature due to AAI cannot be ruled out and so human life will be replaced by another form of life. Then the attribution of legal personality on AAI creatures will not be on the hands of humans and AAI society will attribute the needed legal personality for the function of its inhabitants accordingly.

[17] Massimo Renzo, "Revolution and Intervention" (2020) 54 Nous 233, 243.